F6

TAXATION (UK)

STUDY TEXT

ACCA

Edition 5, Version 1

ISBN 978-1-84808-385-1

Published by

Get Through Guides Ltd.
5, Blake Mews, Richmond
Surrey TW9 3GA
UK

Website: www.GetThroughGuides.com

Email: info@GetThroughGuides.com

Online content feedback form: http://gtgtraining.com/studymaterialfeedback/

For suggestions: feedback@GetThroughGuides.co.uk

Student Support Forum: http://GetThroughGuides.co.uk/forum

Copyright and acknowledgment

Tax returns and other related information are the copyright of HMRC (Her Majesty of Revenue and Customs). With the kind permission of HMRC we have referred to the contents of its website in our book.

The publisher is grateful to the Association of Chartered Certified Accountants for permission to reproduce past examination questions and their answers.

Please check the back of this book for any updates / errata. Further live updates / errata may also be found online on the Get Through Guides Student Support Forum at: http://GetthroughGuides.co.uk/forum. Students are advised to check both of these locations.

STUDY CONTENTS

F6-TAXATION (UK)

STUDY CONTENTS

F6-TAXATION (UK)

Section G

Value added tax

Section H

The obligations of tax payers and/or their agents

The Study Guide includes features like:

- ❑ **'Get Through Intro':** explains **why** the particular Study Guide is important through real life example.
- ❑ **'Case study'**: an introductory article / case study illustrating the Study Guide.
- ❑ **'Definition':** explains the meaning of important terminologies.
- ❑ **'Example':** makes easy complex concepts.
- ❑ **'Tip':** helps to understand how to deal with complicated portions.
- ❑ **'Important':** highlights important concepts, formats, Acts, sections, standards, etc.
- ❑ **'Summary':** highlights the key points of the Learning Outcomes.
- ❑ **'Diagram':** facilitates memory retention.
- ❑ **'Exam focus'**: highlights how the syllabus of each Study Guide has been examined by ACCA in the past.
- ❑ **'Must Read'**: contains references to the technical articles published by ACCA.
- ❑ **'Test Yourself'**: helps check whether students have assimilated a particular Learning Outcome.
- ❑ **'Quick Quiz'**: helps students for quick revision of the Study Guide
- ❑ **'Self Examination Questions'**: exam standard questions at the end of each Study Guide.

SYLLABUS

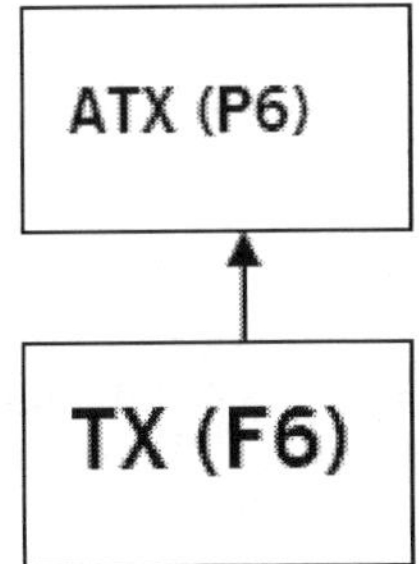

AIM

To develop knowledge and skills relating to the tax system as applicable to the individuals, single companies, and groups of companies.

MAIN CAPABILITIES

On successful completion of this paper candidates should be able to:

A Explain the operation and scope of the tax system

B Explain and compute the income tax liabilities of individuals

C Explain and compute the corporation tax liabilities of individual companies and groups of companies

D Explain and compute the chargeable gains arising on companies and individuals

E Explain and compute the inheritance tax liabilities of individuals

F Explain and compute the effect of national insurance contributions on employees, employers and the self employed

G Explain and compute the effects of value added tax on incorporated and unincorporated businesses

H Identify and explain the obligations of tax payers and/or their agents and the implications of non-compliance

RELATIONAL DIAGRAM OF MAIN CAPABILITIES

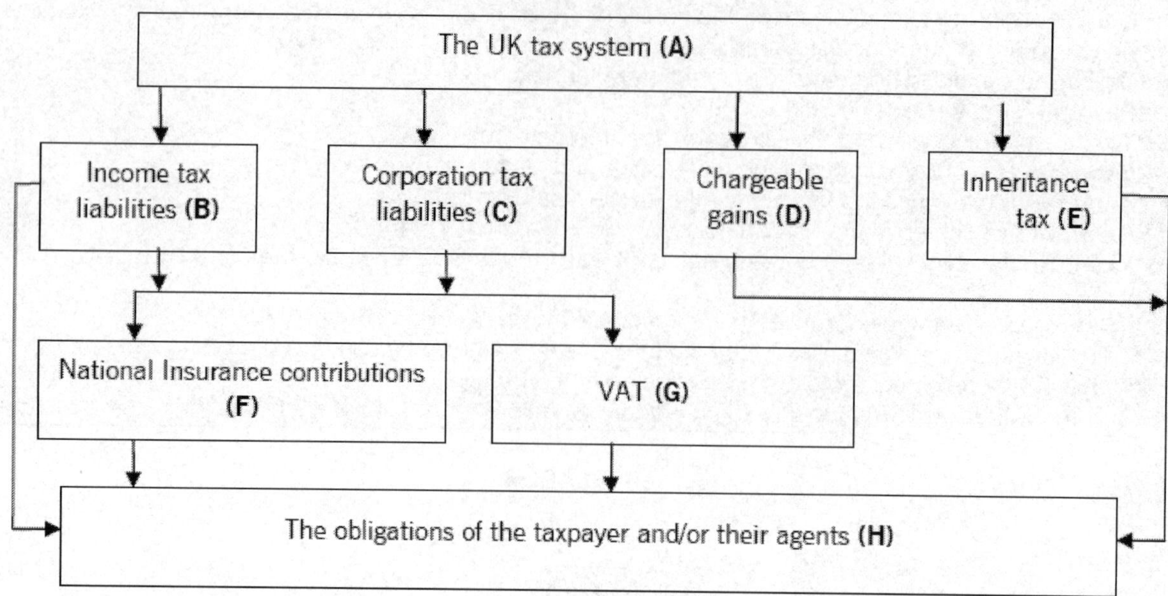

RATIONALE

The syllabus for Paper F6, Taxation, introduces candidates to the subject of taxation and provides the core knowledge of the underlying principles and major technical areas of taxation as they affect the activities of individuals and businesses.

Candidates are introduced to the rationale behind – and the functions of – the tax system. The syllabus then considers the separate taxes that an accountant would need to have a detailed knowledge of, such as income tax from self-employment, employment and investments, the corporation tax liability of individual companies and groups of companies, the national insurance contribution liabilities of both employed and self employed persons, the value added tax liability of businesses, and the chargeable gains arising on disposals of investments by both individuals and companies.

Having covered the core areas of the basic taxes, candidates should be able to compute tax liabilities, explain the basis of their calculations, apply tax planning techniques for individuals and companies and identify the compliance issues for each major tax through a variety of business and personal scenarios and situations.

INTELLECTUAL LEVELS

The syllabus is designed to progressively broaden and deepen the knowledge, skills and professional values demonstrated by the student on their way through the qualification.
The specific capabilities within the detailed syllabuses and study guides are assessed at one of three intellectual or cognitive levels:

Level 1: Knowledge and comprehension
Level 2: Application and analysis
Level 3: Synthesis and evaluation

Very broadly, these intellectual levels relate to the three cognitive levels at which the Knowledge module, the Skills module and the Professional level are assessed.

Each subject area in the detailed study guide included in this document is given a 1, 2, or 3 superscript, denoting intellectual level, marked at the end of each relevant line. This gives an indication of the intellectual depth at which an area could be assessed within the examination. However, while level 1 broadly equates with the Knowledge module, level 2 equates to the Skills module and level 3 to the Professional level, some lower level skills can continue to be assessed as the student progresses through each module and level. This reflects that at each stage of study there will be a requirement to broaden, as well as deepen capabilities. It is also possible that occasionally some higher level capabilities may be assessed at lower levels.

EXAMINATION STRUCTURE

The syllabus is assessed by a three-hour paper-based examination.

Assessment: Taxation (UK)

The paper will be predominantly computational and will have five questions, all of which will be compulsory.

Question	Topic	Marks
1	Income Tax	55
2	Corporation Tax	
3	Chargeable gains	15
4	Any area of syllabus	15
5	Any area of syllabus	15

There will always be at a minimum of 10 marks on value added tax. These marks will normally be included within question one or question two, although there might be a separate question on value added tax.

National insurance contributions will not be examined as a separate question, but may be examined in any question involving income tax or corporation tax.

Groups and overseas aspects of corporation tax may be examined in either question two or question five,

Questions one or two might include a small element of chargeable gains.

Any of the five questions might include the consideration of issues relating to the minimisation or deferral of tax liabilities.

READING AND PLANNING TIME

For all three hour examination papers, ACCA has introduced 15 minutes reading and planning time.

This additional time is allowed at the beginning of each three-hour examination to allow candidates to read the questions and to begin planning their answers before they start writing in their answer books. This time should be used to ensure that all the information and exam requirements are properly read and understood.

During reading and planning time candidates may only annotate their question paper. They may not write anything in their answer booklets until told to do so by the invigilator.

DETAILED SYLLABUS

A The UK tax system

1. The overall function and purpose of taxation in a modern economy
2. Different types of taxes
3. Principal sources of revenue law and practice
4. Tax avoidance and tax evasion

B Income tax liabilities

1. The scope of income tax
2. Income from employment
3. Income from self-employment
4. Property and investment income
5. The comprehensive computation of taxable income and income tax liability
6. The use of exemptions and reliefs in deferring and minimising income tax liabilities

C Corporation tax liabilities

1. The scope of corporation tax
2. Taxable total profits
3. The comprehensive computation of corporation tax liability
4. The effect of a group corporate structure for corporation tax purposes
5. The use of exemptions and reliefs in deferring and minimising corporation tax liabilities

D Chargeable gains

1. The scope of the taxation of capital gains
2. The basic principles of computing gains and losses
3. Gains and losses on the disposal of movable and immovable property
4. Gains and losses on the disposal of shares and securities
5. The computation of capital gains tax payable by individuals
6. The use of exemptions and reliefs in deferring and minimising tax liabilities arising on the disposal of capital assets

E Inheritance tax

1. The scope of inheritance tax
2. The basic principles of computing transfers of value
3. The liabilities arising on chargeable lifetime transfers and on the death of an individual
4. The use of exemptions in deferring and minimising inheritance tax liabilities
5. Payment of inheritance tax

F National insurance contributions

1. The scope of national insurance
2. Class 1 and class 1A contributions for employed persons
3. Class 2 and class 4 contributions for employed persons

G Value added tax

1. The scope of value added tax (VAT)
2. The VAT registration requirements
3. The computation of VAT liabilities
4. The effect of special schemes

H The obligations of tax payers and/or their agents

1. The system for self-assessment and the making of returns
2. The time limits for the submission of information, claims and payment of tax, including payments on account
3. The procedures relating to enquiries, appeals and disputes
4. Penalties for non-compliance

STUDY GUIDE

A THE UK TAX SYSTEM

1. The overall function and purpose of taxation in a modern economy

a) Describe the purpose (economic, social etc) of taxation in a modern economy.[2]

2. Different types of taxes

a) Identify the different types of capital and revenue tax.[1]
b) Explain the difference between direct and indirect taxation.[2]

3. Principal sources of revenue law and practice

a) Describe the overall structure of the UK tax system.[1]
b) State the different sources of revenue law.[1]
c) Appreciate the interaction of the UK tax system with that of other tax jurisdictions.[2]

4. Tax avoidance and tax evasion

a) Explain the difference between tax avoidance and tax evasion.[1]
b) Explain the need for an ethical and professional approach.[2]

Excluded topics

- Anti-avoidance legislation.

B INCOME TAX LIABILITIES

1. The scope of income tax

a) Explain how the residence of an individual is determined.[1]

Excluded topics

- The treatment of a person who comes to the UK to work or a person who leaves the UK to take up employment overseas.
- Foreign income, non-residents and double taxation relief.
- Income from trusts and settlements.

2. Income from employment

a) Recognise the factors that determine whether an engagement is treated as employment or self-employment.[2]
b) Recognise the basis of assessment for employment income.[2]
c) Compute the income assessable.[2]
d) Recognise the allowable deductions, including travelling expenses.[2]
e) Discuss the use of the statutory approved mileage allowances.[2]
f) Explain the PAYE system.[1]
g) Identify P11D employees.[1]
h) Compute the amount of benefits assessable.[2]
i) Explain the purpose of a dispensation from HM Revenue & Customs.[2]
j) Explain how charitable giving can be made through a payroll deduction scheme.[1]

Excluded topics

- The calculation of a car benefit where emission figures are not available.
- The exemption for zero emission company motor cars.
- Share and share option incentive schemes for employees.
- Payments on the termination of employment, and other lump sums received by employees.

3. Income from self-employment

a) Recognise the basis of assessment for self-employment income.[2]
b) Describe and apply the badges of trade.[2]
c) Recognise the expenditure that is allowable in calculating the tax-adjusted trading profit.[2]
d) Recognise the relief that can be obtained for pre-trading expenditure.[2]
e) Compute the assessable profits on commencement and on cessation.[2]
f) Change of accounting date
   (i) Recognise the factors that will influence the choice of accounting date.[2]
   (ii) State the conditions that must be met for a change of accounting date to be valid.[1]
   (iii) Compute the assessable profits on a change of accounting date.[2]
g) Capital allowances
   (i) Define plant and machinery for capital allowances purposes.[1]
   (ii) Compute writing down allowances, first-year allowances and the annual investment allowance.[2]

(iii) Compute capital allowances for motor cars, including motor cars already owned at 6 April 2009 (1 April 2009 for companies).[2]
(iv) Compute balancing allowances and balancing charges.[2]
(v) Recognise the treatment of short life assets.[2]
(vi) Explain the treatment of assets included in the special rate pool.[2]

h) Relief for trading losses
(i) Understand how trading losses can be carried forward.[2]
(ii) Explain how trading losses can be carried forward following the incorporation of a business.[2]
(iii) Understand how trading losses can be claimed against total income and chargeable gains.[2]
(iv) Explain and compute the relief for trading losses in the early years of a trade.[1]
(v) Explain and compute terminal loss relief.[1]

i) Partnerships and limited liability partnerships
(i) Explain how a partnership is assessed to tax.[2]
(ii) Compute the assessable profits for each partner following a change in the profit sharing ratio.[2]
(iii) Compute the assessable profits for each partner following a change in the membership of the partnership.[2]
(iv) Describe the alternative loss relief claims that are available to partners.[1]
(v) Explain the loss relief restriction that applies to the partners of a limited liability partnership.[1]

Excluded topics

- The 100% allowance for expenditure on renovating business premises in disadvantaged areas, flats above shops and water technologies.
- Capital allowances for industrial buildings, agricultural buildings, patents, scientific research and know how.
- Enterprise zones.
- Investment income of a partnership.
- The allocation of notional profits and losses for a partnership.
- Farmers averaging of profits.
- The averaging of profits for authors and creative artists.
- Loss relief for shares in unquoted trading companies.

4. Property and investment income

a) Compute property business profits.[2]
b) Explain the treatment of furnished holiday lettings.[1]
c) Describe rent-a-room relief.[1]
d) Compute the amount assessable when a premium is received for the grant of a short lease.[2]
e) Understand how relief for a property business loss is given.[2]
f) Compute the tax payable on savings income.[2]
g) Compute the tax payable on dividend income.[2]
h) Explain the treatment of individual savings accounts (ISAs) and other tax exempt investments.[1]

Excluded topics

- The deduction for expenditure by landlords on energy-saving items.
- Junior ISAs.

5. The comprehensive computation of taxable income and income tax liability

a) Prepare a basic income tax computation involving different types of income.[2]
b) Calculate the amount of personal allowance available generally, and for people aged 65 and above.[2]
c) Compute the amount of income tax payable.[2]
d) Explain the treatment of interest paid for qualifying purpose.[2]
e) Explain the treatment of qualifying charitable donations.[1]
f) Explain the treatment of property owned jointly by a married couple, or by a couple in a civil partnership.[1]

Excluded topics

- The blind person's allowance and the married couple's allowance.
- Tax credits.
- Maintenance payments.
- The income of minor children.

6. The use of exemptions and reliefs in deferring and minimising income tax liabilities

a) Explain and compute the relief given for contributions to personal pension schemes, using the rules applicable from 6 April 2011.[2]

b) Describe the relief given for contributions to occupational pension schemes, using the rules applicable from 6 April 2011.[1]
c) Explain how a married couple or a couple in a civil partnership can minimise their tax liabilities.[2]

Excluded topics

- The conditions that must be met in order for a pension scheme to obtain approval from HM Revenue & Customs.
- The enterprise investment scheme.
- Venture capital trusts.

C CORPORATION TAX LIABILITIES

1. The scope of corporation tax

a) Define the terms 'period of account', 'accounting period', and 'financial year'.[1]
b) Recognise when an accounting period starts and when an accounting period finishes.[1]
c) Explain how the residence of a company is determined.[2]

Excluded topics

- Investment companies.
- Close companies.
- Companies in receivership or liquidation.
- Reorganisations.
- The purchase by a company of its own shares.
- Personal service companies.

2. Taxable total profits

a) Recognise the expenditure that is allowable in calculating the tax-adjusted trading profit.[2]
b) Explain how relief can be obtained for pre-trading expenditure.[1]
c) Compute capital allowances (as for income tax).[2]
d) Compute property business profits.[2]
e) Explain the treatment of interest paid and received under the loan relationship rules.[1]
f) Explain the treatment of qualifying charitable donations.[2]
g) Understand how trading losses can be carried forward.[2]
h) Understand how trading losses can be claimed against income of the current or previous accounting periods.[2]
i) Recognise the factors that will influence the choice of loss relief claim.[2]
j) Explain how relief for a property business loss is given.[1]
k) Compute taxable total profits.[2]

Excluded topics

- Research and development expenditure.
- Non-trading deficits on loan relationships.
- Relief for intangible assets.

3. The comprehensive computation of corporation tax liability

a) Compute the corporation tax liability and apply marginal relief.[2]
b) Explain the implications of receiving franked investment income.[2]

4. The effect of a group corporate structure for corporation tax purposes

a) Define an associated company and recognise the effect of being an associated company for corporation tax purposes.[2]
b) Define a 75% group, and recognise the reliefs that are available to members of such a group.[2]
c) Define a 75% capital gains group, and recognise the reliefs that are available to members of such a group.[2]
d) Compare the UK tax treatment of an overseas branch to an overseas subsidiary.[2]
e) Calculate double taxation relief.[2]
f) Explain the election for the exemption of profits from overseas branches.[2]
g) Explain the basic principles of the transfer pricing rules.[2]

Excluded topics

- Relief for trading losses incurred by an overseas subsidiary.
- Consortia.
- Pre-entry gains and losses.
- The anti-avoidance provisions where arrangements exist for a company to leave a group.
- The tax charge that applies where a company leaves a group within six years of receiving an asset by way of a no gain/no loss transfer.
- Controlled foreign companies.
- Foreign companies trading in the UK.
- Expense relief in respect of overseas tax.
- Election for the exemption of profits from an overseas branch.
- Transfer pricing transactions not involving an overseas company.

5. The use of exemptions and reliefs in deferring and minimising corporation tax liabilities:

a) The use of such exemptions and reliefs is implicit within all of the above sections 1 to 4 of part C of the syllabus, concerning corporation tax.

D CHARGEABLE GAINS

1. The scope of the taxation of capital gains

a) Describe the scope of capital gains tax.[2]
b) Explain how the residence and ordinary residence of an individual is determined.[2]
c) List those assets which are exempt.[1]

Excluded topics

- Assets situated overseas and double taxation relief.
- Partnership capital gains.

2. The basic principles of computing gains and losses.

a) Compute capital gains for both individuals and companies.[2]
b) Calculate the indexation allowance available to companies.[2]
c) Explain the treatment of capital losses for both individuals and companies.[1]
d) Explain the treatment of transfers between a husband and wife or between a couple in a civil partnership.[2]
e) Compute the amount of allowable expenditure for a part disposal.[2]
f) Explain the treatment where an asset is damaged, lost or destroyed, and the implications of receiving insurance proceeds and reinvesting such proceeds.[2]

Excluded topics

- Small part disposals of land.
- Losses in the year of death.
- Relief for losses incurred on loans made to traders.
- Negligible value claims.

3. Gains and losses on the disposal of movable and immovable property

a) Identify when chattels and wasting assets are exempt.[1]
b) Compute the chargeable gain when a chattel is disposed of.[2]
c) Calculate the chargeable gain when a wasting asset is disposed of.[2]
d) Compute the exemption when a principal private residence is disposed of.[2]
e) Calculate the chargeable gain when a principal private residence has been used for business purposes.[2]
f) Identify the amount of letting relief available when a principal private residence has been let out.[2]

Excluded topics

- The disposal of leases and the creation of sub-leases.

4. Gains and losses on the disposal of shares and securities

a) Calculate the value of quoted shares where they are disposed of by way of a gift.[2]
b) Explain and apply the identification rules as they apply to individuals and to companies, including the same day, nine day, and 30 day matching rules.[2]
c) Explain the pooling provisions.[2]
d) Explain the treatment of bonus issues, rights issues, takeovers and reorganisations.[2]
e) Explain the exemption available for gilt-edged securities and qualifying corporate bonds.[1]

Excluded topics

- A detailed question on the pooling provisions for shares as they apply to limited companies.
- The small part disposal rules applicable to rights issues.
- Substantial shareholdings.
- Gilt-edged securities and qualifying corporate bonds other than the fact that they are exempt.

5. The computation of capital gains tax payable by individuals

a) Compute the amount of capital gains tax payable.[2]

6. The use of exemptions and reliefs in deferring and minimising tax liabilities arising on the disposal of capital assets

a) Explain and apply entrepreneurs' relief as it applies to individuals. [2]

b) Explain and apply rollover relief as it applies to individuals and companies.[2]
c) Explain and apply holdover relief for the gift of business assets.[2]
d) Explain and apply the incorporation relief that is available upon the transfer of a business to a company.[2]

Excluded topics

- Reinvestment relief.
- Entrepreneurs' relief for associated disposals.

E INHERITANCE TAX

1. The scope of inheritance tax

a) Describe the scope of inheritance tax. [2]
b) Identify and explain the persons chargeable. [2]

Excluded topics

- Pre 18 March 1986 lifetime transfers.
- Transfers of value by close companies.
- Domicile, deemed domicile, and non-UK domiciled individuals.
- Trusts.

2. The basic principles of computing transfers of value

a) State, explain and apply the meaning of transfer of value, chargeable transfer and potentially exempt transfer. [2]
b) Demonstrate the diminution in value principle. [2]
c) Demonstrate the seven year accumulation principle taking into account changes in the level of the nil rate band. [2]

Excluded topics

- Excluded property.
- Related property.
- The tax implications of the location of assets.
- Gifts with reservation of benefit.
- Associated operations.

3. The liabilities arising on chargeable lifetime transfers and on the death of an individual

a) Understand the tax implications of chargeable lifetime transfers and compute the relevant liabilities. [2]
b) Understand the tax implications of transfers within seven years of death and compute the relevant liabilities. [2]
c) Compute the tax liability on a death estate. [2]
d) Understand and apply the transfer of any unused nil rate band between spouses.[2]

Excluded topics

- Specific rules for the valuation of assets (values will be provided).
- Business property relief.
- Agricultural relief.
- Relief for the fall in value of lifetime gifts.
- Quick succession relief.
- Double tax relief.
- Variation of wills and disclaimers of legacies.
- Grossing up on death.
- Post mortem reliefs.
- Double charges legislation.

4. The use of exemptions in deferring and minimising inheritance tax liabilities

a) Understand and apply the following exemptions:
(i) small gifts exemption[2]
(ii) annual exemption[2]
(iii) normal expenditure out of income[2]
(iv) gifts in consideration of marriage[2]
(v) gifts between spouses.[2]

Excluded topics

- Gifts to charities.
- Gifts to political parties.
- Gifts for national purposes.

5. Payment of inheritance tax

a) Identify who is responsible for the payment of inheritance tax. [2]
b) Advise on the due date for payment of inheritance tax. [2]

Excluded topics

- Administration of inheritance tax other than listed above.
- The instalment option for the payment of tax.
- Interest and penalties.

F NATIONAL INSURANCE CONTRIBUTIONS

1. The scope of national insurance

a) Describe the scope of national insurance.[1]

2. Class 1 and Class 1A contributions for employed persons

a) Compute Class 1 NIC.[2]
b) Compute Class 1A NIC.[2]

Excluded topics

- The calculation of directors' national insurance on a month by month basis.
- Contracted out contributions.

3. Class 2 and Class 4 contributions for self-employed persons

a) Compute Class 2 NIC.[2]
b) Compute Class 4 NIC.[2]

Excluded topics

- The offset of trading losses against non-trading income.

G VALUE ADDED TAX

1. The scope of value added tax (VAT)

a) Describe the scope of VAT.[2]
b) List the principal zero-rated and exempt supplies.[1]

2. The VAT registration requirements

a) Recognise the circumstances in which a person must register for VAT.[2]
b) Explain the advantages of voluntary VAT registration.[2]
c) Explain the circumstances in which pre-registration input VAT can be recovered.[2]
d) Explain how and when a person can deregister for VAT.[1]
e) Explain the conditions that must be met for two or more companies to be treated as a group for VAT purposes, and the consequences of being so treated.[1]

3. The computation of VAT liabilities

a) Explain how VAT is accounted for and administered.[2]
b) Recognise the tax point when goods or services are supplied.[2]
c) List the information that must be given on a VAT invoice.[1]
d) Explain and apply the principles regarding the valuation of supplies.[2]
e) Recognise the circumstances in which input VAT is non-deductible.[2]
f) Compute the relief that is available for impairment losses on trade debts.[2]
g) Explain the circumstances in which the default surcharge, a penalty for an incorrect VAT return, and default interest will be applied.[1]
h) Explain the treatment of imports, exports and trade within the European Union.

Excluded topics

- VAT periods where there is a change of VAT rate.
- Partial exemption.
- In respect of property and land: leases, do-it-yourself builders, and a landlord's option to tax.
- Penalties apart from those listed in the study guide.

4. The effect of special schemes

a) Describe the cash accounting scheme, and recognise when it will be advantageous to use the scheme.[2]
b) Describe the annual accounting scheme, and recognise when it will be advantageous to use the scheme.[2]
c) Describe the flat rate scheme, and recognise when it will be advantageous to use the scheme.[2]

Excluded topics

- The second-hand goods scheme.
- The capital goods scheme.
- The special schemes for retailers.

H THE OBLIGATIONS OF TAX PAYERS AND/OR THEIR AGENTS

1. The systems for self-assessment and the making of returns

a) Explain and apply the features of the self-assessment system as it applies to individuals.[2]
b) Explain and apply the features of the self-assessment system as it applies to companies, including the use of iXBRL.[2]

2. The time limits for the submission of information, claims and payment of tax, including payments on account

a) Recognise the time limits that apply to the filing of returns and the making of claims.[2]
b) Recognise the due dates for the payment of tax under the self-assessment system.[2]
c) Compute payments on account and balancing payments/repayments for individuals.[2]

d) Explain how large companies are required to account for corporation tax on a quarterly basis.[2]

e) List the information and records that taxpayers need to retain for tax purposes.[1]

Excluded topics

- The payment of CGT by annual instalments.

3. The procedures relating to compliance checks, appeals and disputes

a) Explain the circumstances in which HM Revenue & Customs can make a compliance check into a self-assessment tax return.[2]

b) Explain the procedures for dealing with appeals and disputes.[1]

4. Penalties for non-compliance

a) Calculate late payment interest.[2]

b) State the penalties that can be charged.[2]

ACCA RESOURCES

ACCA provides a number of online resources to help students with their studies. They include detailed syllabus, study guides, examiners' reports, examiners' guidance, past exam papers, technical articles.

They can be found at http://www.accaglobal.com/en/student/qualification-resources/acca-qualification/acca-exams/f6-exams.html

SECTION A

THE UK TAX SYSTEM

STUDY GUIDE A1: THE OVERALL FUNCTION AND PURPOSE OF TAXATION IN A MODERN ECONOMY

Get Through Intro

Tax is a financial charge imposed by the government. The fundamental purpose of taxation is to finance government expenditure. Any money the government expends mostly comes from taxation.

You will agree that having to pay tax from your earnings is a painful experience. You must also have wondered why the government needs to collect taxes. What is the purpose behind collecting a part of our hard-earned money? Most of the tax payers feel that paying taxes is a waste of their money.

This Study Guide explains the various economic and social purposes of taxation. You are advised to understand the Study Guide thoroughly so that you can encourage your clients to pay taxes regularly and help your country to grow.

Learning Outcomes

a) Describe the purpose (economic, social etc.) of taxation in a modern economy.

Introduction

Case Study

This man is counting money. How happy he looks! If the income of this man is £100, some part of this £100 will go to the government in the form of tax on his income.

The fundamental purpose of taxation is to finance government expenditure. The tax system can be used for purposes other than raising revenue. In certain situations, imposing a tax may potentially increase efficiency if markets fail to price factors such as pollution or congestion, or the health costs of particular types of behaviour such as cigarette smoking. The government uses the process of taxation to encourage or discourage public activity in specific ways.

So, even if this man has to pay tax, i.e. money goes from his pocket, he should not feel bad because the government uses this tax money for the economic and social benefits of the country as a whole. Therefore, it is the taxpayer himself who ultimately enjoys the benefits of paying taxes.

(Source: http://comparativetaxation.treasury.gov.au/content/report/html)

---

1. Describe the purpose (economic, social etc) of taxation in a modern economy.[2]

[Learning Outcome a]

General introduction

The UK tax system has developed over the years as each successive government makes changes to the legislation to reflect its political objectives. The UK tax system is managed by Her Majesty's Revenue and Customs (HMRC). These are officers appointed by the government to administer and collect taxes. They are charged with the responsibility of implementing and enforcing the legislation of the government.

The imposition of taxation by governments withdraws money from the economy, and their expenditure returns the money to the economy. The overall position of the UK economy is affected by the tax policies and in turn will influence the success or failure of the country's economy.

The level of economic activity in the UK is affected by:

- the government's net position regarding taxation and expenditure, and
- public sector borrowing policies

1.1 Economic purpose of taxation

The government used to change its taxation policies in response to short-term changes in, for e.g., levels of employment, imports and exports. This was not always effective, and the current government prefers to plan ahead over a longer term. It publishes a plan for its expenditure over the next three years. This plan shows the proportion of the economy's resources that will be left for the private sector to make decisions on, after the government has fulfilled its spending plans.

The government's spending plans will influence the demand for health and education, the demand for consumer goods is influenced by private spending. Changing levels of demand will affect employment and profitability.

The government imposes taxation policies to:

1. Encourage

a) saving by individuals
b) taking risks in investments by entrepreneurs
c) entrepreneurs building their own businesses
d) donations to charities
e) investment in industrial buildings (e.g. factories, warehouses)

2. Discourage

a) Too many vehicles motoring on the road to minimise pollution etc.
b) smoking and alcohol

A government does not intend taxes to be neutral but to encourage or discourage certain activities. The objectives will change over time and successive governments. Increasingly the UK government tax policy is influenced by worldwide economic influences such as international defence policy and overseas aid.

1.2 Social purpose of taxation

Politicians use taxation policies to encourage social justice; however, there are many different ideas as to what constitutes social justice. The taxation system within the UK would suggest that it operates on an equitable basis. The taxation policies are intended to redistribute income and wealth. In a bid to direct funds away from the rich and towards the poor, the UK government adopts a process of redistributing wealth through its taxation policies. This is the Robin Hood Principle.

There are various principles to consider when debating the social justice of taxation:

1. The progressive / regressive principle

a) **Progressive:** a tax such as the income tax demonstrates the progressive principle. As income rises so does the proportion of tax i.e. the rate of tax rises as well as the amount of tax. This can be considered as just and fair, as the higher tax payments are made by those with higher incomes. Taxes which take a higher percentage of the incomes of higher income earners are said to be progressive.

b) **Regressive:** as income rises, the proportion of tax decreases, e.g. the tax on a packet of cigarettes remains the same, regardless of the income of the consumer. Regressive taxes can be justified as smokers are likely to require additional hospital care, which is the reason why they should contribute towards the cost of it. Taxes which take a higher proportion of the incomes from lower income earners are said to be regressive.

2. The income / capital / expenditure principle

a) **Income:** tax on income is just, because it is only paid by people who have higher income. People who have very low incomes can be taken out of the tax net by the use of personal allowances and effective tax rates.

b) **Capital:** tax on capital is just, as it ensures that people are not avoiding tax by having no income and living off the disposal of capital assets.

c) **Expenditure:** tax on expenditure is just, because it is only incurred by those who spend, not those who save.

3. The ability to pay / benefit principle

a) **Ability to pay:** tax is only paid by people who have the income to pay.

b) **Benefit:** people should only contribute to those types of government expenditure from which they are going to benefit.

SUMMARY

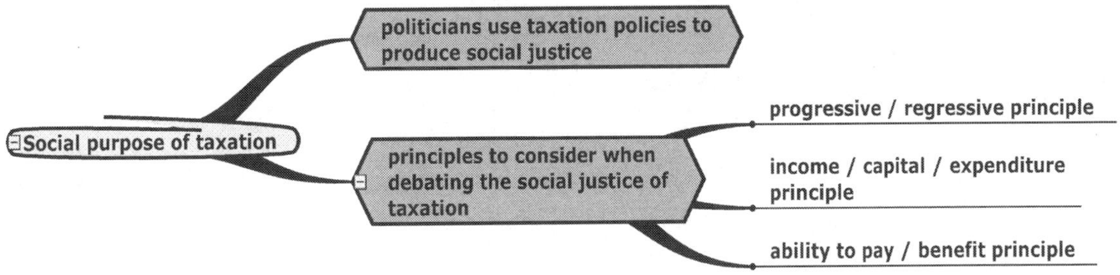

1.3 Environmental concerns

A specific use of taxation in influencing behaviour is in relation to the environment. These are commonly referred to as “Green Taxes”. Currently there are environmental concerns about renewable and non-renewable energy and global warming.

It is considered unlikely that individuals will contribute voluntarily to protect the environment as they are unlikely to be affected in their lifetime by the changes taking place. As a result, the government aims to protect the environment through taxation and spending policies.

These policies include:

a) **Taxation on vehicles and fuel provided by companies:** taxable benefits are based on the CO_2 emission.
b) **Climate change levy** which relates to the proportion of energy consumed by businesses.
c) **Landfill tax** charged on operators of landfill sites to encourage recycling.

These taxes are part of the UK’s Climate Change Programme published by the Government on 17 November 2000.

Tax policies are formulated with an aim to increase government revenues. They are framed on the basis of clear principles such as:

a) savings and investments
b) fairness
c) equality
d) enhancing work efficiency

SUMMARY

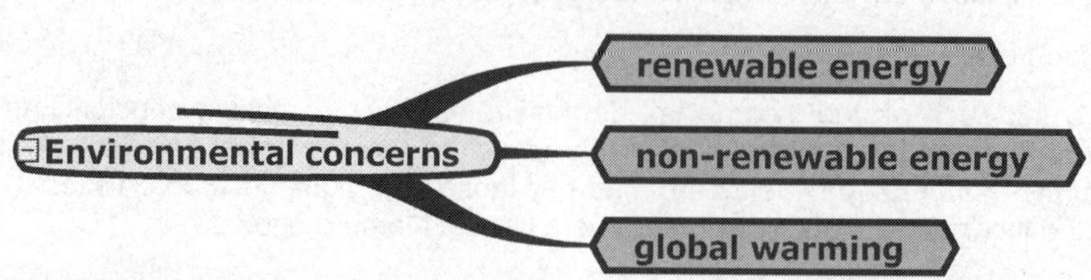

Quick Quiz

Fill in the blanks.

1. The UK tax system is managed by_______________.

Answer to Quick Quiz

1. Her Majesty's Revenue and Customs (HMRC).

Self Examination Question

Question 1

What are the various principles to consider when debating the social justice of taxation?

Answer to Self Examination Question

Answer to SEQ 1

The various principles to consider when debating the social justice of taxation are:

- the progressive / regressive principle
- the income / capital / expenditure principle
- the ability to pay / benefit principle

STUDY GUIDE A2: DIFFERENT TYPES OF TAXES

Get Through Intro

In this Study Guide we will discuss the different types of taxes which are levied on the public. It is essential to have knowledge of the nature of taxes because the law provides various provisions relating to deductible expenses, exemptions and different rates of taxes etc.

This Study Guide introduces you to capital and revenue taxes so that the relevant provisions in other Study Guides are easily understood.

This Study Guide also introduces you to the core difference between direct and indirect taxation.

As a tax consultant you should have thorough knowledge of the types of taxes and also the difference between direct and indirect taxes so that the chargeability of tax can be calculated accordingly.

Learning Outcomes

a) Identify the different types of capital and revenue tax.
b) Explain the difference between direct and indirect taxation.

Introduction

Case Study

Taxation is a mechanism used by the UK government to raise funds to pay for public spending in providing basic amenities in the UK, such as social welfare and health care systems.

Taxation is a compulsory charge imposed by the government on income, expenditure or assets owned by individuals and companies. The method of raising tax is determined by statute and case law. It is administered by Her Majesty's Revenue and Custom's (HMRC).

The taxes of note can be split into two categories as follows:

Direct taxes: either deducted at source or paid directly to the tax authorities.

Examples of direct taxes are Income Tax, Capital Gains Tax and Inheritance Tax (all paid by **individuals**), and Corporation Tax (paid by **companies**).

Indirect taxes: charged when a taxpayer buys an item, and are paid to the vendor as part of the purchase price.

Examples of indirect taxes include VAT (value-added tax), stamp duty, customs duties and the excise duties levied on alcohol, tobacco and petrol.

---

1. Identify the different types of capital and revenue tax.[1]

[Learning Outcome a]

The government raises revenue from many different types of taxes. The main taxes employed within the UK are as follows:

Tax	Suffered by
Revenue taxes	
Income tax	Individuals Partnerships
Corporation tax	Companies
National Insurance contributions	Individuals Partners Employers Self employed
VAT	Final consumer
Capital taxes	
Capital gains tax	Individuals Partnerships (Companies pay corporation tax on their gains)
Inheritance tax	Individuals

1.1 Revenue Tax

1. Income tax

It is a tax levied on the income of an individual.

Income can be from any sources such as:
a) income from earnings (e.g. employment income / trade profit)
b) income from pensions
c) income from other benefits (e.g. rental income)
d) income from savings (e.g. interest income)
e) income from investments (e.g. dividend income)

Income Tax is calculated on earned income, i.e. from employment, and unearned income, i.e. income from savings. Income from various sources is pooled together and tax is charged on the aggregate income after deducting the relevant personal allowance. Taxpayers, who are employed, pay income tax on their earnings under the statutory Pay As You Earn (PAYE) scheme.

2. Corporation tax

It is the tax payable by companies on their 'chargeable profits'. There are numerous provisions relating to corporation taxes which are dealt with at length in section D.

3. National insurance Contributions (NIC)

After the Second World War, National Insurance Contributions were introduced to fund the establishment of retirement pensions, sickness benefit and the National Health System. National Insurance Contributions are a system of taxes which are paid by employees and employers on the basis of their weekly earnings. The money generated is used to provide social security.

4. VAT

VAT is Value Added Tax. It is the tax which is paid on the value added. This tax is levied at each stage of production. VAT is a consumption tax paid by customers in addition to the price of the product.

1.2 Capital taxes

1. Capital Gains Tax

When a person sells an asset that is in his / her possession, the profit arising from such sale is chargeable to tax as capital gains.

Therefore, capital gains tax liability arises when a 'chargeable person' makes a chargeable disposal of a chargeable asset.

Example

Adam sells his business asset at a profit of £5,000. So, the amount of profit i.e. £5,000 is chargeable to capital gains tax.

2. Inheritance Tax

When a person is in possession of an asset and on his death the ownership of such an asset is transferred, the value of the transferred asset is chargeable to inheritance tax, subject to certain tax free thresholds.

Therefore, inheritance tax liability arises when the value of chargeable property is transferred by a chargeable person.

Such tax liability also arises when, during the lifetime of the owner, the asset is given as a gift to any other person unless the person holds the asset for a period of seven years or more, in which case it becomes an exempt transfer.

SUMMARY

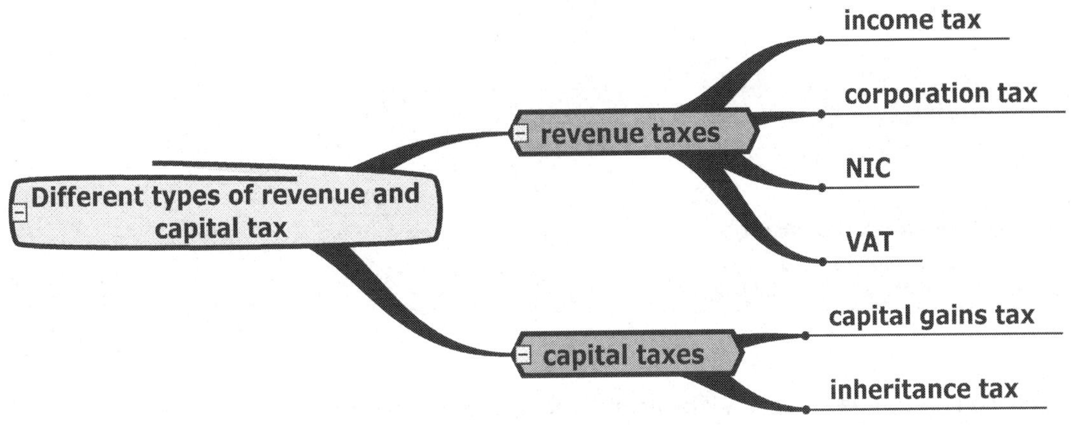

…in the difference between direct and indirect taxation.[2]

[Learning Outcome b]

In order to function effectively, the tax system divides taxes into the following two types:

1. direct taxes
2. indirect taxes.

2.1 Direct Taxes are either deducted at source or paid directly to the tax authorities.

- Tax on income or capital.
- Tax imposed directly on taxpayers (individual / company).
- Direct taxes can be progressive i.e. the more you earn, the higher rate you pay.
- Examples
  - ✓ Income tax
  - ✓ Corporation tax
  - ✓ National insurance contributions

2.2 Indirect Taxes are charged when a taxpayer buys an item, and are paid to the vendor as part of the purchase price. The vendor in turn passes the tax element on to the government, acting as a collector of tax.

- Tax on what people spend, rather than on what they earn.
- People with low incomes pay a higher proportion of their income on indirect taxes than wealthier people.
- Example: VAT, stamp duty, duties levied on tobacco, alcohol and petrol.

Quick Quiz

1. State whether the following are Capital or Revenue taxes

   (a) Inheritance tax
   (b) Income tax
   (c) Value Added tax
   (d) Capital Gains tax
   (e) National Insurance contributions
   (f) Corporation tax

Answer to Quick Quiz

1.

(a) Capital tax
(b) Revenue tax
(c) Revenue tax
(d) Capital tax
(e) Revenue tax
(f) Revenue tax

Self Examination Question

Question 1

What are the different sources of income?

Answer to Self Examination Question

Answer to SEQ 1

Income tax is levied on the income earned by an individual. The different sources of income are

(a) income from employment
(b) income from pensions
(c) income from trading
(d) income from other benefits
(e) income from savings
(f) income from investments

STUDY GUIDE A3: PRINCIPAL SOURCES OF REVENUE LAW AND PRACTICE

Get Through Intro

In this Study Guide we will discuss different sources of revenue law.

It is essential to have knowledge of the overall structure of the UK tax system because it is the government bodies that collect tax from the general public.

This Study Guide introduces you to way the UK tax system interacts with other tax jurisdictions.

As a tax consultant you should have a thorough knowledge of the overall structure of the UK tax system so that tax matters can be effectively handled with government authorities.

Learning Outcomes

a) Describe the overall structure of the UK tax system.
b) State the different sources of revenue law.
c) Appreciate the interaction of the UK tax system with that of other tax jurisdictions.

Introduction

Tax law is the body of law that establishes how taxes are imposed and regulated by the government. Taxes are used to produce government revenue and support government programmes and initiatives. While a variety of taxes exist, the most significant taxes within tax law include income tax, social security tax, estate and gift taxes, property tax and value added tax.

In this Study Guide, we will study the overall structure of the UK tax system.

1. Describe the overall structure of the UK tax system.[1]

[Learning Outcome a]

Diagram 1: Overall structure of the UK tax system

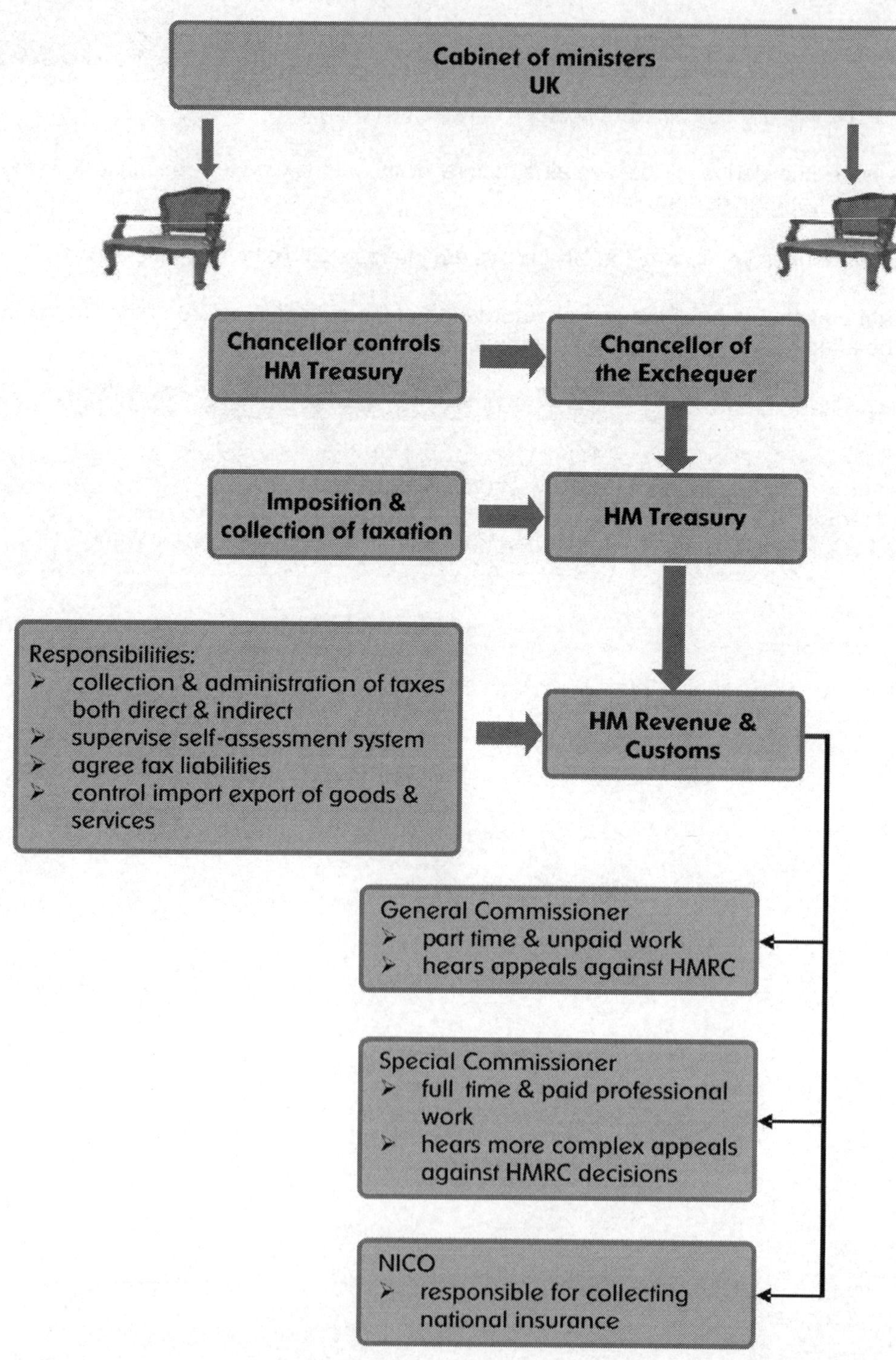

2. State the different sources of revenue law.[1]

[Learning Outcome b]

The sources of revenue law are
1. Statute law
2. Case law
3. Statements and documents issued by HMRC

1. Statute law

a) Acts of parliament contain the basic rules of the UK taxation system.
b) This legislation is altered and added to by the Annual Finance Act and consolidating statutes.
c) Some detailed legislation is made by Statutory Instruments, which do not necessitate the parliamentary procedure required to pass an Act of Parliament.

2. Case law

Case law serves to interpret and clarify statute and is continually evolving.

3. Statements and documents issued by HMRC

HMRC issues the following documents to explain how the law is to be implemented in practice:

a) Statements of practice set out how the law will apply in practice.
b) Extra-statutory concessions detail circumstances under which the statute will not be applied or whether it would be unfair to do so.
c) Mutual Assistance Recovery Directive (MARD) lays down detailed rules to implement mutual assistance with other member states to exchange the relevant information and to ensure that all the taxes are properly collected.
d) Press releases and explanatory notes giving the views and interpretations of the inspectors.
e) Internal guidance manuals commonly known as the inspectors manuals.
f) Pamphlets.

A good source of up to date information can be found at www.HMRC.gov.uk. This is the website for Her Majesty Revenue and Customs.

SUMMARY

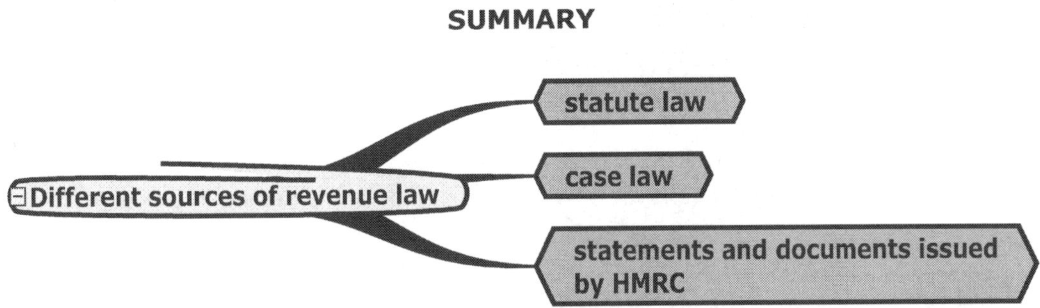

3. Appreciate the interaction of the UK tax system with that of other tax jurisdictions.[2]

[Learning Outcome c]

Parliamentary supremacy has been affected by membership of the European Union. In certain circumstances European law has supremacy over domestic law.

It is not intended that each member state has a common system of taxation, but states may agree to pass laws which provide a common code of taxation in a certain area of taxation, as they have done with VAT. These are known as Directives and set down a common approach to a specific area of taxation.

The UK must follow EU treaties which promise the freedom of movement of workers and capital and to establish business operations in the UK. The European Court of Justice has held that taxation provisions which show prejudice against non-residents are not allowed under European law. Information sharing between European Union revenue authorities takes place.

Double Tax Treaties

The UK has agreements with a number of countries which avoid income being taxed twice. For e.g., an individual earns income in France, and pays tax on the income under the local taxation rules. The individual returns the earned income to the UK where upon the double tax treaty prevents the income being taxed for a second time.

Quick Quiz

1. What are the different sources of revenue law?
2. What is the relevance of Case Law with regard to taxation practice?
3. Where would you look to find up to date press releases or publications relating to taxation?
4. What is MARD?

Answers to Quick Quiz

1. The different sources of revenue law are

   (a) Statute law
   (b) Case law
   (c) Statements and documents issued by HMRC.

2. The case law provides clarification of the statute and demonstrates the practical application of the legislation.

3. We can find up to date press releases or publications relating to taxation on the website www.HMRC.gov.uk

4. MARD is Mutual assistance recovery directive issued by HMRC which gives the detailed rules for mutual assistance among the member states for recovery of taxes.

Self Examination Questions

Question 1

List the documents which are issued by HMRC to explain how the law is to be implemented in practice.

Question 2

What are the main responsibilities of HMRC?

Answers to Self Examination Questions

Answer to SEQ 1

HMRC issues the following documents to explain how the law is to be implemented in practice:

(a) Statements of practice
(b) Extra-statutory concessions
(c) Mutual assistance recovery directive (MARD)
(d) Press releases and explanatory notes
(e) Internal guidance manuals
(f) Pamphlets

Answer to SEQ 2

The main responsibilities of HMRC are:

(a) collection & administration of taxes both direct & indirect
(b) supervise self-assessment system
(c) agree tax liabilities
(d) control import export of goods & services

STUDY GUIDE A4: TAX AVOIDANCE AND TAX EVASION

Get Through Intro

In this Study Guide we will discuss the meaning and difference between tax avoidance and tax evasion.

It is essential to know the difference between the two because the law makes various provisions relating to the taxability of different types of income. You should be aware of the risk associated with tax evasion and avoidance. Committing either one of these is likely to have different consequences.

This Study Guide highlights the importance of understanding the difference between the two, because tax avoidance is permitted by law but tax evasion is illegal.

As a tax consultant, you should have thorough knowledge of the difference between them so that your client does not unwittingly commit tax evasion. In addition, you should advise your client on how to effectively and legally reduce the tax liability.

Learning Outcomes

a) Explain the difference between tax avoidance and tax evasion.
b) Explain the need for an ethical and professional approach.

Introduction

For many years individuals have found imaginative ways of avoiding liability to tax. Large companies employ highly skilled tax planners in a bid to legally reduce their overall tax liability. There have been many instances of individual's under-declaring their income to reduce their tax liability. The question is one of whether these activities constitute tax avoidance or tax evasion.

Tax evasion is a deliberate act by an individual or company to mislead, misinform or otherwise mis-state their tax position to HMRC in order to evade taxes. Tax evasion is illegal and is punishable by hefty fines and imprisonment.

Tax avoidance is legal. It involves the arrangement of individuals' or companies' tax affairs in a way which reduces the tax liability. For example, using incentivised tax savings schemes such as ISA's or Enterprise Investment Schemes. More complex tax avoidance examples would include establishing an offshore company in a tax haven or by forming a limited company to avail of more favourable tax deductions.

---

1. Explain the difference between tax avoidance and tax evasion.[1]

[Learning Outcome a]

Tax avoidance is any **legal way** of reducing the amount of tax payable – involving a sensible arrangement of the taxpayers' affairs so as to minimise the liability to tax. All activities must remain legal at all times. It is the **utilisation of "tax loopholes"** within the legislation in an ingenious way, thereby affording the tax payer, legally, a favourable tax position.

Tax evasion is the intention **to deliberately mislead** HMRC and is illegal. It involves dishonest conduct or behaviour by the taxpayer.

It could consist of:

- providing HMRC with false information
- not giving HMRC information to which they are entitled
- concealing a source of income

SUMMARY

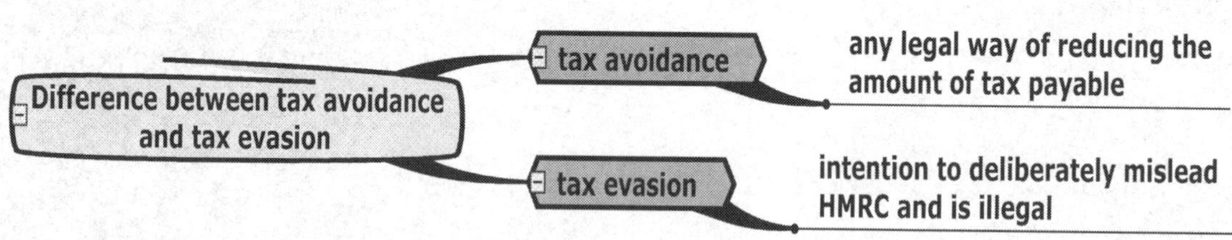

2. Explain the need for an ethical and professional approach.[2]

[Learning Outcome b]

An accountant has responsibilities to

1. individual clients
2. employer
3. HMRC

In addition, he has a responsibility to act in the public interest.

From time to time these duties may conflict. Questions of judgement may be involved in resolving these conflicts. An accountant may suspect that a taxpayer, for whom he is acting, is not being honest with regard to declarations of income or in the provision of information. The accountant will have to act with integrity and uphold the following Code of Ethics and Conduct.

The Code of Ethics and Conduct provides a framework within which to make these judgements.

The Code requires **members to comply** with the following **principles**:

a) integrity
b) objectivity
c) professional competence and due care
d) confidentiality
e) professional behaviour.

Quick Quiz

1. Which is legal and permitted, tax avoidance or tax evasion?

Answer to Quick Quiz

1. Tax avoidance is legal and permitted whereas tax evasion is illegal.

Self Examination Question

Question 1

What are the principles which a member has to comply with?

Answer to Self Examination Question

Answer to SEQ 1

The Code of ethics requires members to comply with the following principles:

(a) integrity
(b) objectivity
(c) professional competence and due care
(d) confidentiality
(e) professional behaviour

SECTION B

INCOME TAX LIABILITIES

B1

STUDY GUIDE B1: THE SCOPE OF INCOME TAX

Get Through Intro

The **residence** of an individual is **very important** because it **determines the income chargeable to UK tax**.

An individual's **nationality makes no difference** when determining **his / her residential status in the UK.** This means that no matter which country a person is a citizen of, if the individual satisfies the conditions of being a resident of the UK, they have to pay UK tax for that year.

Individuals who are **resident in the UK** for any tax year are liable to **pay UK tax on their entire income** for that year i.e. on their UK income and also on their overseas income.

This Study Guide explains the basic conditions which determine the residential status of an individual and also the circumstances in which an individual is said to be ordinarily resident in the UK.

A tax payer should consider the effect of his residence and ordinary residence on his tax liability as this is a major factor in an individual's tax planning. You need to understand this concept thoroughly for success in the examination, and for success in your professional life after you become ACCA qualified.

Learning Outcomes

a) Explain how the residence of an individual is determined.

Introduction

Residence is a question of fact, and usually requires physical presence in a country. In today's increasingly global business environment, there are a considerable number of individuals who usually live in the UK but make frequent and regular business trips abroad which may affect their residence. It is possible that an individual is resident in more than one country for tax purposes.

Determining the residential status of individuals is very important to decide their tax liability. UK residents are liable to income tax on worldwide income, non-UK residents are liable to income tax only on the income generated in the UK.

This Study Guide explains the various conditions which determine whether a person is a resident of the UK.

1. Explain how the residence of an individual is determined.[1]

[Learning Outcome a]

The basic conditions for residency are as follows:

1. An individual who is **physically present in the UK for at least 183 days or more (> half of 365 days)** during a **tax year** (excluding days of arrival and departure) is deemed to be resident in the UK **for the whole of that tax year**. This can be a single continuous period, or spread over a number of visits during the tax year.

2. An individual, who **is present in the UK for an average of 91 days or more in a year, for four or more consecutive tax years**, is deemed to be a resident in the UK from the earlier of:
   a) the start of the fifth tax year, or
   b) the start of a tax year where an intention to continue long-term visits is apparent.

The period of four years is reduced to three years for a person who is emigrating from the UK.

An individual fulfilling **either of these conditions** is a **resident** of the UK for tax purposes.

Tip

A UK resident is liable to income tax on **worldwide income** and a **non-UK resident** is liable to income tax **only on his / her UK income.**

Test Yourself 1

Pearl, has lived in Germany her entire life, arrives in the UK on 15 April 2012 and stays there until 15 March 2013. On that date she goes back to Germany. What is her residential status for 2012-13?

It is important to note that the concept of **UK residence** normally applies **to a whole tax year**. In other words, an individual is deemed to be a UK resident for the whole tax year or none of it. It is usually **not possible to apportion a tax year** into periods of residence and non-residence.

Income tax is charged for a **tax year**. The tax year runs **from 6 April to the following 5 April.**

SUMMARY

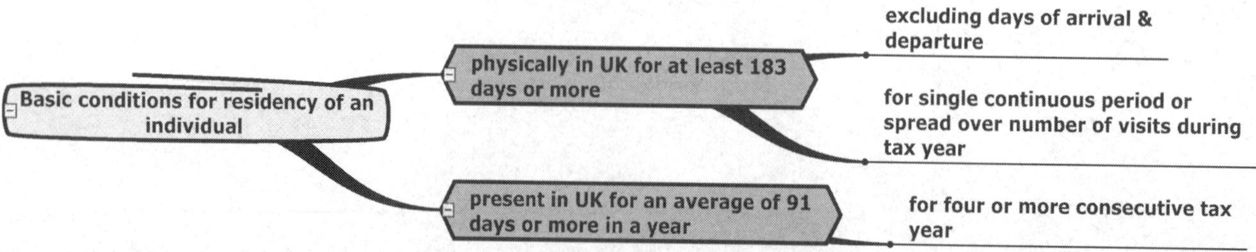

Income tax is payable by an individual on his / her total income which comprises of income from different sources. In one tax year he / she may have, for e.g., employment income, property income and dividends – all these are chargeable to income tax.

In a nutshell, we can say that an individual's taxable income is the total of the different types of income. A personal tax computation of an individual's total income may be presented in the following format.

Computation of taxable income of an individual

	Non-saving Income	Saving Income (excluding dividends)	Dividend Income	Total
	£	£	£	£
Income from employment	X	-	-	X
Income from business	X	-	-	X
Income from UK dividends	-	-	X	X
Property income	X	-	-	X
Bank interest	-	X	-	X
Total income	**X**	**X**	**X**	**X**
Less: Loss relief and interest payments	(X)	-	-	(X)
Net income	**X**	**X**	**X**	**X**
Less: Personal allowance	(X)	-	-	(X)
Taxable income	**X**	**X**	**X**	**X**

Computation of income tax liability of an individual

	£
Tax borne (Using Tax Tables)	X
Total tax liability	**X**
Less: Tax credit on dividends	(X)
Less: Tax deducted at source	(X)
Tax payable	**X**

In order to calculate an individual's income tax liability, we need to learn how each different type of income is taxed. Therefore, income of an individual includes various types of income which are covered in Section B of the Study Guide:

1	Income from employment:	this source of income is explained in Study Guide.
2	Income from business:	this source of income is explained in Study Guide.
3	Income from dividends:	this source of income is explained in Study Guide.
4	Property income:	this source of income is explained in Study Guide.
5	Interest income:	this source of income is explained in Study Guide.

After aggregating all the income, the appropriate rate of tax is applied to calculate the final tax liability. The different sources of income may attract tax at different rates, which is why we show the income split into the three main sources. The calculation of income tax liability is explained in detail in Study Guide B5.

Section B deals with the calculation of an individual's tax liability for the year.

Answer to Test Yourself

Answer to TY 1

Pearl is a **resident in the UK** for the tax year 2012-13 as she has spent more than 183 days in the UK during the year (15 April to 15 March = 11 months i.e. more than 183 days).

Quick Quiz

State in the following cases the residential status of an individual

1. Konjit, a resident of Kenya, arrives in the UK on 24 August 2012. She stays till 4 April 2013, and then returns to Kenya.

2. Gladius is a UK resident, but for the year 2012-13 she was in India.

Answers to Quick Quiz

1. **Konjit will be classified as a UK resident,** because an individual who is **physically present in the UK for at least 183 days** during a tax year (excluding days of arrival and departure) is deemed to be a resident of the UK **for the whole tax year**. Konjit is present in the UK for (24 August 12 to 4 April 13) 222 days i.e. more than 183 days.

2. **Gladius is a non-resident** because although she is ordinarily resident, she is absent from the UK for the whole of 2012-13, and therefore she is not resident for that year.

Self Examination Questions

Question 1

Why is residential status important?

Question 2

In what circumstances will an individual be treated as a UK resident for UK tax purposes?

Answers to Self Examination Questions

Answer to SEQ 1

Liability to income tax depends on whether an individual is resident in the UK. An individual is broadly liable to income tax on worldwide income if he / she is a UK resident. On the other hand, he / she is liable to income tax only on his / her UK income if he / she is non-UK resident.

Answer to SEQ 2

An individual will be treated as resident for a tax year if:

1. he / she is in the UK for 183 days or more in the tax year,

   OR

2. his / her visits to the UK average 91 days or more per tax year for four or more consecutive tax years.

STUDY GUIDE B2: INCOME FROM EMPLOYMENT

Get Through Intro

Employment income is an income in the form of salary or wages. Legislation allows an employee to make **various deductions** from the employment income when determining the amount subject to tax.

This Study Guide discusses how employment income is assessed to tax, the various deductions allowed by the legislation, the PAYE system and the rules relating to tax deducted under the PAYE system.

As an aspiring tax consultant, you are expected to understand all the employment income aspects thoroughly, as you will be required to advise your clients on their employees. Moreover, you will want to ensure that the tax charged on your salary is calculated correctly.

Learning Outcomes

a) Recognise the factors that determine whether an engagement is treated as employment or self-employment.
b) Recognise the basis of assessment for employment income.
c) Compute the income assessable.
d) Recognise the allowable deductions, including travelling expenses.
e) Discuss the use of the statutory approved mileage allowances.
f) Explain the PAYE system.
g) Identify P11D employees.
h) Compute the amount of benefits assessable.
i) Explain the purpose of a dispensation from HM Revenue & Customs.
j) Explain how charitable giving can be made through a payroll deduction scheme.

Introduction

Case Study

Cynthia is a fashion designer. During the year 2012-13, she started working for Beauty Designs Ltd. The terms of her contract include:

1. Beauty Designs Ltd will pay Cynthia a fixed fee of £20,000 for each contract she works on. She is under no obligation to accept all of the contracts offered. Cynthia reports directly to the MD of the company.

2. Cynthia will procure the equipment and materials required for her work; the company does not provide her with any such tools of the trade.

3. Cynthia will visit the company only when she has a meeting with Suzy, the MD of the company regarding the patterns and style of dresses; otherwise she works from home at her convenience.

Cynthia is unsure whether she will be treated as employed or self-employed.

This Study Guide explains the various factors that are considered in determining whether an individual, such as Cynthia, is employed or self-employed. It then goes on to explain how an employed person is taxed.

1. Recognise the factors that determine whether an engagement is treated as employment or self-employment.[2]

[Learning Outcome a]

Usually it is very clear whether a particular person is employed or self-employed. However, sometimes there are borderline cases. For example, in the case of an employee with a number of part-time jobs it is difficult to decide whether they are employed or self-employed. For tax purposes they will usually prefer to be self-employed, because a self-employed person enjoys the followings tax advantages over an employed person:

- A much **wider range** of expenses are allowed against the income of self-employed people, than against the income of employees.

- Self-employed people pay their tax later, as they pay their income tax by **instalments.** However, in the case of employees, tax is **deducted at source** under the PAYE system. (This will be explained in more detail later in this Study Guide).

- An individual's employment status also affects his national insurance contribution. Self-employed people can pay **less** National Insurance contributions than employees (because self-employed people are not eligible for some statutory benefits, such as sick pay or maternity pay).

One important test to be applied in deciding whether a person is employed or self-employed is the nature of the contract **between the taxpayer and the person who is paying for the work done.**

Employment involves a contract of service whereas self-employment involves a contract for services.

The **factors** that help to determine whether an engagement is treated as employment or self-employment are as below. You need to consider the relationship as a whole; the factors are not simply a checklist.

1.1 Distinction between an employee and a self-employed person

Basis of distinction	Employee	Self-employed person
Control	Employees are under the control of the employer to a higher degree. They have to report to work on specific dates, given times and have to obey the instructions of the employer to deliver the result expected by the employer.	Self-employed persons are not subject to anyone else's control. They take their own decisions regarding their work. They have a greater degree of freedom to decide and plan their work and schedule their time and the manner in which they will work.
Financial risk involved	Employees do not invest their own capital in the business, so there is no financial risk for them. Even if an organisation incurs a loss, it has an obligation to pay salaries to employees.	Self-employed persons may not be paid if their performance does not meet the expectation of their customer. They also run the risk of losing their capital if the business fails as they invest their own capital in the business. However, they can increase their profit by sound management (e.g. work faster, earn more).
Equipment	Equipment necessary to carry out the work is provided to an employee by the employer.	Self-employed persons have to use their own equipment.
Substitution	An employment contract is personal to that individual; they cannot instruct someone else to perform their services.	Generally, self-employed persons can allocate or delegate the work to their staff, although they remain responsible for the work.
Work correction	If there are any mistakes in an employee's work, the employee makes the corrections during their working hours.	A self-employed person is responsible for putting right any unsatisfactory work, at their own expense and in their own time.
Holidays	Employees are entitled to paid annual leave.	Self-employed persons do not get paid annual leave; they get remuneration only for the days they work.
Number of persons contracted with	Normally, employees work for a single employer company or firm.	Self-employed people generally deal with more than one company at a time.
Employment protection	An employee is protected under the contract of service i.e. there is a minimum period of notice.	There is no employment protection for a self-employed person.
Mode of payment	Employees are paid weekly / monthly / yearly.	Self-employed individuals are paid per contract.
Position	An employee is an integral part of the business.	Self-employed individuals are not an integral part of the business.
Obligation	Employees are under an obligation to accept the work allotted to them by the employer.	There is no obligation on self-employed individuals to accept every project offered to them.
Wording used in the contact	According to the wording of the contract, there is a contract **of service** between both the parties.	According to the wording of the contract, there is a contract **for services** between both the parties.

Example

The terms self-employed and an employee differ in a very simple way. The conceptual difference is easily understood by considering the example of hiring a plumber.

1. If your project moves from one stage to another then the customer needs to consider and source appropriate expertise for different project phases.

Continued on the next page

ers will agree a convenient time to complete the work, which indicates that they are self-employed.

mers have to specify what problems need fixing. There is no obligation on the plumber to agree to do ork, which indicates self-employment.

4. Customers do not have to pay towards holiday entitlement, which also indicates self-employment.
5. Plumbers will invoice customers for specific project jobs. There is no ongoing contractual arrangement for services. If there is no work available, there is no liability to pay the plumber. This indicates self-employment.
6. Customers don't supervise plumbers; the customer has made a contract "for" the specialist services provided by the plumber; a contract for services is usually self-employment.
7. The plumber carries all their own tools and equipment as they need them for running their business, indicating self-employment.
8. All financial risks are borne by the plumber in so far as maximizing profit by working quickly, or incurring costs to correct errors.

McMillan Byte is a computer programmer who started working for Web-Designs Ltd on 6 April 2012.

The following information is available in respect of the year ended 5 April 2013:

1. McMillan received income of £60,000 from Web-Designs Ltd. He is paid a fixed fee for each contract that he works on, and each contract lasts an average of two weeks. McMillan is under no obligation to accept any of the contracts offered, and carries out the work under his own control. He is, however obliged to do the work personally.
2. McMillan works from home, and never visits the premises of Web-Designs Ltd. He uses one room of his private residence exclusively for business purposes (there are five rooms in his house).
3. McMillan's telephone bills are £500 per quarter. This is £400 per quarter higher than they were prior to the commencement of his working from home.
4. McMillan is required to provide all of his own equipment.

Required:

From the information above, list the factors that indicate that McMillan is self-employed.

2. Recognise the basis of assessment for employment income.[2]

[Learning Outcome b]

2.1 What is employment income?

Income that a person receives as the holder of an office or employment is charged to income tax as "employment income". The salary, wages or remuneration arising under a **contract of service** received by the employee in respect of employment is considered income from employment. The "earnings" received in any one tax year include the employee's earnings plus the "cash equivalent" of any taxable non-monetary benefits.

Earnings include

1. Bonus
2. Commission
3. Fees
4. Round sum expenses allowances
5. Payments on the termination of employment
6. Pensions arising from the employment and
7. Benefits

It is important to note that **all income generated from employment** is considered employment income i.e. income which is not received directly from the employer, but received as a result of employment, is considered employment income.

Example

A restaurant waiter receives £2 as a tip from a customer. The employer does not **directly** pay this income. However, he has received this income as a **result** of his employment. This income is, therefore, taxable as employment income for the waiter.

The income of directors is also treated as employment income.

2.2 When is employment income taxable?

An individual's employment income for a tax year is the income actually received in that year i.e. income from employment is taxable on a **receipt basis.**

Example

An employee is awarded a bonus for the year ended 31 March 2012. The amount of the bonus depends on the company's results for that year. The company's accounts for the year ended 31 March 2012 are finalised on 31 October 2012, and the employee's bonus of £5,000 is paid on 30 November 2012.

The bonus relates to 2011-12, however, as it is received in 2012-13 the bonus is taxable in full in 2012-13.

2.3 When is employment income received?

Income from employment is treated as received on the **earlier** of:

1. **For individual employees**

a) The date when payment is made. For example, the date when the salary cheque is received.

b) The date when an employee becomes entitled to payment.

Example

Stuart Anderson, an employee, is entitled to a bonus for the year ended 31 December 2012. The amount of the bonus depends upon the company's financial results for that year. The company's accounts for the year ended 31 December 2012 are finalised on 31 March 2013, and Stuart's bonus of £5,000 is paid on 7 April 2013.

Here,

- the employee became entitled to the bonus on 31 March 2013 i.e. during the tax year 2012-13.
- the employee received payment on 7 April 2013 i.e. during the tax year 2013-14.

Stuart became entitled to the bonus before the bonus was paid to him. Hence, the bonus received by Stuart will be treated as received during the tax year 2012-13.

2.4 For directors

Bonuses, Salaries and Director fees are treated as received on the earlier of:

a) The date that the earning (bonus) has been paid.

b) The date that entitlement to the earning (bonus) arises.

a) and b) are the same as the ones discussed for the employees above.

c) The date on which the income is **credited** to the director in the accounting records of the company.

d) The end of the period of accounts, if the director's income for that period is determined **by then**.

e) The date on which the amount is determined, **after the end** of the company's **period of accounts.**

SP International Ltd is an advertising company. It prepares its accounts up to 31 March every year. It appointed David as its director on 1 January 2013. His remuneration was agreed to be £60,000 per calendar year, payable monthly in arrears in equal instalments.

On 31 March 2013, the company accounted for £15,000 in David's account showing it as payable. On 2 April 2013, it was decided to increase David's remuneration to £84,000 per calendar year retrospectively. The company had actually paid £12,000 to David on 5 May 2013.

Required:

When is David's employment income treated as received and how much is it?

The income of a director is considered to be received **at earliest of** the following:

1. The date on which the income is actually **received** by the director i.e. **5 May 2013** when David received £12,000.
2. The date on which the **right to receive** the income is established i.e. on **31 March 2013** when the right to receive £15,000 (3/12 x £60,000) crystallises.
3. The date on which the income is **credited** to the director in the records of the company i.e. on **31 March 2013** when £15,000 is credited to his account in the company's records.
4. The end of the period of accounts, if the director's income for that period is determined **before the end of the period of accounts** of the company i.e. on **31 March 2013** as before that date, it was decided to pay him £5,000 per month. Hence £15,000 is income to be treated as received on the accounts date.
5. The date on which the director's income is determined, if the director's income is determined **after the end** of the company's **period of accounts** i.e. on **2 April 2013** when David's remuneration was increased to £84,000 retrospectively. The increase of £24,000 is determined after the end of the company's period of account. **Hence on 2 April 2013, he is entitled to a salary of £21,000 (3/12 x £84,000).**

The **earliest date among all above dates is 31 March 2013.** The amount to be treated as income on that date is **£15,000.**

The remaining **£6,000** will be taxed as income on **2 April 2013**.

The receipt basis does not apply to pension income. Pensions are taxed on an **accrual basis.**

2.5 Some other relevant points

1. An individual is taxed on his net taxable earnings for a tax year. Net taxable earnings are equal to **total taxable earnings less total allowable deductions.**

Net taxable earnings = Total taxable earnings – Total allowable deductions

1. Deductions are allowed to the **maximum** extent of the amount of **taxable earnings** i.e. deductions cannot create a loss; they can only reduce the net taxable earnings to nil.
2. If there is more than one employment in the year, separate calculations are required for each employment.

Example

Pearl worked for three companies during the tax year 2012-13. In this situation, separate calculations of earnings and deductions are required. Her net earnings from all these companies are to be calculated as follows:

Particulars	Company A £	Company B £	Company C £
Period of work	10 April 2012 to 15 June 2012	7 July 2012 to 5 December 2012	25 December 2012 to 15 March 2013
Total earnings	1,250	1,620	1,480
Less: Deductions			
Donations to charity made under the payroll deduction scheme operated by an employer	(310)	(180)	-
Mileage allowance	(120)	(340)	(120)
Contribution to approved pension scheme	(45)	-	(65)
Net earnings	**775**	**1,100**	**1,295**

SUMMARY

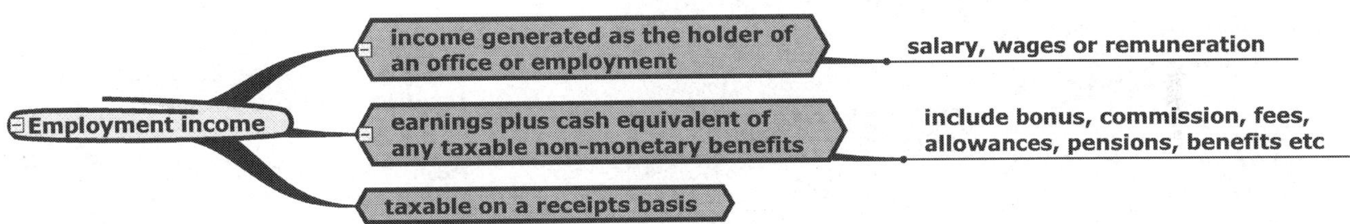

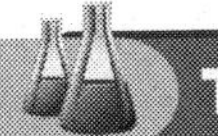

Test Yourself 2

Jo received a basic salary of £35,700 in 2012-13. She also receives an annual bonus (received in January) based on her performance in the previous calendar year.

Bonuses for the last three calendar years are as follows:

	£
Year ended 31 December 2010 (received in January 2011)	5,300
Year ended 31 December 2011 (received in January 2012)	6,550
Year ended 31 December 2012 (received in January 2013)	7,100

Required:

Compute her total income in 2012-13.

Test Yourself 3

State the rules that determine when a bonus paid to a director is treated as being received for tax purpose.

3. Identify P11D employees.[1]

[Learning Outcome g]

Employment income includes the value of benefits, i.e. income received in the form of goods and services, rather than money. Employees are divided into two classes for the purpose of assessing benefits:

1. **P11D (higher paid) employees:** employees whose earnings are £8,500 or more are called "higher paid employees". P11D employees are taxed on any benefit regardless of whether or not it is convertible into cash. They are assessed on the marginal cost incurred by the employer providing that benefit.

Directors and employees who earn £8,500 or above are referred to as P11D employees because their benefits are reported to HMRC on form P11D.

P11D employees **are those who:**

a) earn at least £8,500 per annum: for calculating this £8,500,

- all earnings are totalled, including benefits valued as if the employee were a P11D employee,
- no expenses are to be deducted from earnings except contributions to an occupational pension scheme or to a payroll-giving scheme.

b) Company directors: company directors are P11D employees regardless of their earnings unless they:

- earn less than £8,500 per annum and work full-time **AND**
- have no material interest in the company i.e. control not more than 5% of ordinary share capital of the company.

The employer has to submit form P11D to HMRC for each P11D employee for the tax year, listing the employee's benefits and any reimbursed expenses.

SUMMARY

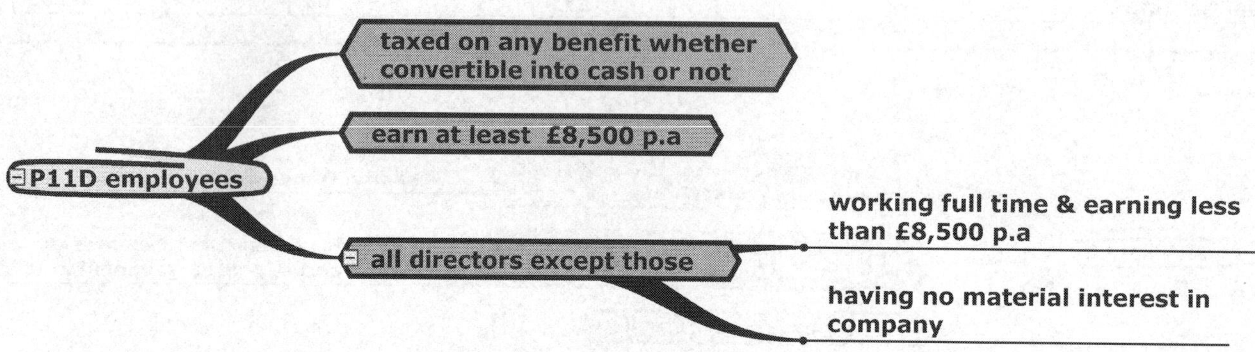

2. **P9D (lower-paid) employees:** all employees other than P11D employees are called "lower-paid employees". Lower paid employment is where earnings for the tax year are less than £8,500. Lower paid employees are taxed only on those **benefits that are convertible into cash.**

SUMMARY

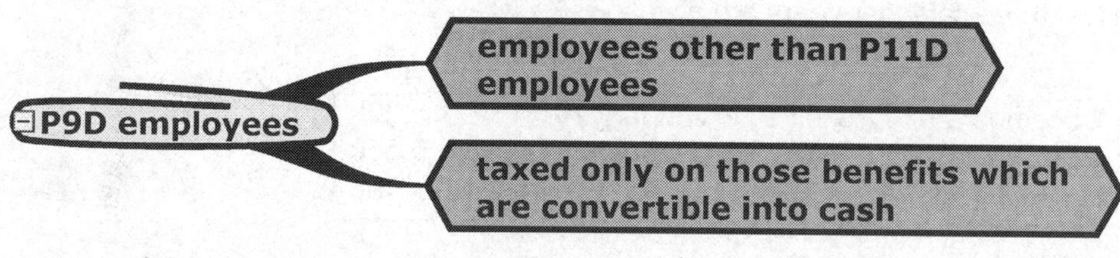

George retires from his job and joins Titan Ltd as a full time director in which he holds 25% of ordinary shares. His annual income from Titan Ltd is £7,000. Is he a P11D employee?

4. Compute the amount of benefits assessable.[2]

[Learning Outcome h]

The benefits are categorised as follows:

- exempt benefits
- benefits assessable on all employees
- benefits assessable on P11D employees

4.1 Exempt benefits

Exempt benefits include:

1. Meal vouchers up to 15p per day.
2. Free or subsidised meals in a staff canteen, if available to all employees.
3. The cost of staff parties, which are open to staff generally, up to £150 per person per year. The £150 limit may be split between several parties. However, if a function costs more than £150, **the whole amount is taxable,** not just the excess over £150.
4. The provision of a parking place at or near an employee's place of work.
5. Contributions by an employer towards additional household costs incurred by an employee who works at home (supporting evidence required if these costs exceed £3 per week).
6. The payment by an employer of an **employee's personal incidental expenses** when the employee is staying away from home overnight on business, of up to:

   - £5 per night within the UK; or
   - £10 per night outside the UK.

   If the limit is exceeded, the whole amount becomes taxable.
7. Reasonable removal expenses (up to a maximum of £8,000) paid for by an employer when an employee first takes up employment or transfers to a new location within the organisation.
8. An award of up to £5,000 made under a staff suggestion scheme (there are strict conditions to be met for this relief).
9. Payments of up to £15,000 per academic year to an employee who is attending a full-time course at a recognised educational establishment. If the limit is exceeded the whole amount is taxable.
10. The provision of **one mobile phone** for an employee's use. If **more than one mobile phone** is provided then that is **taxable**.

Example

Excellent Plc provided Rower with two mobile phones throughout the tax year 2012-13 for her personal use. The mobile phones cost £180 each.

Benefits assessable for the tax year 2012-13 in respect of the second mobile = £180 x 20% = £36 (explained in point 4.3 under assets loaned for private use.) Rower will also be taxed on the ongoing costs paid by Excellent Plc in respect of the second mobile telephone.

---

11. The provision of workplace childcare or childcare vouchers up to

    - £55 per week for basic rate taxpayers,
    - £28 per week for higher rate taxpayers, and
    - £22 per week for additional rate taxpayers.

(Taxpayers categories is discussed in detail in Study Guide B5)

12. The provision of qualifying sports or recreational facilities.
13. The provision of welfare counselling service for employees generally.
14. The provision of pension information and advice if available to all the employees and costing less than £150 per employee per year.
15. Entertainment provided by a third party.
16. Gifts from third parties up to £250 per donor (if exceeded all taxable).
17. Long service awards.
18. Concessional interest on small loans not exceeding £5,000.
19. Job-related accommodation.
20. Contributions to employees' pension fund.

Jacqueline received an amount of £7 a day for 50 days of business trips in the UK and £9 a day for 70 days of business trips abroad. All of these trips required overnight stays away from home and the amounts paid were used to cover the costs of incidental expenses such as laundry and telephone calls home.

Required:

Calculate the amount of taxable benefit.

4.2 Benefits assessable on all employees

This includes:

- Living accommodation
- Vouchers exchangeable for goods or services

1. Living accommodation

If an employee is provided with living accommodation such as a house or flat there are two possible benefits assessable on **ALL** employees.

Diagram 1: Taxable value for living accommodation

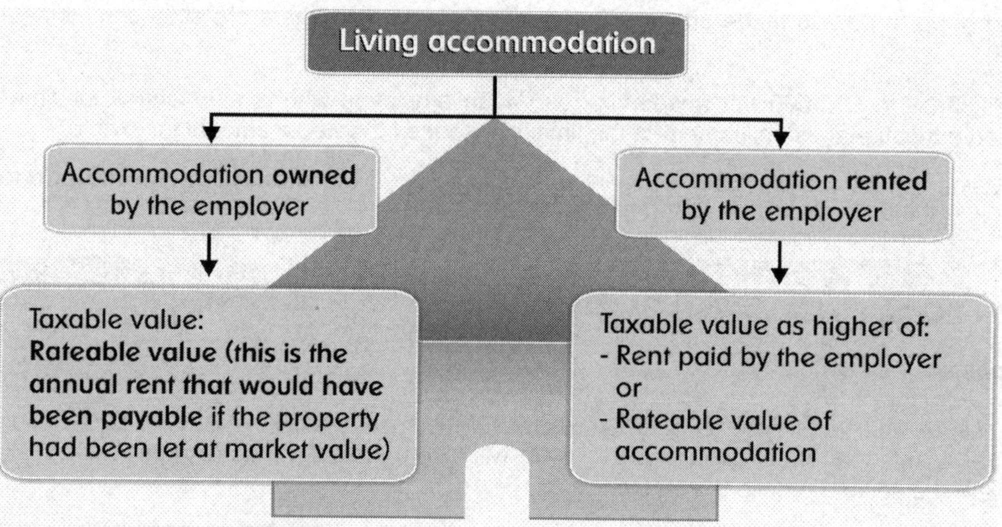

Rateable value may also be called 'annual value' and this figure will be given to you in the exam.

a) Rented accommodation

Taxable benefit for rented living accommodation is calculated as:

	£
Higher of:	
Rent paid by employer }	X
Annual value of property }	
Less: Employee contribution	(X)
Taxable benefit	**X**

Example

Honey is provided with living accommodation from 1 April 2012, which has a rateable value of £6,200. The employer pays rent of £7,400 for the property annually. Honey pays her employer £850 per annum towards the accommodation. the taxable benefits in 2012-13 is:

		£
Rent paid by employer = £7,400 Annual value of property = £6,200	higher	7,400
Less: Employee contribution		(850)
Taxable benefit for living accommodation		**6,550**

b) Employer owned accommodation: taxable value in this case is the rateable value of the property.

i. **Expensive accommodation benefit:** if the employer owns the accommodation and it **cost more than £75,000** when bought, then there is an additional charge on the employee. **This is in addition to the rateable value of the accommodation.**

The amount of the expensive accommodation benefit is:

(Cost of providing the accommodation - £75,000) x official rate of interest

The official rate of interest for 2012 - 13 is 4.00%.

Tip

Official rate of interest will be provided in the exam paper. However, limit for expensive accommodation of £75,000 will not be provided in the exam and you will have to memorise it.

ii. **Cost of providing the accommodation**

- Where the accommodation was purchased by the employer **less than six years** before being made available to an employee, the cost of providing the accommodation is:

Cost of providing the property + improvement expenditure up to the start of the tax year

- Where the accommodation was acquired **more than six years before** being made available to an employee, the cost of providing the accommodation is:

Market value of the property when first occupied by an employee

+ any subsequent improvements up to the start of the tax year

The taxable benefit for employer-owned living accommodation is calculated as:

	£
Rateable Value	**X**
Add: Expensive accommodation benefit (£Cost - £75,000) x official rate of interest	X
Total	**X**
Less: Employee contribution	(X)
Taxable benefit	**X**

The benefit will be **time apportioned** if it is available only for **part of the year**.

Example

Henry is provided with living accommodation from 1 January 2012 which has a rateable value of £6,200. The employer purchased the property in December 2009 for £80,000 and spent £10,000 on improvements in August 2010. Henry pays his employer rent of £850 per annum. Calculate Henry's taxable benefit in 2012-13. The official rate of interest is 4.00% per annum.

	£
Rateable value	6,200
Add: Expensive accommodation benefit (note)	600
	6,800
Less : Employee contribution	(850)
Taxable benefit	**5,950**

Note: the **property costs more than £75,000,** hence the **expensive accommodation** benefit must also be calculated. The expensive accommodation is calculated as:

(Cost of providing the accommodation - £75,000) x official rate of interest

As the accommodation was purchased by the employer less than six years before being made available to the employee, the cost of providing the accommodation is:

Cost of providing the property + Improvement expenditure up to the start of the tax year

= £80,000 + £10,000 = £90,000

Therefore, expensive accommodation benefit is:

(Cost of providing the accommodation - £75,000) x official rate of interest

= (£90,000 - £75,000) × 4.00%

= £15,000 × 4.00%

= £600

Example

Jack was provided with a house by his employer in June 2012. He pays £125 per month for the use of the house. The house had been purchased for £120,000 in 2003 and has an annual rental value of £1,200. The house had a market value of £150,000 in June 2012. Calculate the taxable benefit in 2012-13, assuming an official interest rate of 4.00% per annum.

	£
Rateable value	1,200
Add: Expensive accommodation benefit (£150,000 – £75,000) @ 4.00% (note)	3,000
Total	**4,200**
For ten months (£4,200 x 10/12)	3,500
Less: Employee contribution (£125 x 10 months)	(1,250)
Taxable benefit	**2,250**

Note: the house was acquired by Jack's employer more than six years before being provided to Jack. Hence, the market value of the house on the date when it was first occupied by Jack will be considered for calculating the expensive accommodation benefit.

---

c) Job related accommodation

No taxable benefit arises in respect of job related accommodation if it is:

i. **Necessary** for the employee to reside in the accommodation for the **proper performance** of his duties.

Example

It is necessary for a warden of sheltered housing to live in his employer's premises for proper performance of his duties. Hence it will be treated as job related accommodation. Similarly, wardens of schools or prisons would also be within the exemption. The exemption only applies if it is **essential** that the employee lives in the accommodation, not simply that it is convenient to do so.

---

ii. The accommodation is provided for the **better performance** of the employee's duties and the employment is of the type where it is **customary** for accommodation to be provided (e.g. Prime Minister's / Arch Bishop's residence).

iii. The accommodation is provided as a part of a **security** arrangement because there is a special threat to the employee's security.

Test Yourself 6

An employee lives in accommodation which is owned by his employer. The house cost the employer £100,000 and has a rateable value of £1,200. The employee pays monthly rent of £120. The official rate of interest is 4.00%.

Required:

Calculate the taxable benefit.

Test Yourself 7

Nick lives in a company owned flat. The flat cost the company £120,000 in November 2008. The rateable value of the flat is £1,000 and Nick pays rent of £100 per month. Nick moved out of the flat on 1 January 2013 and bought his own house.

Required:

Calculate Nick's taxable benefit. The official rate of interest is 4.00%.

---

d) Homeworking

Employees who work from home are allowed a weekly tax – free allowance of £4. This covers the light and heat expenses incurred by the employee as he is working from home. The employee does not have to provide any bills or evidences to claim this allowance.

2. **Vouchers for goods or services:** Employees are taxed on the expense incurred by the person providing the vouchers. An employee may receive from his employer:

   a) credit token (such as a credit card) to obtain money, goods or services or

   b) exchangeable vouchers (such as gift vouchers).

In such cases, the employer is taxed on the cost of providing the benefit, less any amount the employee contributes towards it.

The assessable value of the above vouchers for goods or services for all the employees, whether P9D (lower paid) or P11D, is the cost of these vouchers to their employer.

It is also possible to have cash vouchers (vouchers exchangeable for cash). These are rarely used in practice now but, for example, used to be a way of paying holiday pay. Such vouchers are taxable under PAYE on their face value.

Example

Jimmy, an employed person, received a £120 book token from his company. The company paid £110 for the book token. In this case, £110 will be added to Jimmy's employment income. If Jimmy pays £20 to the employer for the book token then only £90 (£110 - £20) will be added to his employment income.

Exceptions

i. **First 15p per day** of meals vouchers are **not taxable**.

ii. Entertainment and hospitality vouchers provided by a person **other than the employer** or someone connected with the employer **are not taxable.**

4.3 Benefits assessable on P11D employees

This includes:
- cars provided for private use
- fuel provided for private use
- vans provided for private use
- beneficial loans
- assets loaned for private use
- ancillary services connected with living accommodation

Important rule about benefits

a) Benefits are time apportioned if only available for part of the year.
b) Benefits are reduced by any contribution made by employee (except fuel benefit).

1. Cars provided for private use

a) If a car is provided to an employee or members of his family for private use a taxable benefit arises.

The charge for the private use is based on the manufacturer's list price, and is calculated as follows:

	£
(Manufacturer's list price – Employee **capital** contribution) x Appropriate %	X
Less: Employee contribution for the private use of the car	(X)
Assessable benefit	**X**

Note: the maximum employee's capital contribution deductible is £5,000.

The **manufacturer's list price** of the car is the standard list price, plus the price of any accessories originally provided, and the price of any accessories provided at a later date costing at least £100. The list price that was capped at £80,000 for these purposes is no longer applicable from 2012-2013 onwards.

George is employed as an accountant at a salary of £50,000 and is provided with a company car by his employer for his private use. His car is a Mercedes with a list price (when new) of £95,000, but his employer purchases the car second hand for £40,000. At the same time, accessories worth £2,000 were fitted in the car for George.

Calculate the list price of the car.

To calculate the taxable benefit, the list price of the car is:
£95,000 + £2,000 = £97,000

b) If the car is a "classic car" and its current market value is greater than the manufacturer's list price, then the market value is used.

What is a classic car?

A "classic car" is one which is more than 15 years old and whose market value at the end of the tax year is more than £15,000.

c) Where an employee contributes towards the **capital** cost of the car, (to enable a more expensive car to be purchased) the capital contribution is deducted from the manufacturer's list price, subject to a maximum of £5,000.

If in the above example, George contributed £3,000 towards the cost of car, the list price will be £97,000 - £3,000 = £94,000.

d) **Appropriate percentage**

The appropriate percentage used to calculate the benefit depends on the carbon dioxide (CO_2) emissions rate of the car, and ranges from 11% to 35%. It is expressed in grams per kilometre (g/km).

The 11% rate is increased by 1% for each 5g/km over the threshold (which is 100 g/km for 2012-13) up to a maximum of 35%. The appropriate percentage, therefore, is calculated as:

$$15\% + \frac{(CO_2 \text{ emissions of the car - 100})}{5}$$

There are two lower rates for low emission motor cars: 5% for cars with emissions exactly 75g/km or less and 10% for motor cars with CO_2 emissions rates between 76g/km and 99 g/km. Cars which do not produce any emission benefit at 0%.

The threshold for 2011-12 for petrol cars is:

75 g/km or less	→	5%
76g/km to 99 g/km	→	10%
100 g/km	→	11%
Each additional 5 g/km	→	1% increase
Maximum (225 g/km or more)	→	35%

3% is added to the appropriate percentage for each threshold if the car runs on diesel. However, the 3% supplement cannot take the appropriate percentage above 35%.

Tip

If the CO_2 emissions rate of the car is above 100 g/km and is not in multiples of five, it is **rounded down to the nearest 5 g/km level** for calculating the appropriate percentage.

Example

Suppose, in George's case, (adjusted list price £54,000), the CO_2 emissions is 208g/km, the appropriate percentage will be calculated as:

(The CO_2 emissions rate of the car, i.e. 208g/km is not in multiples of five, so it is rounded down to the nearest multiple of 5, i.e. 205g/km.)

$$11\% + \frac{(205 - 100)}{5} = 32\%$$

The assessable benefit is = £54,000 x 32% = £17,280

If the car provided to George runs on diesel, the appropriate percentage will be 32% + 3% = 35% and the assessable benefit will be £54,000 x 35% = £18,900.

If the car provided to George had CO_2 emissions of 90 g/km the percentage would be 10% as this is below the 100g/km limit but above 76 g/km

Similarly, if the car provided to George had CO_2 emissions of 68g/km, then the lower rate of 5% will apply as this is below 75g/km.

e) Any **contributions made by the employee** to the employer **for the private use of the car** will be **deducted** from the taxable benefit.

f) If a car is not available for the whole of the tax year or is unusable for a continuous period of at least 30 consecutive days, the benefit is pro-rated accordingly. Calculations are done to the nearest month.

Example

Judi is employed with a salary of £45,000 and is provided with a petrol-driven car with a list price of £90,000 and CO_2 emissions of 56 g/km. The car was made available from 6 November 2012. She contributes £120 per month for the private use of the car. Calculate the benefits assessable in 2012-13.

List price = £90,000

Relevant percentage is 5% as the CO_2 emission rate of the car is less than 75g/km.

Benefit assessable = £90,000 x 5% x 5 months/12 months = £1875 (since there is no cap on the list price)

As she contributes £120 per month (for 5 months) for the private use of the car, the taxable benefit will be: £1875 – (£120 x 5) = £1275.

---

g) **More than one car:** if the employee is provided with more than one car then he is assessed on all cars provided.

h) **Cars used for business only:** if there is **no** private use of the car, there is no benefit.

i) **Pool cars:** no assessable benefit arises from the use of a pool car. A pool car is one which satisfies all the following criteria:

- It is available for use by more than one employee and is not ordinarily used by one employee exclusively.
- It is not normally kept at an employee's residence overnight.
- Any private use is incidental to its use for business purposes.

Test Yourself 8

Lily, a P11D employee, is provided with a car by her employer. The list price of the car is £15,300. Lily made a capital contribution of £1,200 and pays her employer £30 per month for the private use of the car. The car is available throughout 2012-13.

Required:

Calculate the benefits assessable in 2012-13 if the car is petrol driven and has an emissions rate of

1. 70 g/km
2. 90 g/km

The **car benefit** assessable on the employee **covers the provision of the car by his employer and any running costs** (i.e. insurance, road fund licence and maintenance). It does not cover the provision of private fuel.

Test Yourself 9

During the tax year 2012-13, Tip-Top Plc provided the following employees with company motor cars:

1. Neil was provided with a new diesel-powered company car throughout the year 2012-13. The motor car has a list price of £15,500, and an official CO_2 emissions rate of 192 grams per kilometre.

2. Bob was provided with a new petrol-powered company car from 5 September 2012. The motor car has a list price of £12,400, and an official CO_2 emissions rate of 99 grams per kilometre.

3. Simi was provided with a new petrol-powered company car throughout the tax year 2012-13. The motor car has a list price of £25,800, and an official CO_2 emissions rate of 292 grams per kilometre. Simi paid Tip-top Plc £1,600 during the tax year 2012-13 for the use of the motor car.

4. Michelle was provided with a new petrol powered company car throughout the tax year 2012-13. The motor car has a list price of 85,000 and an official CO_2 emissions rate of 153 grams per kilometre.

Required:

Calculate the value of assessable benefits.

---

2. Fuel provided for private use

A separate benefit arises on the provision of **private fuel**, and is calculated as follows:

Fixed amount set by HMRC x	Appropriate %
£20,200 for 2012 - 13	Same % as for car benefit

The benefit is calculated as above where there is any fuel provided for private use; the actual amount is irrelevant. Therefore any **partial reimbursement** by the employee will **not** affect the taxable benefit.

Key points regarding fuel benefit are:

a) **No benefit will arise if:**

- the employee **fully reimburses** the employer **for any private fuel** provided, or
- the fuel is **only provided for business use**.

b) If the fuel is not provided for the whole tax year, the benefit is pro-rated.

c) If the employee does not fully reimburse the cost of the private fuel, the full fuel benefit is assessable.

d) If the employee makes a partial contribution towards the cost of private fuel, the benefit is not reduced by the contribution. This is an **exception to the general rule**.

Test Yourself 10

Mark is provided with a car on 1 July 2012 by his employer. The list price of the car is £24,000 and the CO_2 emissions are 162 g/km. The car runs on unleaded petrol, and the employer pays for all fuel.

Mark contributes £100 per month for the private use of the car and a further £25 per month towards the cost of private fuel (which actually amounts to £45 per month on average).

Required:

Calculate the car benefit and fuel benefit assessable on Mark for 2012-13.

Test Yourself 11

Fernando is employed, earning £30,000 per annum. In January 2012 he was provided with a Renault car that runs on petrol (list price £12,000 and CO_2 emissions 142g/km).

On 1 July 2012, his employer exchanged the Renault for a Ford Focus (list price £14,000 and CO_2 emissions 95 g/km). The Ford Focus runs on diesel. The company reimburses Fernando for his business fuel costs.

Required:

Calculate Fernando's taxable benefit for 2012-13.

---

3. Vans provided for private use

a) A P11D employee is assessed on the private use of a van.
b) The benefit is a fixed amount of £3,000. The benefit is proportionately reduced if a van is unavailable for part of the tax year.
c) Unlike car benefit, while determining whether the van is available for private use, the journey between home and work is not considered.
d) If a van is for private use by more than one employee, then the amount of benefit is divided equally among all the employees who use the van for private purposes irrespective of the amount of private use by each of the employee.
e) There will also be an additional benefit of £550 if fuel is provided for private mileage. The fuel benefit is proportionately reduced if a van is unavailable for part of the tax year, or if fuel is only provided for part of the tax year.

4. Beneficial loans

A beneficial loan is one made to an employee by the employer which is **either interest free or the interest paid is less than the official rate of interest.**

The **taxable benefit** is as follows:

	£
Interest on outstanding amount at the official rate of interest	X
Less: Interest actually paid (if any)	(X)
Assessable benefit	**X**

Loans made in the ordinary course of the employer's **money-lending business are not taxable,** if made on the same terms and conditions as loans made to the general public.

No assessable benefit arises if the total amount outstanding does not exceed £5,000 at any time during the tax year.

A benefit arises on interest on the whole loan, if the loan exceeds £5,000 and not just on the excess of the loan over £5,000.

If any amount of the loan is written off a benefit equal to the amount written off arises.

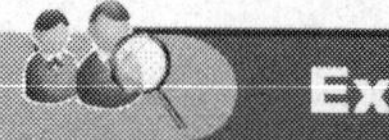

Example

Alan has an annual salary of £30,000. He has taken a loan from his employer of £20,000 at 3% interest to purchase a yacht. The loan was outstanding for the whole 2012-13 tax year.

As the loan is more than £5,000, the assessable benefit is calculated as £20,000 x (4.00% - 3.00%) = £200.

There are two methods of calculating the assessable benefit:

a) Average method

The official rate of interest is applied to the average of the balance at the beginning and at the end of the year. If the loan was repaid before the year end, then the balance at the time of repayment is taken.

b) Strict method

The official rate of interest is applied to the amount outstanding on a month by month basis.

The average method is applied unless either the taxpayer or HMRC elects for the strict method to be used.

Example

Right Plc provided Lai with an interest free loan of £30,000 on 1 January 2009. She repaid £20,000 of the loan on 30 June 2012, with the balance of £10,000 being repaid on 31 December 2013. Calculate the amount of benefit for the tax year 2012-13 using:

a) The average method
b) The strict method

Average method

(£30,000 + £10,000)/2 = £20,000 x 4.00% x 9/12
= £600

Strict method

	£
£30,000 x 4.00% x 3/12	300
£10,000 x 4.00% x 6/12	200
Total	**500**

Hence, it is beneficial for the employee to have the taxable benefits calculated according to the strict method.

Test Yourself 12

An employee availed of a taxable cheap loan from his employer on 10 April 2012 of £38,000. On 31 December 2012, he repaid £22,000. The employee's earning is £16,000 per annum. The remaining balance of £16,000 was outstanding at 5 April 2013. Interest paid during the year was £380.

Required:

What was the taxable benefit for 2012-13, assuming that the official rate of interest was 4.00%?

---

5. Assets loaned to employee for private use

When an employer makes an asset available to an employee for his private use, the employee is **assessed annually on 20% of the market value of the asset** when first provided to the employee.

Example

Excellent Plc provided Rower with a computer throughout the tax year 2012-13 for her personal use. The computer cost £1,500.

Benefits assessable for the tax year 2012-13 in respect of the computer = £1,500 x 20% = £300.

If the asset is subsequently gifted or sold to the employee, the assessable benefit is the greater of:

a) The market value at the date of the gift / sale less employee contribution (if any).

b) The market value when first provided to the employee less annual 20% assessments less employee contribution (if any).

The loan of a bicycle and cycling safety equipment is exempt from tax if used wholly or mainly for the travel between office and home.

If an employee is gifted or sold a bicycle which is used privately by an employee, the benefit is the market value **on the date of the gift / sale** less employee contribution (if any) i.e. (b) above does not apply.

Example

On 6 April 2010 a P11D employee was provided by his employer, for his private use, a new camera costing £600. On 5 September 2012 he buys the camera from his employer for £70 when its value was £200. Calculate the assessable benefits for 2010-11 to 2012-13.

	£	£
2010-11		
20% of £600		120
2011-12		
20% of £600		120
2012-13		
20% of 600 x 5/12		50
Add: greater of (1) or (2) below		
1. £200 - £70	130	
2. £600 - £120 - £120 - £50 - £70	240	240
Total benefits assessed		**530**

On 6 April 2011 an employee was provided by his employer, for his private use, with a new music system costing £800. On 6 April 2012 he bought the music system from his employer for £180 when its value was £350.

Required:
Calculate assessable benefits in 2011-12 and 2012-13.

6. Ancillary services connected with living accommodation

P11D employees are taxed on **related expenses paid by the employer**, in addition to the benefit of living accommodation. These related expenses are:

a) Heating, electricity, cleaning, decorating etc.
b) Repairs and maintenance, but not structural repairs: these are assessed according to the cost to the employer.
c) The use of furniture: this is calculated according to the rules in 5 above.

If the accommodation is job related, the assessable benefit of ancillary services and use of furniture **cannot exceed 10% of employee's net earnings** for the tax year. Net earnings mean total earnings for the year **without** considering ancillary services and use of furniture **less** allowable expenses.

Jack, whose salary was £12,000 for 2012-13, is given living accommodation by his employer. His employer pays the electricity bill of £1,240, a gas bill of £300 and the gardener's salary of £600. Jack contributes £30 per month towards the cost of these services.

Computation of the assessable benefit of the ancillary services, assuming the accommodation is:

✓ not job-related
✓ job-related

➢ **Assuming the accommodation is not job-related**

The ancillary benefits provided along with the living accommodation are taxable.

	£
Electricity bill	1,240
Gas bill	300
Gardener's salary	600
Total benefits	**2,140**
Less: Jack's contribution (£30 x 12)	(360)
Assessable benefit	**1,780**

➢ **Assuming the accommodation is job-related**

If the accommodation is job related, the assessable benefit of ancillary services **cannot exceed 10% of the employee's net earnings** for the year.

Jack's net earnings for 2012-13 are £12,000.

	£
10% of Jack's net earnings	**1,200**
(10% of 12,000)	
Less: Jack's contribution	(360)
Assessable benefit	**840**

Harry has a salary of £62,850 in 2012-13. He is provided with job-related accommodation, which has a rateable value of £2,720. In 2012-13 the company pays an electricity bill of £1,320, a gas bill of £420, gardener's salary of £680 and redecoration costs of £1,280. The company has also provided furniture costing £15,000 along with the accommodation. Harry makes a monthly contribution of £50 for his accommodation.

Required:

Calculate Harry's taxable employment income for the year 2012-13.

Diagram 2: Summary of benefits assessable on P11D employees

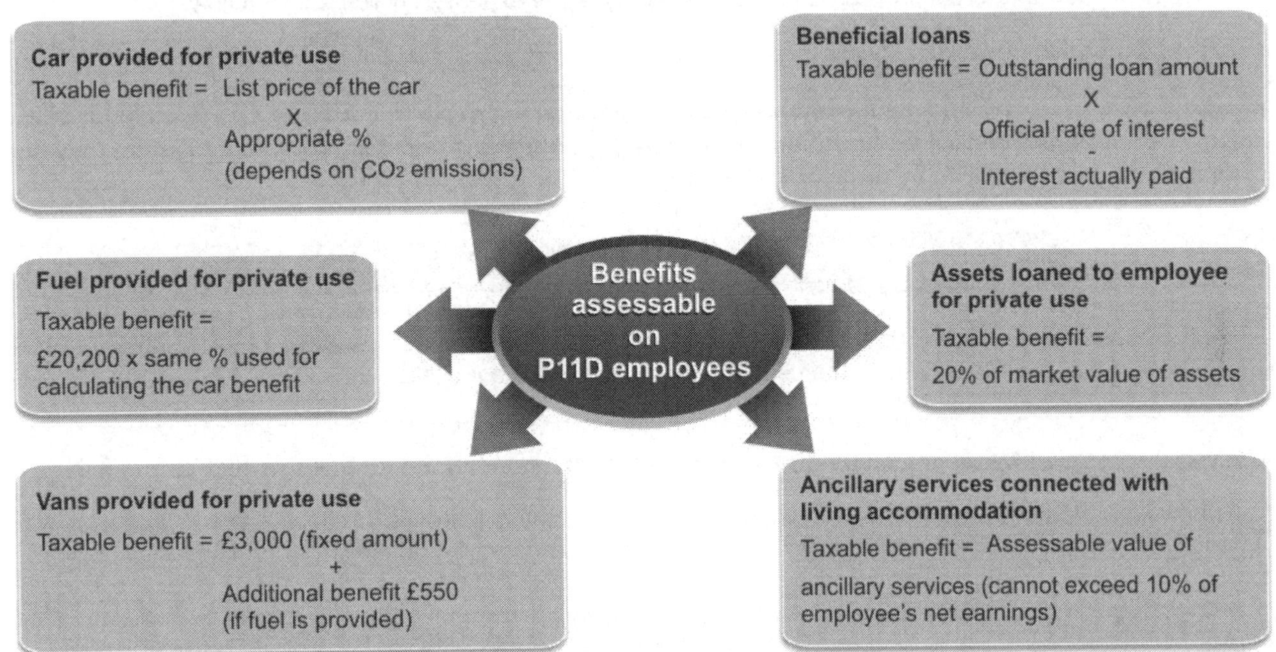

5. Recognise the allowable deductions, including travelling expenses.[2]

[Learning Outcome d]

Deductions allowable from taxable pay can be categorised as:

- expenses that are always deductible
- expenses that are deductible only on proving to be employment related

1. Always deductible

These include:

a) **Contributions to a registered occupational pension**.

b) **Subscriptions to professional bodies** approved by HMRC, if relevant to duties of employment.

The annual subscription to the ACCA paid by a finance manager of a company is deductible from his employment earnings.

---

c) **Donations to charity made under the payroll deduction scheme operated by an employer.** Such donations are **deducted** from the employee's **gross earnings** to arrive at his net taxable earnings.

d) **Mileage allowance** relief (explained in Learning Outcome 6 in this Study Guide)

e) Payment of employment related liabilities and premiums for insurance against them. If an employee or a director of a company incurs a liability related to his employment or pays for insurance against such liability, the cost incurred by him is allowable as deduction from his taxable pay. If such a liability is paid by the employer, on behalf of the employee then no taxable benefit arises to the employee.

A company sued its manager for negligence. He was ordered to make good the losses of £5,000 caused by the manager due to his negligence. He incurred legal costs of £5,000 while defending his case. Thus, these expenses of £10,000 are employment related liabilities and are deductible from his taxable employment income.

---

2. Expenses deductible only on proving to be employment related

These types of allowable deductions are **limited to three** types of expenses which are as follows:

a) Travel expenses

The expenses incurred for **travelling from home to the employee's place of work** are **not deductible.** This is because expenses are deductible if incurred for **performing duties** and generally you cannot perform any duty of employment until you reach the place of employment.

Jessica is a finance manager of a company in London and works at the London office. On occasion she is required to travel to meetings at the company's head office in Southampton. As the journey is undertaken in performance of duties of employment, the cost of these journeys is deductible.

However, the **costs of travel between home and work are allowable in the following situation:**

i. Travel costs incurred by an employee when undertaking business journeys which start from home. However relief will not be available if the journey is substantially the same as the employee's normal journey to work.

Rita is a finance executive of a company. She resides in city A and has to go to city B where the office of the company is situated. However on every Monday and Friday, she has to go to city C to meet the company's bankers. On those days she goes directly to city C from city A. The distance between city A and city C is almost three times the distance between city A and city B.

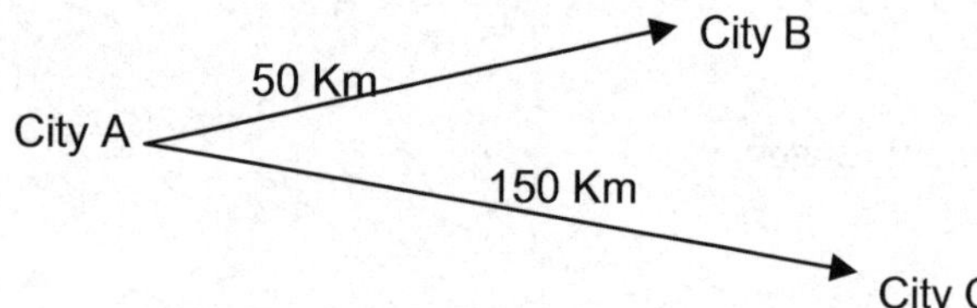

In this case, the travelling costs from city A to city C are deductible.

However, instead of going to city C, if she has to attend a meeting in another part of city B, then as the journey is substantially the same, relief will not be available.

---

ii. Travelling costs **incurred by a "site-based" employee** travelling from home to the site are deductible. Site based employees are those who do not have a permanent workplace.

However there is a **condition** that the employee does **not spend more than twenty-four months of continuous work** at any one site.

iii. Travel costs incurred by an employee who is seconded to a temporary workplace are deductible, provided it is expected that he will return to the normal workplace within **twenty-four months.**

If the secondment is initially expected to last up to twenty-four months, but it is extended, relief ceases to be due from the date the employee becomes aware of the change of period.

Quick revision of the rules relating to travelling expenses

a) Allow relief for the full cost of business travelling expenses.
b) There is no relief for any costs relating to ordinary commuting (i.e. travel between home and a permanent workplace).
c) There is no relief for any costs relating to private travel.
d) Allow relief for travel in the performance of the employee's duties. It covers:

i. Travel costs incurred by an employee when undertaking business journeys which start from home.
ii. Travelling costs **incurred by a "site- based" employee** for travel from home to the site.
iii. If the employee is working at a particular workplace over a period of more than 24 months, that place is treated as his permanent workplace so travel between the work place and home is ordinary commuting for which there is no relief.

b) **Expenses incurred wholly, exclusively and necessarily in the performance of duties of employment** i.e. expenses without which the duties of employment cannot be effectively performed. For example, cost of protective work clothes for a mining job.

The word "wholly and exclusively" emphasises that any expenditure incurred for private purposes is not deductible. Whether expenditure is **"necessary"** for the performance of the duties of employment depends on if they could be **performed without this expenditure.**

Test Yourself 15

Which of the following expenses incurred by an employee would be deductible from his income for tax purposes?

1. The cost incurred by a production manager for a suit to wear for an office meeting.
2. The bank manager pays an annual subscription to the Association of Bankers.
3. A sales manager voluntarily pays an annual subscription to City Club. He visits the club only for the purpose of conducting meetings with clients.
4. An officer pays to attend study courses in the evenings so as to improve his prospects for promotion.

c) **Capital allowances:** Where plant or machinery is **necessarily provided** by an employee for use in the performance of his duties, capital allowances may be claimed for its business use.

Employees may not obtain capital allowances for cars, motorcycles or cycles.

Example

An employee uses his personal computer for performing his official duties. He can claim capital allowances on the computer, which will be deducted from his taxable employment income.

SUMMARY

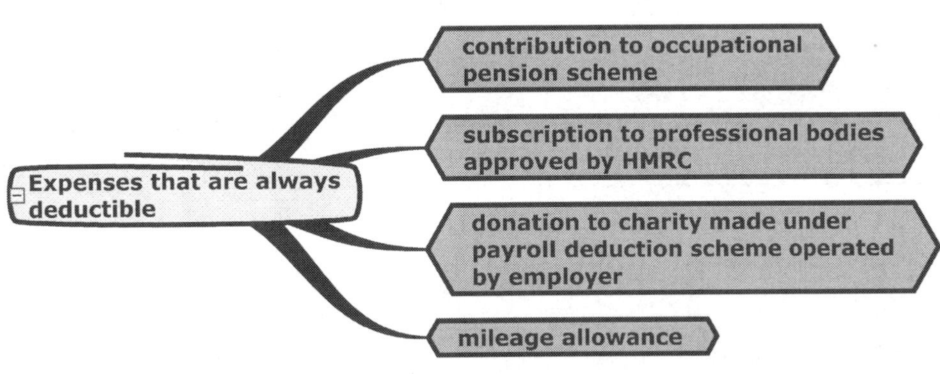

Diagram 3: Expenses deductible only on proving to be employment related

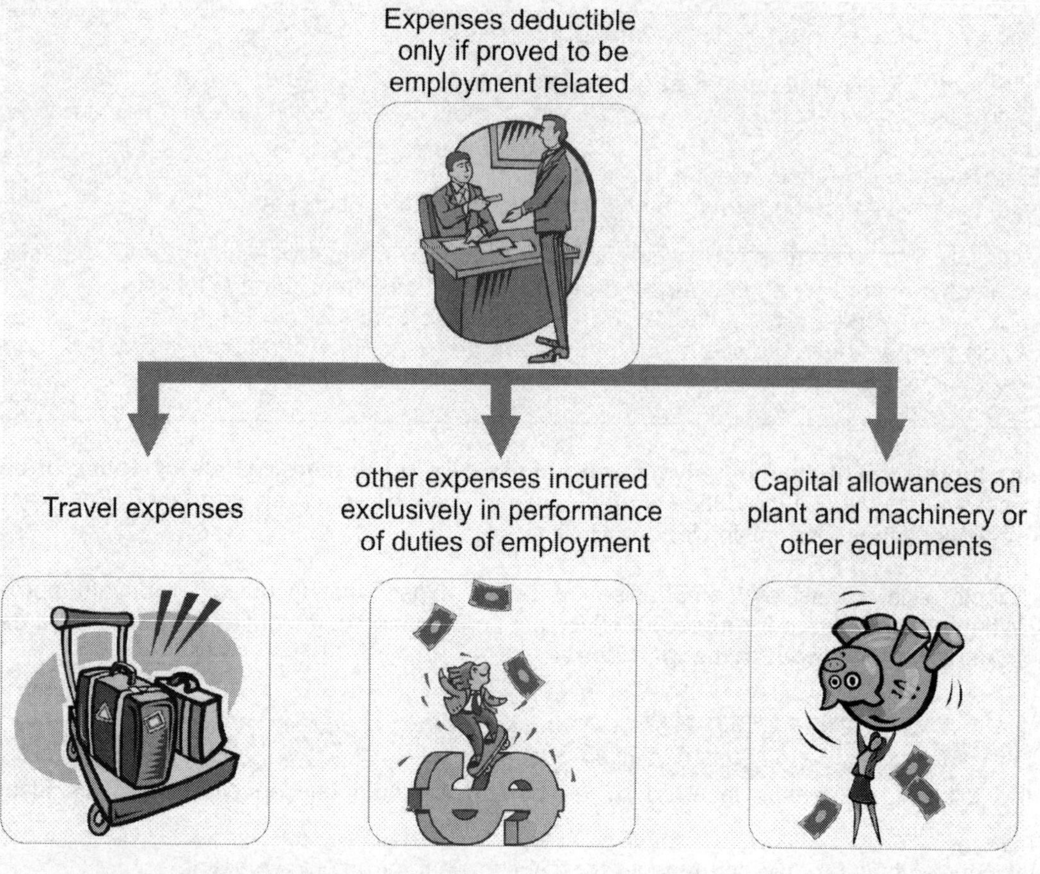

Test Yourself 16

Joy Ltd spent £120 per employee on a Christmas party for all staff. What is the tax position for?

1. Joy Ltd
2. Each employee

Test Yourself 17

Susan is a chartered certified accountant working for TGT Ltd. Her annual salary is £15,000. She incurred the following expenses in the year ended 5 April 2013.

1. Her annual subscription fees for ACCA were £200.
2. She received an award of £150 under the staff suggestion scheme.
3. She received a bonus of £5,000 in the year in addition to her annual salary.
4. She threw a party on her birthday for all her colleagues in the office and incurred costs of £300.
5. She started contributing £300 per month to an occupational pension scheme from 1 August 2012.
6. She paid £200 as a deposit and £250 annual rent for her accommodation in the city.

Required:

What is Susan's taxable employment income for 2012-13?

---

6. Discuss the use of the statutory approved mileage allowances.[2] [Learning Outcome e]

The employer gives a mileage allowance to those employees who use their own vehicles for business. These allowances are tax-free to the extent of the amount approved by HMRC. For 2012-13 the approved mileage rates are:

	First 10,000 miles in the tax year	Each mile over 10,000 miles in the tax year
Motor cars and vans	45p per mile	25p per mile
Motor cycles	24p per mile	24p per mile
Bicycles	20p per mile	20p per mile

Tip

These allowances will be given to you in the rates and allowances in the exam.

If the mileage allowance paid to an employee exceeds the above amount the **excess** is taxable.

Example

An employee uses his own car for business travel. In 2012-13 he travelled 10,000 miles in the duties of his employment. The tax-free mileage allowance is (10,000 miles at 45p per mile) £4,500.

However, if his company paid him a mileage allowance of 60p per mile, the **excess i.e. £6,000 - £4,500 = £1,500 is taxable.**

On the other hand, if the mileage allowance paid to an employee is less than the sum calculated using these rates; the **deficit** is an allowable expense.

Example

Continuing with the above example, assume that he is paid 30p per mile. This is below the approved mileage allowance, and the deficit (£4,500 - £3,000 = £1,500) is deducted from his employment income.

If the employee **carries a passenger** on a **business trip**, the employer may pay the employee up to **5p per passenger per mile tax free**. However the employee cannot claim tax relief if the employer pays less than 5p per passenger per mile or pays nothing at all.

Test Yourself 18

Alan is employed with a salary of £25,000. He uses his own car when travelling, and in 2012-13 he drives 10,200 miles for business purposes.

Required:

Calculate his taxable employment income if his employer pays him:

(a) Nothing
(b) 40p per mile
(c) 50p per mile

Test Yourself 19

Lora is employed with Flex Plc. She used her private motor car for both business and private purposes during the period from 6 April 2012 to 31 December 2012. She received no reimbursement from Flex Plc for any of the expenditure incurred.

Lora's total mileage during this period was 17,480 miles, made up as follows:

Continued on the next page

	Miles
Normal daily travel between home and permanent workplace	6,650
Travel between home and permanent workplace in order to turn off a fire alarm	330
Private travel	5,950
Travel between home and a temporary workplace for a period of two months	3,800
Travel between permanent workplace and Flex plc's suppliers	750
	17,480

Required:

State which of the above travelling costs are deductible from employment income.

---

7. Compute the income assessable.[2]

[Learning Outcome c]

The knowledge gained in the previous Learning Outcomes will now be tested.

Test Yourself 20

Jack works for LLH Ltd, and is in charge of controlling the sales activities in three cities (City B, C and D) in northern England and his annual salary is £36,000.

For the year 2012-13 he received a bonus of £1,500 and a performance incentive of £3,000 in December 2012. Jack contributes £500 to an occupational pension scheme every month.

Jack resides in city A and the company is based in city B. He works from city B and visits other cities in relation to his work. He has incurred the following travelling expenses during the year.

Travelling expenses incurred from:

City A to city B - £800
City B to city C - £700
City B to city D - £900
City D to city C - £1,000

LLH Ltd has provided him with a mobile phone. The company has incurred £2,500 for mobile phone expenses excluding rental charges.

Required:

Calculate Jack's taxable employment income for 2012-13.

Test Yourself 21

Which of the following are exempt from income tax?

(a) Meal vouchers of £1.30 per working day
(b) Free meals in the company canteen
(c) Removal expenses of £4,000
(d) A cheque for £1,200 given to an employee on completing 25 years of service with his employer.

Test Yourself 22

Which of the following expenses incurred by an employee would be deductible?

(a) Travel cost between work and home
(b) Travel cost between employment sites
(c) The cost of a suit to wear at the office
(d) Subscription to professional bodies

---

8. Explain the PAYE system.[1]

[Learning Outcome f]

PAYE stands for **P**ay **A**s **Y**ou **E**arn. An employer deducts income tax from his employees' wages / salaries throughout the year and pays it to HMRC. This system of collecting income tax is known as PAYE.

PAYE is a way of spreading income tax over the tax year. The tax year starts on 6 April of one year and ends on 5 April in the next. Under PAYE, the employer deducts tax from weekly or monthly earnings and pays it over to HMRC. The employer is effectively acting as a collector of taxes on behalf of HMRC.

8.1 Features

The main features of the PAYE system:

1. Under the PAYE system, the employer has to deduct both **Income tax and National Insurance Contributions** (NIC) (refer Study Guide E1 and E2) from the employee's employment income.

2. Income tax and NIC must be paid to HMRC within **14 days** of the **end of the tax month**. In the case of electronic payment, payment must be made within 17 days. A tax month runs from the 6 of one month to the 5 of next month, so payment must be made on or before the **19 / 22** of every month (for electronic payment).

Example

Zed Ltd pays its employees on the last day of every month. In January 2013, the total amount of tax deducted by the employer under PAYE was £36,000. The tax month ends on 5 February 2013, hence the amount must be paid within 14 days of the end of tax month i.e. on 19 February 2013.

---

3. The employers whose monthly PAYE payments do not exceed **£1,500 per month on average** are allowed to make **quarterly** payments instead of monthly payments. Tax quarters end on 5 July, 5 October, 5 January and 5 April. The employer can continue making payments quarterly during a tax year even if the monthly average payments reach or exceed £1,500.

   However, a new estimate of average payments must be made at the start of each tax year.

4. If an employer fails to apply PAYE wherever it is applicable, **he must pay the tax that he should have deducted.** Such an employer may also be liable to penalties. Interest will be charged from **14 days after** the end of the tax month concerned on any underpaid PAYE.

Example

Roger, an employer fails to apply PAYE on the employment remuneration he paid to his employees. If the PAYE would have been applied, the tax that would have been deductible from the employees' employment income under PAYE is £4,500. In this case, he has to pay the tax of £4,500, which he should have deducted from the employees income.

---

5. The officers of HMRC are given wide powers to inspect employer's records in order to satisfy themselves that the correct amounts of tax are being deducted and paid over to HMRC.

8.2 How does PAYE work?

To operate PAYE, an employer needs:

1. Tax codes
2. Tax tables
3. Deduction working sheets

1. Tax codes

a) The PAYE system is based upon the concept of "tax codes". The employer uses a tax code to calculate the amount of tax to deduct from wages / salaries. These codes are determined and amended by the Revenue.

b) A tax code is usually made up of one letter and several numbers. For example, 117L or K497

The tax code represents the employee's tax free allowance. The figure is the employee's total allowances, **without the last digit.**

If an employee's tax free allowances are £4,615, the code will be 461 followed by a letter (the number is the total allowances without the last digit, the letter represents the type of allowances or benefits accounted for in the tax code). The tax code is issued by HMRC to each employee for each tax year.

In order to decide the tax code, all the factors affecting the employee's income tax liability are to be considered. These factors include:

i. the personal allowance to which the employee is entitled. Personal allowance for 2012-13 for an individual between 0 to 64 years of age is £8,105.

ii. allowable expenses (for example, professional subscriptions etc.)

iii. adjustments made for benefits

iv. adjustments for income against which tax was overpaid or underpaid in previous years (see Test Yourself 24 below)

Remember, the tax code allotted to an employee is equal to the total of the above items, without the last digit e.g. if the aggregate of the above items is 5,682, then the tax code will be 568 followed by a letter.

How do you work out tax codes?

Diagram 4: Steps for working out tax codes

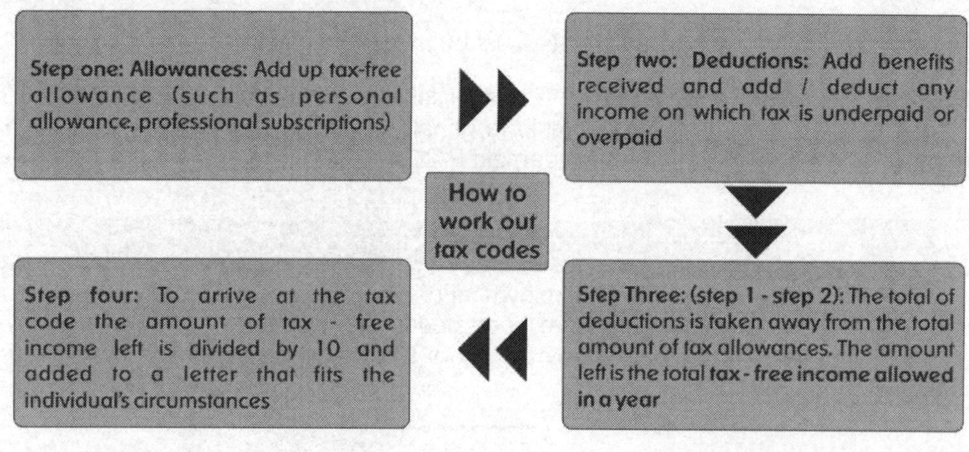

Example

Jimmy earns a salary of £18,000. He pays an allowable professional subscription of £138 and has taxable employment benefits of £520 in 2012-13. His tax of £52.50 remains unpaid for the year 2009-10 and is being collected through his tax code. Jimmy is a basic rate taxpayer.

Required:

Calculate Jimmy's tax code for 2012-13. Assume that the basic tax rate for the tax year 2009-10 is 22%.

Answer

Taking into account Jimmy's personal allowance, allowable expenses and adjustment for unpaid tax in the previous year, the tax code can be worked out as follows.

Continued on the next page

	£
Personal allowance	8,105
Add: Allowable expenses	138
Total	**8,243**
Less: Income on which tax was unpaid in 2008-09 (£52.5 x 100/22) (W1)	(239)
Less: Assessable benefits	(520)
Tax free income	**7,484**

Workings

W1

To collect unpaid tax, the amount must be grossed up by the individual's marginal rate of tax.
Tax code = 1/10 of £7,484 rounded down to a whole number. Therefore, tax code is **748 followed by a letter.**

---

1. Tax code suffixes

The tax code suffix indicates the type of allowance available to each employee.

Suffix	Explanation
L	Indicates that the employee is entitled to the basic personal allowance.
K	Denotes a negative code, which means the employee's benefits exceed their tax-free allowance.
T	A temporary code which is used until the employee's tax office can establish their tax status.
BR, D0, OT	Used when the individual has a second source of income; for example, when an employee has a second job. BR = Basic Rate i.e. tax is deducted at the basic rate D0 = Tax is deducted at 40% 0T = The tax free allowances have been allocated to a different source of income and no allowances are available for this source.

Generally, the codes are determined and notified by the HMRC. An employer may only apply the codes as issued. If they are considered to be incorrect, the employee must contact HMRC and request a new tax code be issued.

2. Tax Tables

Tax tables are used with the code to deduct the correct amount of tax each month.

The tables are designed in such a way that tax is computed on a cumulative basis. The employer is required to maintain a record of each employee's earnings, national insurance and tax on each pay day. This will enable computation of:

- the running total of tax paid and tax due on each pay date; and
- the difference between the tax due and the tax paid.

3. Deduction working sheets

PAYE deduction working sheets contain information on the income paid to employees.

This is required to be maintained in respect of employees who are paid between £95 and £110 a week; provided:

a. they are not employed elsewhere;
b. they do not get any other taxable income; and
c. there is neither tax or National Insurance Contributions due.

8.3 Need to operate PAYE

The PAYE system must be used:

- for employees who are paid more than £110 a week
- for employees who have another job / other taxable income(irrespective of their earnings)

The PAYE system need not be used:

- for employees who are paid less than £95 a week, provided they have no other job / other taxable income

8.4 PAYE Forms

Various forms are given to employees. Here is a summary of the most common.

Form	Contents	Date	To be given by the employer to
P9D	A year-end return showing the benefits and expenses of lower-paid employees.	**6 July** following the end of the tax year	HMRC
P11D	An end of year return showing the benefits and expenses of a director or employee earning at least £8,500.	**6 July** following the end of the tax year	HMRC and copy to employee
P14	An end of year return showing an **individual employee's** gross pay, tax paid and National Insurance paid for the year.	**19 May**	HMRC
P35	An end of year return showing and summarising **all employees'** gross pay, tax paid and National Insurance paid for the year.	**19 May**	HMRC
P45	This form has four parts and is used when an employee leaves employment. It shows the employee's tax code, gross pay to date and tax paid to date. Part 1 is sent to HMRC and Parts 2, 3 and 4 are given to the leaving employee. The employee gives Parts 2 and 3 to his or her new employer who retains Part 2 and sends Part 3 to HMRC. The employee retains Part 4	**19 May**	HMRC
P60	Certificate of gross pay and tax deducted.	**31 May** following the end of the tax year	employee

Test Yourself 23

Julian is the finance director of Solution Ltd. What are the forms that Solution Ltd must provide to him following the end of the tax year 2012-13 in respect of his earnings and benefits for that year? State the dates by which these forms have to be provided to him.

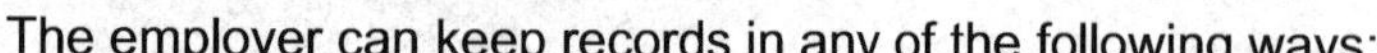

8.5 Records

The employer must keep records of each employee's pay and tax at each payday. The records containing details of National Insurance must also be maintained.

The employer can keep records in any of the following ways:

a) By using the official deductions working sheet (form P11).
b) By incorporating the figures in pay records prepared by the employer using a substitute document.
c) By retaining the figures on a computer.

8.6 Penalties on late submission of forms

a) A form P35 is due for submission to HMRC on **19 May** after the end of the tax year. However, in practice, a 7 day extension to the due date of 19 May is allowed. Thus practically the due date is **26 May.**

b) If an employer fails to submit form P35 on or before the due date, there is an automatic penalty of **£100 for every month or part-month per 50 employees.** This penalty cannot be mitigated.

This penalty applies for late submission in the 12 months after the due date.

Example

A firm with 51 employees filed its P35 for the tax year 2012-13 on 20 June 2013. The penalty amount would be calculated as if the submission was two months late. The fine would accordingly be £400.

c) If form P35 is not submitted within 12 months after the due date, a penalty of up to **100% of income tax plus National Insurance Contributions (NIC)** which remain unpaid at 19 April of following year may be charged. This penalty can be mitigated by HMRC.

d) For incorrect forms P35, there is a maximum penalty of 100% of any additional tax found to be due. This penalty can be mitigated.

Diagram 5: Summary of penalties

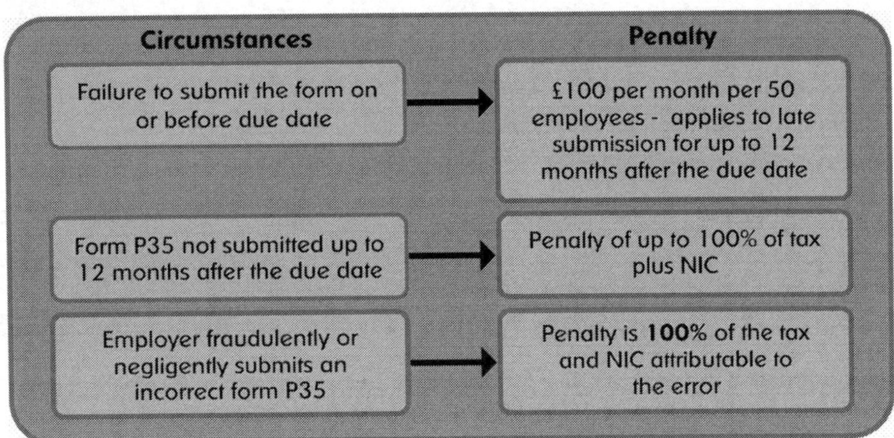

8.7 PAYE settlement agreements:

This is an arrangement **for minor benefits** under which employers can make a single payment to settle their employees' income tax liabilities. It is typically used if staff parties exceed the £150 tax free limit.

The items covered by a PAYE settlement agreement do not have to be included on either Form P9D or P11D or on an employee's tax return.

The **due date** under the PAYE settlement agreement is **19 October following the end of the tax year.**

SUMMARY

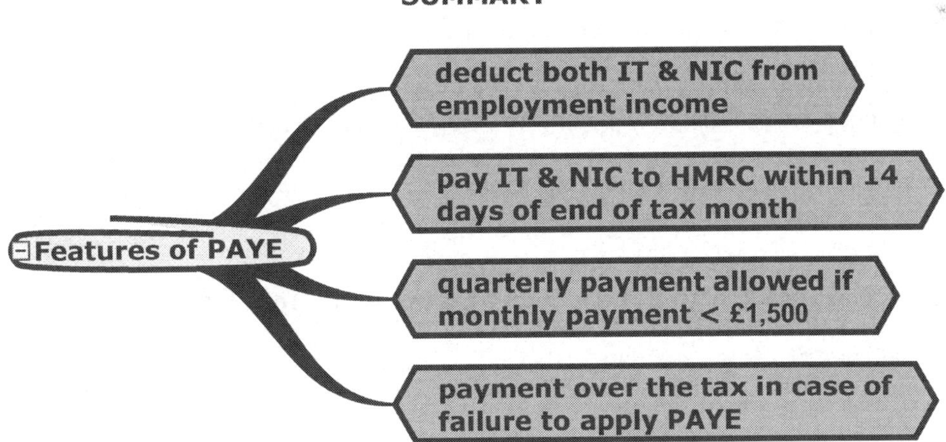

Test Yourself 24

Sam earns a salary of £36,000. He pays an allowable professional subscription of £276 and has benefits of £1,040 in 2012-13. He paid excess tax of £105 in the year 2009-10 which is being repaid through his tax code. Sam is a basic rate taxpayer.

Required:

What is the tax code of Sam for the tax year 2012-13?

9. Explain the purpose of dispensation from HM Revenue & Customs.[2]

[Learning Outcome i]

Employers can save themselves the burden of completing forms P11D in respect of **deductible expense payments** made to directors or employees by applying to HMRC for a Dispensation.

While the dispensation remains in force, the employer need not return the expense payments on form P11D, and they do not need to be included on the employee's tax return.

The purpose of a dispensation is to reduce the administrative burden of completing and filing P11D returns on

- the person completing the returns on behalf of the employer,
- the person handling the returns in the tax office, and
- the employee who is required to complete a self-assessment tax return.

Dispensations may now be applied for via the HMRC website at any point in the tax year to which they relate.

10. Explain how charitable giving can be made through a payroll deduction scheme.[1]

[Learning Outcome j]

Employees can make donations to charities through a payroll deduction scheme, which allows them tax relief at their highest marginal rate. The charitable payment is deducted from employment income. Income tax is then calculated on earnings after deduction of the donation, through PAYE.

The charitable payment is paid gross, and deducted from employment earnings in the calculation of taxable income.

Answers to Test Yourself

Answer to TY 1

1. McMillan carries out the work under his own control.
2. McMillan procures his own equipment when working on the contracts for Web-Designs Ltd.
3. McMillan is paid a fee for each contract; payment is not made on an hourly, weekly or monthly basis.
4. There is a financial risk for McMillan.
5. McMillan can earn increased profit from sound management.
6. The contracts are all for short periods.
7. McMillan is not an integral part of Web-Designs Ltd's business.
8. McMillan is not under any obligation to accept work that is offered to him.

The above factors indicate that McMillan is self-employed.

Answer to TY 2

The assessment of employment income is made on a receipt basis. Therefore, Jo's assessable employment income for 2012-13 is £42,800 i.e. (£35,700 + £7,100). The bonus received in January 2013 is assessed in 2012-13, even though part of it was earned in 2012-13.

Answer to TY 3

The bonus to director is treated to be received at the earliest of:

1. The date on which the bonus was received by the director.
2. The date on which the right to receive the bonus was established.
3. The date when the bonus is credited in the company's accounts
4. The end of the period of account if the bonus relates to that period, and has been determined before the end of the period.
5. The date that the bonus is determined if the period of account it relates to has already ended.

Answer to TY 4

A director, **in order not to be considered as a P11D employee,** has to fulfil the following two conditions:

1. he has to be a director who earns **less than £8,500** per annum **and**
2. he should **not control more than 5% of ordinary share capital** of the company.

Both conditions have to be complied with simultaneously.

As George fulfils only the first condition, but not the second, **he is a P11D employee.**

Answer to TY 5

The payment by an employer of an **employee's personal incidental expenses** when the employee is staying away from home overnight on business, of up to £5 per night within the UK and £10 per night outside the UK is exempt. If the limit is exceeded, the whole amount becomes taxable.

Jacqueline receives £7 a day for business trips in the UK, which is above the exempt limit of £5 per night. As the limit is exceeded, the whole amount will be taxable. Therefore, the taxable benefit is £7 x 50 days = £350.

For business trips outside the UK, Jacqueline receives £9 per day, which is within the exempt limit, so the whole amount will be exempt.

Answer to TY 6

	£
Rateable value	1,200
Add: Expensive accommodation benefit (£100,000 - £75,000) x 4.00%	1,000
Total	**2,200**
Less: Employee contribution (£120 x12)	(1,440)
Taxable benefit	**760**

Answer to TY 7

	£
Annual value	1,000
Add: Expensive accommodation benefit (£120,000 - £75,000) x 4.00%	1,800
Total	**2,800**
For nine months (6/4/2012 to 1/1/2013) (£2,800 x 9/12)	2,100
Less: Employee contribution (£100 x 9)	(900)
Taxable benefit	**1,200**

Answer to TY 8

1. **CO_2 emissions rate of 70 g/km**

(a) Lily's capital contribution is deducted from the list price
£15,300 - £1,200 = £14,100
(b) As the CO_2 emissions rate of the car is less than 75 g/km, the appropriate percentage is 5%.
(c) The assessable benefit is:

	£
£14,100 x 5%	705
Less: Employee contribution (30 x 12)	(360)
	345

2. **CO_2 emissions rate of 90 g/km**

As the CO_2 emissions rate of the car is less than 99g/km but more than 75 g/km, the appropriate percentage applicable is 10%.

The assessable benefit is:

	£
£14,100 x 10%	1,410
Less: Employee contribution (30 x 12)	(360)
	1,050

Answer to TY 9

Neil

The list price of the car is £15,500

The CO_2 emissions are above the base level figure of 100 grams per kilometre. The CO_2 emissions figure of 192 is rounded down to 190 so that it is divisible by five.

Appropriate percentage:

$$11\% + \frac{(190 - 100)}{5} = 29\%$$

Therefore, the relevant percentage is 32% (29% plus a 3% charge for a diesel car). The motor car was available throughout the tax year.
Therefore, the benefit assessable = £15,500 x 32% **= £4,960**

Bob

The list price of the car is £12,400

The CO_2 emissions are below the base level figure of 100 grams per kilometre but more than the lower level figure of 99 grams per kilometre. Therefore, the relevant percentage is 11%.

The motor car was available for seven months during the tax year 2012-13.

Therefore, the assessable benefit = £12,400 x 11% x 7/12
= **£796**

Simi

The list price of the car is £25,800

The CO_2 emissions are above the base level figure of 100 grams per kilometre. The CO_2 emissions figure of 292 is rounded down to 290 so that it is divisible by five.

Relevant percentage

$$11\% + \frac{(290 - 100)}{5} = 49\%$$

However, the relevant percentage is restricted to a maximum of 35%.

The motor car was available throughout the tax year 2012-13.

Therefore the assessable benefit is:

	£
£25,800 x 35%	9,030
Less: Employee contribution (note)	(1,600)
	7,430

Note: The contributions made by Simi towards the use of the motor car reduce the benefit.

Michelle

The list price of the car is £85,000

The CO_2 emissions are above the base level figure of 100 grams per kilometre. The CO_2 emissions figure of 153 is rounded down to 150 so that it is divisible by five.

Relevant percentage

$$11\% + \frac{(150 - 100)}{5} = 21\%$$

The motor car was available throughout the tax year 2012-13.

Therefore the assessable benefit is:

	£
£85,000 x 21%	17,850
	17,850

Note: There is no cap on the list price of a motor car.

Answer to TY 10

Assessable benefit for the car

The appropriate percentage is:

$$15\% + \frac{(160 - 125)}{5} = 22\%$$

	£
List price x appropriate %	
£24,000 x 22%	5,280
Less: Employee contribution (£100 x 12)	(1,200)
	4,080
Available for 9 months	
Benefit £4,080 x 9/12	**3,060**

Assessable benefit for fuel

Assessable benefit for fuel = £20,200 x 22% = £4,444

As the car is provided only for 9 months, reduce the assessable benefits proportionately
£4,444 x 9/12 = £3,333

Total car and fuel benefits = £6,393 (£3,060 + £3,333)

Note: any partial reimbursement made by the employee towards the cost of the private fuel will not affect the taxable benefit for the fuel.

Answer to TY 11

	£
Renault (3 months from April 2012 to June 2012)	
List price of the car is £12,000	
Assessable benefit (note 1)	570
£12,000 x 19% x 3/12	
Ford Focus (9 months from July 2012 to March 2013)	
List price of the car is £14,000	
Assessable benefit	
£14,000 x (10% + 3%) x 9/12	1,365
Total benefit	**1,935**

Notes

1. Appropriate percentage for the Renault is:

$$11\% + \frac{(140 - 100)}{5} = 19\%$$

2. The CO_2 emissions rate of the Ford is less than 99 g/km but more than 75 g/km, therefore the appropriate percentage is 10%. Moreover, it is a diesel car, so 3% will be added to the appropriate percentage for calculating the car benefit.

3. No fuel benefit is available as the employer pays for the business fuel and not for the private fuel.

Answer to TY 12

Average method

	£
(£38,000 + £16,000)/2 x 4.00%	1,080
Less: Interest paid	(380)
Benefit	**700**

Strict method

	£
£38000 x 4.00% x 9/12	1,140
£16000 x 4.00% x 3/12	160
Total	**1,300**
Less: Interest paid	(380)
Benefit	**920**

It is beneficial for the employee to have the taxable benefits calculated according to the average method.

Answer to TY 13

The benefit in 2011-12 is £800 × 20% = £160

The benefit in 2012-13 is **£460**, being the greater of (1) or (2) below:

	£
1. Market value at date of purchase	350
Less: Price paid	(180)
	170
2. Original market value	800
Less: Assessed in 2011-12	(160)
	640
Less: Price paid	(180)
	460

Answer to TY 14

Harry's taxable employment income for 2012-13 is calculated as follows:

	£	£
Salary		62,850
Accommodation benefits		
Rateable value: exempt (being job related)		
Ancillary services		
Electricity	1,320	
Gas	420	
Gardener salary	680	
Redecoration expenses	1,280	
Furniture (£15,000 x 20%)	3,000	
	6,700	
Restricted to 10% of £62,850 (note)	6,285	
Less: employee's contribution (£50 per month)	(600)	5,685
Taxable employment income		**68,535**

Note: the value of ancillary services is £6,700. However, if the accommodation is job related, the assessable benefit of ancillary services **cannot exceed 10% of employee's net earnings** for the year.

Answer to TY 15

1. The cost of the suit is not deductible, even if worn for office meetings. A suit provides warmth and is appropriate for his work. It therefore has a dual purpose. The expenditure is not wholly and exclusively for business purposes.
2. The cost of the subscription will be allowed as relevant professional subscriptions of this nature are specifically allowed by statute.
3. The subscription is not deductible although it is used wholly and exclusively for business purposes. It was not necessary for performing his duties.
4. The cost of the course is disallowed, as it was not incurred in the performance of his duties.

Answer to TY 16

1. **Joy Ltd:** the cost of the Christmas party is deductible.
2. **Each employee:** the party is a taxable benefit as the cost is less than £150 per person.

Answer to TY 17

	£	£	£
Annual employment income			15,000
Add: 1. Bonus		5,000	
2. Award under staff suggestion scheme (exempt)		-	
		5,000	
Less: Deductions			
1. Subscription to ACCA	(200)		
2. Contribution to retirement scheme (8 months x £300)	(2400)		
	(2,600)	(2,600)	
		2,400	2,400
Taxable employment income			**17,400**

Notes

1. The annual subscription fee to ACCA, being relevant to duties of employment, is fully deductible.
2. An award up to £5,000, received under a staff suggestion scheme is an exempt benefit.
3. Bonus received is taxable and hence added to employment income.
4. Expenses incurred on a birthday party, are not employment related expenses, and are not deductible.

5. Contribution to an occupational pension scheme is deductible from employment income. Susan started contributing to the scheme from 1 August 2012; therefore, contributions for eight months (from August 12 to April 13) are deductible from her employment income.

6. Annual rent and deposit paid for accommodation is her personal expense and hence not deductible from employment income.

Answer to TY 18

1. As no amount is received by Alan, an allowable expense is calculated as follows:
   For first 10,000 miles @45p per mile = £4,500
   Next 200 mile @25p per mile = £50
   Total **allowable expense** = **£4,550**
   Total employment income = £25,000 - £4,550 = **£20,450**

2. Tax-free mileage allowance = £4,550(as calculated in (1) above)
   Mileage allowance received from employer = 10,200 miles x 40p per mile = £4,080
   The deficit of **£470** (£4,550 - £4,080) can be set off against the total income from employment.
   Employment income £25,000 - £470 = **£24,530**

3. Tax-free mileage allowance = £4,550
   Mileage allowance received from employer = 10,200 miles x 50p per mile = £5,100. Excess received **£550** (£5,100 - £4,550) is taxable.
   Employment income £25,000 + £550 = **£25,550**

Answer to TY 19

Ordinary commuting (travel between home and the permanent workplace, including the journey to turn off the fire alarm) is not deductible from employment income.

Cost of private travel is not deductible from employment income.

The travel to a temporary workplace is deductible from employment income as it is for a period lasting less than 24 months.

The amount of deduction is (3,800 miles @ 45p per mile) = £1,710

Cost of travel between permanent workplace and Flex plc's suppliers is deductible from employment income.

The amount of deduction is (750 miles @ 45p per mile) = £337.5

Answer to TY 20

Jack's employment income for 2012-13 is as follows:

	£	£
Employment income		36,000
Add: Bonus (W1)		1,500
Performance incentive (W2)		3,000
Mobile phone expenses incurred by company (W3)		-
		40,500
Less: Deductions		
Contribution to occupational pension scheme (W4) (12 x £500 = £6,000)	(6,000)	
Business traveling expenses (W5) (£700 + £900 + £1,000)	(2,600)	**(8,600)**
Taxable employment income		**31,900**

Workings

W1 and W2 Bonus and performance incentives are part of employment income. They are assessed on receipt basis.

W3 The provision of a mobile is exempt.

W4 Contributions to an occupational pension scheme are deductible.

W5 Travel expenses for business purposes are deductible. Here travelling expenses from city A to city B (£800) are **not deductible** as travelling expenses from home to office are not deductible. However, other expenses are related to his work as a sales officer hence those are deductible.

Answer to TY 21

1. 15p per day would be exempt. The remaining £1.15 i.e. (£1.30 - £0.15 = 1.15p) per day would be taxable.
2. Free meals in the company canteen are exempt if available to all employees
3. Removal expenses of up to £8,000 are exempt.
4. Long-service award made in cash is taxable.

Answer to TY 22

1. Not allowable.
2. Allowable.
3. Not allowable even if worn only at office. A suit provides warmth and is appropriate attire. It is not wholly, exclusively and necessarily for the duties of employment.
4. Allowable if relevant to the employment.

Answer to TY 23

Solution Ltd must provide the following forms to Julian.

1. Form P60 employee's certificate of pay, income tax and NIC must be given to Julian. Form P60 must be given by 31 May 2013.
2. A copy of form P11D detailing expense payments and benefits in kind. This must be given to Julian by 6 July 2013.

Answer to TY 24

Taking into account Sam's personal allowance, allowable expenses and adjustment for overpaid tax in the previous year, the tax code can be worked out as follows:

	£
Personal allowance	8,105
Add: Allowable expenses	276
Add: Income on which tax was overpaid in 2009-10 £105 x 100/20 (W1)	525
Total	**8,906**
Less: Assessable benefits	(1,040)
Tax free income	**7,866**

Workings

W1

To collect unpaid tax, the amount must be grossed up by the individual's marginal rate of tax.
Tax code = 1/10 of £7,866 rounded down to a whole number. Therefore, the tax code is **786** followed by a letter.

From the given information, the letter appears to be 'L' as Sam is entitled to personal allowance and his benefits do not exceed his allowance. Therefore, Sam's tax code is 723L.

Quick Quiz

1. What is the basis on which income from employment is taxable?
2. Are the expenses incurred for travelling from home to employee's place of work deductible?
3. What is the chargeable value of free meals provided to employees in a staff canteen?
4. If an employee travels 12,000 miles in a tax year by motor car, how much mileage allowance is he entitled to?

Answers to Quick Quiz

1. Income from employment is taxable on receipt basis.
2. No, as they are not considered to be incurred for performing duties of employment.
3. Benefits for free meals in a staff canteen are exempt from tax.
4.

10,000 miles x 45p per mile	£4,500
2,000 miles x 25p per mile	£500
Total mileage allowance	£5,000

Self Examination Questions

Question 1

When is the employment income received in case of:

1. an employee?
2. a director of a company?

Question 2

What are the tests which might be used to distinguish employment and self-employment?

Question 3

State the general rule which determines whether or not an employee's expenditure is deductible.

Question 4

Which of the following expenses incurred by an employee would be deductible when computing employment income?

1. The travelling cost from home to work place
2. The cost of business calls on a private telephone
3. The travelling cost between employment sites
4. Subscriptions to professional bodies
5. Donations to charity made under payroll deduction scheme operated by an employer

Question 5

Pillsbury is employed and earns a salary of £25,000. His employer reimbursed the following expenses incurred by Pillsbury in 2012-13:

	£
Entertaining expenses	444 (wholly for business)
Rail and taxi fares	326 (wholly for business)
Home telephone cost	182 (50% private use)

His employer provided the following benefits:

1. Private medical insurance costing £650 in 2012-13.
2. A car with a list price of £13,650. The company paid all the costs of the car, including fuel. The car runs on petrol and the CO_2 emissions rate is 160 g/km.

Required:

Calculate Pillsbury's taxable employment income for 2012-13.

Question 6

On 5 July 2012 Harry resigned from Men-city plc, where he had been employed for some years. The following information is available for 2012-13:

1. Harry's gross salary was £36,000 per annum, PAYE of £2,680 was deducted in 2012-13.
2. Men-city Plc had provided Harry with a petrol driven car with a list price of £16,500. The CO_2 emissions rate was 278 g/km. Men-city Plc had also provided Harry with fuel for private journeys. Harry contributed £2,500 towards the cost of the motor car when it was first provided to him and paid £100 per month to Men-city Plc for the use of the car.
3. On 1 January 2011 Men-city Plc provided Harry an interest- free loan of £70,000 to purchase a boat. Harry repaid £45,000 of loan on 5 May 2012, and repaid the balance of the loan of £25,000 on 6 July 2012.
4. The company had provided Harry with free meals in the company staff canteen which is open to all employees. The total cost of these meals to the company was £280.
5. Harry has no other source of income in 2012-13.

Required:

Calculate Harry's total income for 2012-13.

Answers to Self Examination Questions

Answer to SEQ 1

1. Employee

The earlier of:

(a) the date when payment is made
(b) the date when an employee becomes entitled for payment

2. Director

The earliest of:

(a) the two alternatives given in the rule for employees
(b) the date on which the income is **credited** to the director in the accounting records of the company
(c) the end of period of accounts, if the director's income for that period is determined by then
(d) the date on which the amount is determined, if after the end of the company's period of accounts

Answer to SEQ 2

1. Control
2. Financial risk involved
3. Equipment
4. Substitution
5. Work correction
6. Holidays
7. Number of persons contracted with
8. Mode of payment
9. Position
10. Obligation

Answer to SEQ 3

Employee's expenses are allowed only if they are incurred **wholly, exclusively and necessarily** in the **performance of the duties** of employment.

Answer to SEQ 4

1. Not deductible
2. Deductible
3. Deductible
4. Allowable if relevant to the duties of employment
5. Specifically deductible

Answer to SEQ 5

Calculation of Pillsbury's taxable employment income for 2012-13

Earned income		£	£	£
	Employment income			25,000
Add:	Reimbursed expenses			
	Entertaining		444	
	Rail and taxi fares		326	
	Home telephone		182	
			952	
Less:	Allowable expenses			
	Entertaining (W1)	(444)		
	Rail and taxi fares (W1)	(326)		
	Home telephone: 50% (W2)	(91)	(861)	91
Add:	Assessable value of benefits			
	Car (W3)		3,140	
	Fuel: £20,200 X 23%		4,646	
	Private medical insurance		650	8,436
Taxable employment income				**33,527**

Workings

W1 Entertaining expenses and rail and taxi fares incurred wholly for business purposes are deductible from employment income.

W2 Home telephone cost is allowed only up to 50% as any expenditure incurred for private purposes is not deductible.

W3 Assessable benefit of car

The list price of the car is £13,650

The appropriate percentage is: $11\% + \frac{(160 - 100)}{5} = 23\%$

Therefore, assessable benefit =£13,650 x 23%= £3,140

Answer to SEQ 6

Calculation of income tax payable / repayable by Harry for 2012-13

	£
Salary (£36,000 x 3/12)	9,000
Car benefit (W1)	925
Fuel benefit (W2)	1,767
Beneficial loan (W3)	400
Staff canteen (Note)	-
Total Income	**12,092**

Workings

W1 Assessable car benefit

The list price of the car is £16,500. Harry made a capital contribution of £2,500.

The appropriate percentage is:

$$11\% + \frac{(275 - 100)}{5} = 46\%$$

However, the percentage is restricted to a maximum of 35%.

The car was available for 3 months in 2012-13. Harry contributed £100 per month for the private use of the car.

Therefore the assessable car benefit is:

	£
(£16,500 – £2,500) x 35% x 3/12	1,225
Less: Employee contribution (3 x £100)	(300)
	925

W2 Fuel benefit

£20,200 x 35% x 3/12 = £1,767

W3 Assessable value of beneficial loan

Average method

((£70,000 + £25,000)/2 x 4.00% x 3/12) = £475

Strict method

(£70,000 x 4.00% x 1/12) + (£25,000 x 4.00% x 2/12) = £400

Harry will elect to use the strict method, as this gives a lower assessment.

Note: the provision of meals in a staff canteen does not give rise to a taxable benefit.

SECTION B

INCOME TAX LIABILITIES

B3

STUDY GUIDE B3: INCOME FROM SELF-EMPLOYMENT (PART 1)

Get Through Intro

If an individual is trading on his own via an unincorporated business, he is termed as a sole trader. He is the sole proprietor of his business.

We calculate the profits of the business as if it were separate from the proprietor. However, whereas the profits of a company are charged to corporation tax, the profits of an unincorporated business must be included in the calculation of the proprietor's taxable income.

This Study Guide discusses the calculation of taxable profits, the allowable deductions, the relief available for pre-trading expenses and the assessment of the profits of self-employed individuals, including the rules on commencement and cessation of a business.

As a tax consultant, you will need to ensure that your clients **compute their taxable profits correctly** and **make use of all available deductions and exemptions**. You will also need to ensure that your own taxable income is correct.

A question on this topic appears in nearly every paper, and so you **must** have a thorough understanding of this Study Guide.

Learning Outcomes

a) Recognise the basis of assessment for self-employment income.
b) Describe and apply the badges of trade.
c) Recognise the expenditure that is allowable in calculating the tax-adjusted trading profit.
d) Recognise the relief that can be obtained for pre-trading expenditure.
e) Compute the assessable profits on commencement and on cessation.
f) Change of accounting date
   i. Recognise the factors that will influence the choice of accounting date.
   ii. State the conditions that must be met for a change of accounting date to be valid.
   iii. Compute the assessable profits on a change of accounting date.

Introduction

The rules on deductions of expenses are more generous than for employed individuals, and a much **wider range** of expenses are allowed against the income of self-employed individuals. The self-employed pay their tax later than employed individuals, **as they are required to make payments on account, and then a balancing payment after the end of the tax year.** An individual's employment status also affects his national insurance contributions. Self-employed individuals may pay **less NIC** than employees.

As a result, you must determine, when advising clients, whether they are employed or self–employed.

1. Recognise the basis of assessment for self-employment income.[2]

[Learning Outcome a]

Income tax is charged for a **tax year**. A tax year is also called a "year of assessment". The tax year runs **from 6 April to the following 5 April**. However, traders may prepare their accounts to any date. They are not required to prepare them to 5 April.

Example

Lilly, a bookseller may prepare her accounts for the twelve months to 31 December every year.

Each individual trader may have a different period end. It would be very difficult for HMRC to determine the tax liability of different traders for different years. Hence it is necessary to establish a link between the accounting periods for which trading profits are calculated and the tax year in which those profits are charged to tax.

For tax purposes, the trading profits must be calculated in accordance with generally accepted accounting principles. An important point which must be noted here is that **the accrual basis** of accounting must be followed.

The accrual basis means profits and expenses are recognised when they are earned / incurred and accrued in the year, whether or not they are **actually received / paid** in that year.

Individuals are charged tax for the period 6 April to the following 5 April. If the accounts are not prepared to 5 April, special rules are needed to link the period of account to the tax year. Basis periods are used to link periods of account to tax years. The profits are taxed in the corresponding tax year.

The basic rule for taxing trading profits is the current year basis of assessment (CYB). The basis period (the period of profits taxed) for a tax year is the twelve month accounting period ending in the tax year.

Tip

What is a basis period?

The basis period for a tax year is the twelve month accounting period ending in the tax year.

Example

A trader prepares accounts to 31 December each year. The twelve month period of account from 1 January 2012 to 31 December 2012 ends in the tax year 2012-13. The basis period for tax year 2012-13 will be the 12 month period ended on 31 December 2012.

Special rules apply on commencement of trade, on change of accounting date and on cessation. These rules are studied in Learning Outcomes 5 and 6 of this Study Guide.

SUMMARY

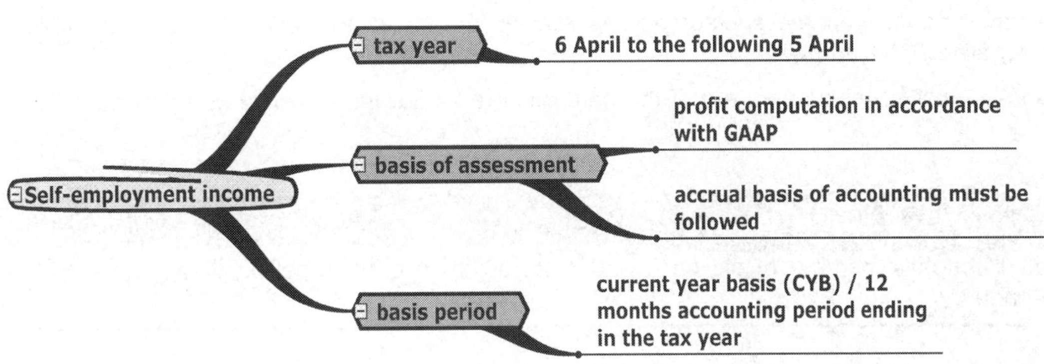

2. Describe and apply the badges of trade.[2]

[Learning Outcome b]

All the **trading** profits of a person who is a UK resident are chargeable to income tax.

When an individual disposes of assets, it is not always clear if those transactions constitute a trade or not. If an individual disposes of an asset, should that transaction be:

- treated as a **capital gain**, or
- treated as **trading income?**

The courts have interpreted what is meant by 'trade' and how to determine if a trade exists in a given situation. Where there is doubt as to whether an activity constitutes a trade, a number of **key factors** have been identified through judicial decisions, known as the **badges of trade**. The badges of trade give guidance where it is not clear if certain activities constitute a trade.

2.1 Badges of trade

1. Subject matter of the transaction

There are three main reasons for purchasing an asset:

a) for personal use
b) as an investment, either to yield income, or for a long-term gain
c) to resell at a profit, which constitutes trading.

The **intentions** of the purchaser **at the time of purchase** regarding the resale of the article are relevant.

If the asset is **held as an investment or for personal use**, any profit on a later sale will be treated as a **capital profit.**

If an asset is **not held as an investment or for personal use**, any profit on its sale will be treated as a **trading profit.**

2. Length of period of ownership

Assets purchased for personal use or as an investment are normally held for a long period, whereas assets purchased as trading inventory are usually held for a shorter term. The shorter the period of ownership, the more likely the activity constitutes a trade.

3. Frequency of similar transactions

The number of similar transactions and the frequency of those transactions suggest that the activity constitutes trading.

A taxpayer bought clothes at the local market each week, and sold them at a profit. The taxpayer is regularly performing the same transaction. This is likely to constitute trading.

4. Supplementary work and marketing

Where a taxpayer performs some supplementary work on the asset, to make it more marketable, it is **more likely to be regarded as trading.**

If steps are taken to find purchasers e.g. if the sale occurred following advertising, this would also suggest a trading activity.

Example

If an individual bought a number of old cars, and restored them prior to selling them, the activity is likely to constitute a trade.

5. Reason for the sale

The circumstances giving rise to the sale of the asset are also important factors to decide if trading has occurred. If a person sold an asset due to personal financial problems, it is unlikely to be regarded as a trade.

Example

An individual sells one of his three motorcars to raise funds to pay for his mother's healthcare is unlikely to be regarded as trading.

6. Profit motive

The presence of a profit motive in the mind of the taxpayer **at the time of buying the asset** is a strong indication that a person is trading. An asset acquired other than by purchase, e.g. inheritance on the death of a relative, is unlikely to indicate a trading activity.

The badges of trade cannot be used as a checklist as no one factor is conclusive in deciding whether or not trading has occurred. All of the badges of trade are to be considered. It depends on the facts of the particular case to determine whether the transaction is a trade or not.

Tip

How do you remember these six elements?

Make some meaningful sentence by using words from each of them.
Like, **Frequency** and **length** of **profit** are **subject matter** not **supplementary reasons.**

where,

Frequency: frequency of transactions
Length: length of ownership
Profit: profit motive.
Subject matter: subject matter of transaction
Supplementary: supplementary work and marketing
Reason: Reason for sale

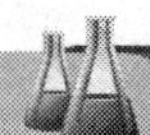

Test Yourself 1

State the six main badges of trade.

Diagram 1: Badges of trade

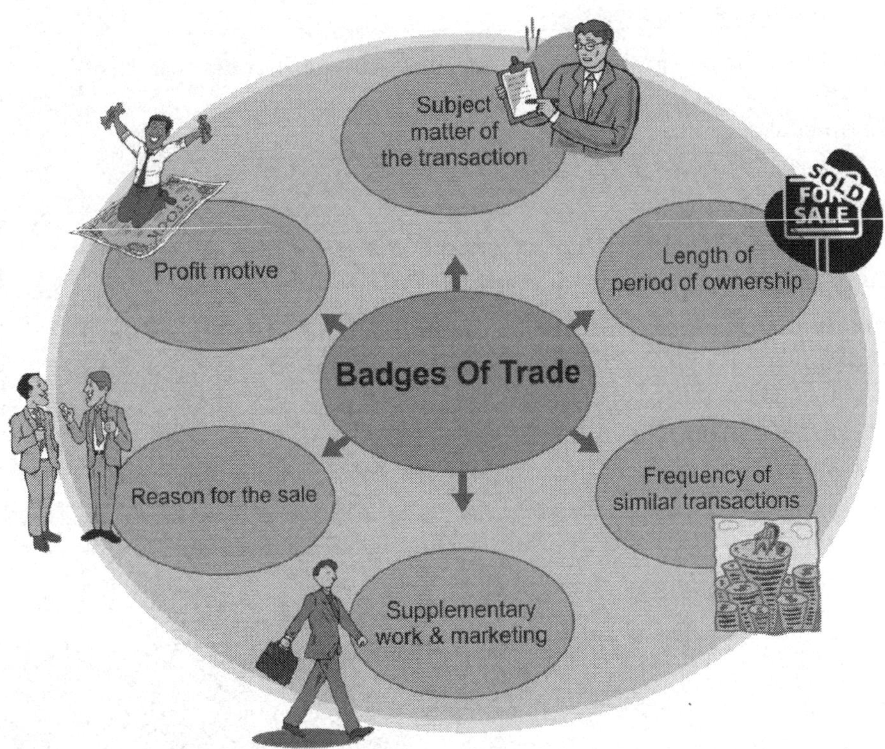

3. Recognise the expenditure that is allowable in calculating the tax-adjusted trading profit.[2]
[Learning Outcome c]

In order to ascertain the taxable trading profits for an accounting period, the net profit shown in the income statement must be adjusted as the accounting conventions are different from the rules of taxation.

Adjustments to profits shown in the financial accounts would include:

1. **Add:** Adding back depreciation, client entertaining, etc. which **are not allowable for tax purposes.**

AND

2. **Deduct:** Deducting capital allowances, (which **are allowable for tax purposes).**

Capital allowances are a statutory form of depreciation giving relief on capital purchases.

After making these adjustments, we arrive at the trading profit for tax purposes.

Some examples of the types of adjustments required to the net profit per accounts are given in the overview below. The detailed rules are explained subsequently:

	Pro forma for calculation of adjusted profit	£
	Net trading profits per accounts	X
Add:	**(I) Expenditure shown in the accounts but not deductible for tax purposes**	
	Customer entertaining	X
	Purchases of asset (capital expenditure)	X
	Increases in general provision	X
	(II) Trading income taxable but not included in the accounts	
	Goods taken for own consumption (at market value)	X
Less:	**(I) Expenditure deductible for tax purposes but not shown in the accounts**	
	Business use of private telephone	(X)
	Short term lease premium paid by the trader	(X)
	(II) Income included in the accounts but not taxable as trading income	
	Dividends	(X)
	Property income	(X)
	Adjusted profit before capital allowances	**X**

These are only some of the examples and are not an exhaustive list of adjustments.

Tip

Remember, you start with **net trading profits** per accounts, not gross profits

The general rule is that only **expenditure which is wholly and exclusively for the purposes of trade is allowable.**

Example

Income tax paid by a trader is not allowed as it does not relate to the trade. It is a personal expense of the person carrying on the trade.

Tip

As a general rule, expenditure incurred wholly and exclusively for the purposes of trade is allowable, and expenditure, which does not relate to the trade, is not allowable.

Allowable and non-allowable deductions for calculating tax-adjusted trading profits

Here we look at the main categories of business expenditure and their treatment, when calculating tax adjusted trading profits.

☑ This **denotes deductible**.

☒ This **denotes non deductible**.

1. Appropriation of profit ☒

Tax must be paid on all the profits of the business, so any amount taken out of the business by the owner must be added back. This includes drawings, owner's salary (although a reasonable salary paid to the spouse may be allowable), interest on capital, the owner's personal income tax and NICs.

2. Salaries to family members ☒

Salary to family members in excess of market rates is not deductible.

3. Expenses attributable to private use by owner ☒

Expenses attributable to private use by the owner e.g. telephone is **not allowable.**

4. Depreciation / amortisation ☒

Depreciation gives relief for the cost of an asset (such as machinery) over its useful life. As the accounting rules (depreciation) are different from the prescribed tax rules (capital allowances), depreciation is added back and capital allowances are deducted.

A detailed discussion on capital allowances is covered in the next section of this Study Guide.

5. Provisions ☒

A specific provision, that relates to revenue expenditure and is specifically quantifiable, is allowable.

General provisions are disallowable.

Example

A general provision for repairs would not be deductible as it is an estimated amount. A provision for a £500 repair to a leaking roof would be allowed if this specifically relates to a building quote received.

Tip

Remember, FRS 26 states that a general allowance cannot be made for debtors. Therefore, all allowances relating to debtors made in the accounts are deductible as they are specific allowances.

---

6. Capital expenditure 

Capital expenditure is specifically disallowed. Capital expenditure is not normally charged to the income statement. However repairs and maintenance expenditure charged to the income statement may contain items that are of a capital nature.

Expenditure on repairs (returning the asset to its original condition) and maintenance (redecoration) is allowable. If the expenditure relates to improvement or enhances the value of the asset, it is a capital expenditure and disallowed.

Example

The rebuilding of a wall that was damaged in an accident is repair expenditure and allowable.

The building of an entirely new wall is capital expenditure and disallowable.

Expenditure which relates to a capital asset is not allowable, **e.g.**

a) Legal and professional fees relating to the acquisition of a capital asset.
b) Losses on the disposal of fixed assets.
c) Purchase of a used asset: If an asset is purchased in a state of disrepair and is not useable, and the purchase price reflects the state of disrepair, any expenditure incurred in bringing the asset into a useable condition is treated as capital expenditure and disallowed.

7. Gifts ☑

a) Gifts to employees are allowable (but may be taxable on the employee).
b) Gifts to customers are not allowable **unless:**
   i. They **cost no more than £50** per person per year.
   ii. They are **not food, drink, tobacco or vouchers** exchangeable for goods.
   iii. They **carry a conspicuous advertisement** for the business.

Expenditure on coffee mugs that cost £20 each, with the business name printed on them would be allowable.

---

8. Entertaining ☑ **and** ☒

- Entertaining employees is allowable.
- Entertaining **customers, suppliers** or anyone else is **not allowable.**

9. Donations ☒

A donation to a **national charity** is **not allowable.** Similarly, donations to a political party are not allowable.

A donation of £5,000 to UNICEF is not allowable, as it is given to a national charity.

However, reasonably **small** gifts or donations to a **local charity** are **allowable.**

Anthony, a trader, made a cash donation of £200 to a local charity, and received free advertising in the local magazine. This is allowable because the amount is small, is given to a local charity, and the business benefits from it.

Qualifying charitable donations are not allowable as a deduction from trading income. This is because the basic rate tax relief is given at the time the payments are made and by extension of the basic rate band for higher rate taxpayers. This is discussed in more detail in Study Guide B5.

Gifts of trading inventory or used plant and machinery to charities and UK educational establishments are allowable by statute.

10. Subscriptions ☑

a) Subscriptions to professional and trade associations are allowable if they relate to the trade.

A trader's subscription to the Chamber of Commerce is allowable.

---

b) Political subscriptions and donations: not allowable

11. Legal and professional charges ☑

Allowable if they relate to revenue expenditure and incurred for the purposes of trade.

Allowable expenses include:

a) fees relating to an action for breach of contract.
b) fees paid to a lawyer in relation to trade debt collection.
c) fees incurred in defending the title to a fixed asset.
d) fees for audit and accountancy work, and agreeing tax liabilities with HMRC.

However, fees incurred in relation to tax appeals and investigations are not allowable.

Legal and professional fees relating to the following capital expenses are specifically allowable:

- legal costs incurred in **the renewal of a short (50 years or less) lease.**
- incidental costs relating to the **raising of long-term finance** (even if the loan is not obtained).
- costs incurred relating to the **registration of a patent or copyright**.

12. Interest ☑

Interest, including interest on business bank overdrafts, hire purchase and credit cards is allowable.

Note: interest paid as a **result of the late payment of tax is disallowed.**

13. Bad debts ☑

a) Trade bad debts are allowable.
b) **Employee bad debts** or other non-trade loans written off are **not allowable.**

14. Penalties and fines ☒

Fines or penalties imposed due to infringements of the law are disallowed, e.g. penalties for late registration of VAT, speeding fines of the owner, fines for infringement of health and safety regulations.

An **exception is parking fines incurred by employees whilst on business, which** are allowable (because they are taxable on the employee).

15. Staff- related expenses ☑

Staff-related expenses are deductible, and include the following:

a) gross salaries and employer's National Insurance Contributions.
b) employer's contributions into an occupational or personal pension scheme.
c) redundancy payments and compensation for loss of office. If payment is made on the cessation of trade, payments up to three times the statutory amount, in addition the statutory redundancy payments are allowed (i.e. four times the statutory redundancy amount in total).
d) counselling services for employees leaving employment.
e) educational courses arranged for staff, if related to the trade.
f) contributions to local enterprise agencies etc.

16. Removal expenses to new business premises ☑

Allowable, provided it is **not due to the expansion** of the business.

17. Illegal payments ☒

Payments, which constitute a criminal offence such as a bribe or illegal payments such as payments to blackmailers or extortionists, are not allowable.

18. Irrecoverable VAT ☑

Irrecoverable VAT is allowable if it relates to an item of allowable expenditure.

19. Staff defalcations ☑

Losses as a result of employee dishonesty are allowable. However, losses resulting from the owner's dishonesty are not allowable.

20. Travelling expenses ☑

The costs of business travel by the owner are allowable, but not travel from home to the office.

21. Car leasing and rental costs ☑

The cost of hiring, leasing or renting a car is allowable irrespective of its price. However, there is a restriction on the allowable expenditure where the CO_2 emissions of the car exceed 160g/km. 15% of the leasing costs are disallowed and 85% are allowed while calculating taxable profits where the CO_2 emissions of the car exceed 160g/km.

A trader pays hire charges of £3,800 per annum for a car with CO_2 emissions of 185g/km.
Compute the allowable amount.

Answer

As the CO_2 emissions of the car exceed 160g/km, 15% of the hire charges will be disallowed and 85% will be allowed while calculating taxable profits.

Amount of hire charges disallowed = £3,800 x 15% = £570

Therefore, **the allowable amount is (£3,800 - £570) = £3,230.**

---

22. Short term lease premiums ☑

When a trader pays a short term lease premium, the deduction of lease premium paid is allowable from their trading profits.

The amount of deduction is the **lease premium assessable on the landlord divided by the number of years.** This amount is deductible each year for the period of lease.

The rent premium deductible per year is calculated by using the following formula:

$$\frac{\text{Lease premium assessable on the landlord}}{\text{Number of years of lease}}$$

The lease premium assessable on the landlord **is equal to the amount of premium reduced by 2% for each year of the lease, except for the first year, and is calculated as:**

Premium assessable to property business income
= P – P (2% x (n- 1))
Where,
P = Premium
n = no. of years of lease

Era pays a premium of £25,000 on 1 April 2012 to her landlord, Gracy, for granting a 20 year lease in respect of an office building, in the accounting period ending on 31 March 2013.

If the lease is granted for a period of 50 years or less, then it is termed a short lease.

The amount to be assessed as income for Gracy (the landlord) is:
= P – P x (2% (n -1)
= £25,000 – £25,000 x (2% x (20 – 1)
= £15,500

The lease premium deductible for Era from her trading profits is calculated as follows:

$$= \frac{\text{Lease premium assessable on the landlord}}{\text{Number of years of lease}} = \frac{£15{,}500}{20 \text{ years}} = £775$$

Therefore, Era can deduct **£775** per year for 20 years of the lease period.

Diagram 2: Summary of allowable expenses

Type of expense	Deductible
Salaries to family members at market rates	✓
Gifts to employees	✓
Gifts to customers (provided cost not more than £50, not food, drink etc)	✓
Staff entertainment	✓
Trade subscriptions	✓
Trade-related legal and professional charges	✓
Interest (trading purposes)	✓
Staff training	✓
Removal expenses, unless an expansionary move	✓
Redundancy pay in excess of statutory limit	✓
Contribution to pension schemes	✓
Short term lease premium	✓
Irrecoverable VAT, if relates to an item of allowable expenditure	✓
Staff defalcations	✓
Travelling expenses (business)	✓
Lease and rent payments for equipment	✓
Registration of patents and trademarks	✓

Type of expense	Deductible
Expenses attributable to private use by owner	✗
Depreciation / amortisation	✗
Increase in general allowance	✗
Capital expenditure	✗
Customer / supplier entertainment	✗
Political donations	✗
Penalties and fines	✗
Appropriation of profit	✗
Illegal payments	✗

Test Yourself 2

Nick runs a restaurant. His income statement for the year ended 31 March 2013 is as follows:

	£	£
Gross profit		27,430
Expenses		
Salaries	6,300	
Depreciation	2,500	
Bad debts written off	180	
Legal fees relating to the purchase of a new restaurant	350	
Increase in general provision	50	(9,380)
Net profit before taxation		**18,050**

Required:

Compute the trading profit for tax purposes.

3.1 Trading income not shown in the accounts

The main example of trading income not shown in the accounts is goods taken by the trader for his personal use. The owner should be taxed on the profit as if the goods had been sold at market value. If he takes goods either without paying for them or accounting for them at cost rather than the normal selling price, the trading profit must be adjusted.

Tip

- If the goods have been adjusted at cost, the profit must be added back.
- If no adjustment has been made, the selling price must be added back.

Example

Thomas, a sports car dealer, gives one of the cars to his son. Its cost was £6,125 and normally sells for £8,000. Thomas does not account for the transaction in his books. £8,000, the selling price of the car, must be added to the accounting profit.

Test Yourself 3

Macho, a trader manufacturing cutting tools, incurred the following expenditure in the year to 31 December 2012. Explain the treatment of each of the following expenses to calculate tax-adjusted trading profits.

	£
Depreciation	3,160
Repairs to machinery	1,390
Construction of a new rest room for staff	9,600
Purchase of a car for the factory manager	2,000
General provision for repairs	1,890
Christmas lunch for staff	120
Christmas lunch for 50 customers	1,510
Wedding gift to staff	320
Wedding gift to a customer	680
Gifts to customers (20 pens, costing £45 each, with business name engraved)	900
Qualifying charitable donation to a local charity	1,000
Legal fees for the collection of trade debts	1,000
Costs of renewing a 40 year lease	2,300
Costs of registering a business trademark	5,500

4. Recognise the relief that can be obtained for pre-trading expenditure.[2]

[Learning Outcome d]

A trader may incur expenses before actually starting the trade, e.g. rent of business premises, interest on a loan for the purchase of machinery, legal charges etc. These expenses are known as pre-trading expenditure, and are treated as if incurred on the first day of trade. They are allowable provided they were incurred within seven years of the commencement of trade, and are related to the trade. These expenses must be of a type which, if incurred after trading had commenced, would be allowable i.e. capital expenditure incurred before the commencement of trade is not allowable as a revenue cost.

Example

John started trading on 1 January 2012, incurring the following expenses before that date:

Expenses	Date	£
Legal fees for transferring the business premises to his name	12 August 2008	1,200
Rent for a workshop for the business	5 May 2008	300
Fees for a market survey	1 January 2007	1,450
Fees for making a project report and feasibility study	15 June 2000	620

Required:

Which expenses are allowable and which are not allowable?

Answer

Expenses	Allowable / Not Allowable	Reason
Legal fees for transferring the business premises to his name	Not allowable	Relates to a capital asset
Rent for a workshop for the business	Allowable	Normal trading expenditure incurred within seven years of the commencement of trade
Fees for a market survey	Allowable	Normal trading expenditure incurred within seven years of the commencement of trade
Fees for making a project report and feasibility study	Not allowable	Incurred more than seven years before the commencement of trade

SUMMARY

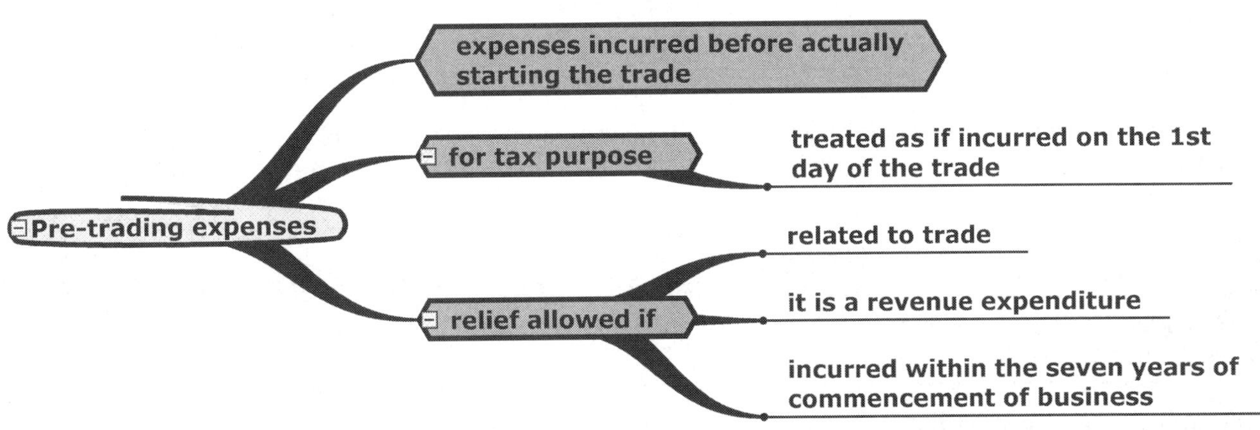

5. Compute the assessable profits on commencement and on cessation.[2]

[Learning Outcome e]

5.1 Assessable profits

The owner of a business is charged to income tax on his trading profits. In order to determine the assessable amount, the following three steps are required:

1. **Adjust the net profit figure per the accounts**

The net profit per the accounts has been arrived at using accounting rules; this figure now needs to be adjusted according to the tax rules (refer to Learning Outcome 3).

2. **Calculation of capital allowances**

The trader has added back the depreciation charge in his accounts, and now calculates the relief for capital expenditure according to HMRC's prescribed rules (refer to Study Guide B3 Part 2).

3. **Determine in which tax year the trading profits will be taxed**

The adjusted profit is charged as trading income in the owner's income tax calculation. Special rules apply to determine the period assessed in each tax year (the basis period).

The trading income calculation

	£
Net profit per accounts	X
Add: Expenditure not allowable	X
Less: Income not taxable as trading income	(X)
Adjusted profits before capital allowances	**X**
Less: Capital allowances on plant and machinery	(X)
Capital allowances on industrial buildings	(X)
Adjusted profits after capital allowances	**X**

The individual pays income tax on the income in a tax year (the year 6 April to following 5 April). If a business prepares accounts to 5 April, then the profits for the year to 5 April 2013 will be taxed in 2012-13.

If an individual prepares the accounts to any other date, the accounts to the chosen date have to be linked to a tax year. The basic rule is to tax the twelve month period ending in the tax year. A trader preparing accounts for the year to 31 August 2012 will have those profits taxed in 2012-13. This is called the current year basis (CYB).

5.2 Commencement of trade

In the first years of trade, we cannot use the current year basis, and so special rules are needed.

1. **The first tax year:** The period charged to tax (the basis period) in the first tax year of trade is determined according to the date the trade commences. It runs from **the date of the start of trade to the following 5 April.**

Example

Annie started trading on 1 January 2013, annually preparing accounts to 31 December. She started trading in 2012-13. The basis period is 1 January 2013 to 5 April 2013.

If the trade ceases to exist before 5 April, the basis period is from the date of start of trade to the date of cessation of trade.

Example

Jimmy started trading on 1 May 2012 and closed down the business on 31 January 2013. The basis period for 2012-13 is 1 May 2012 to 31 January 2013.

2. **The second tax year:** The basis period for the second tax year depends on the length of the accounting period that ends in the second tax year.

a) If the accounting period ending in the second tax year is **at least, or exactly twelve months** long, tax the **twelve months ending on that accounting date.**

Example

Rosy commenced her business on 1 January 2012 and prepares accounts to 31 March each year. Her first accounts are for the period to 31 March 2013.
What is the basis period for 2011-12 and 2012-13?

Rosy started trading in 2010-11. The basis period for the first tax year 2011-12 is 1 January 2012 to 5 April 2012.

There is an accounting period of at least twelve months ending in the second tax year 2012-13 on 31 March 2013, thus the basis period is the twelve months ending on that accounting date i.e. 1 April 2012 to 31 March 2013.

---

b) If the accounting period ending in the second tax year is **less than twelve months** long, tax the **first twelve months of trading.**

Example

Lisa commenced trading on 1 November 2011 and prepares accounts to 30 June each year. Her first accounts are for the period to 30 June 2012.

Lisa's basis period for the first tax year 2011-12 is 1 November 2011 to 5 April 2012.

There is an accounting period from 1 November 2011 to 30 June 2012 ending in the second tax year of 2012-13, but it is less than 12 months.

Therefore, in this case the basis period is the first twelve months of trading, i.e. from 1 November 2011 to 31 October 2012.

---

c) If there is **no accounting period ending in the second tax year**, tax the **period 6 April to 5 April of the second tax year.**

Example

Garry commences trading on 1 February 2012 and prepares accounts to 30 June each year. His first accounts are for the period to 30 June 2013. What are the basis periods for 2011-12 and 2012-13?

The basis period for the first tax year 2011-12 is 1 February 2012 to 5 April 2012.

No accounting period ends in tax year 2012-13 as the accounting date 30 June 2012 falls in tax year 2013-14. Thus, the basis period for the second tax year 2012-13 is 6 April 2012 to 5 April 2013.

---

3. **The third tax year:** The basis period for the third tax year is:

a) If a twelve months accounting period **ends in the third tax year**, tax that period **(CYB).**
b) If (a) is not possible, tax **twelve months to the accounting date in the third tax year.**

Example

Continuing with the example of Garry
The accounting period ending in the tax year 2013-14 on 30 June 2013 is for 17 months. As no twelve months accounting period ends in the third tax year, the basis period for the third tax year 2013-14 is twelve months to the accounting date in 2013-14 i.e. year ended 30 June 2013.

A trader commenced trading on 1 May 2010 and prepares his first accounts to 30 September 2011 and then 30 September thereafter. Here, the basis periods for the first three years are as follows:

Tax year	Basis period
2010-11 (note 1)	1 May 2010 to 5 April 2011
2011-12 (note 2)	1 October 2010 to 30 September 2011
2012-13 (note 3)	1 October 2011 to 30 September 2012

Notes:

1. For the first tax year the basis period runs from the commencement of trade to the following 5 April.
2. **There is an accounting period of at least 12 months ending in the second tax year**, so the basis period is 12 months to the accounting date in the second tax year.
3. Current year basis.

Exam tip: Errors frequently arise, when deciding on the basis periods for the opening years. You must learn these rules. Expect to see these rules tested frequently in the exam.

4. Subsequent tax years

The basis period for the following tax years is the twelve month accounting period ending in the tax year – the current year basis.

Merry has been trading for many years and prepares accounts to 31 October each year.
What is the basis period for 2012-13?

The year ended 31 October 2012 ends in 2012-13.
The basis period for 2012-13 is the year to 31 October 2012.

Diagram 3: Summary of basis periods for the opening years of assessment

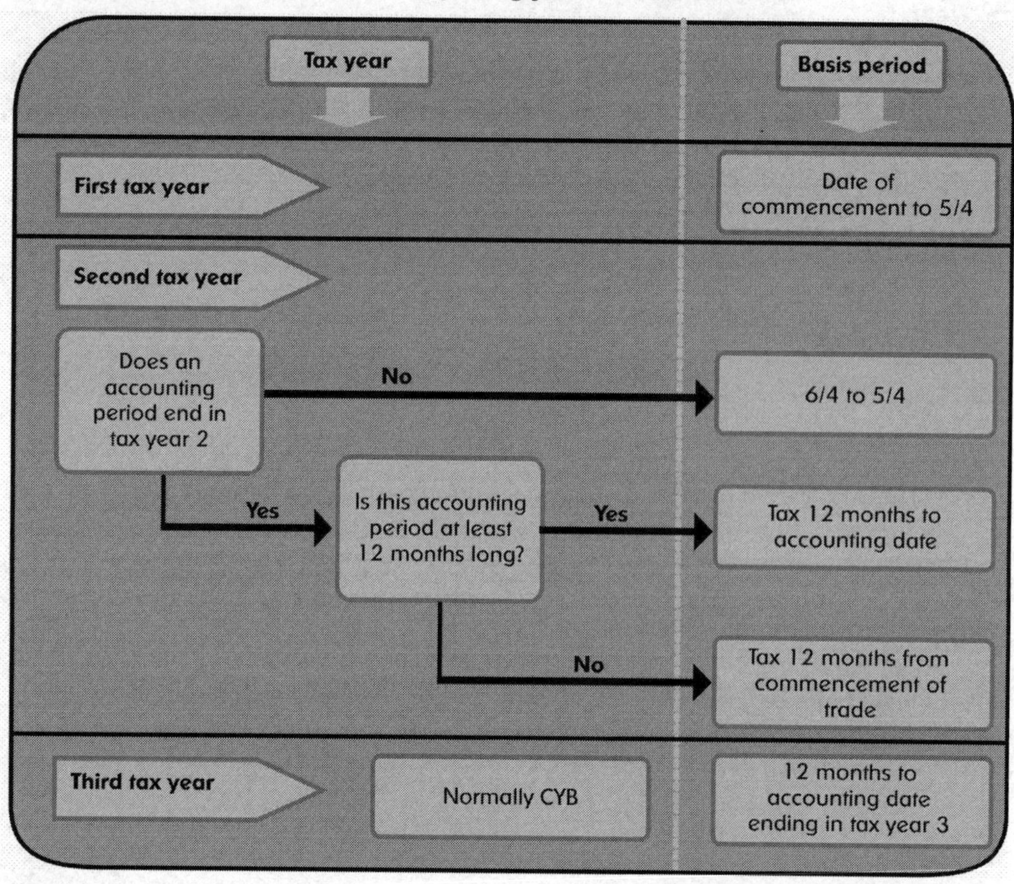

A trader commences trading on 1 January 2012 and prepares accounts to 31 December each year.

Required:

Give the basis periods for the first three tax years.

A trader commences trading on 1 January 2012 and prepares accounts to 30 April. His first accounts are for the period to 30 April 2013.

Required:

Give the basis periods for the first four tax years.

---

5. Overlap profits

If a trader prepares accounts to 5 April each year, all the profits will be taxed only once. If any other year end date is chosen, **some profits will be taxed more than once** in the opening tax years. We call these profits 'overlap' profits.

Vicky started to trade on 1 January 2010 and prepares her first accounts to 30 June 2010 and annually thereafter. Her results are as follows:

	£
Six months to 30 June 2010	13,000
Year to 30 June 2011	27,000
Year to 30 June 2012	42,000

Calculate her taxable profits for the first four tax years, and show the overlap profits.

Answer

Year	Basis Period	Working	Taxable (£) Profit
2009-10	Actual (01/01/2010 - 05/04/2010)	£13,000 x 3/6	6,500
2010-11	First 12 months (01/01/2010 - 31/12/2010)	£13,000 + (£27,000 x 6/12)	26,500
2011-12	CYB (year to 30/06/2011) (01/07/2010 – 30/6/2011)		27,000
2012-13	CYB (year to 30/06/2012) (01/07/2011 – 30/06/2012)		42,000

Overlap profits	£
01/01/2010 – 05/04/2010 (3 months) (W1) (£13,000 x 3 months/ 6 months)	6,500
01/07/2010 – 31/12/2010 (6 months) (W2) (£27,000 x 6months/12 months)	13,500
Total	**20,000**

Notes

1. Profits during the period 01/01/2010 to 05/04/2010 are taxed twice, once in 2009-10 and again in 2010-11. The profits taxed more than once are overlap profit.

2. Profits during the period 01/07/2010 to 31/12/2010 are taxed twice, once in 2010-11 and also in 2011-12.

Sharon commenced trading on 1 June 2011, and has the following results:

17 months to 31 October 2012	£25,500
Year to 31 October 2013	£18,500

Required:

Calculate Sharon's trading income assessments for the first three tax years. How much is the overlap profit?

Ilyas started to trade on 1 January 2010 and makes up his first accounts to 30 June 2010, and then 30 June annually thereafter. His results are as follows:

	£
Six months to 30/06/2010	40,000
Year to 30/06/2011	60,000
Year to 30/06/2012	74,000

Required:

Calculate his trading income assessments for 2009-10 to 2012 - 13 and identify any overlap profits.

6. Cessation of trade

The final assessment of a sole trader is the tax year in which there is a cessation of trade. A cessation of trade may occur when the sole trader retires, sells the business or dies. The basis period for the tax year in which the cessation occurs is determined as follows:

a) If the trade commences and ceases in the same tax year, the basis period is the whole life of the business.

b) If the trade ceases in the second tax year, the basis period runs from 6 April at the start of the second year to the date of cessation. This rule overrides the usual commencement rules.

c) If the trade ceases in the third tax year or any subsequent year, the basis period runs from the end of the basis period for the previous tax year to the date of cessation of trade.

The basis period for the last tax year could be less than 12 months, exactly 12 months or more than 12 months.

7. Overlap relief

a) Relief is available for the overlap profits arising on commencement, by deducting them from the final tax year assessment when a business ceases to trade. This ensures that the assessments over the life of the business equal the total tax-adjusted profits earned by the business. **If overlap profits are greater than the assessment for the final tax year, relief is available for the resulting loss.**

Cinderella has been trading for many years, preparing accounts to 31 December each year. She ceases to trade on 31 May 2012, profits for the 5 months to that date are £12,300.The overlap profits from the opening years of her trade were £7,100.

Required:

Calculate her trading income assessment for 2012-13.

Continued on the next page

Answer

	£
Profit for five months: 01/01/2012 - 31/05/2012	12,300
Less: Overlap relief	(7,100)
Taxable profit	**5,200**

b) Overlap profits may also arise or be deducted on a change of accounting date, depending on the situation. The rules regarding change of accounting date are dealt with in detail in Learning Outcome 6 of this Study Guide.

Overlap profits will arise in all cases other than where the accounting date is 5 April.
Don't forget to calculate overlap profits, and remember how they can be relieved.

SUMMARY

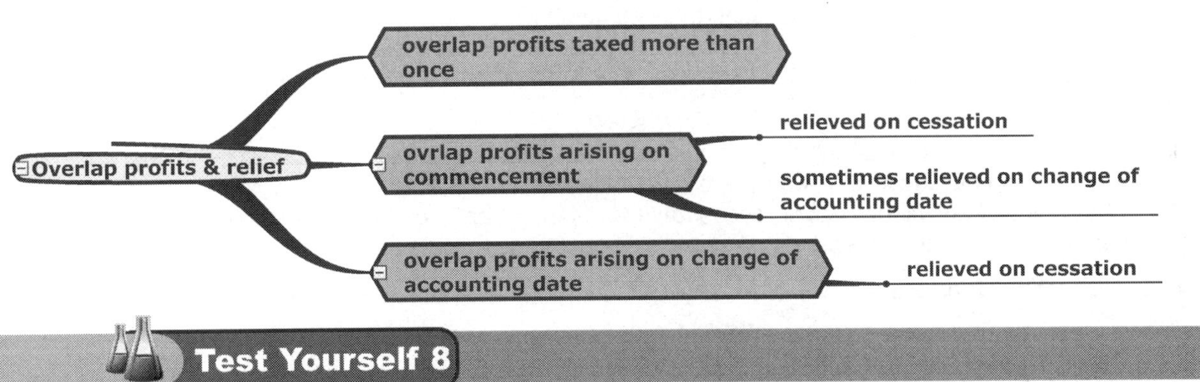

Brian has been trading for many years, preparing accounts to 30 November each year. He ceases to trade on 30 June 2012 and prepares his final accounts for the 7 months to that date.

Required:

What is the basis period for the tax year of cessation?

Test Yourself 9

Simi has been trading for many years, preparing accounts to 31 January each year. She ceases to trade on 31 July 2012 with recent profits as follows:

	£
Year to 31/01/2012	32,000
Six months to 31/07/2012	9,000

The overlap profits from commencement were £7,000.

Required:

Give the assessments for 2011-12 and 2012-13.

What is the basis period for the tax year

1. in which trade commences, and
2. in which trade ceases?

6. Change of accounting date
  - i. **Recognise the factors that will influence the choice of accounting date.**[2]
  - ii. **State the conditions that must be met for a change of accounting date to be valid.**[1]
  - iii. **Compute the assessable profits on a change of accounting date.**[2]

[Learning Outcome f]

6.1 Factors influencing the choice of accounting date

The choice of accounting date is important for a sole trader for tax purposes as it affects the amount of overlap profits and the delay between earning the profits, and making the final tax payment (the balancing payment is due 31 January after the end of the tax year).

31 March accounting date end

- No overlap profits on commencement.
- Application of the basis period rules will be simplified.
- Time between earning the profits and the balancing payment is minimised (10 months).
- The maximum period of assessment in the final tax year will be 12 months.

30 April accounting date end

- Maximum period of overlap, with no relief until cessation (or possibly on future change of accounting date).
- Time between earning the profits and the balancing payment is maximised (21 months).
- The period of assessment in the final tax year could be up to 23 months long, less any relief for overlap profits.

1. If the profits are rising, a 30 April year end date will give lower assessable profits in the year 2, as 11 months of profit allocated to the basis period were those earned in the previous tax year. If profits are falling, a 31 March year end will give lower assessable profits in year 2 as the basis period for the tax year is the profits earned in the second tax year.
2. The accounting year affects the time between earning the profits and the payment of the balancing payment.

Example

Year ended	Tax year	Balancing payment due on
31/03/2012	2011-12	31/01/2013
30/04/2012	2012-13	31/01/2014

Tip

For details of due dates and balancing payments refer Study Guide G2.

Summary:

1. If profits fall, then 31/03 gives no overlap period. Higher profits are not taxed twice.
2. If profits rise, then 30/04 gives overlap profits and earlier lower profits are taxed twice.

6.2 Conditions that must be met for a change of accounting date to be valid

If a trader finds his current accounting date inconvenient, for any reason, he may change it.

The following conditions must be met:

- The change of accounting date **must be notified to HMRC by 31 January** following the tax year in which the change is made.
- The first accounts to the **new date must not exceed 18 months.**
- There must not have been a **change of accounting date in any of the 5 previous tax years**, or, if there has, the latest change is made for **genuine commercial reasons.**

6.3 Computation of assessable profit on change of accounting date

On a change of accounting date, **overlap will either be created or relieved**. No profits should escape tax on a change of accounting date.

On a change in accounting date there will be either an accounting period of less than 12 months, or an accounting period of more than 12 months. The basis periods are determined by applying the following rules:

1. **When a change of accounting date results in an accounting period of less than 12 months ending in a tax year,** the basis period for that tax year will be 12 months to the new accounting date. In this situation, overlap profits are created.

Example

Alan prepares his accounts to 31 December every year. He decides to change his accounting date to 30 June and prepares the accounts for the six months to June 2012. In this case, Alan's basis period for 2012-13 is the 12 month period ending on 30 June 2012. However, the basis period for 2011-12 was the year to 31 December 2011, which means that the six months to 31 December 2011, have been taxed twice. Overlap profits are for the period from 1 July 2011 to 31 December 2011.

---

2. **When a change of accounting date results in an accounting period of more than twelve months ending in a tax year,** the basis period for that tax year ends on the new accounting date. The basis period starts from the end of the basis period for the previous tax year and ends on the new accounting date. This means the basis period will exceed twelve months. In this situation, overlap profits brought forward can be relieved. The overlap can reduce the number of months of profit taxed down to twelve, but no further.

Example

A trader prepares his accounts to 31 May each year. He changes his accounting date to 31 August, and prepares the accounts for 15 months to 31 August 2012.

The basis period for 2012-13 is the 15 month period from 1 June 2011 to 31 August 2012. Three months of overlap profits brought forward (if any) can be relieved in 2012-13.

Example

John prepares his accounts to 31 December each year. He has overlap profits of £6,000 from a 3 month period of overlap. John changed his accounting date to 28 February preparing accounts for the period from 1 January 2012 to 28 February 2013. The profit for this period was £15,000.

Required:

Calculate John's trading income assessment for 2012-13.

Answer

Determine which tax year the change of accounting date falls into.
28 February 2013 falls into 2012-13.
The basis period for 2012-13 is 14 months to 28 February 2013.

The trading income assessment is:

	£
Fourteen months: 01/01/2012 -28/02/2013	15,000
Less: Overlap relief (W1)	(4,000)
Trading income assessments for 2012-13	**11,000**

Workings

W1 Overlap relief used

Overlap profits brought forward relate to a 3 month period.

Continued on the next page

The basis period is 14 months long, which exceeds 12 months by 2 months.

Overlap relief therefore is 2/3 x £6,000 = £4,000

John still has 1 month overlap profits of £2,000 (2/3 x £6,000) to carry forward.

---

3. When a **change** of accounting date **results in no period of account ending in the tax year,** then the basis period is found by **deducting 12 months from the new accounting date, and taking 12 months to the resulting date.**

Example

Akash prepares his accounts up to 31 March 2012. He changed his accounting date to 30 April and prepares the accounts for thirteen months to 30 April 2013.

Step 1: In which tax year does the change of accounting date fall?
2012-13

Step 2: Does an accounting period end in the tax year?
There is **no accounting period ending in 2012-13.**

Step 3: Deduct 12 months from the new accounting date i.e. 30 April 2013 less 12 months = 30 April 2012

Step 4: The basis period for 2012-13 is 12 months ending on 30 April 2012.

Overlap profits arise for the period 1 May 2011 to 31 March 2012 i.e. 11 months overlap profits, which can be carried forward for relief on cessation, or possibly on a future change of accounting date.

---

4. **When a change in the accounting date results in two sets of accounts ending in a year,** the basis period starts from the end of the previous basis period and ends on the new accounting date. Overlap relief can reduce the number of months of profit taxed down to 12.

Example

Andrew prepares his accounts to 31 October. He changed his accounting date and prepares the accounts for 5 months to 31 March 2013.

There are two accounting periods ending in 2012-13, the 12 months to the old date i.e. 31 October 2012 and the five months to the new accounting date 31 March 2013.

The basis period for 2012-13 is the period from 1 November 2011 to 31 March 2013 i.e. 17 months.

Example

Arnold commenced trading on 1 October 2010 and prepares his first accounts to 30 September 2011. His results show a profit of £24,000 (£2,000 per month). The profits assessable in 2010-11 and 2011-12 are as follows:

2010-11: 1 October 2010 to 5 April 2011 = £24,000 x 6/12 = £12,000

2011-12: 1 October 2010 to 30 September 2011 = £24,000

The period 1 October 2010 to 5 April 2011 (6 months) has been taxed twice, resulting in overlap profit of 12,000.

Arnold decides to change his year end to 5 April and prepares accounts for the 18 months to 5 April 2013. The profits for the period are £20,000.

Continued on the next page

The assessable trading profits for 2012-13 are as follows:

	£
18 months to 5 April 2013	20,000
Less: Overlap relief b/f (note)	(12,000)
Assessable trading profit for 2012-13	**8,000**

Note: 18 months' worth of profit is taxed in 2012-13 and so overlap relief b/f of 6 months may be used, to reduce the period taxed to 12 months.

SUMMARY

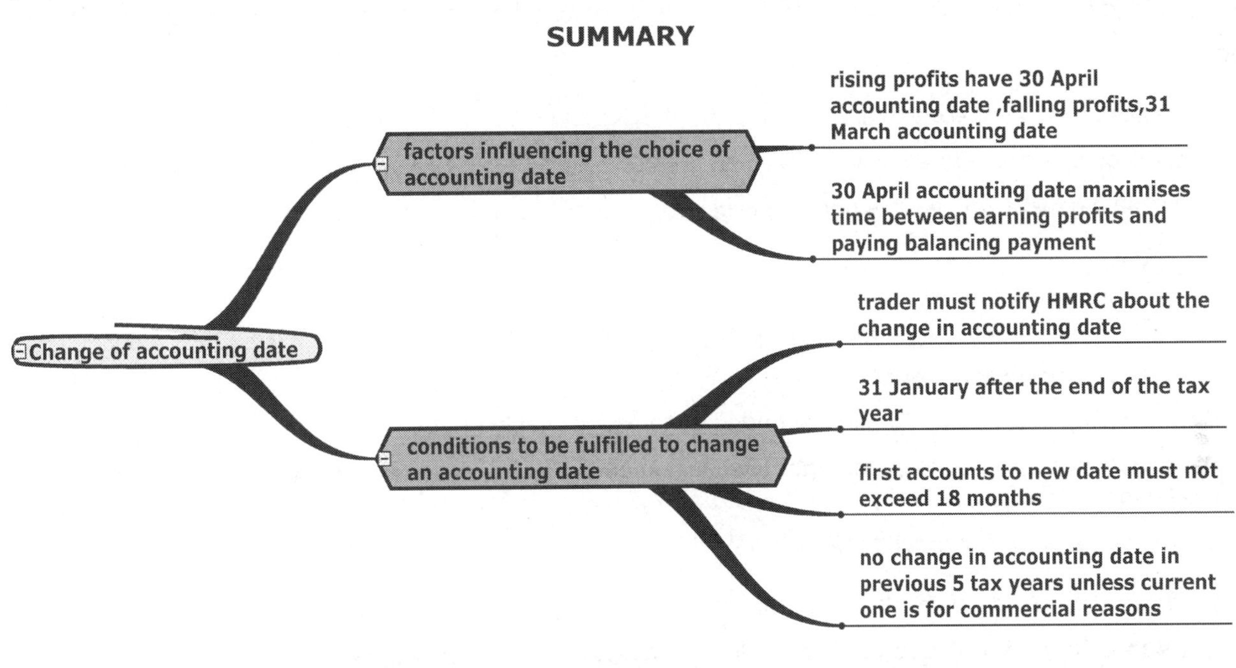

Test Yourself 11

1. Mary prepares accounts to 31 May each year. She changes her accounting date to 31 August and prepares the accounts for the period 1 June 2011 to 31 August 2012. The conditions necessary for a change of accounting date were all satisfied. Identify the basis period for 2012-13.

2. Bob began trading on 1 March 2009, preparing the accounts to 31 January 2010, and annually thereafter. He changed his accounting date to 30 April and prepares the accounts for the period 1 February 2012 to 30 April 2013. The conditions for change of basis period were all satisfied. Identify the basis periods for 2008-09 to 2014-15 inclusive.

Answers to Test Yourself

Answer to TY 1

Badges of trade are:

1. **Subject matter of transaction:** If the property is held for personal enjoyment or if the property yields income, this generally indicates an investment rather than a trading transaction.
2. **Frequency of transactions:** The repetition of a transaction generally indicates the existence of a trade.
3. **Length of ownership:** An intention to re-sell the asset in the short term might be a pointer towards a trading transaction, as opposed to an investment.
4. **Profit motive:** A transaction undertaken with the motive of realising a profit suggests trading.
5. **Supplementary work and marketing:** Work carried out on an asset prior to sale to make it marketable indicates trading.
6. **Reason for sale:** A forced sale to raise cash for an emergency indicates that the transaction is not trading.

Answer to TY 2

	£	£
Net profits per accounts		18,050
Add: Expenditure shown in the accounts but not deductible for tax purpose		
Depreciation (note 1)	2,500	
Legal expenses relating to the purchase of a capital asset (note 2)	350	
Increase in general provision (note 3)	50	2,900
Adjusted trading profits for tax purposes		**20,950**

Notes

1. Depreciation is never allowable.
2. Legal expenses relate to a capital asset, and are not deductible.
3. Increase in general provision is not deductible.

Answer to TY 3

i. **Depreciation:** Not allowable, although capital allowances may be available.
ii. **Repairs to machinery:** Allowable.
iii. **Constructing rest room:** Capital expenditure, so not allowable.
iv. **Purchase of car for factory manager**: Capital expenditure, so not allowable, but capital allowances will be available.
v. **General provision for repairs:** Not allowable.
vi. **Christmas lunch for staff:** Staff entertaining is allowable.
vii. **Christmas lunch for 50 customers:** Customer entertaining is not allowable.
viii. **Wedding gift to staff:** Allowable.
ix. **Wedding gift to customers:** Not allowable.
x. **Gift of 20 pens to customers, costing not more than £50 per person, not food, drink, tobacco or vouchers exchangeable for goods and has business logo engraved on it:** Allowable.
xi. **Qualifying charitable donation to local charity:** Not deductible but eligible for qualifying charitable relief for the individual donor.
xii. **Legal fees incurred for collecting trade debts:** Allowable as connected with the trade.
xiii. **Costs of renewing 40 year lease:** Allowable as cost of renewing a short lease (50 years or less).
xiv. **Costs of registering business trademark:** Allowable.

Answer to TY 4

Tax year	Basis period
2011-12 (note 1)	1 January 2012 to 5 April 2012
2012-13 (note 2)	12 months to 31 December 2012
2013-14 (note 3)	12 months to 31 December 2013

Notes

1. For the first tax year the basis period runs from the commencement of trade to the following 5 April.
2. There is an accounting period of at least 12 months ending in the second tax year, so the basis period is 12 months to the accounting date in the second tax year.
3. Current year basis.

Answer to TY 5

Tax year	Basis period
2011-12 (note 1)	1 January 2012 to 5 April 2012
2012-13 (note 2)	6 April 2012 to 5 April 2013
2013-14 (note 3)	1 May 2012 to 30 April 2013
2014-15 (note 4)	1 May 2013 to 30 April 2014

Notes

1. For the first tax year the basis period runs from the commencement of trade to the following 5 April.
2. No accounting period ends in the second tax year, so the basis period is 6 April to following 5 April.
3. Basis period is 12 months to the accounting date in the third tax year.
4. Current year basis.

Answer to TY 6

Sharon's trading income assessments for the first three tax years are as follows:

Tax year	Basis period	Workings	Trading Income (£)
First tax year 2011-12 (note 1)	1 June 2011 to 5 April 2012	£25,500 x10/17	15,000
Second tax year 2012-13 (note 2)	1 November 2011 to 31 October 2012 (12 months to a/c date in year 2)	£25,500 x12/17	18,000
Third tax year 2013-14	Year to 31 October 2013	-	**18,500**

Notes

1. The basis period for the first tax year runs from 1 June 2011 to 5 April 2012 i.e. 10 months.
2. There is an accounting period of at least 12 months ending in the second tax year, so the basis period is 12 months to the accounting date, i.e. 31 October 2012.

Overlap profits

Profits during the period 1 November 2011 to 5 April 2012 (5 months) are taxed twice; therefore **overlap profit** is **£7,500** (£25,500 x 5/17).

Answer to TY 7

Trading income assessments	£
2009-10	
Actual (1 January 2010 to 5 April 2010)	
£40,000 x 3/6	20,000
2010-11	
First 12 months (1 January 2010 to 31 December 2010)	70000
£40,000 + £30,000 (£60,000 x 6/12)	
2011-12	
Current Year Basis (year to 30 June 2011)	60,000
2012-13	
Current Year Basis (year to 30 June 2012)	74,000

Overlap profits	£
1 January 2010 to 5 April 2010 (£40,000 x 3/6)	20,000
1 July 2010 to 31 December 2010 (£60,000 x 6/12)	30,000
Total overlap profit	**50,000**

Answer to TY 8

Step one: Determine the tax year of cessation.
2012-13

Step two: Determine the period of assessment for the previous tax year.
2011-12 year ended 30 November 2011

Step three: The remaining profits are taxed in the final tax year.
2012-13: 1 December 2011 to 30 June 2012 less any overlap profits b/f.

Answer to TY 9

The date of cessation is 31 July 2012, which falls in 2012-13.
The assessment for 2011-12 is therefore on the CYB.

2011-12

Year to 31/01/2012 £32,000

2012-13

In the final tax year the basis period runs from the end of the basis period for the previous tax year to the date of cessation of trade.

	£
Six months: 01/02/2012 – 31/07/2012	9,000
Less: Overlap relief	(7,000)
Assessable trading profits	**2,000**

Note: overlap profits on commencement are relieved **when the trade ceases.**

Answer to TY 10

1. The basis period for the first tax year runs from **the date of commencement to the following 5 April.**

2. The basis period for the tax year in which trade ceases:

(a) If the trade ceases in the **first tax year,** the basis period is the **whole lifespan of the trade.**
(b) If the trade ceases in the **second tax year,** the basis period runs from **6 April at the start of the second year to the date of cessation.** This rule overrides the normally applicable second year rule.
(c) If the trade ceases in the **third year or any subsequent year,** the basis period runs from **end of basis period for the previous tax year to the date of cessation of trade.**

Answer to TY 11

1. As the change of the accounting date results in an accounting period of more than 12 months, the new basis period is from the end of the previous basis period to the new accounting date. The new accounting date i.e. 31 August 2012 is more than 12 months after 31 May 2011, so the basis period for 2012-13 is 1 June 2011 to 31 August 2012. As this is a 15 month period, 3 months of overlap profits (if any) may be relieved in 2012-13, to reduce the number of months charged to tax to twelve.

2. The accounting date is changed in the tax year 2012-13. The basis period for the previous tax year 2011-12 is the year to 31 January 2012.

The new accounting date, 30 April 2013 falls in 2013-14, so the basis period for 2012-13 is determined by going back 12 months from 30 April 2013 i.e. 30 April 2012, and taking the 12 months to that date.

Basis periods for 2008-09 to 2014-15 are as follows:

2008-09	1 March 2009 to 5 April 2009
2009-10	1 March 2009 to 28 February 2010 (First 12 months)
2010-11	1 February 2010 to 31 January 2011 (year ended 31 January 2011)
2011-12	1 February 2011 to 31 January 2012 (year ended 31January 2012)
2012-13	1 May 2011 to 30 April 2012 (year ended 30 April 2012)
2013-14	1 May 2012 to 30 April 2013 (year ended 30 April 2013)
2014-15	1 May 2013 to 30 April 2014 (year ended 30 April 2014)

Overlap on commencement is 01/03/2009 – 05/04/2009 and 01/02/2010 – 28/02/2010 i.e. 2 months.
On change of accounting date, 9 additional months of overlap profits are created 01/05/2011 – 31/01/2012.

Quick Quiz

1. Explain the concept of badges of trade.
2. Bill started trading on 1 August 2012 and prepared his first set of accounts to 31 December 2011, and annually thereafter.

   What is the basis period for 2011-12?
3. State the general rule which determines whether expenditure is deductible when computing the trading income.
4. Brown starts trading on 1 July 2009 and prepares accounts to 30 June each year. Show the basis periods for the first three tax years, and identify the period of overlap profits.
5. What is the basis of assessment for the final tax year on cessation of trading?
6. Explain overlap profit and overlap relief.

Answers to Quick Quiz

1. Badges of trade are a set of various criteria, which may be used to distinguish between trading activities and non-trading activities.
2. **2012-13**
   01/08/2012 – 05/04/2013

   Profits assessed:
   5 months to 31 December 2012 plus 3/12 of year to 31 December 2013.
3. The expenditure incurred must be wholly and exclusively for the purposes of trade.
4. **2010-11**
   1 July 2010 to 5 April 2011

   2011-12
   1 July 2010 to 30 June 2011

   2012-13
   1 July 2011 to 30 June 2012

   Period of overlap: 1 July 2010 to 5 April 2011.
5. Tax year in which cessation occurs: basis period is from the end of the basis period for the previous tax year to the date of cessation.
6. In the opening years, and sometimes on change of the accounting date, some profits are taxed twice. The basis periods for consecutive tax years contain a common period. The profits which are taxed twice are referred to as overlap profits.
   In the opening years of a business it is possible to have an overlap between tax year 1 and tax year 2.

Relief for overlap profits:

Overlap profits are relieved by deducting them from the assessable trading income of the year of cessation, or sometimes on a change of accounting date.

Self Examination Questions

Question 1

Jessica began trading on 1 January 2012 and prepares the accounts to 30 June. Her first accounts are prepared for the 18 months to 30 June 2013 and show an adjusted trading profit of £43,200. Compute Jessica's trading income for the first three tax years and calculate the amount of any overlap profits.

Question 2

Explain, with suitable examples, the rules for assessing profits in the first tax year of trade.

Question 3

Explain the rules for assessing profits in the second tax year of trade.

Question 4

Explain the rules for assessing profits in the third tax year of trade.

Question 5

Bill started trading on 1 January 2012, and prepared his first set of accounts to:

1. 30 June 2013
2. 31 December 2012
3. 30 June 2012
4. 31 March 2013

Give the basis periods for 2011-12 and 2012-13 for each of the above accounting dates.

Question 6

Bill Brown started trading on 1 January 2011, and prepares his accounts as follows:

1. to 30 June 2012 and annually to 30 June thereafter
2. to 31 December 2011 and annually to 31 December thereafter
3. to 30 June 2011 and annually to 30 June thereafter
4. to 31 March 2012 and annually to 31 March thereafter

Give the basis period for 2012-13 in each of the above cases.

Question 7

Juhi, a sole trader, started trading on 1 January 2012, preparing accounts up to 30 June 2012 and annually thereafter.

Her income statement for the period ended 30 June 2012 was as follows:

	£	£
Gross sales revenue		75,380
Other income		
Dividend received (net)		5,000
Interest on bank deposit		2,100
Goods taken for own use (at cost) (2)		8,000
Expenses		
Salary to self	1,360	
Salary to husband as Manager (1)	2,000	
Rent, business rates and insurance	3,120	
Repairs and maintenance (3)	6,220	
Motor expenses	1,650	
Depreciation on car	300	
Depreciation on equipment	250	
Loss on sale of equipment	960	
Car purchased for employee	12,000	
General repairs provision	1,800	
Legal fees for renewing a 40 year lease	2,490	(32,150)
Finance costs		
Interest on bank overdraft (4)	3,560	
Hire purchase interest	1,230	(4,790)
Net profit		**53,540**

Notes

1. The salary paid to her husband is at the market rate.
2. The goods taken for own use have a market value of £12,000.
3. Repairs to office building includes:
   - alterations to flooring in order to install a new machine £4,300
   - redecoration of offices £1,920
4. The overdraft was necessary to purchase inventory.
5. Recovery from a debtor, previously written off not included in the income statement £2,300.
6. She paid a trade subscription personally which is not included in the income statement £1,000.

Required:

Compute Juhi's adjusted trading profits for tax purposes for the period ended 30 June 2012. Ignore capital allowances.

Question 8

John is a self-employed trader. His income statement for the year ended 5 April 2013 is as follows:

	£	£
Gross profit		173,500
Expenses		
Depreciation	1,210	
Motor expenses (note 1)	6,250	
Professional fees (note 2)	3,090	
Repairs and renewals (note 3)	3,825	
Entertainment expenses (note 4)	4,860	
Wages and salaries (note 5)	68,530	
Other expenses (note 6)	67,370	**(155,135)**
Net profit		**18,365**

Notes

1. **Motor expenses**
   During the year John drove a total of 20,000 miles, of which 40% was private.

2. **Professional fees consist of:**
   £1,020 for accountancy,
   £1,620 for personal financial planning advice,
   £450 for debt collection

3. **Repairs and renewals:** this is made up of £525 for repairing the fence, and £3,300 for a new computer.

4. **Entertainment:** this is made up of £1,610 for entertaining suppliers and £3,250 for entertaining employees.

5. **Wages and salaries:** this includes a salary of £20,000 paid to John's wife. She works in the shop as a sales assistant. Other sales assistants doing the same job are paid a salary of £15,000 p.a.

6. **Other expenses:** this includes £125 for a wedding present to an employee, £125 for John's health club subscription, £125 as a donation to a political party, and £1,800 for a trade subscription.

7. **Business use of house:** John uses one of the six rooms in his house as an office. The total running costs of the house for the year were £8,720.

8. **Private telephone:** the total cost of John's private telephone for the year was £1,850, 45% of this related to business telephone calls. The cost of the private telephone is not included in the income statement.

9. **Goods for own use:** during the year ended 5 April 2013 John took goods out of the shop for his personal use without paying for them, and no entry has been made in the accounts to record this. The goods cost £750, and have a selling price of £1,550.

Required:

Calculate John's tax adjusted trading profit for the year ended 5 April 2013. Ignore capital allowances.

Answers to Self Examination Questions

Answer to SEQ 1

Tax year		Basis Period		£
2011-12	Actual	1 January 2012 to 5 April 2012	£43,200 x 3/18	7,200
2012-13	Tax year itself	6 April 2012 to 5 April 2013	£43,200 x 12/18	28,800
2013-14	12 months to accounting date	1 July 2012 to 30 June 2013	£43,200 x 12/18	28,800

Overlap period is of 9 months from 1 July 2012 to 5 April 2013. This period is taxed in 2012-13 and 2013-14.

Overlap Profits = £43,200 x 9/18 = **£21,600**

Answer to SEQ 2

The taxable profit for the tax year in which a sole trader starts to trade is the amount **arising from the date of commencement of the trade to the end of that first tax year (i.e. 5 April).**

If a trader starts to trade on 1 July 2012, then the first tax year is 2012-13. In 2012-13 he will be assessed on the taxable profit for the period 1 July 2012 to 5 April 2013.

If a trader starts to trade on 1 August 2012, and prepares his first set of accounts to 31 December 2012, then he started trading in 2012-13, and the basis period is 1 August 2012 to 5 April 2013.

Answer to SEQ 3

For the second tax year of trading, the amount of the taxable profit depends upon whether or not there is an accounting date ending in the second tax year.

The following three situations may arise:

1. **No accounting period ends in the second tax year.**
   The basis period is the tax year itself (i.e. 6 April to following 5 April).

2. **The accounting period ending in the second tax year is at least 12 months long.**
   The basis period is the 12 months to the accounting date in the second tax year.

3. The **accounting period ending in the second tax year is less than 12 months long.**
   The basis period is the first twelve months of trade.

Answer to SEQ 4

In the third tax year of trade, the basis period is:

a) 12 month accounting period ending in the third tax year.
b) If there is no 12 month accounting period ending in the third tax year, take 12 months to the accounting date in the third tax year.

Answer to SEQ 5

First tax year

Bill starts trading in 2011-12.

The basis period will be 1 January 2012 (i.e. the date the trade started) to 5 April 2012 (i.e. the end of that tax year in which the trade started) in all situations.

Second tax year 2012-13

1. Accounts prepared to 30 June 2013

There is no accounting period ending in 2012-13 as the first set of accounts is prepared to 30 June 2013.

Therefore the basis period for 2012-13 is 6 April 2012 to 5 April 2013.

2. Accounts prepared to 31 December 2012

There is an accounting period ending in 2012-13 (31 December 2012) and it is exactly 12 months long.

Therefore the basis period for 2012-13 is 12 months to the accounting date i.e. 1 January 2012 to 31 December 2012.

3. Accounts prepared to 30 June 2012

There is an accounting period ending in 2012-13 (30 June 2012) and it is less than 12 months long.

Therefore the basis period for 2012-13 is the first twelve months of trading i.e. 1 January 2012 to 31 December 2012.

4. Accounts prepared to 31 March 2013.

There is an accounting period ending in 2012-13 (31 March 2013) and it is more than 12 months long.

Therefore the basis period for 2012-13 is the twelve months to 31 March 2013 i.e. 1 April 2012 to 31 March 2013.

Answer to SEQ 6

2012-13 is the third tax year of trading:

1. 12 months to 30 June 2012 (as no accounting period ended in the second tax year).

   In answers 2, 3 and 4 below an accounting period ends in the second tax year, so the basis period for the third tax year is the current year basis.

2. 1 January 2012 to 31 December 2012
3. 1 July 2011 to 30 June 2012
4. 1 April 2012 to 31 March 2013

Answer to SEQ 7

	£	£
Net trading profits given per accounts		53,540
Add : (I) Expenses shown in accounts but not deductible for tax purposes		
Car purchase (capital expenditure)	12,000	
Salary to self	1,360	
General repairs provision	1,800	
Alteration to the flooring to install a new machine	4,300	
Depreciation (£300 + £250)	550	
Loss on sale of equipment	960	20,970
(II) Trading income taxable but not included in the accounts		
Goods taken for own use (at Market value) (£12,000 - £8,000)	4,000	
Recovery from a debtor, previously written off	2,300	6,300
Less: (I) Expenditure deductible for tax purposes but not shown in the accounts		
Trade subscriptions	(1,000)	(1,000)
(II) Income not taxable included in the accounts		
Dividend	5,000	
Income which is taxable under another heading such as interest, property inco	2,100	(7,100)
Trading profits for tax purposes		**72,710**

Answer to SEQ 8

Calculation of John's tax adjusted trading profits for the year ended 5 April 2013

	£	£
Net trading profits per accounts		18,365
Add : (I) Expenses shown in accounts but not deductible for tax purposes		
Depreciation	1,210	
Motor expenses (40% private use) (£6,250 x 40%)	2,500	
Fees for personal financial planning advice (private)	1,620	
Purchase of new computer (capital)	3,300	
Entertaining suppliers	1,610	
Salary to wife (the excess over market rate added back) (£20000 - £15000 = £5000)	5,000	
Health club subscription (private)	125	
Donation to a political party	125	15,490
(II) Trading income taxable but not included in the accounts		
Goods taken for own consumption (at MV)	1,550	1,550
Less:(I) Expenditure deductible for tax purposes but not shown in the accounts		
Use of home as office (W1)	1,453	
Telephone expenses (W2)	833	(2,286)
Trading profits for tax purposes		**33,119**

Workings

W1 Share in total running cost of house

Number of rooms is six; one is used for business purposes
Total running cost is divided proportionately
£8,720 x 1 room/6 rooms = 1,453

W2 Telephone expenses

Out of the total cost of private telephone, 45% is used for business purposes
Total telephone cost = £1,850
45% of £1,850 = £833

STUDY GUIDE B3: INCOME FROM SELF-EMPLOYMENT (PART 2)

Get Through Intro

Capital expenditure cannot be deducted when computing taxable income and no allowance is available for the accounts depreciation of the value of assets. However, legislation allows **relief for capital expenditure** in the form of a **deduction, known as capital allowances, from taxable trade profits**.

It is necessary to understand the different provisions for the calculation of capital allowances in order to give proper guidance to your clients when calculating **'trading income'** in your capacity as a chartered certified accountant.

Capital allowances are a very important part of your syllabus as they will be examined, for a significant number of marks, in every exam.

Learning Outcomes

g) Capital allowances
   i. Define plant and machinery for capital allowances purposes.
   ii. Compute writing down allowances, first-year allowances and the annual investment allowance.
   iii. Compute capital allowances for motor cars.
   iv. Compute balancing allowances and balancing charges.
   v. Recognise the treatment of short life assets.
   vi. Explain the treatment of assets included in the special rate pool.

Introduction

Byron set up his business, and purchased a machine for £122,000. He anticipates that the machine will need replacing in about 6 years, and at that time he should be able to sell it for £5,000. The machine has cost him £117,000 over 6 years, and he is unsure how he will be given relief for this expenditure.

This Study Guide explains the relief available for different categories of capital expenditure, and the provisions for the disposal of assets.

---

1. Define plant and machinery for capital allowances purposes.[1]

[Learning Outcome g (i)]

1.1 Definition of plant and machinery for capital allowances purposes

As discussed above, in this section, capital allowances are expenses that are deducted from profits in the financial accounts to arrive at trading profit for tax purposes. In other words, capital allowances are a type of depreciation giving relief for tax purposes on qualifying capital expenditure. The most common type of capital allowances are those available on plant and machinery and industrial buildings (although industrial buildings allowance is being phased out).

Legislation does not define the term plant and machinery. The definition of 'machinery' is not a problem; it includes all machines, vehicles, computers etc. However, the meaning of 'plant' is not so straightforward. Office furniture and equipment are plant and machinery, but expenditure on structures is not so easily dealt with.

In a leading case it was stated that plant includes whatever tool or apparatus is used by a businessman for carrying on his business, other than his stock in trade, but all goods and chattels, fixed or movable, live or dead, which he keeps permanently employed in the business.

Later case law has considered the 'functional test'.

a) If an asset is actively used in the business, then it is considered apparatus **with which** the business is carried on, and so is considered to be plant and machinery.

Example

- Storage platforms built in a warehouse are considered plant and machinery as the inventory cannot be stored without the platforms.
- Swimming pool of a health club is plant and machinery too, as clients probably would not come to the club if it didn't have a pool.

---

b) If an asset is **passively used in the business**, then it is considered to be the setting **in which** the business is carried on, and so it is not considered to be plant and machinery.

Example

The following are not considered to be plant and machinery:

- waste disposal or drainage systems of the building. However, they are considered part of the building.
- a false ceiling built to hide the electrical fittings, or floor of the restaurant making it attractive.

Hence, to identify plant for capital allowance purposes, a distinction must be made between **the setting in which the business is carried on** and **the apparatus with which the business is run**. However, some of the items seem to be part of the setting, but qualify as plant. For example, lifts and escalators qualify as plant for capital allowance purposes. On the other hand, expenditure on flooring and ceilings in office premises will be considered part of the business setting and will not qualify as a plant.

1.2 Different case laws for interpreting the definition of plant

In Jarrold v John Good and Sons Ltd (1963) a dispute arose as to whether moveable partitions were part of the setting and not part of the premises in which the trade was carried on. The **moveable partitions qualified** as capital expenditure as it was apparatus required by the company to carry out its business. For running the daily operations of the business, it was necessary for the partitions to possess mobility and flexibility.

In Leeds Permanent Building Society v Proctor (1982), a dispute arose when a society's claim for decorative screens used for **window displays** as plant was rejected. The purpose of the screens was to increase the business of the society by attracting the attention of passers-by. The High Court held that the screens **qualified** as 'plant' because:

- the screens were part of the shop furniture with which the trade of the society was carried on in the branch office concerned.
- significant modifications to the screens were required to make them capable of being useful to any other business.
- some screens were of such a character that they were really only of use in the particular branch.
- the screens were specifically designed for the society and they were removed by the society when it left the branch office.

In C.I.R. v Scottish and Newcastle Breweries Ltd (1982), a dispute arose whether light fittings and wiring, and **decorative items** such as wall plaques, tapestries, murals, prints and sculptures are eligible for claim as plant or machinery allowance. It was held that they **were plant** because these items were used to create an **atmosphere** which was conductive to the comfort and well being of the customers.

In Wimpy International Ltd and Warland (1988), a dispute arose whether an attractive floor in a restaurant is plant or not. It was held that the function of the floor was to make the restaurant attractive to the customers and so it does not qualify as a plant. In such a case, the **floor is part of the premises** and hence, **ineligible** for capital allowances.

A statue in a tax consultant's office is not plant because selling atmosphere is not a part of a consultant's business. However, taxation books used by the tax consultant will be considered 'plant' because in Munby v Furlong (1977) it was held that plant includes a man's tool of trade. It extends to what a man uses in the daily course of his profession.

Tip

In order for a setting to qualify as plant, it must contribute to the ambience and atmosphere of the business, not merely be the setting of a business".

1.3 Expenditure which specifically qualifies as plant and machinery

Legislation lists the following expenditure as qualifying for relief:

1. Expenditure on the thermal insulation of any building used for a qualifying activity (e.g. a trade).
2. Expenditure incurred to comply with fire and safety regulations for premises used in trade.
3. Expenditure on building operations, incidental to the installation of plant and machinery.
4. Expenditure on sports ground which is necessary to comply with safety regulations.
5. Expenditure on a license to use computer software.
6. Expenditure on assets necessary to safeguard an individual's personal physical security.

Tip

Note that **'land' does not qualify** as plant and machinery.

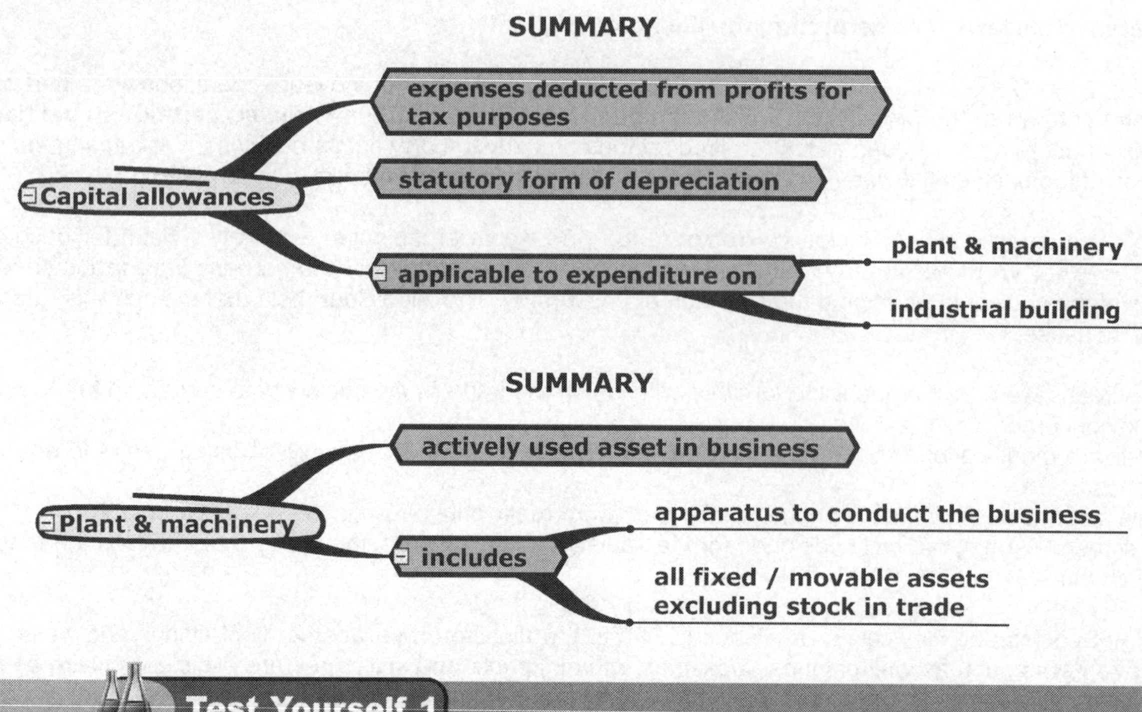

Test Yourself 1

Can the following assets be considered plant and machinery?

1. An old ship used as a restaurant.
2. Central heating system in an office building.

2. Compute writing down allowances, first year allowances and the annual investment allowance.[2]

[Learning Outcome g (ii)]

The allowances available on plant and machinery are:

- annual investment allowance (AIA)
- first year allowance (FYA)
- writing down allowances (WDA)

Capital allowances are not calculated separately for each item of plant and machinery purchased by a business. Instead, capital expenditure is categorised and capital allowances are given at different rates on different types of assets, in a way similar to accounting depreciation charges. When assets are grouped in the same category, it is known as 'pooling'.

2.1 Categories of assets for calculation of capital allowances

The categories and the calculation of capital allowances are as follows:

	General pool £	Expensive Car £	Private use asset £	Short life asset £	Special rate pool £	Capital Allowances £
TWDV b/f	X			X	X	
Additions	X	X	X		X	
Disposals	(X)				(X)	
	X				**X**	
Less: Allowances	(X)	(X)	(X)	(X)	(X)	X
TWDV c/f	**X**	**X**	**X**	**X**	**X**	
Allowances for the period						**X**

TWDV means tax written down value.

2.2 The categories contain the following assets:

1. General pool

The pool groups together:

- plant and machinery, furniture and equipment etc.
- vehicles
- all low emission cars

2. Cars

This is divided into three categories on the basis of CO_2 emissions rate:

- CO_2 emissions rate not exceeding 110g/km (low emission cars)
- CO_2 emissions rate between 110g/km and 160g/km (included in the general pool)
- CO_2 emissions rate exceeding 160g/km (single asset category)

3. Special rate pool

The pool groups together:

- all long-life assets with a useful life of at least 25 years on which total overall expenditure incurred within a year is at least £100,000.
- features that are integral to a building.
- thermal insulation.

4. Single asset categories

- Cars with CO_2 emissions rate exceeding 160g/km
- Private use asset (an asset used partly for private purposes by the owner)
- Short life asset (an asset with a useful life of less than 5 years)

2.3 Annual investment allowance (AIA)

The annual investment allowance (AIA) is available to all kinds of businesses and allows a business to immediately write off the first £25,000 of expenditure on plant and machinery

This limit of £25,000 is applicable annually. Expenditure above £25,000 will be eligible for WDA at the normal rates for the year 2012-2013.

Tip

The AIA limit was same during the previous tax year 2011-12, therefore the examiner has stated that a question can be set where the accounting period spans 6 April 2012 for individuals and 1 April 2012 for companies.

The annual investment allowance is available to all expenditure on plant and machinery, **but not for cars**.

Example

Jake started trading on 6 April 2012 and prepares accounts to 5 April each year. On 10 April 2012, Jake purchased qualifying plant for £170,000. Calculate the amount of annual investment allowance available to Jake for the year ended 5 April 2013.

The AIA available for the year ended on 5 April 2013 is as follows:

	General pool (£)	Allowances (£)
Year ended 05/04/2013		
TWDV b/f		
Additions qualifying for AIA		
Plant	170,000	
Less: AIA (maximum)	(25,000)	25,000
Balance after AIA but before WDA	**145,000**	
Allowances		**25,000**

Important

Where the period of accounts is more or less than 12 months the limit of £25,000 is proportionately increased or decreased.

Example

Mary commenced trading on 1 July 2012 and prepares accounts to 31 March each year. Her first accounts are for the period to 31 March 2013. Mary incurred total expenditure of £164,000 on plant and machinery on 1 July 2012. Therefore the AIA would be £18,750 (25,000 x 9/12) for the nine month period of accounts.

	General pool £	Allowances £
9 months period ended on 31/03/2013		
Additions qualifying AIA	164,000	
Less: AIA	(18,750)	18,750
Balance after AIA but before WDA	**145,250**	
Allowances		**18,750**

2.4 Writing down allowance (WDA)

Writing down allowance (WDA) is given for an accounting period **at 18% per annum** on reducing balance basis.

This is calculated as follows:

- Any balance on the pool is brought forward (the tax written down value TWDV).
- Expenditure on plant and machinery qualifying for AIA is added.
- AIA is deducted.
- Expenditure on plant and machinery not qualifying for AIA is added (this includes cars except low emission cars).
- Disposal proceeds (lower of cost and sale proceeds) are deducted.
- The WDA is deducted from the pool.
- The figure remaining (the TWDV) is carried forward to the next period.

	AIA £	General pool £	Allowances £
TWDV b/f		X	
Additions qualifying for AIA	X		
Less: AIA	(X)	X	X
Additions not qualifying for AIA		X	
Less: Disposals (lower of cost and sale proceeds)		(X)	
		X	
Less: WDA @ 18%		(X)	X
TWDV c/f		**X**	
Allowances			**X**

Tip

The rate of WDA (18%) will be given to you in the examination.

Jack prepares accounts to 31 March each year. Information for the year ending 31 March 2013 is as follows:

		£
1 April 2012	TWDV brought forward	65,000
10 April 2012	Bought plant	59,500
1 May 2012	Bought machinery	112,500
1 July 2012	Sold plant (original cost £38,000 on 01/06/2009)	15,000

Capital allowances for the year ended to 31 March 2013 are as follows.

	AIA £	General pool £	Allowances £
Year ended 31/03/2013			
TWDV b/f		65,000	
Additions qualifying for AIA			
Plant	59,500		
Machinery	112,500		
	172,000		
Less: AIA	(25,000)	147,000	25,000
Additions not qualifying for AIA		-	
Less: Disposals (lower of cost and sale proceeds)		(15,000)	
		197,000	
WDA (£197,000 x 18%)		(35,460)	35,460
TWDV b/f		**161,540**	
Allowances			**60,460**

WDA when an accounting period is 12 months long

WDA is given for an accounting period. If the period is 12 months long the capital allowances will be 18% of the TWDV of the pool after making adjustments for additions and disposals. Whether the asset was bought on the first day of the accounting period or the last day of the accounting period the same allowances are available. It is the length of the accounting period that determines the allowance, not the date of purchase within the accounting period.

WDA when an accounting period is more or less than 12 months

Where a trader prepares accounts for a period longer or shorter than twelve months, the **WDA is increased or decreased accordingly.**

Linda prepares accounts to 31 December each year. In March 2013, she decided to change her accounting date to 31 March, and prepares the accounts for 15 months to 31 March 2013. The tax written down value of the plant and machinery pool as at 1 January 2012 was £10,000.

Her accounting period for the tax year 2012-13 is 15 months ending on 31 March 2013.

Capital allowances for the 15 month accounting period are calculated as follows:
£10,000 x 18% x 15/12 = £2,250

SUMMARY

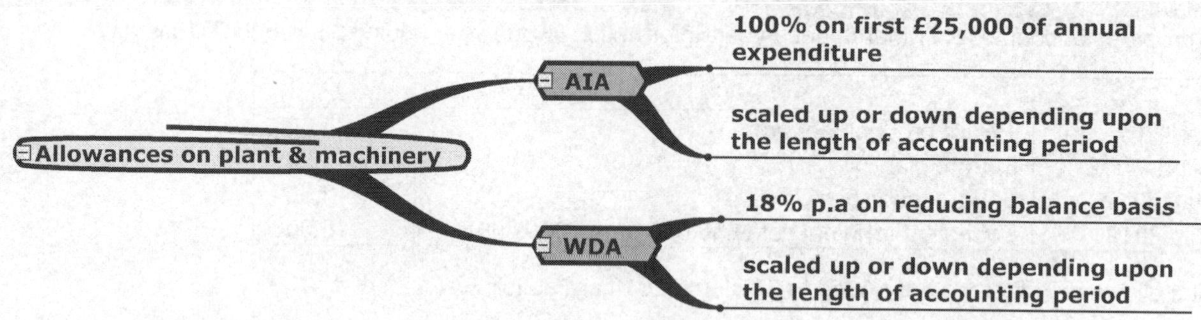

Eric prepares accounts to 31 March each year. Information for the year ending 31 March 2013 is as follows:

	£
TWDV brought forward 1 April 2012	28,000
1 June 2012 purchased machinery	158,000
1 July 2012 sold plant (original cost £10,500)	12,000

Required:

1. Calculate the capital allowances for the year to 31 March 2013.
2. Calculate the capital allowances for the period to 31 March 2014, assuming there are no sales or purchases in the year.

Malcolm started trading on 1 October 2011 and prepares accounts to 31 December each year. His first accounts are for the period to 31 December 2012. The only transaction in the period to 31 December 2012 was on 10 October 2012 when he bought machinery for £168,000.

Required:

Calculate the capital allowances for the period to 31 December 2012.

3. Compute capital allowances for motor cars.[2]

[Learning Outcome g (iii)]

The Finance Act 2009 introduced a new basis for calculation of capital allowances for motor cars. Before 6 April 2009 (1 April 2009 for limited companies), the calculation of capital allowances on motor cars was based upon the cost of the car. However, from the tax year 2009-10, the calculation of capital allowance is based upon the CO_2 emissions rate of the car.

The capital allowances for motor cars purchased on or after 6 April 2009 (1 April 2009 for limited companies) are based on the following categories:

- Cars with CO_2 emissions rate not exceeding 110g/km (low emission cars)
- Cars with CO_2 emissions rate between 111g/km and 160g/km
- Cars with CO_2 emissions rate exceeding 160g/km

Note that these rules only apply to cars. Any other type of vehicle, such as a motorcycle, lorry or van, is treated as plant and machinery with AIA available for the first £25,000.

1. Low emission cars

- A low emission car is one with a **CO_2 emission rate of 110g/km** or less.
- Low emission cars are **eligible for a 100% first year allowance regardless of the cost of the car.**

Tip

FYA at 100% is available on low emission cars irrespective of the length of the accounting period and date of purchase of the car.

2. Cars with CO_2 emissions rate between 111g/km and 160g/km

- If such cars are purchased on or after 6 April 2009 (1 April 2009 for limited companies), they will be included in the **general pool**.
- Writing down allowance (WDA) at the rate of 18% per annum will be available on these cars.
- These cars do not qualify for AIA and FYA.

3. Cars with CO_2 emissions rate exceeding 160g/km

- If these cars are purchased on or after 6 April 2009 (1 April 2009 for limited companies), they are **not pooled in the general pool** of plant and machinery.
- Each of these cars is allocated to the **special rate pool** and will **have its own capital allowance calculation.**
- These cars **do not qualify for AIA and FYA.**
- The **WDA** on these cars is calculated at the **rate of 8%** per annum on a reducing balance basis.

Example

Jack started trading on 1 April 2012 and prepares accounts to 30 May each year. His first accounts covered the period from 1 April 2012 to 31 May 2013. Jack's expenditure on plant and machinery qualifies for capital allowances. In the period he made the following purchases:

		£
1 April 2012	Bought plant	159,467
1 May 2012	Bought motor car (CO_2 emissions rate of 120g/km)	12,500
21 July 2012	Bought motor car (CO_2 emissions rate of 185g/km)	16,210
16 November 2012	Bought motor car (CO_2 emissions rate of 90g/km)	18,000

Capital allowances for **14 months to 30 May 2013** are as follows:

	AIA and FYA £	General pool £	Special rate car £	Allowances £
TWDV b/f				
Additions qualifying for AIA				
Plant	159,467			
Less: AIA (£25,000 x 14/12) (note 3)	(29,167)	130,300		29,167
Additions qualifying for FYA				
Low emission car	18,000			
Less: FYA 100% (note 4)	(18,000)	nil		18,000
Additions not qualifying for AIA				
Car (note 2)		12,500	16,210	
		142,800		
Less: WDA 18%/8% for 14 months (note 3)		(29,988)	(1,513)	31,501
TWDV c/f		**112,812**	**14,697**	
Allowances				**78,668**

Notes

1. AIA applies to all expenditure on plant and machinery with the exception of cars.
2. The CO_2 emissions rate of the car purchased on 1 May 2012 is between 111g/km and 160g/km, therefore it will be included in the general pool and the WDA at the rate of 18% per annum will be available. However, the CO_2 emissions of the car purchased on 21 July 2012 exceeds 160g/km, so it will not be included in the general pool and will have its own column. The WDA at the rate of 8% is available on such cars.

Continued on the next page

3. As the AP is more than 12 months, AIA and WDA will be scaled up proportionately.
4. Jack can claim a 100% FYA on the car purchased on 16 November 2012 as the emission rate of the car is less than 110g/km.

Important

From the June 2013 exams onwards questions will no longer be set involving motor cars purchased before 6 April 2009 (1 April 2009 for limited companies)

The rules for calculating capital allowance on motor cars were different prior to Finance Act 2009; they were based upon the cost of the car.

According to the old provisions, cars costing less than £12,000 were included in the general pool and WDA was calculated on them at the rate of 20% per annum.

Cars costing more than £12,000 were termed expensive cars and each expensive car had its own column. The WDA on an expensive car was calculated at 20% per annum but was restricted to a maximum of £3,000 per annum. If the accounting period is not 12 months long, this limit of £3,000 was scaled up or down **according to the length of the accounting period.**

Example

Ivy prepares accounts to 5 April each year. The written down value of plant and machinery on 6 April 2012 was as follows:

	£
General pool	28,000
Expensive car	18,000

She made the following transactions during the year:

		£
30 May 2012	Purchased car (CO_2 emissions rate of 185g/km)	12,500
20 August 2012	Bought plant	170,000

The capital allowances available to Ivy for the year to 5 April 2013 are as follows:

	AIA	General Pool	Expensive car	Special rate car	Allowances
	£	£	£	£	£
TWDV b/f		28,000	18,000		
Additions qualifying for AIA					
Plant	170,000				
Less: AIA	(25,000)	145,000			25,000
		173,000			
Additions not qualifying for AIA					
Car				12,500	
Less: WDA 18%/w1/8%		(31,140)	(3,000)	(1000)	35,140
TWDV c/f		141,860	15,000	11,500	
Allowances					**60,140**

Workings

W1

WDA on an expensive car is available at the rate of 18%.
WDA = £18,000 x 18% = £3,240
However, it is restricted to a maximum of £3,000 per annum.

Continued on the next page

W2

The car purchased with a CO_2 emission rate of more than 160g/km is not included in the general pool and has its separate column. WDA on such cars is available at the rate of 8%.

Diagram 1: Capital allowance for motor car

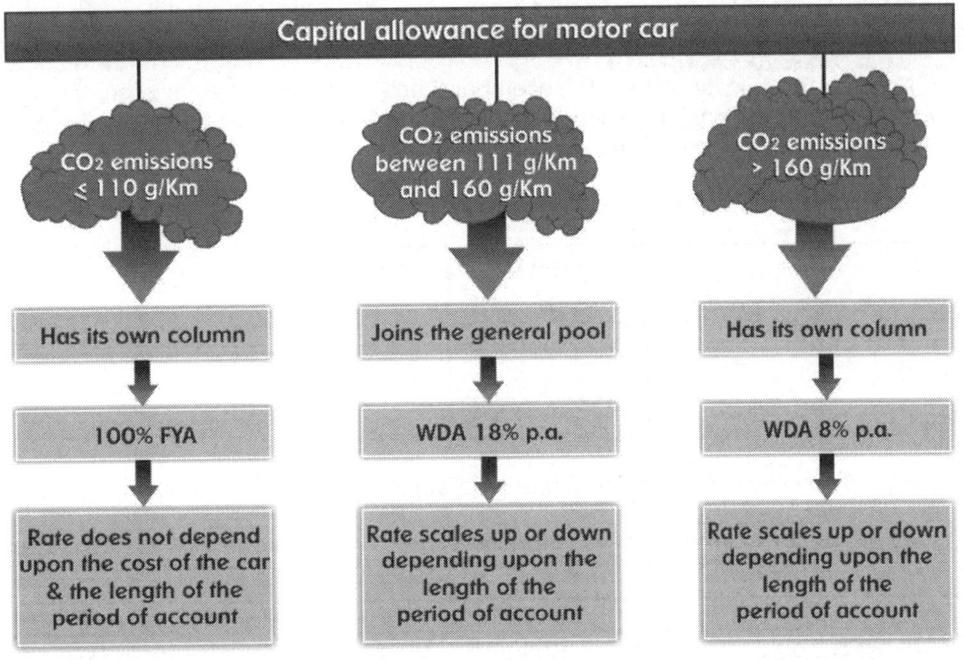

Test Yourself 4

Robert has been trading for many years, preparing accounts to 31 December each year. The TWDV on his general pool on 1 January 2012 was £20,000. On 5 November 2012 he purchased a car for £15,000 with CO_2 emissions rate of 192g/km.

Required:

Calculate the capital allowances for the accounting period to 31 December 2012.

Test Yourself 5

Mack started trading on 1 June 2012 and prepared accounts to 31 March 2013 and annually thereafter. In this period, he made the following purchases:

		£
1 August 2012	Bought motor car (CO_2 emissions rate of 196g/km)	14,000
2 September 2012	Bought motor car (CO_2 emissions rate of 105g/km)	12,500
16 November 2012	Bought equipment	91,400

Required:

Compute the capital allowances for the 10 months to 31 March 2013.

4. Compute balancing allowances and balancing charges.[2]

[Learning Outcome g (iv)]

The aim of capital allowances is to compensate the business for the net cost of owning the asset. Capital allowances would have been given over the life of the asset. They may be greater or less than its **net cost (original cost less sale proceeds)**. On the disposal of an asset, adjustments are made in such a way that the total allowance given equals the net cost of the asset. This is referred to as a **balancing adjustment**.

If insufficient allowances have been claimed, then additional allowances may be given by means of a **balancing allowance**. If the allowances claimed exceed the net cost of the asset, a **balancing charge** may arise, recovering some of the allowances already given.

The treatment of the disposal depends upon whether the asset was in a general pool, or in a pool of its own.

4.1 Balancing adjustments on the general pool

1. If the **disposal value** of an asset **exceeds the TWDV** on the general pool, it means too many allowances have been given in the past, and a **balancing charge arises. A balancing charge is simply a negative capital allowance, and is added to the tax adjusted trading profits.** A balancing charge can arise at the end of any accounting period.

Ross, a trader, prepares his accounts to 31 December each year. The balance on the general pool on 1 January 2012 was £17,450. The only transaction in the year to 31 December 2012 was the sale of machinery for £19,000. The original cost of the machinery was £25,000.

Capital allowances for the year ended 31 December 2012 are as follows:

	General pool (£)	Allowances (£)
TWDV b/f	17,450	
Less: Disposals	(19,000)	
Balancing charge	**(1,550)**	**(1,550)**

The machinery is sold for more than the TWDV of the general pool, giving rise to a balancing charge of £1,550.

This balancing charge is a negative capital allowance and will be added to the tax adjusted trading profits.

2. If the **disposal value** of the asset is **less than the TWDV** on the general pool, it means **insufficient allowances have been given**. However, no balancing allowance occurs on the general pool unless the business is ceasing to trade. If the business is continuing, a WDA of 18% is available and the TWDV on the general pool is carried forward as normal.

Stephen, a trader, prepares accounts to 30 September each year. The balance on the general pool on 1 October 2012 was £24,250. He ceased trading on 31 December 2012, and sold all items in the general pool for £20,000.

Capital allowances for the period ending 31 December 2012 are as follows:

	General pool £	Allowances £
	(£)	(£)
TWDV b/f	24,250	
Disposal proceeds	(20,000)	
Balancing allowance	**4,250**	**4,250**

The machinery is sold for less than the TWDV of the general pool. As the business is ceasing to trade, a balancing allowance of £4,250 arises.

The balancing allowance is deducted from tax adjusted trading profits.

However, if it is a continuing business, then no balancing allowance will arise and a WDA at the rate of 18% will be calculated in the normal way.

4.2 Balancing adjustments on single column assets e.g. expensive car or a special rate pool car

a) If the **disposal value** of the asset **exceeds the TWDV**, then excess allowances have been given, so a **balancing charge arises.**

b) If the **disposal value** of the asset is **less than the TWDV**, then insufficient allowances have been given, and a **balancing allowance arises**.

A balancing allowance on a single asset column can arise at any point in the life of a business, not just on cessation as for the general pool.

No WDAs, FYAs or AIAs are available in the final accounting period, i.e. in the year of cessation.

Diagram 2: Balancing adjustments

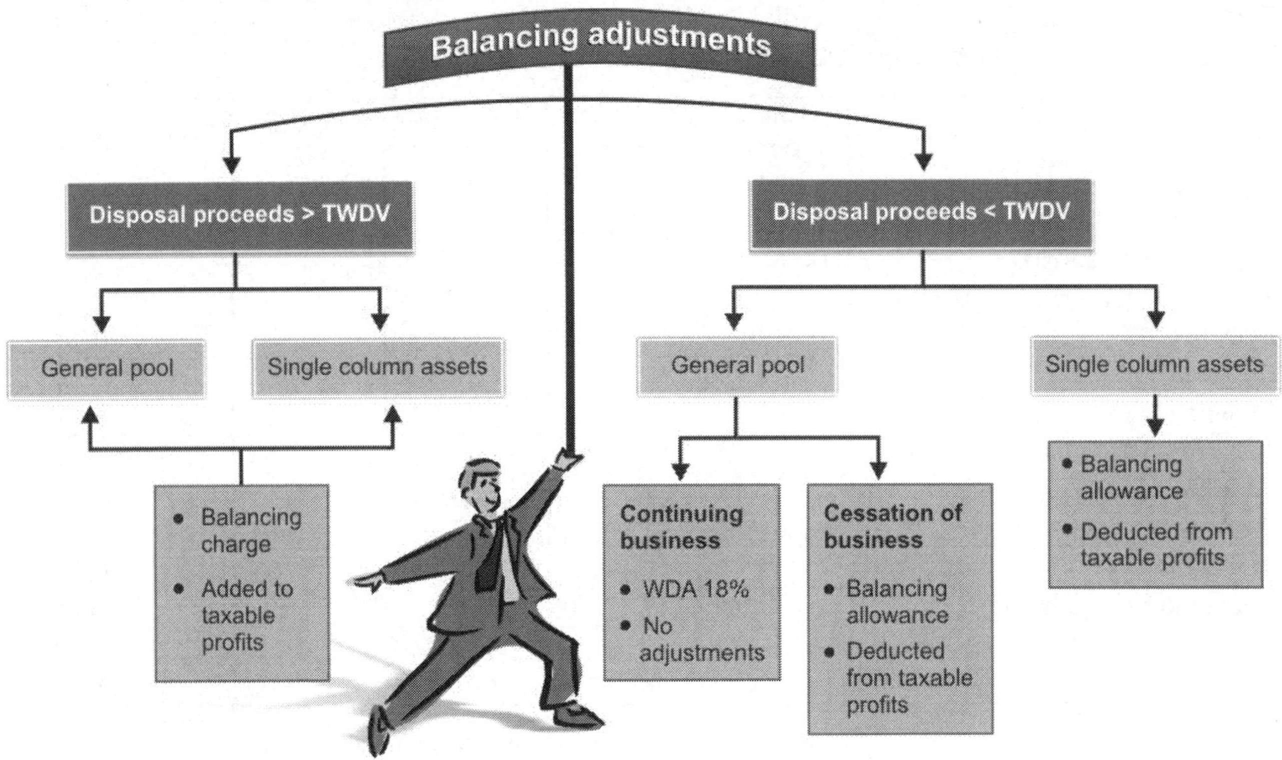

Glenda has been trading for many years, preparing accounts to 31 October each year. The TWDV of her general pool on 1 September 2012 is £28,000. On 1 October 2012, she purchased a car for £8,000 with CO_2 emissions rate of 146 g/km. Due to illness, she decided to close the business on 31 January 2013, and sold all the general pool items (including her car) for £32,100.

Required:

Calculate the capital allowances for the period to 31 January 2013.

4.3 Private use of assets by the owner

Capital allowances are restricted where there is some private use **by the owner**. Capital allowances **can only be claimed on the business proportion.**

An asset which is used **partially** for **business purposes** and partially for **private purposes** does not join the general pool but has its **own column.**

When the asset is disposed of balancing adjustments apply, but **only the business proportion is taken into account.**

Remember, capital allowances are **not restricted** in this way if the private use of **an asset** is **by an employee (not the owner).**

Michael, a trader, prepares accounts to 31 March every year.
He purchased a motor car with CO_2 emissions rate of 128g/km on 1 April 2011 for £5,000, with 60% private use agreed with HMRC. On 1 May 2011 he purchased a motor car for £15,000 with CO_2 emissions rate of 180g/km with 40% private use agreed with HMRC. No FYAs or AIA are available. On 1 November 2012 he sold the asset purchased in April 2011 for £4,800.

Compute the capital allowances for the two years to 31 March 2013.

Answer

The capital allowance available to Michael for the two years is as follows:

	General pool (£)	Business use 40% (£)	Special rate car (£)	Business use 60% (£)	Allowances (£)
Year ended 31/03/2012					
Addition not qualifying for AIA (Car)	5,000		15,000		
WDA 18%/8%	(900)	360	(1,200)	720	1,080
TWDV c/f	**4,100**		**13,800**		
Allowances					**1,080**
Year ended 31/03/2013					
TWDV b/f	4,100		13,800		
Disposal	(4,800)				
Less: WDA 8%			(1,104)	662	662
Balancing charge (W1)	**(700)**	**(280)**			(280)
TWDV c/f			**12,696**		
Allowances					**382**

Note that only the business portion is allowable for tax purposes.

Note: the car with CO_2 emissions rate between 111g/km and 160g/km joins the general pool and WDA on it is available at the rate of 18%. However, if the CO_2 emissions of the car exceed 160g/km, it does not join the general pool and has its own column. The WDA on these cars is available at the rate of 8%.

Workings

W1

The private use asset in the general pool is disposed of in the year ended 31 March 2013. Disposal proceeds are greater than the TWDV, therefore a balancing charge of £800 arises. Only the business proportion of the asset is taken into consideration, therefore the balancing charge is: £800 x 40% = £320.

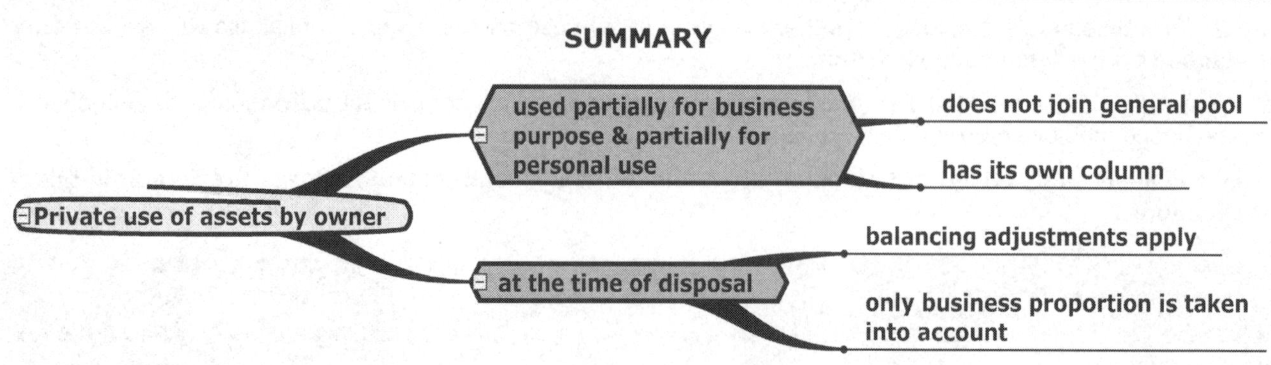

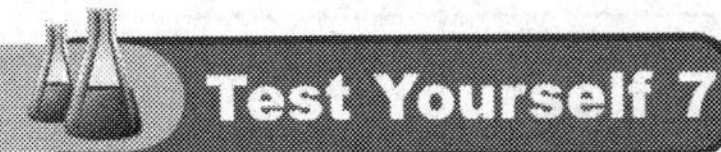

Lucy starts trading on 1 April 2011, preparing accounts to 30 April each year. On 10 April 2011 she purchased a car for £9,000 with CO_2 emissions rate of 152g/km. She agreed private use of 30% with HMRC.

Required:

Calculate the capital allowances for the two years to 30 April 2013.

5. Recognise the treatment of short life assets.[2]

[Learning Outcome g (v)]

A short life asset is an asset which the taxpayer **elects** to treat as a short life asset and which is **not specifically excluded** from being classed as a short life asset. Typically this election may be beneficial where the taxpayer expects the asset to have an expected life of **less than eight years from the end of the period of account in which the asset was purchased** (i.e. less than nine years from the date of acquisition). The effect of an election is to **de-pool such assets, which would otherwise be accounted for in the general pool.**

Earlier, the cut-off point was five years. It has increased to eight years from FY 2012-13. Therefore, the eight year cut-off point is applicable only to short life assets that are purchased after 6 April 2012 for individuals and 1 April 2012 for companies.

Short life asset purchased before these dates will not be examined.

1. The election is **not available** for **cars and private use assets.** (see above)
2. Each short life asset has **its own column for capital allowances.**
3. Expenditure on short life assets qualifies for the annual investment allowance of £25,000.
4. The availability of WDAs is the same as for the general pool. A balancing adjustment arises when the asset is disposed of.
5. If the asset is **not disposed** of by the end of the **eighth year** after the end of the period of account in which the asset was purchased, then the **TWDV of the asset is transferred to the general pool.**
6. The election **accelerates capital allowances** if the **asset is disposed of within eight years** for a **price less than the TWDV.**

If the AIA limit covers the cost of a short life asset, making the short life asset election will not be beneficial as it could result in a balancing charge when the asset is sold.

However, if the expenditure on a short life asset exceeds the £25,000 limit covered by AIA and the asset is likely to be disposed of for less than the TWDV, then it may be beneficial to make a short life asset election for that asset.

Rob has been trading for many years, preparing accounts to 31 December each year. The TWDV on his general pool on 1 January 2012 was £48,000. On 5 November 2012 he purchased plant for £175,000. Rob made a short life asset election for the new plant purchased.

In March 2013, Rob sold the plant purchased in November 2012 for £25,000.

The calculation of capital allowances is as follows:

Continued on the next page

	General pool £	Short life asset £	Allowances £
Year ended 31/12/2013			
TWDV b/f	48,000		
Additions qualifying AIA: Plant	-	175,000	-
Less: AIA	-	(25,000)	25,000
		150,000	
Less: WDA 18%	(8,640)	(27,000)	35,640
TWDV c/f	**39,360**	**123,000**	
Allowances			**60,640**
Year ended 31/12/2014			
TWDV b/f	39,360	123,000	
Less: WDA 18%	(7,085)		7,085
Less: Disposals		(25,000)	
Balancing allowance		98,000	98,000
TWDV c/f	**32,275**	**-**	
Allowances			**105,085**

The value of the short life asset is more than £25,000 (i.e. not covered by the AIA) and was sold for less than the TWDV, hence it was beneficial to make a short life asset election as it resulted in a balancing allowance of £98,000 when the asset was sold.

Example

Matthew started trading on 7 April 2012 and prepares his accounts to 31 March each year. On 10 April 2012, he purchased plant for £12,400, and on 31 October 2013, he purchased additional plant for £130,000. In February 2014 Matthew sold the plant purchased in April 2012 for £1,985.

Matthew made a short life asset election for the plant purchased in April 2012. The **calculation of capital allowances is as follows:**

	General pool (£)	Short life asset (£)	Allowances (£)
Period ended 31/3/2013			
TWDV b/f	Nil		
Additions qualifying for AIA			
Plant		12,400	
Less: AIA		(12,400)	12,400
TWDV c/f		-	
Allowances			**12,400**
Year ended 31/3/2014			
TWDV b/f	-	-	
Additions qualifying for AIA			
Plant	130,000		
Less: AIA	(25,000)		25,000
	105,000		
Less: WDA 18%	(18,900)		18,900
Less: Disposals		(1,985)	
TWDV c/f	**86,100**		
Balancing charge		**(1,985)**	
Allowances			**43,900**

The short life asset is not pooled in the general pool with the other assets; it has its own column.

Continued on the next page

Matthew opted for a short life asset election but it was not beneficial as it has resulted in a balancing charge in the second year. Hence, the net capital allowances for the year ended 31/3/2014 are £41,915 (£43,900 – £1,985).

If Matthew doesn't make a short life asset election, the calculation of capital allowances will be as follows:

	General pool (£)	Allowances (£)
Period ended 31/03/2013		
TWDV b/f		
Additions qualifying for AIA	12,400	-
Less: AIA	(12,400)	12,400
TWDV c/f		
Allowances		**12,400**
Year ended 31/3/2014		
Additions qualifying for AIA	130,000	
Less: AIA	(25,000)	25,000
	105,000	
Less: WDA 18%	(18,900)	18,900
Less: Disposals	(1,985)	
TWDV c/f	**84,115**	
Allowances		**43,900**

In this case, the net capital allowances for the year ended 31/3/2014 are £43,900. It is therefore beneficial not to make the election in this case.

SUMMARY

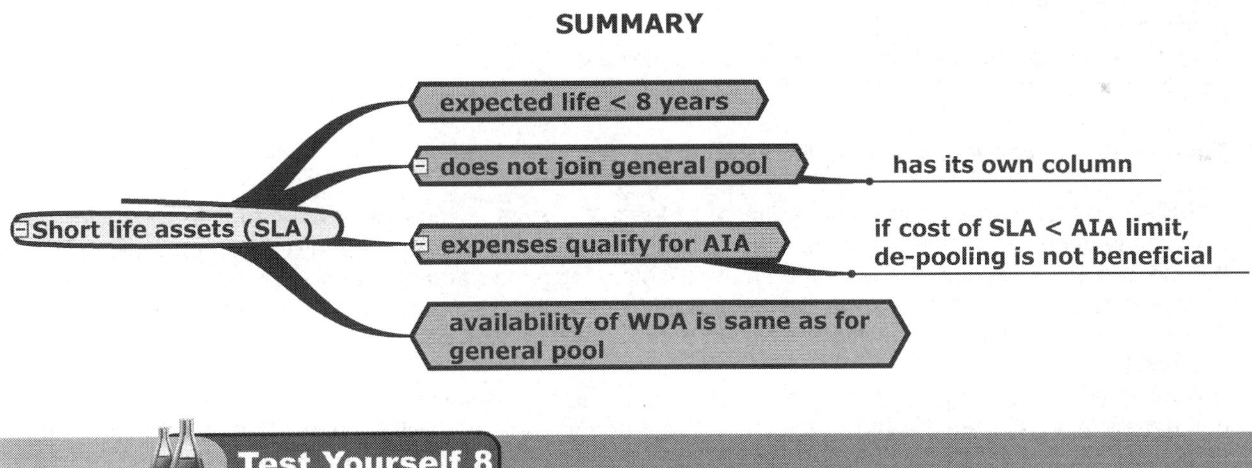

Test Yourself 8

Alice started her manufacturing business on 1 April 2012. She chose 31 March as her annual accounting date. On 10 April 2012, she purchased machinery for £154,800, and in May 2013 she purchased additional plant for £168,500. In August 2014, she sold the asset purchased on 10 April 2012 for £25,000.

Alice made a de-pooling election for the machinery purchased in April 2012.

Required:

Calculate the capital allowances for the three years to 31 March 2015 assuming that the rates and allowances are the same for the next three years.

---

6. Explain the treatment of assets included in the special rate pool.[2]

[Learning Outcome g (vi)]

6.1 Special rate pool

The treatment of a special rate pool is similar to that of a general pool with the exception that the WDA is available at the rate of 8% instead of 18%. The AIA is available on special rate pool assets.

This special rate pool is available for expenditure on:

- long-life assets
- features integral to a building
- thermal insulation

Definition

A **long life asset** is defined as:

- **an asset which, when new** has an **expected economic working life of at least 25 years, and**
- **TOTAL** expenditure on this type of asset **exceeds £100,000 in a 12 month period.**

The following are not treated as long-life assets

a) Motor cars
b) Ships
c) Plant and machinery used in retail shops, showrooms, offices, hotels and dwelling houses

A number of items of plant and machinery are treated as being integral to a building, particularly:

- electrical and lighting systems
- cold water systems
- space or water heating systems
- powered systems of ventilation, cooling, or air purification
- lifts and escalators

6.2 Treatment of expenditure on long life assets

1. If the expenditure on an asset with a life of at least 25 years is **less than £100,000** (pro-rata for short accounting periods), then they are not long life assets, and the assets go into the **general pool** as usual.
2. If the expenditure **exceeds £100,000**, then the assets go into the **special rate pool.**
3. Expenditure on assets in the special rate pool **qualifies for annual investment allowance.**
4. The WDA is also available on the special rate pool and is calculated at the rate of 8% on the reducing balance basis
5. Balancing adjustments apply to the special rate pool in the same way as for the general pool.
6. It is beneficial to allocate the AIA to the special rate pool initially as it will convert 8% WDA into 100% relief (which is more beneficial than converting 18% WDA into 100% relief).

Important

AIA must be allocated against expenditure on assets in the following sequence to claim the maximum benefit

1. Special rate pool
2. General pool
3. Short life asset
4. Private use asset

Example

Patrick has been trading for many years preparing accounts to 31 March every year. The TWDV on his special rate asset pool and general pool on 1 April 2012 was £38,000 and £54,800 respectively.

Patrick has purchased the following assets during the accounting period ending on 31 March 2013:

		£
15 May 2012	Office Furniture	15,600
20 August 2012	Motor car with CO_2 emission rate of 192g/km	12,800
22 January 2013	Machinery	38,000

He also incurred expenditure on his office building which qualifies as an integral feature of a building.

	£
Electrical and lighting systems	14,600
Fire alarm system	12,900
Escalators	38,400

In March 2013, Patrick sold equipment for £8,500 from the general pool. The original cost of that equipment was £15,600.

Capital allowances available for the year ended 31 March 2013 are as follows:

	Special rate pool £	**General pool** £	**Allowances** £
TWDV b/f	38,000	54,800	
Additions qualifying for AIA			
Integral features in a building			
(£14,600 + £12,900 + £38,400)	65,900		
Less: AIA	(25,000)		25,000
Additions not qualifying for AIA			
Office furniture		15,600	
Machinery		38,000	
Motor car	12,800		
Less: Disposal proceeds		(8,500)	
	91,700	99,900	
Less: WDA 8%/18%	(7,336)	(17,982)	25,318
TWDV c/f	**84,364**	**81,918**	
Allowances			**50,318**

Note: AIA should be claimed against the special rate pool asset first as this result in claiming the maximum amount of capital allowances. This is because the WDA available on the special rate pool is only 8% but on the general rate pool is 18%. Hence, converting 8% relief into 100% relief is more beneficial than converting 18% relief into 100% relief.

Patrick has been trading for many years preparing accounts to 30 June every year. The TWDV on his special rate asset pool on 1 April 2012 was £74,200. In June 2013, he sold one of the long life assets for £82,000.

Capital allowances for the two years are as follows:

	Special rate pool (£)	Allowances (£)
Year ended 31/3/2013		
TWDV b/f	74,200	-
Less: WDA 8%	(5,936)	5,936
TWDV c/f	**68,264**	
Allowances		**5,936**
Year ended 31/3/2014		
TWDV b/f	68,264	
Less: Disposal proceeds	(82,000)	-
Balancing charge	**(13,736)**	**(13,736)**

SUMMARY

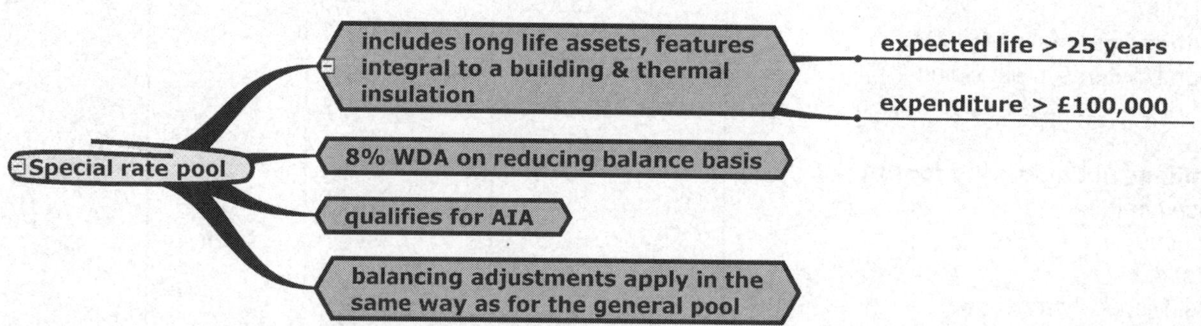

Jack is a trader preparing accounts to 31 March each year. The TWDV of the general pool on 1 April 2012 is £40,000. He purchased an asset on 15 March 2013 with an expected economic working life of 30 years.

Required:

Calculate the capital allowances for the year to 31 March 2013 assuming the purchase price of the asset is

(a) £90,000
(b) £190,000

6.3 Other important points

1. Second hand assets

The same allowances are available for a second hand asset as they are for a new one, including the annual investment allowance.

Long life assets are those with a life expectancy of over 25 years **when new**, not from when purchased.

Short life asset elections may still be made if there is a life expectancy of less than 5 years from the date of acquisition.

2. Part exchange transactions

A part exchange transaction is when a new asset is purchased, but instead of the asset being purchased for cash, the purchase is partly funded by trading a used asset. The remaining balance is paid in cash.

In other words, a new asset is purchased with a combination of an existing asset and cash.

For the capital allowances calculation, this is treated as two separate transactions. First, the disposal of one asset with the part exchange allowance being the disposal proceeds and second, the purchase of the new asset for the full amount.

Example

Jerry has been trading for many years, preparing accounts to 31 March each year. The balance on the general pool on 1 April 2012 is £24,000. He part exchanged a car used by an employee (original cost £7,750) for a new one with a CO_2 emissions of 140g/km. He was given a part exchange allowance of £4,150 on the old car, and paid an additional £6,700.

Capital allowances for the year to 31 March 2013 are as follows:

	General Pool £	Allowances £
Year ended 31/03/2013		
TWDV b/f	24,000	
Additions (£4,150 + £6,700)	10,850	
	34,850	
Less: Disposals	(4,150)	
	30,700	
Less: WDA 18%	(5,526)	5,526
TWDV c/f	**25,174**	
Allowances		**5,526**

Note: WDA at the rate of 18% will be available on the car as the CO_2 emissions rate of the car is between 111g/km and 160g/km.

3. Hire purchase assets

According to the terms of hire purchase agreement, the payer becomes the legal owner of the asset only on making the final payment. However, for capital allowance computation purposes, plant and machinery bought on hire purchase are treated in the same way as assets bought for cash. Therefore the treatment for such assets is as follows:

a) capital allowances are available for the **cash price (excluding interest)** on the date of the hire purchase agreement.

b) interest included in the instalments is deductible as an expense from the trading income.

Example

John has been trading for many years and prepares his accounts to 31 July each year. The balance on the general pool on 1 August 2012 is £16,000.

John bought plant under a hire purchase agreement on 1 August 2012. He paid a deposit of £3,200 and 20 monthly instalments of £250. The price of the plant if purchased for cash is £7,000.

John's trading profits for the year to 31 July 2013, before deducting the capital allowances and interest from the hire purchase agreement are £80,000.

To calculate the adjusted trading profits, first calculate the capital allowances, assuming that the rates and allowances are the same for the year 2012-2013.

Continued on the next page

	AIA £	General Pool £	Allowances £
Year ended 31/07/2013			
TWDV b/f		16,000	
Additions qualifying for AIA	7,000		
Less: AIA	(7,000)	-	7,000
Less: WDA 18%		(2,880)	2,880
TWDV c/f		**13,120**	
Allowances			**9,880**

The interest element of the HP agreement is:

Total payments £3,200 + (20 x £250) = £8,200

Cash price £7,000
Interest element £1,200

The interest is an allowable expense, spread over the period of the contract.
Interest allowable in year ended 31 July 2013 is £1,200 x 12 instalments/20 instalments = £720

Adjusted trading profits for year ended 31 July 2013

	£
Trading profit (given)	80,000
Less: Interest	(720)
Less: Capital allowances	(9,880)
Adjusted trading profits	**69,400**

---

4. Leased assets

A lease is an arrangement by which a person / entity (the lessee) can acquire the right to use an asset from **another person / entity** (the lessor), without making a full payment for the asset when **the arrangement** (the lease) commences.

The lessee pays for the use of the asset in instalments, over the period of the lease. The **lease rentals** which the **lessee pays** periodically are **allowable as an expense from their trading income on accrual basis.**

However, unlike assets purchased on hire purchase, capital allowances are not available to the lessee on the leased asset as the title of ownership of the asset remains with the lessor.

The treatment of leasing a car with a CO_2 emissions rate exceeding 160g/km is different and is discussed in detail in Study Guide B3 (Part 1), Learning Outcome 3.

6.4 Capital allowances at the commencement and cessation of businesses

1. Allowances in opening years

a) A trader will generally prepare accounts for a 12 month period, but it is not unusual for the first accounting period to be of a different length.

b) Capital allowances are calculated for an accounting period. If this period is not 12 months long, the allowances must be scaled up or down.

c) WDAs (8% / 18% and £3,000) must be pro-rated.

d) AIA is pro-rated, according to the length of the accounting period.

e) FYAs are NEVER pro-rated, regardless of the length of the accounting period.

Example

Michael started trading on 1 July 2012 and prepares accounts to 31 March every year.
The following transactions took place over 3 years.

	(£)
1 August 2012, bought car (CO_2 emissions rate of 156g/km)	8,800
1 September 2012, bought plant	125,000
1 May 2013, sold car	6,200

The tax adjusted trading profits before capital allowances are as follows:

	(£)
Period ended 31/3/2013	250,000
Year ended 31/3/2014	100,000
Year ended 31/3/2015	200,000

We first compute the capital allowances for the accounting periods, assuming that the allowances and rates remain the same for the next two years.

9 months to 31/03/2013

	AIA (£)	General pool (£)	Allowances (£)
Additions qualifying for AIA			
Plant	125,000		
Less: AIA (note)	(18,750)	106,250	18,750
Additions not qualifying for AIA			
Car		8,800	
		115,050	
WDA (£115,050 x 18% x 9/12)		(15,532)	15,532
TWDV c/f		**99,518**	
Allowances			**34,282**

Note: AIA is scaled down to £18,750 (£25,000 x 9/12) according to the length of the accounting period.

Year ended 31/03/2014

	General Pool (£)	Allowances (£)
TWDV b/f	99,518	
Less: Disposal	(6,200)	
	93,318	
Less: WDA 18%	(16,797)	16,797
TWDV c/f	**76,521**	
Allowances		**16,797**

Year ended 31/3/2015

	General Pool (£)	Allowances (£)
TWDV b/f	76,521	
Less: WDA 18%	(13,774)	13,774
TWDV c/f	**62,747**	
Allowances		**13,774**

Continued on the next page

The adjusted **trading profits** for the three periods are as follows:

	Period ended 31/03/2013 (£)	Year ended 31/03/2014 (£)	Year ended 31/03/2015 (£)
Trading profits given	250,000	100,000	200,000
Capital allowances	(34,282)	(16,797)	(13,774)
Adjusted trading profits after capital allowances	**215,718**	**83,203**	**186,226**

2. **Pre-trading capital expenditure**

a) Expenditure incurred on plant and machinery before trading commences is treated as if it was incurred on the first day of trading.

b) However, the rate of allowances goes by the **ACTUAL date of expenditure.**

3. **Allowances on cessation**

When trade ceases, all the plant and machinery is disposed of. Capital allowances in the final accounting period are calculated as follows:

a) Any purchases made in the final period are added to the TWDV b/f.

b) There are **no WDAs, FYAs or AIAs in the final period**.

c) Disposal proceeds (limited to cost) are deducted, giving rise to a balancing charge or balancing allowance. If the trader takes over an asset himself, then it is treated as sold at market value.

Sunny has been trading for many years and prepares accounts to 31 March each year. The TWDV on the general pool on 1 April 2012 is £26,000.

On 1 May 2012 he bought plant for £10,600.

He ceased trading on 30 September 2012, and sold all general pool items for £29,800. The tax adjusted profits, before capital allowances, for the period to 30 September 2012 were £28,200.

Sunny has overlap profits brought forward of £2,600.

Calculate Sunny's trading income assessment for 2012-13.

First calculate the capital allowances for the final period of trading.

	General Pool £
6 months to 30/09/2012	
TWDV b/f	26,000
Additions	10,600
	36,600
Less: Disposal	(29,800)
Balancing allowance	**6,800**

Continued on the next page

Note: no AIA, FYA or WDA available in the final period of trading.

2012-13	**£**
Basis period 01/04/2012 - 30/09/2012	
Adjusted trading profits before capital allowances	28,200
Less: Balancing allowance	(6,800)
Less: Overlap relief	(2,600)
2012-13 trading income assessment	**18,800**

Answers to Test Yourself

Answer to TY 1

1. The old ship is the setting for the business to be conducted. The structure used for carrying on the business is not considered as plant and machinery.
2. The central heating system will be considered plant and machinery as it is essential for proper functioning of the office.

Answer to TY 2

1. Capital allowances for the year ended 31 March 2013

	AIA **£**	**General pool** **£**	**Allowances** **£**
Year ended 31/03/2013			
TWDV b/f		28,000	
Additions qualifying AIA (machinery)	158,000		
Less: AIA	(25,000)	133,000	25,000
Disposal (lower of cost and sale proceeds)		(10,500)	
		150,500	
Less: WDA 18%		(27,090)	27,090
TWDV c/f		**123,410**	
Allowances			**52,090**

2. Capital allowances for the year ended 31 March 2014

	General pool **(£)**	**Allowances** **(£)**
Year ended 31/03/2014		
TWDV b/f	123,410	
Less: WDA 18%	(22,214)	22,214
TWDV c/f	**101,196**	
Allowances		**22,214**

Answer to TY 3

Capital allowances for the period to 31 December 2012

	General pool (£)	Allowances (£)
15 months to 31/12/2012		
TWDV b/f	-	
Additions qualifying AIA (machinery)	168,000	
Less: AIA (W1)	(31,250)	31,250
	136,750	
Less: WDA 18% for 15 months (W1)	(30,769)	30,769
TWDV c/f	**105,981**	
Allowances		**62,019**

Working

W1 AIA and WDA are scaled up or down according to the length of the accounting period.

Malcolm began trading on 1 October 2011. He prepares his first accounts to 31 December 2012. His first accounting period is fifteen months long, so the AIA is scaled up for 15 months.

Hence, AIA = £25,000 x 15/12 = £31,250

WDA = £136,750 x 18% x 15/12 = £30,769

Answer to TY 4

	General pool £	Special rate car £	Allowances £
Year ended on 31/12/2012			
TWDV b/f	20,000		
Additions not qualifying for AIA: Car		15,000	
WDA 18%/8%	(3,600)	(1,200)	4,800
TWDV c/f	**16,400**	**13,800**	
Allowances			**4,800**

Note: the car with CO_2 emissions rate of more than 160g/km is not included in the general pool and WDA on the car is calculated at the rate of 8%.

Answer to TY 5

	FYA £	General pool £	Special rate car £	Allowances £
10 month period ended on 31/3/2013				
TWDV b/f				
Additions qualifying for AIA				
Equipment	91,400			
Less: AIA (£25,000 x 10/12)	(20,833)	70,567		20,833
Additions qualifying for FYA				
Low emission car	12,500			
Less: FYA 100%	(12,500)	-		12,500
Additions not qualifying for AIA				
Car			14,000	
Less: WDA at 18%/8% (reduced proportionately for 10 months)		(10,585)	(933)	11,518
TWDV c/f		**59,982**	**13,067**	
Allowances				**44,851**

Answer to TY 6

	General pool £
Period ended 31/1/2013	
TWDV b/f	28,000
Additions not qualifying for AIA Car	8,000
	36,000
Less: Disposal proceeds	(32,100)
Balancing allowance	**3,900**

Note: no WDA is given for the period in which the business ceases trading.

Answer to TY 7

	General pool (£)	Business use 70% (£)	Allowances (£)
Year ended 31/03/2012			
Additions not qualifying for AIA			
Car	9,000		
Less: WDA 18% (W1)	(1,620)	1,134	1,134
TWDV c/f	**7,380**		
Allowances			**1,134**
Year ended 31/3/2013			
TWDV b/f	7,380		
Less: WDA 18% (W1)	(1,328)	(930)	**930**
TWDV c/f	**6,052**		
Allowances			**930**

Working

W1

Motor cars are not eligible for AIA; the WDA is 18% per annum for cars with CO_2 emissions rate between 110g/km and 160g/km. Hence, allowances are £1,620 (£9,000 x 18%).

As Lucy has made private use of 30%, only the business proportion of the allowance (70%) can be claimed.

A Tax year is always from 6 April to 5 April so the capital allowances would be calculated to year ended 31.3.2012 and 31.3.2013

Answer to TY 8

	General pool (£)	Short life asset (£)	Allowances (£)
Year ended 31/3/2013			
TWDV b/f	-	Nil	
Additions qualifying for AIA			
Machinery		154,800	
Less: AIA		(25,000)	25,000
		129,800	
Less: WDA 18%		(23,364)	23,364
TWDV c/f	-	**106,436**	
Allowances			**48,364**
Year ended 31/03/2014			
TWDV b/f		106,436	
Additions qualifying for AIA: plant	168,500		
Less: AIA	(25,000)		25,000
	143,500		
Less: WDA 18%	(25,830)	(19,158)	44,988
TWDV c/f	**117,670**	**87,278**	
Allowances			**69,988**
Year ended 31/03/2015			
TWDV b/f	117,670	87,278	
Less: WDA 18%	(21,181)		21,181
Disposal proceeds		(25,000)	
Balancing allowance		**62,278**	62,278
TWDV c/f	**96,489**		
Allowances			**83,459**

Note: the short life asset election made by Alice for the asset purchased in April 2012 is beneficial as it exceeds the limit of £25,000 covered by AIA.

Answer to TY 9

1. Purchase price is £90,000

	AIA (£)	General Pool (£)	Allowances (£)
Year ended 31/3/2013			
TWDV b/f		40,000	
Additions qualifying for AIA	90,000		
Less: AIA	(25,000)	-	25,000
Less: WDA 18%		(7,200)	7,200
TWDV c/f		**32,800**	
Allowances			**32,200**

2. Purchase price is £190,000

	Special rate pool (£) £	General pool (£) £	Allowances (£) £
Year ended 31/03/2013			
TWDV b/f		40,000	
AIA additions	190,000		
Less: AIA	(25,000)		25,000
	165,000		
Less: WDA 8% / 18%	(13,200)	(7,200)	20,400
TWDV c/f	**151,800**	**32,800**	
Allowances			**45,400**

Note: an asset with a life of 25 years or more is only treated as a long life asset if the expenditure exceeds £100,000 in the accounting period.

Quick Quiz

1. How does a 9 month accounting period affect a WDA?
2. How does a 9 month accounting period affect an AIA?
3. What is a long life asset?

Answers to Quick Quiz

1. The WDA must be pro-rated in a 9 month accounting period.
2. The AIA is pro-rated in a 9 month accounting period.
3. A long life asset is one with an economic working life of more than 25 years, and where more than £100,000 has been spent on the asset in a year.

Self Examination Questions

Question 1

Della started business on 1 May 2012 and prepares accounts to 30 June 2013 and annually thereafter. Her adjusted trading profit before capital allowances for this period was £148,000.

She purchased the following assets:

		£
10 May 2012	Bought machinery	175,000
10 May 2012	Bought car (CO_2 emissions of 122g/km)	18,000
18 November 2012	Bought car (CO_2 emissions of 90g/km)	7,500

Compute the trading profits after capital allowances for the 14 months to 30 June 2013, assuming that the rates and allowances remain unchanged for the next two years.

Question 2

Ivy prepares accounts to 5 April each year. The written down value of plant and machinery on 6 April 2012 was as follows:

	£
General pool	28,000
Expensive car	7,000

She made the following transactions during the year:

		£
30 May 2012	Sold car (acquisition cost £13,000)	2,500
20 August 2012	Bought plant	10,000

Required:

Calculate the capital allowances available to Ivy for the year to 5 April 2013.

Question 3

Sharon has been trading for many years, preparing accounts to 30 June each year. She ceased trading on 10 March 2013. Her TWDVs on 1 July 2012 were as follows:

	£
Main pool	18,200
Expensive car	12,800

Her transactions in the period to 10 March 2013 are:

		£
10 March 2013	Sold all general pool items	21,200
10 March 2013	Sold car	8,500

Required:

Calculate the capital allowances for Sharon's final accounting period.

Question 4

Raja prepares his accounts to 31 March each year. He purchased a motor car on 1 December 2012 for £81,000 with a CO_2 emissions rate of 140g/km. He agreed with HMRC to make 50% private use of the motor car. The motor car was sold on 1 September 2014 for £35,000.

Required:

Calculate the capital allowances available for the 3 years to 31 March 2015, assuming that the rates and allowances remain unchanged for next three years.

Question 5

Amanda started trading on 1 April 2012 and prepared her first accounts for the 13 months to 30 April 2013.
She made the following purchases in the period:

		£
1 May 2012	Bought car (CO_2 emissions rate of 135g/km)	14,000
1 August 2013	Bought car (CO_2 emissions rate of 105g/km)	12,200

Required:

Calculate the capital allowances available to Amanda for the 13 months to 30 April 2013, assuming that the rates and allowances remain the same for the next two years.

Question 6

Jack has been trading for many years, making up accounts to 31 March each year.
The TWDV of his plant and machinery on 1 April 2012 were:

	(£)
General pool	50,000
Expensive car (60% private use by Jack)	20,000
Short life asset (purchased 1 April 2009)	55,000

Jack bought plant and machinery as follows:

		(£)
1 May 2012	Bought car with CO_2 emissions of 143g/km	10,800
10 May 2012	Bought machinery	60,000
31 May 2012	Bought equipment	62,000
1 June 2012	Bought van	15,000
1 July 2012	Bought car (CO_2 emissions of 187g/km) for employee (60% private use)	16,000

Jack makes a short life asset election for the equipment bought on 30 May 2012.

Required:

Calculate the capital allowances available to Jack for the year to 31 March 2013.

Question 7

Mia prepares accounts to 31 December each year. On 1 January 2012 the TWDV of his plant and machinery are as follows:

	CO_2 emissions	(£)
General Pool		15,800
Motor Car (1)	179 grams per km (purchased on 12 January 2010)	19,200
Motor Car (2)	136 grams per km (purchased on 5 June 2011)	22,800

During the year ended 31 December 2012, the following transactions took place:

		CO_2 emissions	(£)
1 January 2012	purchased motor car (3)	180 grams per km	20,325
15 May 2012	purchased equipment		136,200
8 August 2012	purchased motor car (4)	160 grams per km	25,100
20 October 2012	purchased motor car (5)	107 grams per km	15,400
5 December 2012	sold motor car (3)		(11,060)

15% of the mileage of Motor car (2) was for private purpose.
Required:

Calculate the capital allowances available to Mia for year ended 31 December 2012.

Answers to Self Examination Questions

Answer to SEQ 1

Capital allowances computation

	AIA (£)	General pool (£)	Allowances (£)
14 months to 30/06/2013			
Additions qualifying for AIA (machinery)	175,000		
Less: AIA (for 14 months) (W1)	(29,167)	145,833	29,167
Additions not qualifying for AIA (Car)	7,500	18,000	
Less: FYA 100% (W2)	(7,500)	-	7,500
		163,833	
Less: WDA 18% (for 14 months) (W3)		(34,405)	34,405
TWDV c/f	-	**129,428**	
Allowances			**71,072**

Calculation of adjusted trading profits

	£
Trading profits	148,000
Less: Capital allowances	(71,072)
Adjusted trading profits for 14 months ended 30/06/2012	**76,928**

Workings

W1

Expenditure on plant and machinery (with the exception of cars) incurred by any business is eligible for AIA at the rate of 100% on the first £25,000 of such expenditure.

AIA is scaled up or down according to the length of the accounting period.

AIA for 14 months = £25,000 x 14/12 = £29,167

W2

Cars with CO_2 emissions rate less than 110g/km are eligible for 100% FYA.

W3

Cars with CO_2 emissions rate between 110g/km and 160g/km are included in the general pool and are eligible for WDA at the rate of 18%. WDA is scaled up when the accounting period is more than twelve months.

The AP is 14 months, hence WDA for car is £163,833 x 18% x 14/12 = 34405

Answer to SEQ 2

Capital allowances computation

	FYA (£)	General Pool (£)	Expensive car (£)	Allowances (£)
Year ended 05/04/2013				
TWDV b/f		28,000	7,000	
Additions qualifying for AIA (Plant)	10,000			
Less: AIA	(10,000)	-		10,000
Less: Disposals			(2,500)	
Less: WDA @ 18%		(5,040)		5,040
TWDV c/f		**22,960**		
Allowances				**15,040**
Balancing Allowance			**4,500**	**4,500**

Total capital allowance available for the year to 5 April 2013 = £15,040 + £4,500 = £19,540

Notes

1. The expenditure incurred by any business on plant and machinery on or after 6 April 2011 is eligible for AIA up to a limit of £25,000.

2. As the disposal proceeds of the car (£2,500) are less than the TWDV (£7,000), a balancing allowance of £4,500 is given.

Answer to SEQ 3

Calculation of balancing adjustments

	General Pool (£)	Expensive car (£)	Allowances (£)
Period ended 10/03/2013			
TWDV b/f	18,200	12,800	
Disposal proceeds	(21,200)	(8,500)	
(Balancing charge)/allowance (W1)	**(3,000)**	**4,300**	**1,300**

Working

W1

No WDA and AIA are available in the final accounting period.

When the disposal proceeds are **more** than the TWDV, there is a **balancing charge** (i.e. negative capital allowance) which is added to the tax adjusted trading profits.

If the disposal proceeds are **less** than the TWDV, then a **balancing allowance** is given.

Answer to SEQ 4

Calculation of capital allowances until the date of the sale

	Motor car (£)	Business use 50% (£)	Allowances (£)
Year ended 31/03/2013			
Additions not qualifying for AIA	81,000		
WDA @ 18% (note 2)	(14,580)	7,290	7,290
TWDV c/f	**66,420**		
Allowances			**7,290**
Year ended 31/03/2014			
TWDV b/f	66,420		
WDA 18% (note 2)	(11,956)	5,978	5,978
TWDV c/f	**54,464**		
Allowances			**5,978**
Year ended 31/03/2015			
TWDV b/f	54,464		
Disposal proceeds	(35,000)		
Balancing allowance (note 3)	**19,464**	9,732	9,732

Notes

1. A car that is used for both private as well as business purposes should not be included the general pool. It should be dealt with on an individual basis.
2. As the asset is used 50% for private use, the WDA allowance is also given at 50%.
3. If the disposal proceeds are less than the TWDV, then a balancing allowance is given.

Answer to SEQ 5

Computation of capital allowance

	FYA (£)	General pool (£)	Allowances (£)
Period ended 30/04/2013 (13 months)			
Additions not qualifying for AIA (Car)	12,200	14,000	
Less: FYA 100%	(12,200)		12,200
Less: WDA 18% (W1)	-	(2,730)	2,730
TWDV c/f	-	**11,270**	
Allowances			**14,930**

Workings

W1

A car with CO_2 emissions between 110g/km and 160g/km is included in the general pool. The WDA on these cars is calculated at the rate of 18% per annum.

£14,000 x 18% = £2,520
The accounting period is 13 months, so scaled up accordingly.
£2,520 x 13/12 = £2,730.

W2

Cars with CO_2 emissions of less than 110g/km are eligible for 100% FYA.

Answer to SEQ 6

Computation of capital allowance

Remember, this car is used by the **employee** for private use, so capital allowance is **not restricted**.

	General pool (£)	Expensive car (1) (£)	Business use 40% (£)	Special rate car (2) (£)	Short life asset (1) (£)	Short life asset (2) (£)	Allowances (£)
Year ended 31/03/2013							
TWDV b/f	50,000	20,000			55,000		
AIA additions (60,000 + 15,000)	75,000					62,000	
Less: AIA	(25,000)						25,000
Non-AIA additions	10,800			16,000		-	
	110,800					62,000	
Less: WDA 18%/8%	(19,944)	(3,000)	(1,200)	(1,280)	(9,900)	(11,160)	43,484
TWDV c/f	**90,856**	**17,000**		**14,720**	**45,100**	**50,840**	
Allowances							**68,484**

Notes

1. Car purchased before 6 April 2009 and costing more than £12,000 is termed an expensive car and each expensive car has its own column.

2. The maximum WDA for an expensive car is £3,000 per annum and allowance for business use is only allowed.

3. AIA is available to all businesses and provides 100% allowance on the first £25,000 of expenditure on plant and machinery.

4. The expensive car provisions do not apply to lorries or vans.

Answer to SEQ 7

Mia's capital allowance claim for the year ended 31 December 2012 is as follows:

		Main Pool	Expensive Motor Car (1)	Motor Car (2)	Business use 85%	Special rate pool	Allowances
	£	£	£	£	£	£	£
TWDV brought forward		15,800	19,200	22,800			
Addition qualifying for AIA							
Equipment	136,200						
AIA - 100%	(25,000)	111,200					25,000
Addition qualifying for FYA							
Motor car (5)	15,400						
FYA - 100%	(15,400)						15,400
Other additions							
Motor car (3)						20,325	
Motor car (4)		25,100					
Less: Disposals						(11,060)	
		152,100	19,200	22,800			
Balancing allowance						9,265	9,265
WDA 18%/restricted/18%		(27,378)	(3,000)	(4,104)	(3,488)		33,866
TWDV c/f		**124,722**	**16,200**	**18,696**		-	
Allowances							**83,531**

Notes:

1. Motor car (1) was purchased before 6 April 2009 and it's cost is more than £12,000, therefore it is an expensive car. These cars have their own column. The writing down allowance on these cars is calculated at 18%, but is restricted to a maximum of £3,000.
2. Motor car (2) was purchased after 6 April 2009 but is recorded separately because Mia has used it for private purposes. This motor car has **CO_2** emission between 111 and 160 grams per km and therefore it qualifies for writing down allowances at the rate of 18%.
3. The car purchased after 6 April 2009 and with a CO_2 emission rate of more than 160g/km is not included in the general pool and has its separate column. WDA on such cars is available at the rate of 8%. However, the car is sold in the same year, therefore no allowance will be available in the year and a balancing allowance will arise.
4. Motor car (4) has **CO_2** emissions between 111 and 160 grams per km and therefore qualifies for WDV at the rate of 18% and will be included in the general pool.
5. Motor car (5) has **CO_2** emissions of less than 110 grams per km and therefore qualifies for 100% FYA.

STUDY GUIDE B3: INCOME FROM SELF-EMPLOYMENT (PART 3)

Get Through Intro

An important **job of an accountant** is to advise his client on how to make the best **use** of **all the statutory provisions** which are available to help the client **minimise his tax liability.**

A thorough knowledge of all the possible uses for losses is essential, if trading losses are to be relieved in the most beneficial way.

As a tax consultant, you should gain a good understanding of the loss relief provisions to ensure that they are used to the best advantage.

Learning Outcomes

h) Relief for trading losses
   i. Understand how trading losses can be carried forward.
   ii. Explain how trading losses can be carried forward following the incorporation of a business.
   iii. Understand how trading losses can be claimed against total income and chargeable gains.
   iv. Explain and compute the relief for trading losses in the early years of a trade.
   v. Explain and compute terminal loss relief.

Introduction

A trading loss occurs when a trader's adjusted profit after capital allowances gives a negative figure. A trading loss can also arise through capital allowances either creating a loss (turning a trading profit into a loss) or increasing a loss.

Points to note:

- The trading income assessment for the tax year of the loss will be nil. Never put a negative figure as trading income in the calculation of taxable income.
- Relief is available for the loss.

Different reliefs are available to a trader:

- in the previous tax year (thus generating a refund of tax)
- in the current tax year (reducing the current liability)
- in the future tax years (reducing a future liability, and thus delaying relief).

Special reliefs are available in the opening years of trade, in the final 12 months of trade and on incorporation.

Overview:

Main reliefs

Section 83 ITA 2007 – Ongoing Trade – Carry forward losses

The trading loss is carried forward and relieved against the first available future profits of the same trade.

Section 64 ITA 2007 – Ongoing Trade – Offset against other income and gains

The trading loss is relieved against total income (TI) of the current year and/or the preceding years.
A s.64 claim can be extended and any unrelieved trading loss can be set against a trader's capital gains by a claim under s.261B TCGA 1992.

Section 72 ITA 2007 – New Trades – Carry back of losses

A trading loss incurred in any of the first 4 tax years of trade can be relieved against TI of the previous 3 years, taking the earliest year first.

Section 89 ITA 2007 – Cessation of trade – Losses carried back

A trading loss in the last 12 months of trading can be relieved against trading income of the previous 3 years taking the latest year first.

Section 86 ITA 2007 – Losses on incorporation

A trading loss incurred by an unincorporated business may be relieved against income received from a new company on incorporation.

Section numbers are from the Income Tax Act (ITA) 2007 and have been given for ease of identifying loss reliefs, but candidates will not be expected to quote section numbers as part of their answer in the exam.

All these provisions are discussed in more detail in this Study Guide.

1. Understand how trading losses can be carried forward.[2]

[Learning Outcome h (i)]

1.1 Section 83 ITA 2007 – relief against future trading income

If no specific loss relief is claimed, the loss will be carried forward automatically, and relieved against the first available future trading profits.

The main provisions are:

1. the loss carried forward can only be set against **future trading profits**, not against any other income.
2. the set off must be against the **first available trading profits**.
3. it is not possible to restrict the set off of the loss, e.g. in order to avoid wasting personal allowances.
4. the relief is against future trading profits of the **same trade.**
5. there is **no time limit** on the carry forward – the loss can be carried forward indefinitely, until there are future trading profits.
6. it is not necessary to claim this relief - the loss will be carried forward automatically if **a trader does not choose to claim other reliefs, or if** a loss remains after other reliefs have been claimed.

Example

Larry has been trading for many years preparing accounts to 31 December each year. He made a trading loss of £32,600 in the year to 31 December 2011.

His anticipated taxable trading profits for the next three years are as follows.

	£
Year ended 31 December 2012	12,600
Year ended 31 December 2013	10,800
Year ended 31 December 2014	52,600

Larry also has property income of £2,000 every year.
If Larry makes no specific loss relief claim, his taxable income for 2011-12 to 2014-15 is as follows:
(Assume allowances continue unchanged in the future).

	2011-12 £	2012-13 £	2013-14 £	2014-15 £
Trading profits	0	12,600	10,800	52,600
Less: s.83 relief	0	(12,600)	(10,800)	(9,200)
	0	**0**	**0**	**43,400**
Property income	2,000	2,000	2,000	2,000
Total Income	**2,000**	**2,000**	**2,000**	**45,400**
PA (restricted)	(2,000)	(2,000)	(2,000)	(8,105)
Taxable income	**0**	**0**	**0**	**37,295**

Never take loss a negative figure instead take zero

Notes

1. The trading income assessment for the tax year 2011-12 is nil as the business incurred a loss.
2. The trading loss of year ended 31 December 2011 is carried forward and set against future trading profits until the entire loss is relieved.
3. Under s.83, the loss is set off against future trading profits, and not against any other income (i.e. not against the property income). The maximum amount must be set off each year.
4. Personal allowances of £6,105 (£8105 - £2,000) are wasted in 2012-13 and 2013-14.

Continued on the next page

Loss memorandum

	£
Loss for the year 2011-12	32,600
Set off:	
2012-13 (s.83)	(12,600)
	20,000
2013-14 (s.83)	(10,800)
	9,200
2014-15. (s.83)	(9,200)

7. It is necessary to establish the amount of the loss with HMRC. This must be done within 5 years of 31 January following the tax year in which the loss arose (i.e. if a loss was incurred in year ended 31 December 2012, it falls in the tax year 2012-13, and the claim must be made by 31 January 2019).

8. Under s.83 the relief is delayed, as it is given by means of a reduction in a future liability.

Martin has been trading for many years, preparing accounts to 30 November each year. He made a trading loss of £37,550 in the year to 30 November 2011.

His anticipated taxable trading profits for the next three years are as follows:

Year ended	£
30 November 2012	9,600
30 November 2013	11,650
30 November 2014	39,750

Martin also had property income of £2,000 and building society interest of £1,800 (gross) each year.

Required:

Assuming Martin makes no specific loss relief claim, calculate his taxable income for 2011-12 to 2014-15. (Assume allowances continue unchanged in the future).

1.2 Drawbacks of relief under s.83

1. Relief must be taken **to** the **maximum amount possible, and as soon as possible. It is not possible to restrict the relief, so** in some situations **personal allowances may be wasted.**
2. In future years if there is insufficient trading income from the same business, then **relief is delayed** until sufficient profits are earned by the business.
3. It is possible that there may never be profits of the same trade to offset losses against; losses are lost if the trade ceases.

SUMMARY

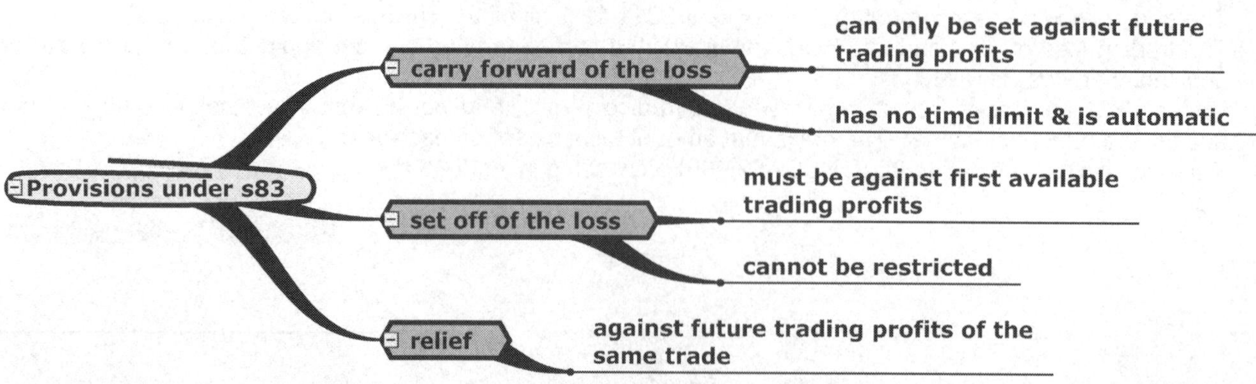

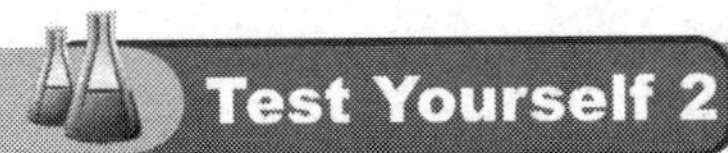

Jack has been trading for many years, preparing accounts to 31 December each year. He has the following results:

	£
Year ended 31/12/2011 trading loss	(4,750)
Year ended 31/12/2012 trading profit	58,250

In 2012-13 he pays interest charges of £7,000 on a loan for a qualifying purpose. He has building society interest of £3,750 (gross) in both 2011-12 and 2012-13.

No specific loss relief claim is made.

Required:

Calculate his taxable income for 2011-12 and 2012-13.

---

2. Understand how trading losses can be claimed against total income and chargeable gains.[2]

[Learning Outcome h (iii)]

2.1 Section 64 ITA 2007 – relief against TI of the current tax year and/or the previous tax year.

1. A trading loss arising in a tax year may be set against the trader's **total income (TI)** of the **current tax year and/and/or the previous tax year.**

Jade has been trading for many years preparing accounts to 31 December. She incurs a loss in the year ended 31 December 2012.

This loss arises in the tax year in which the loss-making accounting period ends (2012-13) and so may be relieved against TI of the current year (2012-13) and/or previous year (2011-12).

---

2. These are **two separate claims** – a trader who incurs a loss in 2012-13 may claim against TI of:

a) 2012-13 only
b) 2011-12 only
c) 2012-13 and then 2011-12
d) 2011-12 and then 2012-13

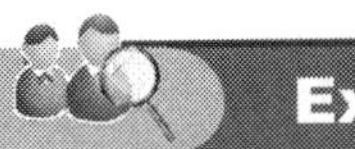

Jack has been trading for many years, preparing accounts to 31 December each year. He made a profit of £4,200 in the year to 31 December 2010 and incurred a loss of £20,000 in the year to 31 December 2012. He receives property income of £15,000 in 2011-12 and £17,000 in 2012-13. Assume a personal allowance of £8,105 each year.

He has the following options:

i. Claim against TI of 2012-13 only.

	2011-12 £	2012-13 £
Trading income	4,200	0
Property income	15,000	17,000
Less: s.64 2012-13 only	0	(17,000)
Net Income	19,200	0
PA	(8,105)	0
Taxable income	**11,095**	**0**

Continued on the next page

The balance of the loss, (£3,000) will be carried forward and relieved against future trading profits under s.83. The relief under s.83 is delayed, and the future profitability is uncertain.
The personal allowance is wasted in 2012-13.

ii. Claim against TI of 2011-12 only.

	2011-12 £	**2012-13 £**
Trading income	4,200	0
Property income	15,000	17,000
	19,200	17,000
Less: s.64 2011-12 only	(19,200)	0
Net Income	0	17,000
PA	0	(8,105)
Taxable income	**0**	**8,895**

The balance of the loss, (£800) will be carried forward and relieved against future trading profits under s.83. The relief under s.83 is delayed, and the future profitability is uncertain. The personal allowance is wasted in 2011-12.

iii. Claim against TI of 2012-13 and then 2011-12.

	2011-12 £	**2012-13 £**
Trading income	4,200	0
Property Income	15,000	17,000
	19,200	17,000
Less: s.64 2012-13 then 2011-12	(3,000)	(17,000)
Net Income	**16,200**	**0**
PA	(8,105)	0
Taxable income	**8,095**	**0**

The personal allowance is wasted in 2012-13. All the loss is relieved.

iv. Claim against 2011-12 and then 2012-13.

	2011-12 £	**2012-13 £**
Trading income	**4,200**	**0**
Property income	15,000	17,000
	19,200	17,000
Less: s.64 2011-12 then 2012-13	(19,200)	(800)
Net Income	**0**	**16,200**
PA	0	(8,105)
Taxable income	**0**	**8,095**

The personal allowance is wasted in 2011-12. All the loss is relieved. There is a slight advantage of (iv) over (iii) as the taxpayer gets a refund of the tax paid for the year 2011-12 along with the interest.

---

3. If there are **losses in two consecutive years**, and a s.64 claim is made for both the years, the first year's loss is dealt with first.

Example

Ian has been trading for many years, preparing accounts to 31 March each year. In the years ending 31 March 2012 and 31 March 2013 he incurred a loss of £6,800 and £1,900 respectively. He receives property income of £18,000 each year.

Ian claims relief under s.64 for the loss for the year ended 31 March 2012 against TI of 11-12. He also claims relief against TI of 2011-12 for the loss for the year ended 31 March 2013. Assume a personal allowance of £8,105 each year.

His taxable income for 2011-12 and 2012-13 is as follows:

	2011-12 £	**2012-13** £
Property income	18,000	18,000
Less: s.64 loss of year ended 31/03/2012	(6,800)	0
s.64 loss of year ended 31/03/2013	(1,900)	0
Net Income	**9,300**	**18,000**
PA	(8,105)	(8,105)
Taxable income	**1,195**	**9,895**

In 2011-12 the loss for the year ended 31/03/2012 is relieved in priority to the loss for the year ended 31/03/2013. Alternatively, Ian may elect to carry forward this loss and set it off against his future trading income under s.83.

4. It is **not possible to restrict the set off of the loss**, for example to avoid wasting personal allowances. However, the taxpayer has a choice to make a claim in one year, in both years, or not to make a claim at all.
5. If no s.64 claim is made, or a loss remains unrelieved after a claim is made, the loss is **carried forward under s.83** to be offset against future trading profits.

Example

Mike has been trading for many years, preparing accounts to 31 August each year.

His recent taxable profits and (losses) have been as follows:

	£
Year ended 31 August 2009	3,000
Year ended 31 August 2010	(45,000)
Year ended 31 August 2011	18,000
Year ended 31 August 2012	20,000

He received property income of £10,000 each year.
Show Mike's taxable income for the years 2009-10 to 2012-13 **assuming he claims relief for the loss as soon as possible.**

Assume a personal allowance of £8,105 throughout.

Tip

In the exam it may be asked to claim relief as soon as possible or to maximise the relief given - make sure you take the approach asked for!

Continued on the next page

	2009-10	2010-11	2011-12	2012-13
	£	£	£	£
Trading income	3,000	0	18,000	20,000
Less: s.83	**0**	**0**	(18,000)	(4,000)
Property income	10,000	10,000	10,000	10,000
	13,000	**10,000**	**10,000**	**26,000**
Less: s.64 2009-10 then 2010-11	(13,000)	(10,000)	0	0
Net Income	**0**	**0**	**10,000**	**26,000**
PA	0	0	(8,105)	(8,105)
Taxable income	-	-	**1,895**	**17,895**

Mike will make a s.64 claim against TI of 2009-10 and 2010-11, relieving a total of £23,000 of the loss. There is still a loss of £22,000 (£45,000 - £23,000) unrelieved, which will automatically be carried forward and set against future trading profits under **s.83.**

Loss memorandum

Year	**£**
Loss for the year ended 31/08/2012	45,000
Less: s.64 2009-10	(13,000)
	32,000
Less: s.64 2010-11	(10,000)
	22,000
Less: s.83 2011-12	(18,000)
	4,000
Less: s.83 2012-13	(4,000)
	0

If no s.64 claims were made, the entire loss of £45,000 would have been carried forward and set off against future trading income.

6. Claim for relief under s.64 must be made **within 12 months of 31 January following the tax year in which the loss arose.**

Example

If a loss arose in 2012-13, a s.64 claim must be made by 31/01/2015.

7. A s.64 claim will **reduce a current liability to tax**, or, if the loss is relieved in the **previous tax year** will lead to a **repayment of tax. A s.64 claim has a cash flow advantage over relief against future trading profits, as s.64 leads to a reduction in the current liability whereas s.83 reduces a future liability.**

Important factors to consider

a) the rates of tax saved by the claim
b) any loss of personal allowance
c) cash flow as a result of the relief
d) future anticipated profits

Tip

In the exam check whether, in each year, the individual is a basic rate or higher rate taxpayer - this will help to decide which claim is the most beneficial.

Test Yourself 3

Henry has been self-employed since 2005. He has the following taxable income and qualifying interest payments for the years 2009-10 to 2012-13.

	2009-10 £	2010-11 £	2011-12 £	2012-13 £
Trading profit / (loss)	15,000	10,000	(12,500)	22,500
Building society interest (gross)	700	1,500	1,800	1,000
Interest paid	(2,000)	(2,500)	(2,500)	(2,600)

Required:

Calculate his taxable income for each of the tax years 2009-10 to 2012-13, assuming that Henry claims loss relief **as early as possible**. Assume a personal allowance of £8,105 throughout.

2.2 Temporary Extension of loss relief carry back

Relief against trading income of the previous three tax years

1. A temporary extension of the carry back period for **loss relief** was available for set off of trading losses for the tax years 2009-10 and 2010-11 only.
2. This extension allows trading loss arising in 2010-11 to be set off against the trader's trading income of the previous three tax years taking the latest year first. Therefore, trading losses for the tax year 2010-11 will be set off first against the **trading profits** of the tax year 2009 - 10, then against the trading profits of 2008- 09 and finally of 2006-07 if extended loss relief is claimed.
3. If a claim is made against the trading profits of the tax years 2008–09 and 2007-08, it is restricted to £50,000 in total for the amount to be claimed as relief i.e. only £50,000 of the loss may be carried back to the first 2 of the 3 years covered by the claim.
4. If a claim is made against the trading profits of the tax year 2009 – 10, there is no such restriction i.e. any balance may be offset against the latest of the 3 years.
5. This relief is in addition to the trading loss relief under s.64 against the trader's total income of the current year and/or previous year. **It can only be made if a s.64 claim has already been made**.
6. It is not possible to restrict the set off of the loss, e.g. to avoid wasting personal allowances. However, the taxpayer has a choice to make a claim in one year, in both years, or not to make a claim at all (assuming that losses arose in both years).

Important

The examiner has stated that from the June 2012 exam, no question will be set involving the extended loss relief.

2.3 Section 261B Taxation of Chargeable Gains Act (TCGA) 1992 – relief against capital gains

1. After a s.64 claim has been made against TI in a tax year, any remaining trading loss may be relieved by making a further claim under s.261B TCGA 1992 to set it against the trader's capital gains for the same year.
2. The trading loss is effectively treated as a current year capital loss.
3. Relief is only available if a s.64 claim has already been made against TI in the same tax year.
4. If the claim is made, the loss must be set off as far as possible, it cannot be restricted in order to preserve the annual exemption.
5. A claim for relief under s.261B must be made within 12 months from 31 January following the tax year in which the loss arose.

6. Important factors to consider

a) the rates of tax saved by the claim
b) any loss of annual exemption
c) cash flow as a result of the relief
d) future anticipated profits.

Todd commenced trading on 1 April 2011 and prepares accounts to 31 March each year. In 2012-13 Todd incurred a loss of £12,000. He had no other income. His 2011-12 financial position is as follows:

	£
Trading income	6,400
Bank interest (gross)	1,200
Capital gains	12,650

The most beneficial way of calculating the losses to be relieved under s.64 and s.261B is as follows:

1. set off loss first against TI
2. determine amount of loss remaining
3. set off unrelieved loss against capital gains.

Calculation of income after relief under s.64 and s.261B

Step 1: Set off of loss first against TI

In the tax year 2012-13, Todd has no other income. So, if he makes claim for loss relief under s.64, he will have to set the loss against previous year's (i.e. 2011-12) total income.

Calculation of set off of loss against total income of the year 2011-12:

	2011-12 £
Trading income	6,400
Bank interest (gross)	1,200
	7,600
Less: Relief s.64	(7,600)
Total Income	**0**

First set off loss under s64 and then under s261B

Step 2: Determine amount of loss remaining

	£
Loss for 2012-13	12,000
Less: s.64	(7,600)
Unrelieved loss	**4,400**

Step 3: Claim to set off unrelieved losses under s.261B

Relief under s.261B is before annual exemption

	£
Capital gains 2011-12	12,650
Less: Relief s.261B	(4,400)
	8,250
Less: Annual exemption (restricted) (Refer to Learning Outcome 3, Study Guide C2)	(8,250)
Total chargeable capital gains	**0**

In this case it may not be beneficial to make any claim as most of the income and gains would have been covered by the personal allowance and annual exemption. Todd would need to decide whether he would prefer to receive a small tax refund for 2011-12 or whether he would prefer to carry the loss forward to offset against future profits.

A taxpayer may claim relief under s.261B to relieve a trading loss against capital gains:

1. in the tax year in which the loss is incurred **OR**
2. the previous year **OR**
3. both the tax years.

But remember that a s.261B claim may only be made after the trading loss has first been set against TI in the year the s.64 claim refers to.

Any remaining loss will be set against future trading income under s.83.

The following summary gives details of relief under s.64 against TI and s.261B against capital gains:

SUMMARY

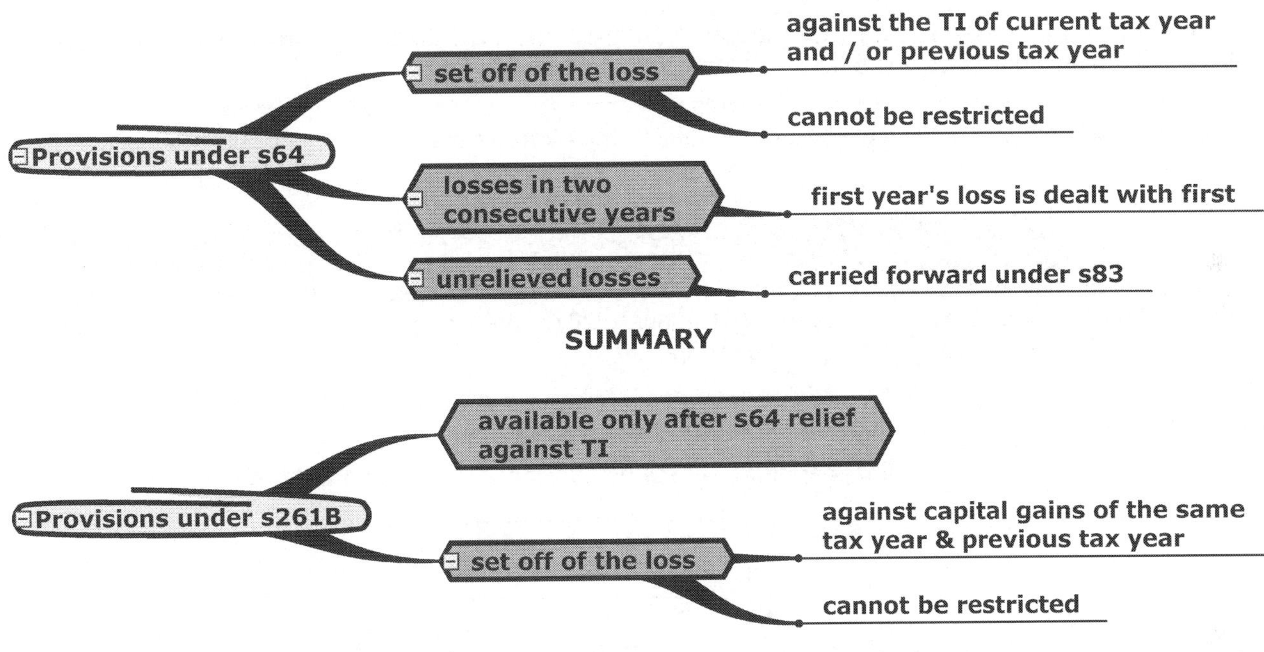

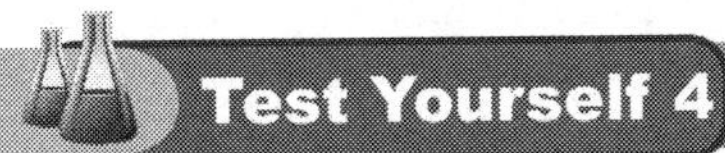

Michael has been self-employed since 2002.
The following information is available for the years 2010-11, 2011-12 and 2012-13.

	2010-11 £	2011-12 £	2012-13 £
Trading profits / (loss)	9,000	(28,000)	23,500
Property income	1,000	1,600	3,000
Bank interest (gross)	500	600	400
Capital gains	17,000	8,000	11,000
Interest paid on loan for qualifying purposes	(2,500)	(2,200)	(3,000)

The capital gains are before the annual exemption.

Required:

Compute Michael's taxable income and chargeable gains for the three years on the assumption that he claims to relieve the trading loss against TI for 2010-11 under s.64 and then against capital gains of the same year under s.261B.

Assume rates and allowances for 2012-13 apply throughout.

3. Explain and compute the relief for trading losses in the early years of a trade.[1]

[Learning Outcome h (iv)]

3.1 Section 72 ITA– relief against TI of the previous 3 years on a first in first out (FIFO) basis, available in the first four years of trade.

1. In the opening years of a business, a trading loss may be set against TI of the year of the loss and/or the previous year (s.64) or it may be carried forward against future trading income under s.83. In addition, there is a special loss relief available for trading losses arising in any of the first four tax years of a business.
2. A trading loss arising in any one of the first four tax years of trade may be set against the trader's total income (TI) of the previous 3 tax years, taking the earliest year first.

Example

Bill started a business on 6 April 2010 and prepares accounts annually to 5 April. He incurs a loss in the year to 5 April 2013.

Bill started trading in 2010-11, as his loss arose in 2012-13, the third tax year of trade, he may relieve it against TI of the previous three years (2009-10 then 2010-11 then 2011-12).

3. If a s.72 claim is made, relief must be taken against TI of **all three years**, it is not possible to make a partial claim.

Example

Mike has been employed for several years, earning £3,000 per month. He ceased employment on 31 December 2012 and started business as a sole trader on 1 January 2013, preparing accounts to 5 April each year. He incurs a loss of £100,000 in the period ended on 5 April 2013.

He has unearned income of £5,000 (gross) each year. Mike claims relief for the loss against the TI of the previous three years under s.72.

The loss arose in 2012-13, so relief is against TI of 2009-10 then 2010-11 then 2011-12.

	2009-10 **£**	**2010-11** **£**	**2011-12** **£**	**2012-13** **£**
Employment income	36,000	36,000	36,000	27,000
Unearned income	5,000	5,000	5,000	5,000
Total Income	**41,000**	**41,000**	**41,000**	**32,000**
Less: s.72	(41,000)	(41,000)	(18,000)	0
Total income	**0**	**0**	**23,000**	**32,000**

	£	
Loss for 2012-13	100,000	(carry back to 2009-10, then 2010-11 and then 2011-12)
Set off s72 2009-10	(41,000)	
	59,000	
s.72 2010-11	(41,000)	
	18,000	
s.72 2011-12	(18,000)	
	0	

Tip

Note that as the relief is against TI, the loss may be set against income earned before trade commenced.

4. The maximum relief possible must be taken for the loss; it is not possible to restrict the set off to preserve personal allowances.

5. If no claim is made in the opening years, or a loss remains after any claim is made, it is carried forward under s.83 against future trading profits.
6. A claim for relief under s.72 must be made within 12 months of 31 January following the tax year in which the loss arose.

If a loss arose in 2012-13, the claim must be made by 31/01/2015.

7. Loss relief claimed under s.72 will reduce the liability of earlier years and this will lead to a repayment of tax.
8. Important factors to consider:
   a) the rate of tax saved by the claim.
   b) any loss of personal allowances.
   c) cash flow as a result of the relief.
   d) future anticipated profits.
9. Losses arising on the commencement of trade are allocated to tax years using the basis period rules for opening years of a business. When these rules are applied to a profitable business, some profit periods overlap and are taxed twice, with relief being given for those profits on cessation. Losses can only be relieved once. If a loss period overlaps, relief is given for the loss in the earlier period only.

Tip

When there is overlap in the basis periods, then any loss arising during that period is treated as a loss of the earlier tax year.

Anna ceased employment on 31 August 2010, and started her own business on 1 September 2010, preparing accounts to 31 August each year.

She incurred losses for the first two years as follows:

	£
Year ended 31/08/2011	34,140
Year ended 31/08/2012	18,900

Her employment income for the past four years was as follows:

	£
2007-08	12,900
2008-09	17,800
2009-10	27,500
Up to 31 August 2010	8,500

Anna claims relief for the losses against TI of the previous 3 years under s.72.

The losses must be allocated to the tax years, using the opening year rules:

	Basis period	Workings	Trading loss £
2010-11	01/09/2010 to 05/04/2011	(£34,140) x 7/12	19,915
2011-12	Year ended 31/08/2011	(£34,140 – £19,915) (W1)	14,225
2012-13	Year ended 31/08/2012	(£18,900)	18,900

Workings

W1

The basis period for 2011-12 is the year ended 31/08/2011, which allocates the loss of £34,140 to tax year 2011-12. However, £19,915 of the loss has already been allocated to 2010-11, therefore only the loss remaining is treated as arising in 2011-12.

Continued on the next page

Relief under s.72 is taken for the loss allocated to 2010-11 first, and then for the loss allocated to 2011-12.

	2007-08 £	2008-09 £	2009-10 £	2010-11 £
Employment income	12,900	17,800	27,500	8,500
Less: s.72 relief for loss arising in 2010-11 first against 2007-08, then 2008-09	(12,900)	(7,015)	0	0
	0	10,785	27,500	8,500
Less: s.72 relief for loss arising in 2011-12 first against 2008-09, then 2009-10		(10,785)	(3,440)	
	0	0	24,060	8,500
Less: s.72 relief for loss arising in 2012-13 against 2009-10			(18,900)	0
Total income	**0**	**0**	**5,160**	**8,500**

Loss memorandum

	£	
Loss for the year 2010-11	19,915	(carry back to 2007-08 then 2008-09 then 2009-10)
Set off in 2007-08	(12,900)	
	7,015	
Set off in 2008-09	(7,015)	
	0	

	£	
Loss for the year 2011-12	14,225	(carry back to 2008-09 then 2009-10 then 2010-11)
Set off in 2008-09	(10,785)	
	3,440	
Set off in 2009-10	(3,440)	
	0	

	£	
Loss for the year 2012-13	18,900	(carry back to 2009-10 then 2010-11 then 2011-12)
Set off in 2009-10	(18,900)	

Example

James started trading on 1 January 2010, preparing his first accounts for 18 months up to 30 June 2011 and annually thereafter. His results for the first two accounting periods are as follows:

	£
Period ended 30 June 2011 – Trading loss	(28,500)
Year ended 30 June 2012 – Trading profit	7,500

James' other gross income for the years 2006-07 to 2012-13 is as follows:

	Employment Income £	Bank interest £
2006-07	42,000	1,000
2007-08	40,000	1,200
2008-09	43,000	1,500
2009-10	36,000	1,800
2010-11	14,500	2,500
2011-12	-	2,600
2012-13	-	2,900

Continued on the next page

Losses can be relieved only once. Hence, the losses must be allocated to tax years, using the opening year rules:

	Basis period	Workings	Trading loss (£)	s72 relief
2009-10	01/01/2010 to 05/04/2010	£28,500 x 3/18	4,750	TI 2006-07, 2007-08 and then 2008-09
2010-11	06/04/2010 to 05/04/2011 (note)	£28,500 x 12/18	19,000	TI 2007-08, 2008-09 and then 2009-10
2011-12	Year ended 30/06/2011	(£28,500 - £19,000 - £4,750)	4,750	TI 2008-09, 2009-10 and then 2010-11

Note: If there is no accounting period ending in the second tax year, the basis period is 6 April to 5 April of the second tax year.)

James claims loss relief as early as possible against his TI, under s.72.

His TI for the tax years 2006-07 to 2012-13 is as follows:

	2006-07 £	2007-08 £	2008-09 £	2009-10 £	2010-11 £	2011-12 £	2012-2013 £
Employment income	42,000	40,000	43,000	36,000	14,500	0	0
Trading income	0	0	0	0	0	0	7,500
Bank interest	1,000	1,200	1,500	1,800	2,500	2,600	2,900
	43,000	**41,200**	**44,500**	**37,800**	**17,000**	**2,600**	**10,400**
Loss relief s.72	(4,750)	(19,000)	(4,750)	0	0	0	0
Total income	**38,250**	**22,200**	**39,750**	**37,800**	**17,000**	**2,600**	**10,400**

SUMMARY

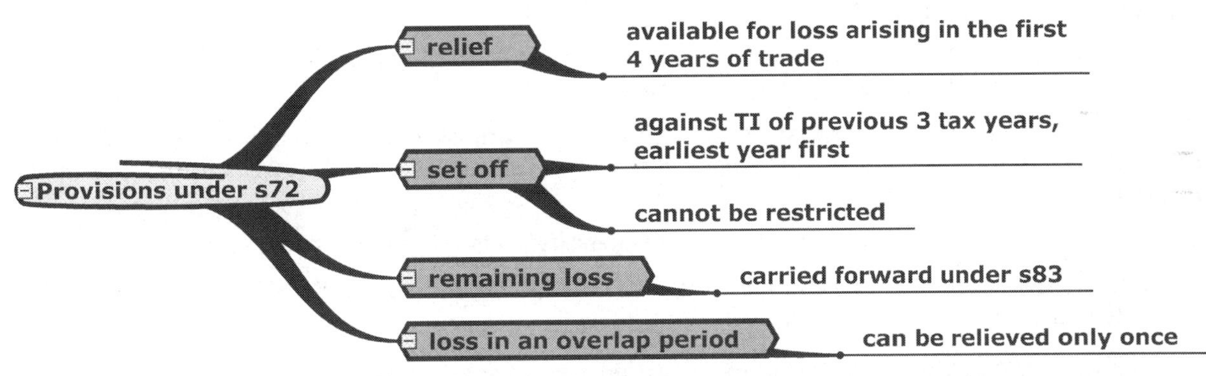

Test Yourself 5

Jerry started trading on 1 November 2010, preparing accounts to 31 October each year. The results for first two years of trading are as follows:

	£
Year ended 31 October 2011 – Trading loss	(27,000)
Year ended 31 October 2012 – Trading profit	5,200

Jerry also had the following gross income for the tax years 2006-07 to 2012-13.

	Employment Income £	Property income £
2006-07	43,000	1,000
2007-08	40,200	1,200
2008-09	41,500	1,500
2009-10	36,500	1,800
2010-11	15,000	2,400
2011-12	-	2,500
2012-13	-	2,900

Continued on the next page

Required:

Compute his TI for each of the tax years 2006-07 to 2012-13, assuming that Jerry **claims loss relief as early as possible** against his TI under s.72.

4. Explain and compute terminal loss relief.[1]

[Learning Outcome h (v)]

4.1 Section 89 ITA 2007 – on cessation of trade, a loss arising in the last 12 months may be set against trading income of the final tax year and the previous 3 years, providing relief against the last year first.

In the case of a continuing business, a trader can relieve his loss by:

- carrying it forward and **setting it against future trading income** from the same trade (s.83) **OR**
- relieving it against the TI of the current tax year **AND/OR** the previous year.

However, if there is a trading loss in the final 12 months of trade, it will not be possible to carry the loss forward against future trading income, and so there is a special loss relief allowing the loss of the last 12 months of trade to gain relief in earlier years.

1. The **terminal loss** is the **loss of the final 12 months of trade** and is calculated by adding:

a) the trading loss after making adjustments for the profits, if any, for the period starting from the 6 April of the final tax year to the date of cessation of trade
b) the trading loss for the period from the previous tax year which falls in the final 12 months of trade after making adjustments for the profits, if any, during that period, and
c) any overlap profits brought forward.

If the period to the date of cessation is a 12 month accounting period, the terminal loss will always be the loss for the period plus any overlap profits.

2. The terminal loss is set against:

a) the **trading profits** of the **tax year in which the trader ceases trading** and
b) the **trading profits** of the **previous three tax years,** latest first.

3. The **claim** for relief under s.89 **must be made within 5 years of 31 January following the tax year in which the cessation occurs**. For example, if cessation occurs in 2011-12, a claim must be made by 31/01/2018.

4. A claim for terminal loss relief will reduce prior year liabilities; this will lead to **repayment of tax**.

5. On cessation, it is possible to claim relief against TI of the current tax year and/or the previous tax year (s.64) instead of, or as well as terminal loss relief.

Brian has been trading for many years, preparing accounts to 31 December each year. He ceased trading on 31 December 2012. Any loss incurred in the twelve months from 1 January 2012 to 31 December 2012 can be relieved under terminal loss relief.

The loss of the last 12 months of trade may be set against the trading profits of the tax year 2012-13, then 2011-12, 2010-11 and 2009-10, in that order.

Monica has been trading for many years, preparing accounts to 31 July each year. She ceased trading on 31 July 2012. Her results for the last 5 years of trading were as follows:

	£
Year to 31 July 2008	17,200
Year to 31 July 2009	21,600
Year to 31 July 2010	18,000
Year to 31 July 2011	900
Year to 31 July 2012	(16,600)

Continued on the next page

She has overlap profits of £3,600 which have been brought forward.

Monica claims terminal loss relief.
Terminal loss is the loss of the final 12 months of trading, and is calculated as follows:

	£
Trading loss of the final 12 months of trading	
Final tax year 2012-13	
(6 April 2012 to 31 July 2012) (4 months) (£16,600 x 4/12)	5,533
Previous tax year 2011-12	
(1 August 2011 to 5 April 2012) (8 months) (£16,600 x 8/12)	11,067
Unused overlap profits b/f	3,600
Terminal loss	**20,200**

Terminal loss relief is against the trading income for the year of the loss and the three preceding years, with the latest first.

	2008-09 £	2009-10 £	2010-11 £	2011-12 £	2012-13 £
Trading income	17,200	21,600	18,000	900	0
Loss relief s.89	0	(1300)	(18000)	(900)	0
TI	**17,200**	**20,300**	**0**	**0**	**0**

Loss memorandum

	£
Terminal loss	20,200
Set off in 2011-12	(900)
	19,300
Set off in 2010-11	(18,000)
	1,300
Set off in 2009-2010	(1,300)
	0

4.2 Some general points

1. Availability of loss reliefs

a) In the opening years of a business, the following loss reliefs are available.

i. **Section 72 i.e.** loss arising in any of the **first 4 tax years of trade,** may be **set against TI of the previous 3 years (FIFO).**

ii. **Section 64** i.e. **set off** of trading loss against **total income** of the current tax year **AND/OR** previous tax year. If a section 64 claim is made, then losses may also be offset against **capital gains** of the same year.

iii. **Section 83** i.e. carried forward and **set off** against **trading income** of the same trade.

Tip

In the opening years it is possible to make both a s.72 and a s.64 claim, if the loss is large enough.

b) **In the continuing years of a business, the following loss reliefs are available**

i. s.64 against the TI of the current and/or previous tax years (and, by extension, against capital gains).
ii. s.83 against the future trading income.

c) **In the closing year of the business, the following loss reliefs are available**

i. s.64 against the TI of the current and/or previous tax year.

ii. s.89 i.e. loss of the last 12 months is set against trading income for the year of the loss and the preceding three tax years, latest first.

2. Disclaiming capital allowances

A trading loss automatically includes capital allowances. It is possible to reduce the capital allowances claimed. The reduced amount claimed is deducted from the pool, leaving a higher tax written down value to carry forward to the next period.

This would be useful if, for example, personal allowances would otherwise be wasted.

SUMMARY

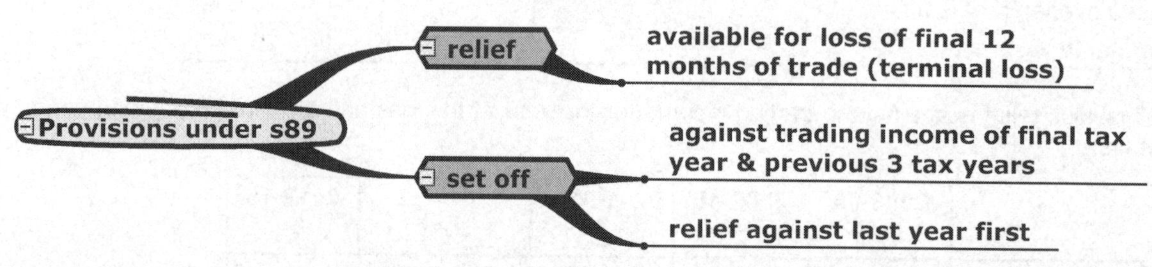

Edwina has been trading for many years, preparing accounts to 31 March each year. She ceased trading on 31 March 2013.

Her trading results for the last five years were as follows:

Year ended	Trading profit / (loss) (£)
31 March 2009	14,000
31 March 2010	15,000
31 March 2011	11,200
31 March 2012	1,000
31 March 2013	(9,800)

Edwina has unused overlap profits brought forward of £4,500.

Required:

Calculate total income for each of the tax years 2008-09 to 2012-13 assuming that Edwina claims terminal loss relief under s.89.

Jane has been trading for many years, preparing accounts to 31 December each year. She ceased trading on 31 August 2012. Her results for the last 5 years of trading were as follows:

	£
Year to 31 December 2008	27,400
Year to 31 December 2009	22,500
Year to 31 December 2010	20,000
Year to 31 December 2011	1,200
Eight months to 31 August 2012	(25,200)

Overlap profits of £2,200 arose when Jane started her business.

Required:

Assuming that Jane wants to claim terminal loss relief under s.89, calculate her income for the tax years 2008-09 to 2012-13.

5. Explain how trading losses can be carried forward following the incorporation of a business.[2]

[Learning Outcome h (ii)]

Section 86 ITA 2007 – relief of trading losses against future income received from a new company

1. When a trader incorporates his business, relief for the losses of an unincorporated business is available under
   a) Section 64: against TI of the current year and/or the previous year
   b) Section 89: against trading income of final and previous 3 tax years.

2. In addition, losses can be relieved under s.86 against future income received by the taxpayer from the company to which the business is sold.

3. Relief under Section 86 is available only if:
   a) the business is sold to a company.
   b) the consideration for the transfer is wholly or mainly the shares of the company to which the business is sold.

4. Relief is available for all the losses at the time of incorporation of a business.

5. To claim the relief under section 86 for any tax year, the following conditions need to be fulfilled:
   a) the previous owner must retain his shares throughout the tax year in which the relief is claimed.
   b) the company to which the business was sold must be carrying on the same trade.

6. The set off must be against the first available income from the company which may be salaries, director's fees, interest or dividends.

Robin has been trading for many years, preparing accounts to 31 March each year. He incorporated his business on 31 March 2012. He incurred a loss in the twelve months of trade prior to incorporation of £32,000 but did not relieve this against other income at the time.

In the tax year 2012-13 he received a salary of £25,000 and interest of £10,000 (gross) from the company.

The trading loss of £32,000 was carried forward on the incorporation and will be relieved against income from the company. In 2012-13, £25,000 of the loss will be offset against his salary and the remaining £7,000 against interest income.

SUMMARY

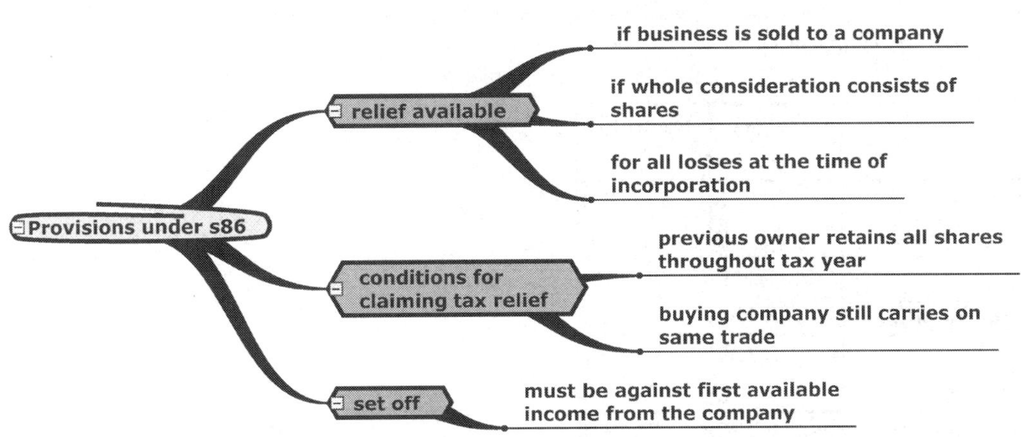

Answers to Test Yourself

Answer to TY 1

Calculation of taxable income of Martin

	2011-12	2012-13	2013-14	2014-15
	£	£	£	£
Trading profits	0	9,600	11,650	39,750
Less: s.83 relief	0	(9,600)	(11,650)	(16,300)
	0	**0**	**0**	**23,450**
Building society interest	1,800	1,800	1,800	1,800
Property income	2,000	2,000	2,000	2,000
Total Income	**3,800**	**3,800**	**3,800**	**27,250**
PA (restricted)	(3,800)	(3,800)	(3,800)	(8,105)
Taxable income	**0**	**0**	**0**	**19,145**

Notes

1. The trading loss arising in 2011-12 is carried forward to and set against future trading income until the whole loss is relieved. There is no need to claim to offset against other income as that is within the personal allowance for 2011-12.
2. Under s.83, the loss is set off against trading profits only, not against any other income.

Loss memorandum

	£
Loss for the year 2011-12	37,550
Set off: 2012-13 (s.83)	(9,600)
	27,950
2013-14 (s.83)	(11,650)
	16,300
2014-15 (s.83)	(16,300)
	0

Answer to TY 2

Taxable income of Jack is as follows:

	2011-12	2012-13
	£	£
Trading income	0	58,250
Less: s.83 relief	0	(4,750)
	0	53,500
Building society income	3,750	3,750
Total Income	**3,750**	**57,250**
Less: Interest Paid	0	(7,000)
Net Income	**3,750**	**50,250**
Less: PA	(3,750)	(8,105)
Taxable income	**0**	**42,145**

Answer to TY 3

	2009-10 £	2010-11 £	2011-12 £	2012-2013 £
Trading income	15,000	10,000	0	22,500
Less: Loss relief s.83 (W2)	0	0	0	(3,500)
	15,000	10,000	0	19,000
Building society interest	700	1,500	1,800	1,000
	15,700	11,500	1,800	20,000
Less: Interest paid	(2,000)	(2,500)	(1,800)	(2,600)
Total Income	**13,700**	**9,000**	**0**	**17,400**
Loss relief s.64	0	(9,000)	0	0
Net Income	**13,700**	**0**	**0**	**17,400**
PA	(8105)	0	0	(8105)
Taxable Income	**5,595**	**0**	**0**	**9,295**

Workings

W1 The earliest relief for the loss is to set it off against TI of the previous tax year under s.64.

W2 The remaining loss of £3,500 (£12,500 - £9,000) is carried forward and set against future trading profits under s.83.

W3 Interest payments of £1,800 are relieved in 2011-12. The balance is unrelieved.

Answer to TY 4

	2010-11 £	2011-12 £	2012-13 £
Trading income	9,000	0	23,500
Less: s.83 relief (W1)	0	0	(3,000)
	9,000	0	20,500
Property income	1,000	1,600	3,000
Bank interest	500	600	400
Total income	**10,500**	**2,200**	**23,900**
Less: Interest charges	(2,500)	(2,200)	(3,000)
	8,000	**0**	**20,900**
Less: s.64 relief (W1)	(8,000)	-	-
Net income	0	0	20,900
Less: PA	0	0	(8,105)
Taxable income	0	0	**12,795**
Relief under s.261B			
Capital Gains	17,000	8,000	11,000
Less: s.261B relief (W1)	(17,000)	0	0
	0	8,000	11,000
Less: Annual Exemption (Refer to Learning Outcome 3, Study Guide C2)	0	(8,000)	(10,600)
Chargeable Gains	**0**	**0**	**400**

Workings

W1

In 2010-11 £8,000 of the loss is relieved against TI under s.64, £17,000 of the loss is relieved against capital gains, and the remaining loss of £3,000 (£28,000 - £8,000 - £17,000), is relieved against future trading profits under s.83.

Loss Memorandum

	£
Loss of 2011-12	28,000
2010-11 s.64	(8,000)
	20,000
2010-11 s.261B	(17,000)
	3,000
2012-13 s.83	(3,000)
	0

Answer to TY 5

	2006-07 £	2007-08 £	2008-09 £	2009-10 £	2010-11 £	2011-12 £	2012-13 £
Employment income	43,000	40,200	41,500	36,500	15,000	0	0
Trading income	0	0	0	0	0	0	5,200
Property income	1,000	1,200	1,500	1,800	2,400	2,500	2,900
	44,000	**41,400**	**43,000**	**38,300**	**17,400**	**2,500**	**8,100**
Loss relief s.72	0	(11,250)	(15,750)	0	0	0	0
Total income	**44,000**	**30,150**	**27,250**	**38,300**	**17,400**	**2,500**	**8,100**

Workings

W1

The losses must be allocated to tax years, using the opening year rules

	Basis period	Workings	Trading loss (£)	S72 relief
2010-11	1 November 2010 to 5 April 2011	£27,000 x 5/12	11,250	TI 2007-08, 2008-09 and then 2009-10
2011-12	Year ended 31 October 2011	£27,000 – £11,250	15,750	TI 2008-09, 2009-10 and then 2010-11

Note: Relief is given under s.72 for losses allocated to the tax year 2010-11 against TI of 2007-08, 2008-09 and 2009-10 (i.e. previous three tax years, FIFO).

Answer to TY 6

	2008-09 £	2009-10 £	2010-11 £	2011-12 £	2012-2013 £
Trading income	14,000	15,000	11,200	1,000	0
Less: Loss relief s.89	0	(2,100)	(11,200)	(1,000)	0
Total income	**14,000**	**12,900**	**0**	**0**	0

Workings

W1 Calculation of terminal loss

	£
Trading loss of the final 12 months of trading	9,800
Overlap profits b/f	4,500
Terminal loss	**14,300**

W2 Loss memorandum

	£
Terminal loss	14,300
Set off in 2011-12	(1,000)
	13,300
Set off in 2010-11	(11,200)
	2,100
Set off in 2009-10	(2,100)
	0

Answer to TY 7

Calculation of terminal loss

	£	£
Trading loss of the final 12 months of trading (i.e. 1 September 2011 to 31 August 2012)		
Period falling in the final tax year 2012-13		
6 April 2012 to 31 August 2012 (5 months) (£25,200 x 5/8)		15,750
Period falling in the previous tax year 2011-12		
1 September 2011 to 5 April 2012 (7 months)		
Loss for the period from 1 January 2012 to 5 April 2012 (£25,200 x 3/8)	9,450	
Less: Profit for the period from 1 September 2011 to 31 December 2011 (£1,200 x 4/12)	(400)	9,050
Add: Unused overlap profits b/f		2,200
Terminal loss		**27,000**

Relief of terminal loss

	2008-09 £	2009-10 £	2010-11 £	2011-12 £	2012-2013 £
Trading income	27,400	22,500	20,000	1,200	0
Less: Loss relief s.89	0	(5,800)	(20,000)	(1,200)	0
Total income	**27,400**	**16,700**	**0**	**0**	**0**

Loss memorandum

	£
Terminal loss	27,000
Set off in 2011-12	(1,200)
	25,800
Set off in 2010-11	(20,000)
	5,800
Set off in 2009-10	(5,800)
	0

Quick Quiz

1. What happens to a trading loss if no specific claim is made to relieve it?
2. Give two loss reliefs available in the continuing years of a business.
3. Describe the loss relief available in the opening years of trade.
4. A trader has been trading for many years and incurs a loss. He wishes to claim relief against TI under s.64. What are the options available to him?
5. A trader has been trading for many years and incurs a loss. He wishes to relieve the loss against his capital gains of the previous tax year. How may he achieve this?
6. What is the relief available for a trading loss on the cessation of a business?

Answers to Quick Quiz

1. The loss is automatically carried forward and set against future trading profits of the same trade.
2. i. Set off against TI of the current year and/or previous year.
   ii. Set off against future trading profits of the same trade.
3. A loss occurring in any of the first 4 tax years of trade may be set against TI of the previous three years, against the earliest year first.
4. He may claim against:
   - TI of the current year only
   - TI of the previous year only
   - TI of the current year and then the previous year
   - TI of the previous year and then the current year
5. He may claim against his capital gains of the current year and/or the previous year, but only after a claim has been made against TI of the year of the claim under s.64.
6. The loss of the last 12 months of trade (terminal loss) may be set against trading income for the tax year of cessation and the previous 3 tax years, latest first.

Self Examination Questions

Question 1

For the year ended 31 March 2013, Jack, a soft-drinks trader, incurred a loss of £22,000. Every year, apart from this trading income, he receives interest of £12,000 (gross). Last year he had no trading income.

Jack is not sure whether his business will be profitable in the future and wishes to claim relief for the loss as early as possible.

Required:

Calculate his taxable income for 2011-12 and 2012-13 assuming he claims relief under s.64.

Question 2

Lisa runs a fish and chip shop. In the year 2011-12 she incurred a loss of £18,200 due to the recession. She is confident that her business will be profitable again in the future.

Required:

(a) State under which section of the legislation she could make a claim for loss relief.
(b) Show the calculation of total taxable income of 2012-13 assuming that she earned a profit of £11,000.
(c) Explain what will happen to the unrelieved loss.

Question 3

Sabrina started trading on 1 November 2010 preparing accounts to 31 December each year.

Her results are as follows:

	£
14 months to 31 December 2011	(28,000)
Year to 31 December 2012	21,000

Sabrina received property income as follows:

	£
2007-08	15,000
2008-09	14,000
2009-10	21,000
2010-11	20,000
2011-12	19,000
2012-13	18,000

She had no other sources of income.

Required:

Assuming Sabrina claims loss relief as early as possible against TI (under s.72) calculate her TI for the tax years 2007-08 to 2012-13.

Question 4

Thornton has been running a wholesale chocolate business for the past three years. In the year 2012-13 he incurred a loss of £21,000. Other information for 2012-13 is as follows:

	£
Savings income (gross)	15,600
Capital gains	14,200

Show the calculations of the loss to be relieved, assuming Thornton has made claim for relief under s.64 against total income and s.261B against capital gains.

Question 5

Michael has been trading for many years. He has the following income and qualifying interest payments for the years 2010-11, 2011-12 and 2012-13.

	2010-11 £	2011-12 £	2012-13 £
Trading profits/(loss)	10,000	(22,000)	23,500
Property income		1,600	3,000
Building society interest (gross)	500	600	400
Interest paid (gross)	(2,500)	(3,500)	(3,000)

Required:

Calculate Michael's taxable income for all three years, assuming that he makes no specific claim to relieve the loss, and that tax rates for 2012-13 apply throughout.

Answers to Self Examination Questions

Answer to SEQ 1

Calculation of Jack's taxable income after relief under s.64

Under s.64, Jack can claim relief against the TI of 2012-13 or total income of 2011-12 or both. As the claim under s.64 is not automatic, Jack must elect for relief.

	2011-12 £	2012-2013 £
Trading income	0	0
Interest	12,000	12,000
Total income	**12,000**	**12,000**
Less: Relief under s.64 (W1)	(12,000)	(10,000)
Net income	**0**	**2,000**
Less: Personal allowance	0	(2,000)
Taxable income	0	0

Workings

W1 Loss memorandum

	£
Loss for the year 2012-13	22,000
Less: Relief under section 64 against 2011-12 income	(12,000)
	10,000
Less: Relief under section 64 against 2012-13 income	(10,000)
Balance	**0**

Note: Jack should first set the loss against the income of the year 2011-12, as he will get a repayment of tax paid for the previous year, along with the repayment supplement on it.

Answer to SEQ 2

1. Lisa has no other income but is confident about earning profits in future. The loss will be carried forward to be offset against future income under s.83.
2. Computation of total income

	2012-13 **£**
Trading income	11,000
Less: Loss for the year 2011-12	(11,000)
Balance trading income	**0**

3. Loss memorandum

	£
Loss for the year 2011-12	18,200
Less: Set off against income of 2012-13	(11,000)
Balance unrelieved loss	**7,200**

The unrelieved loss of £7,200 can be carried forward to future years to be set against future profits from the same trade.

Answer to SEQ 3

Step 1 - In the opening years of a trade we need to allocate the profit/ (loss) to tax years

	Basis period	**Workings**	**Trading (loss)/profit £**	**s72 relief**
2010-11	01/11/2010 to 05/04/2011	(£28000) x 5/14	(10,000)	TI 2007-08, 2008-09 then 2009-10
2011-12	01/01/2011 to 31/12/2011	(£28,000) x12/14	(24,000)	TI 2008-09, 2009-10 then 2010-11
2010-11	01/01/2011 to 05/04/2011	Less: Loss used (£28,000 x 3/14)	6,000	
			(28,000)	
2012-13	Year ended 31/12/2012		21,000	

Step 2 - Calculate TI for years 2007-08 to 2012-13

	2007-08 £	2008-09 £	2009-10 £	2010-11 £	2011-12 £	2012-2013 £
Trading income	0	0	0	0	0	21,000
Property income	15,000	14,000	21,000	20,000	19,000	18,000
	15,000	**14,000**	**21,000**	**20,000**	**19,000**	**39,000**
Loss relief s.72	0	0	0	0	0	0
Loss of 2010-11	(10000)	0	0	0	0	0
Loss of 2011-12	0	(14000)	(4000)	0	0	0
Total income	**5,000**	**0**	**17,000**	**20,000**	**19,000**	**39,000**

Workings

W1 Loss Memorandum

	2010-11 (£)	2011-12 (£)
Trading loss	10,000	18,000
Less: Set against TI of		
2007-08	(10,000)	0
2008-09	0	(14,000)
2009-10 (balance)	0	(4,000)
	0	**0**

Answer to SEQ 4

Thornton has loss in the year 2012-13. However he has income from other sources. Therefore, he can claim to offset the loss against the current year's total income (under s.64).

	£
Step 1 Set off loss against TI of the year 2012-13	
Trading income	0
Savings income	15,600
TI	**15,600**
Less: Relief for trading loss (s.64)	(15,600)
TI after relief	**0**
Step 2 Find out the unrelieved amount of loss	
Total loss for the year	21,000
Less: Loss set off under section 64	(15,600)
Unrelieved loss	**5,400**
Step 3 Set off against capital gains.	
Total available capital gain	14,200
Less: Relief under section 261B	(5,400)
Balance capital gains before annual exemption	**8,800**
Less: Annual exemption	(8,800)
Chargeable gains	**0**

W1 Loss memorandum

	£
Loss for the year 2012-13	21,000
Less: Set off against s.64	(15,600)
Less: Set off against s.261B	(5,400)
Balance unrelieved loss	**0**

Answer to SEQ 5

	2010-11 £	2011-12 £	2012-13 £
Trading income	10,000	0	23,500
Less: s.83 relief (W1)	0	0	(22,000)
	10,000	0	1,500
Property income	0	1,600	3,000
Building society interest	500	600	400
	10,500	**2,200**	**4,900**
Less: Interest paid	(2,500)	(2,200)	(3,000)
Total income	**8,000**	**0**	**1,900**
Less: PA (restricted)	(6,475)	-	(1,900)
Taxable income	**1,525**	**-**	**-**

Working

W1

As Michael has not made a specific claim to relieve the loss, it is carried forward and set against the first available trading profits under s.83.

Note: The PA for 2010-11 was £6475.

STUDY GUIDE B3: INCOME FROM SELF-EMPLOYMENT (PART 4)

Get Through Intro

This Study Guide deals with the income tax rules relating to partnerships. A partnership is a collection of individuals carrying on a business together. Accounts are prepared for the partnership, and the profits are allocated between the partners. Each partner's share of the profits is taxed in their individual income tax computation.

The partnership itself is not taxed. The profits are allocated to the individual partners, and they are each taxed as if they were a sole trader running their own business.

Professionals, like doctors or lawyers often work in a partnership. As an accountant you may yourself become a partner in a partnership. However, you will need to know how your share of profits from the partnership will be assessed for tax. If you have clients operating their businesses as a partnership, you will need to be able to advise them.

Learning Outcomes

i) Partnerships and limited liability partnerships
   i. Explain how a partnership is assessed to tax.
   ii. Compute the assessable profits for each partner following a change in the profit sharing ratio.
   iii. Compute the assessable profits for each partner following a change in the membership of the partnership.
   iv. Describe the alternative loss relief claims that are available to partners.
   v. Explain the loss relief restriction that applies to the partners of a limited liability partnership.

Introduction

Case Study

Apple, Mango and Banana have been trading for many years preparing accounts to 5 April each year. Their profit sharing ratio is 1:2:3.

The profit for the year to 5 April 2012 is £1,800,000.

The profits are allocated to the partners as follows:

	£
Apple	300,000
Mango	600,000
Banana	900,000

Mango retires from the partnership on 5 April 2012, and Apple and Banana share profits in the ratio of 2:3. In the year to 5 April 2013 the profit is £1,500,000.

The profits are allocated to the partners as follows:

	£
Apple	600,000
Banana	900,000

The principles which apply to sole traders also apply to partnerships, once the profits have been allocated to the individual partners. This Study Guide will help you appreciate how this operates.

1. Explain how a partnership is assessed to tax.[2]

[Learning Outcome i (i)]

1.1 How a partnership is assessed to tax

A partnership is a single trading entity, preparing accounts and computing tax adjusted trading income. However, the partnership is not a separate entity for tax purposes, and the partnership is not subject to tax.

Tip

Partnerships and Limited Liability Partnerships (LLPs) are taxed in the same way – they have a different legal status but are the same for tax purposes.

The profits of the partnership are calculated, adjusted for tax purposes, and then allocated to the partners who are each taxed as sole traders in their income tax computations.

1. The tax adjusted trading income of the partnership is calculated in the same way as for a sole trader.
2. The tax adjusted trading income is then allocated to each partner in their profit sharing ratios (PSR).
3. Each partner is then taxed as a sole trader in the tax year determined on the basis of assessment rules.

Example

Alan and Bob have been trading for many years, preparing accounts to 31 December each year. They share profits in the ratio 2:3.

Adjusted profits for the year to 31 December 2012 were £100,000.

This figure is then allocated to the partners, in their profit sharing ratio. Alan's share is £40,000 and Bob's share is £60,000. Each partner is treated as a sole trader, so Alan has profits of £40,000 for the year ended 31 December 2012, which will be assessed as trading income in his income tax computation for 2012-13, and Bob will be assessed on £60,000 in his income tax computation.

1.2 Allocation of profit or loss

A profit sharing agreement may specify that the partners are to be paid an annual "salary", or a fixed percentage of "interest" on their capital, before the balance of the profits are shared between them in their profit sharing ratios.

In this case, the "salary" is not an employment income for the partners, and similarly the "interest" will also not be taxed as their savings income. They are both simply part of the **arrangement for sharing profits**. Therefore, these are **not deductible** expenses while calculating taxable profits of the partnership. They are considered to be drawings and are therefore **added back** to calculate the profits.

Edwin, Fergus and George have been trading for many years, preparing accounts to 30 September each year. Adjusted profits for the year to 30 September 2012 were £160,000.

Profits were shared as follows:
Edwin was paid an annual salary of £10,000,
Interest was paid at 10% on their capital accounts.
Capital account balances:

	£
Edwin	50,000
Fergus	60,000
George	30,000

The remaining profits were shared:

Edwin	Fergus	George
20%	30%	50%

The profit for the year ended 30 September 2012 is shared as follows:

	Total £	Edwin £	Fergus £	George £
Year ended 30 September 2012	**160,000**			
Salary	(10,000)	10,000		
Interest (10% on capital)	(14,000)	5,000	6,000	3,000
	136,000			
Remaining profit in PSR (20:30:50)		27,200	40,800	68,000
	136,000	**42,200**	**46,800**	**71,000**

1.3 Capital allowances

As previously explained, the tax adjusted trading income of the partnership is calculated in the same way as for a sole trader. Similarly, calculation of **capital allowances** for partnerships is also done in the same way as for a sole trader. The adjustment / deduction for capital allowances on partnership assets is made before allocating profits to each partner.

Moreover when a partner personally, owns an asset **e.g. his car,** capital allowances may be claimed **for that, with** adjustments for any private use. **However, the allowances are not set against the partner's share of the partnership profits; instead they are deducted from the partnership profits.**

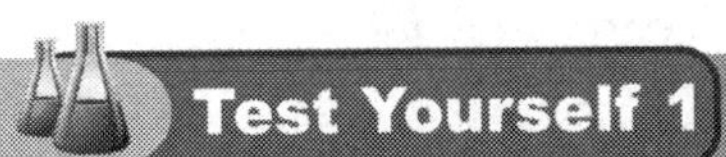

Fiona, Gertrude and Henrietta started a business on 1 May 2011 in partnership, preparing accounts up to 31 December annually. They decided to share the profits and losses on the following basis:

	Salary p.a. £	Interest p.a. £	Balance
Fiona	14,400	1,800	2/5
Gertrude	7,200	1,500	2/5
Henrietta	-	1,500	1/5

Continued on the next page

The firm's adjusted trading profits for the year ended 31 December 2012 were £72,600.

Required:

Show how the profits will be divided between the partners for the year ended on 31 December 2012.

---

2. Compute the assessable profits for each partner following a change in the profit sharing ratio.[2]
Compute the assessable profits for each partner following a change in the membership of the partnership.[2]

[Learning Outcomes i (ii and iii)]

2.1 Change in profit sharing ratio

Profits are allocated to the partners according to their profit sharing arrangements during the accounting period. If the arrangements change during the accounting period, the profits must be allocated accordingly.

The change in the profit sharing ratio can take place due to the following reasons

1. Change in the profit sharing arrangement by the existing partners
2. Changes in the membership of the partnership
   a. 1a new partner joins the partnership
   b. an existing partner leaves the partnership

2.2 Change in the profit sharing arrangement by the existing partners

While calculating the profit of each partner in case of a change in the profit sharing ratio, the accounting period is divided and the profits are allocated accordingly for each period.

Example

Harry, Ian and James have been trading for many years, preparing accounts to 30 June each year. Their recent tax adjusted profits have been as follows:

	£
Year ended 30 June 2012	147,000
Year ended 30 June 2013	171,000
Year ended 30 June 2014	180,000

They shared profits equally, until 31 October 2012 when they decided on the following arrangement:

	Harry	Ian	James
Salary	£19,500	£39,000	£49,500
Profit sharing %	50%	30%	20%

The date from which the change in profit sharing ratio is effected, i.e. 31 October 2012, falls in the second accounting period (year ended on 30 June 2013). Therefore, this accounting period will be divided into two periods, first up to the old PSR, i.e. from 1 July 2012 to 31 October 2012 and the second from 1 November 2012 to 30 June 2013 (the remaining period). The profits will be allocated accordingly for each period on the basis of the old and new PSRs.

Continued on the next page

The allocation of profit among the partners for the three years is as follows:

	Total £	Harry £	Ian £	James £
2012-13 (Year ended 30 June 2012)				
PSR 1:1:1	**147,000**	**49,000**	**49,000**	**49,000**
2013-14 (Year ended 30 June 2013)				
1 July 2012 to 31 October 2012 (4 months)				
PSR (1:1:1)	57,000	19,000	19,000	19,000
1 November 2012 to 30 June 2013 (8 months)				
Salary (for 8 months)	72,000	13,000	26,000	33,000
Remaining profit PSR (50:30:20)	42,000	21,000	12,600	8,400
	171,000	**53,000**	**57,600**	**60,400**
2014-15 (Year ended 30 June 2014)				
Salary	108,000	19,500	39,000	49,500
Remaining profit PSR (50:30:20)	72,000	36,000	21,600	14,400
	180,000	**55,500**	**60,600**	**63,900**

2.3 Changes in the membership of the partnership

A situation may arise where the business of the partnership continues, but the partners change. Can you think of any such situations?

1. A partner leaves the partnership.
2. A new partner joins the partnership.

In the above cases what is the basis period for individual partners?

a) The commencement rules are applicable only to new members of the partnership.

Tip

The basis period for each partner starts from the date that they commence trading as a partner up to the following 5 April.

Example

Alan and Bob were in a partnership. The accounting period of the partnership is twelve months to 31 October each year.

Cathy joins the partnership on 1 January 2012. She is considered to have started her business on 1 January 2012. Hence her period of account will be from 1 January 2012 to 31 October 2012. The basis period for the first tax year runs from the date the trade started to the following 5 April. Thus, her basis period for the tax year 2011-12 will be 1 January 2012 to 5 April 2012. Her basis period for the second tax year, 2012-13, will be twelve months from the commencement of trade i.e. from 1 January 2012 to 31 December 2012.

b) The last year rules are applicable only to partners who have left partnership.

Example

Continuing the above example of Alan, Bob and Cathy

If Alan leaves the partnership on 31 May 2012, it will be treated as if he has ceased his business on that date. Alan's basis period for the tax year 2012-13 will start from the end of the basis period of the previous tax year, i.e. 1 November 2011, and will end on the day he leaves the partnership, i.e. 31 May 2012.

c) Partners who carry on business in partnership continuously (ignoring the other partners who join or leave) carry on using the period of account ending in each tax year as the basis period for the tax year (current year basis).

d) When a partnership transfers its trade to a completely new owner or set of owners, the last year rules for basis period apply to old partners, while commencement rules apply to new owners.

2.4 Basis of trading income assessment for partnership profits

1. Continuing partners

Partners who were partners both before and after the change in membership continue to be taxed on the current year basis as if a change had not occurred.

2. Partners joining

A new partner joining will be assessed under the commencement rules. If a partner joins part way through an accounting period, he will have a period which begins on the day he joined. The other partners continue to be assessed on the current year basis.

3. Partners leaving

A partner leaving the partnership will be assessed under the cessation rules. If a partner leaves part way through an accounting period, he will have a period which ends on the day he left. The other partners continue to be assessed on the current year basis.

Example

Chris and Evan began a partnership on 6 April 2008, preparing accounts to 5 April. Chris resigned as a partner on 31 December 2012, and Greg joined as a partner on 1 January 2013. The partnership's trading profit for the year ended 5 April 2013 is £80,000.

Profits were shared as follows:

1. Evan was paid an annual salary of £5,000.
2. Interest was paid at the rate of 10% on the partners' capital accounts, the balances on which were:

	£
Chris	30,000
Evan	60,000
Greg (from 1 January 2013)	10,000

Chris's capital account was repaid to him on 31 December 2013.

3. The balance of profits were shared as follows:

	Chris %	Evan %	Greg %
6 April 2012 to 31 December 2012	60	40	
1 January 2013 to 5 April 2013		70	30

Required:

Calculate the trading income assessments of Chris, Evan and Greg for the tax year 2012-13.

Answer

Trading income assessment for the year ended 5 April 2013

Continued on the next page

	Total £	Chris £	Evan £	Greg £
Nine months to 31 December 2012 (£80,000 x 9/12)				
Salary (£5,000 x 9/12)	3,750		3,750	
Interest (W1)	6,750	2,250	4,500	
Balance (60%/40%)	49,500	29,700	19,800	
	60,000	31,950	28,050	
Three months to 5 April 2013 (£80,000 x 3/12)				
Salary (£5,000 x 3/12)	1,250		1,250	
Interest (W1)	1,750		1,500	250
Balance (70%/30%)	17,000		11,900	5,100
	20,000		14,650	5,350
Total assessment	**80,000**	**31,950**	**42,700**	**5,350**

Note: the allocation of profit and trading income assessment of each of the partners is same in this case as the accounting period and the tax year both are the same, i.e. 6 April 2012 to 5 April 2013.

Workings

W1 Interest on capital

Nine months to 31 December 2012

Chris: (£30,000 x 10% x 9/12) = £2,250
Evan: (£60,000 x 10% x 9/12) = £4,500

Three months to 5 April 2013

Evan: (£60,000 x 10% x 3/12) = £1,500
Greg: (£10,000 x 10% x 3/12) = £250

SUMMARY

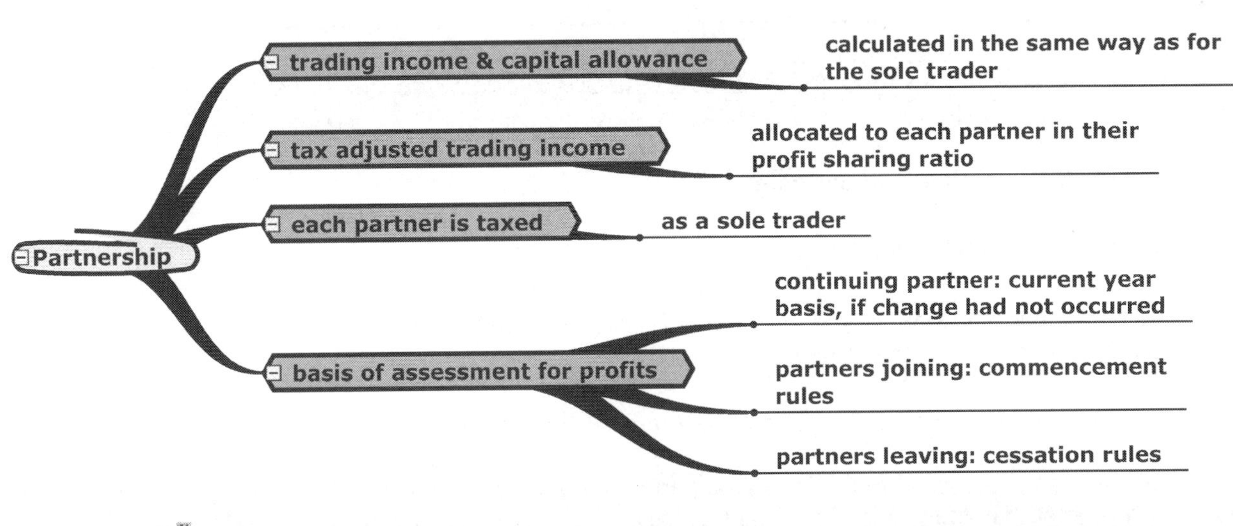

Test Yourself 2

Cindy, Barbie and Cinderella began trading as a partnership on 1 January 2011, sharing profits in the ratio 1:2:3.

From 1 January 2012, the partners decided that:

1. Cinderella should receive a salary of £50,000 per annum.
2. all the partners should be entitled to interest on capital at 4% per annum.
3. the remaining profits should be shared in the ratio of 2:3:5.

Continued on the next page

The adjusted trading profits of the partnership are:
year ended 31 December 2011 £240,000
year ended 31 December 2012 £280,000

The fixed capital of the partners is as follows:
Cindy £120,000, Barbie £160,000 and Cinderella £210,000

Required:

Calculate the trading income assessments and the overlap profits for each of the partners for the years 2011-12 and 2012-13.

Test Yourself 3

Kelly and Millie started a business in partnership on 1 September 2011, sharing profits equally. They decided their accounting date as 31 December. Lily joined their partnership on 1 October 2012 and the three partners decided to share profits equally amongst themselves.

The partnership made their first accounts for 16 months up to 31 December 2012 with a trading profit of £80,000. The trading profits of the partnership for the year ended 31 December 2013 were £120,000.

Required:

What is the amount of profits on which Lily will be assessable for the tax year 2012-13?

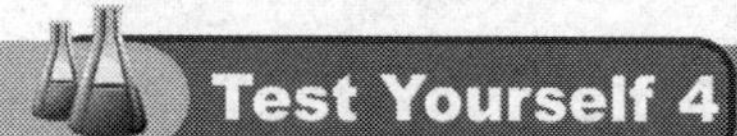

Test Yourself 4

Dean, Jerry and Dick have been trading for many years, preparing accounts to 31 December each year. They share profits equally. The partnership made a profit of £60,000 for the year ended 31 December 2011. Dean resigned as a partner on 31 December 2012. Jerry and Dick continued, and decided to share profits equally. The partnership made a loss of £90,000 in the year ended 31 December 2012. Dean's overlap profit relief brought forward was £9,000.

Required:

What is the amount of trading income on which Dean will be assessable for 2012-13?

3. Describe the alternative loss relief claims that are available to partners.[1]

[Learning Outcomes i (iv)]

2.1 Loss relief claims available to partners

The two steps for a partnership are

Step 1: share the profits between the partners in the profit sharing ratio of the accounting period.
Step 2: treat each partner as a sole trader.

These rules continue to be applied when the partnership incurs a loss.

The partnership loss is allocated to the individual partners in their profit / (loss) sharing ratio of the accounting period. Each partner may then claim their share of loss, as a sole trader. He may claim whatever loss relief is most beneficial to him.

Continuing partners may claim

- **Section 64:** against TI of the current and/or previous tax year
- **Section 83:** against future trading income

Partners joining may claim

- **Section 72:** a loss in any of the first four tax years may be set against TI of the previous three years, earliest first.
- **Section 64:** against TI of the current and / or previous tax year
- **Section 83:** against future trading income

Partners leaving may claim

- **Section 89:** a loss of the last twelve months may be set against trading income of the last and previous three tax years, latest first.
- **Section 64:** against TI of the current and/or previous tax year.
- **Temporary Extension of loss relief:** against trading income of the previous three years, latest first (it is available only for any trading loss incurred during the tax years 2010-11 and 2011-12).

Test Yourself 5

Hira and Mira have been trading for many years, preparing accounts to 31 December each year. They share profits equally. Tara joined the partnership on 1 January 2011 and it was agreed to share profits equally among all the three partners. The partnership made a profit of £60,000 for the year ended 31 December 2011. Hira resigned as a partner on 31 December 2012. Mira and Tara continued and decided to share profits equally. The partnership made a loss of £90,000 in the year ended 31 December 2012.

Required:

Give the possible ways in which Hira, Mira and Tara can relieve their share of the trading loss. Assume Hira's overlap profit relief brought forward was £9,000.

---

4. Explain the loss relief restriction that applies to the partners of a limited liability partnership.[1]

[Learning Outcome i (v)]

4.1 Limited Liability Partnerships (LLP)

1. This type of partnership has a distinct legal existence, separate from its partners. It can own property and sue or can be sued in the name of the corporation. It enjoys perpetual succession even if anything happens to the partners i.e. additions or departure of partners, death or insolvency of partners. It will have no effect on its continuation.

   With a "normal" (unlimited) partnership there is no limit to the amount that each partner is required to contribute towards partnership losses, debts and liabilities.

2. It is possible to form a limited liability partnership where the contribution to losses, debts and liabilities by each partner is limited by agreement (similar to with a limited company).

3. The limited liability partnership is taxed in the same way as other partnerships.

4. Normal loss reliefs are available.

However, the amount of loss (relief under s.64 and s.72), which a partner of a limited liability partnership can set off against his non-partnership income, is restricted to the capital contributed by him in the partnership.

Example

Robert has been a member of an LLP for many years, introducing capital of £100,000 when he joined. The partnership prepares accounts to 5 April each year. The partnership incurred a loss in the year ended 5 April 2012 and 2013.

Robert's share is as follows:

Year ended 5 April 2012	£60,000
Year ended 5 April 2013	£72,000

Continued on the next page

What is the maximum relief that Robert may claim against his TI under s.64?

Answer

Robert is entitled to s.64 relief against his other income or gains as follows:

2011-12	£60,000	(£60,000 of contributed capital has been used up, £40,000 remaining)
2012-13	£40,000	(s.64 relief limited to capital contribution of £100,000. Loss of £40,000 relieved)

Note: The balance of the loss, £32,000 (£72,000 - £40,000), can be carried forward and set against Robert's share of the LLP's profits from the same trade for later years. Alternatively, if Robert makes a further capital contribution in a later year, the balance of the loss can be set against his other income or gains, not arising from the partnership.

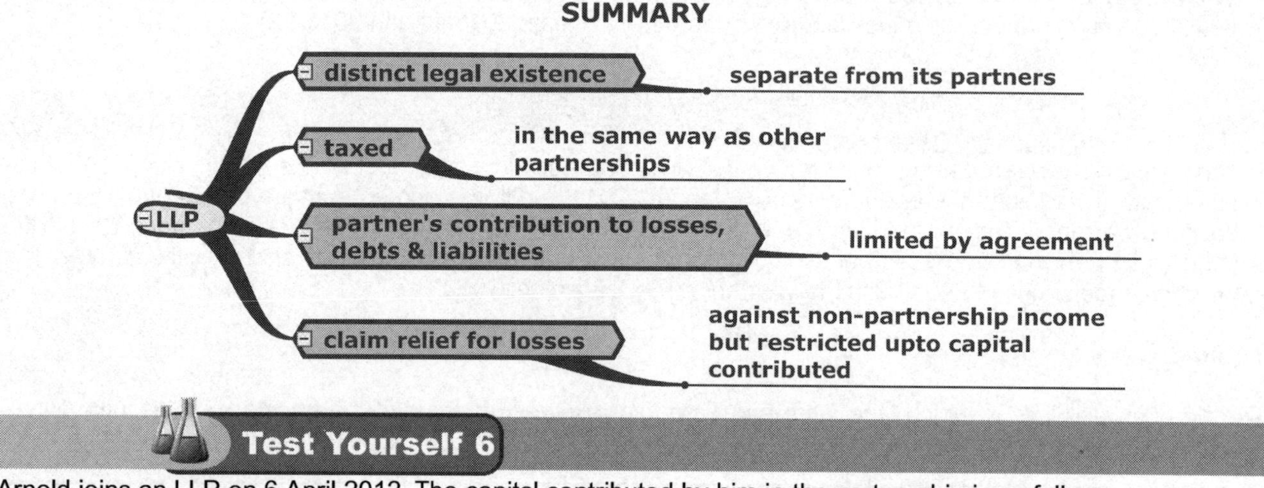

Arnold joins an LLP on 6 April 2012. The capital contributed by him in the partnership is as follows:

6 April 2012	£90,000
6 April 2013	£25,000

Arnold's share of the partnership's trading profits and losses are:
Year ended 5 April 2013: Loss (£140,000)
Year ended 5 April 2014: Profit £60,000

Required:

Explain how loss relief can be claimed.

Test Yourself 7

Tom and Dick began trading as a partnership on 1 October 2009, sharing profits equally. They prepared accounts to 30 September each year.

On 1 January 2011 they agreed to admit Harry as a partner, and decided on the following profit sharing ratio:

Tom	Dick	Harry
50%	30%	20%

The adjusted trading profits of the partnership are as follows:

	£
Year ended 30/9/2010	220,000
Year ended 30/9/2011	250,000
Year ended 30/9/2012	300,000

Required:

Calculate the trading income assessment for each partner for the years 2009-10 to 2012-13 and the overlap profits for each of the partners.

Answers to Test Yourself

Answer to TY 1

Allocation of profits among the partners

	Total £	Fiona £	Gertrude £	Henrietta £
Year ended 31 December 2012				
Salary	21,600	14,400	7,200	-
Interest on capital	4,800	1,800	1,500	1,500
	26,400			
Balance (2:2:1)	46,200	18,480	18,480	9,240
Total profit allocated to each partner	**72,600**	**34,680**	**27,180**	**10,740**

Answer to TY 2

The allocation of trading profit for each accounting period is as follows:

	Total £	Cindy £	Barbie £	Cinderella £
Year ended 31 December 2011				
PSR (1:2:3)	240,000	40,000	80,000	120,000
Year ended 31 December 2012				
Salary	50,000			50,000
Interest on capital	19,600	4,800	6,400	8,400
	69,600			
Remaining profits (2:3:5)	210,400	42,080	63,120	105,200
Total profit allocated to each partner	**280,000**	**46,880**	**69,520**	**163,600**

Each partner is treated as a sole trader who started trading on 1 January 2011, preparing accounts to 31 December each year.

The trading income assessment for the three partners is as follows:

Tax year	Basis period	Cindy £	Barbie £	Cindrella £
2010-11	1 January 2011 to 5 April 2011 (3 months) (note 1)	10,000	20,000	30,000
2011-12	Year ended 31 December 2011 (note 2)	40,000	80,000	120,000
2012-13	Year ended 31 December 2012 (CYB)*	46,880	69,520	163,600

* Current year basis

Notes

1. The basis period for the first tax year runs from the first day of the trade to the following 5 April.
2. There is an accounting period of 12 months ending in the second tax year; therefore the basis period is 12 months to the accounting date, i.e. year ended 31 December 2011.

Overlap profits

The overlap period is from 1 January 2011 to 5 April 2011.
The overlap profits therefore for each partner are:

	£
Cindy	10,000
Barbie	20,000
Cinderella	30,000

Answer to TY 3

Commencement rules are applicable for the partner who joins part way through an accounting period. Therefore, the basis period for Lily for the tax year 2012-13 will be the day on which she joins the partnership, i.e. 1 October 2012 to 5 April 2013.

Lily's trading income assessment for the tax year 2012-13 is as follows:

	Workings	£
1 October 2012 to 31 December 2012 (3 months)	£80,000 x 3 months/16 months x 1/3	5,000
1 January 2013 to 5 April 2013 (3 months)	£120,000 x 3 months/12 months x 1/3	10,000
		15,000

Answer to TY 4

The trading income assessment of all the partners for each accounting period is as follows:

Tax year	Basis period	Total	Dean	Jerry	Dick
		£	£	£	£
2011-12	Year ended 31 December 2011 PSR (1:1:1)	60,000	20,000	20,000	20,000
2012-13	Year ended 31 December 2012 PSR (1:1:1)	(90,000)	(30,000)	(30,000)	(30,000)

Dean is a leaving partner, so he will be assessed under the cessation rules. Therefore, his final assessment is a loss of £30,000 plus an overlap profit relief of £9,000. This will increase his loss to £39,000.

Answer to TY 5

The profits / (losses) will be divided as follows:

	Total £	Hira £	Mira £	Tara £
Year ended 31 December 2011 PSR (1:1:1)	60,000	20,000	20,000	20,000
Year ended 31 December 2012 PSR (1:1:1)	(90,000)	(30,000)	(30,000)	(30,000)

Mira is a continuing partner, Tara is a joining partner and Hira is a leaving partner.

Tara joined the business on 1 January 2011. Her basis period assessments will be as follows:

2010-11	01/01/2011 - 05/04/2011	3/12 x £20,000	£ 5,000
2011-12	01/01/2011 - 31/12/2011	Year ended 31 December 2011	£20,000
2012-13	01/01/2012 - 31/12/2012	Year ended 31 December 2012	£(30,000)

Tara will have an overlap period of 3 months from 1 January 2011 to 5 April 2011. Her overlap profit for this period is 3/12 x £20,000 = £5,000

Mira will have losses of £30,000 for the year ended 31 December 2012.

Hira ceases to trade and her final assessment is a loss of £30,000 plus an overlap profit relief of £9,000. This will increase her loss to £39,000.

Hence, the relief available to each partner is as follows:

Mira (continuing partner)

1. Section 64: Mira can claim the loss of £30,000 against TI of 2012-13 and/or 2011-12.
2. Section 83: Mira can carry forward the loss of £30,000, to set off against future trading profits.

Tara (joining partner)

1. Section 72: Tara can claim the loss of £30,000 against TI of 2009-10 to 2011-12.
2. Section 64: Tara can claim the loss of £30,000 against TI of 2012-13 and/or 2011-12.
3. Section 83: Tara can carry forward the loss of £30,000 to set off against the future trading profits.

Hira (resigning partner)

1. Section 89: Hira can claim the loss of £39,000 against trading profits of 2011-12, then 2010-11 then 2009-10.
2. Section 64: Hira can claim the loss of £39,000 against TI of 2012-13 and/or 2011-12.

Answer to TY 6

Arnold's capital contributions for the purposes of loss relief restrictions are:

At 5 April 2013	£90,000
At 5 April 2014	£115,000 (£90,000 + £25,000)

Loss relief that may be claimed against other income is restricted to the amount of Arnold's capital contribution on 5 April 2013 (£90,000). Thus, Arnold is entitled to claim relief either under section 64 or section 72 against his other income or gains as follows:

Relief under	Against other income	Year
Section 72	£90,000	2009-10
Section 64	£90,000	2012-13 and 2011-12

Note: The remaining loss of £50,000 out of a total loss of £140,000 suffered in 2012-13, for which relief cannot be given against Arnold's other income or gains, can be carried forward under s.83, and set against his share of the partnership's trading profits for 2013-14 and later years.

Answer to TY 7

The allocation of trading profit for each accounting period is as follows:

	Total £	Tom £	Dick £	Harry £
Year ended 30/09/2010				
(1:1)	220,000	110,000	110,000	
Year ended 30/09/2011				
01/10/2010 to 31/12/2010 (3 months)				
£250,000 x 3/12				
PSR (1:1)	62,500	31,250	31,250	
1/1/2011 to 30/09/2011 (9 months)				
£250,000 x 9/12				
PSR (5:3:2)	187,500	93,750	56,250	37,500
	250,000	**125,000**	**87,500**	**37,500**
Year ended 30/09/2012				
PSR (5:3:2)	300,000	150,000	90,000	60,000

Each partner is treated as a sole trader.
Each partner's assessment is as follows:

Tom

	Basis period	Workings	Assessment £
2009-10	01/10/2009 to 05/04/2010	£110,000 x 6/12	55,000
2010-11	Year ended 30/09/2010		110,000
2011-12	Year ended 30/09/2011		125,000
2012-13	Year ended 30/09/2012		150,000

Dick

	Basis period	Workings	Assessment £
2009-10	01/10/2009 to 05/04/2010	£110,000 x 6/12	55,000
2010-11	Year ended 30/09/2010		110,000
2011-12	Year ended 30/09/2011		87,500
2012-13	Year ended 30/09/2012		90,000

Harry

	Basis period	Workings	Assessment
			£
2010-11	01/01/2011 to 05/04/2011	£37,500 x 3/9	12,500
2011-12	01/01/2011 to 31/12/2011	£37,500 + (£60,000 x 3/12)	52,500
2012-13	Year ended 30/09/2012		60,000

Overlap profits

For Tom and Dick, the overlap period is 1 October 2009 to 5 April 2010; the overlap profit for both of them is £55,000.

For Harry, the overlap period is 1 January 2011 to 5 April 2011 and 1 October 2011 to 31 December 2011.

Overlap profits are £12,500 + (£60,000 x 3/12) = £27,500.

Quick Quiz

1. What are the two steps to follow when dealing with a partnership?

2. Explain the basis by which partners are assessed for tax when they join a partnership.

3. Arnold and Bob have been in partnership for many years, preparing accounts to 31 December each year. They always shared profits equally until 1 October 2012 when they decided that Arnold should have a salary of £12,000 per annum and the balance of the profits should be shared 2:3.

   The partnership profits for the year to 31 December 2012 were £100,000.

   Required:

   Show the partners' trading income assessments for 2012-13.

4. Candice and Diane have been in partnership for many years, preparing accounts to 30 June each year. Ethel joins them on 1 January 2013.

   Required:

   What will be the basis period for each partner for 2012-13?

5. Iris and Jade have been trading for many years, preparing accounts to 31 December each year. Kerry joined the partnership on 1 June 2012, and Jade resigned from the partnership on 31 October 2012. The partnership incurred a loss in the year to 31 December 2012.

   Required:

   What loss reliefs are available to each partner?

Answers to Quick Quiz

1. Step 1: allocate the profits between the partners in the profit sharing ratio of the accounting period.
   Step 2: treat each partner as a sole trader.

2. Each partner is treated as a sole trader running a business. The commencement rules apply when a partner joins the partnership, with the first year of assessment being on an actual basis.

3. Partner's trading income assessments

	Total £	Arnold £	Bob £
Year ended 31 December 2012			
01/01/2012 to 30/09/2012 (9 months)			
(£100,000 x 9/12 = £75,000)			
PSR (1:1)	75,000	37,500	37,500
01/10/2012 to 31/12/2012 (3 months)			
(£100,000 x 3/12 = £25,000)	25000		
Salary x 3/12	3,000	3,000	
Balance PSR (2:3)	22,000	8,800	13,200
	100,000	**49,300**	**50,700**

4. Candice and Diane: year ended 30 June 2012 (CYB)

   Ethel: 1 January 2013 – 5 April 2013 (opening year rules)

5. **Iris:**
   - Section 64 against TI of 2012-13 and/or 2011-12.
   - Section 83 against future trading income.

   Jade:
   - Section 64 against TI of 2012-13 and/or 2011-12.
   - Section 89 against trading profits of 2012-13 then 2011-12, 2010-11 and 2009-10.

   Kerry:
   - Section 72 against TI of 2009-10, 2010-11 and 2011-12.
   - Section 64 against TI of 2012-13 and/or 2011-12.

Self Examination Questions

Question 1

Edwin and Frank began trading as a partnership on 1 August 2009, sharing profits in the ratio 60:40. They prepared accounts to 31 December 2008 and annually thereafter. George joined the partnership on 1 May 2011 and they shared profits equally from that date. On 31 December 2012, Edwin resigned; Frank and George continued to share the profits equally.

The trading profits earned by the partnership are as follows:

	£
1/08/2009 to 31/12/2009	18,900
Year ended 31/12/2010	48,000
Year ended 31/12/2010	120,000
Year ended 31/12/2012	99,000

Required:

Show the allocation of profits to the partners for each accounting period.

Question 2

Continuing with Edwin, Frank and George calculate the trading income assessments for 2009-10 to 2012-13 and identify any overlap profits.

Answers to Self Examination Questions

Answer to SEQ 1

Allocation of profits to the partners

	Total (£)	Edwin(£)	Frank (£)	George (£)
01/08/2009 to 31/12/2009				
PSR (60:40)	18,900	11,340	7,560	
Year ended 31/12/2010				
PSR (60:40)	48,000	28,800	19,200	
Year ended 31/12/2011				
01/01/2011 – 30/4/2011 (4 months)				
(£120,000 x 4/12)				
PSR (60:40)	40,000	24,000	16,000	
01/05/2011 – 31/12/2011 (8 months)				
(£120,000 x 8/12)				
PSR (1:1:1)	80,000	26,667	26,667	26,667
	120,000	50,667	42,667	26,667
Year ended 31/12/2012				
PSR (1:1:1)	99,000	33,000	33,000	33,000

Answer to SEQ 2

	Basis period	Working	Edwin £	Frank £	George £
2009-10	01/08/2009 - 05/04/2010	01/08/2009 – 31/12/2009	11,340	7,560	
		01/01/2010 – 05/04/2010 3/12 x Year ended 31/12/2010	7,200	4,800	
		Trading income assessment	18,540	12,360	
2010-11	01/01/2010 – 31/12/2010	Trading income assessment	28,800	19,200	
2011-12	01/01/2011 – 31/12/2011		50,667	42,667	
	01/05/2011 – 05/04/2012	01/05/2011 – 31/12/2011			26,666
		1/01/2012 – 5/04/2012 3/12 x Year ended 31/12/2012			8,250
		Trading income assessment	50,667	42,667	34,916
2012-13	01/01/2012 – 31/12/2012		33,000	33,000	33,000
		Less: Overlap (01/10/2011 to 05/04/2011)	(7,200)		
		Trading income assessment	25,800	33,000	33,000
		Overlap carried forward		4,800	8,250

Note: the basis period for the first tax year runs from the date of the start of trade, to the following 5 April. Hence, the basis period for Edwin and Frank is 1 August 2009 to 5 April 2010 for their first tax year 2009-10. For George it is 1 May 2011 to 5 April 2012 for his first tax year 2011-12.

Closing year rules will be applicable to a partner leaving the partnership. Hence, the basis period for the tax year of cessation 2012-13 for Edwin is from 1 January 2012 to 31 December 2012. He is also eligible to deduct overlap profits from the profits earned during this period.

The overlap period for Edwin and Frank is 1 January 2010 – 5 April 2010, the overlap period for George is 1 January 2012 – 5 April 2012.

Edwin resigned on 31 December 2012, so he may relieve his overlap in 2012-13.

SECTION B

INCOME TAX LIABILITIES

B4

STUDY GUIDE B4: PROPERTY AND INVESTMENT INCOME

Get Through Intro

Property income, received from letting out properties, is taxed according to specific rules. **Income from investments** consists of **dividends received** from company shares and **interest received** on savings.

This Study Guide discusses the provisions for the computation of property income, income from investments and tax exempt investments.

As a tax consultant, you need to be aware of all these provisions in order to compute the correct tax liability of your clients on their property income and investment income. A **thorough knowledge of all these provisions** will **ensure that the best use is made of all the benefits and reliefs available**

This knowledge will help you to solve the questions in your examination with confidence.

Learning Outcomes

a) Compute property business profits.
b) Explain the treatment of furnished holiday lettings.
c) Describe rent-a-room relief.
d) Compute the amount assessable when a premium is received for the grant of a short lease.
e) Understand how relief for a property business loss is given.
f) Compute the tax payable on savings income.
g) Compute the tax payable on dividend income.
h) Explain the treatment of individual savings accounts (ISAs) and other tax exempt investments.

Introduction

Case Study

On the death of her father, Jane inherited his house which she decided to rent it out to generate additional income.

Now Jane has the following questions:

- How will the rental income be calculated?
- What would be the allowable deductions?
- What would be the rate of tax?
- If the property was let out only for a part of the year, how will that affect the computations?

This income is known as unearned income. Most income received from land and property in the UK is taxed under the property income rules.

In the following Study Guide we shall see how to compute income from lettings, what expenses are allowable against the income and the specific deductions available for the tax payer.

1. Compute property income profits.[2]
Compute the amount assessable when a premium is received for the grant of a short lease. [2]

[Learning Outcomes a and d]

1.1 What is property income?

Income from land and buildings

Example

Wilson rents out his flat to William at an annual rent of £12,000. In this case, rent received by Wilson (i.e. £12,000 per annum) is his property income.

1.2 Main classes of property income are as follows:

1. Rents received

Example

Sally lets out her flat to Mike for a monthly rent of £880. The rent received is her property income.

Rented property can be either furnished or unfurnished. There are two different methods that may be used to calculate the profits from furnished property lettings and the taxpayer needs to opt for one of them.

a) Renewal basis: no deductions are allowed for the cost of the original furniture. However, if the furniture is subsequently replaced, the full cost of the replacement of the furniture is treated as revenue expenditure, and is fully deductible as an expense. It is very important to note here that if the replacement cost includes any component attributable to improvement, as opposed to simple replacement, then the improvement portion is not deductible.

b) 10% wear and tear basis: the actual cost of furniture is ignored but 10% of the "net rent" is allowed as a deduction. "Net rent" means that if any liabilities of the tenant are paid by the landlord, e.g. council tax and water rates, then such amounts are first deducted from the rent received; 10% of the remaining balance is allowed as a wear and tear allowance.

2. Lease premiums on short leases

A premium refers to lump sum payments made by a tenant to the landlord on the grant of a lease to the tenant. The tax treatment of these premiums depends upon the nature of the lease i.e. whether it is a short lease or a long lease.

Short Lease: if the lease is granted for a period of 50 years or less **then it is termed a short lease.**

Income element of premium for landlords: **Part of a premium received for granting a short lease is** taxable as property income. **The amount to be assessed as property income is equal to the amount of the** premium reduced by 2% for each year of the lease, except for the first year.

Premium assessable as property income
$= P - P\,(2\% \times (n-1))$

Where, P = Premium
n = no. of years of lease

Tip

If the tenant of a short lease sells their interest in the property to a new tenant, this calculation does not apply to adjust any premium they receive.

Deductible expenses for tenants

Premiums paid by tenants of short leases can be claimed as deductible expenses. The amount which can be claimed each year is $\frac{P - P(2\% \times (n-1))}{\text{number of years of lease}}$

Diagram 1: Short lease

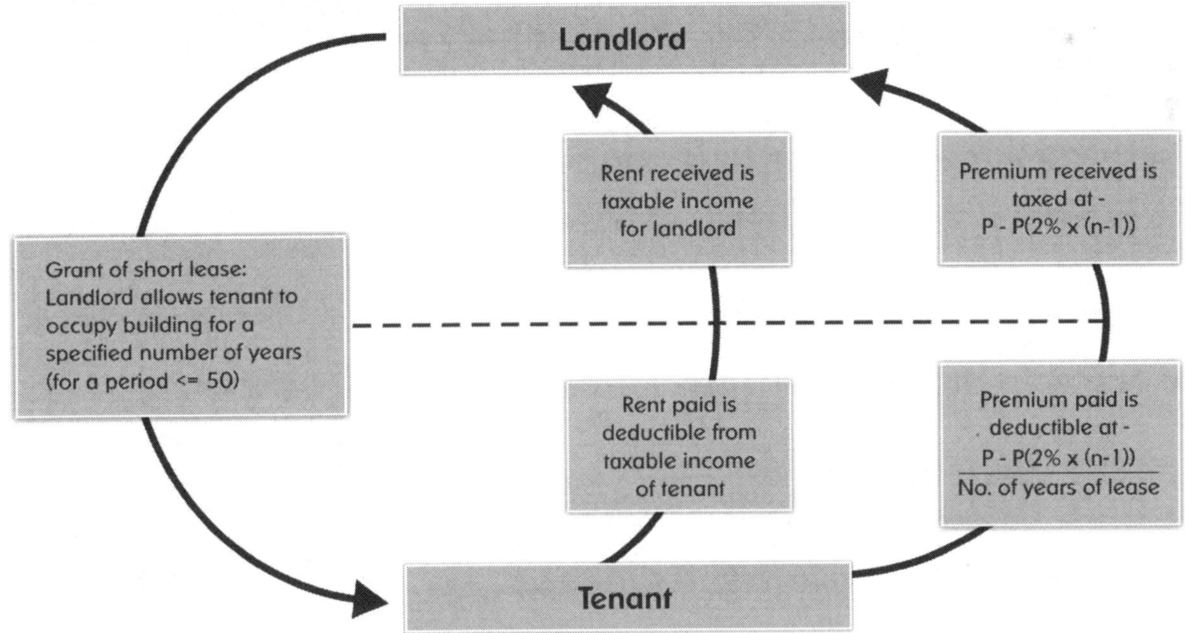

Example

Frank, a trader, receives a premium of £20,000 from his tenant for the grant of a 20 year lease, in 2012-13. What is Frank's property income in respect of this premium?

Property income element of premium = P – P (2% x (n- 1))
= £20,000 – £20,000 (2% x (20 – 1))
= £12,400

The premium is reduced by 2% for property income computation purposes. By reducing 2% each year except for the first year, ((20-1) years x 2%) = 38% of the premium is deductible. Thus, the remaining 62% is taxable in the year of receipt, i.e. £20,000 x 62% = £12,400 (same as calculated above).

The property income element for 2012-13 of the premium is £12,400.
The amount of premium paid which can be claimed as a deductible expense by the tenant (for the tax year 2012-13) would amount to

$$\frac{P - P(2\% \times (n-1))}{\text{no. of years of lease}}$$

$$\text{i.e., } \frac{\text{Property business income assessable on the landlord}}{\text{Number of years of lease}}$$

$$= \frac{£12{,}400}{20} = £620$$

The following points are extremely important

1. **Accrual basis:** the income should be computed on an accruals basis.

Example

Arnold, a trader, buys a new property on 1 July 2012. He let out the property for an annual rent of £12,000 payable in advance.

Rent due for 2012-13 is £12,000 (being annual rent payable in advance).

Rent accrued on 5 April 2013 is £12,000 x 9/12 = £9,000.

---

2. **Aggregation of expenses / income if more than one property:** when rent is generated from letting more than one property, all the rents and expenses for all the properties let out are pooled together, and a single amount is calculated.

The expenses which are deductible are explained in Learning Outcome 2!

Example

John lets out one office for an annual rent of £5,000 and one shop for an annual rent of £6,000. He paid insurance of £300 for the office and £200 for the shop.

The property income will be calculated as:

	£
Rent from office	5,000
Rent from shop	6,000
Total	**11,000**
Less: Insurance expenses (£300 + £200)	(500)
Property income	**10,500**

SUMMARY

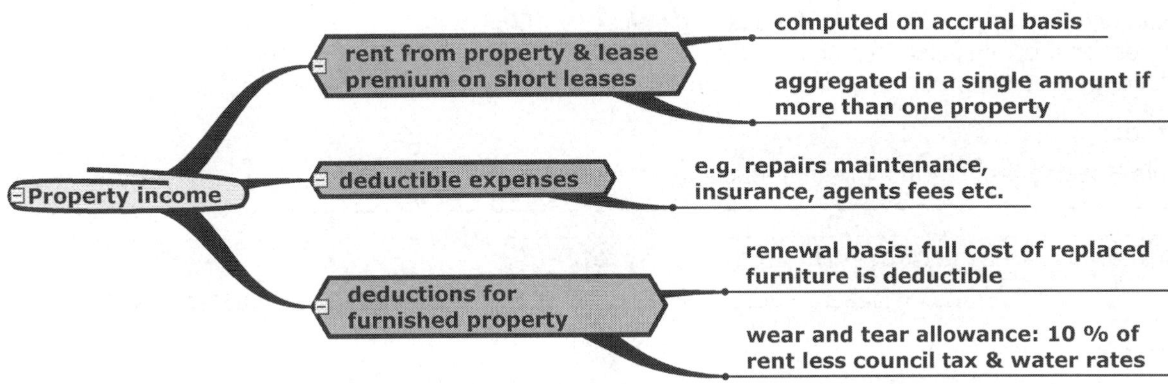

1.3 Deductible expenses from rental income

As we have seen for a trading business, **expenses incurred wholly and exclusively in respect of the property letting** are deductible from rental income, to arrive at the taxable property income. Some examples of allowable expenses are:

a) expenses towards repairs and maintenance
b) insurance
c) agents fees
d) interest on loans to purchase / improve the property
e) the cost of providing services to the tenants
f) administrative and management costs
g) bad debts (if rents are not paid)

Capital expenditure is not generally a deductible expense from rental income although the wear and tear allowance or the renewals basis will provide some relief for certain capital costs of furnishings.

1.4 Private use of residence

When a taxpayer lets their private residence for part of a tax year (e.g. if they occupy the property themselves for part of the year) the deductible expenses would relate to the proportion of the period when the property was available for letting out. For example, if an insurance of £600 is paid for the year 2012-13, and the property is available for letting for a period of 10 months, £500 would be deductible (£600/12 x 10).

However, expenses which relate wholly to the letting would be fully deductible. For example, advertising charges, agent's commission etc.

Fenny, a trader receives a premium of £12,000 from her tenant for the grant of a 12 year lease, in 2012-13. What is Fenny's property income in respect of this premium?

Robert prepares his accounts up to 31 March every year. He owns three shops, a furnished flat and an office building, which he has rented out. Rent on the property is due monthly in advance on the 1st of every month.

The details of the property rented out during the year ended 31 March 2013 are:

1. Shop 1 was let out at £5,500 p.a. throughout the year.
2. Shop 2 was let out at £6,600 p.a. from 1 December 2012.
3. Shop 3 was let out at £7,500 p.a. to 30 June. On 31 May 2012, £1,000 was received. The tenant has since been declared bankrupt and the balance of the rent was not received.
4. The furnished flat was let out throughout the year for £2,500 p.a.
5. The office building was let out unfurnished on 1 October 2012 with a 10 year lease granted for a premium of £20,000 and annual rent of £6,000. The rent for one year was received in advance.

Continued on the next page

Robert incurs the following expenses:

a) repairs of shop 1 in June 2012, £2,000.
b) insurance per shop £500 p.a., for flat £200, for office £2,100.
c) interest on the loan taken to purchase shop 2, £1,500.
d) advertisement expenses for obtaining tenants for shop 2, £1,200 and for the office £1,000.

Required:

Compute Robert's property income chargeable to tax for 2012-13.

---

2. Explain the treatment of furnished holiday lettings.[1]

[Learning Outcome b]

2.1 Meaning

Furnished holiday letting is also known as qualifying holiday accommodation.

If the letting of furnished property satisfies certain conditions, it qualifies as income from the "commercial letting of furnished holiday accommodation". **Such income is treated as income from a trade for certain tax purposes** (although it is not actually taxed as trading income) and furnished holiday lettings are eligible for **capital allowances on furnishings.**

2.2 In order to qualify as a holiday let, the property:

- Must be **available for commercial letting** to the public for **at least 210 days in a tax year,** and
- Must be **actually let commercially** in this period for **at least 105 days** (excluding periods of long term occupation – explained below), and
- If it is let for periods of longer-term occupation (more than 31 consecutive days) this should not exceed more than 155 days during the year.

Example

Jack owns a cottage, which was **originally** purchased **as a holiday h**ome for his personal use. This cottage is furnished and has been available for holiday rentals since the summer of 2007, at which time Jack ceased using it privately. The cottage was let on a commercial basis for 23 weeks in 2012-13 with each individual letting not exceeding 2 weeks in duration. The letting generated a total rental income of £7,850.

If the letting of furnished property satisfies certain conditions, it qualifies as income from "commercial letting of furnished holiday accommodation."

To qualify as a furnished holiday letting, the property must satisfy the following conditions:

- Must be available for commercial letting to the public for at least 210 days in a tax year, and
- Must be actually let commercially in this period for at least 105 days (excluding periods of long term occupation, and
- If it is let for periods of longer-term occupation (more than 31 consecutive days) this should not exceed more than 155 days during the year.

The cottage passes all three conditions. Therefore, it will be regarded as furnished holiday accommodation.

If a taxpayer owns two properties, out of which one satisfies the **210 day** condition, whereas the other satisfies the **105 day condition, then** the properties will be regarded as satisfying the 70 day rule, **if the average number of days let is at least 105 days.**

2.3 The benefits of qualifying as a furnished holiday letting

- **Income is regarded as earned income and qualifies as "net relevant earnings" when determining the extent to which tax relief is available on contributions to pension scheme.** (Net relevant earnings and pension contributions are discussed in detail in Study Guide B6).
- **Losses arising from furnished holiday letting were treated as trading losses,** (not as property losses), and therefore relief was available against any other income of the taxpayer up to tax year 2010-2011. However, from 6 April 2011 losses arising from a furnished holiday letting cannot be relieved against any other income of a taxpayer. These losses can only be carried forward to set off against future profits from the furnished holiday letting.
- **Capital gains are eligible for rollover relief**, entrepreneur's relief and holdover relief.

- **Capital allowances are permitted in respect of furniture** (wear and tear allowances and the renewals basis of allowances do not apply).

SUMMARY

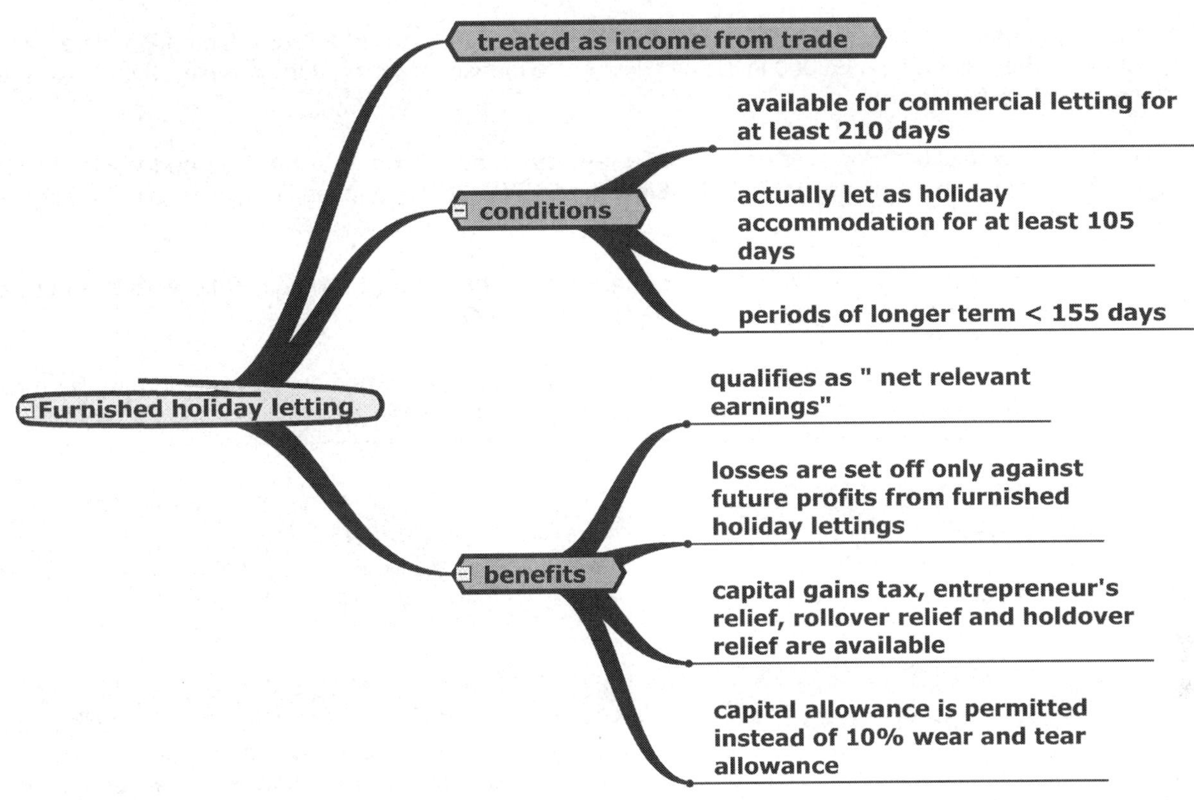

Test Yourself 3

Jane owns a furnished cottage, which has been available for holiday rental since 1 December 2012. The cottage was let on a commercial basis for 12 weeks in 2012-13 with each individual letting not exceeding 2 weeks in duration. The letting generated a total rental income of £5,850.

Required:

Determine whether the rent earned from this property would qualify as income from the "commercial letting of furnished holiday accommodation'.

---

3. Describe rent- a- room relief.[1]

[Learning Outcome c]

Gross rents (i.e. rents with no deduction for expenses) up to a specified limit (£4,250 for 2012-13) are exempt from income tax if they relate to the letting of furnished accommodation, **which is part of an individual's main residence** If it is let out by the joint owners (i.e. if more than one person are getting the rent from letting the same house), then the limit will be £2,125 (half of the normal limit) for each owner.

Example

Ming owns a house, which has 8 rooms. She rents out one of the rooms for £4,000 per annum. As income of up to £4,250 is exempt from tax, the full £4,000 received will be exempt.

If the gross rent exceeds £4,250, the taxpayer may elect to either:

a) be assessed on the excess of gross rents over £4,250 with no expense deductions, or
b) apply normal property income rules with no deduction for rent-a-room relief (i.e. deduct expenses).

Terri owns a house, which has 8 rooms. She rents out one of the rooms for £6,000 per annum. Terri has the following two options:

1. Either to apply normal property income rules i.e. not to take up the rent-a-room exemption. The income assessable in this case will be £6,000 less any allowable expenses incurred, for example, repairs, wear and tear allowance, council tax etc.

2. To take up the exemption. However, in this case, any expenses incurred will not be deductible. In other words, the income assessable will be £6,000 - £4,250 = £1,750. Any expenses, for e.g. repairs incurred, will not be deductible.

This option is to be exercised by the taxpayer **by 31 January in the second tax year following the tax year to which the option relates** (i.e. one year from the tax return filing date).

For the tax year 2012-13 the taxpayer has until 31 January 2015 to elect whether he wants to use the rent-a-room exemption or whether he wants to apply normal property income rules.

Full exemption (i.e. £4,250) is available even if the property is not let out throughout the whole tax year. The exemption is not apportioned.

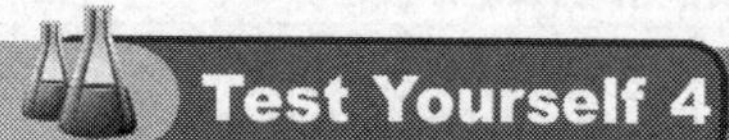

Burley rented out a room in his home to a tenant on 1 June 2012 for £7,000 p.a. He prepares his personal accounts to the year ended 31 March 2013 and noted that he had incurred the following expenses for the let portion of the property:

	£
Agent commission for obtaining tenant	350
Repairs to the staircase	420
Insurance	600

Required:

Calculate his property income by comparing rent-a-room relief and applying normal property income rules for the year-ended 31 March 2013 to decide which is more beneficial.

4. Understand how relief for a property business loss is given.[2]

[Learning Outcome e]

1. All property receipts and all property expenses are pooled to give an overall profit or loss figure for the year. The losses from the running of one property are automatically offset against other property income.

2. Any surplus losses are carried forward to the next tax year.

3. Losses carried forward may only be offset against future profits from the same property rental business; it is necessary that the property business must continue i.e. if the property business ceases to exist, the carried forward losses are not allowed against any other income.

4. The carried forward loss is automatically offset against the first available property income, arising in subsequent tax years.

Example

Glenda prepares accounts up to 31 March every year. She owns a shop and two flats, which she has rented out. Rent on the property is due quarterly, in advance, on 1 January, 1 April etc. The details of the business property profits for the tax year 2012-13 are as follows:

	Shop 1 £	Flat 1 £	Flat 2 £	Total £
Rent accrued (a)	**2,500**	**3,700**	**7,000**	**13,200**
Less: Expenses				
Repairs	5,000			5,000
Agent's fees		2,500		2,500
Insurance	500	300		800
Bad debts		900		900
Rent a room relief			4,250	4,250
Total expenses incurred (b)	**5,500**	**3,700**	**4,250**	**13,450**
Property business profit (a - b)	**(3,000)**	**0**	**2,750**	**(250)**

The losses from the running of one property are automatically **offset against other property income.** Therefore the net loss on property is £250. This loss will be carried forward to the next tax year i.e. 2013-14.

The carried forward loss must be set off against the **first available property income** arising in the subsequent tax years.

For the carry forward of property losses, it is necessary that the **property business should be continued.** Therefore, if Glenda ceases the property letting business, the losses carried forward would not be allowed against any other income.

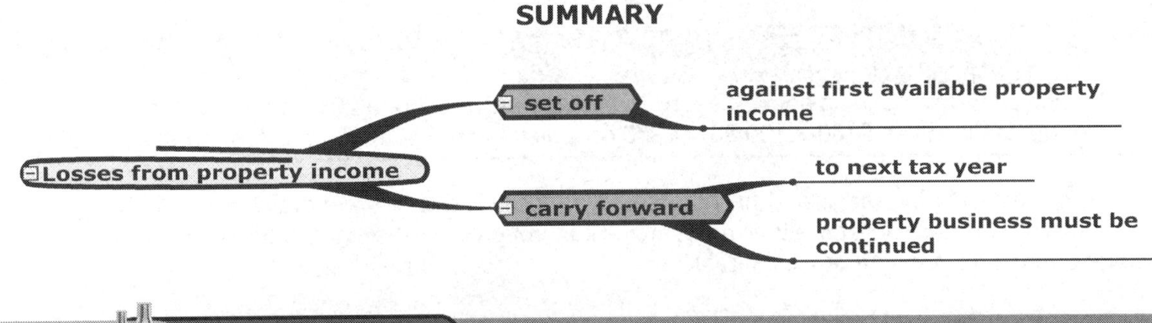

Test Yourself 5

Ronny prepares his accounts up to 31 March every year. He owns two shops, and a flat, which he has rented out. Rent on the property is due quarterly, in advance, on 1 January, 1 April etc. The details of the property rented out during the year ended 31 March 2013 are:

- Shop 1 was let out at £1,800 p.a. throughout the year.
- Shop 2 was let out at £3,400 p.a. from 1 May 2012.
- The flat was let throughout the year at £1,300 p.a., and was unfurnished.

Ronny incurs the following expenses:

- Repairs to shop 1 in January 2013, £5,300.
- Insurance per shop £900 p.a., for flat £350.
- Interest on loan taken to purchase shop 2, £2,100.
- Advertisement expenses for obtaining tenants for shop 2, £200.

Required:

Compute property income / loss. In the case of a loss, explain the loss relief provisions.

5. Compute the tax payable on savings income.[2]

[Learning Outcome f]

Many people have savings (such as bank savings accounts). Savings income consists of:

- Interest on debentures and loan stock paid by UK companies to individuals
- Bank interest
- Building Society interest

Tip

Building society: A building society is very similar to a bank. It is an organisation which offers customers the opportunity to invest their money in a variety of accounts for a given rate of interest. Building societies typically offer services such as mortgage lending and investment planning.

Savings income is usually received **net of tax at 20%, which** means that at the time of receiving the income the basic rate tax is already deducted at source. The amount received has to be grossed up, by multiplying it by **100/80** to include it as gross income in the income tax computation. The tax deducted at source is deducted while computing tax payable.

Tip

In the exam, make sure you read the question carefully to assess whether the amount of saving income is given gross or net.

If the net amount received or credited is given, you should gross up the figure at the rate of 20%, for the tax computation.

Example

The interest received from a building society is £160. This amount is net of a 20% tax deduction.
The equivalent gross income is £160 × 100/80 = £200 on which tax of £40 (20% of £200) has been suffered.

Although the interest paid by banks and building societies to individuals is generally paid net of 20% tax, if a recipient is not liable to tax, he can either recover the tax suffered, or he can certify in advance that he is a non-taxpayer and can receive the gross interest.

Tax on savings income

Savings income is taxed after non-savings income.
Income tax is charged first on non-savings income, which is income from employment, self-employment and property, then on savings income and finally on dividend income. Tax rates and income tax calculations are covered in detail in Study Guide B5.

When is interest taxable?

Interest is taxable in the **tax year that it is paid to the taxpayer,** or credited to his account, **even if part of it has been earned in the previous tax year.** So, the taxpayer does not have to include the gross interest earned in the current year if it has not been paid yet.

SUMMARY

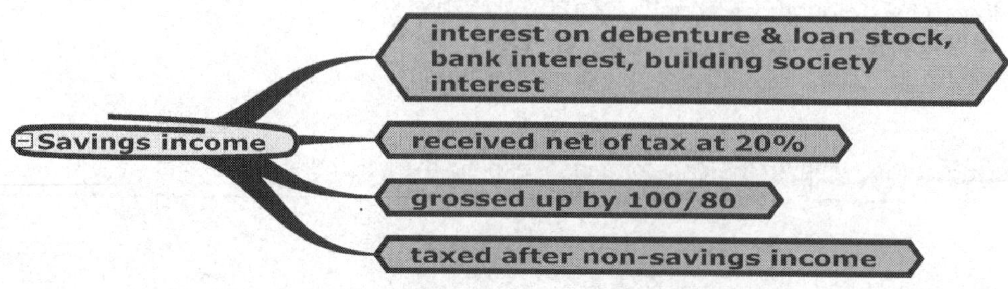

Test Yourself 6

John Smith has the following income and payments for the tax year 2012-13.

- Salary £32,500 (gross; PAYE deducted of £2,500)
- Bank interest £2,400 (net)
- Building society interest £800 (net)
- Interest paid on loan for qualifying purposes £2,000 (net)

Required:

Compute his total income for 2012-13.

6. Compute the tax payable on dividend income.[2]

[Learning Outcome g]

6.1 Dividend income

Dividends from UK shares are deemed to be received **net of a 10% tax credit. Therefore any dividend received needs to be grossed up by 100/90 for inclusion in income tax computation.**

Example

You receive £180 as a dividend from a UK company. Dividends are received net of a 10% tax credit. To find the gross amount of the dividend, multiply the net amount by 100/90.

In this case, the gross dividend is 180 x 100/90 = £200, which is the amount entered into the income tax computation, with a tax credit of £20 (£200 - £180).

The amount of dividend received from UK company shares is grossed up by multiplying it by **100/90.** The gross amount is included in the income tax computation. The tax credit can be **deducted** in computing tax payable, **but any excess tax credit cannot be repaid under any circumstances.** Therefore, tax credits on dividends should always be deducted first to reduce an individual's tax liability and to ensure that the credit is not lost.

The government provides a 'tax credit' to shareholders amounting to 10% of the dividend income, to take account of the fact that dividends are paid out of profits that have been already taxed (the company which is paying the dividend must have already paid tax, and a dividend is paid from profits remaining after paying corporation tax). Therefore, when dividends are issued, you will receive a statement showing how much was paid and the amount of the tax credit.

6.2 Tax on Dividend Income

There are three levels of tax on dividends. Basic rate taxpayers are taxed at 10%, which is covered by the tax credit issued, so there is no further tax to pay. Higher rate taxpayers pay 32.5% less 10% tax credit (i.e. effective rate of tax of 22.5% of the gross dividend). Additional rate taxpayers pay a 42.5% less 10% tax credit (i.e. effective rate of tax of 32.5% of the gross dividend income).

The rate at which tax is payable depends on whether the overall taxable income (after allowances) falls within or above the basic rate (£34,370) or higher rate (£150,000) income tax limit. Tax rates on dividends have been discussed in detail in Study Guide B5.

SUMMARY

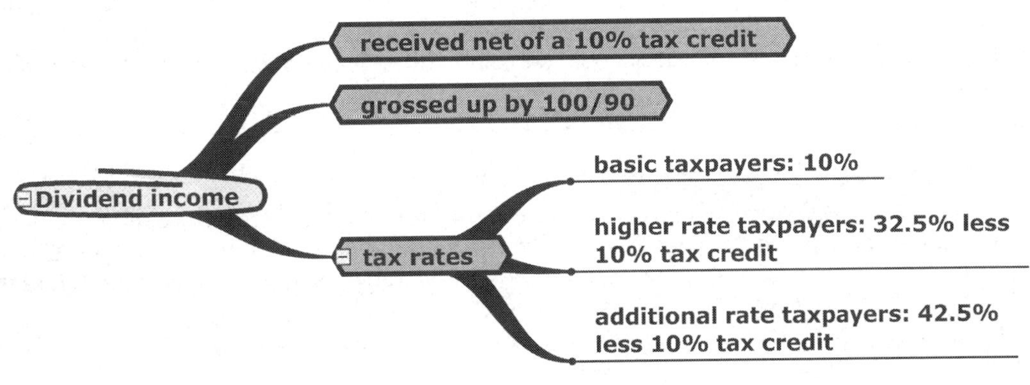

Jack has taxable Income as follows:

- £52,500 Employment income (Gross, PAYE deducted £4,500)
- £4,000 Interest income (net)
- £4,200 Dividend income (net)

Required:

Compute Jack's total income.

---

7. Explain the treatment of individual savings accounts (ISAs) and other tax exempt investments.[1]

[Learning Outcome h]

7.1 Individual Savings Account (ISA)

What is an Individual Savings Account (ISA)?

An ISA is a financial product available in the UK. It is a **tax efficient** way of **saving or investing**. An ISA investment will be free from UK income tax and capital gains tax.

An ISA can contain **two components**

1. **A cash component:** cash ISAs' allow savers to invest their money to accrue interest just like it would in an ordinary bank or building society account, but with the advantage of receiving interest tax-free. Cash ISAs can be a useful place to put money in order to receive tax-free interest and have easy access at relatively short notice.

2. **A stocks and shares component:** share ISAs' will invest in the stock market. As a consequence, the risk profile of the ISA may be anything from low to high. Share ISAs' should, like all stock market investments, may be volatile.

Subscription limits for ISA

There are restrictions on how much an individual can invest in an ISA in each tax year (6 April to the following 5 April).

The amounts which may be deposited in an ISA in a tax year are fixed by law. The overall limit for investment in ISA in 2012-13 is £11,280.

The individual limits for cash ISAs' and stocks and shares ISAs' are:

a) Cash ISA: up to a maximum of £5,640.
b) Stocks and shares ISA: up to a maximum of £11,280.
c) The overall limit for investment in both ISA's is £11,280.

Example

Nikon Ltd offers an ISA that contains a cash component and a stocks and shares component. Their investors can subscribe up to £5,640 to the cash component ISA, and can subscribe the remaining £5,640 to the stocks and shares component. Alternatively, investors could subscribe an overall amount of £11,280 to the stocks and shares component.

Example

Jones invests £2,000 in cash ISA in the year 2012-13. In that same year he can invest up to £9,280 in a stocks and shares ISA. Alternatively, he can also invest a further £3,640 in his cash ISA, and up to £5,640 in a stocks and shares ISA.

Important points to note

i. Any UK resident individual of at least **eighteen years of age** can invest in **one ISA,** with both components provided by a single financial institution.

ii. Alternatively, a person can invest in **two ISAs,** one for each component i.e. cash component and a stocks and shares component. The two ISAs' may be with two different providers if the investor wishes.

iii. UK resident individuals aged between 16 and 18 can also open cash ISAs', but they cannot invest in stock and shares ISA until they reach the age of 18 years. For children under the age of 18 a new junior ISA has been introduced. Junior ISAs are not examinable.

Tax treatment of income arising from ISA

- All income (dividends, interest and bonuses) received from ISA investments are free of any further tax (although the 10% tax credit will still attach to any dividends received).
- All capital gains arising on ISA investments are exempt from capital gains tax.

7.2 Other tax-exempt investments

National Saving Certificates

It is a tax efficient way of saving money. National saving products are a popular mode of investment mainly because of their risk-free nature.

National savings offer various investment products, some of which are tax-free e.g. national savings certificates, children's bonus bonds etc. The income from these investments is exempt from income tax as well as capital gains tax.

National savings also offers some taxable investment products e.g. investment accounts, easy access savings accounts etc. The income on these investments is usually paid gross and taxed as savings income.

SUMMARY

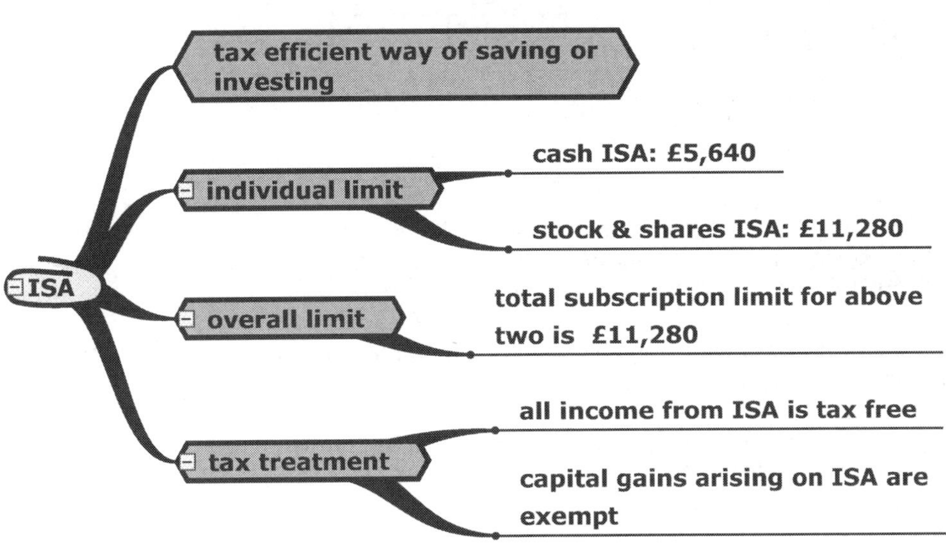

Answers to Test Yourself

Answer to TY 1

	£
Gross premium	12,000
Less: £12,000 (2% x (12 -1))	(2,640)
Property income for premium	**9,360**

Answer to TY 2

		Shop 1 £	Shop 2 £	Shop 3 £	Flat £	Office £	Total £
Rent accrued							
Shop 1		5,500					5,500
Shop 2 (1/12/12 to 31/03/13) (£6,600/12 x 4)			2,200				2,200
Shop 3 (1/04/12 to 30/06/12) (£7,500/12 x 3)				1,875			1,875
Furnished flat					2,500		2,500
Office building							
Rent £6,000/12 x 6						3,000	3,000
Lease premium							
Gross premium	20,000					16,400	16,400
Less: £20,000 x (2% x (10 - 1))	(3,600)						
Net lease premium	**16,400**						
Total rent accrued (a)		**5,500**	**2,200**	**1,875**	**2,500**	**19,400**	**31,475**
Less: Expenses							
Repairs		2,000					2,000
Bad debts (note 4)				875			875
Insurance		500	500	500	200	2,100	3,800
Interest on loan			1,500				1,500
Advertising expenses for obtaining tenants			1,200			1,000	2,200
10% wear and tear on furnished flat (£2,500 x 10%) (note 3)					250		250
Total expenses incurred (b)		**2,500**	**3,200**	**1,375**	**450**	**3,100**	**10,625**
Property business profit (a - b)		**3,000**	**(1,000)**	**500**	**2,050**	**16,300**	**20,850**

Net property business profit is **£20,850.**

Notes

1. All property receipts and all property expenses are pooled to give an overall profit or loss figure for the year. The losses from the running of one property business are automatically set-off against the income from other property businesses.

2. The property business loss of shop 2 is automatically set off against other property business income. (Refer to Learning Outcome 4).

3. 10% wear and tear allowance is allowed as a deduction for the furnished property. It is calculated at the rate of 10% of rent less any liabilities of the tenant paid by the landlord.
4. Only £1,000 could be recovered out of £1,875, so £875 is a bad debt.

Answer to TY 3

To qualify as a furnished holiday letting, the property must satisfy the following conditions:

(a) available for commercial letting to the public for at least 210 days in a tax year,
(b) is actually so let in this period for at least 105 days, and
(c) is not normally in the same occupation for more than 31 days at a time, any longer term occupation must not exceed 155 days.

The cottage does not satisfy the first condition as the property was available for commercial use only for 126 days (1 December 2012 to 5 April 2013). Therefore, it will not be considered furnished holiday accommodation. The rent earned from this property would be assessed under normal property income rules and would not qualify as income from “commercial letting of furnished holiday accommodation’.

Answer to TY 4

1. **By applying rent-a-room relief**

	£
Rent	5,833
Less: Rent-a-room relief	(4,250)
Property business income assessable to tax	**1,583**

House rented on 1/06/2012 to 31/03/2013 i.e. 10 months. So, rent = £7,000 x 10/12 = £5,833

2. **By applying normal property business income rules**

	£	£
Rent		5,833
Less: Expenses		
Agent commission for obtaining tenant	(350)	
Repairs of the staircase	(420)	
Insurance	(600)	(1,370)
Property business income assessable to tax		**4,463**

Thus, as income assessable to tax is lower in option 1, it is advisable to obtain rent-a-room relief and show £1,583 as income chargeable to tax.

Answer to TY 5

	Shop 1 £	**Shop 2** £	**Flat** £	**Total** £
Rent accrued				
Shop 1	1,800			1,800
Shop 2 (1/05/2012 to 31/03/2012) (£3,400/12 x 11)		3,117		3,117
Flat			1,300	1,300
Total rent accrued (a)	**1,800**	**3,117**	**1,300**	**6,217**
Less: Expenses				
Repairs	5,300			5,300
Interest on loan to purchase property		2,100		2,100
Insurance	900	900	350	2,150
Advertising expenses for obtaining tenants		200		200
Total expenses incurred (b)	**6,200**	**3,200**	**350**	**9,750**
Property business profit (a - b)	**(4,400)**	**(83)**	**950**	**(3,533)**

Net loss is £3,533. This loss of the property business can be carried forward to the next tax year i.e. tax year 2013-14.

The carried forward loss must be set off against the first available property income arising in the subsequent tax years. For example in 2013-14, if Ronny's property business income is £6,500, then the carried forward loss of £3,533 will be first set off against this, so the taxable income for 2013-14 will be (£6,500 - £3,533 = £2,967).

For the carry forward of property business losses, it is necessary that the **property business should be continued.** Therefore, if Ronny ceases the property letting business, then the carry forward of property business losses is not allowed.

Answer to TY 6

While calculating John's total income, ensure all his income has been grossed up.

John Smith's total income calculation for 2012-13 is as follows:

	Non savings £	Savings income £	Total income £
Income from employment	32,500		32,500
Building society interest (£800 x 100/80)	-	1,000	1,000
Bank interest (£2,400 x 100/80)	-	3,000	3,000
	32,500	**4,000**	**36,500**
Less: Interest paid	(2,000)		(2,000)
Total Income	**30,500**	**4,000**	**34,500**

Note: the building society and bank interest received were £800 and £2,400 respectively. They have each been grossed up by multiplying by 100/80 to take account of the 20% tax withheld at source.

Answer to TY 7

Jack's total income is computed as follows:

	Non savings income £	Savings income £	Dividend income £	Total income £
Income from employment	52,500			52,500
Interest income (W1)		5,000		5,000
Dividend income (W1)		-	4,667	4,667
Total Income	**52,500**	**5,000**	**4,667**	**62,167**

Workings

W1

Jack's interest income and dividend income needs to be grossed up to take account of income tax deducted at source:

Savings income = £4,000 x 100/80 = £5,000
Dividend income = £4,200 x 100/90 = £4,667

Quick Quiz

State whether true or false

1. Rent a room relief is available in full even if the property was not let out throughout the year.
2. A short lease is a lease granted for a period of 30 years or less.
3. Non-savings income is taxed after savings income.

Answers to Quick Quiz

1. True, rent a room relief is never apportioned on a time basis.
2. False, a short lease is a lease granted for a period of 50 years or less.
3. False, savings income is taxed after non-savings income.

Self Examination Questions

Question 1

What are the advantages of property income being treated as income from furnished holiday accommodation?

Question 2

What is the treatment of a premium received on short lease?

Question 3

When is interest taxable?

Question 4

In 2012-13 Thelma received income from property. Details of the income and corresponding expenses were:

1. Rent from letting out a room in her house for £2,600. The repairs expenditure incurred on this room was £3,200.

2. Rent from a furnished flat. The flat had been let on a lease which expired on 30 June 2012 at an annual rent of £5,500. The property was re-let from 1st July 2012 on a nine-year lease, at an annual rent of £6,000. In addition, the incoming tenant was required to pay a premium of £4,000. Thelma elects to claim wear and tear allowance on this property.

   Expenditure in the year ended 5 April 2013 was:

   a) insurance of £350 was paid.
   b) water rates and council tax £1,400.
   c) sundry repairs £650.

   The rent on both leases was paid in advance on the usual quarter days, 25 March, 24 June, 29 September and 25 December.

3. The rent received from a furnished cottage was £5,200 and the following expenditure was incurred:

	£
Insurance	600
Water rates and council tax	900
Sundry repairs and decorating	350
Cleaning	240
Bad debts	200
Advertising	300
Capital allowances on furniture and fittings, adjusted for private use	500
	3,090

Thelma stayed in the cottage for the whole of August, but it was let out for the remainder of the year.

Required:

Calculate Thelma's property income for the year 2012-13.

Question 5

Sally received the following investment income for the tax year 2012-13:

- Salary £63,000 (gross; PAYE £7,200 deducted)
- Building society interest £2,400 (net)
- UK dividend income of £1,800
- Interest of £700 from an Individual Savings Account (ISA)
- Interest paid on loan for qualifying purposes £1,000

The above amounts are considered to be the cash amounts received.

Required:

Compute her total income for 2012-13.

Question 6

Pharoh has let out two properties in 2012-2013

Property one

It is a freehold house and is let out as a furnished holiday letting for 18 weeks at £325 per week.
In June 2012, £2,925 was spent on furniture and kitchen equipment.
Other allowable expenses incurred comes to £9,995

Property two

It is a freehold house and is let out as furnished property for the whole of tax year 2012-13 at £515 per month payable in advance
Other allowable expenses incurred comes to £10,200

Required:

(a) Compute Pharoh's furnished holiday letting loss 2012-13
(b) Compute Pharoh's property business loss 2012-13 and state how it can be set off.

Answers to Self Examination Questions

Answer to SEQ 1

The tax advantages of property income being treated as income from furnished holiday accommodation are:

1. the income qualifies as 'net relevant income' for the purpose of pension contributions,

2. certain capital gains tax reliefs, e.g. rollover relief, entrepreneur's relief and holdover relief are available and

3. capital allowances may be claimed on furniture and fittings.

Answer to SEQ 2

If the lease is granted for a period of 50 years or less then it is termed a short lease. Premiums received on a short lease are assessable to property business income. The amount to be assessed to property income is equal to the amount of the premium reduced by 2% for each year of the lease, except for the first year.

Premium assessable to property business income
= P – P (2% x (n- 1))

Where, P = Premium
n = no. of years of lease

Answer to SEQ 3

Interest is taxable in the **tax year that it is paid to the taxpayer,** or credited to his account, **even if part of it has been earned in the previous tax year.** So a taxpayer does not have to include the gross interest earned in the current year when working out his taxable income if it has not been paid yet.

Answer to SEQ 4

		Room £	Furnished flat £	Cottage £	Total £
Rent accrued					
Room in house (note)		2,600			2,600
Furnished flat:					
Rent (£5,500/12 x 3)			1,375		1,375
Rent (£6,000/12 x 9)			4,500		4,500
Lease premium					
Gross premium	4,000				
Less: £4,000 x (2% x (9 - 1))	(640)		3,360		3,360
Net lease premium	**3,360**				
Cottage				5,200	5,200
Total rent accrued (a)		**2,600**	**9,235**	**5,200**	**17,035**
Less: **Expenses**					
Repairs (W1)		3,200	650	321	4,171
Water rates and council rates (W1)			1,400	825	2,225
Insurance (W1)			350	550	900
Cleaning (W1)				220	220
Advertising				300	300
Bad debts				200	200
10% wear and tear (W2)			448	438	886
Total expenses incurred (b)		**3,200**	**2,848**	**2,854**	**8,902**
Property business profit (a - b)		**(600)**	**6,387**	**2,346**	**8,133**

Net property business profit is **£8,133.**

Note: if rent a room relief is claimed, the amount up to £4,250 is exempt. As the rent received is less than £4,250, if rent a room relief is claimed, the taxable income will be nil.
However, it is beneficial not to claim rent a room relief as a loss arising after deduction of allowable expenses, i.e. (£2,600 - £3,200 = £600) can be claimed to offset against other income.

Total expenses for one year are £350. Therefore for 1 month they are 350/12 = £29

Workings

W1

It is stated that the cottage was occupied by Thelma for the month of August. Hence the following expenses will be proportionately reduced for private use.

	Total expenses £	Deduction for private use £	Expenses allowed £
1) Repairs	350	29 (350/12 x 1)	321
2) Water rates and council rates	900	75 (900/12 x 1)	825
3) Insurance	600	50 (600/12 x 1)	550
4) Cleaning	240	20 (240/12 x 1)	220

W2 Wear and tear allowance

The wear and tear allowance is available on letting out the furnished property, hence it will be available on both furnished flat and furnished cottage.
The 'wear and tear' allowance is 10% of the rent (excluding lease premium) less the items which would normally be the tenant's responsibility, i.e. water rates and council tax.

	Furnished flat £	Cottage £
Rent:		
Furnished flat (£1,375 + £4,500)	5,875	
Cottage		5,200
Less: Water rates and council tax	(1400)	(825)
	4,475	**4,375**
Wear and tear allowance 10%	**448**	**438**

Answer to SEQ 5

Sally's total income calculation for 2012-13 is as follows:

	Non savings £	Savings income £	Dividend income £	Total income £
Income from employment	63,000			63,000
Building society interest (£2,400 x 100/80)		3,000		3,000
Dividend (1,800 x 100/90)			2,000	2,000
ISA interest - exempt				
	63,000	3,000	2,000	68,000
Less: Interest paid	(1,000)			(1,000)
Total Income	**62,000**	**3,000**	**2,000**	**67,000**

Note: Income from ISAs is exempt from income tax

Answer to SEQ 6

(a) Pharoh – Furnished holiday letting loss 2012-13

	£	£
Rent receivable (325 x 18)		5,850
Expenses	9,995	
Capital allowances - FYA (2,925 x100%)	2,925	(12,920)
Furnished holiday letting loss		(7,070)

(b) Pharoh – Property business loss 2012-13

	£	£
Rent receivable (515 x 12)		6,180
Expenses	10,200	
Wear and tear allowance (6180 x 10%)	618	(10,818)
Furnished holiday letting loss		(4,638)

Property business loss

- The loss incurred in the furnished holiday letting can be carried forward and relieved against the first available profit from furnished holiday letting only.
- The loss incurred in property business is carried forward and relieved against the first available profit from property business only.

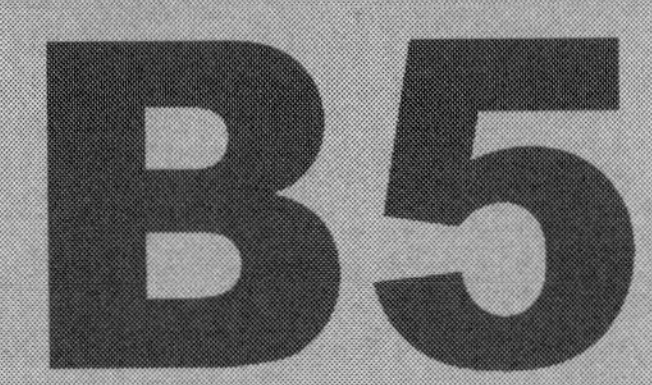

STUDY GUIDE B5: THE COMPREHENSIVE COMPUTATION OF TAXABLE INCOME AND INCOME TAX LIABILITY

Get Through Intro

In this Study Guide we look at how the different types of an individual's income are classified, and the types of expenditure that can obtain tax relief. The sum of the different types of income, less allowable deductions gives the taxable income figure. We will then see how to calculate the income tax on this figure, noting that different types of income are taxed at different rates of income tax.

In your work as an accountant, you will need to calculate the income tax liability of clients, and also give advice on how to minimise their tax liability.

This Study Guide is very important from an exam point of view. The first question in your exam will be on income tax. In addition, aspects of this Study Guide are likely to be examined in other questions.

You need to make sure that you have a thorough understanding of this Study Guide.

Learning Outcomes

a) Prepare a basic income tax computation involving different types of income.
b) Calculate the amount of personal allowance available generally, and for people aged 65 and above.
c) Compute the amount of income tax payable.
d) Explain the treatment of interest paid for a qualifying purpose.
e) Explain the treatment of qualifying charitable donations.
f) Explain the treatment of property owned jointly by a married couple, or by a couple in a civil partnership.

Introduction

McMilan is a sole trader, earning trading income. In addition he receives bank interest and dividends. These three different types of income are all charged income tax at different rates.

You are given the rates in your tax rates and allowances in the exam, but it is essential that you know how to apply the rates.

This Study Guide explains the steps to follow in order to get the calculation correct.

1. Prepare a basic income tax computation involving different types of income.[2] [Learning Outcome a]

Income tax is a tax on the earnings or income of individuals which they receive in different ways from different sources. Not all the income is taxable. Individuals are taxed only on 'taxable income' above a certain level. Income tax assessments of a taxpayer are computed for a tax year, taking into consideration his aggregate income for that year from all sources, and ignoring any income which is exempt from tax. Some basic concepts are as follows:

1. All adults and children are charged to income tax if they receive sufficient income to pay tax.

2. They are liable to income tax on their taxable income in a tax year.

3. A tax year runs from 6 April to the following 5 April. The exam will cover the period from 6 April 2012 to 5 April 2013, written as 2012-13.

4. Taxable income is made up of:

- income from all sources
- payments that are tax deductible
- personal allowances

The basic calculation of income tax payable is as follows:

Calculation of income tax payable	£
Earned income	X
Investment income	X
Total Income	**X**
Less: Payments that are tax deductible	(X)
Net income	**X**
Less: Personal allowances	(X)
Taxable income	**X**
Income tax liability	**X**
Less: Tax suffered	(X)
Income tax payable	**X**

1.1 Taxable persons

Each individual is liable for tax on his own income. In general, a UK resident is liable to pay income tax for all his income arising during the tax year (whether it arises in the UK or abroad). Individuals who are not UK residents are generally only liable to pay tax on their UK source income. Income tax is payable by:

1. **adults:** on their income and on their share of income of a partnership.
2. **children:** if they have taxable income.

1.2 Income tax computation

The total income of an individual comprises:

1. earned income
2. investment income

Earned income consists of:

- income from employment
- income from self-employment (as a sole trader or partner)

Investment income consists of:

- savings income (e.g. bank interest, building society interest)
- dividend income
- other income from investments (property income)

In order to calculate taxable income, we need to look at the various types of income.

Income is either:

- exempt from income tax, or
- taxable.

Taxable income is either:

- taxed before it is received by the taxpayer (taxed at source), or
- tax is paid by the taxpayer through self assessment (income received gross).

In order to calculate taxable income, earned and investment income is aggregated. Exempt income is excluded.

Income taxed at source

All taxable income is included in the calculation of an individual's taxable income, whether it is received gross (and taxed by self assessment) or received net (tax already deducted before being paid to the individual).

The statement of taxable income consists of the gross amount of income from all sources as the amount of tax already deducted may be too small or too large. The gross amount is charged to tax, and then the tax already deducted is taken into account.

Income taxed at source may have different rates of tax deducted:

	Received net of
Building society interest	20% tax
Bank interest (except National Savings Bank interest)	20% tax
Debenture interest	20% tax
Patent royalties	20% tax
UK dividends	10% tax
Employment income	Various rates (paid net under PAYE – Pay As You Earn scheme)

Important point to note

- Most interest is received net of 20% tax.
- Building society interest is treated in the same way as bank interest.
- Care must be taken in the exam to determine if the income given to you is gross, or net (after the tax has been deducted).
- If bank interest, for example is given net, then multiply this figure by 100/80 to find the gross figure for the calculation of taxable income.
- If you are given the net figure for bank interest, to find the tax deducted, multiply the net figure by 20/80.

Income taxed by self assessment

Some income is received gross. The individual is liable to pay tax to HMRC via self-assessment at a later date.

The main types of income received gross are:

- trading income (income from self-employment or partnership income)
- property income (income from letting out land and buildings)
- interest received gross

Interest received gross

Most of the interest income is received net of 20% tax.

The main types of interest received gross are:

- National Savings Bank interest (NSB)
- Interest from Government securities

Total income is the total figure charged to tax, however, different categories of income are charged at different rates, so the total income needs to be categorised.

The categories are as follows:

- non-savings income
- savings income
- dividend income

Non-savings income	Savings income	Dividends
Employment income Pension income Trading income Property income Patent royalties	Interest received gross Interest received net	UK dividends

The total income, less any tax deductible payments is known as **net income**.

Every individual is entitled to a personal allowance (explained in detail later in this Study Guide), and this is deducted from the **net income** to give the **taxable income.** Thus, the taxable income is net income less the personal allowance.

1.3 Income exempt from tax

Certain types of income are completely exempt from income tax. Some of the important sources of non-taxable income are:

1. scholarship income
2. interest on National Saving Certificates.
3. winnings from betting, national lottery and premium bond prizes.
4. income of up to £4,250 per annum received under the "rent–a-room" scheme (see Study Guide B4 for more details).
5. statutory redundancy pay and the first £30,000 of compensation received for loss of employment.
6. interest received from HMRC (repayment supplement).
7. certain social security benefits like child benefit and housing benefit.

2. Calculate the amount of personal allowance available generally, and for people aged 65 and above.[2]

[Learning Outcome b]

2.1 Personal Allowance (PA)

Every individual is entitled to a personal allowance. **The standard personal allowance for 2012-13 is £8,105.** However, this limit is reduced if the taxpayer's adjusted net income exceeds £100,000. The personal allowance is reduced by one half of the excess if the taxpayer's adjusted net income exceeds £100,000. Therefore, if the adjusted net income of a taxpayer is £116,210 or more, the personal allowance available to them will be nil i.e. (£8,105 - ½ x (116,210 – 100,000)).

The adjusted net income is calculated as follows:

	£
Earned income	X
Investment income	X
Total income	**X**
Less: Amounts that are tax deductible	
Loss reliefs	(X)
Interest payments	(X)
Net income	**X**
Less: Personal pension contributions (gross)	(X)
Less: Qualifying charitable donations (gross) (discussed in detail in Learning Outcome 5)	(X)
Adjusted net income	**X**

Personal pension contributions are discussed in detail in Study Guide B6.

Therefore, to claim the maximum amount of personal allowance, an individual can make the higher contributions into their personal pension scheme and qualifying charitable donations to enable their adjusted net income figure to be below £100,000.

The standard personal allowance and the income limit for it is given to you in the rates and allowances section in the exam. The personal allowance is deducted from net income. If there is insufficient income to absorb the allowance, it is lost.

The personal allowance is never time apportioned. It is always allowed in full.

Tip

Personal allowance cannot be carried forward to the next year or be used to create a tax loss.

Income is categorised into non-savings, savings and dividend income. The personal allowance must be set off against non-savings income, then, if it is not fully utilised, against savings income and finally dividend income.

Example

John, a taxpayer aged 40 has an adjusted net income of £108,250 for 2012-13. The maximum net income limit for 2012-13 is £100,000. John's net income exceeds the limit by £8,250 (£108,250 - £100,000).
The standard personal allowance of £8,105 will be reduced by one half of the excess. Therefore, the personal allowance available to John is (£8,105 - ½ x £8,250) = £3,980.

Test Yourself 1

Calculate the personal allowances available to each of the following taxpayers, all below the age of 65 for the tax year 2012-13.

	Employment Income £	Trading Income £	Savings Income (Net) £	Personal pension contribution (net) £	Qualifying charitable donations (net) £
Greg	48,750		800	1,200	-
Adam		102,650	3,400		1,400
Fred		157,800	10,400	-	3,200
Ivan	146,000			25,600	1,600

2.2 Personal Age Allowance (PAA)

As older people living off a pension are likely to have a smaller income than people working, they are given a higher age allowance, instead of the standard personal allowance. The amount of the allowance is dependent on their age and their net income.

A personal age allowance is available to a taxpayer who is **65 or over** at any time in the tax year. The amounts of allowances available are as follows:

	2011-12 £
Personal allowance for people aged 65 - 74	10,500
Personal allowance for people aged 75 and over	10,660
Income limit for age-related allowances	25,400

These figures are given to you in the exam in the rates and allowances section, so you don't need to memorise them.

Tip

A taxpayer is considered to be:

- 65 if his 65th birthday falls anywhere in the tax year.
- 75 if his 75th birthday falls anywhere in the tax year.

The personal age allowances are reduced if the taxpayer's net income exceeds a set limit. The set limit for 2012-13 is £25,400. If a taxpayer's net income **exceeds £25,400**, the **personal age allowance** is **reduced by one half of the excess**. It is important to note that this reduction may only reduce the personal age allowance to the basic amount of £8,105.

Example

John, a taxpayer aged 67 has a net income of £25,500 for 2012-13. The maximum net income limit for 2012-13 is £25,400. John's net income exceeds the limit by £100. Therefore, the personal age allowance of £10,500 available to him will be reduced by one half of the excess.

Hence, the personal age allowance available to John is (£10,500 - ½ x £100) = £10,450.

However, the income limit of £100,000, which is applicable to personal allowances, is also applicable to taxpayers over 65 years of age. Therefore, this limit of personal age allowance is further reduced if the adjusted net income of the taxpayer exceeds £100,000. Thus, despite an individual being 65 years or more, no personal allowance is available if their income is £116,210 or above.

SUMMARY

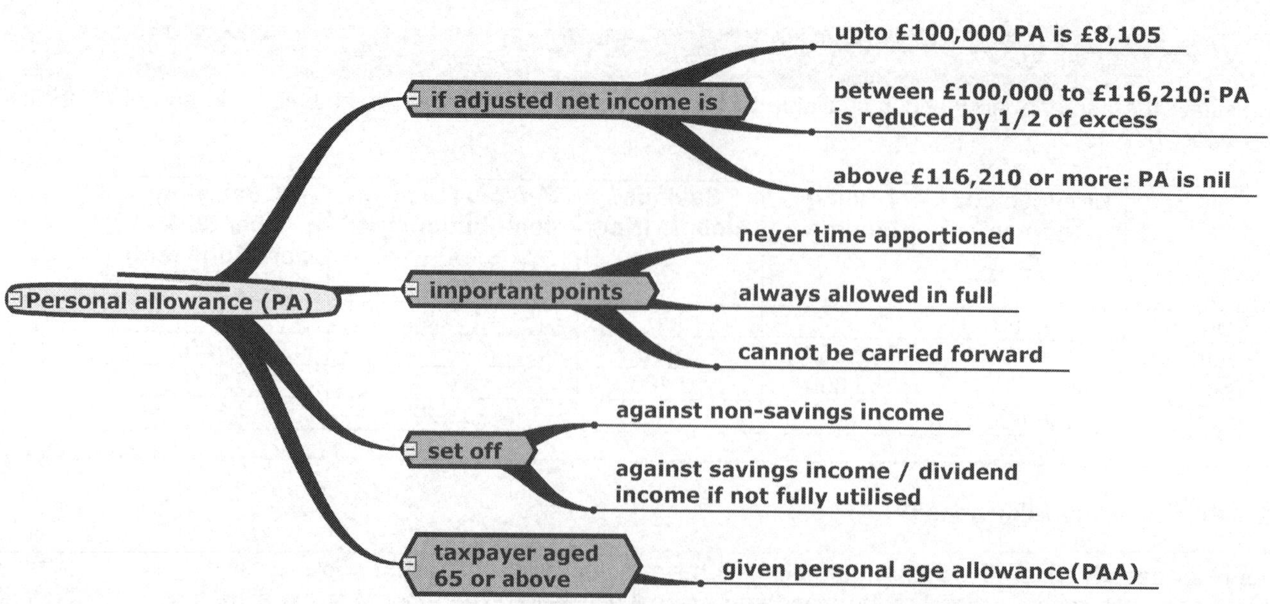

Test Yourself 2

Calculate the personal allowances available in 2011-12 for the following taxpayers:

1. Barry, born on 12 January 1949 with net income of £32,000 in 2012-13.
2. Charles, born on 23 August 1947 with net income of £14,300 in 2012-13.
3. David, born on 10 July 1937 with net income of £9,800 in 2012-13.
4. Edwin, born on 5 October 1946 with net income of £26,100 in 2012-13.
5. Adam, born on 1 November 1934 with net income of £104,200 in 2012-13.

---

3. Compute the amount of income tax payable.[2]

[Learning Outcome c]

Once the income has been categorised and the personal allowance deducted (from non-savings income, then savings income and dividends) the income tax liability can be calculated.

Previously, the tax rates were mainly divided into three categories:
- the starting rate of 10% (applicable only for savings income on fulfillment of certain criteria);
- the basic rate of 20%; and
- the higher rate of 32.5% and 40%.

However, from the tax year 2011-12, a new rate of 50% has been introduced as an additional rate where the taxable income of an individual exceeds £150,000.

For the computation of income tax liability, it is necessary to arrange the taxable income in 'slices', with non-savings income at the bottom, followed by savings income and then dividend income.

Allocation of tax bands and tax rates against different categories (slices) of taxable income is as follows:

3.1 Non-savings income

For the tax year 2012-13, non-savings income, which is the bottom slice of taxable income, is taxed at the following rates:

Income tax band	Income tax rate
£1 - £34,370	Basic rate of 20%
£34,371 to £150,000	Higher rate of 40%
Over £150,000	Additional rate of 50%

Example

In 2012-13 Arthur, Edwina and Cordelia receive the following trading income:

	£
Arthur	78,560
Edwina	109,800
Cordelia	174,200

Assuming that they receive no other income and had made no contributions towards pension schemes, their tax liability for 2012-13 will be as follows:

Arthur	**£**
Trading income	78,560
Less: Personal allowance (Note 1)	(8,105)
Taxable income	**70,455**
Income tax liability	
Basic rate band: £1 to £34,370 at 20%	6,874
Higher rate band: £34,371 to £70455 at 40%	14,434
Income tax liability	**21,308**

Continued on the next page

Edwina	£
Trading income	109,800
Less: Personal allowance (Note 2)	(3,205)
Taxable income	**106,595**
Income tax liability	
Basic rate band: £1 to £34,370 at 20%	6,874
Higher rate band: £34,371 to £106,595 at 40%	28,890
Income tax liability	**35,764**

Cordelia	£
Trading income	174,200
Less: Personal allowance	nil
Taxable income	**174,200**
Income tax liability (Note 3)	
Basic rate band: £1 to £34,370 at 20%	6,874
Higher rate band: £34,371 to £150,000 at 40%	46,252
Additional rate band: £150,001 to £174,200 at 50%	12,100
Income tax liability	**65,226**

Notes

1. As Arthur's adjusted net income is below £100,000, he is entitled to a standard personal allowance of £8,105.
2. Edwina's adjusted net income is above £100,000 but below £116,210, therefore her personal allowance of £8,105 is reduced to: £8,105 – 1/2(£109,800 – £100,000) = £3,205.
3. Cordelia's adjusted net income is above £116,210; therefore she is not entitled to any personal allowance.

3.2 Savings income

The tax rate bands for the savings income are as follows:

Income Tax Band	Savings income
Starting rate band: £1 to £2,710	10%
Basic rate band: £2,711 to £34,370	20%
Higher rate band: £34,371 to £150,000	40%
Additional rate band: £150,001 and above	50%

Savings income is the second slice of income; it is taxed after non-savings income but before dividend income. A starting rate of 10% is applicable for the first £2,710 of savings income. However this **10% rate applies only where savings income falls within the first £2,710 of total taxable income.**

To determine the applicable tax band for savings income, first check the total of non-savings income. If it is nil or less than £2,710, then the starting rate of 10% will be applicable for the savings income which falls within the starting rate limit of £2,710. But if the non-savings income exceeds the starting rate threshold of £2,710, the starting rate of 10% for savings will not come into the picture at all. In that case the savings income will be taxed at the basic rate of 20% if it falls below the higher rate threshold of £34,370, and at the higher rate of 40% if it exceeds this threshold.

Example

Sophie earns a salary of £8,185, and bank interest of £3,900 (net). Her income tax liability is as follows:

	Total	Non-savings income	Savings income
	£	£	£
Salary	8,185	8,185	
Bank Interest (£3,900 x 100/80)	4,875		4,875
Total / Net income	**13,060**	**8,185**	**4,875**
Less: Personal allowance	(8,105)	(8,105)	-
Taxable income	**4,955**	**80**	**4,875**
Income tax			
Non-savings income	16		
Basic rate: £1 to £80 at 20%			
Savings income			
Starting rate: (falling within first £2,710 of taxable income)	263		
£81 to £2,710) = £2630 at 10%			
Basic rate: £2630 to £4,875 = £2,245 at 20%	449		
Income Tax liability	**728**		

Note: Non savings income does not exceed the starting rate threshold of £2,710, so £2630 (£2,710 - £80) of the savings income is taxed at the starting rate of 10%, and the balance of the savings income, £2,245 (£4,875 - £2,630), is taxed at the basic rate of 20%.

3.3 Dividend income

Dividend income is the top slice of income; it is taxed after non-savings and savings income. To the extent that dividend income falls in the basic rate band it is taxed at 10%. However, if it falls in the higher rate band, it is taxed at 32.5% and if it falls in the additional rate band, it is taxed at 42.5% (not 40% or 50% as for savings income and non-savings income).

Dividend is declared by companies after they have paid corporation tax. Therefore when the dividend is received by an individual there is a 10% tax credit. This is why it is grossed up by 100/90. As long as the dividend income is below the base band of £34,370 it is taxed at 10%. Thus, the individual does not have to pay any further tax on the dividend with the 10% tax credit offsetting the tax payable. If the dividend income falls between £34,370 and £150,000, it will be taxed at the higher rate of 32.5% so that the individual will have to pay an additional tax of 22.5% (32.5% - 10%). If the dividend income exceeds £150,000, then it will be taxed at 42.5% in which case the individual will have to pay additional tax of 32.5% (42.5% - 10%).

Important

The personal allowance is always set off against non-savings income first. If non-savings income does not exceed the personal allowance, then the personal allowance is set off against savings income and finally dividend income.

Summary of tax rates

Income Tax Band	Non-savings income	Savings income	Dividend income
Basic rate band: £1 to £34,370	20%	20%	10%
Higher rate band: £34,371 to £150,000	40%	40%	32.5%
Additional rate band: over £150,000	50%	50%	42.5%

A starting rate of 10% is applicable for savings income that falls within the first £2,710 of taxable income. However, if the non-savings income, which is the bottom slice of income itself, exceeds £2,710, then the starting rate of 10% for saving income will not come into the picture.

Diagram 1: Summary of tax rates

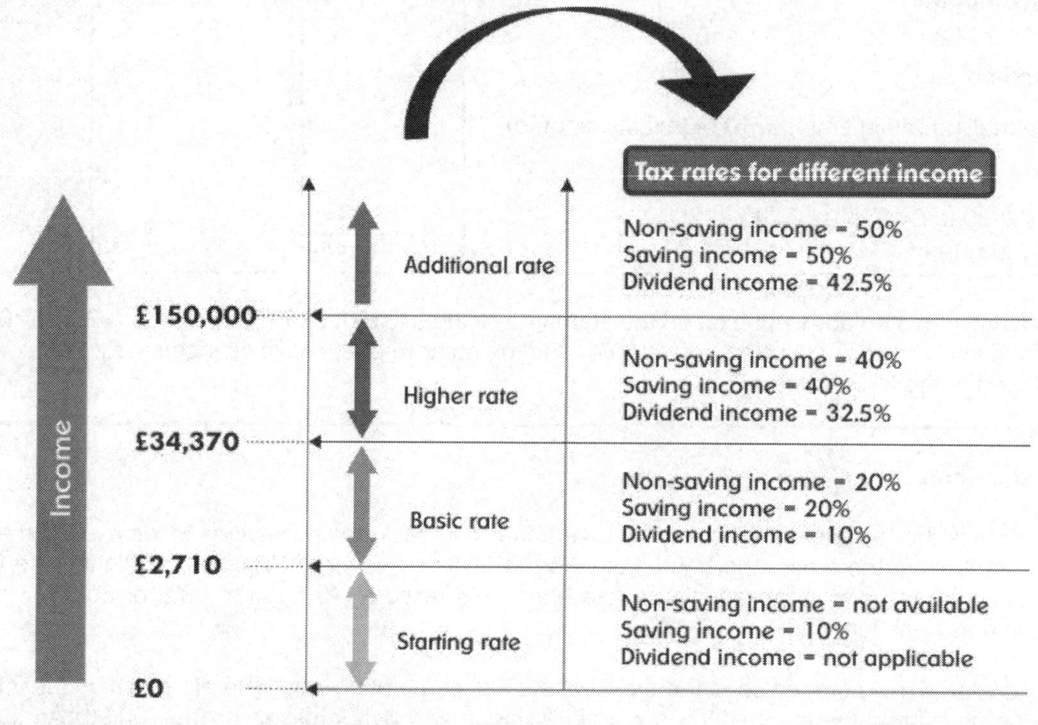

Example

James aged 35 has received the following income in 2012-13:

	£
Salary	22,500
Building society interest (cash amount received)	3,800
Dividends (cash amount received)	18,900

James's income tax liability for 2012-13 is computed as follows:

Continued on the next page

	Total £	Non-savings £	Savings £	Dividends £
Employment income	22,500	22,500		
Building society interest (£3,800 x 100/80)	4,750		4,750	
Dividend income (£18,900 x 100/90)	21,000			21,000
Total / Net Income	**48,250**	**22,500**	**4,750**	**21,000**
Less: PA	(8,105)	(8,105)		
Taxable income	**40,145**	**14,395**	**4,750**	**21,000**
Income tax				
Non-savings: basic rate band (£14,395 x 20%)	2,879			
Savings: basic rate band (£4,750 x 20%)	950			
Dividends: basic rate band (£15,225 x 10%)	1,523			
£ 34,370				
Dividends: higher rate band (£5,775 x 32.5%)	1,877			
Income tax liability	**7,229**			

Steps for calculation of income tax liability

Step 1
Ensure that all James's income has been grossed up if any income tax has been deducted before James received it:

Salary £22,500 (this is the gross amount).
Building society interest: £3,800 x 100/80 = £4,750 (tax of 20% has been deducted).
Dividend income: £18,900 x 100/90 = £21,000 (cash amount of dividends must be grossed up by 100/90).

Step 2
Deduct personal allowance. This is always deducted from non-savings income first, leaving £14,395 (£22,500 - £8,105) of taxable non-savings income.

Step 3

Compute the income tax liability for each category of income, starting with non-savings income, then savings and finally dividend income.

- **Non-savings income**

The first £34,370 of non-savings income is taxed at the basic rate of 20%.
£14,395 x 20% = **£2,879**

- **Savings income**

The savings income of £4,750 is taxed at 20%.
£4,750 x 20% = **£950**

(This is because the sum of non-savings income of £14,395 plus savings income of £4,750 i.e. £19,145 is still within the basic rate band of £34,370).

- **Dividend income**

The dividend income falls partly in the basic rate band and partly in the higher rate band.

The amount falling in the basic rate band is £15,225 (£34,370 - £19,145) and is taxed at 10%.
£15,225 x 10% = **£1,523.**

The amount falling in the higher rate band is £5,775 (£21,000 - £15,225) and is taxed at 32.5%.
£5,775 x 32.5% = £1,877

The figure of £7,229 is the income tax liability.

3.4 Difference between income tax liability and income tax payable

Total income tax liability is calculated by applying the tax rates as discussed above.

Income tax payable / repayable is calculated by deducting the tax already suffered on the income, for example, PAYE deducted from salary income or tax credit on savings income and dividend income.

"Income tax liability" means the total tax due, **"Income tax payable"** means after offsetting any amounts deducted at source" Therefore, if asked for the income tax payable, then PAYE and tax suffered will be deducted from the income tax liability figure.

In 2012-13 Jo, aged 35 years, has trading income of £117,450, receives bank interest of £28,640 and dividend income of £36,000 (amount received).

Required:

Calculate Jo's income tax payable for 2012-13.

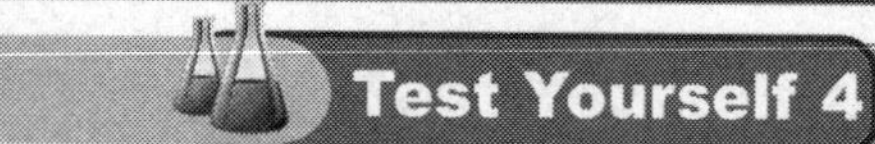

Harry, aged 62 years, receives the following income in 2012-13:

	£
Pension	8,200
Bank deposit interest (amount received)	3,200

Required:

Calculate the amount of income tax payable / repayable.

4. Explain the treatment of interest paid for a qualifying purpose.[2]

[Learning Outcome d]

Certain payments of eligible interest made by a taxpayer are entitled to tax relief. These payments are deducted from taxable income.

Eligible interest

Eligible interest is paid gross, and deducted in the calculation of taxable income.

The loan must be used for a qualifying purpose, which includes:

1. the purchase of plant and machinery by an employee which is used in the performance of his duties.
2. the purchase of plant or machinery by a partner which is used in the business.
3. the purchase of an interest in a partnership or contribution to the partnership by way of capital or loan. However, such partner should not be a limited partner.
4. the purchase of an interest in an employee-controlled unquoted trading company resident in the UK. Employee controlled company is one in which at least 50% of the voting shares are held by the employees.
5. the purchase of an interest by way of shares or loan in a co-operative in which the person has worked for a substantial time of their life.

Treatment of interest paid for a qualifying purpose

The gross amount of the interest is deducted from income, to give net income. The interest is deducted first from non-savings income, then savings income and finally from dividend income, in the same way as personal allowances.

The taxpayer will obtain full tax relief as the interest is reducing the amount of income taxed.

Example

In 2012-13 Anthony and Bob both aged 35 years, have trading income of £45,000 and £26,200 respectively. Anthony paid interest on a loan for qualifying purposes of £200 (gross).

Their income tax liabilities are calculated as follows:

	Anthony £	Bob £
Trading income	45,000	26,200
Less: Interest paid	(200)	
Net Income	**44,800**	**26,200**
Less: Personal allowance	(8,105)	(8,105)
Taxable Income	**36,695**	**18,095**
Income tax		
£34,370 / £18,095 at 20%	6,874	3,619
£2,325 at 40%	930	-
	7,804	**3,619**

5. Explain the treatment of qualifying charitable donations.[1]

[Learning Outcome e]

5.1 Qualifying charitable scheme

The qualifying charitable scheme allows tax relief for gifts of money by individuals to charities.

The relief **applies to all charitable donations** other than gifts through the payroll giving scheme.

A donation must be a payment of a sum of money.

The conditions for qualifying charitable relief to apply are as follows:

1. The payment must not be repayable to the individual.
2. The donor must give the charity a qualifying charitable declaration.

Payments of any amount may qualify for qualifying charitable relief; there is no minimum or maximum amount.

5.2 Tax relief for qualifying charitable payments

Tax relief is given at the individual's highest marginal rate of tax. This is achieved as follows:

Basic rate relief:

The payments are treated as if they have been paid net of the basic rate tax (20%) which the charity then recovers from HMRC.

If the taxpayer made a gift of £800 (the amount of cash paid) to a charity, the charity would receive a total (gross gift) of £1,000. This is made up of the cash of £800 from the taxpayer, and the tax of £200 (£800 x 20/80) which the charity would recover from HMRC.

If the individual is a basic rate taxpayer, relief is given at the time of payment (he paid it net of 20% tax) and no further relief is available. The qualifying charitable payment does not feature in the calculation of taxable income or the income tax liability.

Higher rate relief

If the individual is a higher rate taxpayer, he has received relief of 20% as the payment was made net of basic rate tax. He receives the additional relief by extending both the basic rate band of £34,370 and the higher rate band of £150,000 by the gross amount of the payment.

Charles, David and Edgar each have trading income of £157,225 in 2012-13. Charles makes a qualifying charitable payment of £4,320 (amount paid) and David pays an interest of £5,400 on a loan for qualifying purposes. Edgar makes no payments.

Their income tax liabilities are calculated as follows:

				Charles £	David £	Edgar £
Trading income				157,225	157,225	157,225
Less: Interest paid				-	(5,400)	-
Net Income				**157,225**	**151,825**	**157,225**
Less: Personal allowance (Note)				-	-	-
Taxable Income				**157,225**	**151,825**	**157,225**
Income tax						
Charles	**David**	**Edgar**				
£39,770 (W1)	£34,370	£34,370	at 20%	7,954	6,874	6,874
£115,630 (W1)	£115,630	£115,630	at 40%	46,252	46,252	46,252
£155,400 (W1)	**£150,000**	**£150,000**				
£1,825	£1,825	£7,225	at 50%	913	913	3,613
£157,225	**£151,825**	**£157,225**				
Income tax liability				**55,119**	**54,039**	**56,739**

Charles and David both have made the same payments:

	Charles (£)	David (£)
Qualifying charitable payment / interest payment	4,320	5,400
Income tax liability	55,119	54,039
Total	**59,439**	**59,439**

Charles and David both have made tax relievable payments of £5,400 (gross) and are additional rate band taxpayers, therefore their tax bill will be reduced by £2,700 (£5,400 x 50%). The interest paid is deducted as a charge on income, whereas the qualifying charitable relief is given by extending the basic rate tax band. The difference between Edgar's and David's income tax liability is £2,700 (£56,739 - £54,039).

Note: the adjusted net income for determining the amount of personal allowance available is net income less the gross amount of personal pension contributions and qualifying charitable donations. Therefore, adjusted net income of Charles's is £151,825 (£157,225 - £5,400), of David is £151,825 and of Edgar is £157,225. The adjusted net income of all the three taxpayers is above £116,210, therefore personal allowance available to them is nil.

Workings

W1

Charles's basic rate band and higher rate band will be extended by the gross amount of the payment to qualifying charitable donations, i.e. £5,400 (£4,320 x 100/80). Therefore, Charles's extended basic rate band will be £39,770 (£34,370 + £5,400) and the extended higher rate band will be £155,400 (£150,000 + £5,400).

SUMMARY

- Tax relief for qualifying charitable payments
  - basic rate taxpayer
    - relief of 20% given at time of payment
    - not taken into account in calculation of taxable income
  - higher rate taxpayer
    - relief of 20% given at time of payment
    - additional relief is given by extending both basic rate band & higher rate band by gross amount of payment

Test Yourself 5

Mike aged 54 years, earns a salary of £48,250 per annum. He makes a qualifying charitable payment of £2,080 (amount paid) in 2012-13.

Required:

Calculate his income tax liability for 2012-13.

Proforma for tax calculation

	Total	Non-savings	Savings	Dividends
Trading income	X	X	-	-
Employment income	X	X	-	-
Property income	X	X	-	
Bank interest (gross)	X		X	-
Dividends (gross)	X		-	X
Total Income	X	X	X	X
Less: Interest paid for a qualifying purpose	(X)	(X)	-	-
Net income	X	X	X	X
Less: Personal allowance	(X)	(X)	-	-
Taxable income	X	X	X	X
Income tax liability	X			
Less: Tax credits	(X)			
Less: Tax deducted at source	(X)			
Income tax payable	X			

Test Yourself 6

Abraham aged 45 years has the following income in 2012-13:

	£
Salary (gross) (PAYE deducted £5,454)	31,000
Building society interest (amount received)	410
Bank deposit interest (amount received)	500
Dividend income (amount received)	12,600

Required:

Calculate his tax payable or repayable for 2012-13.

Test Yourself 7

Merry started trading on 1 January 2013 and had the following results for the period to 5 April 2013:

	Notes	£	£
Gross profit			66,075
Less:			
Depreciation		910	
Motor expenses	1	4,580	
Professional fees	2	3,090	
Sundry expenses	3	2,695	
Entertaining	4	4,060	
Business rates		3,930	(19,265)
Net profit			**46,810**

Notes

1. **Motor expenses:** it has been agreed with HMRC that 60% of motor expenses relate to business use.
2. **Professional fees** consist of:

	£
Legal costs in defending a claim for allegedly faulty work	1,320
Personal financial planning advice	1,240
Debt collection	530
	3,090

3. **Sundry expenses consist of:**

	£
Merry's health club subscription	125
Donation to local charity (Merry received free advertising in the charity's magazine)	45
Printing and stationery	645
Gifts of 35 umbrellas bearing Merry's logo.	680
Subscription to a trade association	1,200
	2,695

4. Entertaining; £2,311 for entertaining customers, £1,749 for entertaining employees.
5. The cost of Merry's private telephone for the period 1 January 2013 to 5 April 2013 was £2,650. It has been agreed with HMRC that 35% of this related to business calls. Telephone costs are not included in the profit and loss account.
6. Merry took goods from stock that cost £1,250, and had a selling price of £1,550. No entry was made in the accounts.
7. No capital allowances were claimed.

Merry was employed up to 31 December 2012 earning a monthly salary of £4,200.

Her employer provided Merry with a petrol-powered car which had a list price of £18,500. Merry contributed £2,300 towards the capital cost of the car. The official CO_2 emission rate for the car was 272 grams per kilometre. The employer paid for all the fuel for private journeys. Merry paid £110 per month to her employer for the private use of the car.

On 1 January 2011 Merry was given an interest free loan of £65,000 to purchase a residential flat. On 5 May 2012 she repaid £35,000, and the balance of £30,000 was repaid on 31 December 2012. The official rate of interest was 4.00%.

Continued on the next page

PAYE paid during employment was £6,980.

Merry received interest from her bank account of £380 on 31 December 2012.
She also received dividend income of £1,233 (amount received) during 2012-13.

Required:

Calculate the income tax payable by Merry for 2012-13.

---

6. Explain the treatment of property owned jointly by a married couple, or by a couple in a civil partnership.[1]

[Learning Outcome f]

A married couple or civil partners who live together may hold property in their joint names. If the jointly held asset is a building society account or bank account, any income needs to be allocated between the couple.

The couple are treated as if they own the property in equal proportions, and the income is divided equally between them. This happens regardless of the actual ownership.

If couples own the property in unequal proportions, they may make a declaration to HMRC of their actual ownership, and are then taxed on the proportion of income to which they are actually entitled.

Tip

An election can be made in respect of any asset except for shares in family companies, income from furnished holiday lettings or dividends from close companies.

Example

Linda and her husband Jerry deposited £100,000 into a joint building society account.

Linda contributed £40,000 and Jerry £60,000. They received interest of £4,800 in 2012-13.

Linda and Jerry will each be taxed on £3,000 (£4,800 x 100/80 x1/2).

However, if they make a declaration to HMRC as to the actual ownership, Linda will be taxed on £2,400 (£4,800 x 100/80 x 4/10) and Jerry will be taxed on £3,600 (£4,800 x 100/80 x 6/10).

Answers to Test Yourself

Answer to TY 1

To determine the amount of personal allowance available to each taxpayer, we need to first determine their adjusted net income.

The adjusted net income of each of the taxpayer is as follows:

	Greg	Adam	Fred	Ivan
	£	£	£	£
Employment income	48,750	-	-	146,000
Trading income	-	102,650	157,800	-
Savings income (gross)	1,000	4,250	13,000	-
Net income	**49,750**	**106,900**	**170,800**	**146,000**
Less:				
Personal pension contributions	(1,500)			(32,000)
Qualifying charitable donations		(1,750)	(4,000)	(2,000)
Adjusted net income	**48,250**	**105,150**	**166,800**	**112,000**

The amount of personal allowance available to each of the taxpayer is:

- **Greg:** the amount of personal allowance available is £8,105 as his adjusted net income is below £100,000.
- **Adam:** the adjusted net income is £105,150, which is above £100,000 but below £116,210, therefore the amount of personal allowance available to him is:
  = £8,105 – ½ (£105,150 – £100,000)
  = £5,530
- **Fred:** the adjusted net income is £166,800, which is above £116,210, therefore the personal allowance available to Fred is **nil**.
- **Ivan:** the adjusted net income is £112,000, which is above £100,000 but below £116,210, therefore the amount of personal allowance available to him is:
  = £8,105 – ½ (£112,000 – £100,000)
  = £2,105

Answer to TY 2

1. Barry

He is 64 years old at the end of the tax year.

Barry is less than 65 at the end of the tax year and his net income is below £100,000, so he is entitled to a PA of £8,105.

2. Charles

He is 66 years old at the end of the tax year.
Charles reaches the age of 66 years during 2012-13 and his net income is below £25,400 so he is entitled to a PAA of £10,500.

3. David

He is 76 years old at the end of the tax year.

David is above 75 years of age during 2012-13 and his net income is below £25,400 so he is entitled to a PAA of £10,660.

4. Edwin

He is 67 years old at the end of the tax year.

	£
Personal age allowance	10,500
Less: Reduction (Note)	
1/2 (£26,100 – £25,400)	(350)
Personal age allowance	**10,150**

Note: Edwin is 67 at the end of 2012-13 and his net income exceeds the limit by (£26,100 - £25,400) = £700. Therefore, the PAA to which he is entitled will be reduced by one-half of the excess.

5. Adam

He is 79 years old at the end of the tax year.

	£
Personal age allowance	10,660
Less: Reduction (W1)	
1/2 (£104,200 – £25,400) (restricted)(W1)	(2,555)
Personal age allowance	**8,105**
Less: Reduction	
1/2 (£104,200 – £100,000) (W2)	(2,100)
Personal allowance	**6,005**

Workings

W1

Adam has a net income which exceeds the limit by (£104,200 - £25,400) = £78,800. His personal age allowance is reduced by one-half of the excess:

PAA = (£10,660 – (1/2 x £78,800)) = Nil

The PAA cannot be reduced to below the standard personal allowance of £8,105; therefore the reduction is restricted to £2,555 (£10,660 - £8,105).

W2

The allowance available to Adam will be further reduced as his adjusted net income exceeds £100,000. Therefore, Adam is entitled to an allowance of = £8,105 – ½ (£104,200 - £100,000) = £6,005.

Answer to TY 3

Calculation of taxable income

	Total	Non-savings	Savings	Dividend
	£	£	£	£
Trading income	117,450	117,450		
Bank interest (£28,640 x 100/80)	35,800		35,800	
Dividend income £36,000 x 100/90)	40,000			40,000
Net Income	**193,250**	**117,450**	**35,800**	**40,000**
Less: PA	-	-	-	-
Taxable Income	**193,250**	**117,450**	**35,800**	**40,000**

Note: no personal allowance will be available as Jo's adjusted net income exceeds £116,210.

Calculation of income tax payable

	Income	Rate	Tax
	£	£	£
Non-savings income			
Basic rate band: £1 to £34,370 at 20%	34,370	20%	6,874
Higher rate band: £34,371 to £117,450 at 40%	83,080	40%	33,232
	117,450		
Savings income			
Higher rate band: (£150,000 - £117,450) = £32,550 at 40%	32,550	40%	13,020
	150,000		
Additional rate band: (£35,800 - £32,550) = £3,250 at 50%	3,250	50%	1,625
	153,250		
Dividend income			
Additional rate band: £40,000 at 42.5%	40,000	42.50%	17,000
Income tax liability	**193,250**		**71,751**
Less: Tax credits			
Savings income (£35,800 x 20%)			(7,160)
Dividend income (£40,000 x 10%)			(4,000)
Income tax payable			**60,591**

Answer to TY 4

Harry's income tax computation for 2012-13

	Total	Non-Savings income	Savings income
	£	£	£
Pension Income	8,200	8,200	
Building society interest (£3,200 x 100/80)	4,000		4,000
Net income	12,200	8,200	4,000
Less : Personal allowance	(8,105)	(8,105)	
Taxable income	**4,095**	**95**	**4,000**
Income tax liability			
Non-savings income			
Basic rate: £1 to £95 at 20%	19		
Savings income (note)			
Starting rate: (£2,710 - £95) = £2,615 at 10%	262		
Basic rate: (£4,000 - £2,615) = £1,385 at 20%	277		
	558		
Less: Tax credit on saving income (£4,000 x 20%)	(800)		
Income tax repayable	**(242)**		

Note: the starting rate of 10% is applicable for saving income, as Harry's non-saving income does not exceed £2,710. It is applicable on his saving income falling in the first £2,710 of taxable income after deducting non-saving income amount. Balance of saving income not falling in the first £2,710 of taxable income is taxed at the basic rate of 20%.

Answer to TY 5

Mike's income tax liability is as follows:

	£
Employment income	48,250
Less: PA	(8,105)
Taxable income	**40,145**
Income tax	
Basic rate band (W1) £36,970 at 20%	7,394
Higher rate band £3,175 at 40%	1,270
Income tax liability	**8,664**

Workings

W1

Mike's basic rate tax band is extended to £36,970 (£34,370 + £ 2,600) by the gross amount of the qualifying charitable payment i.e. £2,600 (£2,080/80 x 100)

Answer to TY 6

Calculation of Abraham's income tax payable / repayable for 2012-13

	£	Total £	Non-savings £	Savings £	Dividend £
Employment income		31,000	31,000		
Building society income (£410 x 100/80) (Note1)		513		513	
Bank interest (£500 x 100/80) (Note 2)		625		625	
Dividend income (£12,600 x 100/90) (Note 3)		14,000			14,000
Net income		**46,138**	**31,000**	**1,138**	**14,000**
Less: PA		(8,105)	(8,105)		
Taxable income		**38,033**	**22,895**	**1,138**	**14,000**
Income tax					
Non-savings income: basic rate band	22,895 x 20%	4,579			
Savings income : basic rate band (Note 5)	1,138 x 20%	228			
Dividends (Note 6): basic rate band	10,337 x 10%	1,034			
	34,370				
Dividends higher rate band	3,663 x 32.5%	1190			
	38,033				
Income tax liability		**7,031**			
Less: Tax credits / deducted at source					
Dividends (£14,000 x 10%)		(1,400)			
Savings income (£1,138 x 20%)		(228)			
PAYE		(5,454)			
Income tax repayable		**(51)**			

Notes

1. Building society interest is received net of 20% tax. All income must be included gross: the calculation is £410 x 100/80.

2. Bank interest is received net of 20% tax. All income must be included gross: the calculation is £500 x 100/80.

3. Dividend income has a tax credit of 10%. All income must be included gross: the calculation is £9,000 x 100/90.

4. Non-savings income is taxed first.

5. Savings income is taxed next as it falls in the basic rate band it is taxed at 20%.

6. Dividend income falls partly in the basic rate band, partly in the higher rate band. Non-savings and savings income totals £24,033 (£22,895 + £1,138). This leaves £10,337 (£34,370 - £24,033) of the basic rate band. Dividends in the basic rate band are taxed at 10%. The remaining £3,663 (£14,000 - £10,337) falls in the higher rate band and is taxed at 32.5%.

Answer to TY 7

Calculation of Merry's income tax payable / repayable for 2012-13

	Total income £	Non-savings income £	Savings income £	Dividend income £
Trading income (W1)	53,850	53,850		
Employment income (W2)	47,382	47,382		
Bank interest (£380 x 100/80)	475		475	
Dividend income (£1,233 x 100/90)	1,370			1,370
Net income	**103,077**	**101,232**	**475**	**1,370**
Less: Personal allowance (W6)	(6,751)	(6,751)		
Taxable Income	**96,326**	**94,481**	**475**	**1,370**
Income tax				
Non-savings income:				
Basic rate: £1 to £34,370 at 20%	6,874			
Higher rate: £34,371 to £94,481 at 40%	24,044			
Savings income				
Higher rate: £475 at 40%	190			
Dividend income				
Higher rate: £1,370 at 32.5%	445			
Income tax liability	**31,553**			
Less: Tax credits				
Dividends (£1,370 x 10%) (note)	(137)			
Interest (£475 x 20%)	(95)			
PAYE	(6,980)			
Income tax payable	**24,341**			

Note: tax credit of dividends is deducted while computing tax payable. However any excess tax credit cannot be repaid under any circumstances, so it is deducted in priority over other tax credits and PAYE.

Workings

W1 Calculation of Merry's tax adjusted trading profits for the year ended 5 April 2013

Tip

Always start from net profit and add back non-allowable expenses, then deduct additional expenses allowed for tax.

	Notes	£	£
Net profit per accounts			46,810
Add: Disallowable expenditure:			
Depreciation		910	
Private element of motor expenses	1	1,832	
Private element of professional fees	2	1,240	
Health club subscription	3	125	
Entertaining customers	4	2,311	
		6,418	
Add: Goods taken out of business by owner (at market value)	5	1,550	7,968
Less: Business expenditure borne personally by the owner			
Telephone expenses	6		(928)
Adjusted profits for tax purposes			**53,850**

Notes

1. Private element of motor expenses: 40% x £4,580 = £1,832

2. Professional fees:
   - Legal cost in defending a claim for allegedly faulty work is business expenditure, hence allowed.
   - Private financial planning is Merry's personal expenditure: add back £1,240.
   - A professional fee for debt collection is also business expenditure, hence allowed.

3. Sundry expenses:
   - Merry's health club subscription is personal expenditure: add back £125.
   - Donation to local charity is allowable as it benefits the trade through advertising in the charity's magazine.
   - Printing and stationery and subscription to a trade association are allowable expenses.
   - Gifts of 35 umbrellas bearing Merry's logo are allowable as they carry a conspicuous advertisement for the business, and do not cost more than £50 per person (£680 / 35 = £19 per umbrella) and are not food, drink or tobacco vouchers exchangeable for goods.

4. Customer entertaining not allowed: add back £2,311

5. Market value of goods taken are added back: £1,550

6. Business call allowable: 35% x £2,650 = £928.

W2 Employment income

		£
Salary (April 2012 to December 2012 = £4,200 x 9)		37,800
Car benefit	(W3)	3,262
Fuel benefit	(W4)	5,303
Beneficial loan	(W5)	1,017
Employment income		**47,382**

W3 Car benefit

	£
List price of the car when new	18,500
Less: Capital contribution from Merry	(2,300)
	16,200
% based on CO_2 emissions 11% + ((270 -100)/5)) = 45% restricted to 35%	35%
Car benefit (for 12 months)	5,670
Less: Non availability for 3 months (January 2013 to March 2013) £5,670 x 3/12	(1,418)
	4,252
Less: Contribution from employee (£110 x 9)	(990)
Taxable value of car benefit	**3,262**

W4 Fuel benefit

Fuel benefit = £20,200 x % based on CO_2 x number of months available
= £20,200 x 35% x 9/12 = £5,302

W5 Beneficial loan

Average method

	£
(Loan balance at Start of year + Loan balance at end of year) / 2 x official rate of interest x number of months	
= (£65,000 + £30,000) / 2 x 4.00% x 9/12	**1,425**

Alternative method: strict method

	£
April 2012: £65,000 x 4.00% x 1/12	217
May 2012 – December 2012: £30,000 x 4.00% x 8/12	800
	1,017

Merry would elect for the strict method.

W6 Personal allowance

As Merry's net adjusted income (i.e. £102,709) is above £100,000 but below £116,210, her personal allowance will be reduced to: £8,105 – 1/2(£102,709 - £100,000) = £6,751

Quick Quiz

1. What is total income?

2. What is taxable income?

3. How are personal allowances and charges deducted in the income tax calculation?

4. At what rates are the following types of income taxed?

   (a) Non-savings income
   (b) Savings income
   (c) Dividend income

Answers to Quick Quiz

1. **Total income** is the aggregate of all income i.e. savings, non-savings and dividend income less interest paid for qualifying purpose. Note **this is before personal allowances**.

2. It is net income less personal allowances.

3. First from non-savings income, then from savings income, then from dividend income.

4.
(a) Non-savings income 20%, 40% and 50%
(b) Savings income 10%, 20%, 40% and 50%.
(c) Dividend income 10%, 32.5% and 42.5%.

Self Examination Questions

Question 1

Pearl is employed by Pillsbury plc as a manager. The information relevant to her income is as follows:

(a) She is paid a gross annual salary of £36,000.

(b) Throughout 2012-13 Pearl was provided with an 1800 cc petrol powered car, which has a list price of £14,000. Pearl made a capital contribution of £2,000 towards the cost of the car when it was first provided. The official $C0_2$ emission rate for the car is 223 grams per kilometre. Pillsbury plc paid for all the running costs of the car during 2012-13 including petrol used for private journeys.

(c) Pillsbury has provided Nancy with living accommodation since 2012. The property was purchased in 2008 for £110,000. It has an annual value of £4,250. Pearl pays the company £2,800 towards living accommodation.

(d) Pearl pays a gross interest of £705 on a loan for qualifying purposes.

(e) During 2012-13 Pearl received building society interest of £1,800 (net).

(f) During 2012-13, Pearl received dividends of £2,160 (net).

Required:

Calculate Pearl's income tax payable for 2012-13.

Question 2

Farah was born in 1940. The following information is relevant:

(a) Farah owns a cottage, which was originally purchased as a holiday home for her. This cottage, which is furnished, has been let to the public from the summer of 2007 for holiday use. Farah ceased using it privately as from this day. The cottage was let on a commercial basis for 35 weeks in 2012-13 with each individual letting not expected to exceed 2 weeks in duration. The letting generated total rental income of £7,850. She incurred advertising costs of £1,000, maintenance costs of £5,600 and loan interest costs of £1,900 in the tax year. The maintenance costs relate to roof repairs following gale damage. The tax written down value of furniture in the cottage at 5 April 2012 was £3,500.

(b) She received bank interest of £3,800 in 2012-13.

(c) She received net dividends of £2,340 in 2012-13 from a UK Company.

(d) She received net building society interest amounting to £5,400.

(e) She also received a taxable state retirement pension amounting to £5,750.

(f) She pays interest of £1,000 gross on a loan taken for qualifying purposes.

Required:

Calculate Farah's income tax payable or repayable for 2012-13.

Answers to Self Examination Questions

Answer to SEQ 1

Income Tax Computation for Pearl 2012-13

	Total £	Non-saving income £	Saving income £	Dividend income £
Income from Employment (W1)	50,120	50,120		
Income from UK Dividends (£2,160 x 100/90)	2,400			2,400
Income from Building society Interest (£1,800 x 100/80))	2,250		2,250	
Total Income	**54,770**	**50,120**	**2,250**	**2,400**
Less: Interest paid	(705)	(705)		
Net Income	**54,065**	**49,415**	**2,250**	**2,400**
Less: Personal Allowance	(8,105)	(8,105)		
Taxable Income	**45,960**	**41,310**	**2,250**	**2,400**
Income tax liability				
Non-savings income				
Basic rate: £1 to £34,370 at 20%	6,874			
Higher rate: £34,371 to £41,310 at 40%	2,776			
Savings income				
Higher rate: £2,250 at 40%	900			
Dividend income				
Higher rate: £2,400 at 32.5%	780			
Income tax liability	**11,330**			
Less: Tax credit on Dividends (£2,400 x 10%))	(240)			
Less: Tax deducted at source on building society interest (£2,250 x 20%))	(450)			
Income Tax payable	**10,640**			

Workings

W1 Taxable employment income

Employment income		£
Salary		36,000
Car benefit	(W2)	4,200
Fuel benefit	(W3)	7,070
Living accommodation	(W4)	2,850
Taxable employment income		**50,120**

W2 Car benefit

	£
List price of the car when new	14,000
Less: Capital contribution from Pearl	(2,000)
	12,000
% based on CO_2 emissions	35
11% + ((220 -100)/5))	
Taxable value of car benefit	**4,200**

W3 Fuel benefit

Fuel benefit = Base figure x % based on CO_2 x number of months given by HMRC emissions
= £20,200 x 35%
= **£7,070**

W4 Living accommodation

	£
Annual value	4,250
Add: Additional annual rent if cost £75,000 (£110,000 - £75,000) x 4.00%	1,400
Total	**5,650**
Less: Employee contribution	(2,800)
Taxable benefit	**2,850**

Answer to SEQ 2

Income Tax Computation for Farah 2012-13

	Total Income £	**Non-savings Income £**	**Savings Income £**	**Dividend Income £**
Pension	5,750	5,750		
Income from UK Dividends (£2,340 x 100/90)	2,600			2,600
Income from Bank Interest (£3,800 x 100/80)	4,750		4,750	
Income from building society interest (£5,400 x 100/80)	6,750		6,750	
Total Income	**19,850**	**5,750**	**11,500**	**2,600**
Less: Interest paid	(1,000)	(1,000)		
Less: Loss from furnished holiday lettings (W1)	-	-		
Net Income	**18,850**	**4,750**	**11,500**	**2,600**
Less: Personal Allowance (W2)	(10,500)	(4,750)	(5,750)	
Taxable Income	**8,350**	**0**	**5,750**	**2,600**

	£	£	£	£
Income tax liability				
Savings income				
Starting rate: £1 to £2,710 at 10%	271			
Basic rate: £2,711 to £5,750 at 20%	608			
Dividend income				
Basic rate: £2,600 at 10%	260			
Income tax liability	**1,139**			
Less: Tax credits				
Dividends (£2,600 x10%)	(260)			
Bank interest (£4,750 x 20%)	(950)			
Building society interest (£6,750 x 20%)	(1350)			
Tax repayable	**(1421)**			

Workings

W1

If the letting of furnished property satisfies certain conditions, it qualifies as income from the "commercial letting of furnished holiday accommodation." **Such income is treated as income from trade, and not as income from a property business.**

To qualify as a furnished holiday letting, the property must satisfy the following conditions:

- available for commercial letting to the public for at least 210 days in a tax year,
- is actually so let in this period for at least 105 days, and
- is not normally in the same occupation for more than 31 days at a time, any longer term occupation must not exceed 155 days.

The cottage passes all three conditions. Therefore, it will be regarded as furnished holiday accommodation. The net assessable letting income for 2012-13 is calculated as follows:

	£	£
Rental income		7,850
Less: Expenses		
Advertising	(1,000)	
Maintenance (repairs to roof allowable)	(5,600)	
Loan interest	(1,900)	
Capital allowances £3,500 @ 20%	(700)	(9,200)
Loss		**(1,350)**

However, from the Finance Act 2011, it will not be possible now to adjust the loss from furnished holiday lettings against any other income. It can now only be carried forward to set against any future income from furnished holiday lettings.

W2

The taxpayer is over 65 and her net income is below the income limit of £25,400.Therefore, she is entitled to the full PAA of £10,500.

If the personal allowance exceeds the total for non-savings income, deduct the surplus from the savings income and then dividend income.

STUDY GUIDE B6: THE USE OF EXEMPTIONS AND RELIEFS IN DEFERRING AND MINIMISING INCOME TAX LIABILITES

Get Through Intro

Making pension contributions is one of the most efficient ways of obtaining tax relief while also saving for old age.

In this Study Guide we will discuss various pension schemes available to self-employed people, as well as non-earners and those in employment

We will also see how a self-employed person may join either a 'personal pension scheme' or a 'retirement annuity contract.'

As a tax consultant, you should have thorough knowledge of all these provisions so that you can guide your clients through the associated tax planning.

Learning Outcomes

a) Explain and compute the relief given for contributions to personal pension schemes, using the rules applicable from 6 April 2011.
b) Describe the relief given for contributions to occupational pension schemes, using the rules applicable from 6 April 2011.
c) Explain how a married couple or couple in a civil partnership can minimise their tax liabilities.

Introduction

A pension is a means by which you will financially support yourself when you retire from employment. Currently there are **four sources** from which an individual may draw a pension in the UK. These are:

- **The state pension scheme**: a scheme based upon National Insurance contributions.
- **An occupational pension scheme:** one which is based upon an individual's employment and length of service with a particular employer.
- **A personal pension scheme:** a scheme with which an individual may choose to save a part of their earnings for use in their later years.
- **A stakeholder pension:** this is a portable pension fund in which an individual saves and can transfer when they change employment.

The UK government encourages investment in a pension scheme in order to reduce the reliance upon the state pension scheme. Accordingly most investments attract tax relief and contributions are made under very favourable tax incentives.

---

1. Explain and compute the relief given for contributions to personal pension schemes, using the rules applicable from 6 April 2011.[2]

[Learning Outcome a]

A state pension is available when an individual reaches state retirement age, but the government encourages individuals to provide additional funds for their retirement. An individual can save additional funds for their retirement by contributing to pension schemes. Tax relief is given on contributions to a pension fund. However, the tax relief is available only if the pension scheme is registered with HMRC.

There are two types of pension schemes

- Personal pension scheme
- Employer's occupational pension scheme

Discussed in Learning Outcome 2 of this Study Guide

1.1 Personal pension scheme

An **individual can contribute any amount, regardless of their earnings,** into a personal / private pension fund even if they already belong to an occupational pension fund. Personal pensions are generally offered by banks, insurance companies and financial institutions.

There is no restriction on the number of pension schemes into which an individual can contribute. However, the tax relief available on the contribution is subject to certain restrictions such as a limit on the total amount of contribution which an individual can make to the various pension schemes.

1.2 Net relevant earnings

Tax relief is available for pension contributions up to the amount of an individual's net relevant earnings.

'**Net relevant earnings**" is the total of the **employment income, trading income and income from furnished letting.** If the individual does not have any net relevant earnings, relief is available on gross contributions up to **£3,600** (this figure is given in the rates and allowances in the exam).

Hence, the maximum amount of gross pension contribution in a tax year on which an individual can get tax relief is the higher of:

- an individual's earnings for the tax year; and
- £3,600

1.3 Annual allowance

The **annual allowance** is the maximum amount that you can save from pension each year to obtain the benefit. There is no limit for saving in a pension scheme but there is a limit on the tax relief you will get on these savings.

Refer to the example of Mike below!

Up to tax year 2010-11 this annual allowance limit was **£255,000 but for the tax year 2011-12 it has been reduced to £50,000** (given in tax rates and allowances in the exam) and remains unchanged for the tax year 2012-13.

1.4 Method of giving relief

i. Personal pension contributions are made net of basic rate tax of 20% by both employed and self-employed contributors. (Refer to the example given below)

ii. Tax relief has been given to all except higher-rate taxpayers at the time of contribution itself, and hence contributions are ignored in the income tax calculation. From 6 April 2011 tax relief for pension contributions made by high income tax payers is restricted.

iii. Higher rate tax payers have already obtained 20% relief, the additional 20% (40% - 20%) relief is obtained by extending the basic rate band and the higher rate band by the gross contribution when calculating income tax. Hence, in general tax relief for all the pension contributions is given at the marginal rate of income tax, i.e.20% at the time of payment itself.

iv. If the annual allowance limit of £50,000 is not fully used in any tax year then the unused allowance can be carried forward for up to next three years. The carry forward of any unused limit is possible only if the person is a member of a pension scheme for that particular tax year. Hence, if the person is not a member of a pension scheme in any tax year, then the entire annual allowance for that year will be lost.

v. As discussed above, the individual contributes to personal pension schemes net of tax; i.e. the contribution paid is deducted by the amount of basic tax rate. The amount of tax relief offered to the individuals is then contributed by HMRC to the pension scheme.

vi. If the individual is an employee, their employer may make contributions into their personal pension fund.

These contributions:

- are exempt benefits.
- have no limit for the employer.
- count towards the annual allowance.

Tip

The examiner has commented that as the limit of £50,000 and brought forward of any unused limit to the next three years is applicable only from the tax year 2011-12, a notional £50,000 limit can be assumed for the previous three tax years to find out any brought forward figure.

Example

Mike and Jenny had contributed towards personal pension during the years 2009-10, 2010-11 and 2011-12 as follows:

	2009-10 £	2010-11 £	2011-12 £
Mike	49,000	35,000	Nil
Jenny	58,000	Nil	47,000

Mike was not a member of the pension scheme for the tax year 2011-2012 while Jenny was a member in 2010-2011.

Mike

	Annual Allowance limit	Pension contributions	unused allowance
2009-2010	50,000	49,000	1,000
2010-2011	50,000	35,000	15,000
2011-2012	50,000	0	note
carry forward to 2012-2013 (note)			**16,000**

Continued on the next page

Note: Mike was not a member of the pension scheme for the tax year 2011-2012 and so loses the annual allowance for that year

Jenny

	Annual Allowance	Pension contributions	unused allowance
2009-2010	50,000	58,000	nil
2010-2011	50,000	0	50,000
2011-2012	50,000	47,000	3,000
carry forward to 2012-2013			**53,000**

The annual allowance for 2009-2010 is fully utilised and since she was a member of the pension scheme for 2010-2011 the annual allowance for that year is fully available.

---

vii. The annual allowance limit for the current year is utilised first and then any unused brought forward limit from the previous tax years is used, taking the earliest year first.

Example

Brian has contributed to the gross personal pension from 2009-2010 to 2012-2013. The amounts are £28,000, £39000, £22000 and £60000 respectively.

	Annual Allowance	Pension contributions	unused allowance
2009-2010	50,000	28,000	22,000
2010-2011	50,000	39,000	11,000
2011-2012	50,000	22,000	28,000
2012-2013	50,000	60,000	nil
			61,000

Brain has utilised the entire 50000 annual allowance for 2012-2013 and 10000 (60000 – 50000) of the unused allowance of 22000 (50000-28000) from 2009-2010. Brain has now unused allowances of 11000 (50000-39000) from 2010-2011 and 28000 (50000-22000) from 2011-2012 to carry forward to 2013-2014. The remaining unused allowance from 2009-2010 cannot be carried forward to 2013-2014 as this is more than three years.

---

viii. If the contribution is made in excess of the annual allowance, i.e. £50,000 by the contributor and tax relief is given on that contribution, then an annual allowance will be charged on the excess amount at the marginal rates of income tax of that person.

Example

Percy earns a trading profit of 239,000 for the year 2012-13 and contributes 89,000 towards his gross personal pension contributions. He does not have any brought forward unused annual allowances.

The income tax liability of Percy is calculated as below:

	£
Trading profit	239,000
Annual allowance charge W1	39,000
	278,000
Personal allowance W2	0
Taxable income	278,000
Income tax	
123370 at 20% W3	24,674
115630 at 40% W4	46,252
39000 at 50%	19,500
Tax liability	90,426

Workings

W1

Annual allowance charge = Pension contribution – annual allowance
= £89,000 – £50,000
= £39,000

W2

Personal allowance – Percy's net adjusted income is £ (278,000 – 50,000) = £228,000 which is more than £114,950. Therefore the personal allowance will not be available.

W3

Income tax liability – The basic and higher rate tax bands are extended to provide higher and additional rate tax relief.

Extended basic tax band = (£34,370 + £89,000) = £123,370

Extended higher tax band = (£150,000 + £89,000) = £239,000

W4

Income tax liability higher tax band = £239,000 – £123,370 = £115,630

Note: Percy would have to pay towards personal pension company 71,200 (89,000 less 20%)

Tip

The calculations involving annual allowance charge will be straight forward. It will not involve partial restriction of the personal allowance and more complex portions of the pension rules are not examinable. For example, annual allowance charge and the pension contributions on which tax relief is available made arise in different tax years.

Lifetime allowance

The tax treatment of any income arising from the amount contributed and accumulated in the pension schemes is as follows:

- All income (interest and bonuses) received by pension schemes are tax-free.
- All capital gains arising on capital disposal of investments made are exempt from capital gains tax.

The funds contributed to the pension schemes and the subsequent investment growth of the pension fund is tax free up to a certain maximum amount. This maximum amount is known as lifetime allowance and has been reduced from £1,800,000 to £1,500,000 for the tax year 2012-13.

If the value of the pension fund exceeds this amount, there is an **additional tax charge** when funds are **withdrawn** as a pension. The additional charge is as follows:

- If the funds are withdrawn in a single instance (i.e. as a lump sum), the excess fund amount is taxed at the rate of 55%.
- If the funds are used to provide a pension, the excess fund amount is taxed at the rate of 25%.

Tip

The examiner has stated that this rule will not be examined in any detail.

SUMMARY

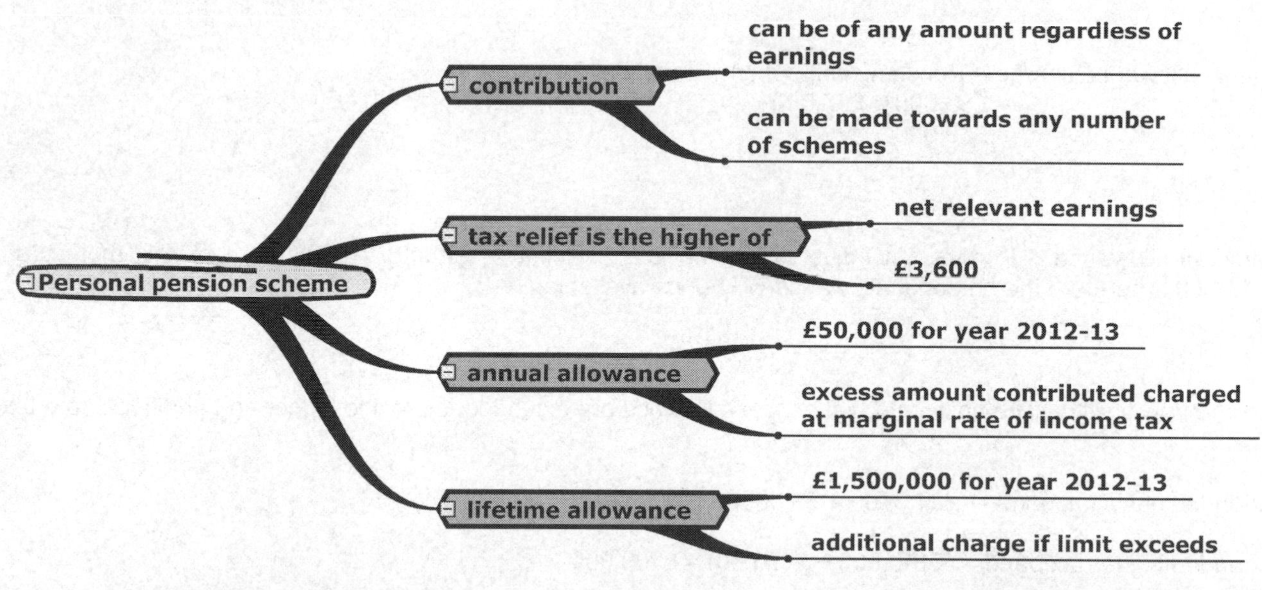

Test Yourself 1

Samson has earnings of £85,000 during the tax year 2012-13. He has contributed £45,000 towards a pension scheme which is recognised by HMRC.

He does not have any brought forward unused annual allowances

Required:

For the tax year 2012-13, compute the following:

a) Tax relief for Samson, on account of his contribution into the pension fund
b) Net contribution to personal pension fund
c) Samson's tax liability

---

2. Describe the relief given for contributions to occupational pension schemes, using the rules applicable from 6 April 2011.[1]

[Learning Outcome b]

An occupational pension scheme is one set up by an employer for his employees. The employer generally contributes to the scheme. Some schemes require the employee to contribute, whereas some are non-contributory.

Occupational pension schemes are of two types:

- **Defined benefit arrangement:** is **related to the employee's 'final pensionable salary'**. Such a scheme guarantees the amount of pension which will be paid to employees on retirement. The pension is determined on the basis of two variables i.e. the 'final pensionable salary' and the number of years of service. Therefore contributions to this scheme would vary each year.

- **Money purchase pension (defined contribution scheme): here, the contribution paid into the scheme is invested by** those operating the scheme / fund. The pension is then paid based on the value of the investments made by the fund. Thus, the amount of pension would not be fixed.

The same tax relief is available for occupational pension schemes as for personal pension schemes but they are administered slightly differently as contributions to this type of pension scheme are typically made via the payroll.

Method of giving relief

1. An occupational scheme will usually **operate net pay arrangements**.
2. The employer deducts the gross pension contributions from the individual's earnings before applying PAYE.

Tax relief is therefore given automatically at the appropriate rate.

Example

Tom and Jerry are employed with Cheese Ltd earning a salary of £50,000. Tom contributes £10,000 into a personal pension scheme and Jerry contributes £10,000 into an occupational pension scheme.

Tom has earnings of £50,000 for the tax year 2012-13 which are higher than his contribution to the pension scheme. Therefore, all of his contributions of £10,000 qualify for tax relief.

Tax relief = £2,000 (£10,000 at 20%).

Amount to be paid to the personal pension company by Tom is £8,000 (£10,000 - £2,000).

Since Tom is a higher-rate taxpayer, he is eligible for higher-rate tax relief. Thus, his basic rate tax band is extended by £44,370 (£34,370 + £10,000).

Jerry contributes to occupational pension scheme. This contribution is deductible from taxable employment income.

Their tax computations will appear as follows:

	Tom (£)	Jerry (£)
Income from employment	50,000	50,000
Less: Contribution to occupational pension scheme	-	(10,000)
Net income	**50,000**	**40,000**
Less: Personal allowance	(8,105)	(8,105)
Taxable income	**41,895**	**31,895**
Income tax liability		
£41,895/ £31,895 at 20%	8,379	6,379

Cash outflow

	Tom (£)	Jerry (£)
Amount paid towards the pension scheme	8,000	10,000
Income tax paid	8,379	6,379
	16,379	**16,379**

Tip

Summary

Personal pension scheme	Occupational pension scheme
Paid net of basic rate tax	Paid gross
The gross contribution is not deducted while calculating taxable income	The gross contribution is deducted while calculating taxable income
Basic rate band and higher rate band are extended by the gross contribution to give additional relief.	No extension of basic rate and higher rate band.

Scarlet is employed with Dixie Ltd and earns a gross salary of £70,000. She instructs her employer to contribute £6,000 to an occupational pension scheme on her behalf. Scarlet has no other source of income.

Required:

Compute Scarlet's income tax liability and cash outflow for the tax year 2012-13.

---

3. Explain how a married couple or couple in a civil partnership can minimise their tax liabilities.[2]

[Learning Outcome c]

Husbands and wives are taxed separately on their income and capital gains. Hence, both have their own allowances, lower and basic rate tax bands for income and capital gains tax purposes and are responsible for their own tax affairs. Since December 2005, the same tax treatment applies to same-sex couples who have entered into a civil partnership under the Civil Partnership Act.

Tax planning opportunities

1. Income tax allowances and tax bands

Everyone is entitled to a personal allowance, which is dependent on their income figure. The standard personal allowance for the tax year 2012-13 is £8,105.

This allowance **cannot,** however, **be transferred between spouses**.

Married couples should try to ensure that they both fully use their allowance since there is no facility to transfer it from one spouse to the other. This can make a difference to the overall income tax liability for the year because:

a) The total taxable income of the couple will be reduced by twice the amount of personal allowance.

Example

If a couple's total income of £80,000 is split between the spouses, each spouse will get a personal allowance of £8,105 for the tax year 2012-13. Thus, the couple's overall taxable income will be £63,790 (£80,000 – (£8,105 + £8,105))

---

b) As the income is split between the spouses, this may result in more income being taxed at the basic rate of tax rather than the higher rate. This can be better understood with the help of the following example.

Example

Nick's total income is £79,895 and his wife, Amy, has no income. In this case, Nick's tax liability will be as follows:

	£
Total income	79,895
Less: Personal allowance	(8,105)
Taxable income	**71,790**
Tax borne	
£34,370 @20%	6,874
£37,420 @ 40%	14,968
Total	**21,842**

Instead, if Nick transfers some of his income, say £25,000 to his wife, their total tax liability will be as follows:

Continued on the next page

	Nick (£)	Amy (£)
Total income	54,895	25,000
Less: Personal allowance	(8,105)	(8,105)
Taxable income	**46,790**	**16,895**
Tax borne		
(£34,370/£16,895) @20%	6,874	3,379
£12,420 @ 40%	4,968	-
Total	**11,842**	**3,379**

Thus, the couple's total tax liability will be £15,221 (£11,842 +£3,379) i.e. reduced by £6,621 as compared to £21,842.

This reduction is because of the following reasons:

- The total income of £79,895 is reduced by £16,210 (£8,105 +£8,105).
- Instead of £37,420 being taxed at 40%, only £12,420 is taxed at 40%. Thus, as the tax band is reduced, the tax is also reduced.

Tip

Whilst it is not possible to simply gift an income stream to a spouse, see below for suggestions as to how taxable income can effectively be transferred to a spouse.

c) In the case of those aged 65 and over

Taxpayers aged at least 65 should consider how to make full use of the available age allowances.

Income tax allowances	2012-13
Personal allowance for people aged 65-74	10,500
Personal allowance for people aged 75 and over	10,660

The higher allowances are gradually withdrawn once income exceeds £25,400 (for tax year 2012-13) (refer to Study Guide B5).

Test Yourself 3

Darren and Lynn have total annual taxable income of £100,000. What will be their tax liability if:

a) The total income is to be taxed on either of the spouses alone.
b) The income is split between the couple equally.

2. Married couple allowance (MCA)

If either of the spouses were born before 6 April 1935, a married couple's allowance is available. This is given to the spouse with higher income, although it is possible, by election, to transfer it to the other spouse.

A married couple allowance is available **only if the following conditions** are fulfilled.

- The couple is legally married and lives together for at least part of the tax year.
- At least one of the spouses was born before 6 April 1935.

In the case of couples married **before 5 December 2005**, the MCA is given to the **husband.** In the case of couples married **on or after 5 December 2005 (and civil partners)**, the MCA is normally given to the **spouse with the higher income.**

a) It is important to note here that:

i. The husband and wife **jointly may decide** that a minimum amount of MCA (£2,960 for 2012-13) should be set against the wife's tax.

ii. The **wife unilaterally may decide** that 50% of the MCA should be set against her tax.

iii. If one spouse is unable to fully utilise the MCA, the **unused MCA can be transferred** to the other spouse.

b) The amount of allowance

i. For 2012-13, the allowance is10% of £7,705.

Remember, MCA is deducted from tax payable and not from TI.

Like age allowance, this allowance also starts to be withdrawn once income goes over the income threshold i.e. £25,400 for tax year 2012-13 (refer Study Guide B5).

Income tax allowances	2012 - 13
Married couple's allowance - aged 75 or more	10% of £7,705
Minimum amount of married couple's allowance	10% of £2,960

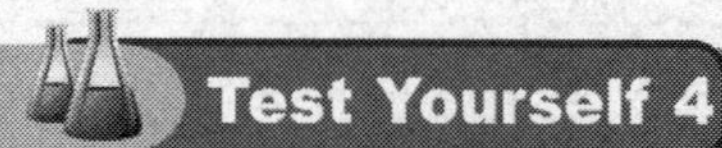

Henry is 74 and is married to Alice who is 72. Henry receives his state pension of £3,470 and also a pension from his former employer of £8,000, from which the employer deducted £443 as tax. He also has £4,500 bank interest that has had tax taken off at 20% leaving him with £3,600.

Required:

Calculate Henry's tax liability and determine whether any tax is repayable to him in 2012-13.

The MCA can be used to minimise the tax liability of the couple overall. Where the person who is entitled to a married couple's allowance is unable to use his full MCA in any tax year he can ask for the balance to be transferred to his spouse.

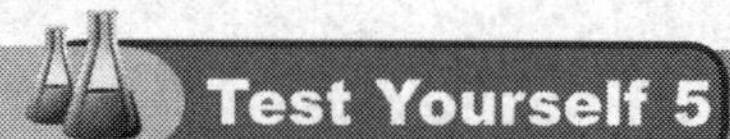

Peter and Susan are married. Peter is 78 and works part-time. Susan is 71 and also works. They have a joint bank account, which pays gross interest of £2,000, from which the bank has taken off 20% in tax leaving them with £1,600. Peter earns £10,000. He also has half of the gross bank interest, £1,000, and half of the tax £200 that the bank has already deducted.

Susan has an income of 20,000 in wages from which her employer deducted £1,395 tax through PAYE, plus half of the gross interest on her joint account with Peter, £1,000.

Required:

Determine how the MCA can be used to reduce the tax liability of the couple.

3. Jointly owned assets

It is often the case that married couples own assets jointly. The normal rule is to split income from such assets equally between them for tax purposes. This applies even where the asset is owned in unequal shares unless an election is made to split the income in proportion to the ownership of the asset.

Example

A let property is owned by a married couple in the proportion 95:5. The rental income arising can be split between them for tax purposes either 50:50 or by election, 95:5. This can be a useful mechanism for achieving a more desirable split of income for tax purposes without needing the underlying capital ownership to follow.

There are two key exceptions to this rule:

i) Dividends from jointly owned shares in 'close' companies (broadly those owned by the directors or five or fewer people) which are taxed according to the actual ownership of the shares.
ii) Income from Furnished Holiday Lettings.

This option can prove to be a very efficient measure to reduce the tax liability of each spouse.

Example

A let out property was owned by a married couple (John and Jenny) in the proportion 90:10. The rent received from this property is £20,000. John's employment income is £30,000 and Jenny has no income.

If the property income is **not split between them 50:50**, the tax liability would be as follows:

	John £	Jenny £
Employment income	30,000	-
Property income (90:10)	18,000	2,000
Net Income	**48,000**	**2,000**
Less: Personal allowance	(8,105)	(2,000)
Taxable income	**39,895**	-
Tax borne		
£34,370 at 20%	6,874	-
£5,525 at 40%	2,210	-
Total tax liability	**9,084**	-

If the property income is **split between them 50:50**, the tax liability would be as follows:

	John £	Jenny £
Employment income	30,000	-
Property income (50:50)	10,000	10,000
Net income	**40,000**	**10,000**
Less: Personal allowance	(8,105)	(8,105)
Taxable income	**31,895**	**1,895**
Tax borne		
(£31,895/ £1,895) at 20%	6,379	379
Total tax liability	**6,379**	**379**

Thus, total tax liability of the couple is £6,758 (£6,379 + £379). **The couple has saved tax of £2,326** (£9,084 - £6,758) by using the 50:50 split of jointly owned property income.

4. Capital gains

Transfers of assets between spouses or persons who are civil partners **and** who are living together will be on a no-gain no-loss basis, and thus not attract an immediate CGT charge.

Each spouse has their own annual capital gains tax (CGT) exemption, currently £10,600. Any gains above this level are taxed on each spouse separately by reference to their own disposals of assets.

So the option of transferring the asset to the spouse and realising the capital gain in the hands of the lower income partner is another measure of a married couple's tax planning. A considerable CGT saving may be made by ensuring that maximum advantage is taken of annual exemptions and to utilise any capital losses the other spouse or partner may have.

Example

Mr Smith bought a non-business asset for £5,000 in March 1988. He sold the asset to his wife for £50,000 in September 2011 when they were living together. The asset is deemed to have transferred for an amount, which gives neither a gain nor a loss on transfer. The actual amount paid by Mrs. Smith is ignored.

The deemed cost to Mrs. Smith for any future disposal of the asset is £50,000 (cost to Mr. Smith when he originally purchased the asset).

Mrs. Smith sells the asset for £80,000 in June 2012.

The gain arising is:

	£
Disposal proceeds	80,000
Less: Cost	(50,000)
Net chargeable gain	**30,000**
Annual exemption	**(10,600)**
Taxable gain	**19,400**

Answers to Test Yourself

Answer to TY 1

(a) Samson has earnings of £85,000 for the tax year 2012-13. His contribution to the fund is less than his earnings. Therefore, the entire amounts of £45,000 of his contributions qualify for the tax relief (as it falls within the annual allowance limit of £50,000).

Therefore, **tax relief = £9,000** (£45,000 at 20%).

(b) Amount to be paid to the personal pension company by Samson is £36,000 (£45,000 - £9,000).

(c) **Computation of Samson's tax liability**

	£
Trading profit	85,000
Less: Personal allowance	(8,105)
Taxable income	**76,895**
Income tax liability	
£76,895 at 20%	15,379

Samson's net adjusted income, after deducting the gross amount of pension contributions, is less than £100,000; therefore he is entitled to standard personal allowance of £8,105.

Note: since Samson is a higher-rate taxpayer, he is eligible for higher-rate tax relief. Thus, his basic rate tax band is extended by £79,370 (£34,370 + £45,000).

Answer to TY 2

Scarlet's tax computation for the tax year 2012-13

	£
Income from employment	70,000
Less: Contribution to occupational pension scheme	(6,000)
Net income	**64,000**
Less: Personal allowance	(8,105)
Taxable income	**55,895**
Income tax	
£34,370 at 20%	6,874
£21,525 @ 40%	8,610
Tax liability	**15,484**

Cash outflow of Scarlet

	£
Amount paid towards the pension scheme	6,000
Income tax paid	15,484
	21,484

Answer to TY 3

(a) If the total income is to be taxed in either of spouse alone:

	£
Income	100,000
Less: Personal allowance	(8,105)
Taxable income	**91,895**
Tax borne	
£34,370 at 20%	6,874
£57,525 at 40%	23,010
Total tax liability	**29,884**

(b) Instead, if the couple split this income equally, the tax liability of each of them would be as follows:

	Darren	**Lynn**
	£	**£**
Income	50,000	50,000
Less: Personal allowance	(8,105)	(8,105)
Taxable income	**41,895**	**41,895**
Tax borne		
£34,370 at 20%	6,874	6,874
£7,525 at 40%	3,010	3,010
Total tax liability	**9,884**	**9,884**

Hence Darren's tax liability is £9,884 and Lynn's tax liability is also £9,884.
The couple's total liability is £19,768.

Thus almost £10,116 (i.e. £29,884 - £19,768) of tax can be saved every year.

Answer to TY 4

Henry's income is calculated for tax as follows:

	Total income	Non-savings income	Savings income
	£	£	£
State pension	3,470	3,470	
Employer's pension	8,000	8,000	
Bank interest	4,500		4,500
Net income	**15,970**	**11,470**	**4,500**
Less: Personal allowance (Note 1)	(10,660)	(10,660)	0
Taxable income	**5,310**	**810**	**4,500**
Tax on taxable income			
Non saving income			
Basic rate £810 at 10%	81		
Saving income			
Starting rate (£2,710 - £810) £1,900 at 10% (Note 3)	190		
Basic rate (4,500-1,900) = £2,600 at 20%	520		
Tax payable	**791**		
Less: Married couple's allowance (£7,705 at 10%) (Note 1)	(771)		
Net tax payable	**20**		
Less: Tax already paid			
Bank interest (£4,500 - £3,600)	(900)		
Employer's pension	(443)		
Repayment due	**(1,323)**		

Notes

1. Henry is entitled to the age related personal allowance of £10,660 as he is aged over 75. He is also entitled to married couple's allowance of 10% of £7,705 as he is aged over 75.

2. As his income is less than £25,400, none of the age-related elements of his allowances needs to be reduced.

3. Non savings income £810 does not exceed the starting rate threshold of £2,710, so £1,900 (£2,710 -£810) of the savings income is taxed at the starting rate of 10% and the balance of the savings income, £2,600 (£4,500 - £1,900), is taxed at the basic rate of 20%.

Answer to TY 5

Peter's income is taxed as follows:

	Total income £	Non-savings income £	Savings income £
Gross bank interest	1,000		1,000
Add: Wages	10,000	10,000	
Net income	**11,000**	10,000	1,000
Less: Personal allowance	(10,660)	(10,000)	(660)
Taxable income	**340**	0	340
Tax on taxable income			
Saving income (£340 at 10%) (Note 2)	34		
Tax Payable	**34**		
Less: MCA (£7,705 at 10%) = £771 but restricted upto amount of tax, i.e. £34	(34)		
Amount of married couple's allowance unused (£771-£34) = £737			
Net Tax payable	-		
Less: Tax already paid (Bank Interest) (£1000 x 20%)	**(200)**		
Repayment due	**(200)**		

Peter's unused MCA can be transferred to Susan, which she can set against her income as follows:

	Total income (£)	Non-savings income (£)	Savings income (£)
Gross bank interest (i.e. before tax is taken off)	1,000		1,000
Add: Wages	20,000	20,000	0
Net income	**21,000**	**20,000**	**1,000**
Less: Personal allowance	(10,500)	(10,500)	0
Taxable income	**10,500**	**9,500**	**1,000**
Tax on taxable income			
Non saving income £9500 x 20%	1,900		
Saving income (£1,000 at 20%) (Note 2)	200		
Total tax due	**2,100**		
Less: Unused MCA from Peter £737	(737)		
Tax payable	**1,363**		
Less: Tax already paid			
Tax deducted from bank interest	(200)		
Tax deducted by employer under PAYE	(1,395)		
Repayment due	**(232)**		

Notes

1. Peter is entitled to the age-related personal allowance of £10,660 and married couple's allowance because he is aged above 75.

2. A 10% starting rate is applicable for the first £2,710 saving income subject to non-saving income not exceeding £2,710.

3. If there is any unused MCA after adjusting the income of both the spouses, then it cannot be carried forward, and is wasted.

Quick Quiz

Fill in the blanks

1. Employee's contribution to a _______ pension scheme is deducted in calculation of taxable income.
2. Personal pension contribution is paid ________of basic rate tax.
3. If the individual does not have any earnings, relief is available on gross contributions of up to _______.
4. Annual allowance for 2012-13 is _______.

Answers to Quick Quiz

1. occupational
2. net
3. £3,600
4. £50,000

Self Examination Questions

Question 1

What is the lifetime allowance?

Question 2

Which two conditions are to be satisfied for the availability of married couple allowance?

Question 3

Harry and Peter are friends. Harry is employed with Best Bakers. He earns a salary of £400,000 and contributes £245,000 into an occupational pension scheme. Peter contributes £45,000 into a personal pension scheme from his earnings of £400,000. Peter does not have any brought forward unused annual allowances

Required

Compute Harry and Peter's tax liability for tax year 2012-13.

Question 4

Jerome and Miriam had contributed towards personal pension during the years 2010-11, 2011-12 and 2012-13 as follows:

	2010-2011	2011-2012	2012-2013
	£	£	£
Jerome	53,000	Nil	42,000
Miriam	Nil	60,000	35,000

Jerome was not a member of the pension scheme for the tax year 2011-2012 while Miriam was a member in 2010-2011.

Required

Compute Jerome and Miriam's unused allowance for the tax year 2012-13.

Answers to Self Examination Questions

Answer to SEQ 1

The maximum value for a pension fund is called the lifetime allowance and is £1,500,000 for the tax year 2012-2013.

Answer to SEQ 2

Married couple allowance is available only if the following two conditions are satisfied:

(a) the couple should be legally married and live together for at least part of tax year.
(b) at least one of the spouses should be born before 6 April 1935.

Answer to SEQ 3

Their tax computations will appear as follows:

	Harry (W1) £	Peter (W2) £
Income from employment/ Trading profits	400,000	400,000
Less: Contribution to occupational pension scheme (W1)	(245,000)	
Net income	155,000	400,000
Less: Personal allowance	0	0
Taxable income	**155,000**	**400,000**
Income tax		
Basic rate: £1 to £34,370 / £1 to £79,370 at 20% (W2)	6,874	15,874
Higher rate: £34,370 to £150,000 / £79,371 to £195,000 @ 40% (W2)	46,252	46,252
Additional rate: £150,001 to £155,000 / £195,001 to £400,000 @ 50% (W2)	2,500	102500
Income tax liability	**55,626**	**164,626**

Cash flow

	Harry £	Peter £
Amount paid towards the pension scheme (W2)	245,000	36,000
Income tax paid	55,626	164,626
	300,626	200,626

Workings

W1

Harry contributes to an occupational pension scheme. This contribution is deductible from employment income.

W2

Peter has earnings of £400,000 for the tax year 2012-13, which are higher than his contribution to the pension scheme. Therefore, his entire contributions of £45,000, which are within the annual allowance limit, qualify for tax relief.

Tax relief = £9,000 (£45,000 at 20%).

Amount to be paid to the personal pension company by Peter is £36,000 (£45,000 - £9,000).

Since Peter is a higher-rate taxpayer, he is also eligible for higher-rate tax relief. Thus, his basic rate tax band is extended by £79,370 (£34,370 + £45,000) and higher rate band is extended by £195,000 (£150,000 + £45,000).
Income which exceeds the higher rate band will be taxable at the additional rate of 50%.

Answer to SEQ 4

Jerome

	Annual Allowance limit	Pension contributions	unused allowance
2010-2011	50,000	53,000	Nil
2011-2012	50,000	Nil	note
2012-2013	50,000	42,000	8,000
carry forward to 2013-2014 (note)			**8,000**

Note: Jerome was not a member of the pension scheme for the tax year 2011-2012 and so loses the annual allowance for that year

Miriam

	Annual Allowance	Pension contributions	unused allowance
2010-2011	50,000	nil	50,000
2011-2012	50,000	60,000	nil
2012-2013	50,000	35,000	15,000
carry forward to 2012-2013			**65,000**

The annual allowance for 2010-2011 is fully available since she was a member of the pension scheme and the annual allowance for 2011-2012 is fully used.

STUDY GUIDE C1: THE SCOPE OF THE TAXATION OF CAPITAL GAINS

Get Through Intro

Capital gains tax is a charge on the increase in the value of an asset over the period of ownership.

'Capital Gains tax' is an important topic of your syllabus. Also, as a tax consultant to companies as well to individuals, you need to possess a **complete and in-depth knowledge of the scope, applicability and requirements of capital gains tax.**

In the course of the next six Study Guides, we will take you through all the related provisions of capital gains tax.

In this Study Guide we shall discuss the **scope of capital gains tax** and how the **classification of individuals** as **resident and ordinarily residents affects** the **applicability** of capital gains tax.

Learning Outcomes

a) Describe the scope of capital gains tax.
b) Explain how the residence and ordinary residence of an individual is determined.
c) List those assets which are exempt.

Introduction

Case Study

During the past ten years, Maria has been a resident of the UK and was living in Manchester. In July 2012, she left Manchester to take a job in Canada. While in Canada, she had to send some money to her parents in the UK. She sold a painting for £30,000 and sent all the money to the UK. This transaction resulted in her making a capital (profit) gain of £20,000.

Maria thought that this gain was neither taxable in the UK nor in Canada and she didn't pay any tax. So, when the UK tax authorities made a demand for capital gains tax, she was surprised.

Maria is liable to capital gains tax on the disposal of the painting as she was, until recently, a resident of the UK.

In this Study Guide we will see how residential status affects the capital gains tax liability of a person, the scope of capital gains tax and the assets which attract capital gains tax.

1. Describe the scope of capital gains tax.[2] List those assets which are exempt. [1]

[Learning Outcomes a and c]

Capital gains tax is a charge on the increase in value of an asset over the period of ownership. If a disposal is made by a company, there is an allowance for inflation.

1.1 Scope of capital gains tax

A liability to tax arises if there is a **chargeable disposal** of a **chargeable asset** by a **chargeable person.**

1.2 Chargeable person

The following are chargeable persons:

1. **Individual:** a liability to capital gains tax arises if an **individual resident or ordinarily resident in the UK** makes a chargeable disposal.

2. **Companies:** pay tax on their chargeable disposals, but pay corporation tax, rather than capital gains tax.

The following are **not** considered as chargeable persons for the purpose of capital gains tax:

- Local authorities
- Registered charities
- Registered friendly societies
- Approved superannuation funds
- Unit trusts
- Investment trusts

1.3 Chargeable disposal

1. The sale of an asset.
2. The sale of part of an asset (e.g. selling a 40% share of a house).
3. The gift of an asset (e.g. giving an expensive necklace to your daughter as a present).
4. The loss or destruction of an asset (e.g. an insurance receipt in respect of a fire damaged property).

The chargeable disposal occurs on the date of the contract.

The following disposals are treated as exempt disposals:

1. Disposal of asset to registered charities and national museums etc.
2. Transfers of assets on death.
3. The sale of trading stock. (it is chargeable to income tax and not capital gains tax)

1.4 Chargeable asset

All capital assets are chargeable, unless specifically exempt. This applies to all assets wherever in the world they may be located.

All assets are chargeable to capital gains tax unless they are specifically exempted by law or other regulation.

Therefore, a chargeable person is liable to capital gains tax on disposals of all assets whether:

- Owned and sold in the UK; or
- Owned and sold outside the UK (overseas assets).

A list of exempt assets is given below

a) **An individual's home** (principal private residence (refer to Study Guide C4). If he owns more than one home then he must elect which property is his principal private residence).

b) **Motorcars** including veteran and vintage cars.

c) **Cash (sterling currency** and **foreign currency** for an individual's own use or maintenance of assets abroad).

d) **Wasting assets** (tangible, moveable property with a predicted life of not more than 50 years (refer to Study Guide C3).

e) **Chattels** which are not wasting assets **if sold (and bought) for £6,000 or less** (refer to Study Guide C3).

f) **Compensation** or **damages** received for personal or professional wrongs or injury.

g) **Prizes and betting** winnings.

h) **Life insurance policies** but only when disposed of in the hands of the original owner or beneficiaries.

i) **Gifts to charities** or certain sports clubs.

j) **SAYE** (save as you earn) deposits, savings certificates and premium bonds.

k) **Government securities** and qualifying companies loan stock.

l) **Gilt edged securities** and qualifying corporate bonds.

m) All **debts** except debts on security.

n) **Pensions** and annuity rights.

Tip

Gains on the sale of the above exempt assets are not liable to capital gains tax. In the same way, a loss arising from the disposal of the above assets is not eligible for set off.

The capital gains of a limited company and an individual have similarities and also differences.

1. A limited company's capital gains are part of profits chargeable to corporation tax (PCTCT) and are charged to corporation tax.

2. An individual's capital gains are charged to capital gains tax which is totally separate from income tax. It has its own rates of tax.

3. An indexation allowance (to allow for inflation) is given for a company in the calculation of its gains. However, this allowance is not applicable for individuals.

4. Reliefs available

To individuals	To a company
i. Rollover relief ii. Holdover relief for the gift of business assets iii. Rollover relief when a business is incorporated	i. Rollover relief

Linda owns an industrial building. She purchased this building in June 2004 for £32,000. She regularly pays an insurance premium for industrial buildings to Max Saver, the Insurance Company.

One morning in May 2012, due to a fire, more than 50% of the industrial building was destroyed. The insurance company made a final payment of £30,000 to Linda.

As Linda's tax consultant, how much would you calculate to be taxable under capital gains tax?

Answer

A gain on the disposal of a chargeable asset is chargeable to capital gains tax. A capital receipt in lieu of an asset is also chargeable to capital gains tax. Hence, the claim settlement by an insurance company on the loss of an asset is also chargeable to capital gain tax.

Calculation of chargeable gains

	£
Insurance claim received	30,000
Less: Acquisition cost of building (50% of £32,000)	(16,000)
Gain on disposal	**14,000**

SUMMARY

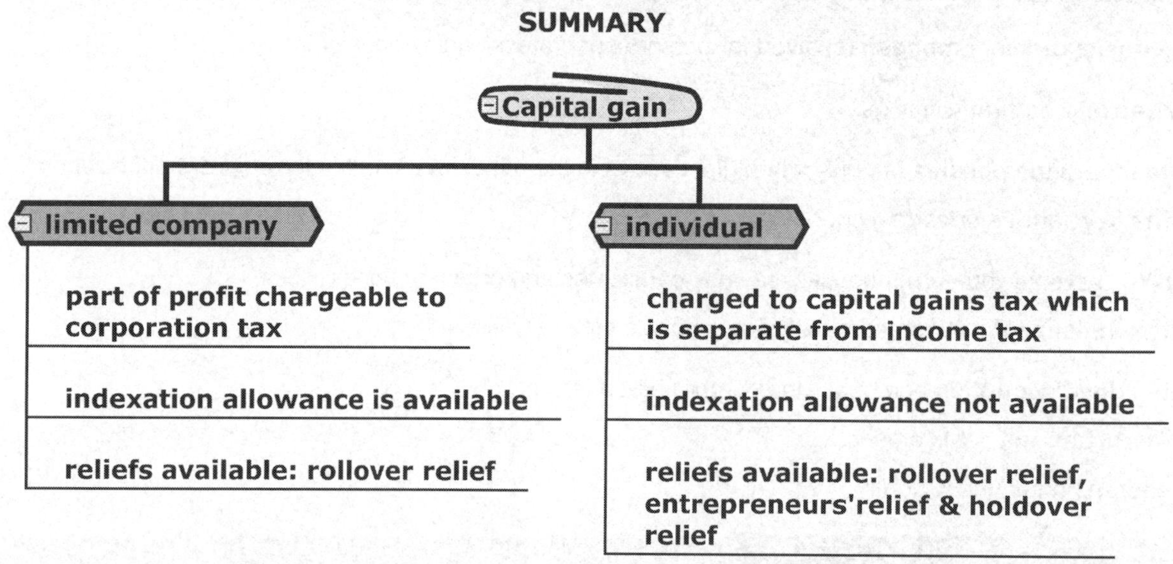

2. Explain how the residence and ordinary residence of an individual is determined.[2]
[Learning Outcome b]

2.1 Residence of an individual

1. An individual **physically present in the UK for at least 183 days** is a UK **resident** for the **whole tax year**.
2. An individual returning to the UK for visits will be UK resident for the whole tax year if he makes regular and substantial (average at least 91 days per tax year) visits to the UK. This is calculated as an average over the last four tax years (or since the date of leaving the UK if less than four years).

   An individual is either resident or a non-resident for the **entire** year of assessment. They **cannot be partly resident** (although there are some circumstances in which HMRC will, by concession, split the tax year for residence purposes).

3. A non-UK resident starting to make regular and substantial visits to the UK will be a UK resident from the earlier of:

a) the start of the fifth tax year, or
b) the start of a tax year where an intention to continue long-term visits is apparent.

2.2 Ordinary residence

The ordinary residence of an individual is the country where he normally resides year after year.

An individual who is ordinarily resident in the UK but who is temporarily abroad during a particular tax year (i.e. not present in the UK for the minimum 183 days but not absent for the entire tax year) is deemed to be a UK **resident** for the whole of that tax year.

Tip

It is possible to be a UK resident but not ordinarily resident, and vice-versa. For more details, refer to Study Guide B1.

2.3 Chargeability to capital gain tax – individuals

An individual resident or ordinarily resident in the UK is liable to capital gains tax on:

- assets owned and sold in the UK
- assets owned and sold outside the UK (overseas assets)

An individual who is non-resident and non-ordinarily resident is not liable to UK capital gains tax on any assets whether sold in the UK or outside the UK. The only exception is where a non-resident carrying on a permanent trade disposes of an asset in the UK.

Example

Tina is a resident of Brazil. She runs a modelling class in London. She sold her classroom building for £70,000 and made a capital gain of £21,000.
Tina is a non-resident individual of the UK but as she carries on a permanent trade in the UK and sells the business asset in the UK, she is liable to capital gains tax on the gain from such a disposal in the UK.

Test Yourself 1

Joydeep has been UK resident since his birth. On 10 May 2012, he leaves the UK to take up a permanent job in the US. However, he didn't like it there, so on 4 March 2013, he returned to the UK.

During the period when he was in the US, he sold his diamond and gold Omega wrist watch which he had purchased there, for £21,000 and made a capital gain of £2,000. Is this capital gain taxable in the UK?

Answer to Test Yourself

Answer to TY 1

Joydeep is a resident of the UK as well as UK domiciled. However, during the tax year 2012-13, he was present in the UK for only 67 days.

6/4/2012 to 30/4/2012	25
1/5/2012 to 9/5/2012	9
5/3/2013 to 31/3/2013	27
1/4/2013 to 5/4/2013	5
Total	**66**

Although, Joydeep was not present in the UK for the minimum 183 days, he was not absent for the whole year. Hence, Joydeep is considered a resident. As a resident and UK domiciled, Joydeep is liable to capital gains tax on all world gains.

As a result, Joydeep is liable to capital gains tax on a gain arising on the disposal of an overseas asset (i.e. his watch).

Quick Quiz

State whether the following disposals are chargeable.

1. James had two plots of land. Out of these he gave one plot of open land to his married daughter as a gift.
2. Garry sold his private motor car for £8,000 and made a gain of £500.
3. Mark sold government securities for £21,000, which originally cost £20,500.

Answers to Quick Quiz

1. The definition of chargeable disposal includes the gift of a chargeable asset. Therefore, the gift to his daughter is a chargeable disposal.
2. Capital gains arise on sale or disposal of a chargeable asset. However, a private motor car is an exempt asset. Hence the gain on disposal of a private motor car is not chargeable to capital gains tax.
3. Government securities are exempt assets; hence the disposal is not a chargeable disposal.

Self Examination Questions

Question 1

John, who is ordinarily resident in the UK, likes to travel. During 2012-13, he spent only one month in the UK. For the remainder of the year he was in Tasmania, Australia. During the year 2012-13 he sold his farmhouse in Tasmania and made a capital gain of £50,100.

Required:

Advise John as to whether he is liable for capital gains tax in the UK on this capital gain of £50,000.

Question 2

Annette grew up in Germany. She arrived in the UK on 15/08/2012 and stayed there until 31/10/2012. After this date she returned to live in Germany permanently. During her stay in the UK, she purchased 100 shares of Sleep-Well Ltd. Over the next 10 days, the share prices of Sleep-Well increased by £7. She sold all the shares she had purchased and made a capital gain of £35,500.

Required:

Advise her as to whether or not she is liable for capital gains tax.

Answers to Self Examination Questions

Answer to SEQ 1

An individual who is ordinarily resident in the UK but who is not present in the UK for the minimum 183 days is deemed to be resident in the UK for the year provided he was not absent for the entire tax year.

Here, John is ordinarily resident in the UK but was not present in the UK for the minimum 183 days during 2012-13. However, he was not absent for the entire tax year. Hence, he is deemed to be resident in the UK for 2012-13.

A person who is ordinarily a resident in the UK is liable for capital gains tax on UK assets as well as on foreign assets.

Hence, John must pay capital gains tax on capital gains arising from the sale of foreign assets.

Answer to SEQ 2

An individual who is physically present in the UK for at least 183 days during a tax year (excluding days of arrival and departure) is deemed to be resident in the UK for the whole tax year.

Annette was present in the UK for (15/8/2012 to 31/10/2012) i.e. 77 days. Therefore, she is a non-resident.

A person who is a non-resident of the UK is not liable to capital gains tax on any asset whether sold in the UK or outside the UK. Hence, Annett is not liable to pay capital gains tax on the gain of £35,500 arising from the disposal of shares in the UK.

SECTION C

CHARGEABLE GAINS

C2

STUDY GUIDE C2: THE BASIC PRINCIPLES OF COMPUTING GAINS AND LOSSES

Get Through Intro

This Study Guide discusses the **computation of capital gains, calculation of capital gains tax for individuals, treatment of capital losses,** and introduces you to the **concept of the indexation allowance.**

It is essential that you pay considerable attention to this Study Guide as proper computation of capital gains and **paying the proper amount** of tax calculated according to the principles of the Act is **important** for both the government and the taxpayer.

The treatment of transfers between a husband and wife, the treatment to be given to an asset which is lost, damaged or destroyed and the computation of allowable expenditure for the part disposal of a chargeable asset is also discussed in this Study Guide.

A thorough understanding of these principles is a must so that in future you can easily take on these complex issues.

Knowledge of these principles is essential both from the examination point of view and also for your future professional life.

Learning Outcomes

a) Compute capital gains for both individuals and companies.
b) Calculate the indexation allowance available to companies.
c) Explain the treatment of capital losses for both individuals and companies.
d) Explain the treatment of transfers between a husband and wife or between a couple in a civil partnership.
e) Compute the amount of allowable expenditure for a part disposal.
f) Explain the treatment where an asset is damaged, lost or destroyed, and the implications of receiving insurance proceeds and reinvesting such proceeds.

Introduction

Case Study

Suzanne had a good collection of antique furniture. It was worth around £200,000. On 4 May 2011, most of the furniture was destroyed in a fire. Fortunately she had insurance cover on the furniture.

In the month of January 2012, the insurance company paid her compensation of £150,000. As it was antique furniture, she could not replace the furniture and she retained the whole amount.

When she received a notice from HMRC to pay tax, she was surprised. From her point of view, she had lost her furniture and had duly received compensation from the insurance company. Why should she then have to pay tax on that?

We will try to understand the provisions relating to compensation for a destroyed or damaged asset in detail, but first let us look at transfers between husband and wife.

In this Study Guide, we will also look at the basics of capital gain calculations, including allowable deductions and the concept of indexation allowance.

1. Compute the capital gains for both individuals and companies.[2]

[Learning Outcome a]

In the previous Study Guide, we discussed the assets chargeable to CGT and the persons liable to capital gains tax. In this Study Guide, we will explain how to calculate capital gains (and losses) for individuals and companies.

1.1 Basis of assessment

A person's CGT liability is calculated on the basis of the assets disposed of during the tax year. In the case of **individuals, the** tax year is the period between **6 April and 5 April** of the following year, whereas in the case of **companies**, the tax year is the period between **1 April and 31 March** of the following year.

Example

On 6 April 2012, Peter sold 1,000 shares of Success Ltd and made a capital gain of £5,000. This gain is chargeable to tax during the tax year 2012-13 (as the tax year for individuals is the period between 6 April and 5 April).

Suppose the asset is sold by Delta Ltd on 6 April 2013. The gain on the disposal of the asset, if any, is chargeable on the basis of the asset disposed of during the tax year. Therefore, in this case, the gain will be chargeable to tax during the tax year 2013-14.

1.2 Basic computation of gain / loss

Pro forma for Individuals

	£
Disposal consideration	X
Less: Incidental costs of disposal	(X)
Net disposal consideration	**X**
Less: Allowable deductions	
Acquisition costs (including incidental costs)	(X)
Enhancement expenditure	(X)
Net gain / (loss)	**X/(X)**

Pro forma for Companies

	£
Disposal consideration	X
Less: Incidental costs of disposal	(X)
Net disposal consideration	**X**
Less: Allowable deductions	
Acquisition costs (including incidental costs)	(X)
Enhancement expenditure	(X)
Unindexed gain	**X**
Less: Indexation allowance	**(X)**
Net indexed gain / (loss)	**X/(X)**

Tip

The indexation allowance is applicable only to companies and was withdrawn for individuals from 6 April 2008.

Let us look at each term in detail.

1. Disposal consideration

This is the cash or cash equivalent value received on disposal of the asset. A gain or loss may be realised on the sale or gift of an asset. However, transfers on death are exempt from CGT.

Method of disposal	Disposal proceeds
Sale	Sale proceeds
Sale to a connected person	Market value
Gift	Market value
Transfer to spouse / civil partner	Special rules (refer to Study Guide C3)

Tip

Market value is the value the asset can expect to realise if sold on the open market.

Connected person

On a disposal to a connected person, the market value is used as disposal proceeds.

a) A person is connected with:

i. His spouse / civil partner.
ii. His relatives (brothers, sisters, ancestors (parents, grandparents etc.) and lineal descendants (children, grandchildren etc.).
iii. His spouse / civil partner's relatives and their spouse / civil partners.

b) A company is connected with

i. The persons controlling it.
ii. Companies under the same control are connected with each other.

Example

Doll Plc and Dot Plc are sister companies (i.e. both companies are managed by the same group of people). During 2012-13, Doll Plc sold its industrial building to Dot Plc for £100,000, when the actual market value of the same building was £150,000.

As the transaction is between two connected persons, the market value on the date of sale (i.e. £150,000) is deemed to be sale proceeds and not the actual amount paid (i.e. £100,000), for the calculation of capital gains.

2. Incidental costs of disposal

Incidental costs of disposal, which are allowable deductions include:

a) legal fees e.g. legal fees paid to lawyers for legal advice when devising agreements
b) estate agent's fees
c) advertising costs e.g. advertisements given in a newspaper
d) auctioneer's fees

Tip

Auction is the sale of an asset by giving public notice; the asset is sold to the person who is ready to give the highest price for the asset.

3. Allowable deductions

a) If purchased, acquisition cost.

b) If acquired as a gift, market value at the date of acquisition.

c) If acquired from a connected person, market value at the date of acquisition.

d) If inherited (acquired as a result of an individual's death), probate value (market value on the date of death).

Example

George's grandfather gave him a gold ring on his eighteenth birthday. On that day, the market value of the ring was £2,000. On 2 May 2012, George sold the ring for £2,100.

In this situation, when calculating chargeable gains, the cost of the ring received by George is considered to be £2,000 i.e. the market value of the ring on the day it was given.

e) Incidental costs of acquisition (valuation fees, legal fees).

f) Enhancement expenditure (capital costs of additions and improvements).

Example

Tracy bought a piece of land in Manchester for £40,000. In May 2012, she constructed a new industrial building on this land. The cost of constructing this industrial building was £20,000.

She disposed of the industrial building in June 2012 for £120,000. The total cost will be the cost of land (£40,000) and the expenditure incurred on the industrial building (£20,000) which is reflected in the value of the asset on the date of its disposal. Tracy can deduct this expenditure from the sales proceeds to calculate the capital gain.

Example

Linda bought a shop in May 2004 for £50,000. She paid £2,000 in legal fees and stamp duty to register the title of the shop in her name. Due to an earthquake in June 2012, the plaster on the walls of the shop cracked. She spent £1,000 repairing the walls. At the same time, she spent £6,500 on redecorating the shop.

In December 2012, Linda sold the shop for £80,000.

Here, the capital gain is calculated as follows:

	£
Disposal consideration	80,000
Less: Incidental costs of disposal	-
Net disposal consideration	**80,000**
Less: Allowable deductions	
Acquisition costs (£50,000 + £2,000)	(52,000)
Enhancement expenditure	-
Net gain	**28,000**

Notes:

1. Repairs and maintenance expenses are not considered to be enhancement expenditure as they are not of a capital nature.
2. Redecoration is not enhancement.

SUMMARY

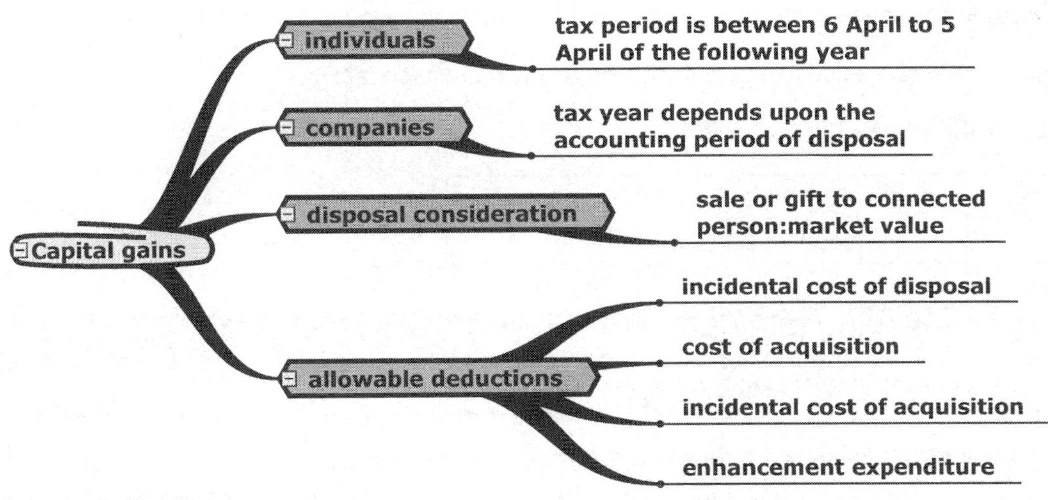

Test Yourself 1

Malcolm purchased a business asset in April 2005 for £40,000. In order to purchase machinery he took out a bank loan. To obtain this bank loan he had to pay £500 for legal and administrative fees.

In June 2009, he spent £10,000 on further machinery to improve the efficiency of the asset. In September 2012, he sold the asset for £30,000. To help him sell the asset, he appointed an agent, whom he paid £500.

Required:

Calculate chargeable gains / losses.

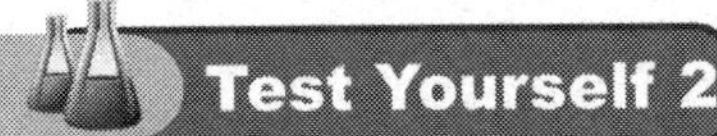

Test Yourself 2

On 20 April 2012, Margaret gave her diamond jewellery to her daughter Iris as a wedding present. On the day of the gift, the market value of the jewellery was £20,000. Margaret had originally purchased the jewellery for £15,000.

Required:

Advise Margaret as to whether she is liable for CGT.

---

2. Calculate the indexation allowance available to companies.[2]

[Learning Outcome b]

2.1 Indexation allowance for companies

The intention is to tax the increase in the capital value of an asset. The indexation allowance was introduced as a relief against inflation, and acts to increase the base cost of an asset for the purposes of calculating a capital gain on a disposal.

It is only available for the purposes of calculating capital gains for **companies**.

Example

In 2011, it was possible to purchase 1 litre of petrol for £1. However in 2012, a litre of petrol cost £1.30. In short, more money was needed to purchase the same quantity of petrol i.e. the purchasing power of money had decreased.

Companies are allowed an indexation allowance from the month of acquisition of an asset to the month of its disposal to take account of this.

2.2 Calculation of indexation allowance

1. The indexation allowance is calculated using the movement in the RPI (Retail Price Index).

2. Each item of allowable expenditure is multiplied by the indexation factor.

The formula for the indexation factor is:

$$\frac{\text{RPI for the month of disposal} - \text{RPI for the month of acquisition}}{\text{RPI for the month of acquisition}}$$

You will be given the RPIs in the exam if you need them.

3. The indexation allowance must be **rounded to three decimal places**.

4. The **indexation allowance cannot** be used to **create or increase a loss**.

5. The indexation allowance is calculated separately for each item of expenditure (such as cost of disposal, enhancement expenditure etc).

Example

Good Ltd purchased an asset in May 1999 (RPI 165.6) for £28,500. The company sold it in March 2012 for £54,100 (RPI 240.8). In this situation, the capital gains after indexation allowances are calculated as follows:

	£
Disposal consideration	54,100
Less: Incidental costs of disposal	-
Net disposal consideration	54,100
Less: Allowable deductions	
Acquisition costs	(28,500)
Unindexed gain	25,600
Less: Indexation allowance	
$\frac{240.8 - 165.6}{165.6}$ = (0.454) x £28,500	(12,939)
Indexed gain	**12,661**

Rounded to three decimal places

Example

Multi Ltd acquired a chargeable asset in April 2003. The cost of acquisition was £20,000. The company sold the asset in March 2012. The calculations of chargeable gain assuming actual sales proceeds were as follows:

1. £27,500
2. £22,800
3. £17,920

(RPI of April 2003 – 181.2, RPI of March 2012 – 240.8)

Continued on the next page

	1 £	2 £	3 £
Disposal consideration	27,500	22,800	17,920
Less: Allowable deductions			
Acquisition costs	(20,000)	(20,000)	(20,000)
Unindexed gain / (loss)	**7,500**	**2,800**	**(2,080)**
Less: Indexation allowance	(6,578) (W1)	(2,800) (note 1)	- (note 2)
Indexed gain / (loss)	**922**	-	**(2,080)**

Working

W1 Indexation allowance = $\frac{(240.8 - 181.2)}{181.2} \times £20,000$

= 0.329 x £20,000

= £6,578

Notes

1. Indexation allowance is restricted to £2,800, as indexation allowance cannot be used to create a loss.
2. The company cannot claim indexation allowance, as indexation allowance cannot be used to increase loss.
3. The amount of capital gain will be charged to corporation tax.
4. The loss will be set off against other capital gains.

Example

Rosary Inc purchased a business asset on 20 August 2003 (RPI 181.6) for £27,800. The company incurred enhancement expenditure of £5,000 in December 2006 (RPI 202.7).

Rosary Inc sold the asset in March 2012 (RPI 240.8) for £43,500. Chargeable gains on the disposal of the business asset are calculated as follows:

Calculation of chargeable gains of Rosary Inc

	£
Disposal consideration	43,500
Less: Allowable deductions	
Acquisition costs	(27,800)
Enhancement expenditure	(5,000)
Unindexed gain	**10,700**
Less: Indexation allowance (W1)	(9,830)
Indexed gain / (loss)	**870**

Note: The amount of gain will be charged to corporation tax.

Working

W1 Indexation allowance

	£
1. On cost of acquisition	
$\frac{240.8 - 181.6}{181.6}$ = (0.326) x £27,800	9,063
2. On enhancement expenditure	
$\frac{240.8 - 202.7}{202.7}$ = (0.188) x £5,000	940
Total	**10,003**

Although you may be required to calculate the indexation allowance, the examiner has said that it is not examinable in detail. In many cases the actual indexation allowance figure will be provided as part of the question, or the figure given for the cost of an asset will already take account of indexation.

SUMMARY

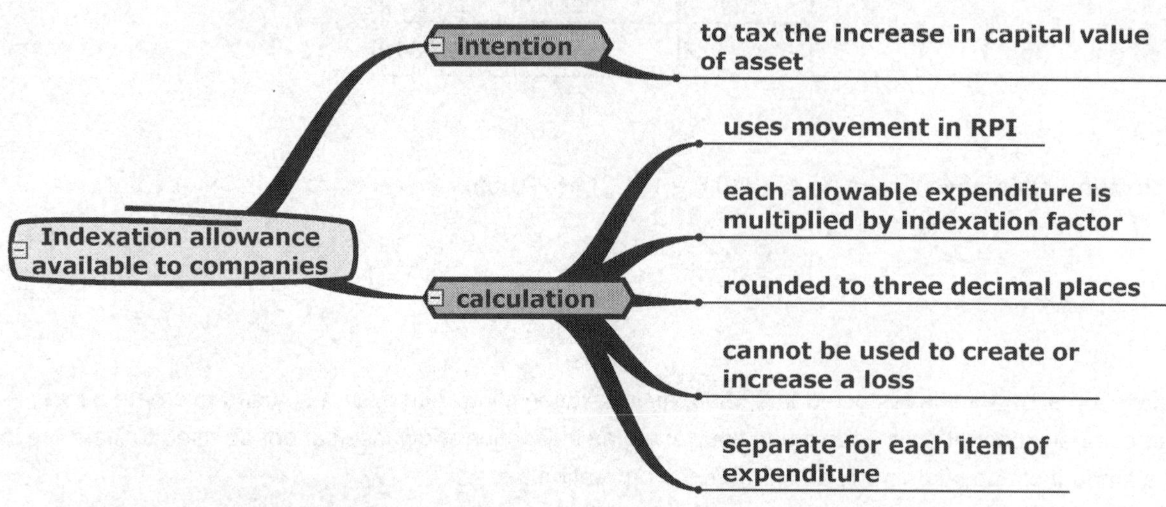

In July 2003 (RPI 181.3) Arc Ltd purchased an asset for £35,300, and disposed of the asset in March 2012 (RPI 240.8) for £38,000.

Required:

a) Show the calculation for capital gains.

b) Suppose Lisa, a professional, owns this asset, what is the chargeable gain on disposal of the asset?

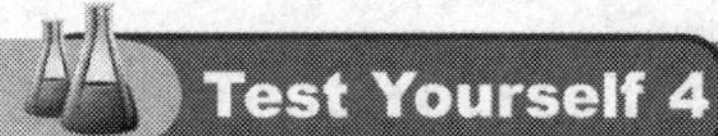

Mars Ltd purchased a factory on 14 October 1999 (RPI 166.5) for £175,000. During March 2001 (RPI 172.2), the company incurred a cost of £40,000 for the extension of the factory.

During May 2002 (RPI 176.2), a fire occurred and the roof of the factory was damaged. So, the roof was repaired and the cost incurred for this purpose was £3,000.

On 25 March 2012 (RPI 240.8), Mars Ltd sold the factory for £400,000.

Mars Ltd incurred the following legal fees both at the time of purchasing the factory and at the time of sale.

Legal fees	£
At the time of purchase	4,000
At the time of sale	7,500

Required:

Calculate the chargeable gains of Mars Ltd.

3. Explain the treatment of capital losses for both individuals and companies.[1]

[Learning Outcome c]

3.1 Treatment of capital losses for companies

1. A capital loss is **first set against any CAPITAL gains in the same accounting period.**
2. **If** any capital loss **remains**, it is **carried forward and set against the first available capital gains in future** accounting periods.
3. When a company incurs a capital loss, the capital gain in the taxable total profits calculation is nil, **(never a negative figure). Capital losses are never set against other income.**

Example

Margaret Ltd has been engaged in a trading business for many years.

The results of its trading and other incomes for two years are as follows:

	Year ended 31 March 2012 £	Year ended 31 March 2013 £
Adjusted trading profit / (loss)	60,000	(20,500)
Property business income	5,000	12,000
Capital gain / (loss)	(10,000)	90,000

The taxable income of Margaret Ltd for the two years is calculated as follows:

	Year ended 31 March 2012 £	Year ended 31 March 2013 £
Adjusted trading profit	60,000	-
Property business income	5,000	12,000
Capital gain (W1)	-	80,000
Total income	**65,000**	**92,000**
Less: Loss relief	-	(20,500)
Taxable total profits	**65,000**	**71,500**

Working

W1 Capital gains

Capital gains for the year ended 31 March 2013 = £90,000 - £10,000 (b/f loss of year ended 31 March 2012) = £80,000.

3.2 Treatment of capital losses for individuals

1. **Current year losses**

a) Must be **set off against current year capital gains**, and **cannot be restricted** to preserve annual exemption.

b) Are set off **before brought forward capital losses and annual exemption.**

Example

Information relating to three friends is shown below.

	Tom £	Dick £	Harry £
Capital gains for 2012-13	12,000	15,000	13,000
Capital losses for 2012-13	13,400	800	10,500

Continued on the next page

Calculation of taxable gains is as follows:

	Tom	Dick	Harry
	£	£	£
Capital gain for 2012-13	12,000	15,000	13,000
Less: Current year capital loss (note)	(12000)	(800)	(10500)
Brought forward capital loss	-	-	-
Chargeable gain	-	**14,200**	**2,500**
Less: Annual exemption	-	(10,600)	(2,500)
Taxable gain / (loss)	-	**3,600**	-

Note: the current year's losses must be **set off against the current year's gains**, and **cannot be restricted** to preserve annual exemption.

Therefore, it is not possible for Tom to restrict the current year's losses to £1,400 (£12,000 - £10,600) to preserve the annual exemption of £10,600. Tom's remaining loss of £1,400 (£12,000 - £13,400) can be carried forward and set against the first available capital gains in future tax years.

Also, it is not possible for Harry to restrict the current year's losses. He has to set off the current year's losses in full, even though his annual exemption to the extent of £8,100 (i.e. £10,600 - £2,500) is wasted.

2. Capital losses b/f

a) Must be set off against the first available net gains in the future.
b) Losses brought forward are only set off to reduce current year capital gains (after current year losses) to the annual exempt amount. Note, this means that the b/f losses are deducted up to the amount which makes up the total net gains equal to the exempt amount.

The following is the available information for the three friends.

	Tom	Dick	Harry
	£	£	£
Capital gains for 2012-13	8,000	15,000	21,000
Capital losses for 2012-13	13,400	800	10,000
Brought forward capital losses from 2011-12	600	1,000	5,000

Calculation of taxable gains is as follows:

	Tom	Dick	Harry
	£	£	£
Capital gain for 2012-13	8,000	15,000	21,000
Less: Current year capital loss	(8,000)	(800)	(10,000)
Current year net capital gain	-	**14,200**	**11,000**
Brought forward capital loss	-	(1,000)	(400)
Chargeable gain	-	**13,200**	**10,600**
Less: Annual exemption	-	(10,600)	(10,600)
Taxable gains / (loss)	-	**2,600**	-

Working

W1 Loss memorandum

	Tom	Dick	Harry
	£	£	£
Brought forward capital losses from 2011-12	600	1,000	5,000
Less: Set off against gains for 2012-13	-	(1000)	(400)
Add: Current year unrelieved capital loss 2012-13 (£13,400 - £8,000)	5,400		
Loss c/f to 2012-13	**6,000**	**0**	**4,600**

Continued on the next page

Note: After set off of current year capital losses of Harry, the balance of the gain remaining is £11,000. Brought forward losses are set off to reduce current year capital gains up to the annual exemption amount, hence loss relief for brought forward losses is restricted to £400, so as to leave net gains exactly equal to the annual exemption amount of £10,600 (£11,000 – £400).

In August 2012, Robin sold a business asset and made a capital gain of £25,000. He also sold gold coins realising a capital loss of £1,500. He has a brought forward capital loss of £3,000. His trading income for the tax year 2012-13 is £30,000. His tax liability is calculated as follows:

Step 1 Computation of income tax liability

	£
Trading profits	30,000
Less: Personal allowance	(8,105)
Taxable income	**21,895**
Income Tax	
£21,895 @20%	4,379

Step 2 Computation of capital gains tax liability

	£
Capital gain	25,000
Less: Current year capital loss	(1,500)
Current year net capital gain	**23,500**
Brought forward capital loss	(3,000)
Net chargeable gains	**20,500**
Less: Annual exemption	(10,600)
Taxable gains	**9,900**
Capital gains tax at 18% (note)	**1,782**

Note: Robin's taxable income is £21,895 (£30,000 -£8,105). Therefore, his unused basic rate band is £12,475 (£34,370 - £21,895). The entire taxable gains of £9,900 fall within the unused basic rate band; therefore it will be taxed at the rate of 18%.

3. Losses on disposal to a connected person

a) Losses on disposals to a connected person **cannot be set off** against all chargeable gains.

b) They can **only be set against gains made on disposals to the same connected person** in the same or future years.

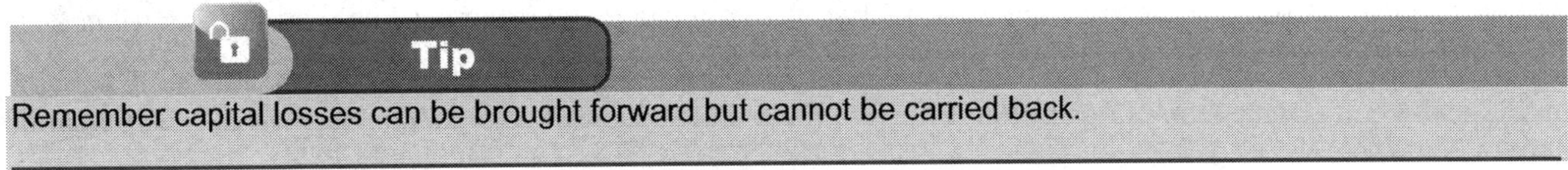

Remember capital losses can be brought forward but cannot be carried back.

SUMMARY

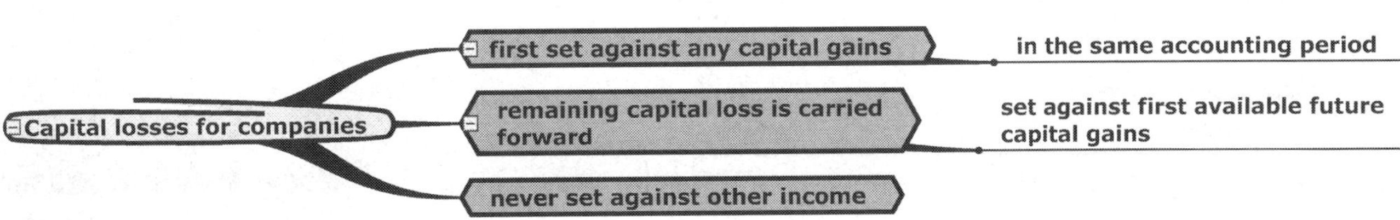

SUMMARY

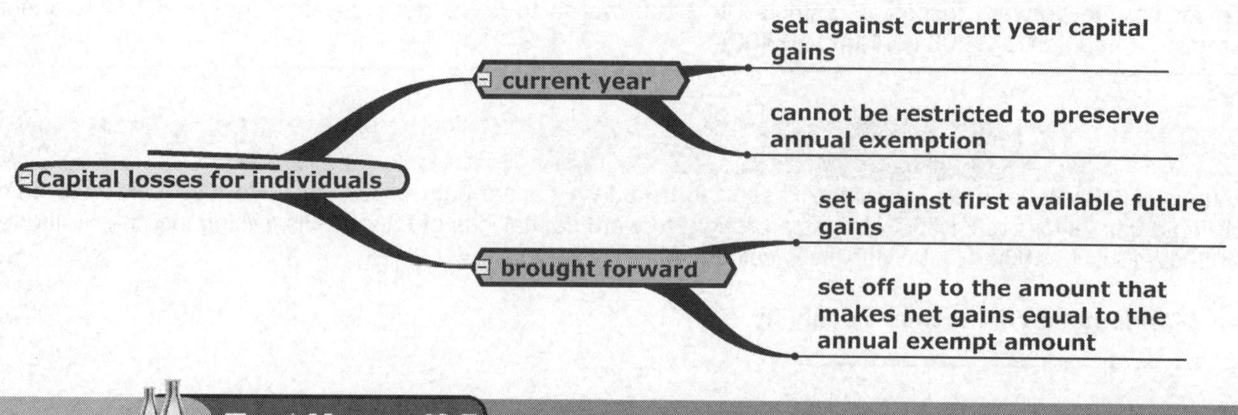

Test Yourself 5

Alan has a loss of £37,100 carried forward from the previous year (2011-12). His current year's (2012-13) capital gain is £33,000, and his capital loss is £2,700.

Required:

Show the calculation of chargeable gains for the tax year 2012-13.

4. Explain the treatment of transfers between a husband and wife or between a couple in a civil partnership.[2]

[Learning Outcome d]

1. A disposal between husband and wife / civil partners is **not exempt**.
2. If transfer is after 6 April 2008, original cost of the asset to the spouse disposing the asset is considered the disposal value for the spouse acquiring the asset so that neither a chargeable gain nor an allowable loss arises. This is known as a "No gain / no loss" transfer.

Tip

Situations before 6 April 2008 are not examinable.

3. The no gain / no loss transfer displaces the usual rule that market value is used if transfer is between connected persons.
4. On a subsequent disposal, the acquisition cost for the spouse making the disposal is the value taken into account to reach a no gain / no loss position on the original transfer.

Example

In January 2004 Roger purchased 2000 shares for £20,000. In May 2011, Roger transferred these shares to his wife, Camilla. The market value of the shares on that date was £35,000.

As the disposal is between husband and wife, neither a chargeable gain nor an allowable loss arises. Hence, it is considered that the shares are transferred to the spouse (wife) at the original cost of £20,000.

In October 2012, Camilla sold these shares for £47,000. Calculation of chargeable gain on this disposal of shares is as follows:

	£
Disposal consideration	47,000
Less: Allowable deductions	
Acquisition costs (note1)	(20,000)
Net chargeable gain	**27,000**

Continued on the next page

Note: in the case of the disposal of an asset between husband and wife, the acquiring spouse is treated as having acquired the asset at its original cost to the other spouse to make a no gain / no loss transfer. In the case of Camilla, it is assumed that she had acquired these shares for £20,000.

Test Yourself 6

Michael sold a piece of land on 10 May 2012 for £250,000. This land had been purchased by Margaret, Michael's wife for £190,000 on 25 July 2009. She later transferred the land to Michael on 20 November 2011 for £225,000. On this date, the market value of the land was £210,000.

Required:

Calculate Michael's chargeable gains.

5. Compute the amount of allowable expenditure for a part disposal.[2]

[Learning Outcome e]

We have already seen in Study Guide C1, that a chargeable disposal **includes the disposal of part of an asset**. As only a part of the asset is sold (e.g. John sold only the first floor of his house and kept the ground floor for himself), only part of the original cost of the entire asset can be used as the acquisition cost.

Important points to note

1. The **original cost** is **allocated** between the **part disposed of** and the **part retained**.
2. The **cost is allocated according to the market values** of the part disposed of and the part retained as.at the date of disposal
3. The cost is **not allocated based on size** (e.g. if part of a plot of land is sold).
4. When the part retained is eventually sold, the balance of the original cost is used.

The cost of the part disposed of is calculated as:

Cost of the part disposed = Total Cost x A/(A+B)

Where:

A is the market value of the part being disposed of, and
B is the market value of the part being retained.

Example

Jack purchased 5 acres of land on 15 July 2010 for £250,000. He sold 3 acres of land for £290,000 on 20 February 2013. The land was never used for business purposes. The market value of the unsold 2 acres of land as on 20 February 2013 was £110,000.

Here, we will have to calculate the cost of the piece of land that was sold.
Out of 5 acres of land, 3 acres were sold.

Therefore, the cost relating to the three acres of land = Total Cost x A/(A+B)

= £250,000 x £290,000/ (£290,000+£110,000)
= £250,000 x £290,000/£400,000
= £181,250

This is how you should present the answer in the examination:

	£
Disposal consideration	290,000
Less: Allowable deductions	
Acquisition costs (including incidental costs)	(181,250)
Chargeable gains	**108,750**

In December 1998 (RPI 164.4), Alistair Ltd bought a chargeable asset for £32,000. In March 2012 (RPI 240.8), it sold 40% of the interest in the asset for £14,000. The cost of disposing the asset was £480.
The market value of the remaining 60% of interest in the asset is £38,000.
The calculation of chargeable gain on part disposal is as follows:

	£
Disposal consideration	14,000
Less: Incidental costs of disposal	(480)
Net disposal consideration	**13,520**
Less: Allowable deductions	
Part acquisition costs	(8,615)
£14,000/(£14,000 + £38,000) x £32,000	
Gain	**4,905**
Less: Indexation allowance (note)	
$\frac{240.8 - 164.4}{164.4}$ = (0.465) x £8,615	(4,006)
Chargeable gain	**899**

Note: companies are eligible for indexation allowance from the date of acquisition until the date of disposal.

In December 2000 (RPI 172.2), Soft Ltd purchased a chargeable asset for £50,000. In February 2012 (RPI 239.9), it sold 35% of the interest in the asset for £22,000. The cost of disposing the asset was £1,400.

The market value of the remaining 65% of interest in the asset was £56,000. In March 2012 (RPI 240.8), Soft Ltd disposed of the remaining part of the asset for £56,000.

Required:

Calculate the chargeable gains of Soft Ltd.

6. Explain the treatment where an asset is damaged, lost or destroyed, and the implications of receiving insurance proceeds and reinvesting such proceeds.[2]

[Learning Outcome f]

6.1 Asset lost / destroyed entirely

Asset lost and asset destroyed receive the same treatment.

This covers the following situations

1. No compensation received
2. Compensation received, but no replacement
3. Compensation received, asset replaced

1. No compensation received

If an asset is entirely lost or destroyed, then there is a **disposal** for capital gains tax purposes, giving rise to an **allowable loss.**

Example

Merry bought a painting for £50,000 in May 2007. It was destroyed by fire in August 2012, and no compensation was received.

Here, she realises an allowable loss of £50,000 (as the proceeds are nil).

---

2. Compensation received, but no replacement

If an asset is totally destroyed, and compensation or insurance proceeds are received, this is treated as a **CGT disposal**, with the **money received being the proceeds**.

Example

Continuing the example of Merry
Assume that she received insurance proceeds of £65,000 in October 2012 as a compensation for the painting.

Here, the transaction will be treated as disposal of the painting. The disposal proceeds are £65,000 and cost of acquisition is £50,000. Accordingly, capital gains will be:

	£
Sale proceeds (insurance proceeds)	65,000
Less Cost of acquisition	(50,000)
Chargeable gain	**15,000**

---

3. Compensation received, asset replaced

a) **Full proceeds used for replacement:** if all the proceeds are used to buy a replacement asset within twelve months, the **gain** arising on destruction of the asset can be **deferred by deducting the gain from the base cost of the replacement asset**.

Example

Continuing the example of Merry
Assume that in March 2013, Merry purchased a replacement asset costing £67,000.

The gain arising on destruction of the painting is:

	£
Sale proceeds (insurance proceeds)	65,000
Less: Cost of acquisition	(50,000)
Deferred gain	**15,000**

Here, as all the insurance proceeds of £65,000 are used to buy a replacement asset within 12 months, the gain of £15,000 can be deferred by deducting it from the base cost of the replacement asset.

Therefore, the deemed or base cost of the replaced asset will be:

	£
Cost of replaced asset	67,000
Less Deferred gain	(15,000)
Deemed cost of the replaced asset	**52,000**

---

b) **Part of the proceeds used for replacement:** if the full proceeds are not used for the replacement asset, the gain (up to the **amount** of proceeds **not reinvested**) is **chargeable now**, and the balance of the gain is deducted from the base cost of the replacement asset.

Glory bought a painting for £45,000 in May 2008. It was destroyed by fire in December 2012. Glory received insurance proceeds of £58,000.

In March 2013, Glory purchased a replacement asset costing £54,000.

	£
Sale proceeds (insurance proceeds)	58,000
Less: Cost of acquisition	(45,000)
Total gain	**13,000**
Less: Amount not re-invested (£58,000 - £54,000) chargeable to capital gains	(4,000)
Deferred gain	**9,000**

Here, out of the total insurance proceeds of £58,000, only £54,000 is used for the replacement asset. Therefore, out of a total gain of £13,000, £4,000 (£58,000 - £54,000) is chargeable to capital gains tax immediately. The balance of the gain (i.e. £9,000) can be deferred by deducting the gain from the base cost of the replacement asset.

Therefore, the base cost of the replaced asset will be

	£
Cost of the replaced asset	54,000
Less: Deferred gain	(9,000)
Deemed cost of the replaced asset	**45,000**

Diagram 1: Asset entirely lost or destroyed

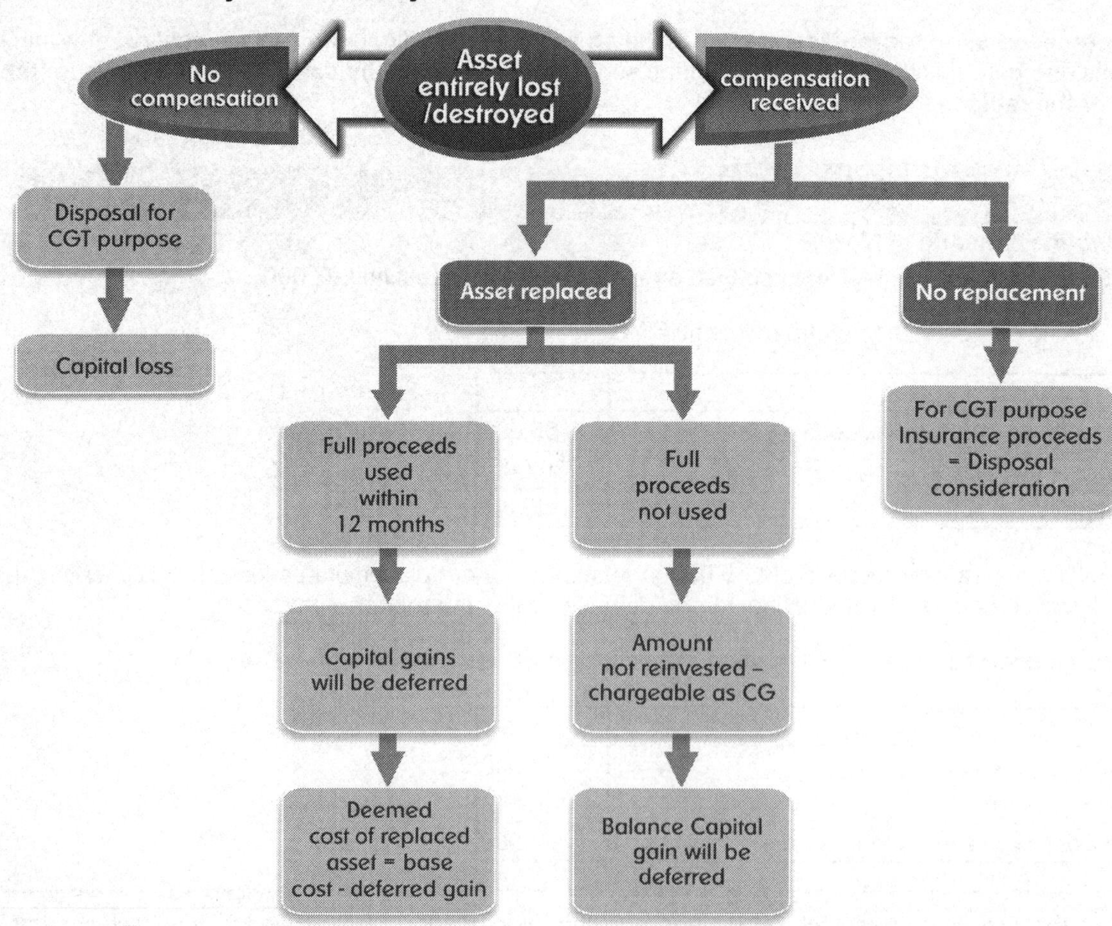

6.2 Asset damaged, compensation received

When an asset has been damaged, and compensation or insurance proceeds are received, this is **treated as a part disposal** (for part disposal, refer to Learning Outcome 2 above).The market value of the asset in its damaged condition is taken as the market value of the part retained.

If compensation is used to restore the asset, the taxpayer may claim that instead of being treated as a part disposal, the sum received can be deducted from the allowable expenditure when the gain is computed on the subsequent disposal of the asset.

To claim this, one of the following conditions must be met

a) All of the sum received must be spent on restoring the asset **OR**
b) The amount not spent on restoring the asset is 'small' **OR**
c) The amount received is **'small'**

Definition of 'small'

For this purpose, the sum is regarded as small, if the sum received / not used for restoration is **less than 5% of the proceeds received,** restricted to **maximum of £3,000**.

Example

If all of the compensation amount is used to restore the asset

Alan bought an asset for £10,000. The asset was damaged and the value of the asset in its damaged condition was £2,000. Alan received compensation of £4,000. He spent all the compensation on restoring the asset.

Here, as all the proceeds were used in restoration, a claim may be made to deduct the proceeds from the cost of the asset i.e. not to treat this as part-disposal.

The allowable expenditure on **subsequent disposal** is £10,000 calculated as follows

	£
Cost of asset	10,000
Less: Compensation receipt	(4,000)
	6,000
Add: Expenditure on restoration	4,000
Adjusted cost	**10,000**

Example

If compensation not used in restoring the asset is small

Alan bought an asset for £10,000. The asset was damaged and the value of the asset in its damaged condition was £2,000, Alan received compensation of £4,000. He spent £3,900 of the compensation on restoring the asset.

Therefore, £100 of the compensation was not used to restore the asset. This does not exceed 5% of the capital sum received and is also less than £3,000, so a claim may be made to deduct the proceeds from the cost of the asset i.e. to not treat this as part-disposal.

The allowable expenditure on **subsequent disposal** is £9,900 calculated as follows:

	£
Cost of asset	10,000
Less: Compensation received	(4,000)
	6,000
Add: Expenditure on restoration	3,900
Adjusted cost	**9,900**

If the compensation remaining is not small, then all proceeds would be treated as part disposal.

If compensation not used in restoring the asset is not small

In April 2006, Winston purchased an antique statue for £100,000. On 5 May 2012, the statue was damaged by fire. In December 2012, the insurance company paid him compensation of £28,000.

Winston did not use the sum received from the insurance company for restoring the statue. The market value of the damaged statue was £150,000.

Here, the capital gains are calculated as follows

	£
Disposal consideration	28,000
Less: Allowable deductions	
Part acquisition costs	
£28,000/(£28,000 + £150,000) x £100,000	(15,730)
Net gain	**12,270**

Note: Winston can carry forward the balance of allowable expenditure, £84,270 (£100,000 - £15,730) and can use the same in the calculation of the gain arising on subsequent disposal.

If the sum received from the insurance company is not used for restoration of the asset, then the taxpayer cannot avoid part disposal.

It is possible to claim to have part of the capital sum which was applied in restoring the asset deducted from the acquisition cost of the asset. The proceeds not applied in restoring the asset are treated as a part-disposal.

Diagram 2: Asset damaged

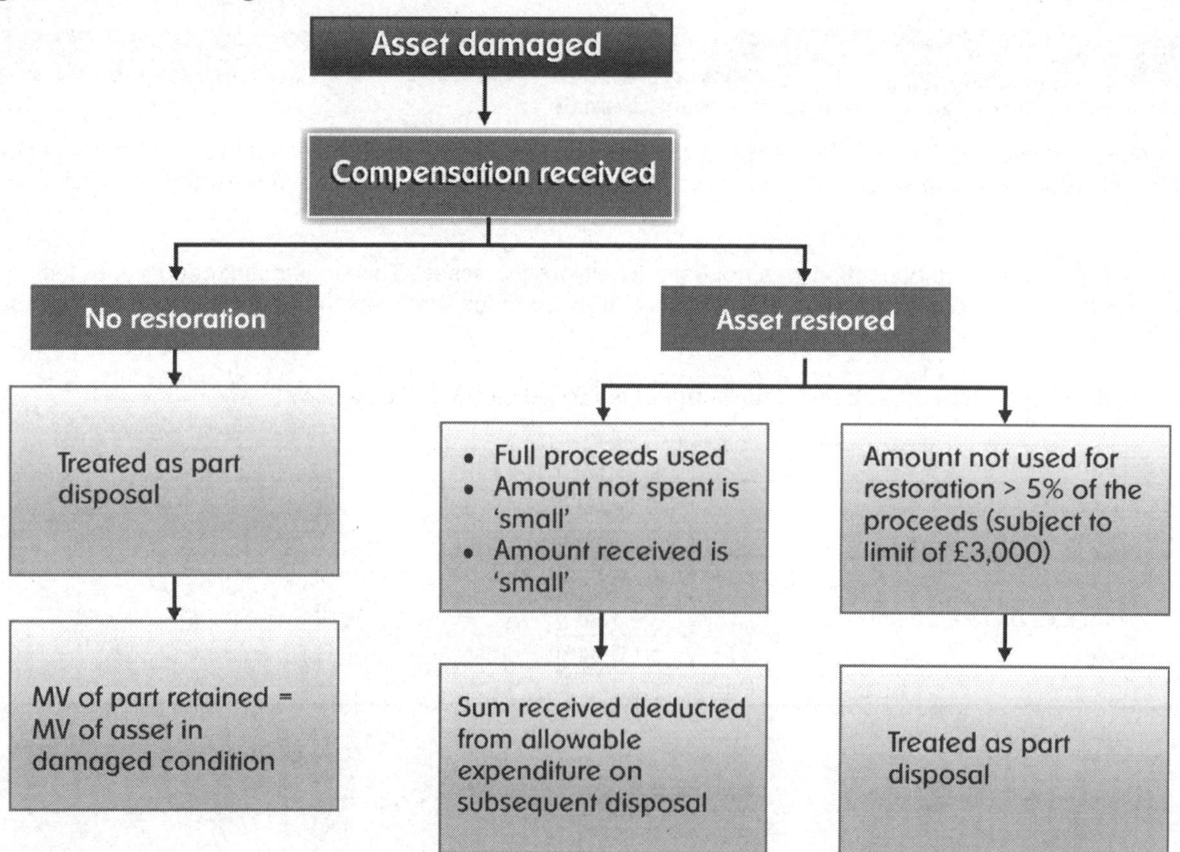

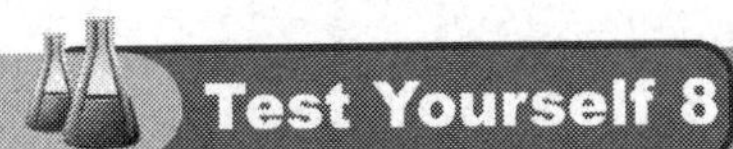

Test Yourself 8

Jill purchased a painting for £41,000 in January 2009. On 3 May 2012, the painting was destroyed due to a fire. In August 2012, she received a sum of £48,000 from the insurance company. She spent £49,000 to replace the painting.

Required:

Show the computation of chargeable gains.

Answers to Test Yourself

Answer to TY 1

Calculation of chargeable gains

	£
Disposal consideration	30,000
Less: Incidental costs of disposal	(500)
Net disposal consideration	**29,500**
Less: Allowable deductions	
Acquisition costs (including incidental costs) (£40,000 + £500)	(40,500)
Enhancement expenditure	(10,000)
Gain / (loss)	**(21,000)**

Note: £10,000 spent on machinery will be treated as enhancement expenditure, as it improves the efficiency of the asset.

Answer to TY 2

Margaret had given her diamond jewellery to her daughter as a present. As the gift of an asset is also considered to be a chargeable disposal, the chargeable gain is calculated as follows:

	£
Disposal consideration (note)	20,000
Less: Incidental costs of disposal	-
Net disposal consideration	**20,000**
Less: Allowable deductions	
Acquisition costs	(15,000)
Gain / (loss)	**5,000**

Note: when an asset is disposed of by way of a gift (i.e. for less than market value), the disposal consideration is the market value of an asset on the day of the gift.

Answer to TY 3

(a) Calculation of indexed capital gains of Arc Ltd

	£
Disposal consideration	38,000
Less: Allowable deductions	
Acquisition costs	(35,300)
Unindexed gain	**2,700**
Less: Indexation allowance (W1)	(2,700)
Indexed gain / (loss)	**-**

Working

W1 Indexation allowance = $\frac{£240.8 - £181.3}{£181.3}$ = (0.328) x £35,300

= £11,585

However, the allowable indexation allowance is £2,700, as indexation allowance cannot convert gain into loss.

(b) Computation of indexed capital gains of Lisa

	£
Disposal consideration	38,000
Less: Allowable deductions	
Acquisition costs	(35,300)
Gain	**2,700**

Note: indexation allowance is withdrawn for individuals from 6 April 2008.

Answer to TY 4

Computation of indexed capital gains / losses

	£
Disposal consideration	400,000
Less: Incidental costs of disposal	(7,500)
Net disposal consideration	**392,500**
Less: Allowable deductions	
Acquisition costs (£175,000 + £4,000)	(179,000)
Enhancement expenditure	(40,000)
Unindexed gain	**173,500**
Less: Indexation allowance (W1)	(95,754)
Indexed gain / (loss)	**77,746**

Working

W1 Indexation allowance

	£
1. On cost of acquisition	
$\frac{240.8 - 166.5}{166.5}$ = (0.446) x £179,000	79,834
2. On enhancement expenditure	
$\frac{240.8 - 172.2}{172.2}$ = (0.398) x £40,000	15,920
Total	**95,754**

Notes

1. Repairs and maintenance expenses are not considered to be enhancement expenditure as they are not of a capital nature.
2. The amount of indexed gain will be charged to corporation tax.

Answer to TY 5

Calculation of taxable gains

	£
Capital gain for 2012-13	33,000
Less: Current year capital loss	(2,700)
Current year net capital gain	**30,300**
Brought forward capital loss (note)	(19,700)
Chargeable gains	**10,600**
Less: Annual exemption	(10,600)
Taxable gains / (loss)	-

Note: relief for brought forward capital losses is restricted to £19,700 so that Alan can take full advantage of annual exemption. The remaining loss of £17,400 (£37,100 – 19,700) can be carried forward to set off against future capital gains.

Working

W1 Loss memorandum

	£
Capital losses b/f from 2011-12	37,100
Less: Set off against gains for 2012-13	(19,700)
Loss c/f to 2013-14	**17,400**

Answer to TY 6

	£
Disposal consideration	250,000
Less: Allowable deductions	
Acquisition costs (note)	(190,000)
Chargeable gains	**60,000**

Note: in the case of the disposal of an asset between husband and wife, the acquiring spouse is treated as having acquired the asset at its original cost to the other spouse. In the case of Michael, it is assumed that he had acquired the land for £190,000. The value at which Michael purchased the asset from his wife and the market value of the land are not relevant where the transfer is between a husband and wife or between civil partners.

Answer to TY 7

Calculation of chargeable gains on disposal of 35% interest in the asset

	£
Disposal consideration	22,000
Less: Incidental costs of disposal	(1,400)
Net disposal consideration	**20,600**
Less: Allowable deductions	
Part acquisition costs	
£22,000/(£22,000 + £56,000) x £50,000	(14,103)
Gain	**6,497**
Less: Indexation allowance	
$\frac{239.9 - 172.2}{172.2}$ = (0.393) x £14,103	(5,542)
Indexed gain	**955**

Note: companies are eligible for indexation allowance from the date of acquisition until the date of disposal. The cost when a part of an asset is sold is allocated according to the market value at the time of the part disposal of the part disposed of and the part that is retained.

Calculation of chargeable gains on disposal of remaining 65% interest in the asset

	£
Disposal consideration	56,000
Less: Allowable deductions	
Part acquisition costs (note)	
(£50,000 - £14,103)	(35,897)
Gain	**20,103**
Less: Indexation allowance	
$\frac{240.8 - 172.2}{172.2}$ = (0.398) x £35,897	(14,287)
Indexed gain	**5,816**

Note: The acquisition cost of 65% interest in the asset is calculated as follows:

Part acquisition cost (65% interest) = Total cost – cost allocated on sale of 35% interest
= £50,000 - £14,103 = £35,897

Answer to TY 8

Computation of chargeable gains

	£
Disposal consideration	48,000
Less: Cost of acquisition	(41,000)
Chargeable gains	**7,000**

£7,000 may be deducted from the cost of the painting purchased to replace the original painting. Thus, the cost of the new painting will be £42,000 (£49,000 - £7,000).

Due to this, Jill's capital gains tax liability is postponed until she sells the painting that she had purchased to replace the original.

Quick Quiz

1. What is market value?
2. What is the purpose of providing indexation to assets?
3. Is indexation allowance given to individuals?
4. Fill in the blanks.

(a) In the case of part disposal of an asset, the original cost is allocated between the part __________ and the __________.

(b) If an asset is totally destroyed, and compensation is received, then this transaction is treated as a _________ for capital gain tax purposes.

5. What is the effect of transfer of assets between spouses or civil partners?

Answers to Quick Quiz

1. The market value is the value the asset can achieve if sold in the open market.
2. The indexation allowance was introduced as a relief against inflation and is available only to companies.
3. For individuals, indexation allowance is not available from 6 April 2008.

4.

(a) disposed of, part retained

(b) disposal

5. When an asset is transferred between spouses or civil partners, it is not a chargeable disposal, as the asset is deemed to be transferred at no gain / no loss. However, the **subsequent disposal** of the asset to another person is a chargeable disposal.

Self Examination Questions

Question 1

Stuart purchased an asset in July 1993 for £28,000.In May 2010, he spent £2,500 on repairs to the asset to improve the working life.

In November 2012, he sold this asset for £40,500. The incidental expenditure of the sale was £800.

Required:

Show the calculation of the capital gains tax for 2012-13, assuming that he carried forward the previous year's capital loss of £8,100.

Question 2

Fire Plc purchased a chargeable asset on 9 January 2006, for £15,000 (RPI 193.4). The company incurred enhancement expenditure of £4,600 on 20 April 2009 (RPI 211.5).

The asset was sold in March 2012 (RPI 240.8) for £51,000.

Required:

Compute the chargeable gains.

Question 3

Canara Ltd purchased an asset in March 2004 for £15,400 (RPI 184.6). In August 2007 (RPI 207.3), the company incurred additional enhancement expenditure of £2,100 on the asset. In March 2012 (RPI 240.8), the company sold this asset for £21,000.

Required:

Calculate the amount of chargeable gains.

Question 4

Henry sold a plot of land on 5 March 2013 for £500,000.

This land was purchased by Jerry, Henry's wife for £200,000 on 20 July 2011. She transferred the land to Henry on 5 November 2012 for £250,000. On this date, the plot of land was valued at £300,000.

Required:

Calculate Henry's chargeable gains.

Question 5

Mack purchased 5 acres of land on 20 July 2011 for £500,000. He sold 3 acres of land for £550,000 on 25 February 2013.The market value of the unsold acres of land on 25 February 2013 was £220,000.

Required:

Calculate Mack's chargeable gains.

Question 6

Lisa purchases a set of diamond necklace and earrings for £120,000 in June 1999.

She sells the diamond earrings for £40,000 in April 2012. The incidental cost of sale is £450. On the date the earrings were sold, the market value of the necklace was £160,000.

Required:

Show the calculation of chargeable gains.

Question 7

Jennifer owns an asset which she purchased in June 2008 for £28,000. It was destroyed in an earthquake in October 2012. Jennifer received an amount of £42,500 as compensation from an insurance company in November 2012 and replaced the asset in February 2013 at a cost of £40,000.

Required:

Calculate the chargeable gains and the base cost of the new asset.

Answers to Self Examination Questions

Answer to SEQ 1

Calculation of capital gain

	£
Disposal consideration	40,500
Less: Incidental cost of disposal	(800)
Net disposal consideration	**39,700**
Less: Cost of acquisition	(28,000)
Net capital gain	**11,700**
Less: Current year capital loss	-
Current year net capital gain	**11,700**
Less: Brought forward capital loss	(1,100)
Chargeable gain	**10,600**
Less : Annual Exemption	(10,600)
Net capital gain	-
Capital gains tax	-

Notes

1. Additional expenditure is allowable expenditure for the calculation of chargeable gains, provided it enhances the utility of the asset (i.e. it is a capital enhancement cost rather than a revenue repair cost).

   Stuart incurred additional expenditure to improve the working life of an asset. As it was a revenue repair expense, it is not capital enhancement expenditure.

2. Relief for brought forward capital losses is restricted to £1,100 i.e. (£11,700 – £10,600) so that full advantage of annual exemption can be taken.

Answer to SEQ 2

Calculation of chargeable gains

	£	£
Disposal consideration		51,000
Less: Allowable deductions		
Cost of acquisition	15,000	
Enhancement expenditure	4,600	(19,600)
Unindexed gain		**31,400**
Less : Indexation allowance		
Cost of acquisition		
(£240.8 – £193.4) = (0.245) x £15,000	3,675	
£193.4		
Enhancement expenditure		
(£240.8 – £211.5) = (0.139) x £4,600	639	(4,314)
£211.5		
Chargeable gain		**27,086**

Answer to SEQ 3

Computation of chargeable gains of Canara Ltd

		£
Disposal consideration		21,000
Less: Allowable deductions		
Cost of acquisition	(15,400)	
Enhancement expenditure	(2,100)	(17,500)
Unindexed gain		**3,500**
Less: Indexation allowance		
Cost of acquisition		
(240.8 – 184.6) = (0.304) x £15,400 (note)	4,682	(3,500)
184.6		
Enhancement expenditure		
(240.8 - 207.3) = (0.162) x £2,100	(339)	
207.3	(4,342)	-
Indexed gain (note)		-

Note: indexation allowance for the actual cost of acquisition is £5,021 (calculated above). However, as indexation allowance cannot be used to create or increase a loss, it is restricted to £3,500.

For the same reason, no indexation allowance is given for enhancement expenditure.

Answer to SEQ 4

	£
Disposal consideration	500,000
Less: Allowable deductions	
Acquisition costs (note)	(200,000)
Chargeable gains	**300,000**

Note: in the case of the disposal of an asset between husband and wife, the acquiring spouse is treated as having acquired the asset at its original cost, along with any incidental costs and enhancement expenditure incurred.

Therefore, the acquisition cost of the land for Henry is £200,000. The price at which Henry purchased the asset (£250,000) from his wife and the market value of the plot of land at the date of acquisition (£300,000) are not considered for calculation of CGT.

Answer to SEQ 5

	£
Disposal consideration	550,000
Less: Allowable deductions	
Acquisition costs (including incidental costs) (W1)	(357,143)
Chargeable gains	**192,857**

Working

W1

Cost is allocated according to the market values of the part disposed of and the part retained at the time of part disposal.

Here, we will have to calculate the cost of the land that was sold. Out of 5 acres of land, 3 acres of land was sold.

The cost relating to three acres of land sold = £500,000 x £550,000/(£550,000 + £220,000)
= £500,000 x £550,000/£770,000
= £357,143

Answer to SEQ 6

Computation of chargeable gains

	£
Disposal consideration	40,000
Less: Incidental cost of disposal	(450)
Net disposal consideration	**39,550**
Less: Cost of acquisition	
£40,000 / (£40,000 + £160,000) x £120,000	(24,000)
Chargeable Gain	**15,550**

Note: cost of acquisition is allocated according to the market values of the part disposed of (diamond earrings) and the part retained (diamond necklace) at the time of part disposal.

Answer to SEQ 7

Computation of chargeable gains

	£
Sale proceeds (insurance proceeds)	42,500
Less: Cost of acquisition	(28,000)
Total gain	**14,500**
Less: Amount not re-invested (£42,500 - £40,000) chargeable to capital gains immediately	(2,500)
Deferred gain	**12,000**

Therefore, the base cost or deemed cost of the replaced asset will be:

	£
Cost of the replaced asset	40,000
Less: Deferred gain	(12,000)
Deemed cost of the replaced asset	**28,000**

SECTION C

CHARGEABLE GAINS

STUDY GUIDE C3: GAINS AND LOSSES ON THE DISPOSAL OF MOVABLE AND IMMOVABLE PROPERTY

Get Through Intro

Capital gains tax has a wide scope and can be split into various sections for the purpose of easy understanding. One **new section** which has been introduced to the syllabus deals with **capital gains tax on the disposal of movable and immovable property.**

Movable and immovable property forms a **major section** of capital assets of both individuals and companies and its disposal normally is a **major component of capital gains tax**.

This Study Guide discusses the principles of identification of chattels and wasting assets and introduces you to the important **concept of a principal private residence**. It also deals with the treatment of capital gains tax on their disposal.

Learning Outcomes

a) Identify when chattels and wasting assets are exempt.
b) Compute the chargeable gain when a chattel is disposed of.
c) Calculate the chargeable gain when a wasting asset is disposed of.
d) Compute the exemption when a principal private residence is disposed of.
e) Calculate the chargeable gain when a principal private residence has been used for business purposes.
f) Identify the amount of letting relief available when a principal private residence has been let out.

Introduction

Case Study

Sam owns various assets such as an antique table, shares in Sun Ltd, a television set and a water colour painting. He has owned these assets for many years.

On 5 May 2011, he sold the antique table, the shares in Sun Ltd and the water colour painting for £500,000, £200,000 and £450,000 respectively.

Are all these assets chargeable to capital gains tax under the same provisions?

The answer to this question is - 'No'. There are different provisions that apply to different classes of assets.

These provisions are explained in depth in this Study Guide.

1. Identify when chattels and wasting assets are exempt.[1]

[Learning Outcome a]

1.1 Chattel

A chattel is tangible, movable property: something touchable and not fixed, for example:

- a painting,
- jewellery

The following are, therefore, **not** chattels - Shares (as they are intangible) or a house (which is immovable)

1.2 Wasting asset

A wasting asset is an asset which has a predictable life of less than 50 years at the time of acquisition, e.g. plant and machinery. Such assets may also include copyrights or registered designs.

Tip

All machinery is automatically treated as having a life expectancy of less than 15 years so, for example, an antique clock would be a wasting asset.

1.3 Types of chattels

Some assets will be both chattels and wasting assets:

- **Wasting chattel:** a wasting chattel is a chattel with an expected life of less than 50 years. Wasting chattels are exempt from capital gains tax e.g. a greyhound, racehorse, antique clock etc.
- **Non-wasting chattel:** a non-wasting chattel is a chattel with an expected life of more than 50 years, e.g. antiques (other than machinery), paintings etc.

1.4 Exempt chattels

The disposal of the following chattels is exempt from capital gains tax:

1. **Wasting chattels** (unless used in a business and eligible for capital allowances).
2. **Non-wasting** chattels when **sold for £6,000 or less, realising a gain.**

Test Yourself 1

1. Katherine sold a painting. Is the gain on disposal of this painting chargeable to CGT?

2. Tina acquired an item of plant for £8,000. The plant has a working life of 20 years. She used the plant for business purposes for 5 years. After 5 years, Tina wanted to sell the plant for £10,000. Advise her as to whether the gain on this disposal will be liable to capital gains tax.

SUMMARY

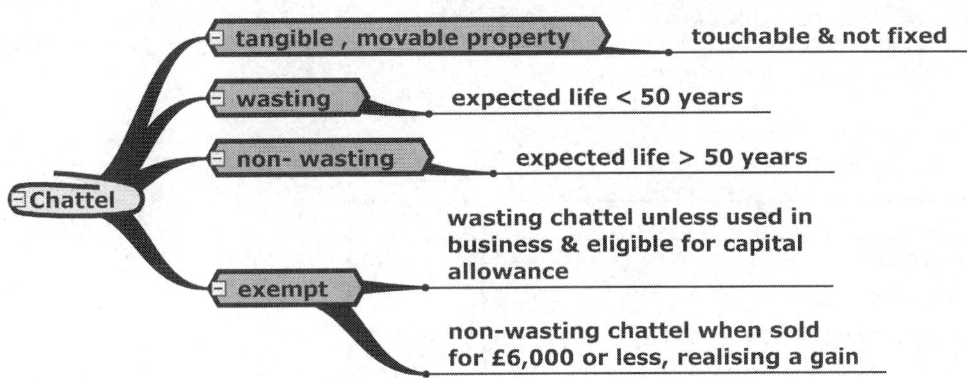

2. Compute the chargeable gain when a chattel is disposed of.[2]

[Learning Outcome b]

2.1 Rules for computing CGT on disposal of non-wasting chattels

1. If **gross sale proceeds** are **£6,000 or less:**

a) any **gain is exempt.**
b) any **loss is allowable**. However, if **gross sale proceeds are less than £6,000**, they are **deemed to be £6,000** for the purpose of calculation.

Tip

You are substituting the gross proceeds in this case, so look at the proceeds before any costs of disposal are taken into account.

Example

Alan bought a painting for £4,250 in January 2010 and sold it in November 2011 for £5,800. As the sale proceeds are less than £6,000, the gain is fully exempt.

Example

Rex bought an antique vase for £7,650 in October 2010 and sold it for £5,250 in February, 2013. As the gross sale proceeds are less than £6,000, when calculating the allowable loss, the sale proceeds are deemed to be £6,000.

Therefore, the allowable loss will be:

	£
Deemed proceeds	6,000
Less: Allowable deductions	
Acquisition costs (including incidental costs)	(7,650)
Allowable loss	**(1,650)**

2. If gross sale proceeds **exceed £6,000**, the gain is the **lower of:**

a) the normal net gain, or
b) 5/3 x (gross proceeds - £6,000)

Important

Learn these rules as they will not be given to you in the exam, and this is a popular exam topic.

Jack bought an antique desk for £4,125 in December 2009 and sold it for £7,200 in January 2012. As the sale proceeds exceed £6,000, the net gain is the **lower of**:

1. the normal net gain, or
2. 5/3 x (gross proceeds - £6,000)

	£
Disposal consideration	7,200
Less: Allowable deductions	
Acquisition costs (including incidental costs)	(4,125)
Normal net gain	**3,075**

Therefore the net gain is the **lower of:**

1. normal net gain = £3,075
2. 5/3 of (£7,200 - £6,000) = £2,000

Hence, the net gain is £2,000.

Continuing the previous example of Jack

Assume the antique desk was sold for £18,600.

In this situation, as the sale proceeds exceed £6,000, the net gain is the lower of:

1. the normal net gain, i.e. (£18,600 - £4,125) = £14,475
2. 5/3 x (gross proceeds - £6,000) = 5/3 x (£18,600 - £6,000) = £21,000

Hence, the net gain is the normal net gain, i.e. £14,475.

Diagram 1: Rules for non-wasting chattels

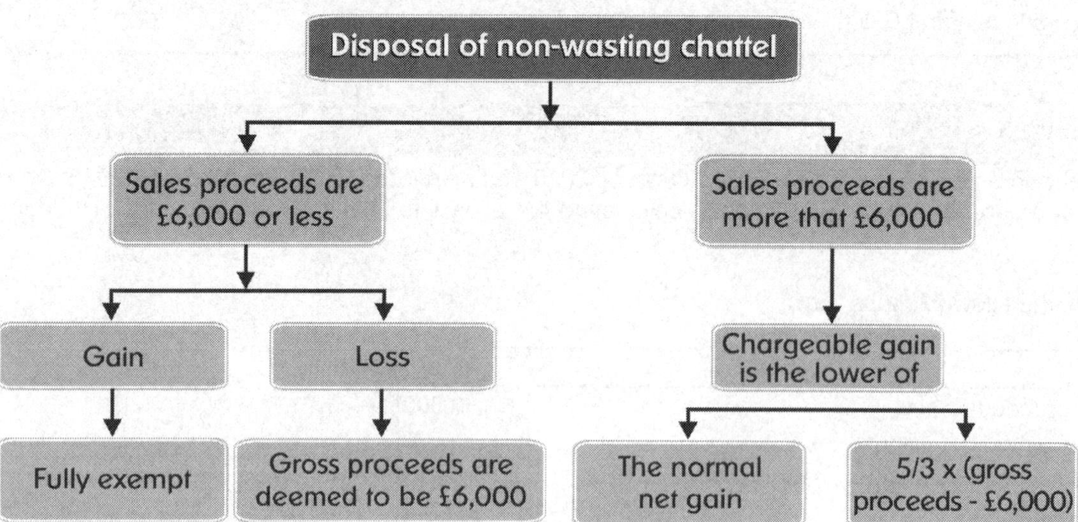

2.2 Rules for computing CGT on disposal of wasting chattel

1. A gain on the disposal of a wasting chattel is **exempt,** unless it is used in a business and eligible for capital allowances (in such a case, it is treated as a non-wasting chattel).

Example

In December 2012, Cathy disposed of a greyhound for £7,250, bought for £3,150 in February 2012. As this is a wasting asset, which is not used in a business and is not eligible for capital allowances, the gains arising on its disposal are exempt from capital gains tax.

2. The rules for computation of CGT on disposal of the wasting chattels used in business and **eligible for capital allowances** (plant and machinery) are as follows:

- If they are sold at a loss, then CGT computation is not considered, as the loss has already been given as capital allowance. While computing CGT, the net amount of capital allowances given (after deducting balancing charges on disposal) are deducted from allowable expenditure so that neither a chargeable gain nor an allowable loss arises.

- If they are sold at a gain, the capital gains are calculated normally by treating them as a disposal of non-wasting chattels. Hence, the rules for computing CGT on the disposal of non-wasting chattels will be applicable.

Example

Peter disposed of machinery which was used in his business, for £7,440 in November 2012. This machinery was originally bought for £15,250 in September 2011.

As the machinery was sold at a loss, the net amount of capital allowances given will be deducted from the allowable expenditure while computing CGT so that neither a chargeable gain nor an allowable loss arises.

The capital allowances on machinery will be computed as follows:

	FYA (£)	Allowances (£)
Year ended 31/03/2012		
Additions qualifying for AIA	15,250	
Less: AIA	(15,250)	15,250
TWDV c/f	-	
Allowances		**15,250**
Year ended 31/03/2013		
TWDV b/f	-	
Less: Disposal	(7,440)	
Balancing charge	**(7,440)**	**(7,440)**

The capital loss on the sale of the machinery will be computed as follows:

		£
Disposal consideration		7,440
Less: Allowable deductions		
Acquisition costs	15,250	
Less: Net capital allowances given	(7,810)	(7,440)
(£15,250 - £7,440)		
Net gain / loss		-

Example

Continuing the previous example of Peter

Assume the machinery was bought for £4,250 in September 2011. In this situation, although the machinery is a wasting chattel (expected life being not more than 50 years), it is treated as a non-wasting chattel as it is used in the business, is eligible for capital allowances and is sold at a gain. Therefore, the capital gain will be calculated normally and the rules for non-wasting assets (as discussed above) will be applicable.

Continued on the next page

Capital allowance computation is as follows:

	FYA (£)	Allowances (£)
Year ended 31/03/2012		
Additions qualifying for AIA	4,250	
Less: AIA	(4,250)	4,250
TWDV c/f	-	
Allowances		**4,250**
Year ended 31/03/2013		
TWDV b/f	-	
Less: Disposal (restricted to cost)	(4,250)	
Balancing charge	**(4,250)**	**(4,250)**

The capital gain on sale of machinery will be computed as follows:

		£
Disposal consideration		7,440
Less: Allowable deductions		
Acquisition costs	4,250	
Less: net capital allowances given (£4,250 - £4,250)	-	(4,250)
Net gain		**3,190**

As the sale proceeds exceed £6,000, the chargeable gain is the lower of:

1. the normal net gain which is £3,190
2. 5/3 of excess proceeds over £6,000 which is 5/3 (£7,440 - £6,000) = £2,400

Hence, the chargeable gain is £2,400.

3. **No losses** are allowable.

Example

Merry disposed of a greyhound for £7,250, in December 2012, originally bought for £8,150 in February 2012. Here, as this is a wasting asset, losses arising on its disposal are not allowable.

Test Yourself 2

Jack purchased antique furniture a few years ago for £2,900. He decided to replace this furniture and sold it for £8,200.

Required:

Show the calculation of chargeable gains on the disposal of furniture.

Test Yourself 3

Jay is a trader. On 9 February 2008, he purchased a machine for £41,000. This machine was eligible for capital allowances. He used this machine for four years for business purposes and then on 20 April 2012 Jay sold the machine.

Required:

Show the calculation of chargeable gains on disposal of machinery assuming the disposal value is:

(a) £25,000
(b) £49,000
(c) £5,000

3. Calculate the chargeable gain when a wasting asset is disposed of.[2]

[Learning Outcome c]

In this section of the Study Guide, the term "wasting asset" is taken to mean a wasting asset (i.e. one which has a predictable life of less than 50 years when acquired) which is not a chattel (those are discussed in the section above on wasting chattels). Such assets may include copyrights or registered designs. The allowable cost to be used in calculating the chargeable gain must be apportioned so that only the part relating to the remaining life of the asset is taken into account.

The asset is depreciated **on a straight line basis over its useful life**.

In practice, wasting assets are either:

1. exempt, or
2. business assets

As any business asset on which capital allowances may be claimed is treated as non-wasting assets, the straight line apportionment of cost only applies to non-capital allowance type business assets. This is typically intangible assets such as options or patents.

Example

Katie sold a registered design of a piece of equipment. This was a business asset with a 35 year life when acquired. It had a remaining useful life of 15 years on disposal. The registered design was sold for £20,000 in January 2013. The design had originally cost £10,000 when purchased.

The calculation of chargeable gain is as follows:

	£
Disposal consideration	20,000
Less: Cost of acquisition (allowable cost 15/35 x £10,000)	(4,286)
Chargeable gain	15,714

Note: The allowable cost represents the 15 years of **life remaining** out of the 35 years predictable total life of the asset.

4. Compute the exemption when a principal private residence is disposed of.[2]

[Learning Outcome d]

4.1 Principal private residence

1. The disposal of an **individual's only or main residence** (principal private residence) **is fully exempt** if the **property** is **occupied** by the owner **throughout the period of ownership.**

   This is known as principal private residence relief **(PPR relief).**

2. If the property has been **unoccupied for a part of the period of ownership,** then **part of the gain** may be **chargeable.**

   The exempt part of the gain (PPR relief) is:

$$\frac{\text{Periods of occupation}}{\text{Total period of ownership}} \text{ x net gain}$$

Tip

The period of residence and the period of ownership are calculated to the nearest month.

3. Periods of occupation include periods of **actual occupation** and periods of **deemed occupation**.
4. Some periods of absence are deemed to be periods of occupation which are as follows:

a) the **last 36 months are always exempt** i.e. the taxpayer will get full PPR relief whether or not, during the last 36 months, the taxpayer was using the property as his residence and whether or not the taxpayer owns another PPR.
b) any length of period whilst the individual is **employed overseas.**

c) a total of up to 4 years where the individual is working (employed or self-employed) elsewhere in the UK.
d) a total of **3 years for any reason.** This period **need not be a consecutive period** of thirty six months but at **some time both before and after the period of absence** there must be a **period of actual occupation**.

For (b) and (c) the general rule is that the individual must re-occupy the property after the period of absence. However if he does not, this must be due to the situation of the individual's place of work in order for the deemed occupation provisions to apply to the period of absence.

Prior to 6 April 2009 relief for deemed occupations was given for absences by reason of employment only where the property was re-occupied after the period of absence. The current rules now reflect an extra statutory concessionary treatment by HMRC.

The periods of occupation mentioned in (b) to (d) above are treated as periods of occupation only if the taxpayer **claims no other property as his principal private residence**.

5. It is the **net gain** that is **exempt.**

Brian owned a house in London. He purchased this house on 1 June 1998 for £35,000. He used this apartment as his main residence until 31 May 2006. On 1 June 2006, he moved to a rented house. The apartment was then unoccupied until it was sold on 31 May 2012 for £75,000.

In this situation the chargeable gain (after PPR exemption) is calculated as follows:

Step -1 Calculate total chargeable gain before PPR
Step -2 Calculate PPR exemption
Step -3 Calculate chargeable gain after PPR

Step 1 Calculate total chargeable gain before PPR

	£
Disposal consideration	75,000
Less: Cost of acquisition	(35,000)
Net gain	**40,000**

Step 2 Calculate PPR exemption

Calculation of periods of occupation by Brian:

Last 36 months are always exempt

	Total (months)	Exempt (months)	Chargeable (months)
1 June 1998 to 31 May 2006 (actual occupation)	96	96	
1 June 2006 to 31 May 2012 (absence- any reason) (Note)	72	36	36
	168	**132**	**36**

Note: Brian's period of absence for any reason will not be considered deemed occupation for principal private residence relief as there should be an actual period of residence both before and after the period of absence. As Brian has not returned after he left his residence on 31 May 2006, PPR relief will not be available for this period. However, the last 36 months of ownership are always exempt.

$$\text{PPR relief} = \frac{\text{Period of actual and deemed residence}}{\text{Period of ownership}} \times \text{net gain}$$

$$= \frac{132 \times £40{,}000}{168}$$

$$\mathbf{= £31{,}429}$$

Continued on the next page

Step 3 Calculate chargeable gain after PPR

	£
Net gain	40,000
Less: PPR relief	(31,429)
Chargeable gain	**8,571**

Test Yourself 4

On 1 February 2013, Melanie sold a residential property for £80,000. She had purchased this property on 1 April 1989 for £15,000 and occupied it as her principal residence from the date of purchase until 31 May 2003. The property was then unoccupied until it was sold on 1 February 2013.

Required:

Calculate chargeable gain (after PPR exemption).

Example

Henry purchased a house in Birmingham on 1 April 1992 for £150,000. He occupied this house as his main residence from the date of purchase until 30 June 1996. On 1 July 1996, he moved to a rented flat in Norwich as his employer asked him to work at their Norwich office temporarily. He re-occupied the house from 1 January 1999 to 31 July 2006 as his main residence. After that, he moved to Canada, again at the request of his employer. Henry retired in October 2011 but decided to remain in Canada for personal reasons. He remained there until he sold his house on 31 December 2012 for £300,000.

Henry's chargeable gains (after PPR exemption) shall be calculated as follows:

Step 1 Calculate total chargeable gain before PPR
Step 2 Calculate PPR exemption
Step 3 Calculate chargeable gain after PPR

Step 1 Calculate total chargeable gain before PPR

	£
Disposal consideration	300,000
Less: Cost of acquisition	(150,000)
Net gains	**150,000**

Step 2 Calculate PPR relief

Calculation of periods of occupation by Henry:

	Total (months)	Exempt (months)	Chargeable (months)
1 April 1992 to 30 June 1996 (Actual occupation)	51	51	
1 July 1996 to 31 December 1997 (employed elsewhere in the UK) (Note 1)	30	30	
1 January 1999 to 31 July 2006 (Actual occupation)	91	91	
1 August 2006 to 31 December 2012 (unoccupied) (Note 2)	77	36	41
	249	**208**	**41**

Notes:

1. A total of up to four years where an individual is employed elsewhere in the UK is deemed to be period of occupation for calculation of PPR relief, only if the property was occupied both before and after the period of absence, or if the individual cannot resume occupation afterwards due to employment.

Continued on the next page

2. Any period where an individual is employed abroad is considered deemed occupation for principal private residence relief but there should be an actual period of residence both before and after the period of absence or, if actual occupation is not resumed, this should be due to employment reasons. As Henry has not returned after he left his residence to work abroad on 1 August 2005 for personal reasons, PPR relief will not be available for this period. However, the last thirty-six months of ownership are always exempt.

$$\text{PPR relief} = \frac{\text{Period of actual and deemed residence}}{\text{Period of ownership}} \text{ x Net gain}$$

$$= \frac{208 \times £150{,}000}{241}$$

= £129,461

Step 3 Calculate chargeable gains after PPR

	£
Net gains	150,000
Less: PPR relief	(129,461)
Chargeable gain	**20,539**

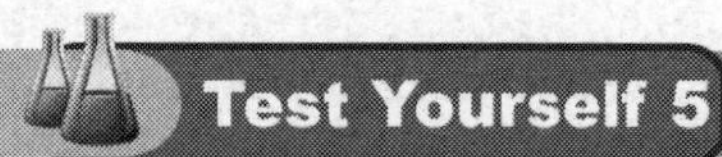

Test Yourself 5

On 1 May 1996, Pinky purchased a residential property in Wick for £28,000. She occupied this house until 30 June 2001. On 1 July 2001 she moved to the USA, to start on a new job there. She was in the USA for 3 years and 4 months. On 1 November 2004 Pinky returned to the property, but on 31 December 2004 she moved to Leeds to be closer to her family. The property in Wick was unoccupied until she sold it for £58,000 on 1 April 2013.

Required:

Calculate Pinky's chargeable gain (after PPR exemption).

4.2 Important points to remember

While computing gain from disposal of principal private residence we must remember the following points:

1. For tax purposes, the taxpayer has only one principal private residence at any one time. If he owns more than one principal private residence then he has to **elect** which property is to be considered his principal private residence.

   This election must be made **within 2 years** of commencing occupation of the second residence.

2. A married couple or civil partners living together may have **only one main principal private residence between them**. If they own more than one main house, then they have to elect which property is to be treated as their PPR.

SUMMARY

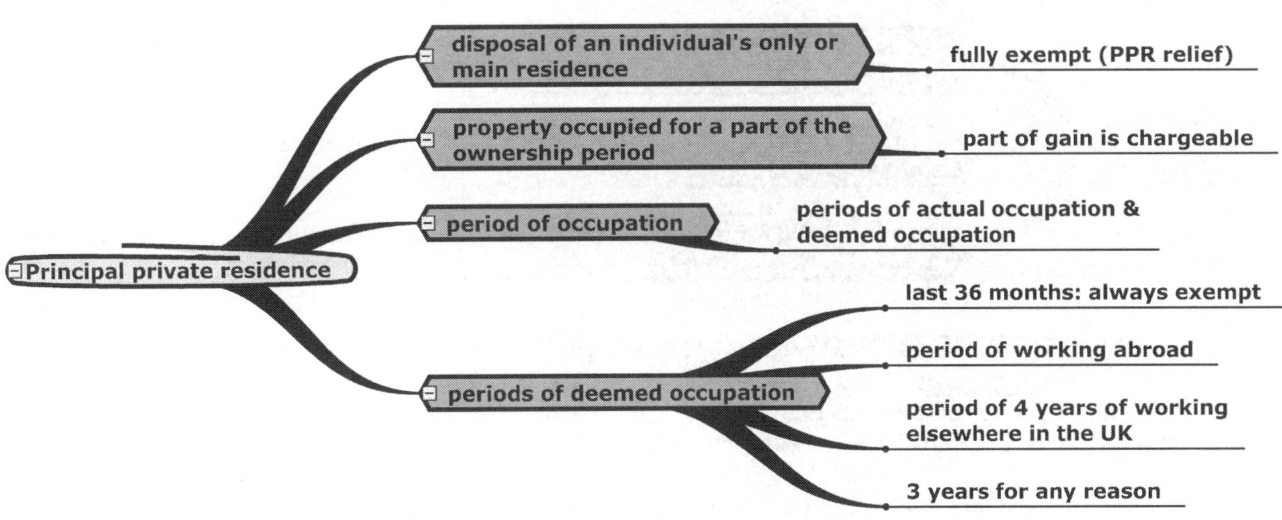

5. Calculate the chargeable gain when a principal private residence has been used for business purposes.[2]

[Learning Outcome e]

If an individual has used the whole or part of his principal private residence for business purposes, then the **business proportion of that gain will be chargeable to CGT.**

The PPR exemption for the **last 36 months** of ownership is **not applicable** to the **part of the property** which is used exclusively for **business purposes throughout the period of the ownership**.

However, if that part of the main residence was used for business purposes for only part of the period of ownership, then the last 36 months of exemption will be **applicable** to the **whole of the property** despite the fact that there has been some business use.

Example

Rick purchased a house on 1 June 1998 for £13,000 and was using half of the house for his business purposes throughout the period of ownership. On 1 April 2013, he sold this house for £65,000.

Here, the chargeable gain is calculated as follows:

Step 1 Calculation of total chargeable gain

	£
Disposal consideration	65,000
Less: Cost of acquisition	(13,000)
Net capital gain	**52,000**
Less: PPR relief (Note)	
£52,000 x 50%	(26,000)
Chargeable gains	**26,000**

Note: the house was occupied by Rick throughout the period of ownership; hence the entire capital gain is eligible for PPR relief.
However, the PPR exemption for the last 36 months of ownership will not be applicable for half of the house used for business purposes as it was used exclusively for business purposes throughout the period of ownership. As the business half of the house was not occupied as a principal private residence, it will be fully chargeable to CGT.

SUMMARY

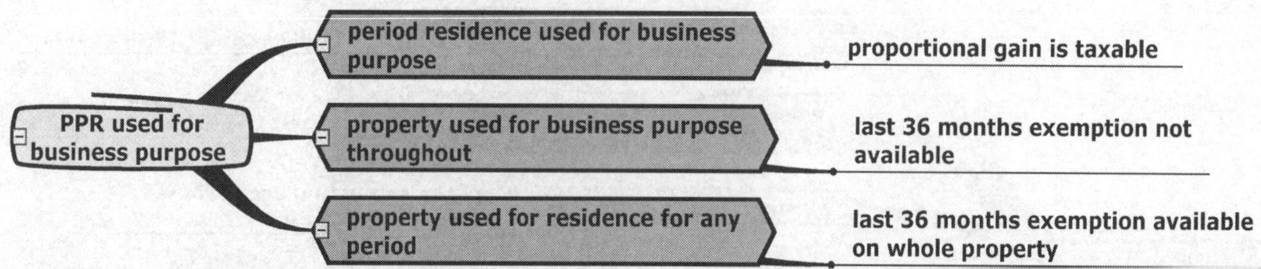

Mohammed was working with Excellence Plc as a marketing manager. During his period of service, he purchased a house for £16,400. The date of purchase of the house was 1 April 1996.

On 1 May 2008, he left the job and started a new business. From that date until the date of sale of the house i.e. 1 May 2012, he used the house for business as well as domestic purposes. He sold the house for £59,200. 35% of the property was used for business purposes.

Required:

Show the calculation of chargeable gain on the disposal of the house.

---

6. Identify the amount of letting relief available when a principal private residence has been let out.[2]

[Learning Outcome f]

- Where a principal private residence has been let out to tenants, **letting relief may be available.**
- Principal private residence relief **(PPR relief**) is deducted from the net gain first, then letting relief is deducted.
- Letting relief is the **lowest of:**
  - ✓ PPR relief
  - ✓ £40,000
  - ✓ the gain that arose in the letting period
- Letting relief can reduce a gain to nil, but **cannot create a loss.**

Proforma

	£	£
Disposal consideration		X
Less: Cost of acquisition		(X)
		X
Less: PPR relief		
Gain x $\frac{\text{Period of actual and deemed residence}}{\text{Period of ownership}}$		(X)
Gain after PPR relief		X
Less: Letting relief		
Lowest of:		
PPR relief	X	
£40,000	X	
The gain that arose in the letting period	X	(X)
Net gain		**X**

There are two situations where letting relief applies:

1. **Where a part of the property is let to tenants**

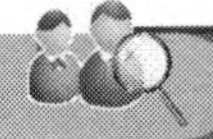

Example

Peter purchased a detached house on 1 April 2006 for £88,000 which was much bigger than he needed for himself. He therefore rented out 40% of the house to a tenant. This arrangement continued until 31 December 2012 when he sold his house for £148,000.

In this situation chargeable gain is calculated as follows:

	£	£
Disposal consideration		148,000
Less: Cost of acquisition		(88,000)
		60,000
Less: PPR relief (W1)		(36,000)
Gain after PPR relief		**24,000**
Less: Letting relief		
Lowest of:		
PPR relief	36,000	
£40,000	40,000	
The gain that arose in respect of the let out portion of the property (W2)	24,000	(24,000)
Chargeable gain		-

Workings:

W1 Calculation of PPR exemption

First calculate the portion of the gain relating to the own occupation:

£60,000 x 60% = £36,000

As Peter occupied this part of the property throughout the period of ownership, it will be a period of actual occupation. The full £36,000 is eligible for PPR relief.

W2 Gain in respect of let out property

The remaining portion of the gain relates to the let part of the property.

---

2. **Where the entire property is let out during periods of absence**

Example

Jeremy owned a house in London, which he bought on 1 April 2003 for £31,740. On 30 June 2008, he purchased a new apartment in Brighton. He moved into the new house immediately. On 1 December 2008, he let out the property in London. The property was let out until it was sold on 1 April 2013.

The London property was sold for £75,000. The calculation of chargeable gain on the disposal of the London property is as follows:

Continued on next page

	£	£
Sale proceeds		75,000
Less: : Cost of acquisition		(31,740)
		43,260
Less: PPR relief (W1)		(35,690)
Gain after PPR relief		**7,570**
Less: Letting relief		
Lowest of:		
PPR relief	35,690	
£40,000	40,000	
The gain that arose in the letting period (£43,260 x 16/120)	5,768	(5,768)
Chargeable gain		**1,802**

Workings

W1

The total period of ownership of 120 months (1 April 2003 to 1 April 2013) needs to be broken down into the following periods:

	Total (months)	Exempt (months)	Chargeable (months)
1 April 2003 to 30 June 2008 (actual occupation)	63	63	
1 July 2008 to 30 November 2009 (unoccupied and not let out)	5		5
1 December 2008 to 31 March 2013 (52 months)(let out)	52	36	16
Total	**120**	**99**	**21**

PPR exemption

Out of the total ownership period of 120 months, the house was actually occupied for domestic purposes for 63 months. The last 36 months are always exempt. No relief is available for the 5 month period when the house was not occupied as Jeremy did not re-occupy the property after the period of absence.

PPR relief = 99/120 x gain = 99/120 x £43,260 = £35,690

SUMMARY

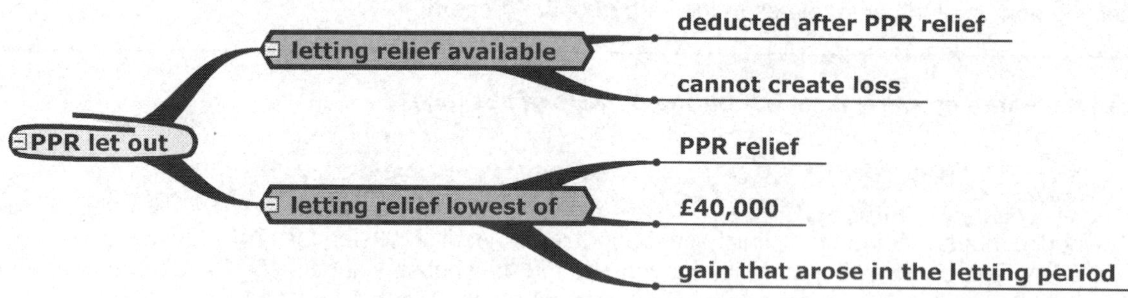

Wendy has an apartment in London which she bought on 1 April 2002. On 1 June 2005, she changed her job and found her residence to be too far from her workplace.

She rented out her apartment and bought a new studio apartment close to her new workplace. On 31 July 2012 she resigned from her job and decided to have a career break. On October 2012, she sold her apartment in London and made a gain of £12,000.

Required:

Calculate her chargeable gain.

Answers to Test Yourself

Answer to TY 1

1. A painting is tangible movable property, therefore can be classified as a chattel. A painting's expected life is more than 50 years hence it is a non-wasting chattel. Therefore, gains arising on disposal of a painting are liable to CGT.
   However, if the disposal value of the chattel is £6,000 or less, then any gain on the disposal is not liable to CGT.

2. The plant is a business asset eligible for capital allowances. Any gain on the disposal of plant and machinery used for business purposes gives rise to capital gains tax. Therefore, Tina is liable to capital gains tax on the gain on the disposal of the plant.

Answer to TY 2

Calculation of chargeable capital gain on the disposal of a non-wasting chattel

	£
Disposal consideration	8,200
Less: Allowable deductions	
Acquisition costs (including incidental costs)	(2,900)
Chargeable gain	**(5,300)**

As the gross sale proceeds are more than £6000, the chargeable gain is the **lower of:**

1. The normal net gain = £5,300
2. 5/3 x (gross proceeds - £6,000) = 5/3 of £2,200 (i.e. £8,200 - £6,000) = £3,667

Therefore, the chargeable gain is restricted to £3,667.

Answer to TY 3

1. As the machinery (wasting chattel eligible for capital allowances) was sold at a loss, the capital gain computation is ignored as the loss had already been given as capital allowance. The net amount of capital allowances given is deducted from allowable expenditure so that neither a chargeable gain nor an allowable loss arises.
   Hence, the net capital gain / loss in this situation is nil.

2. As the machinery was sold at a gain, capital gain will be calculated normally. For CGT purpose, it will be treated as a **non-wasting chattel and** therefore, rules for non-wasting chattels will be applicable.

	£
Disposal consideration	49,000
Less: Acquisition cost	(41,000)
Net gain	**8,000**

As the sale proceeds are more than £6,000, chargeable gain on disposal is restricted to 5/3 of excess disposal value over £6,000.

Therefore, maximum chargeable gain = 5/3 (£49,000 - £6,000)
= £71,667

However, the actual gain is less than maximum chargeable gain. Therefore the chargeable gain is £8,000.

3. The machinery was sold at a loss and it qualifies for capital allowance, therefore the CGT computation is ignored as the loss is given by way of capital allowances.

Hence, the net capital gain / loss in this situation is nil.

Answer to TY 4

Step 1 Calculate total chargeable gain before PPR
Step 2 Calculate PPR exemption
Step 3 Calculate chargeable gain after PPR

Step 1 Calculate total chargeable gain before PPR

	£
Disposal consideration	80,000
Less: Cost of acquisition	(15,000)
Net gain	**65,000**

Step 2 Calculate PPR relief

Calculation of periods of occupation by Melanie:

	Total (Months)	Exempt (Months)	Chargeable (Months)
1 April 1989 to 31 May 2003 (Actual occupation)	170	170	
1 June 2003 to 31 January 2013 (absence- any reason) (Note)	116	36	80
	286	**206**	**80**

Total period of ownership = 206 + 80 = 286 months

Note: Melanie has not returned after she left her residence on 31 May 2003. Hence, PPR relief will not be available for this period. However, the last 36 months of ownership are always exempt.

$$\text{PPR relief} = \frac{\text{Period of actual and deemed residence}}{\text{Period of ownership}} \text{ x Net gain}$$

$$= \frac{206 \text{ x } £65{,}000}{286}$$

= £46,818

Step 3 Calculate chargeable gains after PPR

	£
Net gain	65,000
Less: PPR relief	(46,818)
Chargeable gain	**18,182**

Answer to TY 5

In this situation chargeable gain on disposal of property in Wick is calculated as follows:

	£
Disposal consideration	58,000
Less: Cost of acquisition	(28,000)
Net gain	**30,000**
Less: PPR relief (W1)	(20,690)
Chargeable gain	**9,310**

Workings

W1 Calculation of PPR

Pinky's ownership period of the house in Wick is split into exempt and chargeable periods as follows:

	Total (months)	Exempt (months)	Chargeable (months)
1 May 1996 to 30 June 2001 (Actual occupation)	62	62	-
1 July 2001 to 31 October 2004 (unoccupied -working abroad) (Note 1)	40	40	-
1 November 2004 to 31 December 2004 (Actual occupation)	2	2	
1 January 2005 to 31 March 2013 (unoccupied – any reason) (Note 2)	99	36	63
Total	**203**	**140**	**63**

Notes:

1. The actual period of residence is always exempt when calculating chargeable gain on the disposal of a residence.

   Pinky was working abroad for three years and four months. Any period of absence during which the taxpayer is working abroad is exempt where the property was occupied both before and after the period of absence.

2. The last thirty six months of ownership are always exempt.

   Therefore, out of the 203 months of ownership, 140 months are exempt. Hence, PPR exemption is calculated as follows:

$$\text{PPR relief} = \frac{\text{Period of actual and deemed residence}}{\text{Period of ownership}} \text{ x Net gain}$$

$$= \frac{140 \times £30{,}000}{203} = \mathbf{£20{,}690}$$

Answer to TY 6

	£
Disposal consideration	59,200
Less: Cost of acquisition	(16,400)
Net capital gain	**42,800**
Less: PPR relief (W1)	
Actual occupation (181/193 x £42,800)	(40,139)
	2,661
Less: PPR relief (W1)	
Domestic as well as business use	
(12/193 x £42,800) x 65%	(1,730)
Chargeable gain	**931**

Workings

W1

Out of the total usage of the house, 35% usage is for business purposes and 65% (100% – 35%) is for domestic purposes.

	Total (months)	Exempt (months)	Chargeable (months)
1 April 1996 to 30 April 2008 (only domestic use)	145	145	
1 May 2008 to 30 April 2012 (domestic as well as business use) (Note)	48	36	12
	193	**181**	**12**

The exemption for the final 36 months will be applicable to the whole of the property as the business portion of the property was not used for the business throughout the entire period of ownership. It was used wholly for residential purpose for some part of the period of the ownership.

The period for which the property was used for both domestic as well as business purposes is 48 months. But 35% usage for business purposes for 48 months will be considered only for a 12 month period after deducting the last 36 months' exemption. i.e. (48 months – 36 months).

Of that 12 month chargeable gain, PPR will be available for the 65% proportion used as a private residence, leaving the 35% business element chargeable to CGT.

Answer to TY 7

Calculation of chargeable gains

	£	£
Gain		12,000
Less: PPR relief (W1)		(6,992)
Gain after PPR relief		**5,008**
Less: Letting relief		
Lowest of:		
PPR relief	6,992	
£40,000	40,000	
The gain that arose in the letting period	5,008	(5,008)
Chargeable gain		-

Workings

W1 Total ownership period is broken down as follows:

		Total (months)	Exempt (months)	Chargeable (months)
1 April 2002 to 31 May 2005	Self-occupied	38	38	
1 June 2005 to 31 October 2012 (89 months)	Let out	89	36	53
Total ownership period		**127**	**74**	**53**

Out of a total ownership period of 127 months, Wendy let out the property for 89 months. Out of these 89 months, she will get PPR exemption for the last 36 months. She is not eligible for PPR relief on the period of absence by reason of employment as she did not re-occupy the property, nor was her continued absence due to employment.

PPR relief

Out of a total ownership period of 127 months, gain apportioned to 74 months (38 + 36) will get PPR relief.

Therefore, total PPR relief is calculated as follows:

= 74/127 x £12,000 = £6,992

W2 Calculation of gain that arose during letting period

The only chargeable period is the 53 months during which property was let out. The gain apportioned to these 53 months is calculated as follows:

= 53/127 x £12,000 = £5,008

Quick Quiz

Classify the following assets into chattels and wasting assets.

1. Gold jewellery
2. Leasehold of a building (lease period – 31 yrs)
3. An antique painting
4. Car
5. Trademark (with life of 20 years)

Answers to Quick Quiz

1. Chattels: moveable, tangible property
2. Wasting assets: less than 50 year lifespan
3. Chattels: moveable, tangible property
4. Wasting assets: all cars are classed as wasting assets as they are machinery and deemed to have a lifespan of less than 50 years
5. Wasting assets: less than 50 year lifespan

Self Examination Questions

Question 1

In May 2012, Eric sold his diamond cutting machinery for £8,500 which he had purchased for £4,000. He had used this machinery for three years for business purposes. He wants your help to calculate the chargeable gain on the disposal.

Question 2

On 1 January 2013, Damon sold an antique cutlery set. He had purchased this in March 2003 for £12,000.

Required:

Show the calculation of allowable loss assuming the disposal value of the cutlery set is:
(a) £8,600
(b) £5,600

Question 3

Raj, who is a wholesaler of woollen cloth, purchased a new apartment in Dundee on 1 February 2000 for £38,000. He lived in this apartment until 31 May 2005.

On 1 June 2005, he started a new job in Bristol. Until 31 December 2009, he lived in a rented house in Bristol. On 1 January 2010, he purchased a new apartment in Bristol and elected that apartment as his PPR.

On 1 January 2013, Raj sold his apartment in Dundee for £99,000.

Required:

Show the calculation of capital gain on disposal of the apartment in Dundee.

Question 4

In April 2002, Matthew purchased an antique picture for £1,000. In July 2012, he sold this picture for £8,200 having incurred incidental expenditure of £320.

Required:

Calculate chargeable gain.

Question 5

Linda is a practising chartered accountant. She bought a house for £28,000 on 1 January 2005. From that date she started using one room out of the four rooms of the house for business purposes.

On 31 May 2012, she purchased another house and sold her first house for £98,000.

Required:

What will be the chargeable gain?

Question 6

On 2 April 2002, Jaydeep purchased a house for £73,000. However, from 1 January 2003, he rented out 40% of the house. The tenant vacated the house on 31 March 2012. On 1 April 2013, Jaydeep sold the house for £148,300 in order to work in the USA.

Required:

Show the calculation of chargeable gain.

Question 7

David works in the IT industry. Owing to the nature of his job he travels all over Europe. On 1 June 2005, he purchased a new house for £98,000. He lived in the house until 31 August 2006. He then went to India due to his employment for four years. On 1 December 2012 he sold his house for £258,000.

Required:

Calculate the chargeable gain arising from the transaction.

Answers to Self Examination Questions

Answer to SEQ 1

Calculation of chargeable capital gain on the disposal of chattel

	£
Disposal consideration	8,500
Less: Cost of acquisition	(4,000)
Gain on disposal	**4,500**
Restricted to	**4,167**

Workings

W1

As the machinery has been used for business purposes, the wasting asset rules do not apply (i.e. the gain is taxable as if it were a non-wasting asset).

As the disposal value is more than £6,000, the chargeable gain is the lower of:

(a) the normal net gain = £8,500 - £4,000 = £4,500
(b) 5/3 x (gross proceeds - £6,000) = 5/3 x (£8,500 - £6,000) = £4,167

Hence, the chargeable gain is restricted to £4,167.

Answer to SEQ 2

1. **Disposal value of the cutlery set is more than £6,000** (calculation of capital loss in the usual way)

Calculation of allowable loss

	£
Disposal consideration	8,600
Less: Cost of acquisition	(12,000)
Allowable loss	**(3,400)**

2. **Disposal value is less than £6,000.**

As the disposal value is less than £6,000, for the purposes of calculating the allowable loss we replace the gross proceeds value with £6,000).

Calculation of allowable loss

	£
Disposal value (deemed)	6,000
Less: Acquisition cost	(12,000)
Allowable loss	**(6,000)**

Note: the actual loss is £6,400 (£12,000 - £5,600) but the allowable loss is £6,000 as calculated above.

Answer to SEQ 3

	£
Disposal consideration	99,000
Less: Cost of acquisition	(38,000)
Net gain	**61,000**
Less: PPR relief (W1)	(58,245)
Chargeable gain	**2,755**

Workings

W1 Calculation of PPR

Raj's ownership period of house in Dundee is split into exempt and chargeable periods as follows:

	Total (months)	Exempt (months)	Chargeable (months)
1 February 2000 to 31 May 2005 (note 1)	64	64	-
1 June 2005 to 31 December 2009 (note 2)	55	48	7
1 January 2010 to 31 December 2012 (note 3)	36	36	-
Total	**155**	**148**	**7**

Notes

1. Actual period of residence is always exempt when calculating chargeable gain on the disposal of a residence.
2. A total of up to four years of absence where an individual is employed elsewhere in the UK is deemed to be period of occupation for calculation of PPR relief provided that there is an actual period of occupation both before and after the period of absence. Although Raj has not come back after he left the property in June 2003, up to four years of that period will still be treated as an exempt period as his permanent absence is by reason of his employment.
3. The last 36 months of ownership are always exempt. This is the only exemption that is still available even though Raj had a new PPR for part of that 36 month period.

Therefore, total exemption is available for 148 months and the gain apportioned to the 7 month period is chargeable to tax.

$$\text{PPR relief} = \frac{\text{Period of actual and deemed residence}}{\text{Period of ownership}} \text{ x gain}$$

$$= \frac{148}{155} \text{ x £61,000}$$

$$= \text{£58,245}$$

Answer to SEQ 4

Calculation of chargeable gain

	£
Disposal consideration	8,200
Less: Incidental cost of disposal	(320)
Net disposal consideration	**7,880**
Less: Allowable deductions	
Acquisition cost	(1,000)
Net gain	**6,880**

If the gross sales proceeds of the chattel exceed £6,000 then chargeable gain is the lower of:

(a) the normal net gain = £6,880
(b) 5/3 x (gross proceeds - £6,000) = 5/3 x (£8,200 - £6,000) = £3,667

Hence, the chargeable gain is restricted to £3,667.

Answer to SEQ 5

Calculation of chargeable gain

	£
Disposal consideration	98,000
Less: Allowable deductions	
Acquisition cost	(28,000)
Net gain	**70,000**
Less: PPR exemption (W1)	
(3/4 x £70,000)	(52,500)
Chargeable gain	**17,500**

Workings

W1

Linda used one out of the four rooms of her house for business purposes throughout the period of ownership. To that extent she lost the PPR exemption. As that portion of the house was used solely for business purposes throughout the period of ownership, it is not possible to claim the last 36 month exemption on the business element of the gain.

Answer to SEQ 6

Calculation of chargeable gain

	£	£
Disposal consideration		148,300
Less: Allowable deductions		
Acquisition cost		(73,000)
Net gain		**75,300**
Less: PPR exemption (W1)		(55,448)
		19,852
Less: Letting relief		
Lowest of:		
PPR relief	55,448	
£40,000	40,000	
The gain that arose in the letting period		
£75,300 x 87/132 x 40%	19,852	(19,852)
132		
Chargeable gains		-

Workings

W1 Calculation of total ownership period

Period between dates	Total (months)	Exempt (months)	Chargeable (months)
2 April 2002 to 31 December 2002 (only domestic purpose)	9	9	
1 January 2003 to 31 March 2010 (40% let out) (111 months)	87		87
1 April 2010 to 31 March 2013 (last 36 month exemption)	36	36	
	132	**45**	**87**

PPR exemption

i. Out of his total ownership period of 132 months, for the first 9 months and the last 12 months, the house was used only for domestic purposes

ii. PPR relief is available for the last 36 months of ownership. As there was a period during which the entire property was used by Jaydeep as his PPR, the 36 month exemption is available on the full amount of the gain (i.e. before apportioning for letting periods).

iii. The total **chargeable** period of ownership during which property was used for domestic purposes as well as let out is therefore 87 months. PPR exemption will be available only for the 60% of the property used for his own domestic purposes during that period.

$$\text{PPR relief} = \frac{\text{Period of actual and deemed residence x Gain}}{\text{Period of ownership}}$$

	£
(45/132) x £75,300	25,670
(87/132) x £75,300 x 60%	29,778
	55,448

Answer to SEQ 7

Calculation of chargeable gain

	£
Disposal consideration	258,000
Less: Allowable deductions	
Acquisition cost	(98,000)
Net gain	**160,000**
Less: PPR exemption	
	(160,000)
Chargeable gain	-

Workings

W1

Calculation of total ownership period and exempt and chargeable period

	Total (months)	Exempt (months)	Chargeable (months)
1 June 2005 to 31 August 2006 (actual occupation)	15	15	0
1 September 2006 to 30 November 2009 (Note 1)	39	39	0
1 December 2009 to 30 November 2012 (Note 2)	36	36	0

Notes

1. Any period of absence during which the taxpayer is working abroad is exempt provided that the property was occupied both before and after the period of absence or the continued absence was by reason of employment. The period between 1 September 2006 and 30 November 2012 is therefore covered under the PPR exemption, as the continued absence was due to ongoing employment overseas.
2. The last thirty six months of ownership are always exempt.

SECTION C

CHARGEABLE GAINS

C4

STUDY GUIDE C4: GAINS AND LOSSES ON THE DISPOSAL OF SHARES AND SECURITIES

Get Through Intro

This Study Guide deals with the **calculation of capital gains** that arise because of the **disposal of shares and securities.**

Identification of the share matching rules is the **core ingredient** in the recipe required to prepare the dish called 'capital gains due to disposal of shares and securities'. An **improper identification** will lead to an **incorrect calculation** of capital gains and therefore this principle needs to be understood thoroughly.

This Study Guide discusses how **share matching rules** and **certain exemptions are different** for **companies** and for **individuals.** It also explains the pooling provision and states the treatment applied to bonus issues, rights issues, takeovers and reorganisations.

It is important for you to grasp the principles underlying the calculations as they will help you answer the questions in the examination with confidence, and guide you to give the correct advice in your professional life as a tax consultant.

Learning Outcomes

a) Calculate the value of quoted shares where they are disposed of by way of a gift.
b) Explain and apply the identification rules as they apply to individuals and to companies, including the same day, nine day, and thirty day matching rules.
c) Explain the pooling provisions.
d) Explain the treatment of bonus issues, rights issues, takeovers and reorganisations.
e) Explain the exemption available for gilt-edged securities and qualifying corporate bonds.

Introduction

Case Study

On 5 May 2006, Lily purchased 500 shares of Mega Ltd for £2 each. In May 2011, Mega Ltd made a bonus issue of 1 for 2. At the time of the bonus issue the market price of the shares was £5.

As she received 250 shares free of cost, she gave them to her daughter, Millie. One morning she received a notice from HMRC asking her to pay capital gains tax on the transfer of the shares, by way of a gift.

Lily was confused, she had received the bonus shares free of cost and rather than selling them, she had given them to her daughter as a gift. Why then should she pay capital gains tax?

In this Study Guide let us absorb the various provisions related to capital gains tax on the disposal of shares and securities.

1. Calculate the value of quoted shares where they are disposed of by way of a gift.[2] [Learning Outcome a]

Quoted Shares are the shares **listed on a recognised stock exchange**. These shares are also called listed shares.

We have already seen in Study Guide C1, that disposal of an asset by way of a gift is considered to be chargeable disposal. In the case of disposal by way of a gift, the **market value** of the asset on the day of disposal is considered to be the **sale proceeds**.

Tip

Market value is used when assets are disposed of by way of a gift.

Shares and securities which are listed on the Stock Exchange are valued at the lower of:

1. Lower quoted price +1/4 x (higher quoted price – lower quoted price) ('quarter up' rule), and
2. The average of the highest and lowest recorded bargains.

Example

Kim, a seventy year old lady, gifted 200 shares in Beta Plc to her son, Jim on 5 June 2012. On that day the shares were quoted at £200 - £208 with bargains marketed at £200, £202, £205, £206. In this situation, the market value of these quoted shares on the day of transfer is calculated as follows:

The valuation of quoted shares as on the day of transfer is the lower of the following:

1. Lower quoted price +1/4 (higher quoted price - lower quoted price)
   = £200 + 1/4(£208 - £200) = £202
2. The average of the highest and lowest recorded bargains
   = (£200 + £206)/2 = £203

Therefore, the value per share for CGT purposes is £202 and the value of 200 shares will be charged accordingly.

Tip

On the date of disposal by way of gift, if information relating to transactions or bids or bargains is not given, then the average of the range (the highest and lowest quoted price) is considered for calculating the average of the highest and lowest recorded bargains.

Jack owns 20,000 ordinary shares of Jupiter Ltd. He had purchased these shares on 15 April 1998 for £25,000. On 23 June 2012, he gave all the shares to his son. On that day the shares were quoted on the Stock Exchange at £5.05- £5.13.

The disposal consideration for the purposes of capital gains should be calculated as follows:

As the bargains on the day of disposal by way of gift are not given, highest and lowest quoted price will be used for calculating average of the highest and lowest recorded bargains.

The valuation of quoted shares as on the day of transfer is the lower of the following:

Lower quoted price +1/4(higher quoted price - lower quoted price)
= £5.05 + 1/4(£5.13 - £5.05) = £5.07

The average of the highest and lowest recorded bargains
= (£5.05 + £5.13)/2 = £5.09

Therefore, the value per share for CGT purposes will be £5.07 and the value of 20,000 shares will be charged accordingly.

The disposal consideration will be 20,000 ordinary shares x £5.07 = £101,400

SUMMARY

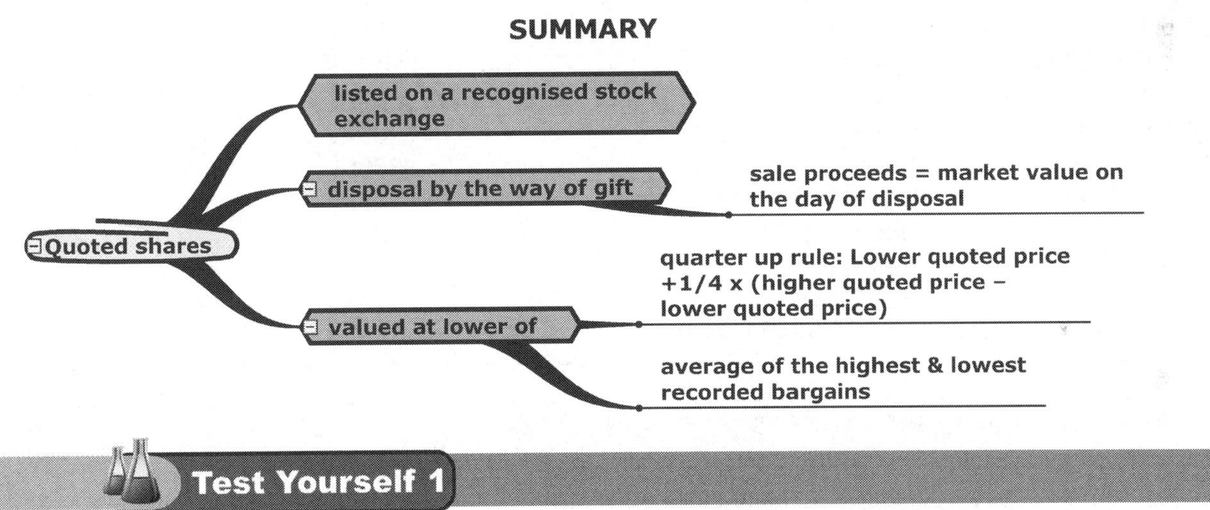

Test Yourself 1

On 1 September 2010 River Plc made a gift of 2,000 shares of Rain Ltd to Sea Plc. On the day of transfer, shares in Rain Plc were quoted at £120 - £130. The highest and lowest marked bargains were £122 and £129.

Required:

What would be the market value for CGT purposes?

---

2. Explain and apply the identification rules as they apply to individuals and to companies, including the same day, nine day, and thirty day matching rules.[2]
Explain the pooling provisions.[2]

[Learning Outcomes b and c]

2.1 Share identification rules applicable for individuals

The disposal of shares from 6 April 2009 onwards by individuals, is matched with purchases, in the following order:

1. Shares purchased on the **same day** as the disposal.
2. Shares purchased within the **following 30 days.**
3. Shares in the share pool.

The above rule 2 of matching against the future purchase is to prevent a person establishing a gain or a loss by selling shares at the close of business and buying them back at the start of business on the following day. This was, in the past, common tax planning intending to trigger a chargeable gain within the annual exemption or to crystallise a loss to offset against other gains. This was known as **bed and breakfasting**, and allowed a gain or a loss to be established without a genuine disposal being made.

The **share pool** aggregates all purchases except for those made on the same day as the disposal, or within the following 30 days. Disposals are taken out at average cost for the shares in the share pool. Therefore, while calculating chargeable gain on the shares sold from the share pool, the number of shares purchased and the cost of those shares should be checked. Indexation allowance is not available to individuals.

The share identification rules were much more complex prior to 6 April 2008. The introduction of the share pool means that any shares owned at 5 April 2008 will be pooled, and later purchases will simply be added to this pool (unless matched with disposals under (1) or (2) above).

The following are the details of acquisitions and disposals of shares by Barber over several years. Show the sequence in which the disposals will be matched against the acquisitions from the following data:

Date of transaction	Transaction acquisition	Number of shares
20 April 1995	Acquisition	200
9 September 2001	Acquisition	200
1 October 2005	Acquisition	1,200
20 March 2011	Acquisition	100
12 April 2011	Acquisition	100
12 April 2011	**Disposal**	**(300)**
30 April 2011	Acquisition	125
5 January 2012	Acquisition	150
15 April 2012	**Disposal**	**(350)**

1. Disposal of 300 shares on 12 April 2011 are matched in the following order:

	No. of shares
Shares purchased on the same day as the disposal (12 April 2011)	100
Shares purchased within next 30 days of the disposal (i.e. up to 12 May 2011)	125
Shares from the share pool acquired before date of disposal	75
Total number of shares sold	**300**

2. The 350 shares disposed on 15 April 2012 are matched in the following order:

	No. of shares
Shares purchased on the same day as the disposal (15 April 2012)	-
Shares purchased within next 30 days of the disposal (i.e. up to 15 May 2012)	-
Shares in the share pool acquired before date of disposal	350
Total number of shares sold	**350**

On 10 May 2012, Mack purchased 2,000 shares in Mars Ltd for £20,500. Mack found that the value of the shares fell drastically, so on 1 December 2012 he sold them for £4,000. He repurchased the shares on 12 December 2012 for £3,500.

Continued on the next page

In this case, the capital gain will be calculated as follows:

The transaction satisfies the condition of the 30 day matching rule. So, the sale of shares for £4,000 on 1 December 2012 will match the purchase made on 12 December 2012 (i.e. within next 30 days of disposal). Therefore, the capital gain for 2012-13 is £4,000 - £3,500 = £500.

Juliet purchased 50,000 ordinary shares in Jumbo Ltd on 20 June 2010 for £150,000. On 8 April 2012, Juliet purchased an additional 2,000 shares in Jumbo Ltd for £8,000, and sold 6,000 ordinary shares in Jumbo Ltd for £30,000 on the same day. She purchased 2,500 more shares in Jumbo Ltd for £12,000 on 30 April 2012.

Disposal of 6,000 shares on 8 April 2012 is matched in the following order:

	No. of shares
Shares purchased on the same day as the disposal (8 April 2012)	2,000
Shares purchased within next 30 days of the disposal (i.e. up to 8 May 2012)	2,500
Shares from the share pool acquired before date of disposal (against acquired on 20 June 2010)	1,500
Total number of shares sold	**6,000**

The capital gain for 2012-13 is computed as follows:

	£	£
Shares (2,000) purchased on same day of disposal		
Disposal consideration (£30,000 x 2,000/6,000)	10,000	
Less: Acquisition cost of shares	(8,000)	2,000
Shares (2,500) purchased within next 30 days of disposal		
Disposal consideration (£30,000 x 2,500/6,000)	12,500	
Less: Acquisition cost of shares	(12,000)	500
Shares (1,500) in the share pool acquired before disposal		
Disposal consideration (£30,000 x 1,500/6,000)	7,500	
Less: Acquisition cost of shares (£150,000 x 1,500/50,000)	(4,500)	3,000
Chargeable gains		**5,500**

SUMMARY

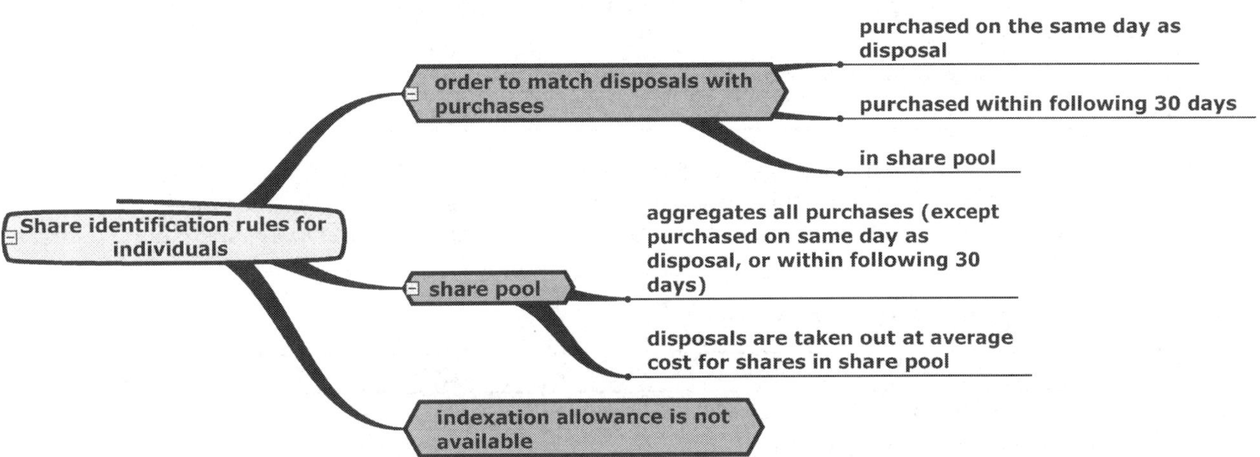

2.2 Share identification rules applicable for companies

When a company makes various acquisitions of shares in the same company over a period of time, and then disposes of some of them, special matching rules are required to determine which shares are being disposed.

1. **The disposal of shares is matched with purchases** in the following **order**:

a) shares purchased on the **same day** as the disposal
b) shares purchased **during the nine days prior to the disposal**
c) the "1985 pool" - shares acquired on or after 1 April 1982
d) the 1982 holding - share acquired between 1 April 1965 and 31 March 1982
e) other shares on a 'last in first out' basis (broadly any shares held pre 31 March 1965)

Tip

In practice most disposals are in respect of shares in (a) to (c) above; those are the rules that we will concentrate on in this Study Guide.

2. **Operation of the 1985 pool**

The 1985 pool includes shares acquired **after 1 April 1982** - it gets its name by virtue of the fact that it was introduced into the tax legislation in 1985.

a) The pool **records** the number of shares, their cost and their indexed cost.
b) The pool must be **indexed up before each 'operative event**.' These events are acquisitions, disposals and rights issues.
c) The movement in the RPI is **not rounded to 3 decimal places**.
d) Disposals are taken out at **average cost and average indexed cost.**

Tip

Indexation allowance is not available for shares purchased on the same day as the disposal, and during the nine days prior to the disposal. Unlike other disposals, the movement in RPI is not rounded to three decimal places when shares are disposed from the 1985 pool.

Example

Sun Ltd purchased 20,000 shares in Moon Ltd on 16 November 2012 for £100,000 and an additional 5,000 shares on 23 November 2012 for £30,000. Sun Ltd sells 12,000 shares in Moon Ltd on 23 November 2012 for £84,000.

First, we will match the disposal of shares with the purchases in the following order:

	No. of shares
Shares purchased on the same day as the disposal (23 November 2012)	5,000
Shares purchased during the nine days prior to the disposal (i.e. from 14 November 2012 to 22 November 2012)	7,000
Shares in the share pool (other than above two)	-
Total number of shares sold	**12,000**

Note: shares purchased on the same day as the disposal and shares purchased during the nine days prior to the disposal are not indexed up, and capital gains or loss on the disposal is calculated normally i.e. sales proceeds less allowable costs. Indexation allowance is available only for the shares in the share pool. (or earlier acquisitions).

The computation of capital gains is made as follows:

	£	**£**
Shares purchased on same day of disposal		
Disposal consideration (£84,000 x 5,000/12,000)	35,000	
Less: Acquisition cost of shares	(30,000)	5,000
Shares purchased nine days prior to the disposal		
Disposal consideration (£84,000 x 7,000/12,000)	49,000	
Less: Acquisition cost of shares (£100,000 x 7,000/20,000)	(35,000)	14,000
Chargeable gains		**19,000**

Example

Saturn Ltd purchased 50,000 shares in Neptune Ltd on 10 June 2001 (RPI 174.4) for £200,000. It purchased an additional 40,000 shares on 22 August 2005 (RPI 192.6) for £190,000. Saturn Ltd sold 60,000 ordinary shares in Neptune on 20 May 2012 (RPI 242.4) for £350,000.

First, we will match the disposals of shares with the purchases in the following order:

	No. of shares
Shares purchased on the same day as the disposal (20 May 2012)	-
Shares purchased during the nine days prior to the disposal (i.e., from 11 May 2012 to 19 May 2012)	-
Shares in the 1985 pool	60,000
Total number of shares sold	**60,000**

The computation of capital gains is as follows:

	£
Disposal consideration	350,000
Less: Acquisition cost of shares (W1) (Note 2)	(260,000)
Un-indexed gain	**90,000**
Less: Indexation allowance (£342,260 - £260,000) (W1)	(82,260)
Chargeable gain	**7,740**

Workings

W1 Indexed cost

	Number of shares	Cost (£)	Indexed cost (£)
Purchased in June 2001	50,000	200,000	200,000
Indexation to August 2005 (192.6 -174.4/174.4) x £200,000			20,872
	50,000	200,000	**220,872**
Purchased in August 2005	40,000	190,000	190,000
	90,000	**390,000**	**410,872**
Indexation to March 2012 (242.4 – 192.6/192.6) x £410,872			106,238
	90,000	**390,000**	**517,110**
Less: Disposal March 2012 (Cost x 60,000/90,000)	(60,000)	(260,000)	(344,740)
Balance c/f	**30,000**	**130,000**	**172,370**

£517,110 x 60,000/ 90,000

Notes

1. As all the shares are related to the 1985 pool, indexation allowance will be available when calculating the capital gain on disposal. The share pool will record the number of shares, their cost and indexed cost and will be indexed up to the date of each operative event. In this case, there is one operative event on 22 August 2005 i.e. the purchase of 40,000 shares, and another on 20 April 2012 i.e. the disposal of 60,000 shares. Hence, indexation is done before each of these events.

2. Disposals are taken out at average cost and average indexed cost.

3. The unindexed cost of sale for 60,000 shares amounting to £260,000 is matched first and then the indexation of £84,740, (£344,740 – £260,000) is deducted from the gain. This is to ensure that the indexation does not give rise to a loss nor increase a loss.

SUMMARY

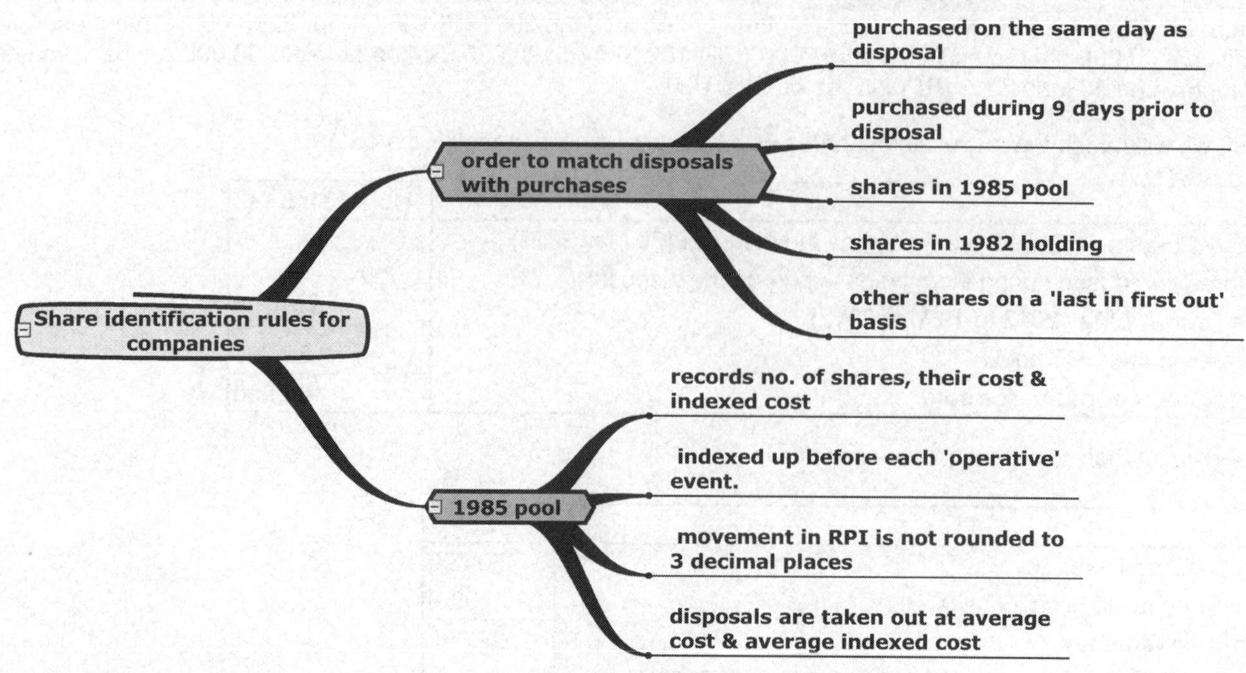

Test Yourself 2

Henry purchased 19,000 shares in Huge Plc on 10 December 2011 for 65,000. As the position of the company was very sound, he purchased another 15,000 shares on 25 August 2012 for £30,000. Henry sold 20,000 shares to his brother, Jerry, on 20 February 2013. On that date the shares were quoted at £6.40 - £6.60.

Required:

Compute Henry's capital gain for 2012-13.

Test Yourself 3

Jerry had the following transactions relating to the sale and purchase of shares of Jupiter Ltd.

5 June 2000	Purchased 4,000 shares for £8,500
25 April 2010	Purchased 2,000 shares for £7,500
20 May 2010	Purchased 1,000 shares for £5,000
20 February 2013	Sold 5,000 shares for £30,000

Required:

Calculate the capital gains.

Test Yourself 4

City Ltd sold 3,850 shares in Country Ltd for £40,000 on 27 March 2012. These shares were purchased by City Ltd as follows:

i. 4,000 shares in April 2004 for £12,000
ii. 5,000 shares in July 2010 for £26,000

The indexation factor from April 2004 to July 2010 is 0.204 and from July 2010 to March 2012 is 0.077.

Required:

Calculate City Ltd's chargeable gains.

---

3. Explain the treatment of bonus issues, rights issues, takeovers and reorganisations.[2] [Learning Outcome d]

3.1 Bonus issue

A bonus issue is a **free issue of shares** to **existing shareholders** in proportion to their existing holding.

A bonus share is given for a certain number of shares previously held.

Tip

A company may issue bonus shares because it wishes to increase the number of shares issued. As this would otherwise dilute the shareholding already held, it issues shares free of charge.

Example

'1 for 4' bonus issue means that one additional share is given for every 4 shares held.

---

1. Individuals

The bonus shares are given based on the original holding. Therefore it is **treated as having been acquired on the same date as the original holding that qualified for the bonus.**

Example

Alan purchased the following shares:

1. 1 June 2010: 800 shares purchased
2. 1 December 2011: 1,200 shares purchased
3. 1 June 2012: bonus issue 1 for 4

He will receive an additional 500 shares on 1 June 2012 ((800 + 1,200) x 1/4)

These bonus shares will be treated as acquired as follows:

1. 200 (800 x 1/4) on 1 June 2010
2. 300 (1,200 x 1/4) on 1 December 2011

Example

On 20 December 2011, Alice acquired 1,000 shares of Orchid Ltd for £5,000. On 18 March 2013, the company made a bonus issue of 3 for 10. Immediately after the bonus issue, Alice sold all the shares for £10 each.

Calculation of capital gains on disposal of all these shares is as follows:

	£
Sale proceeds (W1) (1,300 x £10)	13,000
Less: Acquisition cost	(5,000)
Chargeable gains	**8,000**

Continued on the next page

Workings

W1 Share holding

	Number of shares	Cost (£)
Shares acquired on 20 December 2011	1,000	5,000
Bonus shares (1,000/10) x 3	300	
	1,300	**5,000**

2. Companies

When a bonus issue is received, there is **no additional cost.** This is **not an 'operative event';** hence the 1985 pool is **not indexed up** before adding the bonus issue to the pool.

Example

In May 1996, Cooper Ltd acquired 500 ordinary shares of Metal Plc for £2,500. In June 2001, Cooper Ltd acquired another lot of 500 shares for £3,000. In March 2012, Metal Plc issued one for ten bonus shares. The indexation factor from May 1996 to March 2012 is 1.575 and from June 2001 to March 2012 is 1.381. The shareholding, immediately after bonus issue will be as follows:

	Date of acquisition	Number of shares	Cost (£)	Indexed cost (£)
	May 1996	500	2,500	3,938 (£2,500 x 1.575)
	June,2001	500	3,000	4,143 (£3,000 x 1.381)
Bonus issue	March 2012	100	-	-
Total		**1100**	**5,500**	**8,081**

Original cost of shares remains same. The number of shares increases.

Example

Strong Ltd purchased 50,000 shares in Smart Ltd on 20 June 1994 (RPI 144.7) for £40,000. On 15 October 2009 (RPI 216.0), Smart Ltd made a bonus of 1 for every 4 shares held.

Strong Ltd sold 30,000 shares in Smart Ltd for £125,000 on 25 May 2012 (RPI 242.4).

The capital gains for 2012-13 are calculated as follows:

	£
Disposal consideration	125,000
Less: Acquisition cost of shares (W1)	(19,200)
Un-indexed gain	**105,800**
Less: Indexation allowance	
£32,027 - £19,200	(12,827)
Chargeable gain	**92,973**

Continued on the next page

Workings

W1 Acquisition cost of shares

Share pool is not indexed up before adding bonus issue to the pool as it is not an operative event.

	Number of shares	Cost (£)	Indexed cost (£)
Purchased in June 1994	50,000	40,000	40,000
Bonus issue October 2009 (50,000 x 1/4)	12,500		
	62,500	40,000	40,000
Indexation to May 2012 (242.4 – 144.7/144.7) x £40,000			27,008
	62,500	40,000	67,008
Disposal March 2012 (Cost x 30,000/62,500)	(30,000)	(19,200)	(32,164)
Balance c/f	**32,500**	**20,800**	**34,844**

SUMMARY

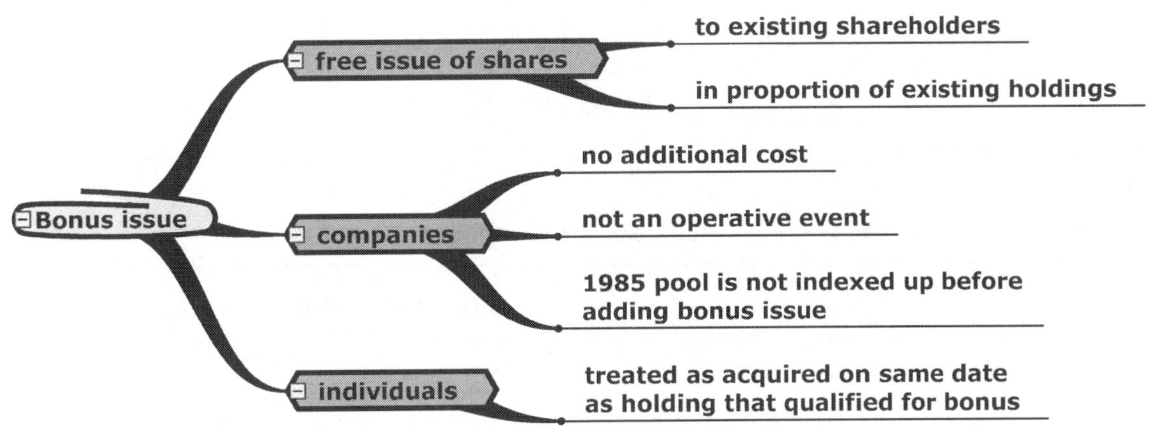

Test Yourself 5

Alice acquired the following preference shares in Square Ltd:

Date	No. of shares	Cost (£)
01/01/1994	2,000	8,000
20/04/1998	500	3,000
09/09/2004	400	2,000

On 1 December 2010, the company made a 2 for 5 bonus issue. On 1 June 2012, Alice sold all the shares of Square Ltd for £28,420.

Required:

Calculate Alice's chargeable gains.

Test Yourself 6

Ivan Ltd purchased 35,000 shares in Koyna Ltd on 15 February 2008 for £100,500. The indexed value of the 1985 pool on 5 January 2013 was £112,000. Koyna Ltd made a bonus issue on 5 January 2013 in the ratio of 1 for 2 shares.

Ivan Ltd sold 35,000 shares in Koyna Ltd on 25 January 2013 for £160,500.

Required:

Calculate the capital gains.

3.2 Rights issue

A rights issue is an offer to existing shareholders to **buy** additional shares in proportion to their existing holdings. These additional shares are purchased; they are not free.

A rights issue is a way for a company to raise additional share capital. The shareholdings of those who do not take up the rights issue will be diluted.

1. Individuals

The rights shares are **treated as** having been **acquired on the same date as the original holding** that qualified for the rights.

Tania's investment folder shows the following transactions:

Date	Transaction	Number of shares (Cool Ltd)	Cost £
5 March 2008	Purchase	500	500
20 May 2011	Purchase	1,000	4,000

On 21 August 2012, the company made a 1 for 5 rights issue at £7 per share. Tania purchased her full quota of rights shares.

Tania's shareholding immediately after the rights issue will be as follows:

	Number of shares	Cost £
Bought 5 March 2008	500	500
Bought 20 May 2011	1,000	4,000
	1,500	**4,500**
Rights issue on 21 August 2012 at £7 per share (1:5 ratio)	300	2,100
	1,800	**6,600**

These rights shares will be treated as acquired as follows:

1. 100 shares (500 x 1/5) on 5 March 2007
2. 200 shares (1000 x 1/5) on 20 May 2009

Continuing the previous example of Tania's investment

In continuation of the above example, assume that Tania sold all the above shares for £16,200 on 28 March 2013.

Calculation of capital gains will be as follows:

	£
Sale proceeds	16,200
Less: Acquisition cost	(6,600)
Chargeable gain	**9,600**

Henry purchased 40,000 shares in Venus Ltd on 15 February 2009 for £120,000.

Venus Ltd made a rights issue of 1 for 2 rights on 5 January 2013. He paid for the rights issue @ £2.00 for each new share issued.

On 25 January 2013, Henry sold 40,000 shares in Venus Ltd for £180,000.

Calculation of capital gains will be as follows:

First of all, we have to calculate the number and cost of the rights shares and the cost of the acquisition of the shares sold.

	Number of shares	Cost (£)
Bought 15 February 2009	40,000	120,000
Rights issue on 5 January 2013 at £2 per share (1:2 ratio)	20,000	40,000
	60,000	**160,000**
Less: Disposal on 25 January 2013 (£160,000 x 40,000 /60,000)	(40,000)	(106,667)
Balance c/f	**20,000**	**53,333**

Therefore, Henry's chargeable gain on disposal of shares is:

	£
Sale proceeds	180,000
Less: Acquisition cost of shares	(106,667)
Chargeable gain	**73,333**

---

2. Companies

The purchase of rights issue shares is an **'operative event'**. The 1985 pool **must be indexed up** to the date of the rights issue, before the shares are added to the pool.

Matthew Ltd purchased 35,000 shares in Michael Ltd on 10 February 2010 for £120,000. The indexed value of the 1985 pool on 4 January 2012 was £150,000.

Michael Ltd made a rights issue of 1 for 2 rights on 4 January 2012. Matthew Ltd paid for the rights issue at £2.20 for each new share issued.

On 26 January 2013, Matthew Ltd sold 35,000 shares in Michael Ltd for £175,000.The indexed value of the 1985 pool on that date was £195,000. As a rights issue is made by one company and exercised by another company, the calculation of capital gains will be made as follows:

First of all, we have to calculate the number and cost of the rights shares.
Number of rights shares = 35,000 x 1/2 = 17,500 shares.
Cost of right shares = No. of shares x rate of one share
= 17,500 x £2.20
= £38,500

Therefore, the chargeable gain on disposal of shares will be as follows:

	£
Sale proceeds	175,000
Less: Acquisition cost of shares (W1)	(105,667)
	69,333
Less: Indexation allowance	
(£130,000 - £105,667) (note 1)	(24,333)
Chargeable gains	**45,000**

Continued on the next page

Workings

W1 Calculation of acquisition cost and indexed cost of shares sold

	No. of shares	Cost (£)	Indexed cost (£)
Purchased on 10 February 2010	35,000	120,000	120,000
Indexation to 4 January 2012			30,000
Indexed value as on 4 January 2012	35,000	120,000	150,000
Rights shares purchased on 4 January 2012	17,500	38,500	38,500
	52,500	158,500	188,500
Indexation to 26 January 2013			6,500
Indexed value as on 26 January 2013	52,500	158,500	195,000
Less: Disposal on 26 January 2013 (note 2)			
(Cost x 35,000/52,500)	(35,000)	(105,667)	(130,000)
Balance c/f	**17,500**	**52,833**	**65,000**

SUMMARY

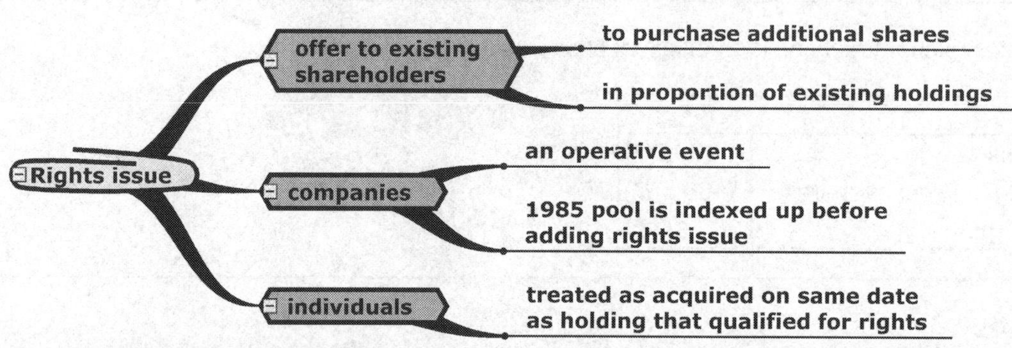

Sun Ltd purchased 10,000 shares in Moon Ltd on 5 March 2013 for £30,000. On 26 March 2013, Moon Ltd made a rights issue of 1 for 1. Sun Ltd paid £3.50 for each new share issued, and sold 15,000 ordinary shares in Moon Ltd on 31 March 2013 for £60,500.

Required:

Calculate chargeable gains.

3.3 Takeovers and reorganisations

1. Companies

a) When **one company takes over another company**, the new company acquires shares in the old company in exchange for shares in the new company.

b) Known as '**paper for paper**' transaction.

c) This transaction does **not give rise to a chargeable gain.**

d) **New shares** take the place of the old shares, and are **treated as having been purchased at the same time and for the same cost.**

e) There is **no gain at the time of the takeover** if all the consideration is in the form of shares in the new company.

f) If the consideration is partly in shares and partly in cash and the consideration received in cash is not 'small', then the gain related to cash consideration will be chargeable immediately. The sum is regarded as 'small' if the cash consideration received is less than 5% of the total consideration received, restricted to **maximum of £3,000**.

While calculating chargeable gains, the part of the cost of the original shares attributable to the cash consideration received will be calculated as follows:

$$\text{Cost of original shares} \times \frac{\text{Cash received}}{\text{Total value of consideration from company}}$$

Where,
Total value of consideration from company = cash received + market value of new shares received

g) There is a **gain when the new shares are disposed of.**

h) If **more than one class of the new share** is acquired (e.g. ordinary shares and preference shares) the **cost of the original shares must be allocated** according to the market value of the new shares at the time of the takeover.

Example to show allocation of original cost

Tip Top Plc bought 10,000 shares in Armco Plc in June 2010 for £25,000. In June 2012 Braun Plc took over Armco Plc.

For every 2 shares in Armco Plc, Tip Top Plc received 3 ordinary shares and 1 preference share in Braun Plc.

At the time of the takeover Braun Plc's ordinary shares were quoted at £2.00, and their preference shares at £3.00.

Allocation of original cost:

Consideration of takeover for Tip Top Plc	£
(10,000 x 3/2) 15,000 ordinary shares in Braun Plc at £2.00	30,000
(10,000 x 1/2) 5,000 preference shares in Braun Plc at £3.00	15,000
	45,000

Original cost allocated to	£
Ordinary shares: £25,000 x £30,000/£45,000	16,667
Preference shares: £25,000 x £15,000/£45,000	8,333
	25,000

Saturn Ltd purchased 20,000 ordinary shares in Sun Ltd on 1 July 2012 for £100,000.

On 15 July 2012, Sun Ltd was taken over by Moon Ltd. Saturn Ltd received one £1 ordinary share and one £1 preference share in Moon Ltd for each £1 ordinary share held in Sun Ltd.

When Sun Ltd was taken over by Moon Ltd, the shares were quoted at different rates. Each £1 ordinary share in Moon Ltd was quoted at £5.10 and each £1 preference share was quoted at £1.75.

Saturn Ltd sold 12,000 £1 ordinary shares in Moon Ltd on 31 March 2012 for £40,000.

The RPI for May 2012 is 242.4.

The calculation of the capital gains of Saturn Ltd is as follows:

Due to takeover, Saturn Ltd receives a number of ordinary shares = 20,000
Number of preference shares = 20,000

Cost attributable to shares in Moon Ltd from the takeover is allocated on the basis of the market value of the new shares at the time of the takeover.
Market value of the shares in Moon Ltd:

- Ordinary shares = 20,000 x £5.10 = £102,000
- Preference shares = 20,000 x £1.75 = £35,000

Continued on the next page

Hence, cost attributable to 20,000 ordinary shares in Moon Ltd
= £100,000 x £102,000/(£102,000 + £35,000)
= £100,000 x £0.74
= £74,000

The cost attributable to 12,000 ordinary shares sold
= £74,000 x 12,000/20,000
= £44,400

	£
Sale proceeds	40,000
Less: Acquisition cost of shares	(44,400)
Capital loss	**(4,400)**

Note: As all the transactions were in the same month, there will be no indexation allowance. Moreover, indexation allowance cannot be used to create or increase a loss.

2. Individuals

The **same principle** is applied where an individual is concerned except indexation allowance, as from 6th April 2008, it is no longer available to individuals.

Also from 5th April 2008, a shareholder who received a paper to paper transaction may elect to have the event treated as a disposal. This is to use their annual exemption or claim entrepreneur's relief.

Example

Roger purchased 20,000 shares in Splendid Ltd on 2 May 2005 for £24,000

Splendid Ltd was taken over by Blue Ltd on 5 March 2013.

Roger received two £1 ordinary shares and one £1 preference share in Blue Ltd for each £1 ordinary share held in Splendid Ltd.

After the takeover each £1 ordinary share in Blue Ltd was quoted at £2.00 and each preference share was quoted at £1.00.

Roger sold his entire holding of £1 ordinary shares in Blue Ltd on 29 March 2013 for £60,000.

The calculation of capital gain is made as follows:

Due to the takeover, Roger receives a number of ordinary shares= 20,000 x 2 = 40,000 shares

Number of preference shares = 20,000 x 1 = 20,000 shares

Value of the shares = Ordinary shares = 40,000 x £2.00 = £80,000

Preference shares = 20,000 x £1.00 = £20,000

Cost attributable to ordinary shares = £24,000 x £80,000/(£80,000 + £20,000)
= £24,000 x £80,000/£100,000
= £19,200

	£
Sale proceeds	60,000
Less: Acquisition cost of shares	(19,200)
Net gain	**40,800**

SUMMARY

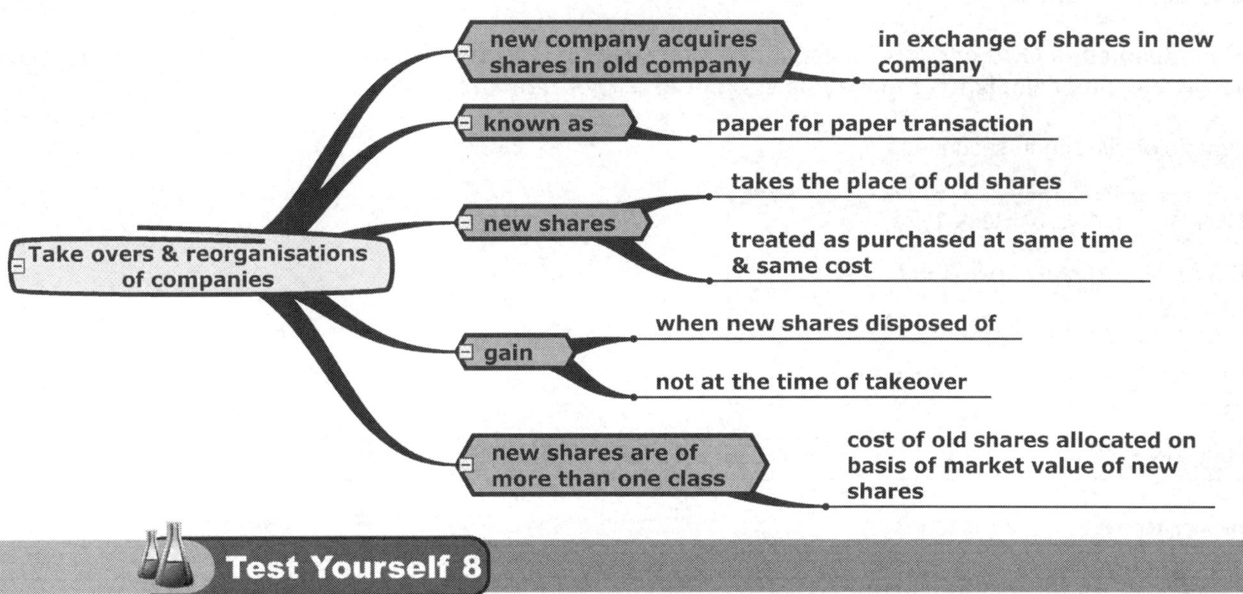

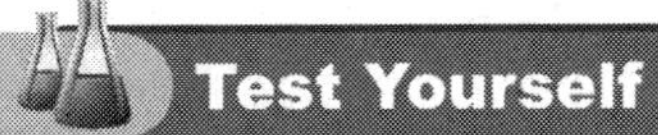

Early Ltd purchased 15,000 shares in Weak Ltd on 2 May 2004 for £20,000. The indexed value of the 1985 pool on 5 March 2013 was £24,500.

On 5 March 2013, Weak Ltd was taken over by Strong Ltd. Early Ltd received two £1 ordinary shares and one £1 preference shares in Strong Ltd for each £1 ordinary share held in Weak Ltd. After the takeover each £1 ordinary share in Strong Ltd was quoted at £3.00, and each preference share was quoted at £2.00.

Early Ltd sold all the £1 ordinary shares in Strong Ltd on 29 March 2013 for £30,000.

Required:

Calculate the chargeable gain of Early Ltd.

Rosy purchased 18,000 shares in Superb Ltd on 2 May 2005 for £20,000. Superb Ltd was taken over by White Ltd on 5 March 2013.

Rosy received two £1 ordinary shares and one £1 preference share in White Ltd and £1.25 in cash for each £1 ordinary share held in Superb Ltd. After the takeover, each £1 ordinary share in White Ltd was quoted at £2.75 and each preference share was quoted at £1.75.

Rosy sold her entire holding of £1 ordinary shares in White Ltd on 29 March 2013 for £60,000.

Required:

Calculate the chargeable gain of Rosy.

4. Explain the exemption available for gilt-edged securities and qualifying corporate bonds.[1] [Learning Outcome e]

Qualifying corporate bonds are basically debentures and other fixed interest securities of companies which represent a normal commercial loan.

Tip

In the exam you will be told whether a disposal is of a qualifying corporate bond or a gilt.

Disposals of **gilt-edged securities** (or "gilts") and **qualifying corporate bonds** (QCBs) are **exempt for capital gains tax for individuals.**

For **companies**, a QCB or gilt is treated in the same way as any other money debt i.e. it is **not subject to a chargeable gain calculation but may be subject to corporation tax**.

Example of gilt-edged securities

2½%	Treasury Stock 1975
12¾%	Treasury Loan 1992
12¼%	Exchequer Stock 1992
10½%	Treasury Convertible Stock 1992

Answers to Test Yourself

Answer to TY 1

The value will be the **lower of:**

1. Lower quoted price +1/4(higher quoted price - lower quoted price)
   = £120 + 1/4 x (£130 – £120) = £122.5

2. The average of the highest and lowest recorded bargains
   = (£122 + £129)/2 = £125.5

Therefore, the value per share for CGT purpose will be £122.5. The value of 2,000 shares will be charged accordingly. The market value of the shares will be 2,000 x £122.5 = £245,000

Answer to TY 2

	£
Disposal consideration (W1)	129,000
Less: Acquisition cost of shares (W2)	(55,882)
Chargeable gain	**73,118**

Workings

W1

As the disposal is to a connected person, the proceeds are deemed to be the market value of the shares at the time of the sale (this is regardless of the actual sale proceeds agreed between the brothers). The valuation of quoted shares as on the day of the transfer is calculated as follows:
The value will be the **lower of:**

1. Lower quoted price +1/4 (higher quoted price - lower quoted price)
   = £6.40 + 1/4 x (£6.60 – £6.40) = £6.45

2. The average of the highest and lowest recorded bargains
   = (£6.40 + £6.60)/2 = £6.50

Therefore, the value per share for CGT purposes will be £6.45. The value of 20,000 shares will be changed accordingly.

Hence, disposal consideration will be 20,000 ordinary shares x £6.45 = £129,000.

W2

Disposal of 20,000 shares on 20 February 2013 is matched in the following order:

Shares purchased on same day as the disposal	-
Shares purchased within next 30 days of disposal	-
Shares in the 1985 pool acquired before disposal	20,000
	20,000

Calculation of acquisition cost of shares sold from the 1985 pool

	No. of shares	Cost
		£
Purchased on 10 December 2011	19,000	65,000
Purchased on 25 August 2012	15,000	30,000
	34,000	95,000
Less: Disposal on 20 February 2013 at average cost (£95,000 x 20,000/34,000)	(20000)	(55,882)
	14,000	39,118

Answer to TY 3

Disposal of 5,000 shares on 20 February 2013 is matched in the following order:

	No. of shares
Shares purchased on the same day as the disposal (20 February 2013)	-
Shares purchased within next 30 days of the disposal (i.e. up to 22 March 2013)	-
Shares from the 1985 pool acquired before date of disposal	5,000
Total number of shares sold	**5,000**

	£
Shares in the 1985 pool:	
Disposal consideration	30,000
Less: Acquisition cost of shares (W1)	(15,000)
Chargeable Gains	**15,000**

Workings

W1 Calculation of the cost of acquisition of shares sold from the 1985 pool is as follows:

	No. of shares	Cost (£) £
Purchased on 5 June 2000	4,000	8,500
Purchased on 25 April 2010	2,000	7,500
Purchased on 20 May 2010	1,000	5,000
	7,000	**21,000**
Less: Disposal on 20 February 2013 (at average cost) (£21,000 x 5,000/7,000)	(5,000)	(15,000)
	2,000	**6,000**

Answer to TY 4

City Ltd's chargeable gain on disposal of shares in Country Ltd is:

	£
Disposal consideration	40,000
Less: Acquisition cost of shares (W1)	(16,256)
Un-indexed gain	**23,744**
Less: Indexation allowance (W1) (£18,635 - £16,256)	(2,379)
Chargeable gain	**21,365**

Workings

W1 Calculation of cost and indexed cost of shares sold

	Number of shares	Cost	Indexed cost
		£	£
Purchased in April 2004	4,000	12,000	12,000
Indexation to July 2010			
(0.204 x £12,000)			2,448
	4,000	12,000	14,448
Purchased in July 2010	5,000	26,000	26,000
	9,000	38,000	40,448
Indexation to March 2012			
(0.077 x £40,448)			3,114
	9,000	38,000	43,562
Less: Disposal in March 2012			
(Cost x 3,850/9,000)	(3,850)	(16,256)	(18,635)
Balance c/f	**5,150**	**21,744**	**24,927**

Answer to TY 5

Alice's chargeable gain for 2012-13

	£
Disposal consideration (4,060 shares)	28,420
Less: Acquisition cost of shares (W1)	(13,000)
Chargeable gain	**15,420**

Workings

W1 Shareholding

	Number of shares	Cost (£)
Purchased on 01/01/1994	2,000	8,000
Purchased on 20/04/1998	500	3,000
Purchased on 09/09/2004	400	2,000
	2,900	13,000
Bonus issue on 1 December 2010 (2,900 x 2/5)	1,160	-
	4,060	**13,000**

Answer to TY 6

	£
Disposal consideration	160,500
Less: Acquisition cost of shares (note 3)	(67,000)
Un-indexed gain	**93,500**
Less: Indexation allowance (note 4)	(7,667)
Chargeable gain	**85,833**

Notes

1. Koyna Ltd made the bonus issue in the ratio of 1 for each 2 shares held.
   Therefore, bonus issue = 35,000 shares x 1/2 = 17,500 shares.

2. Cost of bonus shares is always 0.
   So, £100,500 is the cost of the total number of shares, including bonus shares i.e. 35,000 + 17,500 = 52,500 shares.

3. The cost of 35,000 shares sold = £100,500 x 35,000/(35,000 + 17,500) = £67,000

4. Indexation Allowance is calculated as follows:

   Indexed value – Purchase value
   = £112,000 - £100,500 = £11,500

   For 35,000 shares sold = £11,500 x 35,000/(35,000 + 17,500) = £7,667

Answer to TY 7

A rights issue is made by Moon Ltd and it has been exercised (purchased) by Sun Ltd. The capital gains are therefore calculated as follows:

First of all, we have to calculate the number and cost of the rights shares.
Number of rights shares = 10,000 x 1 = 10,000 shares.
Cost of right shares = No. of shares x rate of one share
= 10,000 x £3.50
= £35,000

	£
Sale proceeds	60,500
Less: Acquisition cost of shares (W1)	(48,750)
Chargeable gain	**11,750**

Workings

W1 Calculation of acquisition cost and indexed cost of shares sold

	No. of shares	Cost (£)
Purchased on 5 March 2013	10,000	30,000
Rights shares purchased on 26 March 2013 (note)	10,000	35,000
	20,000	65,000
Less: Disposal on 31 March 2013		
(Cost x 15,000/20,000)	(15,000)	(48,750)
Balance c/f	**5,000**	**16,250**

Note: shares sold were purchased during the nine days prior to the disposal; hence the cost will not be indexed up. Moreover, all the transactions took place in the same month. In such a case, the RPI will be the same and hence there will be no inflation (indexation allowance).

Answer to TY 8

The capital gain of Early Ltd is calculated as follows:

Due to the takeover, Early Ltd receives:
Number of ordinary shares = 15,000 x 2 = 30,000
Number of preference shares = 15,000 x 1 = 15,000

Market value of these shares at the time of the takeover:
Ordinary shares = 30,000 x £3.00 = £90,000
Preference shares = 15,000 x £2.00 = £30,000

Cost attributable to ordinary shares = £20,000 x £90,000/(£90,000+ £30,000)
= £20,000 x £90,000/£120,000
= £15,000

	£
Sale proceeds	30,000
Less: Acquisition cost of shares	(15,000)
Un-indexed gain	**15,000**
Less: Indexation allowance (W1)	(3,375)
Capital gains	**11,625**

Working

W1

Indexation allowance is calculated as follows:
Indexed value – original cost indexed for total value of ordinary shares.
= £24,500 – £20,000
= £4,500

Indexation allowance attributable to ordinary shares:
= £4,500 x £90,000/(£90,000 + £30,000)
= £3,375

Answer to TY 9

The computation of capital gains is made as follows:

Due to the takeover, Rosy received

Number of ordinary shares = 18,000 x 2 = 36,000 shares

Number of preference shares = 18,000 x 1 = 18,000 shares

Cash consideration = 18,000 x 1.25 = £22,500

Market value of these shares:

Ordinary shares = 36,000 x £2.75 = £99,000

Preference shares = 18,000 x £1.75 = £31,500

Hence, total value of consideration = £22,500 + £99,000 + £31,500 = £153,000

There is no gain at the time of takeover for the consideration received in shares. However, the gain related to cash consideration will be chargeable immediately as the cash consideration received of £22,500 is more than the 5% of the total consideration, i.e. £7,650 (£153,000 x 5%).

Cost attributable to cash consideration = Cost of original shares x cash received / Total value of consideration
= £20,000 x £22,500/(£22,500 + £99,000 + £31,500)
= £20,000 x £22,500/£153,000
= £2,941

The computation of capital gains at the time of takeover is as follows:

	£
Sale proceeds (cash)	22,500
Less: Acquisition cost of shares attributable to cash consideration	(2,941)
Capital gain	**19,559**

The calculation of capital gain on sale of entire holding of ordinary shares is as follows:

Cost attributable to ordinary shares = £20,000 x £99,000/(£22,500 + £99,000 + £31,500)
=£20,000 x £99,000/£153,000
= £12,941

	£
Sale proceeds	60,000
Less: Acquisition cost of shares attributable to ordinary shares	(12,941)
Capital gains	**47,059**

Quick Quiz

1. How is a disposal of shares matched with purchases in the case of a company?

2. How is a disposal of shares matched with purchases in the case of an individual?

3. What is meant by a 'paper for paper' transaction?

Answers to Quick Quiz

1. **The disposal of shares is matched with purchases** in the following **order**:

   (a) shares purchased on the **same day** as the disposal
   (b) shares purchased during the nine days prior to the disposal
   (c) the "1985 pool" - shares acquired on or after 1 April 1982
   (d) the 1982 holding – share acquired between 1 April 1965 and 31 March 1982
   (e) other shares on a last in first out basis (broadly any shares held pre 31 March 1965)

   However in practice, most disposals are in respect of shares in (a) to (c) above.

2. The disposal of **shares is matched** as follows:

   (a) Shares purchased on the **same day** as the disposal.

   (b) Shares purchased in the **following 30 days.**

   (c) Shares in **the share pool.**

   All purchases are aggregated in the share pool except for those purchased on the same day or the following 30 days. They are each treated as single assets.

3. When **one company takes over another company**, the new company acquires shares in the old company in exchange for shares in the new company. This is known as a '**paper for paper'** transaction. It does not give rise to chargeable gain.

Self Examination Questions

Question 1

Lisa acquired shares in CD Plc on different dates. The details regarding the date of acquisition, number of shares and cost are as follows:

Date of acquisition	Number of shares	Cost (£)
01/09/2000	20,000	40,000
09/02/2008	7,200	10,800
10/10/2012	500	500
12/02/2013	1,000	1,500

Date of sale	Number of shares	Sales price (£)
09/02/2013	1,500	4,500

Required:

Show the calculations of capital gains arising on the disposal of shares.

Question 2

Nadia sold 300 qualifying corporate bonds at a loss of £200, which she had purchased in the previous month. Can she adjust this capital loss against the current year's capital gains?

Question 3

In July 2008, Prem purchased 300 shares of Lazy Ltd. In April 2012, Hate Ltd made an offer to the shareholders of Lazy Ltd to acquire their shares on the basis of 1 share of Hate Ltd for each share of Lazy Ltd.

Prem accepted the offer and exchanged his shares in return for 300 shares of Hate Ltd.

Required:

Calculate the amount of capital gains tax Prem is required to pay after this transaction.

Answers to Self Examination Questions

Answer to SEQ 1

Disposal of 1,500 shares on 09/02/2013 are matched in the following order:

	No. of shares
Shares purchased on the same day as the disposal	-
Shares purchased within next 30 days of the disposal	1,000
Shares from the share pool acquired before date of disposal	500
Total number of shares sold	**1,500**

Calculation of acquisition cost of shares sold from the share pool

	No. of shares	Cost (£)
Purchased on 01/09/2000	20,000	40,000
Purchased on 09/02/2008	7,200	10,800
Purchased on 10/10/2012	500	500
	27,700	51,300
Less : Disposal on 09/02/2013 at average cost (£51,300 x 500/27,700)	(500)	(926)
	27,200	**50,374**

The capital gain for 2012-13 is computed as follows:

	£	£
Shares purchased on same day of disposal		
Disposal consideration	-	
Less: Acquisition cost of shares	-	-
Shares purchased within next 30 days of disposal		
Disposal consideration: 1000 shares (£4,500 x 1,000/1,500)	3,000	
Less: Acquisition cost of shares	(1,500)	1,500
Shares in the share pool acquired before disposal		
Disposal consideration: 500 shares (£4,500 x 500 /1,500)	1,500	
Less: Acquisition cost of shares	(926)	574
Chargeable gains		**2,074**

Answer to SEQ 2

For capital gains purposes, the qualifying corporate bonds are not a chargeable asset. Therefore any gain arising from the disposal of qualifying corporate bonds is not a chargeable gain. In the same way, any loss on disposal of these bonds is not an allowable loss.

Therefore, Nadia cannot offset the loss arising out of disposal of qualifying corporate bonds against the current year's capital gains.

Answer to SEQ 3

In the case of a paper for paper transaction, the chargeable gain will arise only at the time when the shares of the acquired company are **sold** by the taxpayer.

Therefore, in the case of Prem, he is not liable to any capital gains tax on unrealised gains arising from the takeover transaction.

SECTION C

CHARGEABLE GAINS

C5

STUDY GUIDE C5: THE COMPUTATION OF CAPITAL GAINS TAX PAYABLE BY INDIVIDUALS

Get Through Intro

This Study Guide deals with the **calculation of capital gains** tax payable by individuals that arise because of the **disposal of shares and securities, disposal of movable and immovable property.**

This Study Guide gives you good practise to calculate the capital gains tax payable.

Learning Outcomes

a) Compute the amount of capital gains tax payable.

Introduction

Capital gains tax (CGT) was introduced with effect from 6 April 1965 to tax the gains of individuals, personal representatives and trustees. Most CGT rules apply to companies as well, except for some important differences. However, a company's gains are charged to corporation tax and not CGT.

In general, CGT applies when a **chargeable person** makes a **chargeable disposal** of a **chargeable asset**. A gain arises where the proceeds received are greater than the cost of acquisition plus any enhancement costs.

A simple example is as follows:

John bought a rental property as an investment for £42,000. He incurred acquisition costs of £3,200 and installed a new bathroom which cost £5,000. He later sold the cottage for £80,000. In simple terms the gain subject to CGT would be £29,800.

---

1. Compute the amount of capital gains tax payable.[2]

[Learning Outcome a]

1.1 Capital gains tax

An individual pays capital gains tax on his taxable gains.

Taxable gains are calculated as follows:

a) **Deduct** current capital losses and brought forward capital losses from net capital gains, to give chargeable gains. Provisions regarding current year capital losses and brought forward capital losses are discussed in detail later in Learning Outcome 4 of this Study Guide.

b) Chargeable gains are **reduced by the annual exemption** to give taxable gains.

Annual exemption

Every individual is entitled to an annual exemption which is deducted from capital gains income. The annual exemption limit for the tax year 2012-13 is £10,600.

Pro forma for calculation of taxable gains

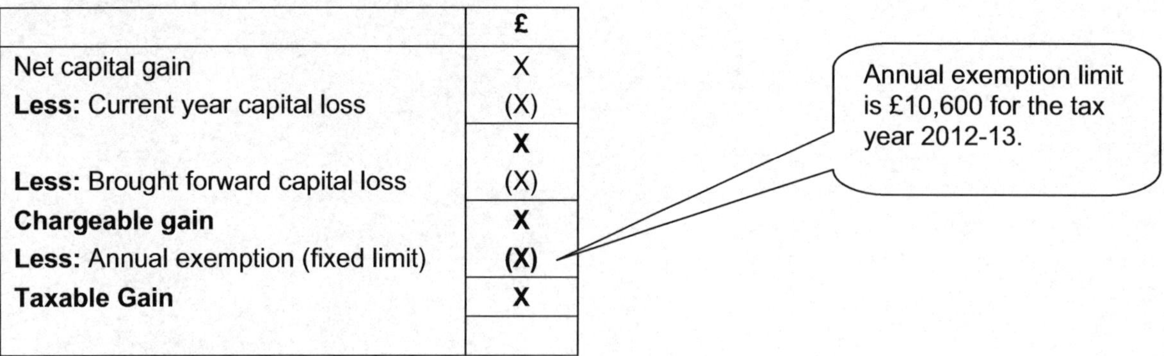

	£
Net capital gain	X
Less: Current year capital loss	(X)
	X
Less: Brought forward capital loss	(X)
Chargeable gain	**X**
Less: Annual exemption (fixed limit)	**(X)**
Taxable Gain	**X**

c) If the sum of the chargeable gains for a year is less than the annual exemption, the assessment is **nil** and any **unused annual exemption is lost.**

d) Once the taxable gains are calculated as discussed above, then the capital gains tax liability can be calculated. Capital gains tax liability is calculated at the lower rate of 18% or the higher rate of 28% depending upon the taxable income of an individual.

If the taxable capital gains of an individual fall within the income tax basic rate band of £35,000, then they are taxed at the rate of 18%. If the taxable gains exceed this threshold, then they are taxed at the higher rate of 28%. This basic rate band of £34,370 is extended where an individual contributes to personal pension scheme or qualifying charitable donations.

e) Capital gains tax is collected as **part of the self-assessment process**. It is **due on 31 January following the tax year.** Payments on account are not needed. So, the capital gains tax liability for the tax year 2012-13 will be payable on 31 January 2014.

Example

During 2012-13, Sweety made a capital gain of £20,000. Her other income for the tax year includes salary income of £38,465 and interest income of £2,400 (net). She has also contributed £3,200 (net) to a personal pension scheme.

Calculation of Sweety's capital gains tax liability

The capital gains tax liability computation of an individual is linked with their taxable income and basic rate tax band. Therefore to determine Sweety's capital gains tax liability, first we need to determine her unused basic rate tax band.

Sweety's taxable income and unused basic rate band is as follows:

Salary income	38,465
Interest income (2,400 x 100/80)	3,000
	41,465
Less Personal allowance	(8,105)
Taxable income	33,360
Basic rate band	34,370
Add: Contribution to pension scheme (3,200 x 100/80)	4,000
Extended basic rate band	38,370
Less: used by taxable income	(33,360)
Unused basic rate band availble for taxable gains	5,010

Sweety's capital gains tax liability is calculated as follows:

Net chargeable gain	20000
Less: Annual exemption	(10600)
Taxable gain	9400
Gains falling within basic rate band taxed at 18%: (5010 x 18%)	902
Gains which exceed basic rate bandL 5011 to 9400 taxed at the higher rate : 28%	1229
Total capital gain tax liability	

Example

Naomi has chargeable capital gains of £14,600 during the tax year 2012-13. Her trading profits for 2012-13 are £38,000. Calculate Naomi's total tax liability.

Calculation of income tax payable

Trading profits	38000
Less: Personal allowance	(8105)
Taxable income	29895
Tax liability	
Basic rate band (29895 x 20%)	5979
Income tax liability	
Unused basic rate band (34370 - 29895)_	4475

Continued on the next page

Calculation of capital gains tax liability

Chargeable capital gains	14600
Less: Annual exemption	(10600)
Taxable capital gains	4000
Capital gain tax (4,000 x 18%) (note)	720

Note: the entire taxable gains fall within the unused basic rate tax band of £34,370, therefore they will be taxed at the lower rate of 18%.

Naomi's total tax liability is £6,699 (£5,979 + £720)

Example

Suzy is a sole trader. She has been running her business since 5 March 2002. Her business was growing at a rapid pace. She decided to sell part of her business to concentrate on running the remaining business.

She sold the following assets on 25 February 2013:

1. Goodwill for £60,000. The goodwill was built up from the inception of the business i.e. from 5 March 2002. The cost of the goodwill was nil.
2. She sold a motor car for £40,000. The motor car was used solely for business purposes. It was purchased on 2 November 2010 for £30,000.
3. A freehold office building was sold for £150,000. The office building was used solely for business purposes. The office building was purchased by Suzy on 2 July 2011 for £120,000.
4. A freehold warehouse was sold for £160,000. This warehouse was never used by her for business purposes. It was purchased on 5 March 2002 for £96,000.

Suzy's property income for 2012-13 was £31,000.

Compute Suzy's total tax liability for 2012-13.

To compute the capital gains for the year, we have to compute the gain derived from each individual transaction as follows:

Goodwill

	£
Sale proceeds	60,000
Less: Acquisition cost	-
Net gain	**60,000**

Freehold office building

	£
Sale proceeds	150,000
Less: Acquisition cost	(120,000)
Net gain	**30,000**

Freehold Warehouse

	£
Sale proceeds	160,000
Less: Acquisition cost	(96,000)
Net gain	**64,000**

Notes

1. Capital gain is calculated separately for each asset disposed.
2. Motor car is exempt from capital gains tax.

Continued on the next page

Computation of total taxable gains

	£
Goodwill	60,000
Freehold office building	30,000
Freehold warehouse	64,000
Chargeable gains	**154,000**
Less: Annual exemption	(10,600)
Taxable gains	**143,400**

Suzy's tax liability is calculated as follows:

Income tax liability	
Property income	31,000
Less: Personal allowance	(8,105)
Taxable income	**22,895**
Income tax	
Basic rate: 22895 @20%	**4,579**
Unused basic rate band (34370 - 22895)	**11,475**
Capital gains tax liability	
11475 at the rate of 18% (note)	2,066
11476 to 143400 at the higher rate of 28%	36,939
	39,005

Note: the amount of taxable gains that fall within the unused basic rate band is taxed at the rate of 18% and the amount which exceeds this threshold is taxed at the higher rate of 28%.

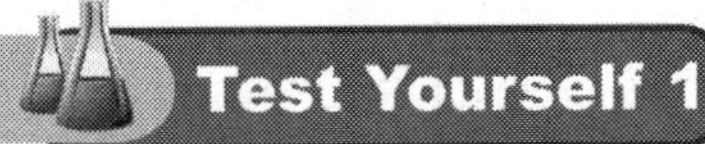

Test Yourself 1

For the year 2012-13, Colin's salary income is £9,935. This income is before deduction of personal allowance. During the tax year, he made a capital gain of £62,000 on disposal of his business asset.

Required:

Calculate the tax payable by Colin during 2012-13.

Answer to Test Yourself

Answer to TY 1

Calculation of Colin's income tax liability for 2012-13

Salary income	9935
Less: Personal allowance	(8,105)
Total taxable income	1830
Tax liability	
Income tax (1830 @ 10%)	183

Note: Colin's unused basic rate band is (£34,370 – £1,830) = £32,540.

Calculation of Colin's capital gains tax liability for 2012-13

Total capital gain	62,000
Less: Annual exemption	(10,600)
Taxable gain	**51,400**
Capital gains tax liability (note)	
32540 at the rate of 18%	5,857
(51400 - 32540) = 18860 at 28%	5,281
Capital gains tax	**11,138**

Note: the amount of taxable gains that fall within the basic rate band is taxed at the rate of 18% and the amount which exceeds this threshold is taxed at the higher rate of 28%.

Self Examination Question

Question 1

The following information of Nob, Bob and Job for the tax year 2012-13 is given:

	Nob	Bob	Job
Salary	42,145		40,250
Trading Profit		62,240	
Personal Pension Contribution	6,200		
Chargeable gains on sale of antique pieces	22,100	20,400	26,200

Required:

Calculate the amount of Capital Gains Tax Liability and state when they will be due.

Answer to Self Examination Question

Answer to SEQ 1

Computation of unused basic rate band

	Nob	Bob	Job
Salary	42145		40250
Trading Profit		62240	
Personal allowance	(8105)	(8105)	(8105)
Taxable income	**34040**	**54135**	**32145**
Basic rate band	34370	34370	34370
Add: Contribution to pensiopn scheme (6200 x 100/80)		7750	
Exetended basic rate band	34370	42120	34370
Less: Used by taxable income	(34040)	(54135)	(32145)
Unused basic rate bankd (available for taxable gains	**330**	**(12015)**	**2225**

Chargeable gains	17,400	20,400	26,200
Less: Annual exemption	(10,600)	(10,600)	(10,600)
Taxable gains	**6,800**	**9,800**	**15,600**
Capital gains tax liability			
Gain falling within basic rate band zt 18%			
330 / nil /2225 at 18%	59		401
Gains which exceed basic rate band at 28%			
6470 / 9800/ 13375 at 28%	1,812	2,744	3,744
Capital gains tax liability	**1,871**	**2,744**	**4,144**

The capital gains tax liability of all Nob, Bob and Job will be due on **31 January 2014**.

SECTION C

CHARGEABLE GAINS

C6

STUDY GUIDE C6: THE USE OF EXEMPTIONS AND RELIEFS IN DEFERRING AND MINIMISING TAX LIABILITIES ARISING ON THE DISPOSAL OF CAPITAL ASSETS

Get Through Intro

Proper tax planning requires an **in-depth knowledge** of all the rules, provisions and reliefs existing in the Tax Law.

This means that for the calculation of capital gains tax, the taxpayers or their consultants should be aware of all the reliefs – such as **entrepreneurs' relief, rollover relief, holdover relief, gift relief, and incorporation relief** that the legislation has made available to them, along with all the other provisions relating to the calculation of capital gains.

This Study Guide explains the calculation of rollover relief (which is available to both individuals and companies) and the calculation of **entrepreneurs' relief, holdover relief** and **incorporation relief**, which is available only to individuals.

Learning Outcomes

a) Explain and apply entrepreneurs' relief as it applies to individuals.
b) Explain and apply rollover relief as it applies to individuals and companies.
c) Explain and apply holdover relief for the gift of business assets.
d) Explain and apply the incorporation relief that is available upon the transfer of a business to a company.

Introduction

Case Study

Kathy owned an industrial building in London. Until January 2012, she used this building for manufacturing toys. However, as she grew old, she was unable to manage the business and her profits started to decline. As her daughter Laura was not interested in running the business, Kathy sold all her business assets except the industrial building.

Kathy wanted to give the industrial building to her daughter, Laura. However, she was avoiding this because she knew that the tax treatment of the transfer of the asset as a gift would trigger a chargeable disposal. This would require her to pay capital gains tax, which she did not want to do.

In this Study Guide we will see all the provisions relating to holdover relief and whether or not Kathy can give her daughter the business asset without having to pay any capital gains tax.

1. Explain and apply entrepreneurs' relief as it applies to individuals.[2]

[Learning Outcome a]

1.1 Entrepreneurs' relief

1. Conditions

a) This relief is available when **an individual disposes of a business or part of a business.**

b) Conditions to qualify for this relief:

- assets disposed of should have been owned for one year, prior to the date of their disposal.
- the asset disposed of must be a qualifying asset **throughout the one year period** (see below).

c) The following are the qualifying disposals to claim this relief:

- disposal of the **whole or part of the business** operated individually or in a partnership. It will include only the capital gains arising from the disposal of the **trading assets** (in use for the purpose of the business) and will exclude capital gains arising from non-trading assets, such as investments.
- disposal of **shares in a trading company** where it is shares in the individual's "personal company". This means that:

  ✓ an individual has a shareholding of 5% in the company, and
  ✓ is also an employee of that trading company.

  In this case, there is no restriction on the amount of relief, even if the underlying assets disposed of are non-trading assets such as investments, subject to the condition that the company is a trading company.

d) In case of **disposal of the trading assets after the cessation of a business**, the disposal needs to be within three years of the cessation of the business, and the asset must have been a qualifying asset for the 12 months up to the date of cessation, not to the date of disposal, in order to claim entrepreneurs' relief.

e) This relief is available before the current year losses, brought forward losses and annual exemption.

2. Method of relief

The relief is available on the **first £10 million of qualifying gains** that a person makes during their lifetime for the tax year 2012-13. Hence, this limit is known as the **lifetime limit**. The £10 million limit is reduced every time an individual makes a qualifying gain.

The CGT is calculated at two rates: 18% and 28% but the gains that qualify for Entrepreneur's relief are **taxed directly at the rate of 10%** without taking into consideration the taxable income of an individual.

Example

Adam sold a 30% shareholding in Jacket Lamb Ltd, an unquoted trading company, on 25 January 2013. There was a capital gain of £505,000. Adam had purchased the shares on 1 March 2007 and was an employee of Jacket Lamb from 1 March 2007 until the date the shares were disposed of.

The taxable income of Adam for the tax year 2012-13 is £32,680.

Adam's capital gains tax liability for the tax year 2012-13 is as follows:

	£
Gain on shareholding in Jacket Lamb Ltd (note 1)	505,000
Less: Annual exemption	(10,600)
Taxable gains	**494,400**
Capital gains tax at 10% (notes 2 and 3)	49,440

Notes

1. Entrepreneurs' relief is available on the disposal of shares in Jacket Lamb Ltd, as Adam was an employee of the company and held more than 5% of the company's shares.
2. Relief is available on the first £10 million of qualifying gains that a person makes during their lifetime. The £10 million limit is reduced every time an individual makes a qualifying gain. Therefore, Adam will have a balance of £9,495,000 (£10,000,000 – £505,000) of qualifying gains to claim entrepreneurs' relief available in the future.
3. The CGT is calculated simply at the rate of 10% on the gains qualifying for entrepreneurs' relief without considering the taxable income of an individual.

3. **Other important points**

The capital gains that qualify for entrepreneurs' relief, although taxed simply at the rate of 10%, are taken into consideration for determining the rate of capital gains tax (18% or 28%) applicable on other gains.

Therefore, the unused basic rate band is reduced by the amount of gains qualifying for entrepreneurs' relief.

Tip

To claim the maximum benefit, the current year and brought forward capital losses as well as the annual exemption should first be offset against the gains that do not qualify for entrepreneur's relief. This will save tax at the rate of 18% or 28% as compared to gains that qualify for entrepreneurs' relief, which are taxed at the rate of 10%.

Example

John sold a business on 30 June 2012, which he had started on 1 January 2006. He made the following capital gains:

	£
Goodwill	234,000
Freehold property	333,000
Freehold warehouse	153,000

The assets were owned prior to one year from the date of disposal. John did not use the warehouse for business purposes at all.

John's other income for the tax year includes trading income of £37,640 and dividend income of £2,700 (net). He also contributed £4,800 (net) under the qualifying charitable scheme.

He sold a freehold shop realising a capital loss of £11,500 and has a brought forward capital loss of £3,000.

Continued on the next page

For ease of computation of CGT liability, the gains that qualify for entrepreneurs' relief should be kept separate from the gains that do not qualify for entrepreneurs' relief.

Therefore, John's capital gains tax liability for the tax year 2012-13 is as follows:

	£	£
Gains that qualify for entrepreneurs' relief (note)		
Goodwill	234,000	
Freehold property	333,000	**567,000**
Gains that do not qualify for entrepreneurs' relief		
Freehold warehouse	153,000	
Less: Current year capital loss	(11,500)	
	141,500	
Less: Brought forward capital loss	(3,000)	
	138,500	
Less: Annual exemption	(10,600)	**127,900**
Taxable gains		**694,900**
Capital gains tax		
Gains that qualify for entrepreneurs' relief at 10% (£567,000 x 10%)		56,700
Gains that do not qualify for entrepreneurs' relief (W1)		
£127,900 at 28%		35,812
Capital gains tax liability		**92,512**

Note: entrepreneurs' relief is available only on trading assets used in the business. Hence, it is available on the disposal of goodwill and freehold office building. However, as the warehouse was not used for business purposes at all, entrepreneurs' relief will not be available on its disposal.

W1 Unused basic rate band

John's taxable income and unused basic rate band is as follows:

	£
Trading income	37,640
Dividend income (£2,700 x 100/90)	3,000
	40,640
Less: Personal allowance	(8,105)
Taxable income	**32,535**
Basic rate band	34,370
Add: Contribution to qualifying charitable scheme (£4,800 x 100/80)	6,000
Extended basic rate band	40,370
Less: Used by taxable income	(32,535)
Unused basic rate band (available for taxable gains)	**7,835**

Although there is unused basic rate band of £7,835 available for taxable gains, it is used up entirely by the gains qualifying for entrepreneurs' relief. Therefore, the gains that do not qualify for entrepreneurs' relief will be taxed at the higher rate of 28%.

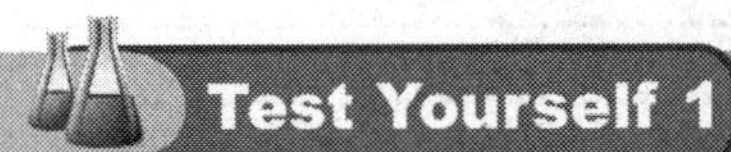

On 1 November 2012, Ben, a toy manufacturer, sold part of his business due to a financial crisis. He had been in the business for many years. His gains from this disposal were:

	£
Moulds	250,000
Goodwill	150,000
Freehold land	200,000
Warehouse	300,000

All these assets were owned by him from the start of the business. Ben held the freehold land as an investment.

He was also employed by Clarks Ltd, an unquoted trading company, for the last 5 years, and held 15% of the company's shares. He sold 10% of his shares in Clarks Ltd at a gain of £200,000.

These were the only disposals made by him in 2011 - 12. He also has a capital loss of £36,000 brought forward from the tax year 2011-12. Ben's taxable income for the tax year 2012-13 is £10,000.

Required:

Calculate Ben's capital gains tax liability for 2012-13.

---

2. Explain and apply rollover relief as it applies to individuals and companies.[2] [Learning Outcome b]

As the name suggests, when an old business asset is replaced by a new business asset, the gain arising on the disposal of the old asset is rolled over (carried forward) against the cost of the new asset.
Rollover relief is **available both to companies and individuals.**

The taxpayer has to claim rollover relief. It is not automatic.

2.1 Rollover relief to companies

1. **Rollover relief:** also known as replacement of business asset relief.
2. **Purpose:** to encourage businesses to re-invest in capital assets.
3. **Problem:** if a business asset is sold and realises a gain, money must be made available to pay tax on the gain, rather than re-investing in new assets.
4. **Solution:** calculate the gain, but no tax charged now as the gain is postponed ('rolled over') until disposal of the replacement asset.
5. **Capital gain is deferred** where the disposal proceeds of the first asset are re-invested in a new asset.
6. The deferral is achieved by deducting the capital gain from the base cost of the new asset.

How this relief operates in the case of companies

Without relief	£	With relief	£
Asset (1) is sold		**Asset (1) is sold**	
Proceeds	270,000	Proceeds	270,000
Less: Cost	(150,000)	**Less:** Cost	(150,000)
Less: Indexation allowance (say)	(20,000)	**Less:** Indexation allowance (say)	(20,000)
Indexed gain	**100,000**	**Indexed gain**	**100,000**
		Less: Rollover relief	(100,000)
		Gain	-
Asset (2) purchased for £300,000		Asset (2) purchased for 300,000. Cost for tax purposes £200,000 (£300,000 - £100,000)	
Asset (2) is sold		**Asset (2) is sold**	
Proceeds	480,000	Proceeds	480,000
Less: Cost	(300,000)	**Less:** Cost	(200,000)
Less: Indexation allowance (say)	(40,000)	**Less:** Indexation allowance (say)	(40,000)
Indexed gain	**140,000**	**Indexed gain**	**240,000**

The total gains are the same in both situations. **With relief, the indexed gain is deferred until the disposal of the replacement asset.**

2.2 Conditions to qualify for claiming rollover relief

1. The old and the new asset **must be qualifying business assets (QBA)**:
   a) Land and buildings
   b) **Fixed** plant and fixed machinery
2. The asset sold and the replaced assets do **not need** to be in the **same category.**
3. **The purchase of the replacement asset must take place in the period one year before and three years after the disposal of the old asset.**
4. The asset sold and replaced assets **must both be qualifying business assets and used for business purposes.**
5. The replaced asset must be brought into **business use at the time it is acquired.**

Example

Victory Ltd purchased a warehouse in August 2004 (RPI 187.4) for £200,000. The company sold the warehouse on 20 May 2012 (RPI 242.4) for £400,000.

The company decided to re-invest the sale proceeds by purchasing a building for £420,000. The company purchased the building on 15 August 2012.

In this example, it is clear that the whole proceeds are reinvested and the purchase is made within three years after the date of sale, so the entire indexed gain realised on sale of the warehouse can be rolled over.

The calculation of **indexed gain** on sale of warehouse is as follows:

	£
Disposal consideration	400,000
Less: Cost of acquisition	(200,000)
Unindexed gain	**200,000**
Less: Indexation allowance	
$\frac{(242.4 - 187.4)}{187.4}$ = (0.293) x 200,000	(58,600)
Indexed gain	**141,400**
Gain Rolled Over	(141,400)
Chargeable now	**NIL**

Continued on the next page

As a result of rollover relief, the gain on the disposal of the warehouse is not immediately chargeable. However, the cost of the new building is reduced by the amount of gain on the disposal of the warehouse.

Hence, the cost of the new building purchased will be £279,000 (£420,000 - £141,000).

2.3 Partial re-investment

Rollover relief is available, as shown above, if all the proceeds of the disposal of the old asset are used to acquire the new asset.

If **only a part** of the proceeds is used, the amount of **rollover relief is restricted.** The amount not re-invested reduces the amount of the capital gain that can be rolled over.

A gain will arise equal to the sale proceeds not re-invested or the actual gain whichever is lower. The balance of the gain can be rolled over.

If the amount not re-invested is greater than the capital gain, no rollover relief is available.

Example

Swing Ltd purchased a freehold factory in September 2003. The company sold the factory in January 2012 for £80,000. This sale transaction gave rise to an indexed gain of £20,500.

In June 2012, a replacement factory was purchased for £70,000.

In this example, it is clear that the total proceeds are not re-invested; therefore, the entire capital gain of £20,500 cannot be rolled over.

The rollover gain is calculated as follows:

	£
Total indexed gain	20,500
Less: Amount not re-invested chargeable immediately	
(£80,000 - £70,000)	(10,000)
Rollover gain	**10,500**

The amount of the proceeds not reinvested i.e. £10,000 will be chargeable immediately. The balance of the gain can be rolled over.

The remaining capital gain will be rolled over and deducted from the base cost of the new building.

The base cost of the replaced factory will be calculated after deducting rollover relief as follows:

	£
Cost of replaced factory	70,000
Less: Rollover gain	(10,500)
Base cost of new factory	**59,500**

2.4 Rollover relief for individuals

Rollover relief for an individual **entitles the individual to defer the net gain,** where the disposal proceeds of the first asset are re-invested in a new asset.

Qualifying assets for individuals

1. Land and buildings
2. Fixed plant and fixed machinery
3. Goodwill

The rules for individuals extend to acquisitions and disposals of goodwill – this is not available to companies as they deal with goodwill under the intangible assets rules.

The deferral is achieved by deducting the capital gains from the base cost of the new asset in the same way as for a company.

Jack sold a freehold factory for £200,000 on 25 November 2008. He had purchased the factory on 5 August 2007 for £140,000. The asset was a business asset.

The disposal of the factory resulted in a gain, which was rolled over against the purchase cost of a freehold warehouse for £200,000 on 20 February 2011. The warehouse was also sold by Jack on 28 March 2012 for £250,000.

Jack had used both the assets for business purposes.

As the sale proceeds from freehold factory of £200,000 were fully re-invested in a freehold warehouse, the whole gain of £60,000 (£200,000 - £140,000) realised on the sale can be rolled over and deducted from the base cost of the warehouse purchased.

Hence, cost of the new warehouse for CGT purposes will be = Base cost of the warehouse – Rolled over gain
= £200,000 - £60,000 = £140,000

Therefore, the calculation of chargeable gain on the sale of the warehouse is as follows:

	£
Disposal consideration	250,000
Less: Cost (£200,000 - £60,000)	(140,000)
Chargeable gain	**110,000**

Diagram 1: Rollover relief on reinvestment of proceeds of old asset in new asset

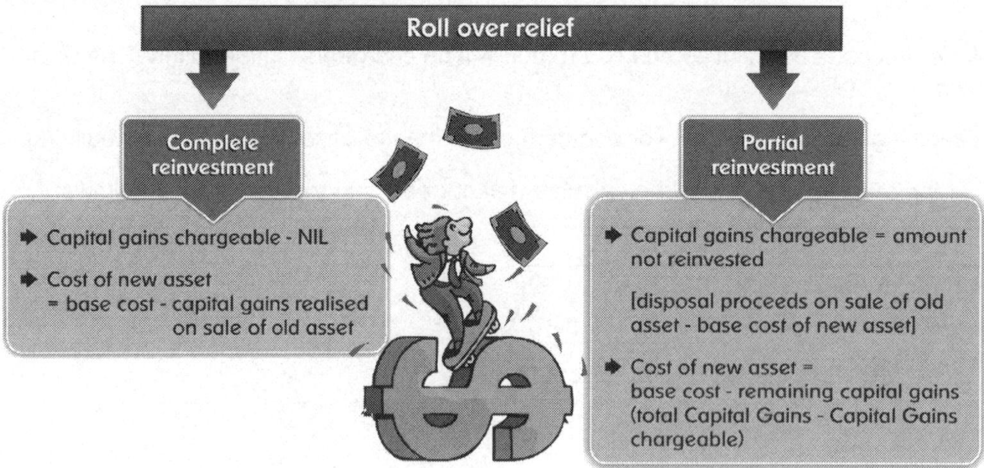

2.5 Re-investment in a depreciating asset

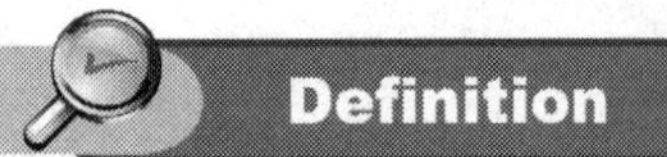

A depreciating asset is one which has an **expected life of 60 years or less.** For example, a leasehold factory on a 35 years lease.

Fixed plant and fixed machinery are **always depreciating assets.**

Where the **replacement asset is a depreciating asset**, the gain on the old asset is not rolled over; instead it is **'held over'**.

A held over gain does not reduce the cost of the replacement asset; instead it is **'frozen'** until the **earliest of the following:**

i. **10 years after the purchase** of the replacement asset,
ii. the **replacement asset stops being used** for the purpose of the business,
iii. the **replacement asset is sold.**

Victory Ltd sold a warehouse on 20 February 2012 for £400,000. The sale resulted in a capital gain of £95,000.

The company decided to re-invest the sale proceeds to acquire a leasehold factory on a 50-year lease for a premium of £550,000. The company purchased the building on 15 May 2012.

In this example, it is clear that the whole proceeds are re-invested, so the complete capital gain can be held over.

As the re-investment is made into a depreciating asset, the base cost of the factory will not be adjusted as a held over gain does not reduce the cost of the replacement asset; instead it is **'frozen'** until the **earliest of the following:**

1. **10 years after the purchase** of the replacement asset,
2. the **replacement asset stops being used** for business purposes,
3. the **replacement asset is sold.**

Thus, the gain is held over until May 2022 (i.e. first condition 10 years from the date of purchase) or the date the replaced asset is sold or stops being used for business purposes, whichever is earlier.

2.6 Non-business use

Rollover relief is available when qualifying assets are used for business purposes.

Where an asset disposed of is **not entirely used for business purposes** then **only the gain relating to the business use qualifies for rollover relief.**

Henry purchased a factory on 20 January 2004. He sold the factory on 15 November 2012 for £200,000. The sale of the factory resulted in a capital gain of £85,000.

Henry used 60% of the factory for business purposes. The remaining 40% was kept for his personal use.

Henry purchased another factory on 20 November 2012 for £250,000. This new factory was wholly used for business purposes.

When we calculate Henry's chargeable gain, we will first calculate the amount of capital gains that are **not** allowed to be rolled over.

Total capital gains = £85,000
Utilisation of factory for non-business purposes is 40%
Therefore, the amount of sale proceeds related to non-business purposes = £200,000 x 40% = £80,000
Similarly, the proportion of capital gains for non-business purposes = £85,000 x 40%
= £34,000.

Thus, the amount of £34,000 does not qualify for roll-over relief and re-investment is not required for the sale proceeds of £80,000 related to non-business purposes.

As 60% of the sale proceeds used for business purposes, i.e. £120,000 (£200,000 x 60%) were fully re-invested, the balance of the capital gain (£85,000 - £34,000 = **£51,000**) can be **rolled over.**

As the sale proceeds are not re-invested into a depreciating asset, the cost of the new asset will be adjusted.

The cost of the new factory = £250,000 - £51,000
= £199,000.

Calculation of the chargeable gain is as follows:

	£
Capital gain	85,000
Less: Roll over relief	(51,000)
Chargeable gain	**34,000**

SUMMARY

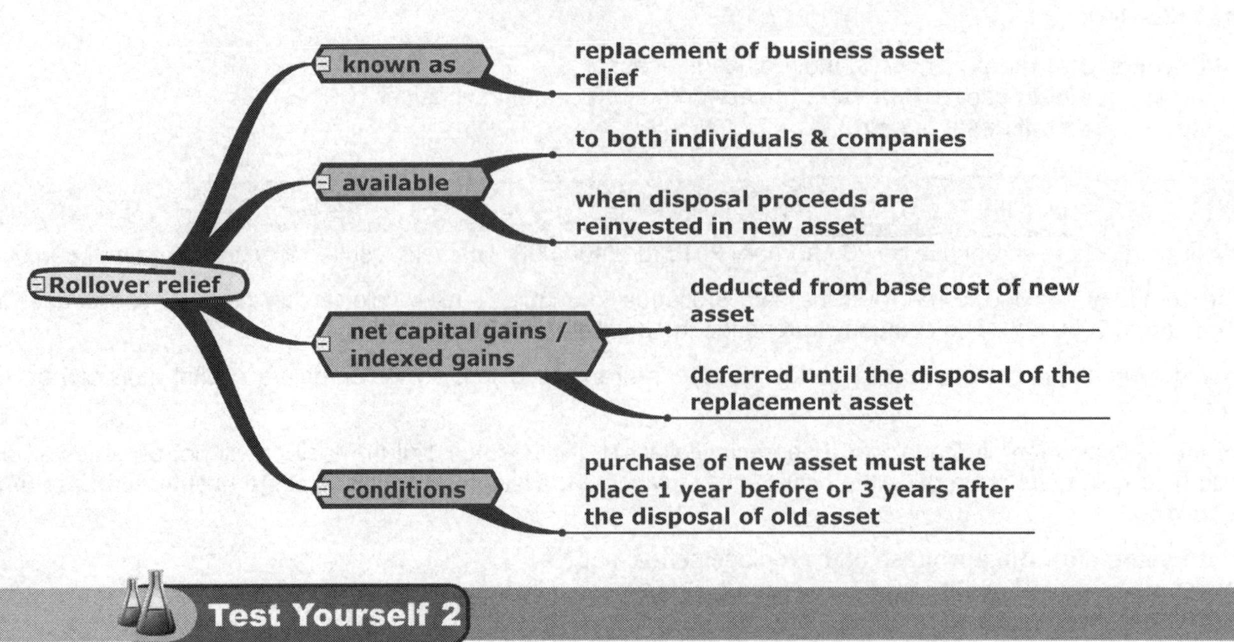

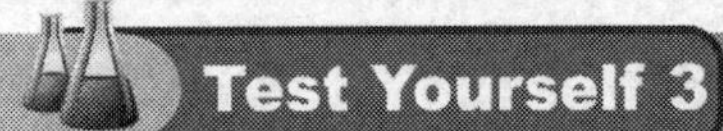

Test Yourself 2

In May 2006 (RPI 197.7) Cargo Ltd purchased an office building for £300,000. Due to its expansion the company decided to purchase a new office building. Therefore, in May 2012 (RPI 242.4), the company sold the old office building for £399,500. The company purchased a new office building for £560,000 in December 2012.

Required:

Calculate the chargeable gains on the disposal of the old office building assuming the company has elected for rollover relief and calculate the base cost for the new office building.

Test Yourself 3

Mack sold a warehouse on 20 April 2012 for £152,000, which he had purchased on 12 November 2006 for £98,000. In May 2012, he purchased an office building for £150,000. He made a claim to roll over the gain resulting from the sale proceeds of the warehouse against the cost of the building. Mack used both the office building and warehouse for business purposes.

Later, he sold the office building on 15 March 2013 for £220,000.

Required:

a) Calculate the chargeable gain on the disposal of the warehouse, and the base cost of the new office building.
b) Calculate the chargeable gain on the subsequent disposal of the office building.

3. Explain and apply holdover relief for the gift of business assets.[2]

[Learning Outcome c]

3.1 Relief for the gift of business assets

We have already discussed in Study Guide C1 that the gift of an asset is a chargeable disposal. This relief is available only **to individuals** and only applies to the gift of business assets.

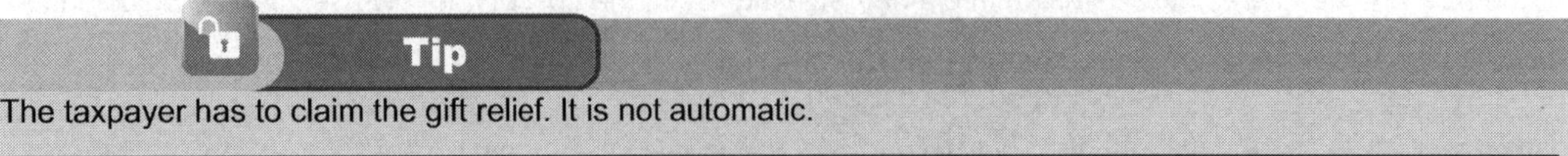

Tip

The taxpayer has to claim the gift relief. It is not automatic.

This relief is available when an individual gives a business asset as an outright gift, or sells it at less than market value. As the person making the gift (donor) receives no proceeds (or less than market value) on such a gift, the market value is deemed to be the disposal proceeds for the purposes of calculating any capital gain on the disposal.

This relief allows a **capital gain on the gift of a qualifying asset to be deferred** (held over); therefore it is also termed a holdover relief. The relief operates by **deferring the gain** of the person making the gift by **deducting it from the base cost** (i.e. **market value**) of the person receiving the gift. **Both parties have to claim the relief.**

3.2 Qualifying assets for gift relief

Assets qualifying for gift relief include the following

1. Assets used for business purposes:

a) by the donor as a sole trader;
b) by the personal company of the donor; or
c) by any company in a trading group in which the holding company should be the donor's personal company.

2. Shares in unquoted trading companies (any size of holding).

3. Shares in a personal company.

Definition

A personal company is one where an individual can exercise at least 5% of the voting rights. It must be a trading company.

Example

Jack purchased a freehold building on 15 August 2003 for £26,000. He used this building solely for business purposes.

He used the building for many years, and then decided to give it as a gift to Mack, his younger brother, on 25 November 2012, when the market value was £75,000.

Both Jack and Mack decided to holdover the gain.

In this case as the asset was given by way of a gift, the market value of the asset on that date will be considered the deemed proceeds for calculation purposes.
Therefore, the chargeable gain is:
This whole gain may be held-over and will be reduced from the deemed acquisition cost to Mack.

	£
Base cost (at market value)	75,000
Less: Deferred gain	(49,000)
Deemed cost to Mack	**26,000**

Thus, the relief operates by **deferring the gain (£49,000)** of the person making the gift (Jack) by **deducting it from** the base cost (i.e. **market value**) (£75,000) of the person receiving the gift (Mack).

3.3 Sale at undervalue

Gift relief is also available when there is a sale at less than the market value.

The market value is used while calculating the gain, **not the actual proceeds.** If the actual proceeds exceed the original cost, the **excess is taxed immediately and the balance of the gain is deferred.**

Gift relief is available before entrepreneurs' relief.

Note that an asset qualifying for gift relief is a business asset.

Susan sold 15,000 £1 ordinary shares in Sun Ltd, an unquoted trading company, to her son, Jack, on 20 April 2012 for £120,000.

On that date, the market value of the shares was £150,000. Susan had purchased the shares on 15 July 2005 for £45,000.

They both decided to holdover the gain as a gift of a business asset.

As both Susan and her son are connected persons, the market value of the shares is used for the purpose of calculating chargeable gain. Hence, **chargeable gain is calculated** as follows:

	£
Deemed proceeds (at market value)	150,000
Less: Cost of acquisition	(45,000)
Net gain	**105,000**
Less: Qualifying charitable payment relief **(W1)**	(30,000)
Chargeable gain	**75,000**

Workings

W1

The consideration of £120,000 paid for the shares is greater than the original cost by £75,000 i.e. (£120,000 - £45,000). Hence, £75,000 is chargeable to tax immediately.

The balance gain of £30,000 (£105,000 - £75,000) will be deferred as gift relief and will be deducted from the base cost of the person receiving the gift, i.e. Jack.

Continuing the above example of Susan and Jack

Let us suppose that Jack, at a later date, sold 15,000 £1 ordinary shares in Sun Ltd for £175,000. Here, the chargeable gain would be calculated as follows:

The cost of Jack's shares would be the market value of the shares less gift relief.
Hence, the cost of the shares for Jack would be (£150,000 - £30,000) = £120,000 (i.e. the actual sales proceeds amount).

	£
Disposal consideration	175,000
Less: Cost of acquisition	(120,000)
Chargeable gain	**55,000**

3.4 Non Business use

Gift relief or holdover relief is available when qualifying assets are used for business purposes. However, if an asset is used for both business as well as non-business purposes by the person giving the gift, then only the gain relating to the business use qualifies for holdover relief.

3.5 Restriction of holdover relief on the gift of the shares.

Holdover relief may be restricted if the shares (quoted or unquoted) are given as a gift and these shares are in the personal company of the person making the gift.

A personal company is one where an individual can exercise at least 5% of the voting rights. It must be a trading company.

The **gain to be deferred (holdover relief) is:**

$$\text{Net gain on the gift} \times \frac{\text{Market value of the company's chargeable business assets}}{\text{Market value of the company's total chargeable assets}}$$

You will be given the values of the chargeable assets and chargeable business assets in the exam.

Chargeable assets are **those assets** (business or non-business) that would be **subject to capital gains** if sold. Hence, stock, debtors and cash are not chargeable assets as no capital gains arise from their sale.

Chargeable business assets are chargeable assets **used for business purposes, excluding investments**.

Jack gave his shareholding of 60,000 shares (65% holding) in Jupiter Ltd (an unquoted trading company) to his brother, Jimmy, on 10 December 2012. On that date the market value of the shares was £300,000. Jack had bought the shares from the company on 10 January 2011 for £90,000.

The market values of Jupiter Ltd's assets on 10 December 2012 were as follows:

	£
Land	65,000
Office Building	105,000
Factory	50,000
Stock	35,000
Cash	10,000
Debtors	40,000
Investment in shares	80,000

Both Jack and Jimmy elected to holdover the gains.

Required:

Calculate Jack's chargeable gain.

Answer

The shareholding is 65%, i.e. Jimmy holds more than 5% of the shares. When a person owns at least 5% of the shares in a trading company (quoted or unquoted), holdover relief is available, but may be restricted depending on the underlying assets of the company.

The gain to be deferred is:

$$\text{Net gain on the gift} \ \text{x} \ \frac{\text{Market value of the company's chargeable business assets}}{\text{Market value of the company's total chargeable assets}}$$

Chargeable assets of Jupiter Ltd on 10 December 2012 were £300,000 i.e. (£65,000 + £105,000 + £50,000 + £80,000)

Chargeable business assets on that day amounted to £220,000 i.e. (£65,000 + £105,000 + £50,000)

Thus, chargeable gain is calculated as follows:

	£
Deemed proceeds	300,000
Less: Cost of acquisition	(90,000)
	210,000
Less: Holdover relief	
(£210,000 x £220,000/£300,000)	(154,000)
Chargeable gain	**56,000**

SUMMARY

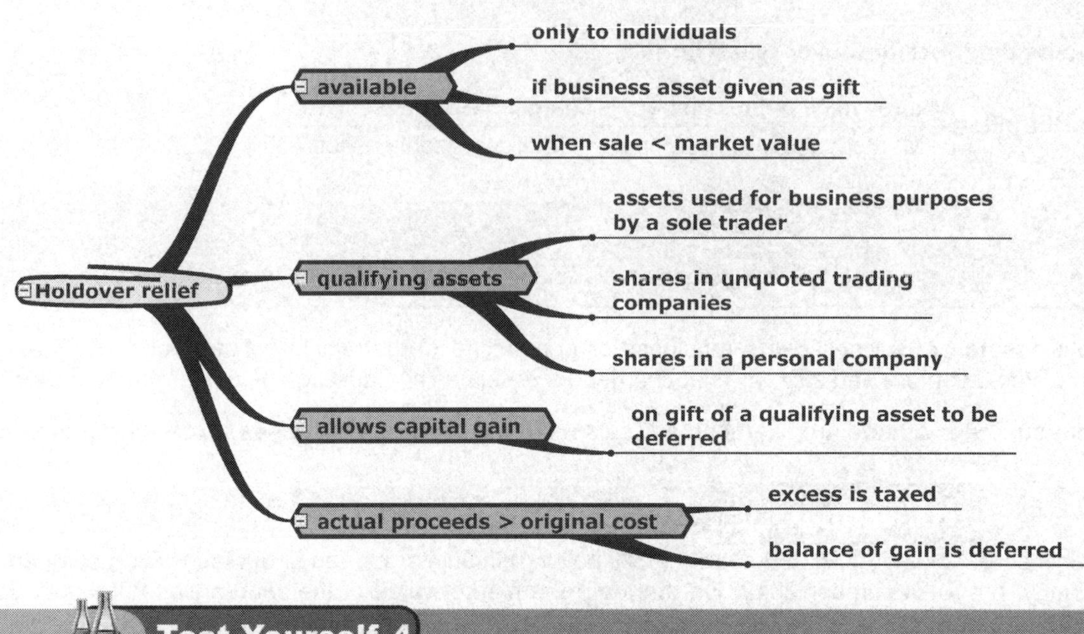

Test Yourself 4

Peter sold a machine to his daughter Shina on 12 November 2012, for £150,000, on cessation of his trade. On the date of sale the actual market price of the machine was £200,000. Peter had originally purchased this machine in May 2008 for £100,000.

Required:
Calculate the chargeable gains for Peter assuming that both Peter and Shina make an election for holdover relief.

Test Yourself 5

Ronny purchased a building for his business on 9 February 2006 for £45,000. He sold the building to his son, Kane on 20 April 2012 on the cessation of his business. On that date the market value of the building was £250,000. Kane paid his father £60,000 for the building.

Kane sold the building on 30 November 2012 for £260,000.

Required:

Calculate the chargeable gains for Ronny and Kane, assuming that they made an election for holdover relief. Assume that the current rules have always been used.

4. Explain and apply the incorporation relief that is available upon the transfer of a business to a company.[2]

[Learning Outcome d]

Incorporation relief is **only available to individuals**; either as sole traders or partnerships.

4.1 General introduction

- An individual is a sole trader who decides to incorporate his business.
- Sole trader ceases to trade, and a new company starts trading.
- Incorporation is achieved by transferring all the assets of the sole trader's business to the company (at market value) in exchange for shares in the company, or a mixture of shares and cash (known as 'consideration').
- The value of the consideration will equal the total value of the sole trader's business transferred to the new company.
- The assets of the sole trader have therefore been disposed of. Capital gains may arise on some of the assets (those chargeable to capital gains tax).

Consider some of the assets that may be transferred:

	Chargeable asset	Non-chargeable asset
Land and buildings	X	
Goodwill	X	
Motor car – exempt		X
Net current assets		X

Incorporation relief allows the capital gains arising on the disposal of the chargeable assets **to be deferred.**

This is achieved by **deducting the gains from the value of the shares received in the new company.**

This defers the gain until the individual disposes of the shares in the company.

4.2 Conditions

1. The transfer must be of a business as a **going concern.**
2. **All** of the assets **apart from cash** must be **transferred.**
3. The **consideration** for the transfer must be **wholly or partly in the form of shares.**

If all of the consideration received from the company is in the form of shares, all of the gains can be deferred.

If only part of the consideration is in the form of shares, only part of the gains can be deferred:

$$\text{Net gains on individual chargeable assets} \times \frac{\text{Value of shares received from the company}}{\text{Total value of consideration from company}}$$

The balance of the gain is taxable.

The gain (or part of the gain) that may be deferred is deducted from the base cost of the shares.

If conditions are satisfied, **incorporation relief can be claimed and given automatically.** There is no need to apply for this relief.

Michael, a sole trader ran a business from 1 March 2009. On 10 April 2012 he incorporated a company, when the market value of the business was £300,000.

Michael transferred his business to Mars Ltd, the consideration being 225,000 ordinary shares valued at £225,000 and cash amounting to £75,000.

Goodwill was the only chargeable asset of the business, valued at £120,000 on 10 April 2012. The cost of goodwill is nil.
Here, the chargeable gain on the goodwill is calculated as follows:

	£
Disposal consideration	120,000
Less: Cost of acquisition	-
	120,000
Less: Incorporation relief (W1)	(90,000)
Chargeable gain	**30,000**

Workings

W1 Incorporation relief

The consideration is in the form of shares and cash. The proportion of the gain relating to the cash consideration is not eligible for incorporation relief.

Continued on the next page

So, the amount of capital gains that can be deferred as incorporation relief is:
= (Gain on chargeable asset) x (Value of shares / Total consideration)
= £120,000 x £225,000/£300,000
= £90,000

The deferred gain will be reduced from the market value of the shares to give the base cost of the shares.

	£
Market value of shares	225,000
Less: Deferred gain	(90,000)
Base cost of shares	**135,000**

Example

Continuing the above example of Michael and Mars Ltd,

Let us suppose Michael sold 75,000 £1 ordinary shares in his new limited company (an unquoted trading company) for £175,000 on 10 May 2012.

As Michael sold the shares in the company, we have to first calculate the base cost of the shares.

Base cost of the shares = Value of shares – Incorporation relief
= £225,000 - £90,000 = £135,000.

Out of a total 225,000 ordinary shares, 75,000 ordinary shares are sold.

Therefore the proportionate cost of 75000 shares = £135,000 x 75,000/225,000 = £45,000

	£
Disposal consideration	175,000
Less: Cost	(45,000)
Chargeable gains	**130,000**

Example

Simran was operating as a sole trader from 5 May 2009. She incorporated a company on 31 January 2013.

On 31 January 2013 the market value of the business assets was £800,000.

	Market value £	Cost £
Goodwill	200,000	-
Freehold warehouse	175,000	150,000
Freehold shop	250,000	185,000
Net current Assets	175,000	100,000
	800,000	**435,000**

The goodwill of the business had been built up from 5 May 2009.

Simran used both the freehold warehouse and the freehold shop solely for business purposes. Both these assets were purchased by her on 5 May 2009.

Simran transferred all the business assets to a new limited company, Sun Ltd, the consideration being made up of 500,000 £1 ordinary shares valued at £550,000 and cash of £250,000.

1. **We assume that Simran does not take advantage of any of the reliefs available.**

The chargeable gains are calculated as follows:

Continued on the next page

	£	£
Goodwill		
Market value	200,000	
Less: Cost	0	200,000
Freehold Warehouse		
Market value	175,000	
Less: Cost	(150,000)	25,000
Freehold Shop		
Market value	250,000	
Less: Cost	(185,000)	65,000
Chargeable gains		**290,000**

2. **We assume that Simran takes advantage of incorporation relief**.

Consideration comprises of shares and cash. So only the proportion of the gain relating to the shares is eligible for incorporation relief.

Therefore, £290,000 x £550,000/£800,000 = **£199,375 of the gain can be deferred by way of incorporation relief.**

Thus, **chargeable gains** = £290,000 - £199,375 = £90,625

3. **Simran sells 400,000 £1 ordinary shares in her newly incorporated company on 31 March 2013 for £420,000.**

Chargeable gain on the disposal of the shares in new company is calculated as follows:

	£
Disposal consideration	420,000
Less: Cost (W1)	(280,500)
Chargeable gains	**139,500**

Workings
W1

Amount of gains rolled over:
= Total gains – Gain to be immediately charged
= £290,000 – £90,625
= £199,375

Base cost of 500,000 shares = £550,000 – £199,375
= £350,625

Therefore, cost of 400,000 shares sold = £350,625 x 400,000/500,000
= £280,500

Example

In April 2012 Martha transferred her business of manufacturing ice cream to Cool-Chill Ltd. In exchange for that the company gave her shares worth £60,000 and paid cash of £20,000. From Before considering any available tax reliefs, Martha had a capital gain of £15,500.
Martha did not make an election in respect of incorporation relief. In this situation calculation of capital gains is as follows:

$$\text{Incorporation relief} = \text{Net gains on individual chargeable assets} \times \frac{\text{Value of shares received from the comapny}}{\text{Total value of consideration from the company}}$$

$$= £15{,}500 \times \frac{£60{,}000}{£(60{,}000 + 20{,}000)}$$

$$= £11{,}625$$

Continued on the next page

Notes

1. In effect, the chargeable gain is £3,875 (£15,500 - £11,625).
2. Incorporation relief is automatic. Even though Martha did not make an election for incorporation relief, she is eligible unless she elects for it to be disapplied.

SUMMARY

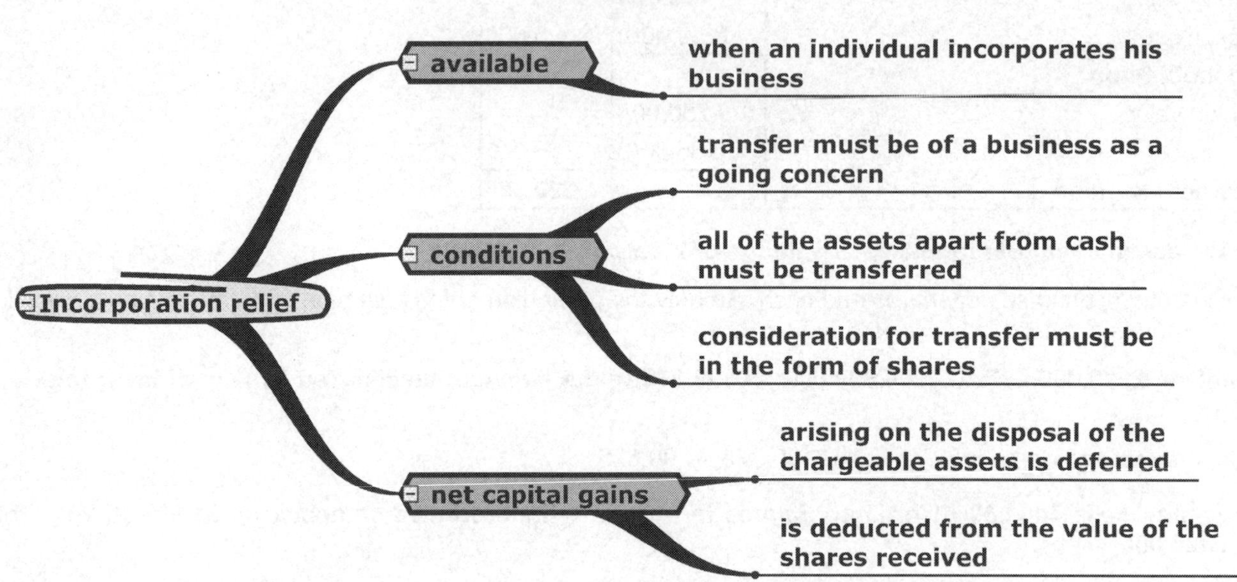

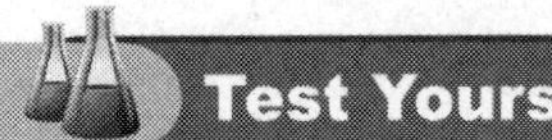

Merry ran a business for 10 years. On 20 April 2012, her business was taken over by Coca Ltd, in return for which Merry received consideration of shares of Coca Ltd worth £90,000. The capital gain from this transfer is £38,000.
Merry may wish to claim incorporation relief. Show the calculations for the amount that can be held over.
How will you answer if the business is exchanged for cash of £10,000 and shares worth £80,000?

Tax planning

- Transfer between husband and wife is a no gain / no loss transaction, so this mechanism could be used to ensure both annual exemptions are used.
- Delaying a disposal until 6 April to use next year's annual exemption, as there is often an increasing trend in the amount of the annual exemption limit. In addition, the capital gains tax liability of an individual will be delayed until the following year.
- The fact that gifts on death are not subject to capital gains tax.
- If a business is to be incorporated, take up to the annual exemption in cash to generate an immediately chargeable gain.

Suzy has been a sole trader from 5 April 1993. Although she is 79 years old, she is a still actively involved with the business and has no intention of retiring.

On 31 March 2013, she transferred her entire business to her son Sam (and continued to work for him). As a result of the transfer, the following assets were sold to Sam:

1. A freehold warehouse that has a market value of £300,000.

This warehouse was purchased on 2 April 1993 for £90,000 and was never used by her for business purposes.

Sam paid £150,000 for the warehouse.

Continued on the next page

A freehold shop that has a market value of £310,000.

This shop was purchased on 2 July 2008 for 120,000, and was always used for business purposes.

Sam paid £175,000 for the shop.

Suzy and Sam have elected to holdover any gains arising.

Required:

a) If Suzy had postponed the transfer of her business until 6 April 2012, explain how it would have been beneficial for capital gains tax purposes.

b) If Suzy had retained the business until her death, explain what the tax implications would be.

Answer

a) If Suzy had postponed the transfer of her business until 6 April 2013, the gains would not be assessed in the 2012-13 but in 2013-14.

   The payment of the capital gains tax liability would not be due on 31 January 2014, but would instead be due on 31 January 2015 (refer Study Guide C2).

   The warehouse is not a business asset, therefore it does not qualify for holdover relief.

   With the shop, this is a business asset and eligible for holdover relief. The gain is £190,000 (£310,000 - £120,000) of which £55,000 (£175,000 - £120,000) is taxable immediately as Sam paid for the shop. The balance of £135,000 may be held over, giving a revised base cost of £175,000 (£310,000 - £135,000) for Sam.

b) If Suzy had retained the business until her death, when the transfer of assets would be made on the death of a person, then the transfer of assets is not subject to capital gains tax (although there may be a charge to inheritance tax on any assets not qualifying for relief from inheritance tax).

   On such a transfer, Sam would have inherited the freehold warehouse and freehold shop at full market value.

Tip

Entrepreneurs' relief is available when an individual disposes of a business or part of a business. If such disposal is made by way of gift, then it can also qualify for gift / holdover relief. However, an individual cannot claim both the reliefs at the same time.

Therefore, if they intend to defer their tax liability by deferring the gain, then they can claim gift / holdover relief. However, if they intend to pay capital gains tax in the same year, then they can opt for entrepreneurs' relief.

In the above example of Suzy and Sam, they may choose the second option if say, Sam had already utilised his lifetime allowance for entrepreneurs' relief and would be taxed at a higher rate than Suzy on a future disposal.

Answers to Test Yourself

Answer to TY 1

Ben's capital gains tax liability for the tax year 2012-13 is as follows:

	£	£
Gains qualifying for entrepreneurs' relief (note)		
Moulds	250,000	
Goodwill	150,000	
Warehouse	300,000	
Shareholding in Clarks Ltd	200,000	**900,000**
Gains that do not qualify for entrepreneurs' relief		
Freehold Land (note 1)	200,000	
Less: Brought forward capital loss (note 2)	(36,000)	
	164,000	
Less: Annual exemption (note 2)	(10,600)	**153,400**
Taxable gains		**1,053,400**
Capital gains tax		
Gains qualifying for entrepreneurs' relief		
(£900,000 at 10%) (note 3)		90,000
Gains that do not qualify for entrepreneurs' relief (note 4)		
(£153,400 at 28%)		42,952
Capital gains tax liability		**132,952**

Notes

1. Entrepreneurs' relief will not be available for freehold land as it is not a business asset.
2. To claim the maximum benefit, the annual exemption and capital losses should be set against the gains that do not qualify for entrepreneurs' relief.
3. The gains that qualify for entrepreneurs' relief are directly taxed at the rate of 10% without considering the taxable income.
4. Ben's unused basic rate band is £24,370 (£34,370 - £10,000), but it is set against the gains that qualify for entrepreneurs' relief. Therefore, the gains that do not qualify for entrepreneurs' relief are taxed at the higher rate of 28%.
5. The relief is available on the first £10 million of qualifying gains that a person makes during their lifetime. The £10 million limit is reduced every time an individual makes a qualifying gain. Therefore, Ben will have a balance of £9,100,000 (£10,000,000 – £900,000) of qualifying gains available in the future.

Answer to TY 2

	£
Disposal consideration	399,500
Less: Cost of acquisition	(300,000)
Unindexed gain	**99,500**
Less: Indexation allowance	
$\frac{(242.4 - 197.7)}{197.7}$ = (0.226) x £300,000	(67,800)
Chargeable gains	**31,700**
Gain Rolled Over	**(31,700)**
Chargeable now	**NIL**

Note: as the entire sale proceeds are invested to purchase the new office building, and the purchase is made within three years after the date of sale, Cargo Ltd is entitled to rollover relief.

As a result of rollover relief, the gain on the disposal of the old office building is not immediately chargeable. However, the cost of the new office building is reduced by the amount of gain on the disposal of the old office building.

Hence, the cost of the new office building is £528,300 (£560,000 - £31,700).

Answer to TY 3

a) Chargeable gain on disposal of warehouse

	£
Sale proceeds	152,000
Less: Acquisition cost	(98,000)
Total gain	**54,000**
Less: Rolled over gain (note)	(52,000)
Chargeable gain	**2,000**

Note: amount not reinvested in office building, £2,000 (£152,000 - £150,000), will be chargeable to CGT immediately. The remaining capital gains of £52,000 (£54,000 - £2,000) can be rolled over, and deducted from the cost of the new office building.

The base cost of the office building will be calculated after deducting roll over relief as follows:

	£
Cost of building	150,000
Less: Rolled over gain	(52,000)
Cost for tax purpose	**98,000**

b) Computation of chargeable gain on disposal of the office building is as follows:

	£
Disposal consideration	220,000
Less: Cost (as calculated above)	(98,000)
Chargeable gain	122,000

Answer to TY 4

Peter's CGT position for 2012-13:

	£
Disposal consideration (market value)	200,000
Less: Acquisition cost	(100,000)
Gain	**100,000**
Less: Gift relief (note)	(50,000)
Chargeable gains	**50,000**

Note: when the transaction is not at an arm's length price, the market value is considered to be the sales proceeds. The difference between the market value of the asset and the actual sale price (i.e. the discount element of the sale) is the maximum gain eligible for gift / holdover relief (£200,000 - £150,000 = £50,000).

Answer to TY 5

1. Computation of Ronny's chargeable gains:

	£
Deemed sale proceeds (market value)	250,000
Less: Cost of acquisition	(45,000)
Gains	**205,000**
Less: Holdover relief (note)	(190,000)
Chargeable gains	**15,000**

2. Computation of Kane's chargeable gains:

	£
Disposal consideration	260,000
Less: Cost (£250,000 - £190,000)	(60,000)
Chargeable gains	**200,000**

Note:

The consideration of £60,000 paid for the building is greater than the original cost by £15,000 i.e. (£60,000 - £45,000). Hence, £15,000 is chargeable to tax immediately.

The balance gain of £190,000 (£205,000 - £15,000) will be deferred as holdover relief will be deducted from the base cost of the person receiving the gift, i.e. Kane.

Answer to TY 6

1. The whole amount of capital gains of £38,000 can be held over, as the whole consideration was received in shares.

2. Where consideration is received partly in cash and partly in shares.

$$\text{Incorporation relief} = \text{Net gains on individual chargeable assets} \times \frac{\text{Value of shares received from the company}}{\text{Total value of consideration from company}}$$

= 38,000 x (£80,000/£90,000)
= £33,778

As such, the gain of £33,778 can be held over until a subsequent disposal takes place. However, the gain of £4,222 (£38,000 - £33,778) is immediately chargeable to tax.

Quick Quiz

1. State which of the following reliefs are automatic (i.e. no claim for relief is required).

   (a) rollover relief
   (b) holdover relief
   (c) incorporation relief

2. What are the required conditions to claim incorporation relief?

3. What are the various business assets for claiming entrepreneurs' relief?

Answers to Quick Quiz

1. Incorporation relief is automatic.

2. To claim incorporation relief the following are the required conditions:

(a) all the business assets, except cash are transferred to the company.
(b) the business is transferred as a going concern.
(c) the consideration is in the form of shares (wholly / partly).

3. The most relevant types of business assets for claiming entrepreneur's relief are as follows:

(a) the whole or part of a business carried on by a sole trader (which includes assets forming "part of" a business, but not assets being sold piecemeal)
(b) assets used for trade purposes by a sole trader at the time at which the business ceases to be carried on.
(c) shares in a personal trading company (quoted or unquoted) i.e. where an individual has a 5% shareholding and is an employee of the company.

Self Examination Questions

Question 1

In June 2000 (RPI 171.1) Mix Ltd acquired a building for business purposes for £48,000. In May 2012 the company sold the building for £89,500 (RPI 242.4). The following month the company purchased another building for use in its business.

Required:

Assuming the company made a claim for rollover relief; show the calculations for chargeable gain if the purchase price of the new building is:

(a) £85,000
(b) £95,000

Question 2

Peter sold his machinery to his daughter Shina on 12 November 2012, for £150,000 on cessation of his trade. On the date of sale the market value of the machine was £200,000. Peter had originally purchased this machinery in May 2008 for £100,000.

Required:

What is the chargeable gain in the hands of Peter assuming he makes a claim for holdover relief?

Question 3

In January 2013 Mica transferred all his business assets to Takeover Ltd and received a total consideration of £75,000. It was decided that he will receive 2/3 of the consideration by way of shares in the company, and the remaining 1/3 in cash.

Assume the gain arising on the transfer was £25,000. Show the amount of capital gains immediately chargeable and the amount which is held over.

Answers to Self Examination Questions

Answer to SEQ 1

Calculation of gain on disposal of original building:

	£
Disposal consideration	89,500
Less: Original cost of building	(48,000)
Un-indexed gain	41,500
Less: Indexation Allowance (W1)	(20,016)
Indexed gains	**21,484**

W1

Indexation Allowance = $\frac{(242.4 - 171.1)}{171.1}$ (0.417) x £48,000
= £20,016,

1. Purchase price of new building is £85,000

Total sale proceeds = £89,500
Purchase price of new building = £85,000
So, company retained = £4,500

£4,500 is immediately chargeable to tax.

Amount of gains rolled over

= Indexed Gains – Gain to be immediately charged
= £21,484 - £4,500
= £16,984, is the remaining amount of chargeable gain, which may be rolled over.

Therefore, the base cost of the new building = £85,000 - £16,984
= £68,016,

2. Purchase price of new building is 95,000

Purchase price of the new building = £95,000
Sale proceeds = £89,500

It is clearly evident that the company has spent the entire sale proceeds for the purchase of the new building. Therefore the entire gains may be rolled over.

Thus, allowable cost of new building = £95,000 - £16,984
= £78,016,

Answer to SEQ 2

Peter's CGT position for 2012-13:

	£
Disposal consideration (market value)	200,000
Less: Acquisition cost	(100,000)
Gain	**100,000**
Less: Holdover relief (W1)	(50,000)
Chargeable gains	**50,000**

Workings

W1

When the transaction is not at an arm's length price, we deem the market value to be the sales proceeds. The difference between the market value of the asset and the actual sale price (i.e. the discount element of the sale) is the maximum gain eligible for holdover relief (£200,000 - £150,000 = £50,000).

Answer to SEQ 3

Mica's total sales consideration:

£75,000 x 2/3 = £50,000	in the form of shares
£75,000 x 1/3 = £25,000	in cash

As Mica receives sales consideration partly in cash and partly in shares, the held over gain is calculated by applying the following formula:

$$\text{Net gains on individual chargeable assets} \times \frac{\text{Value of shares received from the company}}{\text{Total value of consideration from the company}}$$

= (£50,000/£75,000) x £25,000

= £16,667 (can be held over)

Calculation of the amount of gain immediately chargeable to tax:

	£
Total capital gain	25,000
Less: Incorporation relief	(16,667)
Chargeable gains	8,333

CORPORATION TAX LIABILITIES

D1

STUDY GUIDE D1: THE SCOPE OF CORPORATION TAX

Get Through Intro

A tax is a compulsory charge paid by individuals, unincorporated businesses or incorporated businesses (companies) to the government. A company is a separate legal entity. This Study Guide deals with corporation tax i.e. tax paid by companies.

In this Study Guide, we will study the meaning of some basic terms and principles of corporation tax and also the tax rates applicable to companies.

Learning Outcomes

a) Define the terms 'period of account', 'accounting period', and 'financial year'.
b) Recognise when an accounting period starts and when an accounting period finishes.
c) Explain how the residence of a company is determined.

Introduction

Case Study

Bob is the owner and Managing Director of Acme Ltd. However, Bob and Acme Ltd are two different entities in the eyes of law. The chargeability of income of these two entities varies. Bob is liable to pay income tax on his salary, bonus and dividend income from Acme Ltd. At the same time, Acme Ltd is liable to corporation tax on the profits it has made during the accounting period.

Tip

Corporation tax is tax paid by companies on their taxable total profits for each accounting period.

1. Define the terms 'period of account', 'accounting period' and 'financial year'.[1]

[Learning Outcome a]

Before proceeding further, we need to understand some important concepts.

1. Company

Any incorporated body whether limited or unlimited is a company. Any corporate body or unincorporated organisation **chargeable to corporation tax is also a company.** The term also includes unincorporated associations which are not run as partnerships, such as members' clubs, societies and associations, sports clubs or a political associations.

Tip

Remember tax paid by individuals and partnerships is known as income tax and not corporation tax.

2. Period of Account and Accounting Period

We will frequently be using these two terms while calculating the corporation tax liability. So let us first try to understand what "Period of Account" and "Accounting Period" mean and how they differ from each other.

a) **Period of Account:** this is the period for which a company prepares its set of accounts. No specific period of account is specified by law, so companies can prepare their accounts for any period as they see fit. Therefore, the length of a period of account can be 6 months, 12 months, 18 months, 30 months, or any other length that the company decides. However, usually it is 12 months.

Example

Alpha Ltd prepares its accounts for 12 months period from 01/01/2012 to 31/12/2012 (i.e. year ended 31 December 2012).

Beta Ltd prepares its accounts for 9 months period from 01/01/2012 to 30/09/2012 (i.e. 9 months ended on 30 September 2012).

Gamma Ltd prepares its accounts for 15 months from 01/01/2012 to 31/03/2013 (i.e. 15 months ended on 31 March 2012).

b) **Accounting Period:** the accounting period is the period for which the government charges corporation tax. The accounting period can never exceed 12 months. The accounting period may be less than 12 months.

Example

Continuing the above example of Alpha, Beta and Gamma Ltd

Alpha Ltd makes up its accounts to year ended 31 December 2012. The accounting period will be the 12 month period ended on 31 December 2012.

Beta Ltd makes up its accounts for 9 months ended on 30 September 2012. The accounting period will be the 9 month period ended on 30 September 2012. This is less than 12 months.

Gamma Ltd makes up accounts for 15 months ended on 31 March 2013. This period is longer than 12 months. Therefore the accounting period will be divided into two periods. The first period will be the first twelve months from 01/01/2012 to 31/12/2012 (i.e. 12 months ended on 31 December 2012). The next period will be the remaining period from 01/01/2013 to 31/03/2013 (i.e. 3 months period ended on 31 March 2013).

Financial year: the financial year is:

a) the period for which the rates of corporation tax are fixed by the government

b) the period that runs from 1 April to the succeeding 31 March

c) identified by the calendar year in which it begins

Example

The financial year (FY) 2011 covers the period from 1 April 2011 to 31 March 2012 and FY 2012 covers the period from 1 April 2012 to 31 March 2013.

For each FY the government decides the tax rates.

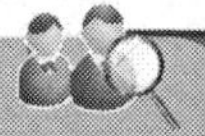

Example

The small profits rate of corporation tax in FY 2012 is 20%.

The main rate of corporation tax for FY 2012 is 24%.

The important point to consider here is which corporation tax rate should you consider to tax the profits if the accounting period does not match with the financial year?

Example

The accounting period of a company is the 12 months ended 31 August 2012.

This accounting period falls in two financial years. The first 7 months fall in FY 2011 (FY starting from 1 April 2011 to 31 March 2012) and the next 5 months fall in FY 2012 (FY starting from 1 April 2012 to 31 March 2013).

Here, the chargeable profits will be apportioned between the two FYs in the ratio of the months falling in each FY. The profits falling into FY 2011 will be taxed at the rates applicable to FY 2011 and the profits falling into FY 2012 will be taxed at the rates applicable to FY 2012.

2. Recognise when an accounting period starts and when an accounting period finishes.[1] [Learning Outcome b]

Diagram 1: Start and end of accounting period

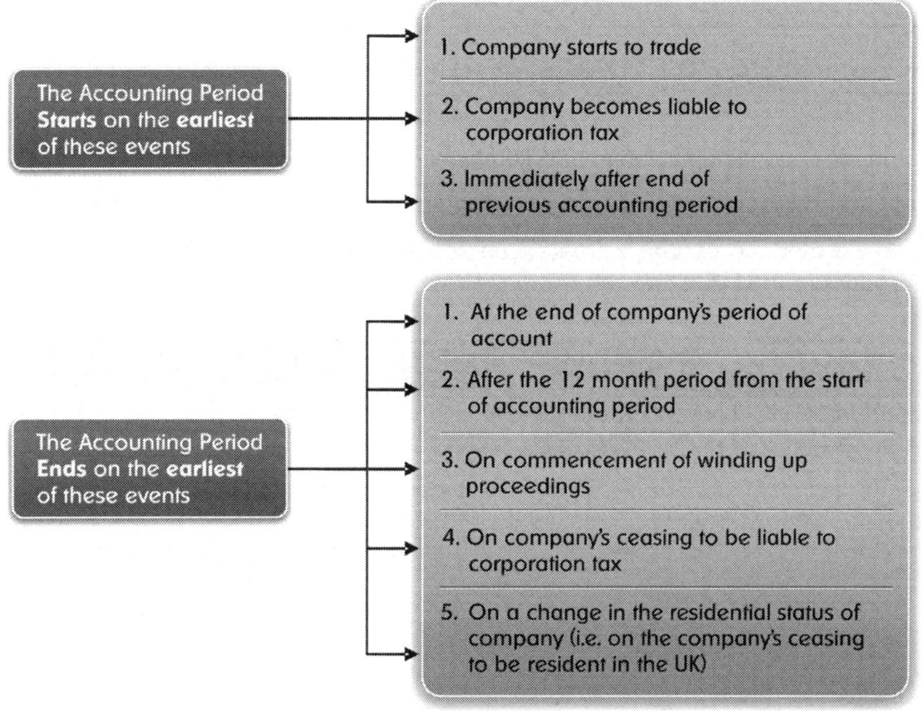

As we have already seen, it is not necessary that a period of account must be 12 months. A company can prepare its set of accounts for any period consisting of any length. **What if, then, the set of accounts covers a period either less than 12 months or more than 12 months?**

Diagram 2: Accounting period

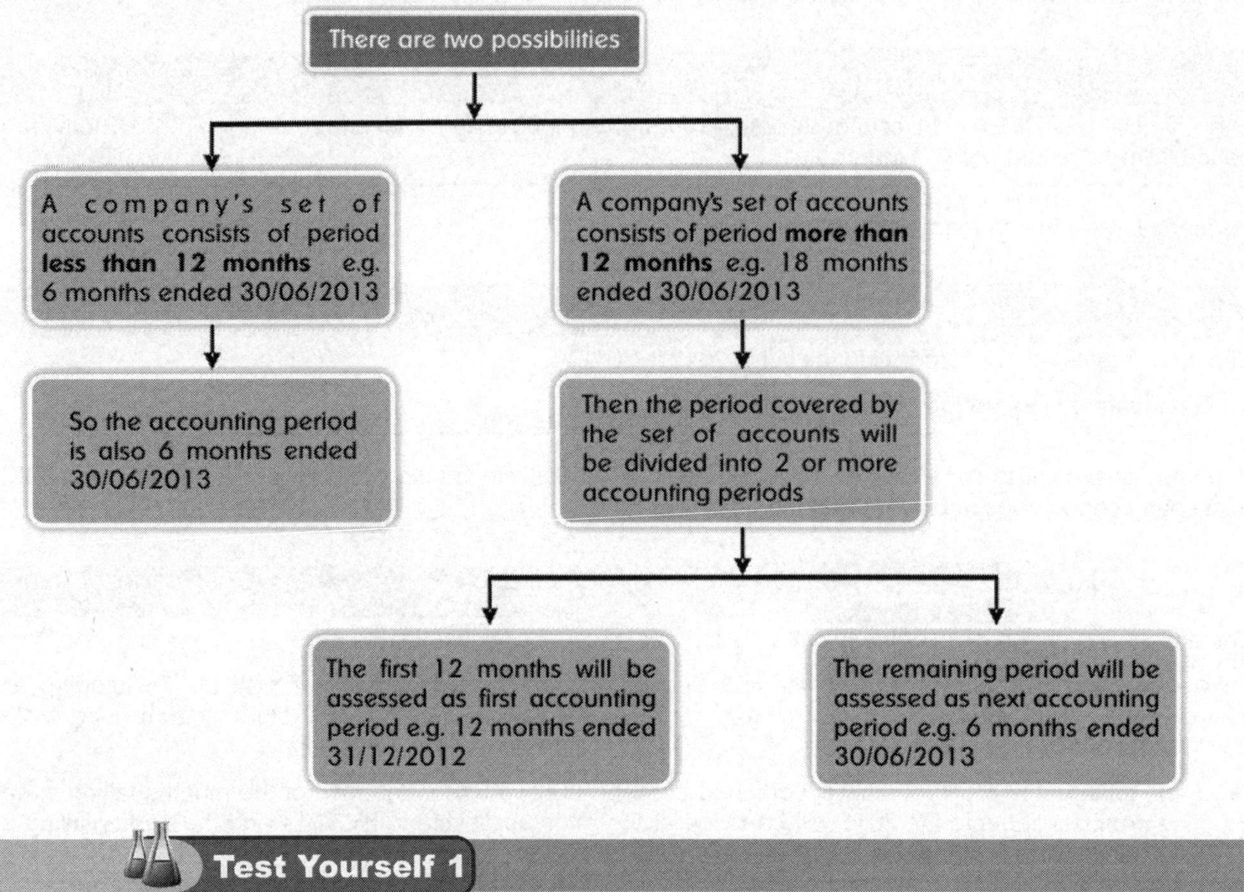

Test Yourself 1

From the given periods of accounts, identify the relevant accounting periods.

(a) The set of accounts of Sun Ltd is prepared for year ended 31/12/2012.
(b) The set of accounts of Kelvin Ltd is prepared for six months ended 30/06/2012.
(c) The set of accounts of Woods Ltd is prepared for sixteen months ended 31/12/2012.
(d) The set of accounts of Shop Zone Ltd is prepared for twenty months ended 31/03/2013.

---

3. Explain how the residence of a company is determined.[2]

[Learning Outcome c]

Residence of a company depends upon where the company is incorporated.

1. If a **company is incorporated in the UK, then it is resident in the UK.**
2. A **non-UK incorporated company** is treated as **resident** in the UK **if its central management and control is exercised in the UK.**

Example

A company is incorporated in a country other than the UK, say France, but its Board of Directors conducts its affairs through meetings held in the UK. In this case, is the company resident in the UK or in France?

The answer is that the company is **resident in the UK** because its affairs are conducted (central management and control) through meetings of Board of Directors in the UK.

Tip

There can be three different situations depending upon the place of incorporation of a company:

Place where the company is incorporated	Whether resident in the UK
Company incorporated in the UK	Resident in the UK
Company incorporated in a place other than the UK	Non-resident in the UK
Company incorporated in a place other than the UK but control and management of the company situated in the UK	Resident in the UK

It is important to determine the residential status of a company as the companies which are **resident in the UK** are **liable to corporation tax on all the profits and chargeable gains arising worldwide**.

Test Yourself 2

Determine whether the following companies are UK residents for the purposes of corporation tax:

(a) Adobe Ltd is incorporated in the UK and operates in Spain.

(b) Bake Ltd is incorporated, managed and controlled from Ukraine.

(c) China Chop Ltd is incorporated in Australia but is managed and controlled centrally from the UK.

Answers to Test Yourself

Answer to TY 1

1. The period of 12 months ended on 31/12/2012 is an accounting period in itself.
2. The period of 6 months ended on 30/06/2012 is an accounting period in itself.
3. The accounting period can never exceed 12 months. Hence, the period of 16 months from 01/09/2011 to 31/12/2012 is divided into two accounting periods - the first period will be the first 12 months from 01/09/2011 to 31/08/2012 and the other will be the remaining 4 months from 01/09/2012 to 31/12/2012.
4. The period of 20 months from 01/08/2010 to 31/03/2013 is divided into two accounting periods - the first 12 months from 01/08/2011 to 31/07/2012 will be the first period and the other will be the remaining 8 months from 01/08/2012 to 31/03/2013.

Answer to TY 2

Company	Whether resident in the UK
1. Adobe Ltd	UK resident, as it is incorporated in the UK.
2. Bake Ltd	Non-resident in the UK, as it is neither incorporated in the UK nor managed and controlled centrally from the UK.
3. China Chop Ltd	UK resident, as it is managed and controlled centrally from the UK.

Quick Quiz

1. Explain the term accounting period.
2. What period is the financial year 2012?
3. The period of accounts of LMN Ltd is of 13 months ended 31 May 2012. Identify its accounting periods.

Answers to Quick Quiz

1. The accounting period is the period for which the government charges corporation tax on the company's profits. The accounting period can never exceed 12 months.
2. 1 April 2012 to 31 March 2013.
3. The period of accounts of 13 months is divided into two accounting periods:

   (a) One for the first 12 months from 01/05/2011 to 30/04/2012 and
   (b) The other for the remaining 1 month i.e. May 2012.

Self Examination Questions

Question 1

When does an accounting period start for corporation tax purposes?

Question 2

When does an accounting period end for corporation tax purposes?

Question 3

The following information is provided in respect of three companies:

1. Red Ltd: the chargeable profits for the year ended on 31 March 2013 are £120,000.
2. Yellow Ltd: the chargeable profits for the year ended on 31 December 2012 are £180,000.
3. Orange Ltd: the chargeable profits for the 15 months period ended on 31 March 2013 are 300,000.

Required:

The corporation tax rates of which financial years are applicable to these profits?

Answers to Self Examination Questions

Answer to SEQ 1

An accounting period starts at the earliest of these events

1. when a company starts to trade
2. when its profits become liable to corporation tax
3. immediately after the end of the preceding accounting period

Answer to SEQ 2

An accounting period ends at the earliest of these events

1. at the end of a company's period of account.
2. 12 months after the beginning of the accounting period.
3. when a company commences winding up proceedings.
4. when its profits otherwise cease to be liable to corporation tax.
5. when a company ceases to be UK resident.

Answer to SEQ 3

1. The accounting period of Red Ltd is the 12 month period ended on 31 March 2013. This entire period falls in the financial year 2012 (i.e. 1 April 2012 to 31 March 2013). Hence, the corporation tax rate of FY 2012 will be applicable to the profits of £120,000 of Red Ltd.

2. The accounting period of Yellow Ltd for the year ended on 31 December 2012 falls in two financial years, i.e. FY 2011 (1 April 2011 to 31 March 2012) and FY 2012 (1 April 2012 to 31 March 2013). The period of 3 months up to 31 March 2012 falls in the FY 2011 and the remaining period of 9 months up to 31 December 2012 falls in the FY 2012.

Accounting period	Corporation Tax Rate applicable (FY 2011)	Corporation Tax Rate applicable (FY 2012)
12 months ended on 31 December 2012 (chargeable profits of £180,000 in the ratio of 3:9)	£180,000 x 3/12 = £45,000	£180,000 x 9/12 = £135,000

3. The accounting period can never exceed 12 months. As the accounting period of Orange Ltd is more than 12 months (15 months), first it will be divided into two accounting periods: first accounting period of 12 months ended on 31 December 2012 and the second accounting period of 3 months ended on 31 March 2013.

   Chargeable profits for the first accounting period of twelve months ended on 31 December 2012 are (£300,000 x 12/15) = £240,000

   Chargeable profits for the second accounting period of three months ended on 31 March 2013 are (£300,000 x 3/15) = £60,000

   The first accounting period (year ended on 31 December 2012) falls into two financial years; hence chargeable profits for this period are required to be split according to the financial year for determining the rates of corporation tax applicable.

   The first 3 months (1 January 2012 to 31 March 2013) fall in FY 2011 and the next 9 months (1 April 2012 to 31 December 2012) fall in FY 2012.

   The second accounting period (3 months period ended on 31 March 2013) falls into FY 2012.

Accounting period	Corporation Tax Rate applicable (FY 2011)	Corporation Tax Rate applicable (FY 2012)
12 months ended on 31 December 2012 (chargeable profits of £240,000 in the ratio of 3:9)	£240,000 x 3/12 = £60,000	£240,000 x 9/12 = £180,000
3 months period ended on 31 March 2013	-	£60,000
	60,000	**240,000**

SECTION D

CORPORATION TAX LIABILITIES

D2

STUDY GUIDE D2: TAXABLE TOTAL PROFITS (PART 1)

Get Through Intro

Corporation tax is charged on the trading profits of companies, and on their other income and chargeable gains. A company's taxable income is charged with reference to income or gains arising in its accounting period. It is essential to correctly identify and calculate the taxable total profits to determine the corporation tax liability. In this Study Guide, we will learn what the taxable total profits are and how to calculate chargeable profits from trade.

Learning Outcomes

a) Recognise the expenditure that is allowable in calculating the tax-adjusted trading profit.
b) Explain how relief can be obtained for pre-trading expenditure.
c) Compute capital allowances (as for income tax).
d) Compute property business profits.
e) Explain the treatment of interest paid and received under the loan relationship rules.
f) Explain the treatment of qualifying charitable donations.

Introduction

Case Study

Superb Ltd is a fast growing company. It deals in the manufacture of personal computers. This is its third year of operation.

It has incurred different types of expenditure during the current year, including the purchase of assets, expenses incurred entertaining customers, gifts to employees, trade subscriptions, political donations, staff training and travelling expenses.

Superb Ltd is not sure which expenses are deductible and which are not, while calculating chargeable profits.

The company approaches you for advice about the calculation of chargeable profits.

This Study Guide will teach you how to calculate the chargeable profits of Superb Ltd and other companies.

1. Recognise the expenditure that is allowable in calculating the tax-adjusted trading profit.[2] [Learning Outcome a]

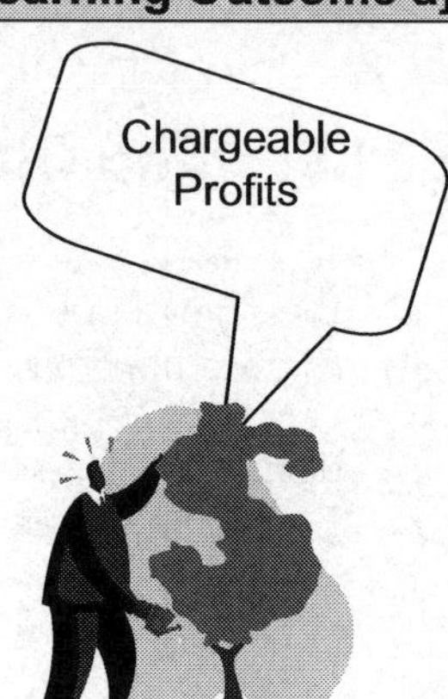

If a company is liable to pay corporation tax, then it must work out its tax liability. In order to calculate the tax liability, you need to know how much taxable or **chargeable profits** you have made in the **accounting period**. Corporation tax is charged on income and gains that fall within certain headings, all of which are defined by legislation. A company's chargeable profits consist of income in the form of trading profits, income from non-trading loans, income from property and chargeable gains. In other words, a company's total income is the addition of the following different categories of income and gains:

1. Trading profits
2. Property income
3. Profits arising from loan relationship (commonly referred to as interest income)
4. Income from foreign securities and possessions
5. Chargeable gains

Tip

1. Dividends received by a company are **not included in the taxable total profits.**
2. Dividends paid by a company are not deductible from chargeable profits.

Taxable total profits of a company are made up as follows:

	£	£
1. Trading profits	X	
Less: Brought forward trading losses	(X)	X
2. Property income		X
3. Income from loan relationship (interest income)		X
4. Profits from foreign securities and possessions		X
5. Chargeable gains	X	
Less: Allowable capital losses brought forward	(X)	X
Total income		**X**
Less: Reliefs		
Property business losses	X	
Trading losses relieved under s 37 CTA 2010	X	
Qualifying charitable payments	X	(X)
Taxable total profits (TTP)		**X**

Now let us see the part **trading profits** in detail.

The profits arising from a company's trade are termed trading profits. The starting point is to take the net profits before tax from the financial statements and make various adjustments which will give the adjusted trading profits. The format you may follow to arrive at the adjusted profits is shown here:

	£
Net Profits given in the accounts	X
Add:	
(i) Expenditure shown in the accounts but not deductible for tax purposes	X
(ii) Income taxable but not included in the accounts	X
Less:	
(i) Expenditure deductible for tax purposes but not shown in the accounts	(X)
(ii) Income included in the accounts but not taxable as trading income	(X)
Adjusted trading profits	**X**

An important step in the calculation of trading profits for tax purposes **is recognising which expenses are deductible and which are non-deductible for tax purposes**. We have already seen the deductible and non-deductible expenses in Study Guide B3 (part 1). Let us quickly revise them here.

Type of expense	Deductible
Depreciation / amortisation	✗
Increase in general allowance	✗
Capital expenditure	✗
Gifts to employees	✓
Gifts to customers (provided cost not more than £50, not food, drink etc)	✓
Staff entertainment	✓
Customer / supplier entertainment	✗
Trade subscriptions	✓
Political donations	✗
Trade-related legal and professional charges	✓
Interest (trading purposes)	✓
Penalties and fines	✗
Staff training	✓
Removal expenses, unless an expansionary move	✓
Redundancy pay in excess of statutory limit	✓
Contribution to pension schemes	✓
Lease premium	✗
Illegal payments	✗
Irrecoverable VAT, if relates to an item of allowable expenditure	✓
Staff defalcations	✓
Travelling expenses (business)	✓
Lease and rent payments for equipment	✓
Registration of patents and trademarks	✓

There are differences in treatment of some of the items while calculating the trading profits for tax purposes for an individual and a company, which are as follows:

1. private use adjustments
2. capital allowances (Learning Outcome 3)
3. interest paid and received under loan relationship (Learning Outcome 5)
4. qualifying charitable payments (Learning Outcome 6)

Private use adjustments

Expenses attributable to private use by a sole trader are not allowable. Adjustments are made for the private use by an owner. But, **in the case of a company, directors are employees and therefore no such adjustments are made for private use**. Hence, any expense attributable to the private use by a director or an employee of the company are fully allowable while calculating tax adjusted trading profits.

Test Yourself 1

Given below is the statement of profit or loss of Sunshine Ltd for the year ended 31 March 2013:

	£	£
Gross profit		74,705
Other income		
Property income		1,300
Expenses		
Entertainment expenses (Note 1)	3,800	
Legal and professional charges (Note 2)	16,400	
Gifts and donations (Note 3)	12,575	
Salaries (Note 4)	26,000	
Depreciation	2,500	
Bad debts written off	220	
Legal expenses relating to issue of shares	1,500	
Increase in general allowance	50	
Loss on sale of non-current assets	70	(63,115)
Net Profit before taxation		**12,890**

Notes

1. Entertainment expenses include:

	£
New Year's dinner for 18 employees	1,800
New Year's dinner for 10 customers	2,000
	3,800

2. Legal and professional charges relate to the following items:

	£
Purchase of a new machine	8,300
Collection from trade debtors	1,100
Obtaining bank loan	1,500
Costs of renewing a 30-year lease	4,000
Costs of registering the company's trademark	1,500
	16,400

Continued on the next page

3. Sunshine made the following gifts and donations during the year:

	£
Christmas gifts for staff (£100 each)	2,500
Christmas gift vouchers for 10 customers of £65 each	650
15 watches, with company name engraved (costing £45 each) as Christmas gifts for customers	675
Cash donation to a political party	5,000
Cash donation to UNICEF	2,500
Cash donation to local charity, for which free advertising for the company was received in the local magazine	250
Qualifying charitable donation to local charity	1,000
	12,575

4. Salaries include remuneration paid to directors of £10,000.

Required:

Calculate trading profits of Sunshine Ltd for the year ended 31 March 2013.

2. Explain how relief can be obtained for pre-trading expenditure.[1]

[Learning Outcome b]

A company may incur expenses before actually starting to trade, e.g. rent of business premises, interest on loan for the purchase of machinery, legal charges etc. These expenses are known as pre-trading expenditure, and are **treated as if incurred on the first day of the trade.** They are **allowable** provided they were incurred **within seven years of the commencement of trade** and are related to the trade. Such expenses must be of the type which, if incurred after commencement of trade, had been allowable i.e. **capital expenditure** incurred before commencement of trade is **not allowable.** However, **capital allowances are available on capital expenditure** incurred before commencement of trade and this expenditure is treated as if it was incurred on the first day of the trade.

SUMMARY

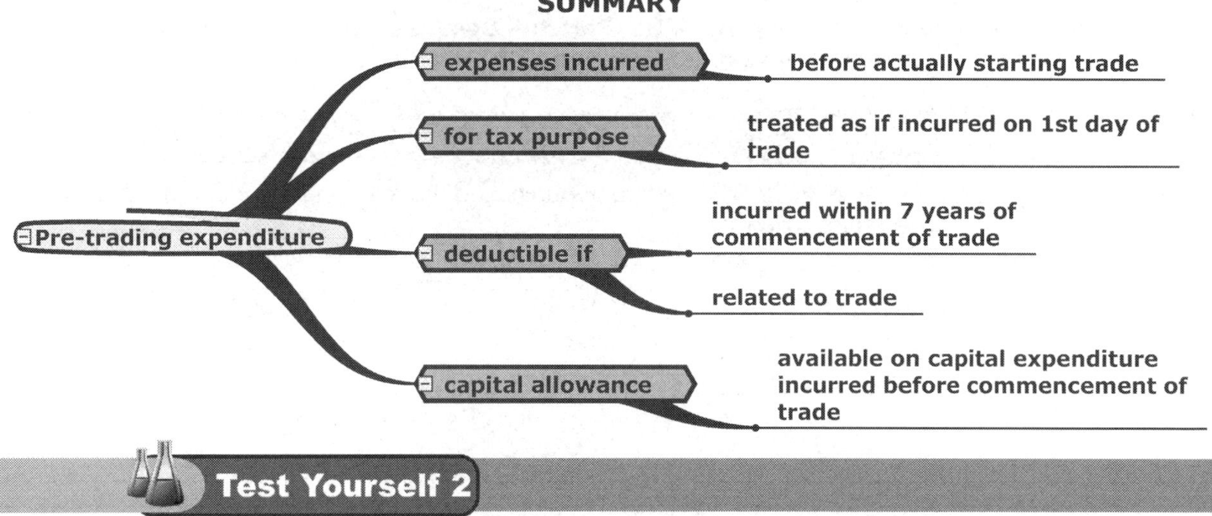

Test Yourself 2

M & C Ltd was incorporated on 1 Jan 2009. The first three years of operation were the research phase and so there was no revenue during this period. The phase of research included the development of products, market research and production setup. M & C Ltd started trading on 1 December 2012 and, by that date, had already incurred the following expenses.

	Date	£
Rent for the office and warehouse for business	15/10/2009 – 15/10/2010	15,000
Purchase of own office place and permanent warehouse	01/10/2010	200,000
Legal charges for purchase of office place and warehouse	10/12/2010	5,000
Marketing and advertising expenses	01/06/2012 – 01/11/2012	46,000
Land purchased for business use	24/05/2002	70,000

Continued on the next page

Required:

Explain with reasons whether the expenses are deductible under relief of pre-trading expenses.

---

3. Compute capital allowances (as for income tax).[2]

[Learning Outcome c]

We have already seen various provisions relating to capital allowances in Study Guide B3 (part 2). All the provisions of capital allowances relating to self-employed individuals are equally applicable to corporate entities except the differences mentioned below:

1. Unlike self-employed individuals, there is **no private use restriction** by a director or an employee, where a company is involved.
2. The AP of a company can't exceed 12 months, so there is **no need to scale up WDAs or the AIAs**. However, if the accounting period of a company is less than 12 months, then WDA or AIA will be scaled down proportionately.

But, the rule for the FYA is the same as it is given in full in the year the asset is purchased, irrespective of the length of the accounting period.

Your knowledge of the capital allowance provisions will be tested below.

Refer to Learning Outcome 1 from Study Guide B3 (Part 2) - Define plant and machinery for capital allowances purposes

Test Yourself 3

State whether the following assets are eligible for capital allowance:

1. computer hardware
2. rented software
3. plant purchased on hire purchase basis
4. old railway wagon used as primary school classroom
5. cold storage room in ice factory

Refer to Learning Outcome 2 from Study Guide B3 (Part 2) – Compute writing down allowances (WDA), first year allowance (FYA) and annual investment allowance (AIA)

Test Yourself 4

Trans Ltd was incorporated on 1 April 2012. The company purchased the following plant and machinery during the year. The dates of purchase are as follows:

		£
10 May 2012	Purchased plant	80,000
1 September 2012	Purchased machinery	42,000
1 October 2012	Purchased car (with CO_2 emissions rate of 125g/km)	9,000

Required:

Show the calculations of capital allowance for the years ended 31 March 2013 and 31 March 2014.

Test Yourself 5

Speed Ltd manufactures sports bikes. The company started operations on 1 January 2012 and decided to prepare its accounts to 31 August each year. Its first accounts are for the period to 31 August 2013. During the first accounting period, the company bought the following plant and machinery:

		£
12 April 2012	Plant	105,000
1 November 2012	Equipment	27,500
10 January 2013	Machinery	78,000

Required:

Show the calculations of capital allowance for the accounting period ended on 31 August 2013.

Refer to Learning Outcome 3 from Study Guide B3 (Part 2) – Compute capital allowances for motor car

On 1 January 2012 Best Ltd started its new business. The company is a dealer of various types of balls. The company chose 30 June as its annual accounting date. However its first accounting period was until 30 June 2013 (i.e. 18 months).

On 1 January 2012 the company purchased a car with CO_2 emissions of 80g/km for £18,000. On 1 June 2012 the company purchased another car with CO_2 emissions of 185g/km for £21,000.

On 10 January 2013, the company purchased another car costing £10,000 with CO_2 emissions of 140g/km for the directors of the company.

Required:

Show the calculation of capital allowance for the accounting period ended 30 June 2013.

Refer to Learning Outcome 4 from Study Guide B3 (Part 2) – Compute balancing allowances and balancing charges

In July 2007 Fat Ltd started its business. The company follows 30 June as its annual accounting date. On 30 June 2012, WDV of plant and machinery was as follows

	£
General Pool	15,200
Expensive car	7,400

The following is the summary of sale and purchase transactions for the period ended 30 June 2013.

			£
1 December 2012	Sell	Expensive car	5,000
10 December 2012	Purchase	Plant	165,000

Required:

Show calculations of capital allowance and balancing adjustments for the company for the year ended 30 June 2013.

Refer to Learning Outcome 5 from Study Guide B3 (Part 2) – Rocognise the treatment of short life asset

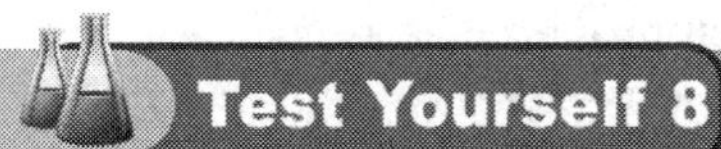

On 5 April 2012, Hot Ltd purchased plant for £112,000. The useful life of the plant was three years. However, in the second year, the company sold the plant for £7,500. The date of sale is 5 June 2013.

Required:

Show the calculations of the balancing adjustment assuming the company prepares its annual accounts to 30 June every year.

Refer to Learning Outcome 6 from Study Guide B3 (Part 2) – Explain the treatment of assets included in the special rate pool

Lucky Plc is a soap manufacturing company. On 15 July 2012 the company purchased new machinery for £150,000. The machinery has a useful life of thirty years.

Required:

Show the calculation of capital allowance for the company assuming that the company prepares its accounts to 31 October every year.

4. Compute property business profits.[2]

[Learning Outcome d]

4.1 We have already seen in Study Guide B4, how property business profits are calculated.

Let us quickly revise some of the following points related to property business profits which are extremely important:

1. The property must be situated in the UK.
2. The income should be computed on an accruals basis.
3. Aggregation of expenses / income if more than one property
4. Deductible expenses from rental income: expenses incurred wholly and exclusively for the property business are deductible from rental income to arrive at the taxable property income. Some examples of allowable expenses are:

   a) expenses towards repairs and maintenance
   b) insurance
   c) agent's fees
   d) bad debts (if rent not paid for some part of the accounting period).

However, the treatment for the companies differs from the individuals in respect of the following points:

1. In the case of a company, the property business profits are calculated on the basis of the accounting periods and not tax years.

2. **Treatment of interest paid on loan taken to buy a property, which is let out**: for individuals, interest on loans to buy or improve properties is treated as an expense (on an accruals basis).

   However, for companies, such interest is dealt with under the loan relationships rules, which is discussed later in this Study Guide. **Such interest is not deductible in calculating property business income of companies.**

3. In the case of an individual, all property receipts and all property expenses are pooled to give an overall profit or loss figure for the year and any balance loss is carried forward to set off against the first available property income.

However, in the case of a company, first all property receipts and all property expenses are pooled to give an overall profit or loss figure for the period and if there is any balance loss, it can be set off against taxable total profits of the current accounting period before qualifying charitable payments. Then, it can be carried forward to set off against taxable total profits of the future accounting period.

Excellent Ltd receives a premium of £25,000 on 1 January 2012 from its tenant Goggle Ltd for granting 20 years lease, in the accounting period ending on 31 December 2012.

The property income of Excellent Ltd is calculated as follows:

If the lease is granted for a period of 50 years or less than 50 years then it is termed a short lease. Premiums received on a short lease are assessable to property business income. The amount to be assessed to property income is equal to the amount of premiums reduced by 2% for each year of the lease except for the first year.

Therefore, property income = P – P x (2% (n -1))
= £25,000 – £25,000 x (2% x (20 – 1))
= £15,500

4.2 Lease premiums paid by the company

When a company pays any short lease premium, then the deduction of lease premiums paid is allowable from the company's trading profits. The amount of deduction is the lease premium assessable on the landlord divided by the number of years. Such a premium is deductible each year for the period of lease.

Continuing the example of Excellent Ltd

The lease premiums deductible for Goggle Ltd are calculated as follows:

(a) Excellent Ltd declared £15,500 as its property lease premium chargeable to tax.
(b) Goggle Ltd can deduct **£15,500/20 years = £775** per year for 20 years of the lease period.

4.3 Assigning a sublease

When a tenant sublets a property, it is termed a lease assignment.

The following are important issues in relation to the sublease:

1. Any premiums received on a sublease are treated as rent received in full.

2. If the tenant originally paid a premium to his landlord for the grant of a lease, the premium received on his sublease is reduced in the following ratio:

Portion of head lease premium treated as rent x sublease duration / head lease duration

Example

Lung Plc got an asset on lease from Kidney Ltd on 1 April 2010 for a period of 25 years at a premium of £50,000. On 1 April 2012, Lung Plc granted a sublease on that asset to Liver Inc for 10 years. The premium for this sublease was £60,000.
The amount assessable as property income for Lung Plc is calculated as follows:

= P - P x (2% x (n -1))
Where, P = Premium and n = period of lease

	£	£
Premium assessable to property business income		
Premium received by Lung Plc	60,000	
Less: £60,000 x (2% x (10 - 1))	(10,800)	49,200
Less: Allowance for premium paid by Lung Plc (W1)		(10,400)
Premium treated as rent		**38,800**

Workings

W1 Allowance for premium paid

	£
Premium paid by Lung Plc	50,000
Less: £50,000 x (2% x (25 - 1))	(24,000)
	26,000

This amount paid will be reduced in the following ratio
= Portion of head lease premium treated as rent x sublease duration / head lease duration
= £26,000 x 10 / 25
= £10,400

Head Ltd granted a lease to Face Ltd on 1 January 2008 for a period of 25 years for a premium of £20,000. On 1 January 2012, Face Ltd granted a sublease to Neck Ltd for 15 years. The sublease premium payable by Neck Ltd was £40,000.

Required:

Calculate the amount assessable as property income for Face Ltd.

Creamy Ltd owns two offices for several years, which it has rented out. The details of property rented out during the year ended 31/03/2013 are as follows:

- Office 1 was let out on lease on 01/08/2012 for 20 years to Icy Ltd. The initial lease premium was £25,000 and annual rent of £5,100 p.a. is payable by Icy Ltd.

- Office 2, a furnished office, was let out at £1,200 p.a. from 01/05/ 2012. The tenant leaves on 31/08/2012 and a new tenant moves in on 01/02/2013, paying £1,800 p.a.

Creamy Ltd incurred the following expenses:

- repairs of Office 2 in January 2013, £600
- insurance per office, £600 p.a.
- interest on loan taken to purchase office, 1, £2,300
- advertisement expenses for finding tenants for office, 2, £150

Required:

Calculate Creamy Ltd's property income for the year ended 31/03/2013.

5. Explain the treatment of interest paid and received under the loan relationships rules.[1] [Learning Outcome e]

5.1 What is a loan relationship?

A company is said to have a loan relationship if the company borrows or lends money.

Diagram 1: Loan Relationship

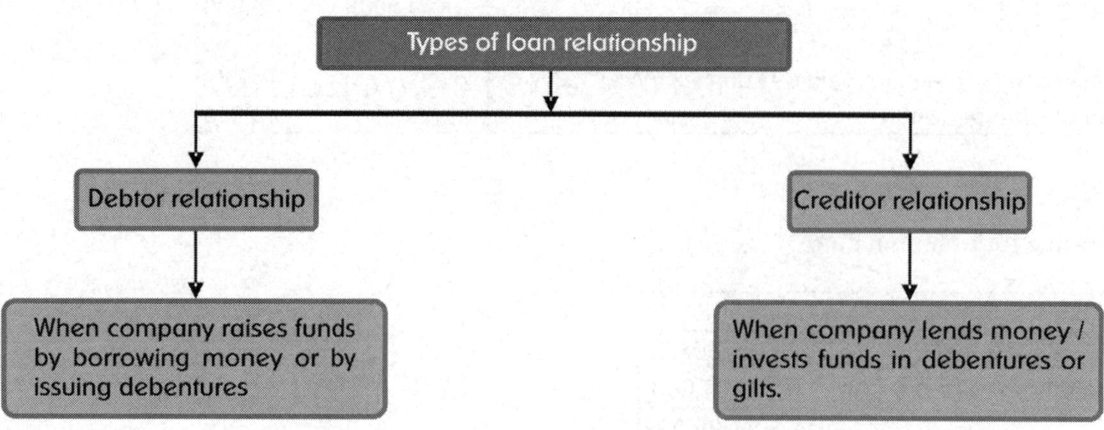

Tax Treatment of loan relationships

The tax treatment of loan relationships depends upon whether the loan relationship entered into is a **trading loan relationship or a non-trading loan relationship.**

1. **Trading loan relationships**: are when a loan is taken or issued for trading purposes.

a) The interest paid or payable on a loan taken for trading purposes is treated as a **trading expense** and hence is **fully deductible.**

b) The interest received or receivable can be of a trading nature only if the company is engaged in the business of lending money. In this case, the interest is treated as **trading income.**

Example

Low Ltd took a bank loan of £20,000 to purchase raw materials for the business. The interest paid on this loan during the year ended 31 March 2013 was £1,260.

As the loan was taken for trading purposes, the interest paid on the loan is a trading expense. Hence, £1,260 will be fully deducted from the company's trading profits.

2. **Non-trading loan relationships:** if a loan is given for purposes other than trading, then any income arising out of such a relationship is **assessable as income from loan relationships. Similarly, if a loan is taken for purposes other than trading then any expenditure (e.g. interest payable) arising** out of such a relationship is **treated as expense from loan relationships.**

Example

Loan to purchase a property intended for letting out is a non-trading loan relationship.

5.2 How is income from loan relationship calculated?

If the **income from non-trading loan relationships** is **more than the expenses relating to non-trading loan relationships** then the **excess income is chargeable as income from loan relationship.**

Some examples of interest income which is assessable as income from loan relationships are

1. Interest received on bank accounts.
2. Interest received on overpaid corporation tax
3. Interest received on government securities

Tip

Companies receive gross interest; hence grossing it up by multiplying it by 100/80 is not required for calculation of corporation tax.

5.3 Accounting methods of loan relationships

While accounting for loan relationships, the company can opt for either of the following two methods:

1. **Accruals basis**: This refers to the practice of recognising income and expenses as soon as they become due. The actual receipt of income or payment of expenses is not relevant. If the income has become receivable, although not actually received by the end of the accounting period, the income is still considered for taxation purposes.

Test Yourself 12

Tree Ltd received gross bank interest of £8,200 for the year ended 31 March 2012. Bank interest owed to the company at the end of the year is £1,900. The corresponding amount at the start of the year was zero.

Required:

Calculate Tree Ltd's taxable interest.

2. **Mark to market basis**: In this method, at the end of each accounting period, the fair value of the loan relationship is determined.

SUMMARY

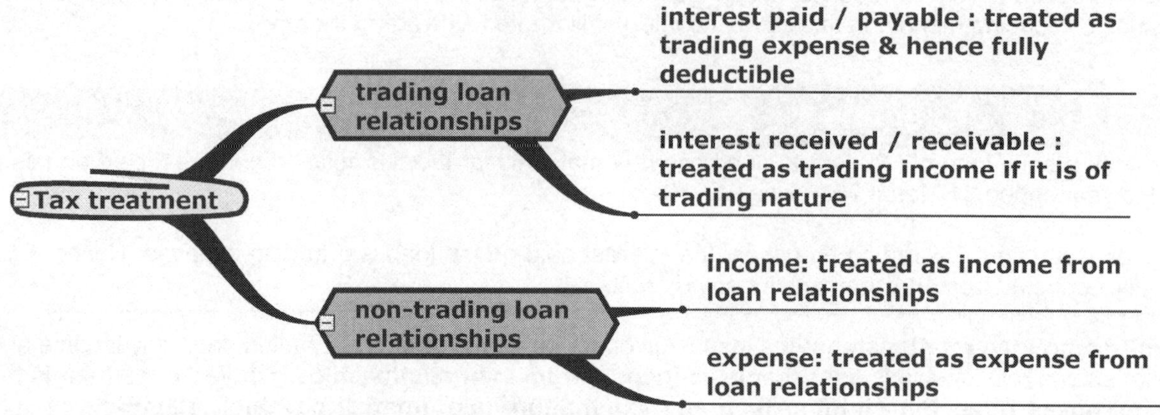

Test Yourself 13

Zebra Ltd's results for the year ended 31 March 2013 are as follows:

	£
Trading income	25,300
Income from property	11,000
Bank interest received (gross)	5,600
Government securities interest received (gross)	12,000
Chargeable gains	40,000

The following information is relevant:

1. Gross bank interest of £5,600 was received during the year and a further £890 was owed to the company at the end of the year. Bank interest of £300 was owed to the company at the start of the year.
2. Zebra Ltd acquired government securities on 30 June 2012. Interest of £12,000 (gross) is payable to the company on 1 January and 1 July every year.

Required:

Calculate Zebra Ltd's taxable total profits for the year to 31 March 2013.

6. Explain the treatment of qualifying charitable donations.[2]

[Learning Outcome f]

Qualifying donations made by Companies (and unincorporated associations) to approved charities under the qualifying charitable donations, can be claimed for tax relief. Tax relief for Qualifying Charitable Donations is available for the accounting period in which the donation is made,

Qualifying charitable donations made by companies are always paid gross. Donations for charities are annual payments that a donor can claim for exemption on tax. If a company deducts tax from a donation incorrectly, the charity cannot reclaim the tax from HMRC but must recover the shortfall from the donor i.e. the company.

Tax treatment of companies making Qualifying charitable donations

The qualifying donation made by a company to a charity is treated as a 'charge on income'. The company sets the amount of donation against its taxable profits to claim in its corporation tax self-assessment (CTSA) return so that it reduces its chargeable profits.

However, in case the company has a trading loss then charitable donations cannot be used to create or augment a company's trading losses. Any excess charges on income cannot be carried forward or back although they have been surrendered as group relief. Therefore such excess charges that cannot be surrendered will not be tax effective.

The declaration or claims on qualifying charitable donation should be supported by proper documentation of such donations, like the receipt from the charity and correspondence with the charity with regards to the donation made like a thank you letter.

Qualifying Charitable donations can also be made by non-resident companies within the UK corporation tax regime and that are trading in the UK through a branch or agency. Whereas non-resident companies that are only chargeable to UK income tax in respect of income arising in the UK cannot get relief on qualifying charitable donations.

Qualifying donations and restrictions on qualifying charitable donations treatment

Only "qualifying donations" would be allowed for claiming relief for donations made by companies for qualifying charity

Definition

A qualifying donation is a payment of a sum of money which is not a distribution of profit.

A payment will not be a qualifying donation if:

- It is subject to repayment, or
- There is a benefit to the company or a connected person from the donation and the value of the benefit exceeds the value of the donation made.
- It is an arrangement where the charity acquires property from the company or a connected person in some business agreement.
- The donation is made by a charity to another charity

Example

Cargo Ltd donates £100 to a museum (charity) on 1 June 2007, The charity gives free entry to four of the directors of Cargo Ltd in one of its events at the museum. The free entry is worth £20 each which is £80 (4 x £20) benefit to the company. The amount of benefit actually a substantial part of the donation therefore cannot be treated as a 'qualifying charitable donation' for relief.

Points to remember:

1. We have already discussed in Study Guide B3(1) that qualifying charitable donations are not allowable as a deduction from trading income. Hence, first add back the qualifiying charitable donations to obtain the adjusted trading profits for tax purposes.
2. Later, while calculating the taxable total income of the company, deduct it from the total income of the company.

Tip

Qualifying charitable donations made by a company are **relieved from chargeable profits** as a **deduction from total income**.

Example

Shady Ltd's statement of profit or loss for the year ended 31 March 2013 shows a trading profit of £215,000. The operating expenses include:

	£
Directors' fees	12,000
Depreciation	2,300
Qualifying charitable donation paid	3,400
Customer entertaining expenses	2,600

All the remaining operating expenses are allowable as trading expenses. Shady Ltd also has property income of £25,000, and chargeable gains of £13,550.

Continued on the next page

Computation of taxable total profits

	£
Trading profits (W1)	223,300
Property income	25,000
Chargeable gains	13,550
	261,850
Less: Qualifying charitable donation	(3,400)
Taxable total profits	**258,450**

Workings

W1 Trading profits

	£
Profits according to the accounts	215,000
Add: Expenditure shown in the accounts but not deductible for tax purposes.	
Depreciation	2,300
Qualifying charitable donation	3,400
Customer entertaining expenses	2,600
Trading income	**223,300**

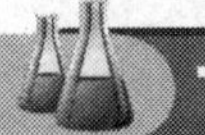

Test Yourself 14

Suppose Zebra Ltd (refer to Test yourself 13) paid a qualifying charitable donation of £12,000. What will be its taxable total profits for the year ended 31 March 2013?

Calculate Zebra Ltd's taxable total profits for the year ended 31 March 2013.

Answers to Test Yourself

Answer to TY 1

Computation of trading profits of Sunshine Ltd for the year ended 31 March 2013

	£	£
Net profits given according to the income statement		12,890
Add: Expenditure shown in the accounts but not deductible for tax purposes		
New year's dinner for 10 customers (Note 1)	2,000	
Legal and professional charges for the purchase of a new machine (Note 2)	8,300	
Christmas gift vouchers of £65 each for 10 customers (Note 6)	650	
Cash donation to a political party (Note 7)	5,000	
Cash donation to UNICEF (note 8)	2,500	
Qualifying charitable donation to a local charity (Note 10)	1,000	
Depreciation (Note 11)	2,500	
Legal expenses relating to issue of shares (Note 12)	1,500	
Increase in general allowance (Note 13)	50	
Loss on sale of non-current asset (Note 14)	70	23,570
Less: Income not taxable but included in the accounts		
Property income		(1,300)
Adjusted trading profits		**35,160**

Notes

These notes are given to explain the reasons for making the adjustments, and need not be given in an examination answer unless specifically requested for by the examiner. However, it is recommended that if there are any workings, you should show them so that the maximum marks can be scored.

1. Entertaining employees is allowable but entertaining **customers, suppliers** or anyone else is **not allowable.**
2. The legal and professional charge for the purchase of new machinery is in relation to an item of capital expenditure, hence disallowed. This will be added to the cost of the new machinery and capital allowance will be allowed on the entire cost of machinery.
3. Legal and professional charges incurred for collection from trade debtors, obtaining bank loan and registering the company's trademark are allowed as they are related to the business and are revenue in nature.
4. Legal costs incurred on renewing a 30-year lease are allowed as they relate to short term lease (less than 50 years).
5. Gifts and entertainment expenditure for the employees are fully allowable.
6. Gifts to customers are deductible as expenses **only if:**

   - they cost less than £50 per recipient per year;
   - they are not food, drink, tobacco or vouchers exchangeable for goods or services; and
   - they carry a conspicuous advertisement for the company making the gifts.

   Christmas gift vouchers for 10 customers are not allowable as they **cost more than £50** per person. However, Christmas gifts to customers of 15 watches, with company name engraved (costing £45 each) is allowable as it fulfills all the above three conditions.
7. Cash donation made to a political party is never deductible.
8. Cash donation to UNICEF is also not deductible as it is not given to a local charity.
9. Cash donation to local charity is deductible as it is small in amount, given to a local charity and benefits the company.
10. Qualifying charitable donation to local charity is not deductible but tax relief is given as a deduction from total income.
11. Depreciation is never deductible and hence, added back.
12. As the legal expenses relate to the issue of shares, these are considered to be capital expenses and hence are not deductible.
13. General allowances are never deductible.
14. Loss on sale of non-current assets is not deductible from trading profits as it is a capital loss. Hence, it is added back.
15. Salaries paid to directors are allowed as no adjustments are made for private use in the case of companies.

Answer to TY 2

Expenses	Deductible / non-deductible	Reason
Rent for the office and warehouse used for business	Deductible	Being incurred not more than 7 years before the date of actual trading and revenue in nature
Purchase of own office place and permanent warehouse	Not deductible	Being capital expenditure. However, capital allowance will be available as it is treated as incurred on 1 December 2012 (first day of trade)
Legal charges for purchase of office place and warehouse	Not deductible	Relates to a capital asset. It will be added to the cost of office and warehouse.
Marketing and advertising expenses	Deductible	Being normal trading expenses
Land purchased for business use	Not deductible	Being capital expenses and incurred more than 7 years before commencement of trade.

Answer to TY 3

1. Expenditure on computer hardware is always eligible for capital allowance.
2. When software forms part of the computer (such as operating systems, utility programs) it is considered plant and machinery for the purposes of capital allowance. However if software is acquired on a rental basis, rent is charged against the profit for the tax year. Hence, it is not eligible for capital allowance purposes.
3. Plant purchased on a hire purchase basis is eligible for capital allowance purposes. The cash price of the plant is considered to be expenditure on plant and machinery and is eligible for capital allowance purposes as soon as the plant comes into use. However, hire purchase charges (e.g. interest) are not eligible for capital allowance purposes as they are charged against the profit.
4. An old railway wagon is used for conducting primary school classes. In effect, it is used merely as a structure. It does not perform an active role in the functioning of the school. Hence, it is not considered to be plant for capital allowance purposes.
5. In an ice factory, a cold storage building is essential for storing ice once it is manufactured. Therefore the cold storage building performs an active role in the functioning of the factory. It is therefore considered to be plant for capital allowance purposes.

Answer to TY 4

	AIA £	General Pool £	Allowances £
Year ended 31 March 2013			
Additions qualifying for AIA			
Plant	80,000		
Machinery	42,000		
	122,000		
Less: AIA (Note 1)	(25,000)	97,000	25,000
Additions not qualifying for AIA			
Car (Note 2)		9,000	
		106,000	
Less: WDA at 18%		(19,080)	19,080
TWDV c/f		86,920	
Allowances			**44,080**
Year ended 31 March 2014			
TWDV b/f		86,920	
Additions		-	
Less: WDA @18%		(15,646)	15,646
TWDV c/f		**71,274**	
Allowances			**15,646**

Notes

1. The expenditure incurred during the year by any business on plant and machinery except cars is eligible for annual investment allowance up to a limit of £25,000.
2. As the CO_2 emissions of the car purchased is between 110g/km and 160g/km, it is eligible for WDA at the rate of 18% per annum.

Answer to TY 5

Speed Ltd's first accounting period is of twenty months (period between January 2012 and August 2013). This period of twenty months must be split into two accounting periods for corporation tax purposes.

The first chargeable period will be of twelve months (ending on 31 December 2012) and the second period will be of eight months (ending on 31 August 2013).

Calculation of the capital allowance is as follows:

	AIA £	General Pool £	Allowance £
Year ended 31 December 2012			
Additions qualifying for AIA			
Plant	105,000		
Equipment	27,500		
	132,500		
Less: AIA	(25,000)	107,500	25,000
Less: WDA 18%		(19,350)	19,350
TWDV c/f		**88,150**	
Total capital allowance			**44,350**
8 months to 31 August 2013			
TWDV c/f		88,150	
Additions qualifying for AIA			
Machinery	78,000		
Less: AIA (£25,000 x 8/12) (note 2)	(16,667)	61,333	16,667
		149,483	
Less: WDA 18% (£149,483 x 18% x 8/12)		(17,938)	17,938
TWDV c/f		**131,545**	
Total allowances			**34,605**

Notes

1. The expenditure incurred by any business on plant and machinery except cars is eligible for annual investment allowance at 100% up to an annual limit of £25,000.
2. AIA and WDA is scaled up or down according to the length of the accounting period.

Answer to TY 6

Best Ltd's first period of account is of eighteen months (period between January 2012 and June 2013). This eighteen month period must be split into two accounting periods for corporation tax purposes.

The first chargeable period will be of twelve months (ended on 31 December 2012) and the second period will be of six months (ended on 30 June 2013).

Calculation of the capital allowance is as follows:

	FYA £	General Pool £	Special rate pool £	Allowance £
Year ended 31 December 2012				
Additions not qualifying for AIA			-	
Low emission car (Note 1)	18,000			
Less: FYA 100% (Note 1)	(18,000)	-		18,000
Car (Note 2)			21,000	
Less: WDA @ 8%			(1,680)	1,680
TWDV c/f	**NIL**	**-**	**19,320**	
Total Capital Allowances				**19,680**
6 months to 30 June 2013				
TWDV b/f			19,320	
Additions not qualifying for AIA				
Car (Note 3)		10,000		
Less: WDA @ 18%/ 8% for 6 months (Note 4)		(900)	(773)	1,673
TWDA c/f		**9,100**	**18,547**	
Total capital allowances				**1,673**

Notes

1. Cars with CO_2 emissions of less than 110g/km are known as low emission cars and are eligible for a 100% first year allowance regardless of the cost of the car and length of the accounting period.

2. Cars with CO_2 emissions exceeding 160g/km are included in the special rate pool and WDA is available at the rate of 8%

3. Cars with CO_2 emissions between 110g/km and 160g/km are included in the general pool and WDA is available at the rate of 18%.

4. WDA is scaled up or down according to the length of the accounting period.

Answer to TY 7

	FYA £	General Pool £	Expensive Motor car £	Allowances £
Year ended 30 June 2013				
TWDV b/f		15,200	7,400	
Additions qualifying for AIA				
Plant	165,000			
Less: AIA	(25,000)	} 140,000		25,000
Less: Disposal (lower of cost and sale proceeds)			(5,000)	
		155,200		
Less: WDA 18%		(27,936)		27,936
TWDV c/f		**127,264**		52,936
Balancing allowance (note 2)			**2,400**	2,400
Total capital allowances				**55,336**

Notes

1. Expensive motor cars do not join the pool. Capital allowance on expensive cars is calculated on an individual basis.

2. On the disposal of an asset, if the disposal proceeds are less than the TWDV, then a balancing allowance is given.

3. The expenditure incurred by any business on plant and machinery except cars in an accounting period is eligible for annual investment allowance at 100% up to an annual limit of £25,000.

Answer to TY 8

	Short life asset £	Allowance £
Year ended 30 June 2012		
Additions qualifying for AIA		
Plant	112,000	
Less: AIA	(25,000)	25,000
	87,000	
Less: WDA 18%	(15,660)	15,660
TWDV c/f	**71,340**	
Allowances		**40,660**
Year ended 30 June 2013		
TWDV b/f	71,340	
Less: Disposal value	(7,500)	
Balancing allowance	**63,840**	

Notes

1. Short life assets are not pooled. For capital allowance purposes, these assets are considered separately.

2. AIA is available to all businesses for expenditure on plant and machinery at 100% up to a limit of £25,000.

3. If the disposal value of the asset is less than TWDV, a balancing allowance arises which is deducted from tax-adjusted trading profits.

Answer to TY 9

Calculation of capital allowance in relation to long life asset

	Special rate pool £	Allowance £
Year ended 31 October 2012		
TWDV b/f	-	
Additions qualifying for AIA		
Machinery	150,000	
Less: AIA	(25,000)	25,000
	125,000	
Less: WDA @ 8%	(10,000)	10,000
TWDV c/f	**115,000**	
Total capital allowance		**35,000**
Year ended 31 October 2013		
TWDV b/f	115,000	
Less: WDA @8%	(9,200)	9,200
TWDV c/f	**105,800**	
Total capital allowance		**9,200**

Notes

1. An asset with a life of 25 years or more is only treated as a long life asset if the expenditure on such asset exceeds £25,000 in the accounting period. For capital allowance purposes, these assets are considered separately in a special rate pool.

2. AIA is available on long life asset (special rate pool asset) at 100% up to a limit of £25,000, and above this limit, it is chargeable for WDA @ 8%.

Answer to TY 10

= P - P x (2% x (n -1))
Where, P = Premium and n = period of lease

	£	£
Premium assessable to property business income		
Premium received by Face Ltd	40,000	
Less: £40,000 x (2% x (15 - 1))	(11,200)	28,800
Less: Allowance for premium paid by Face Ltd (W1)		(6,240)
Premium treated as rent		**22,560**

Workings

W1 Allowance for premium paid

	£
Premium paid by Face Ltd	20,000
Less: £20,000 x (2% x (25 - 1))	(9,600)
	10,400

This amount paid will be reduced in the following ratio
= Portion of head lease premium treated as rent x sublease duration / head lease duration
= £10,400 x 15 / 25
= £6,240

Answer to TY 11

	£
Lease premium received (office 1)	25,000
Less: £25,000 x (2% x (20 - 1))	(9,500)
Premium treated as rent	**15,500**
Rent (office 1) £5,100 x 8/12 (W1)	3,400
Rent (office 2) (W2)	700
	19,600
Less: Expenses	
Repairs	(600)
Insurance (£600 x 2 as 2 offices)	(1,200)
Advertisement expenses	(150)
Property income	**17,650**

Workings

W1 Office 1 was let out for 8 months (from 01/08/2012 to 31/03/2013) during the year.

W2 Office 2

£1,200 x 4/12 (from 01/05/2012 to 31/08/2012) = £400

£1,800 x 2/12 (from 01/02/2013 to 31/03/2013) = £300

£700

Note: The interest on the loan is dealt with under the loan relationship rules. It is not a property business expense.

Answer to TY 12

The bank interest is income from a non-trading loan relationship and is assessed on the accrual basis.

The amount assessable for the year is **£10,100** (£8,200 received + £1,900 receivable)

Answer to TY 13

	£
Trading income	25,300
Property income	11,000
Income from loan relationship (W1)	24,190
Chargeable gains	40,000
Taxable total profits	**100,490**

Workings

W1
Bank interest and interest on government securities is income from a non-trading loan relationship and is assessed on the accrual basis.

	£
Bank interest received	5,600
Add: Receivable at the end of the year	890
Less: Receivable at the start of the year	(300)
	6,190
Government securities interest received	12,000
Add: Accrued (from 1 January 2014 to 31 March 2014)	6,000
	18,000

Total income from loan relationship (£6,190 + £18,000) = **£24,190**

Answer to TY 14

	£
Trading income	25,300
Property income	11,000
Income from loan relationship (W1)	24,190
Chargeable gains	40,000
	100,490
Less: Qualifying charitable donation	(12,000)
Taxable total profits	**88,490**

Quick Quiz

1. Are dividends paid deductible for arriving at the taxable total profits?
2. Better Enterprises Ltd incurred the expenditure below:

	£
Depreciation on building	30,000
Depreciation on machinery	14,000
New office constructed near existing building	21,000
Repairs to machinery	9,000

Which expenditure is deductible for computation of trading profits?

Answers to Quick Quiz

1. No, dividends paid are not included in any calculation.
2. Only repairs to machinery (£9,000) are allowable. The new office constructed is a capital expenditure hence not deductible. Depreciation is never deductible.

Self Examination Questions

Question 1

The statement of profit or loss of OK Ltd for the year ended 31 March 2013 is given below. Calculate trading profits.

	£	£
Gross operating profit		81,050
Expenses		
Office salaries and expenses	16,000	
Advertising and selling expenses	5,000	
Donation to a political party	7,000	
Depreciation on building and furniture	6,500	
Expenses of lunch given to customers on company annual day	6,600	
Professional fees paid for collection from trade debtors	2,350	(43,450)
Net profit before taxation		**37,600**

Question 2

Given below is the statement of profit or loss of Wonderful Ltd for the year ended 31 March 2013. You are required to calculate the trading profits of Wonderful Ltd.

	£	£
Gross operating profit		211,930
Salaries	36,800	
Depreciation	23,070	
Bad debts written off	2,120	
Property income	18,200	
Legal expenses relating to issue of shares	3,500	
Entertainment of customers	5,320	
Loss on sale of non-current assets	710	(53,320)
Net Profit		**158,610**

Question 3

Delicious Ltd prepares its accounts up to 31 March every year. The company owns two warehouses, and an office, which it rents out. Rent of the property is due quarterly in advance on 1 January, 1 April and so on. The details of property rented out during the year ended on 31/03/2013 are as follows:

1. Warehouse 1 was let out at £8,900 p.a. throughout the year.
2. Warehouse 2 was let out at £5,400 p.a. from 1 May 2012. The company received a premium of £50,000 for the grant of 15 years' lease.
3. Office was let out until 31 December 2012 at an annual rent of £3,600 p.a. On that date, the tenant left without paying three months rent which the company is not able to recover.

Delicious Ltd incurs the following expenses:

(a) repairs of warehouse 1 in January 2013, £3,900
(b) insurance per warehouse £1,300 p.a., for office £2,350
(c) interest on loan taken to purchase warehouse 2, £3,200
(d) advertisement expenses for obtaining tenants for warehouse 2, £2,600

Required:

Calculate property business income of Delicious Ltd.

Answers to Self Examination Questions

Answer to SEQ 1

	£	£
Net Profits given in Accounts		37,600
Add:		
(i) Expenditure shown in the accounts but not deductible for tax purposes		
Donation to a political party	7,000	
Depreciation on building and furniture	6,500	
Expenses of lunch given to customers on company annual day	6,600	20,100
Adjusted trading profits		**57,700**

Answer to SEQ 2

	£
Net Profits given in Accounts	158,610
Add:	
(i) Expenditure shown in the accounts but not deductible for tax purpose	
Depreciation (W1)	23,070
Legal expenses relating to issue of shares (W2)	3,500
Entertainment of customers (W3)	5,320
Loss on sale of non-current asset (W4)	710
	191,210
Less:	
(ii) Income not taxable but included in the accounts	
Property income	(18,200)
Adjusted trading profits	**173,010**

Notes

1. Depreciation is never deductible hence added back.
2. As the legal expenses relate to the issue of shares, these are considered to be capital expenses and hence not deductible.
3. Entertaining employees is allowable but entertaining customers, suppliers or anyone else is not allowable.
4. Loss on sale of a non-current asset is not deductible in the calculation of trading profits.

Answer to SEQ 3

		Warehouse 1 £	Warehouse 2 £	Office £	Total £
Rent accrued					
1. Warehouse 1		8,900			8,900
2. Warehouse 2 (01/05/2012 to 31/03/2013)					
(£5,400/12 x 11)			4,950		4,950
Lease premium received	£50,000				
Less: £50,000 x (2% x (15-1))	(£14,000)		36,000		36,000
Office (£3,600 x 9/12)				2,700	2,700
Total rent accrued (a)		**8,900**	**40,950**	**2,700**	**52,550**
Expenses					
1. Repairs		3,900			3,900
2. Insurance		1,300	1,300	2,350	4,950
3. Advertising expenses for obtaining tenants			2,600		2,600
4. Bad debts (£3,600 x 3/12)				900	900
Total expenses incurred (b)		**5,200**	**3,900**	**3,250**	**12,350**
Property business profit (a – b)		**3,700**	**37,050**	**(550)**	**40,200**

The net property business profit is £40,200.

Note: interest on loan taken to purchase warehouse is dealt with under loan relationship.

STUDY GUIDE D2: TAXABLE TOTAL PROFITS (PART 2)

Get Through Intro

The **main job of a tax consultant** is to advise his client on how to make **optimal use** of **all the provisions of the Income Tax Act,** which will help the client **minimise his tax liability.**

A thorough knowledge of all the provisions related to this topic becomes imperative, if 'relief for trading losses' is to be used **as the effective tax planning tool that it is.**

You should devote a considerable amount of time to the study of this topic, so that you become fully aware of all the intricacies of this effective tax planning provision. Needless to say, it is also frequently examined!

Learning Outcomes

g) Understand how trading losses can be carried forward.
h) Understand how trading losses can be claimed against income of the current or previous accounting periods.
i) Recognise the factors that will influence the choice of loss relief claim.
j) Explain how relief for a property business loss is given.
k) Compute taxable total profits.

Introduction

A trading loss occurs when a trader's adjusted profit after capital allowances gives a negative figure. It can also arise by capital allowances either creating a loss (turning a trading profit into a loss) or increasing a loss.

Points to note:

- The trading income assessment for the current accounting period will be nil – never put a negative figure as trading income.
- Relief is available for the loss.

Different reliefs are available in the current accounting period (reducing the current liability) in the previous 12 months (therefore generating a refund of tax) and in future accounting periods (reducing a future liability, and therefore delaying relief).

A special relief is available in the final 12 months of trade.

Overview:

Main reliefs

Section 45 CTA 2010 (previously referred to as Section 393(1) ICTA 1988)

Trading loss carried forward and relieved against future trading profits of the same trade.

Section 37 CTA 2010 (previously referred to as Section 393A (1) ICTA 1988)

Trading loss relieved against total profits before Qualifying charitable donations of the current accounting period and then against total profits of the previous 12 months.

Section 39 CTA 2010 (previously referred to as Section 393A ICTA 1988)

On cessation of trade, the carry back period is extended to 36 months.

The government is under the process of rewriting the Income and Corporation Taxes Act 1988 (ICTA 1988) into plain English. The writing of the part which is relevant for paper F6 is complete, and accordingly, the section numbers and some of the important terminologies have changed. The new act will now be referred to as Corporation Tax Act 2010 (CTA 2010).

Section numbers (both old and new) have been given for ease of identifying loss reliefs, but candidates will not be expected to quote section numbers as part of their answer in the exam.

In this Study Guide we will see various provisions such as carry forward of trading losses, reliefs available for trading losses against incomes of previous or current accounting periods etc.

1. Understand how trading losses can be carried forward.[2]

[Learning Outcome g]

1.1 Section 45 CTA 2010: Relief against future trading profits

1. Loss carried forward can **only be set off against future trading profits**, **not against any other income.**
2. The **set off must** be **against the first available trading profit.**
3. It is **not possible to restrict the set off** of the loss.
4. The relief is against future trading profits of the same trade. If there is any change in the nature of the business or if the company starts a new business then it cannot claim the relief for trading loss against the income from the changed or new business.

Example

Extraction Plc is in the business of extracting oil from various seeds such as coconut and groundnut. In the years ended on 31 March 2012 and 31 March 2013 the company incurred losses of £38,000 and £64,000 respectively.

In October 2012, the company started manufacturing cosmetics. In the first year, the company earned a profit of £51,500 from the cosmetics business.

However, as the activities conducted by both the businesses are different, **Extraction Plc cannot claim relief for loss from the oil business against the cosmetics business.**

---

5. There is **no time limit on the carry forward.** It may be carried forward until there are future trading profits.
6. It is **not necessary to claim** this relief. It **is automatically** done if a loss remains after other reliefs, if any, have been claimed.
7. Loss relief is delayed as it means a reduction in future liability.

Example

For the year ended on 31 March 2011, Citizen Ltd incurred a trading loss of £280,000. The company wants to set off losses under section 45. The company's trading results for the next two years are as follows:

	Year ended 31 March 2012 **£**	**Year ended 31 March 2013** **£**
Trading profits	132,400	144,590
Property income	8,000	8,000
Chargeable gains	-	27,500

The calculation of the company's taxable total profits for the year ended on 31 March 2012 and 31 March 2013 after the set off of the trading losses is as follows-

	Year ended 31 March 2012 **£**	**Year ended 31 March 2013** **£**
Trading profits	132,400	144,590
Less: Relief s 45	(132,400)	(144,590)
	0	0
Property income	8,000	8,000
Chargeable gains	0	27,500
Taxable total profits	**8,000**	**35,500**

Notes

1. The trading loss of the year ended on 31 March 2011 is carried forward and set off against future trading profits.
2. Under section 45, the loss is set off against the future trading profits only and not against any other income (i.e. in this case against property income or chargeable gains).
3. **Loss memorandum**

Year		**£**
Year ended 31 March 2011	Loss for the year	280,000
Year ended 31 March 2012	Loss set off	(132,400)
	Loss c/f	**147,600**
Year ended 31 March 2013	Loss set off	(144,590)
	Loss carried forward	**3,010**

The trading loss of £3,010 is carried forward to the future year to be set off against the first available trading profits of the same trade in the future.

SUMMARY

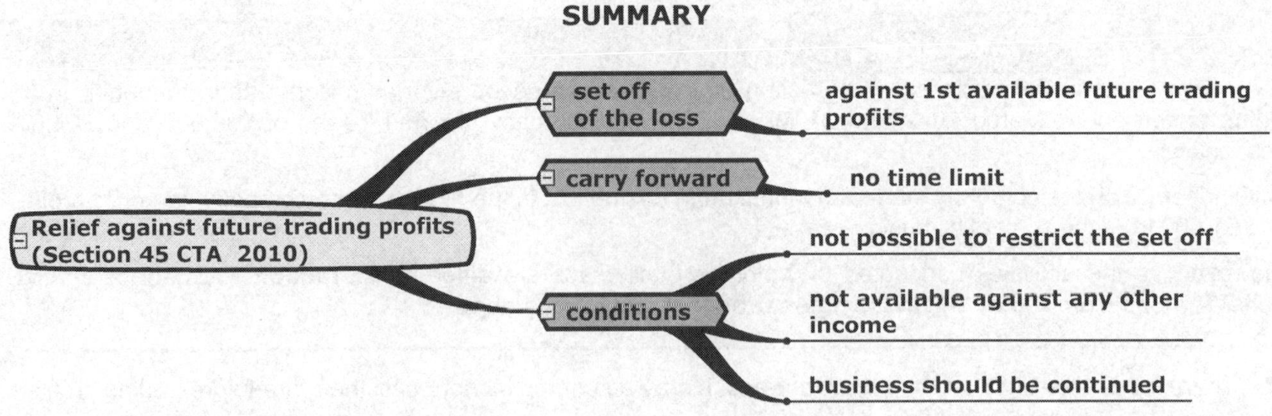

The following are the trading results of Comfort Ltd:

	Year ended 31 December 2010 £	Year ended 31 December 2011 £	Year ended 31 December 2012 £
Trading profits	(347,400)	157,200	248,700
Property income	100,000	100,000	100,000
Chargeable gains	120,000	-	-

Assume that Comfort Ltd wants to carry forward its trading loss under section 45.

Required:

Calculate the taxable total profits of the company for the three years.

---

2. Understand how trading losses can be claimed against income of the current and previous accounting periods.[2]

[Learning Outcome h]

2.1 Section 37 CTA 2010 – relief against total profits of the current accounting period and then against total profits of the previous 12 months

1. Current year loss relief

A trading loss arising in an accounting period may be set off against **total profits before deducting qualifying charitable donations payments of the loss-making accounting period. Qualifying charitable donations** may remain **unrelieved**. In short, the loss should be set off first.

The following are the results of Tamco Ltd for the year ended 31 December 2012

	£
Trading loss before deducting Qualifying charitable donations	(40,000)
Property business profits	10,000
Building society interest receivable	10,000
Chargeable gains	48,000

During the year ended on 31 December 2012, the company paid £32,000 towards Qualifying charitable donations.

In this situation **'total profits'** for section 37 are:

Continued on the next page

	£
Trading profits	-
Property business income	10,000
Income from loan relationship	10,000
Chargeable gains	48,000
Total profits before qualifying charitable donation payments	**68,000**

Taxable total profit calculations will be as follows

	£
Total profits	**68,000**
Less: Relief s.37	(40,000)
	28,000
Less: Qualifying charitable donation	(28,000)
Taxable total profits	0

Note: Qualifying charitable donations of £4,000 (£32,000 - £28,000) are unrelieved.

Test Yourself 2

Zenta Ltd gives its trading results for the year ended to 31 March 2013 as follows:

	£
Trading loss	(32,000)
Building society interest	3,500
Chargeable gains	21,000
Property business profits	20,000
Qualifying charitable donation	2,000

Required:

Calculate the taxable total profits for the year.

2. Carry back loss relief

Once a claim has been made against total profits of the loss-making accounting period, a **further claim** may be made to relieve any remaining loss **against the total profits of the previous 12 months**.

PROFORMA

	£
Trading profit	X
Less: Trading loss brought forward	(X)
	X
Property business profit	X
Chargeable gains	X
	X
Less: Current year loss relief	(X)
Less: Carry back loss relief	(X)
	X
Less: Qualifying charitable donation	(X)
Taxable total profits	**X**

Extended loss relief

The Finance Act 2009 had extended the carry back period of relief for the losses arising during the accounting periods (AP) ending between **24 November 2008 and 23 November 2010**. The relief for losses of these accounting periods can be claimed against the total profits of the previous **36 months** i.e. the carry back period is extended from 12 months to 36 months (i.e. further 24 months), taking the latest accounting period first.

The **maximum amount of relief** that can be claimed against the total profits of the extended period of 24 months is **£50,000.** However, there is no limit for claiming relief against the total profits of the previous 12 months.

The examiner has stated that no question involving extended loss relief will be set in the exams.

While calculating carry back loss relief, the following situations can arise on the basis of the length of the accounting period:

a) If the loss making accounting period and carry back period both are exactly 12 months long

Tetra Pack Ltd has the following results for two accounting periods

	Year ended 31 March 2012 **£**	**Year ended 31 March 2013** **£**
Trading profits / (loss)	150,150	(74,000)
Rental income	20,000	20,000
Chargeable gains	8,000	12,000
Qualifying charitable donation	10,000	10,000

Assuming that the company has made claim under section 37 for both the years, the company's taxable total profits for these two years are as follows:

	Year ended 31 March 2012 **£**	**Year ended 31 March 2013** **£**
Trading profit	150,150	–
Less: Trading loss brought forward	–	–
	150,150	**–**
Property business profit	20,000	20,000
Chargeable gains	8,000	12,000
Total income	**178,150**	**32,000**
Less: Current year loss relief	–	(32,000)
Less: Carry back loss relief	(42,000)	–
	136,150	**–**
Less: Qualifying charitable donation	(10,000)	–
Taxable total profits	**126,150**	**–**

Workings

W1 Loss memorandum

		£
Year ended 31 March 2013	Loss incurred	74,000
Year ended 31 March 2013	Less: Relief s.37	(32,000)
	Balance	**42,000**
Year ended 31 March 2013	Less: Relief s.37	(42,000)
	Balance	**0**

Note: Qualifying charitable donations paid of £10,000 for the year ended 31 March 2013 are unrelieved.

b) If the loss-making accounting period is less than 12 months; the amount carried back is not restricted.

Kiwi Ltd has given the following results:

	Year ended 30 June 2012 £	9 months to 31 March 2013 £
Trading profits	21,000	(18,000)
Property business profits	12,000	10,000
Chargeable gains	6,000	7,000
Qualifying charitable donation	(1,100)	(1,400)

The company has brought forward a trading loss of £4,000 on 1 July 2011.

Calculation of taxable total profits after relief under section 37 is as follows:

	Year ended 30 June 2012 £	9 months to 31 March 2013 £
Trading profit	21,000	-
Less: Trading loss brought forward	(4,000)	-
	17,000	-
Property business profit	12,000	10,000
Chargeable gains	6,000	7,000
	35,000	**17,000**
Less: Current year loss relief s.37	-	(17,000)
Less: Carry back loss relief s.37	(1,000)	
	34,000	-
Qualifying Charitable donations	(1,100)	-
Taxable total profits	**32,900**	-

Workings

W1 Loss memorandum

		£
9 months to 31 March 2013	Loss incurred	18,000
9 months to 31 March 2013	**Less:** Relief section 37	(17,000)
	Balance	**1,000**
Year ended 30 June 2012	**Less:** Relief section 37	(1,000)
	Balance	0

Note: Qualifying charitable donation is paid of £1,400 for the 9 months period ended 31 March 2013 are unrelieved.

---

c) If the carry back period is not 12 months, it may be necessary to apportion the total profits figure.

Moon Plc's results are as follows:

Accounting period	1/05/2011 to 31/7/2012 £	Year ended 31/7/2013 £
Trading profits	30,000	(65,000)
Bank interest	-	5,000

Current year loss is £5,000, Assuming that the company claims relief for trading losses under section 37, unrelieved loss is calculated as follows:

Under section 37, relief is first against the **total profit of the current accounting period.**

Continued on the next page

The unrelieved loss after considering the current year loss relief is: £65,000 - £5,000 **= £60,000**

This unrelieved loss may be **set off against** the **total profit of the 12 months prior to the loss making period** i.e. between the period 1 August 2011 and 31 July 2012.

However, the accounting period in which this 12 months period falls is of fifteen months. Therefore, it will be divided into two accounting periods, first accounting period of 12 months ended on 30/04/2012 and second accounting period of 3 months ended on 31/07/2012.

The loss should first be set off against profits for accounting period of 3 months from 01/05/2012 to 31/07/2012 which is £30,000/15 x 3 = £6,000

Then the balance can be set off against 9 months of the profit for the year ended on 30/04/2012 i.e. (£30,000 x 9/15) = £18,000.

	Year ended 30-Apr-12 £	**3 months to 31-Jul-12 £**	**Year ended 31-Jul-13 £**
Trading profit	24,000	6,000	-
Income from loan relationship	-		5,000
	24,000	**6,000**	**5,000**
Less: Current year loss relief	-	-	(5,000)
Less: Carry back loss relief	(18,000)	(6,000)	-
Taxable total profits	**6,000**	**0**	**0**

Therefore, the total carry back **loss relief** under section 37 is £24,000.

Loss memorandum

		£
Year ended 31 July 2013	Loss incurred	65,000
Year ended 31 July 2013	Less: Relief s.37 (Current year loss relief)	(5,000)
	Balance	**60,000**
3 months to 31 July 2012	Less: Relief s.37 (Carry back loss relief)	(6,000)
	Balance	**54,000**
Year ended 30 April 2012	Less: Relief s.37 (Carry back loss relief)	(18,000)
	Balance carried forward to be set off under section 45	**36,000**

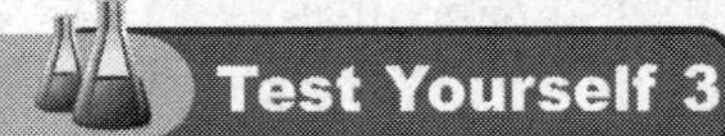

Magic Pot Ltd has given the following results for the three years:

	Year ended 31 March 2011 £	**Year ended 31 March 2012 £**	**Year ended 31 March 2013 £**
Trading profits	24,000	13,000	(45,000)
Property business income	10,000	10,000	10,000
Chargeable gains	--	3,000	-
Qualifying charitable donation	2,000	2,000	2,000

Required:

Assume the company has made claim for relief under section 37. Show the calculation of taxable total profits after set off of loss for the year ended 31 March 2013.

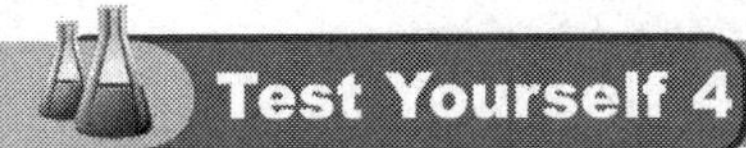

Sonja Ltd has the following financial results for the last three periods:

	Year ended 31 March 2011 £	Period ended 31 December 2011 £	Year ended 31 December 2012 £
Trading profits / (loss)	18,000	8,000	(18,000)
Bank interest	2,000	2,000	2,000

Required:

Show how it will set off its trading losses.

2.2 Other important points regarding relief under section 37 CTA 2010

1. The **carry back claim** is **only possible once a claim against the total profits of the current year has been made.** It is not compulsory to claim carry back relief. The company can claim current year relief and then can opt to carry the balance forward to set off against future trading profits of the same trade.
2. It is not possible to restrict the set off, e.g. to relieve qualifying charitable donations payments.
3. If no claim is made, under section 37 or trading loss remains after a claim, the remaining loss is carried forward under section 45 against future trading profits.
4. Claim for relief under s.37 must be made within 2 years from the end of the accounting period in which the loss arose.

If the loss arose in the year ended 31/12/2012, the claim must be made by 31/12/2014.

SUMMARY

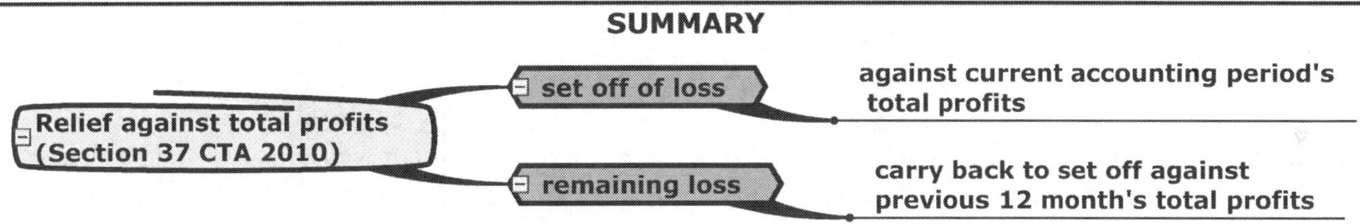

Terminal Loss Relief (Section 39 CTA 2010)

1. If a **loss arises in the last 12 months of trading**, the **carry back period** is **extended to 36 months.** It is referred to as terminal loss relief.

   The loss is set off against the **total profits** before deducting qualifying charitable donations payments **of the same accounting period,** and **then** against the **total profits** before deducting qualifying charitable donations payments of **the previous 36 months,** relieving against **later years first**.

Superior Ltd has been trading for many years, preparing accounts to 31 March every year. It ceased trading on 31 March 2013. The results for the last 5 years of trading were as follows:

	Year ended 31/03/2009 £	Year ended 31/03/2010 £	Year ended 31/03/2011 £	Year ended 31/03/2012 £	Year ended 31/03/2013 £
Trading profit / (loss)	197,000	234,000	176,000	58,000	(647,000)
Property business profits	6,800	12,000	8,000	4,200	4,000
Qualifying charitable donation	(10,500)	(10,500)	(10,500)	(10,500)	(10,500)

Continued on next page

We assume that the company claims the maximum possible relief for its trading losses.

Calculation of the **chargeable profits** is made as follows:

	Year ended 31/3/2009	Year ended 31/3/2010	Year ended 31/03/2011	Year ended 31/3/2012	Year ended 31/03/2013
	£	£	£	£	£
Trading profit	197,000	234,000	176,000	58,000	-
Property business profits	6,800	12,000	8,000	4,200	4,000
	203,800	**246,000**	**184,000**	**62,200**	**4,000**
Less: Current Year Loss relief	-	-	-	-	(4,000)
Less: Terminal loss relief for the loss incurred during the last 12 months of trading (i.e. year ended 31/03/2013)	-	(246,000)	(184,000)	(62,200)	
	203,800	-	-	-	-
Less: Qualifying charitable donation	(10,500)	-	-	-	-
Taxable total profits	**193,300**	0			

Note: terminal loss in the last 12 months of trading can be set off against total profits of the current accounting period and then against the total profits available of previous 36 months without any restriction, relieving the loss against the later years first.

Working

W1 Loss memorandum

		£
Year ended 31 March 2013	Loss incurred	647,000
Year ended 31 March 2013	Less: Current year relief s.37	(4,000)
	Balance	**643,000**
Year ended 31 March 2012	Less: Terminal loss relief s.39	(62,200)
	Balance	**580,800**
Year ended 31 March 2011	Less: Terminal loss relief s.39	(184,000)
	Balance	**396,800**
Year ended 31 March 2010	Less: Terminal loss relief s.39	(246,000)
	Unrelieved losses	**150,800**

2. If there are **losses in different periods**, they are **dealt with chronologically** i.e. claims are made for the **earlier loss before the later loss**.

3. If the **carry back periods before the loss-making period are not 12 months** – it may be necessary to **apportion the total profits figure.**

Example

Yamazaki Ltd prepares its accounts to 31 March every year. In April 2011, it has decided to change its accounting date to 31 July and prepares the accounts for the four months to 31 July 2011 and thereafter to 31 July every year. It ceased trading on 31 July 2012. The trading results for the last five accounting periods are as follows:

Continued on the next page

	Year ended 31/03/2009 £	Year ended 31/03/2010 £	Year ended 31/03/2011 £	Period ended 31/07/2011 £	Year ended 31/07/2012 £
Trading profit / (loss)	246,000	69,500	26,500	(50,200)	(350,200)
Property business profits	7,500	14,000	7,000	5,000	-
Capital gains	-	-	6,000	-	25,500
Qualifying charitable donation	(1,500)	(1,200)	-	-	(1,000)

To calculate the company's chargeable profits for the years ended 31 March 2009, 31 March 2010 and 31 March 2011, the four month period ended 31 July 2011, and the year ended 31 July 2012, we have to first calculate the profits available in the different years.

We assume that the company claims the maximum possible relief for its trading losses.

Calculation of the **chargeable profits** is made as follows:

	Year ended 31/03/2009 £	Year ended 31/03/2010 £	Year ended 31/03/2011 £	Period ended 31/07/2011 £	Year ended 31/07/2012 £
Trading profit / (loss)	246,000	69,500	26,500	-	-
Property business profits	7,500	14,000	7,000	5,000	-
Capital gains	-	-	6,000	-	25,500
	253,500	**83,500**	**39,500**	**5,000**	**25,500**
Less: Current year loss relief s.37 (note 1)	-	-	-	(5,000)	(25,500)
Less: Carry back loss relief s.37 (note 1)			(39,500)		
Less: Terminal loss relief s.39 (for year ended 31 July 2011) (notes 2 and 3)	(169,000)	(83,500)			
	84,500	**-**	-	-	-
Less: Qualifying charitable donation (note 4)	(1,500)	-	-	-	-
Taxable total profits	**83,000**	0	0	0	0

Loss Memorandum

	Period ended 31 July 2011 £	Year ended 31 July 2012 £
Loss for the period	50,200	350,200
Less: Loss relief		
Current year loss relief s.37 (note 1)	(5,000)	(25,500)
Carry back loss relief s.37 (previous 12 months) (note 1)	(39,500)	
Terminal loss relief (previous 36 months) (notes 2 and 3)		
1 April 2011 to 31 July 2011 — 4 months		-
Year ended 31 March 2011 — 12 months		-
Year ended 31 March 2010 — 12 months		(83,500)
1 August 2008 to 31 March 2009 — 8 months		(169,000)
36 months		
Unrelieved losses	**5,700**	**72,200**

Notes

1. Loss for the period ended 31 July 2011 may be set off only against total profits of the current AP and then against total profits of the previous 12 months (year ended 31 March 2011).

Continued on the next page

2. Terminal loss in the last 12 months of trading (year ended 31 July 2012) can be set off against total profits of the current AP and then against total profits available of previous 36 months (without any restriction) relieving the losses against the later years first.

3. For the year ended 31/03/2009, terminal loss relief available is restricted to £253,500 x 8/12 = £169,000.

4. Qualifying charitable donation of £1,200 and £1,000 for the years ended 31/03/2010 and 31/07/2012 respectively are unrelieved.

SUMMARY

Terminal loss relief (Section 39 CTA 2010)
- for loss arising in the last 12 months of trading
- carry back period extended to 36 months

3. Recognise the factors that will influence the choice of loss relief claim.[2]

[Learning Outcome i]

3.1 A company may claim relief for a trading loss under:

1. Section 45 i.e. trading losses are carried forward to be set off against **future trading profits** or

2. Section 37 (a) i.e. trading losses incurred during the accounting year are set off against **total profits of the same accounting period** and

3. Section 37 (b) i.e. trading losses incurred during the accounting year are set off against **total profits of the 12 month period prior to the loss-making period.**

3.2 Some of the **factors that will influence the choice of loss relief claim** are as follows:

a) **Corporation tax rate** in the year the loss was incurred and the future tax rates when the losses are set off (if there is a decreasing trend, companies normally tend to set off trading losses at the lower rates in order to reduce current tax bills).

b) **Expectations about the future trading profits** of the company.

c) **A company's cash flows** (i.e. where a company suffers from cash shortage, generally it is sensible to set off losses at the earliest and avoid cash outflows).

4. Explain how relief for a property business loss is given.[1]

[Learning Outcome j]

1. **All property income, receipts and expenses are pooled to give an overall profit or loss figure for the year. The losses from running one property business are automatically** set off against income from other property business.

2. **The net loss from running a property business is** first set off against non-property income and gains of the same accounting period.

3. **Any excess loss, which could not be set off as above, is carried forward to the next accounting period.**

4. **For the carry forward of property business losses, it is necessary that the property business** should continue **i.e. if a property-letting business has ceased, then the carry forward of the property business loss is not allowed.**

5. **The carried forward loss can be set off against the total profits of subsequent tax years.**

SUMMARY

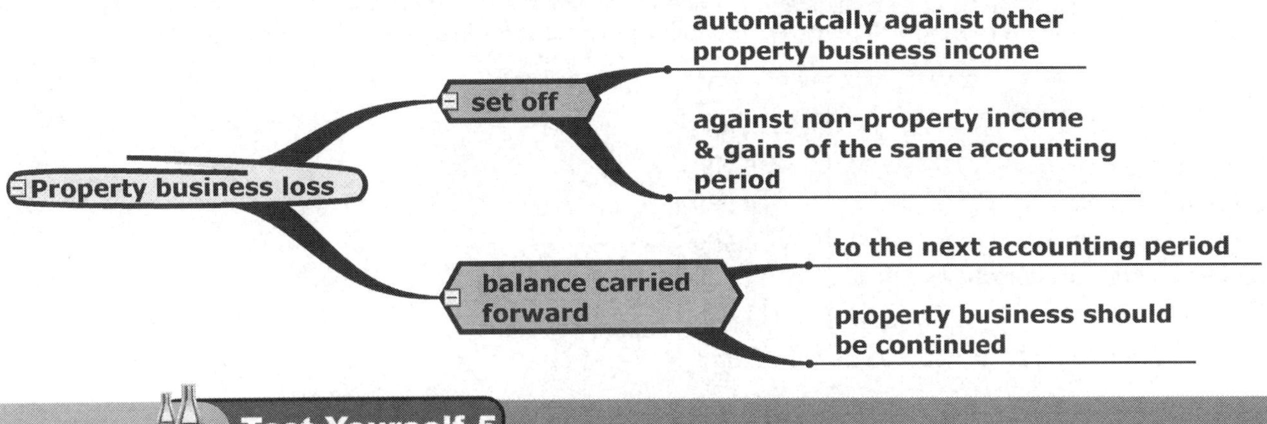

Test Yourself 5

Precious Ltd prepares its accounts to 31 March every year. Its trading profits for the year ended 31 March 2013 are £4,500 and it had received bank interest of £5,000. The company owns two shops, and an office which it had rented out. Rent on the property is due quarterly in advance on 1 January, 1 April and so on.

The details of property rented out during the year ended 31/03/2013 are as follows.

a) Shop 1 was let out at £3,800 p.a. throughout the year

b) Shop 2 was let out at £5,400 p.a. from 1 May 2012

c) Office was let out at £3,300 p.a. throughout the year

Precious Ltd incurs the following expenses.

a) Repairs of shop 1 in January 2013, £7,300

b) Insurance per shop £2,900 p.a., for office £2,350 p.a.

c) Interest on loan taken to purchase shop 2, £4,100

d) Advertisement expenses for obtaining tenants for shop 2, £2,200

Required:

Calculate the property business's income / loss. Explain the loss relief provisions, in the case of loss.

---

5. Compute taxable total profits.[2]

[Learning Outcome k]

After aggregating all trading income, property income, income from loan relationships, chargeable gains net of any capital losses and deducting qualifying charitable donations , the total income is the **taxable total profits (TTP)**.

We can present it as:

	£
1. Trading profits	X
Less: Brought forward trading losses	(X)
2. Property income	
3. Profits from loan relationship	
4. Profits from foreign securities and possessions	
5. Chargeable gains	X
Less: Allowable capital losses brought forward	**(X)**
Total income	
Less: Reliefs	
1. Property business losses	X
2. Trading losses relieved under s.37	X
3. Qualifying charitable donations	X
Taxable total profits (TTP)	

Test Yourself 6

Ding Dong Ltd, a manufacturing company has the following results for the year to 31 March 2013.

	£
Property income	15,500
Trading income	745,200
Bank interest (Note 1)	4,589
Loan interest receivable (Note 2)	2,400
Dividends from UK company	13,500
Chargeable gains	11,200
Qualifying charitable donation	21,000

Notes

1. Bank interest received in the year was £3,232. Of this, £1,000 was owed to the company at the start of the year. The corresponding amount at the end of the year was £2,357 but was not received until March 2013.

2. Gross loan interest of £1,850 was received during the year and a further £550 was owed to the company at the end of the year.

Required:

Calculate Ding Dong Ltd's taxable total profits for the year to 31 March 2013.

Test Yourself 7

Green Plant Ltd's statement of profit or loss for the year to 31 March 2013 is as follows.

	£	£
Gross trading profits		240,000
Other income		
Income from property (Note 4)	6,000	
Bad debts recovered (previously written off)	1,420	
Building society interest (gross)	2,100	9,520
		249,520
Expenses		
General expenses (Note 1)	60,112	
Directors' fees	30,000	
Repairs and renewals (Note 2)	12,000	
Bad debts written off	1,100	
Depreciation	23,100	
Registering patent	6,600	
Legal and accountancy charges (Note 3)	10,000	(142,912)
Net profit for the year before taxation		**106,608**

Notes

1. General expenses include £450 towards customers' entertainment and £1,000 towards donation to a political party.

2. Repairs and renewals include £200 towards refurbishing the premises and £300 towards constructing a new staff room.

3. Legal and accountancy charges are made up as follows.

Continued on the next page

	£
Collections from debtors	2,200
Purchasing land	2,300
Cost of renewing 45 year lease	4,500
Audit and accountancy	1,000
	10,000

4. The property was let out on 1 December 2012 at a rent of £2,000 per month payable in advance on 1 December, 1 March, 1 June and 1 September. There were no allowable expenses in the year to 31 March 2013.

Required:

Calculate Green Plant Ltd's taxable total profits for the year ended 31 March 2013.

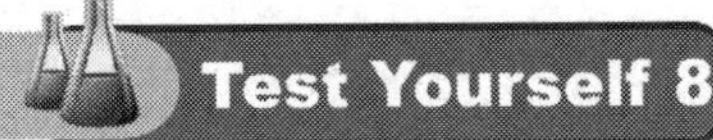

Test Yourself 8

Jasmine Ltd is a manufacturing company. The company's summarised the statement of profit or loss for the year ended 31 March 2013 is as follows:

	£	£
Gross profit		1,919,920
Other income		
Bank interest		14,400
		1,934,320
Expenses		
Bad debts written off (note 1)	14,230	
Professional fees (note 2)	20,150	
Depreciation	95,500	
Rent and rates (note 3)	121,480	
Gifts and donations (note 4)	5,930	
Other expenses (note 5)	197,630	
Qualifying charitable donations paid	12,000	(466,920)
		1,467,400
Finance costs		
Interest on loan notes paid (note 6)		(100,000)
Net profit before taxation		**1,367,400**

Notes

1. Bad debts are as follows

	£
Trade debts recovered from earlier years	(4,020)
Employee bad debts	4,250
Non-trade loans written off	14,000
	14,230

2. Professional fees are as follows

	£
Cost of registering trademark	1,900
Legal fees in connection with share capital	15,000
Audit fees	3,250
	20,150

Continued on the next page

3. Rent and rates include a premium of £45,000 paid on 1 April 2012 for the grant of a 15 years lease on an office building.
4. Gifts and donations include

	£
Gift of pens (£20 each) displaying name Jasmine Ltd	2,600
Donations to a political party	3,330
	5,930

5. Other expenses include Christmas party expenses of £7,500 for entertaining employees and £4,500 for entertaining customers. The remaining expenses are all allowable.
6. Bank interest was received on bank deposit held for non-trading purposes.
7. Loan notes interest was the actual amount paid during the year. The 10% loan notes for £1,000,000 were issued on 1 January 2011 to raise capital to build a new factory for manufacturing. The interest is payable half yearly on 30th September and 31st March each year.

Required:

Calculate Jasmine Ltd's taxable total profits for the year.

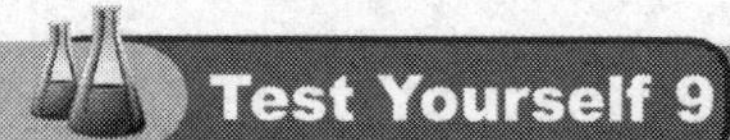

Test Yourself 9

Tasty Ltd's Net trading profits for the year ended 31 December 2012 were £482,500, calculated as follows:

	£	£
Gross profit		550,000
Expenses		
Depreciation	25,000	
Qualifying charitable donation paid	11,000	
Bad debt written off	9,500	
Penalties and fine	10,000	
General allowance for repairs	12,000	(67,500)
Net profit before taxation		**482,500**

Tasty Ltd's other income is as follows:

1. Tasty Ltd owned two warehouses. The first warehouse was let out from 1 April 2012 for an annual rent of £24,000. The company received a premium of £40,000 for grant of a 12 year lease. Rent is payable in advance on the first of every month.

The second warehouse was let until 30 September 2012 at an annual rent of £12,000. On that date, the tenant left without paying three months' rent which the company is not able to recover. The roof of the warehouse was repaired at a cost of £2,500 during October 2012. The company had taken a loan to purchase the warehouse. The interest paid on the loan was £2,000.

2. Loan notes interest received on 31 December 2012 was £35,000. Loan notes interest owed to the company at the end of the year is £5,000.

The details of the income from bank interest are as follows:

	£
Bank interest receivable on 1 January 2012	2,000
Bank interest received	6,000
Receivable on 31 December 2012	3,000

Required:

Calculate taxable total profits for the year ended 31 December 2012.

Answers to Test Yourself

Answer to TY 1

Step 1 Calculation of trading profits after relief under section 45

	Year ended 31-Dec-10 £	Year ended 31-Dec-11 £	Year ended 31-Dec-12 £
Trading profits	-	157,200	248,700
Less: Relief under s.45	-	(157,200)	(190,200)
Trading profits	**-**	**-**	**58,500**
Property income	100,000	100,000	100,000
Chargeable gains	120,000	-	-
Taxable total profits	**220,000**	**100,000**	**158,500**

Working

W1 Loss memorandum

Accounting periods		£
Year ended 31 December 2010	Loss for the year	347,400
Year ended 31 December 2011	Loss set off	(157,200)
	Balance	**190,200**
Year ended 31 December 2012	Loss set off	(190,200)
	Balance	-

Notes

1. The trading loss for the year ended on 31 December 2010 is carried forward to set off against future trading profits.

2. Under section 45, the loss is set off against the trading profits of the same trade only and not against any other income. (such as, in this case, property income, chargeable gains)

Answer to TY 2

Calculation of chargeable profits after set off of trading loss under s.37

	£
Income from loan relationship	3,500
Property business profits	20,000
Chargeable gains	21,000
Total profits	**44,500**
Less: Relief under s.37	(32,000)
Balance	12,500
Less: Qualifying charitable donation	(2,000)
Chargeable profits	**10,500**

Answer to TY 3

Calculation of taxable total profits after relief under section 37

	Year ended 31-Mar-11 £	Year ended 31-Mar-12 £	Year ended 31-Mar-13 £
Trading profit	24,000	13,000	-
Property business profit	10,000	10,000	10,000
Chargeable gains	-	3,000	-
	34,000	**26,000**	**10,000**
Less: Current year loss relief	-	-	(10,000)
Less: Carry back loss relief	-	(26,000)	
	34,000	-	-
Less: Qualifying charitable donation	(2,000)	-	-
Taxable total profits	**32,000**	-	-

Working

W1 Loss memorandum

		£
Year ended 31 March 2013	Loss incurred	45,000
Year ended 31 March 2013	Less: Relief s.37 (current year loss relief)	(10,000)
	Balance	**35,000**
Year ended 31 March 2012	Less: Relief s.37 (carry back loss relief)	(26,000)
	Balance carried forward to be set off under section 45	**9,000**

Note: relief under section 37 is available only against total profits of the current accounting period and then against total profits of previous 12 months .Hence, relief is not available against profits of the year ended 31 March 2011.

Answer to TY 4

	Year ended 31-Mar-11 £	Period ended 31-Dec-11 £	Year ended 31-Dec-12 £
Trading profit	18,000	8,000	-
Income from loan relationship	2,000	2,000	2,000
	20,000	**10,000**	**2,000**
Less: Current year loss relief	-	-	(2,000)
Less: Carry back loss relief	(5,000)	(10,000)	
Taxable total profits	**15,000**	-	-

Workings

W1

Sonja Ltd can claim relief against the profits of twelve months prior to the loss-making period (i.e. the period between 1 January 2011 and 31 December 2011). Out of these twelve months:

- nine months fall in the chargeable period ended 31 December 2011; and
- the remaining three months fall in the chargeable period ended 31 March 2011.

However, the period of the year ended 31 March 2011 is of 12 months. Hence, the proportionate profit for three months needs to be calculated.

The proportionate profit for three months = £20,000 x 3/12 = £5,000

Sonja Ltd can claim loss relief to the extent of £5,000 against the profits of the chargeable year ended 31 March 2011.

W2 Loss memorandum

		£
Year ended 31/12/2012	Trading loss incurred	18,000
Year ended 31/12/2012	Less: Relief s.37	(2,000)
	Balance	**16,000**
Period ended 31/12/2011	Less: Relief s.37	(10,000)
	Balance	**6,000**
Year ended 31/3/2011	Less: Relief s.37	(5,000)
	Balance carried forward s.45	**1,000**

Answer to TY 5

	Shop 1 £	Shop 2 £	Office £	Total £
Rent accrued				
Shop 1	3,800	-	-	3,800
Shop 2 (1/05/2012 to 31/03/2013) (£5,400 x 11/ 12)	-	4,950	-	4,950
Office	-	-	3,300	3,300
Total rent accrued	**3,800**	**4,950**	**3,300**	**12,050**
Less: Expenses				
1. Repairs	7,300			7,300
2. Insurance	2,900	2,900	2,350	8,150
3. Advertising expenses for obtaining tenants		2,200		2,200
Total expenses incurred	10,200	5,100	2,350	17,650
Property business loss	**(6,400)**	**(150)**	**950**	**(5,600)**

Note: the interest on the loan is dealt with under the loan relationship rules. It is not a property business expense.

Net property business loss is £5,600. **This £5,600 of property business loss can be first set off against current year non-property business income.**

Therefore, Precious Ltd's taxable total profits are as follows:

	£
Trading profits	4,500
Income from loan relationship (W1)	900
	5,400
Property income (restricted)	(5,400)
Taxable total profits	-

Excess loss of £200 (£5,600 - £5,400) which was not set off in the current accounting period can be carried forward to the next accounting period.

Such carried forward loss can be set off against the total income arising in subsequent accounting periods. Hence in the next accounting period, if Precious Ltd's total income is £6,500, then the carried forward loss of £200 will be first set off against it and the taxable income will be (£6,500 - £200 = £6,300).

For such carry forward of property business loss, it is necessary that the property business is continued. Therefore, if Precious Ltd ceases its property business then the carry forward of property business loss is not allowed.

W1 Income from loan relationship

	£
Bank interest received	5,000
Less: Interest on loan taken to purchase shop 2	(4,100)
	900

Answer to TY 6

	£
1. Trading profits	745,200
2. Property income	15,500
3. Income from loan relationship (£4,589 +£2,400) (W1 and W2)	6,989
4. Chargeable gains	11,200
	778,889
Less: Qualifying charitable donation	(21,000)
Taxable total profits (TTP)	**757,889**

Workings

W1

Bank interest of (£3,232 - £1,000 + £2,357) = **£4,589** is taxable for the year to 31 March 2013 under loan relationship. Because we follow the accrual basis, £1,000 must be accounted for in the previous year although it is actually received this year. Also, £2,357, although actually not received until March 2013, is accrued for the year and hence to be taken into consideration when calculating the chargeable profits for the year ended 31 March 2013.

W2

Loan interest: it is assumed that the loan was not made for trade purposes. Hence **£2,400** (£1,850 + £550) is part of income from loan relationships.

W3

The dividends from a UK company are franked investment income (discussed in detail in Learning Outcome 2 Study Guide D3) and do not form part of the company's taxable total profits.

Answer to TY 7

Computation of taxable total profits of Green plant Ltd

	£
1. Trading profits (W1)	125,658
2. Property income (W2)	8,000
3. Income from loan relationship	2,100
Taxable total profits (TTP)	**135,758**

Continued on the next page

Workings

W1 Trading profits

	£
Net Profits according to accounts	**106,608**
Add: 1. Expenditure shown in the accounts but not deductible for tax purposes:	
Depreciation (note 1)	23,100
Customer entertainment (note 2)	450
Donation to political party (note 3)	1,000
Construction of a new staff room (note 4)	300
Legal charges for purchasing a property (note 5)	2,300
	133,758
Less: Income not taxable as trading income included in the accounts	
Income from property	(6,000)
Building society interest	(2,100)
Trading profit	**125,658**

Notes

1. Depreciation is never deductible, hence added back.
2. Entertaining customers is not allowable.
3. Donations to a political party are not allowable.
4. Construction of a new staff room is a capital expenditure, hence not allowable.
5. Legal charges for purchasing land are capital expenditure and will be added to the cost of the land.

W2 Property income

Rent: 1 December 2012 to 31 March 2013

(£2,000 x 4) = £8,000

Answer to TY 8

Calculation of taxable total profits for Jasmine Ltd

	£
Trading profits (W1)	1,544,420
Income from loan relationship (W2)	14,400
	1,558,820
Qualifying charitable donation	(12,000)
Taxable total profits (TTP)	**1,546,820**

Workings

W1 Calculation of tax adjusted trading profits

	£	£
Net profit according to accounts		1,367,400
Add: Expenditure shown in the accounts but not deductible for tax purposes		
Employee bad debts and non-trade loans written off	18,250	
Professional fees in connection with issue of share capital (capital expenditure)	15,000	
Depreciation (not allowed)	95,500	
Premium for 25 year lease (W2)	45,000	
Qualifying charitable donations	12,000	
Donation to political party (not allowed)	3,330	
Entertaining customers (not allowed)	4,500	193,580
Less: Income not taxable as trading income included in the accounts		1,560,980
Short lease premium (W2)	(2,160)	
Bank Interest	(14,400)	(16,560)
Trading profits		**1,544,420**

Note: gifts (i.e. pens) displaying the company's name are allowed as they cost less than £50 per person per year and are not food, alcohol, tobacco or vouchers exchangeable for goods and carry a conspicuous advertisement for the business.

W2

The amount of premium assessed under property business income for the landlord is
= P – P x (2% x (n-1))
= £45,000 - £45,000 x (2% x (15 -1)) = £32,400

Jasmine Ltd can deduct £2,160 (£32,400/15) per annum when calculating its trading profits. Hence, the total amount of premium of £45,000 which was deducted as operating expenses from gross trading profits will be added back and the amount of £2160 will be deducted for calculation of tax adjusted trading profits.

Answer to TY 9

Calculation of taxable total profits

	£
Trading profits (W1)	540,500
Property income (W2)	52,700
Income from loan relationships (W3)	45,000
	638,200
Less: Qualifying charitable donation	(11,000)
Taxable total profits (TTP)	**627,200**

Workings

W1 Trading profits

	£	£
Net profit according to accounts		482,500
Add: 1. Expenditure shown in the accounts but not deductible for tax purposes:		
Depreciation	25,000	
Qualifying charitable donations	11,000	
Penalties and fines	10,000	
General allowance for repairs	12,000	58,000
Trading profits		**540,500**

Notes

1. As fines and penalties are not incurred exclusively for purpose of the trade, they are not deductible from trading profits.
2. General allowance for repairs is not allowable.

W2 Property income

	£	£
Property income		
Warehouse 1		
Premium	40,000	
Less: £40,000 x (2% x (12 -1))	(8,800)	
Premium treated as rent	31,200	
Rent (1 April 2012 to 31 December 2012)		
(£24,000 x 9/12)	18,000	**49,200**
Warehouse 2		
Rent (1 January 2012 to 30 September 2012)		
(£12,000 x 9/12)	9,000	
Less: Bad debts (three months' rent) (£12,000 x 3/12)	(3,000)	
Repair of roof	(2,500)	**3,500**
Property income		**52,700**

Note: interest on loan to purchase the warehouse is taken care of under loan relationship.

W3 Income from loan relationship

	£	£
Income from loan relationship		
Interest on loan notes	35,000	
Add: Receivable	5,000	40,000
Bank interest received	6,000	
Less: Receivable on 1 January 2012	(2,000)	
Add: Receivable on 31 December 2012	3,000	7,000
		47,000
Less: Interest paid on loan taken to purchase warehouse 2		(2,000)
Income from loan relationship		**45,000**

Quick Quiz

Fill in the blanks.

1. Under section 45 CTA 2010, trading loss can be carried forward and relieved against ________of the same trade.

2. On cessation of trade, the carry back period is extended to _________months.

3. Claim for relief under section 37 must be made within _________of the accounting period in which the loss arose.

Answers to Quick Quiz

1. future trading profit

2. 36

3. 2 years

Self Examination Questions

Question 1

Twins Ltd provides its financial results for the last three years:

	Year ended 31-Mar-11 £	Year ended 31-Mar-12 £	Year ended 31-Mar-13 £
Trading profits	(30,000)	25,000	47,500
Property income	5,000	10,000	10,000
Income from loan relationship	2,000	2,000	2,000

The company knew that loss was a temporary situation. As a result, the company wanted to claim relief for trading loss under s.45.

Required:

Calculate Twins Ltd's taxable total profits after relief under s.45.

Question 2

Power Ltd gives the following information for the year ended 31 March 2013

	£
Trading income	(90,100)
Rental income	14,000
Non-trade interest	2,000
Chargeable gains	78,400

The company has made Qualifying charitable donations totalling £5,000 during the year.

Required:

Show the calculation of taxable total profits assuming that the company has made a claim for relief under s.37.

Question 3

Sparks Ltd is a UK resident company that commenced trading on 1 July 2011 as a producer of electrical accessories. The company's results for the nine-month period ended 31 March 2012 were as follows

	£
Trading profit	192,500
Income from loan relationship	6,500
Qualifying charitable donations	(1,000)

The company's results for the year ended 31 March 2013 are as follows.

	£
Trading loss	(175,000)
Income from loan relationship	8,500
Chargeable gains	16,000

Required:

Calculate the chargeable profits of the company for both the accounting periods.

Question 4

Thunder Ltd is a manufacturer of ready-to-use electronic goods. The following information is available in respect of the year ended 30 September 2013.

Trading Loss

The trading loss is £85,000. (This amount is after taking account of capital allowances).

Property Income

Property income is £82,500. (This amount is after giving effect to rent receivable and bad debts).

Loan Interest Received

Loan interest of £10,000 was received on 30 June 2013, and £4,500 was accrued on 30 September 2013. The loan was made for non-trading purposes.

Required:

Calculate the company's chargeable profits assuming that the company claims relief for its trading loss against total profits under section 37 CTA 2010.

Question 5

Toss Ltd has the following results for the accounting period ended 30 June 2012.

	£
Trading loss	(41,200)
Bank interest	15,000
Chargeable gains	30,000
Qualifying chargeable donations	2,000

Required:

Assuming Toss Ltd made a claim for loss relief under section 37, calculate the company's taxable total profits for the year.

Question 6

During the accounting period ended on 31 March 2013 Music Ltd incurred a trading loss of £10,000. If the company wants to make a claim for relief under section 37, by which date should the company make this claim?

Answers to Self Examination Questions

Answer to SEQ 1

Calculation of taxable total profits after relief under s.45

	Year ended 31-Mar-11 £	Year ended 31-Mar-12 £	Year ended 31-Mar-13 £
Trading profits	-	25,000	47,500
Less: Relief under s.45	-	(25,000)	(5,000)
	-	-	**42,500**
Property income	5,000	10,000	10,000
Income from loan relationship	2,000	2,000	2,000
Taxable total profits	**7,000**	**12,000**	**54,500**

Working

W1 Loss memorandum

Accounting periods		£
Year ended 31 March 2011	Loss for the year	30,000
Year ended 31 March 2012	Loss set off	(25,000)
	Balance	**5,000**
Year ended 31 March 2013	Loss set off	(5,000)
	Balance	-

Answer to SEQ 2

	Year ended 31 March 2013 £
Trading profit	-
Property income	14,000
Income from loan relationship	2,000
Chargeable gains	78,400
	94,400
Less: Current year loss relief s.37	(90,100)
Less: Carry back loss relief s.37	-
	4,300
Less: Qualifying chargeable donation	(4,300)
Taxable total profits	-

Note: the company was able to relieve the qualifying charitable donations of £4,300. The remaining amount of £700 (£5,000 – £4,300) cannot be relieved.

Answer to SEQ 3

	Period ended 31 March 2012 £	**Year ended 31 March 2013 £**
Trading profit	192,500	
Income from loan relationship	6,500	8,500
Chargeable gains	-	16,000
	199,000	**24,500**
Less: Current year loss relief s.37		(24,500)
Less: Carry back loss relief s.37	(150,500)	
	48,500	-
Less: Qualifying charitable donations	(1,000)	
Taxable total profits	**47,500**	-

Working

W1 Loss memorandum

		£
Year ended 31 March 2013	Loss incurred	175,000
Year ended 31 March 2013	Less: Current year relief s.37	(24,500)
	Balance	**150,500**
Period ended 31 March 2012	Less: Carry back relief s.37	(150,500)
	Balance carried forward to be set off under s.45	-

Answer to SEQ 4

Calculation of chargeable profits of Thunder Ltd for the year ended 30 September 2013

	£
Property income	82,500
Income from loan relationship (£10,000 + £4,500)	14,500
	97,000
Less: Current year loss relief s.37	(85,000)
Taxable total profits	**12,000**

Answer to SEQ 5

	£
Income from loan relationship	15,000
Chargeable gains	30,000
Total profits (note)	**45,000**
Less: Relief under section 37	(41,200)
Balance	**3,800**
Less: Qualifying chargeable donations	(2,000)
Taxable total profits	**1,800**

Note: for set off of trading loss under section 37, total profit should be considered before deducting qualifying charitable donations payments.

Answer to SEQ 6

Music Ltd had incurred a trading loss during the accounting period ended on 31 March 2013. As the company wants to set off its loss under section 37, the company should make an election for loss relief within two years from the end of the accounting period (i.e. 31 March 2013) during which the company incurred the loss. Hence, the company should make this claim up to 31 March 2015.

SECTION D

CORPORATION TAX LIABILITIES

D3

STUDY GUIDE D3: THE COMPREHENSIVE COMPUTATION OF CORPORATION TAX LIABILITY

Get Through Intro

As we discussed earlier, a company's trading and other incomes are charged to corporation tax under different headings. After ascertaining a company's chargeable profits for an accounting period, the next step is to calculate the actual corporation tax liability for that period.

In this Study Guide, we will see how to carry out a complete corporation tax calculation. We will look at how to consolidate the different elements and consider the deductions to be made in calculating a company's corporation tax liability.

Learning Outcomes

a) Compute the corporation tax liability and apply marginal relief.
b) Explain the implications of receiving franked investment income.

Introduction

Case Study

Superb Ltd manufactures personal computers.

In the year ended on 31 March 2013 it has earned trading profits of £290,000, property income of £25,000, dividend income of £12,000 and chargeable gains of £15,000.

The company is of the view that all the above-mentioned incomes will be chargeable to tax at different rates.

The company approaches you to calculate its tax liability for the year ended 31 March 2013.

The calculation of the tax liability of Superb Ltd shall be done taking into consideration the corporation tax rate applicable to the income streams and also the marginal relief which is available.

This Study Guide will guide you through the calculation of corporation tax liability.

1. Compute the corporation tax liability and apply marginal relief.[2] Explain the implications of receiving franked investment income.[2]

[Learning Outcomes a and b]

1.1 Tax rates applicable to Corporation Tax

The rate of corporation tax for the companies is determined on the basis of the financial year i.e. from 1 April to 31 March of the following year and not on the basis of tax years (6 April to the following 5 April) as for individuals. The rate of corporation tax to be applied also depends upon the **augmented profits** of the company.

Augmented profits of the company here mean:

	£
Taxable total profits	x
Franked investment income (FII)	x
Augmented profits (A)	**x**

FII is added only to determine the rate of corporation tax applicable. The rate of tax determined accordingly is then applied to the taxable total profits.

1.2 Franked investment income

We have already discussed in Study Guide D2 that the dividends received from other UK companies are paid out of the profits on which the corporation tax has already been paid. Hence, to avoid double taxation, such dividends are not included in the chargeable profits of the receiving company and are therefore, exempt from corporation tax. However, these are added to the taxable total profits to find out the augmented profits of the company for determining the rate of corporation tax applicable.

The term **franked investment income (FII)** is used to refer to the **UK dividends received by a company, together with the notional 10% tax credits**. Therefore, dividends need to be grossed up by multiplying them by 100/90 for calculation purposes. However, the dividends received from associated companies (companies in the same group) are not included in FII.

The treatment of dividends received from an overseas company has been changed by the Finance Act 2009. Previously, these dividends were not exempt from the UK corporation tax and hence were not included in franked investment income.

But now, **dividends that are received from an overseas company are exempt from corporation tax and hence are considered while calculating FII**. However, the overseas dividends received from any company from the same group (group provisions are discussed in detail in Study Guide D4) are not included in the franked investment income.

Hence, the dividends received from associated companies whether a UK company, or an overseas company, is not included in FII.

It is very important to note here that even though franked investment income is not charged to corporation tax, the FII received by a company is taken into account when determining the rate at which the company is liable to pay the tax.

1.3 Rates of corporation tax

The rates of corporation tax for companies for the financial year ended on 31 March 2013 are as follows.

1. **The small profits rate:** this rate is applicable to companies with profits not exceeding the lower limit (which is £300,000 for FY 2012). **Tax at the small profits rate is charged at 20% for FY 2012.**

2. **Main rate:** this rate applies to companies whose profits are more than the upper limit (i.e. £1,500,000 for FY 2012). **Tax at the main rate is charged at 24% for FY 2012.**

3. **Marginal rate:** this is available to companies whose profits do not exceed the upper limit but are more than the lower limit. The upper limit for FY 2012 is £1,500,000. Hence, for the companies whose **profits lie between £300,000 and £1,500,000**, the tax rate is applicable at the main rate, but the tax liability is reduced by marginal relief. Marginal relief is explained in detail later in this Learning Outcome.

The augmented profits of Sweet Ltd for the year ended 31 March 2013 are £57,500. As the augmented profits are less than £300,000 (lower limit), the tax is assessable at the small profits rate, which is 20%.
Hence, the corporation tax liability of Sweet Ltd is £57,500 x 20% = £11,500

The augmented profits of Candy Ltd for the year ended 31 March 2013 are £2,357,500. As the augmented profits are more than £1,500,000 (upper limit), the tax is assessable at the main rate, which is 24%.
Hence, the corporation tax liability of Candy Ltd is £2,357,500 x 24% = £565,800

Let us summarise the **tax rates** for the financial year ended on 31 March 2013.

Diagram 1: Tax rates

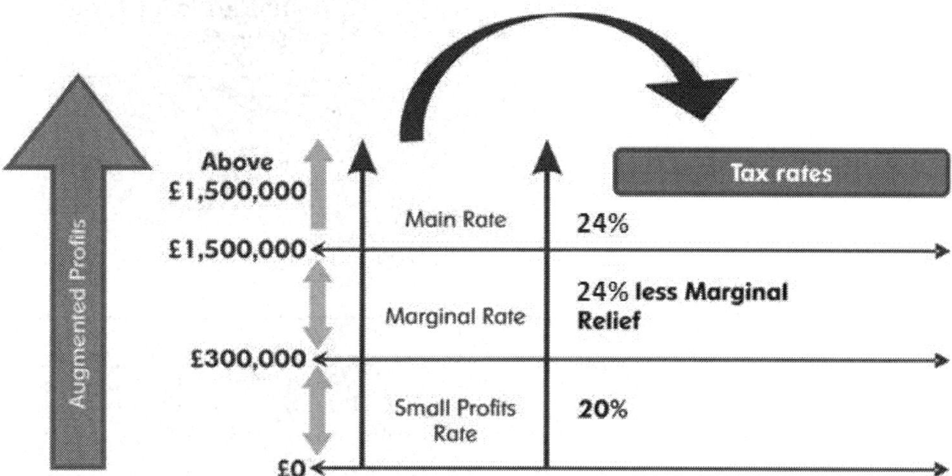

1.4 Marginal relief

A company's corporation tax liability is reduced by an amount known as "marginal relief" if the company's augmented profits fall between the lower and upper limits (i.e. tax liability is calculated at the main rate less marginal relief).

The following formula is applied to calculate marginal relief for the financial year ended 31 March 2013.

Diagram 2: Marginal relief

Where

U = Upper Limit
A = Augmented Profits = TTP + Gross Dividends Received
N = Taxable Total Profits (i.e. TTP)

The fraction is **1/100**

Example

The taxable total profits of Sun Ltd for the year ended on 31 March 2013 are £450,000. Dividends received from UK companies for the year were £10,000. Sun Ltd has also received overseas dividends of £7,280.

Calculation of augmented profits of Sun Ltd for the year ended 31 March 2013 is as follows.

	£
Taxable total profits (N)	450,000
FII (17,280 x 100/90)	19,200
Augmented profits (A)	**469,200**

As the augmented profits of £469,200 are less than the upper limit (£1,500,000 for FY 2012-13) but more than the lower limit (£300,000 for FY 2012-13), the tax is assessable at 24% less marginal relief.

Hence, the corporation tax liability for Sun Ltd is calculated as follows.

	£
(£450,000 x 24%)	108,000
Less: Marginal relief (W1)	(9,886)
Corporation tax liability	**98,114**

FII is added only to determine the rate of corporation tax applicable but the rate determined is then applied to the taxable total profits figure.

Working

W1 Marginal relief = Standard fraction x (U - A) x N/A

$$= \frac{1}{100} \times (£1,500,000 - £469,200) \times \frac{£450,000}{£469200}$$

= £9,886

Important

The corporation tax information will be given in the exams as follows:

Financial Year	2010	2011	2012
Small profits rate	21%	20%	20%
Main rate	28%	26%	24%
Lower limit	£300,000	£300,000	£300,000
Upper limit	£1,500,000	£1,500,000	£1,500,000
Marginal relief fraction	7/400	3/200	1/100

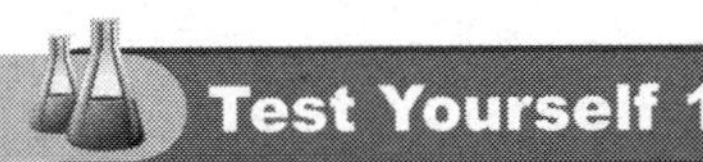

Test Yourself 1

The taxable total profits of three companies for the year ended 31 March 2013 are given below. The three companies are not associated.

Company	Chargeable profits (£)
Jasmine Ltd	3,562,350
Orchids Ltd	1,242,400
Marigold Ltd	215,900

Required:

State the rate at which corporation tax will be calculated for each of these companies.

Test Yourself 2

ABC Ltd has taxable total profits of £297,200 for the year ended 31 March 2013. Total dividends received for the year include dividends received from UK companies amounting to £8,000 and overseas dividend amounting to £5,680. Calculate the corporation tax liability.

Important

Effective marginal rate: the rate of tax on each incremental £ of profits.

£		£
1,500,000 (upper limit)	@ 24%	360,000
(300,000) (lower limit)	@ 20%	(60,000)
1,200,000		**300,000**

Hence, the effective tax rate at marginal rate is $\left(\frac{£300,000}{£1,200,000}\right) \times 100\% = 25.0\%$

1.5 The upper and lower limits are reduced if:

a) the accounting period is **less than 12 months**

Example

Jackson Ltd commenced trading on 1 July 2012 and made up its first accounts to 31 March. As the company's accounting period is 9 months (1July 2012 to 31 March 2013) i.e. less than 12 months, the lower and upper limit will be reduced proportionately (for Jackson Ltd as below).

The lower limit will be £300,000 x 9/12 = £225,000
The upper limit will be £1,500,000 x 9/12 = £1,125,000

---

b) if the company has associated companies (explained in detail in Learning Outcome 1, Study Guide D4)

Example

Strong Ltd has two associated companies. The lower and upper limits will be divided among all the three associated companies (Strong Ltd + two associated companies) as follows:

The lower limit will be £300,000/3 = £100,000
The upper limit will be £1,500,000/3 = £500,000

1.6 Long period of accounts

As discussed earlier, an accounting period can never exceed 12 months. Then how should the taxable profits of the company be calculated if it has prepared its accounts for a period exceeding 12 months?

In such cases the company is required to divide its period of accounts into two or more accounting periods and for each such period, the profit chargeable to corporation tax is to be calculated and tax liability has to be assessed. A company's profits for a long period of account are usually allocated between the accounting periods as follows:

a) Adjusted trading profits **before capital allowances are usually apportioned on a** time basis. **Capital allowances are then allowed for each accounting period separately.** WDAs and AIAs need to be time-apportioned **for the short accounting period.**

b) Property income **is usually apportioned on a** time basis.

c) **A net credit on a** non-trading loan relationship **is generally allocated on an** accrual basis **between the accounting periods.**

d) **The** chargeable gains **are allocated to the** accounting period **in which the** asset giving rise to such gains **is** disposed of.

e) Qualifying chargeable donations **are allocated to the period in which they are** actually paid.

f) Dividends received from other UK companies **are allocated to the** accounting period **in which they are** received **as this is important while determining the rate at which corporation tax is to be paid by the company.**

A long period of account must be split into two accounting periods.

The first accounting period is always twelve months long. The rest of the period of account forms the second accounting period.

Boo Ltd makes up its accounts for 18 months to 31 March 2013. The company's results for this period of account are as follows (all figures are gross):

	£
Adjusted trading profits (before capital allowance)	549,000
Property income	180,000
Non-trade loan interest receivable:	
Received on 31 July 2012	1,800
Received on 31 January 2013	1,800
Accrued to 30th June 2013	1,500
Chargeable gains:	
Disposal on 12 March 2012	1,200
Disposal on 15 September 2012	6,900
Disposal on 2 March 2013	12,200
Qualifying charitable donations:	
Paid on 30 June 2012	2,500
Paid on 30 September 2012	2,500
Accrued to 31 March 2013	2,500
Loan interest receivable relates to a £36,000 loan made on 1 November 2011 at 10%	

Required:

Calculate Boo Ltd's taxable total profits for the above periods.

Continued on the next page

A long period of account must be split into two accounting periods. The first accounting period is always twelve months long. The rest of the period of account forms the second accounting period.

Therefore, there are two accounting periods: the year to 30 September 2012 and the six months to 31 March 2013.
The chargeable profits of Boo Ltd for each accounting period are as follows:

	12 months to 30/09/2012	6 months to 31/03/2013
	£	£
Trading profits (12:6) (note 1)	366,000	183,000
Property income (12:6)	120,000	60,000
Income from loan relationship (note 2)	3,300	1,800
Chargeable gains (note 3)	8,100	12,200
	497,400	257,000
Less: Qualifying chargeable donations (note 4)	(5,000)	-
Taxable total profits	**492,400**	**257,000**

Notes

1. Trading profits before capital allowances and property incomes are apportioned on a time basis.
2. The loan interest is allocated on an accrual basis. Interest accruing on £36,000 per month @ 10% is £300 (£36,000/12 x10%).
   Loan interest accrued for 11 months from 1 November 2011 to 30 September 2012 is £3,300 and for 6 months to 31 March 2013 is £1,800.
3. The chargeable gains are allocated to the accounting period in which the asset giving rise to such gains is disposed of.
   Chargeable gains on asset disposed on 12 March 2012 and on 15 September 2012 fall within the 12 months to 30 September 2012.
   Chargeable gains on asset disposed on 2 March 2013 falls within the next accounting period i.e. the 6 months to 31 March 2013.
4. Qualifying chargeable donations are allocated to the period in which they are actually paid. The Qualifying chargeable payments accrued on 31 March 2013 are ignored for now but will be taken into consideration when calculating the chargeable profits of the subsequent accounting period in which they are paid.

1.7 Accounting period straddles 31 March

If the accounting period of the company straddles 31 March, then the accounting period will fall into two financial years. If the corporation tax rates, the marginal relief fraction or the lower limit and the upper limit of the companies are different for the two financial years, then the corporation tax liability has to be calculated for each financial year separately.

Forward Ltd has profits of £540,000 chargeable to corporation tax for the year ended 31 October 2012. Dividends received from UK companies for the year were £36,000.

Augmented profits of Forward Ltd for the year ended 31 October 2012 are as follows:

	£
Taxable total profits (N)	540,000
FII (£36,000 x 100/90)	40,000
Augmented profits (A)	**580,000**

As the profit of £580,000 is between the upper limit and the lower limit, marginal relief will be available.

As the accounting period of the company straddles 31 March 2012, the accounting period is to be divided according to the financial year. The period from 1 November 2011 to 31 March 2012 (5 months) will fall in the financial year 2011 and the period from 1 April 2012 to 31 October 2012 (7 months) will fall in the financial year 2012. The corporation tax rates will be applied accordingly.

Hence, the corporation tax liability for Forward Ltd is calculated as follows

Continued on the next page

	£	£
Financial Year 2011		
(£540,000 x 5/12) = £225,000 x 26%	58,500	
Less: Marginal relief (W1)	(5,353)	53,147
Financial Year 2012		
(£540,000 x 7/12) = £315,000 x 24%	75,600	
Less: Marginal relief (W2)	(4,997)	70,603
Corporation tax liability		**123,750**

Workings

W1 FY 2011
Marginal relief = 3/200 x (£1,500,000 – £580,000) x £540,000/ £580,000 x 5/12 = £5,353

W2 FY 2012
Marginal relief = 1/100 x (£1,500,000 – £580,000) x £540,000/ £580,000 x 7/12 = £4,997

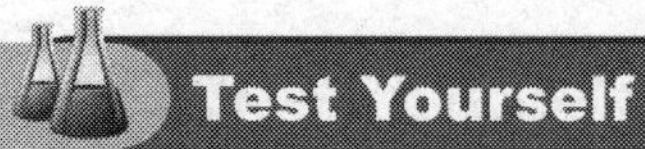

Test Yourself 3

The accounts of Truth Ltd showed the following results for the year ended 31 March 2013. Calculate the corporation tax liability for this period.

	£
Income from UK trade	243,000
UK trade losses brought forward	102,000
Income from land situated in the UK	100,000
Chargeable gains	158,000
Bank interest income (Accrued during the year to 31/03/2013)	92,000
Donations to UK charities	10,000

Test Yourself 4

Tough Ltd commenced trading on 1 April 2012 as a manufacturer of tools, preparing its first accounts for the nine-month period ended 31 December 2012. The following information is available:

Trading profit

Trading profit is £212,000. This figure is before taking account of capital allowances and any deduction arising from the premium paid in respect of leasehold property.

Leasehold property

On 1 April 2012, Tough Ltd acquired two leasehold office buildings. In each case, a premium of £60,000 was paid for the grant of a twenty-year lease. The first office building was used for business purposes by Tough Ltd throughout the period ended 31 December 2012. The second office building was empty until 30 September 2012, and was then sub-let to a tenant. On that date, Tough Ltd received a premium of £40,000 for the grant of a five-year lease, and annual rent of £12,400 which was payable in advance.

Loan interest received

Loan interest of £8,000 was received on 30 September 2011, and £4,000 was accrued at 31 December 2012.The loan was made for non-trading purposes.

Dividends received

During the period ended 31 December 2012, Tough Ltd received dividends of £14,400 from Rough Ltd, an unconnected UK company. This figure is the actual cash amount received.

Qualifying chargeable donation

A Qualifying chargeable donation of £5,000 was made on 31 May 2013.

Continued on the next page

Other information

Tough Ltd has two associated companies.

Required:

Calculate Tough Ltd's corporation tax liability for the nine-month period ended 31 December 2012. Ignore capital
allowances

Test Yourself 5

Apple Ltd has always made up its accounts to 31 December, but has decided to change its accounting date to 31 March. The company's results for the fifteen-month period ended 31 March 2013 are as follows:

1. Trading profit as adjusted for taxation is £220,000. This figure is before taking account of capital allowances.
2. On 1 January 2012, the written down value of plant and machinery was £32,000. Apple Ltd purchased office equipment for £27,000 on 15 March 2013. Assume that the new rules according to Finance Act 2012 have always applied.
3. There is a property income of £43,000 for the fifteen-month period ended 31 March 2013.
4. On 15 April 2012, the company disposed of some investments, and this resulted in a chargeable gain of £29,300. On 18 February 2013, the company made a further disposal, and this resulted in a capital loss of £4,400.
5. Franked investment income of £20,000 (gross) was received on 10 September 2012.
6. A Qualifying chargeable donation of £5,000 was made on 31 March 2013.

As at 1 January 2012, Apple Ltd had unused trading losses of £15,300 and unused capital losses of £2,000. Apple Ltd has no associated companies.

Required:

Calculate Apple Ltd's corporation tax liabilities in respect of the fifteen-month period ended 31 March 2013.

1.8 Timing of capital disposals

If the disposal of a capital asset is expected to realise a gain, care should be taken regarding the date of disposal.

1. Disposal near the end of an accounting period means that profits will be increased by the gain. The company needs to consider if this will increase its profits leading to a higher rate of corporation tax.

2. If the gain is delayed into next accounting period, the company should consider the likely rate of tax. Also, from a timing point of view, tax on gain will be paid 12 months later.

If the asset is expected to realise a loss, then it should be disposed of as soon as possible in order to use the capital loss against any capital gains already realised.

1.9 Choice of loss reliefs

Points to consider:

1. Rate of corporation tax at which relief will be obtained: aim to relieve at 27.5%, then 26% then 20%.

2. Cash flow considerations: applying section 37 will mean a reduction of the current liability and a repayment of the liability of the previous 12 months. On the other hand, applying section 45 means a reduction in a future liability.

3. Extent to which relief for Qualifying chargeable will be lost.

Rate of tax saved is the most important consideration.

In addition, a company with losses should consider claiming less than the maximum amount of capital allowances. If a s.37 claim is to be made, and the current rate of tax is 20%, though it is expected to be 24% in the future, then a reduced claim for capital allowances means a higher TWDV to carry forward, and higher capital allowances in future years. This means that capital allowances will be relieved at a higher rate.

1.10 Rollover relief

If a business asset is disposed of (land and buildings or fixed plant and machinery) and a new asset is to be purchased, care should be taken to ensure the reinvestment is in the period 12 months before the disposal or 36 months after the disposal. This ensures that the gain can be rolled over, providing all the proceeds are reinvested.

Answers to Test Yourself

Answer to TY 1

Jasmine Ltd (Note 1)	24%
Orchids Ltd (Note 2)	24% less Marginal Relief
Marigold Ltd (Note 3)	20%

Notes

1. The profits are more than the upper limit, i.e. £1,500,000.
2. The profits lie between the lower and the upper limit (i.e. between £300,000 and £1,500,000).
3. The profits are less than the lower limit, i.e. £300,000.

Answer to TY 2

	£
Taxable total profits	297,200
Add: Dividend (£8000 + £5,680) x 100/90	15,200
Augmented profits (A)	**312,400**

Notes

1. As the profits are above £300,000 but below £1,500,000 the tax rate applicable is **24% less marginal relief.**
2. Dividends received (both UK dividends and overseas dividends) are not taxable but are added to taxable total profits to arrive at the 'A' figure and to decide the applicable tax rate.

Calculation of corporation tax liability

	£
Corporation tax (£297,200 x 24%)	71,328
Less: Marginal relief (W1)	(11,298)
Corporation tax liability	**60,030**

Working

W1 Marginal relief = Standard fraction x (U - A) x N/A
= 1/100 x (£1,500,000 - £312,400) x £297,200/£312,400 = £11,298

Answer to TY 3

	£	£
Trading Profits	243,000	
Less: Brought forward trading losses	(102,000)	141,000
Property income		100,000
Income from loan relationship		92,000
Chargeable gains		158,000
		491,000
Less: Qualifying chargeable donation		(10,000)
Taxable total profits (TTP)		**481,000**
Tax on TTP (£481,000 x 24%)		115,440
Less: Marginal Relief		
1/100 x (£1,500,000 - £481,000) x £481,000/£481,000		(10,190)
Corporation Tax Liability for the period		**105,250**

Note: donations to UK Charities are deductible as Qualifying chargeable donations.

Answer to TY 4

	£	£
Trading Profits	212,000	
Less: Deduction for lease premium (W1)	(1,395)	210,605
Property income (W2)		30,600
Income from loan relationship (W3)		12,000
		253,205
Less: Qualifying chargeable donation		(5,000)
Taxable total profits (N)		**248,205**
Add: Franked investment income (£14,400 x100/90)		16,000
Augmented profits (A)		**264,205**

Corporation tax liability for the period		
Tax on taxable total profits (£248,205 x 24%)		59,569
Less: Marginal relief (W4)		(1,041)
Corporation tax liability for the period		**58,528**

Workings

W1 Deduction for lease premium

1. The first office building has been used for business purposes, and so a proportion of the lease premium assessed on the landlord can be deducted.

2. The amount assessed on the landlord is £37,200 calculated as follows:

	£
Premium received	60,000
Less: £60,000 x (2% x (20 - 1))	(22,800)
	37,200

3. This is deductible over the life of the lease, so the deduction for the nine-month period ended 31 December 2012 is £1,395 (£37,200/20 = £1,860 x 9/12).

W2 Property income

	£
Premium received for sub-lease	40,000
Less: £40,000 x (2% x (5 - 1))	(3,200)
	36,800
Less: Relief for premium paid for head lease £37,200 (W1) x 5 (duration of sub-lease)/20 (duration of head lease)	(9,300)
Premium treated as rent	27,500
Add: Rent receivable (£12,400 x 3/12)	3,100
Property income	**30,600**

W3 Loan interest

	£
Interest received on 30 September 2012	8,000
Interest accrued at 31 December 2012	4,000
Income from loan relationship	**12,000**

W4 Marginal relief

Tough Ltd's augmented profit of £264,205 for 9 months falls between the lower and the upper limit. These limits are calculated as follows:

Lower limit = (£300,000 x 9/12) = £225,000
Upper limit = (£1,500,000 x 9/12)= £1,125,000

Hence, tax rate applicable is 24% less marginal relief.

These limits are then further reduced to £75,000 (£225,000/3) and £375,000 (£1,125,000/3) as Tough Ltd has two associated companies (refer to Study Guide D4).

Therefore, marginal relief = Fraction x (U - A) x N/A
= 1/100 (£375,000 – £264,205) x £248,205/£264,205
= £1,041

Answer to TY 5

	Year ended 31/12/2012 £	**Period ended 31/3/2013 £**
Trading profits (W1)	176,000	44,000
Capital allowances (W2)	(6,400)	(26,380)
	169,600	**17,620**
Less: Loss relief s.45	(15,300)	-
	154,300	**17,620**
Property income (W3)	34,400	8,600
Capital gains (£29,300 – £2,000)	27,300	
	216,000	**26,220**
less: Qualifying chargeable donations (note 2)		(5,000)
Taxable total profits	**216,000**	**21,220**
Add: Franked investment income	20,000	-
Augmented profits	**236,000**	**21,220**
Corporation tax liability (Note 3)		
Financial Year 2011 (Note 4)		
(£216,000 x 3/12) = £54,000 at 20%	10,800	
Financial Year 2012		
(£216,000 x 9/12) = £162,000 at 20%	32,400	
(£21,220 at 20%)(Note 5)		4,244
Corporation tax liability	**43,200**	**4,244**

Workings

W1

Trading profits are allocated on a time basis: £176,000 (£220,000 x 12/15) to the year ended 31 December 2012 and £44,000 (£220,000 x 3/15) to the period ended 31 March 2013.

W2

Separate capital allowance calculations are prepared for each accounting period as follows.

	AIA £	General Pool £	Allowances £
Year ended 31 December 2012			
TWDV b/f		32,000	
Less: WDA @ 18%		(5,760)	5,760
TWDV c/f		**26,240**	
Allowances			**5,760**
Period ended 31 March 2013			
TWDV b/f		26,240	
Additions qualifying for AIA:			
Office equipment	27,000		
Less: AIA (£25,000 x 3/12)	(6,250)	20,750	6,250
		46,990	
Less: WDA @ 18% for 3 months		(2,115)	2,115
TWDV c/f		**44,875**	
Allowances			**8,365**

Expenditure incurred by any business on plant and machinery (with the exception of cars) is eligible for AIA up to £100,000. However, AIA is scaled up or down according to the length of the accounting period.

Hence, AIA for the period ended 31 March 2013 is £6,250 (£25,000 x 3/12)

WDA is also scaled up or down according to the length of the accounting period.

W3 Property income

Property incomes are allocated on a time basis: £34,400 (£43,000 x 12/15) to the year ended 31 December 2012 and £8,600 (£43,000 x 3/15) to the period ended 31 March 2013.

Notes

1. The capital loss of £4,400 for the period ended 31 March 2013 is carried forward.
2. Qualifying charitable donations are allocated to the period in which they are actually paid.
3. In each case, the franked investment income is considered to determine the applicable tax rate. But actual tax liability is calculated on taxable total profits without considering franked investment income.
4. As the accounting period of the company for the year ended 31 December 2012 straddles 31 March 2012, the accounting period is to be divided according to the financial year. The period from 1 January 2012 to 31 March 2012 (3 months) will fall in the financial year 2011 and the period from 1 April 2012 to 31 December 2012 (9 months) will fall in the financial year 2012. The corporation tax rates will be applied accordingly.
5. The period ended 31 March 2013 is three months long, therefore the lower limit is reduced to £75,000 (£300,000 x 3/12). Augmented profits for the period ended 31 March 2013 are below this limit, so the tax rate applicable is 20%.

Quick Quiz

1. What is franked investment income?
2. What is the treatment for franked investment income in a corporation tax calculation?
3. PQR Ltd's results for the year ended 31 March 2013 are summarised as follows:

	£
Taxable total profits	410,000
Dividend received from a UK company	27,000

Calculate PQR Ltd's corporation tax liability for the year ended 31 March 2013.

Answers to Quick Quiz

1. The UK dividends and overseas dividends received by a company, multiplied by 100/90, are known as franked investment income.

2. FII is not chargeable to corporation tax, however, the amount of FII plus taxable total profits is considered to determine the rate at which the company is liable to pay the tax.

3. PQR Ltd's corporation tax liability for the year ended 31 March 2013 is calculated as follows:

	£
Taxable total profits	410,000
Add: Franked investment income (£27,000 x 100/90) (note 2)	30,000
Augmented profits	**440,000**
Corporation tax (£410,000 x 24%)	98,400
Less: Marginal relief: 1/100 x (£1,500,000 – £440,000) x £410,000/£440,000	(9,877)
Corporation Tax Liability	**88,523**

Notes

1. Dividend from associated companies is not included in the profit for calculating CT liability.
2. UK dividends received (franked investment income) are grossed up by multiplying by 100/90.

Self Examination Questions

Question 1

The following information is given for four companies:

1. A Ltd has taxable total profits of £165,000 and UK dividends of £9,000.

2. C Ltd has taxable total profits of £5,000 and received UK dividends of £148.50.

3. D Ltd has taxable total profits of £1,800,000 and has received no UK dividends.

4. B Ltd has taxable total profits of £295,000 and overseas dividends of £13,500.

Assume that the companies prepare a set of accounts for the year to 31 March 2013 and that none of them have any associated companies.

Required:

Calculate the rate at which corporation tax is liable to be paid by each of these companies and also calculate the corporation tax liability in each case.

Question 2

Bright Ltd commenced trading on 1 October 2011, and its results for the 15-month period ending 31 December 2012 are summarised as follows.

	£
Trading profits	220,000
Chargeable gain in respect of disposal of shares on 9 November 2012	26,000
Franked investment income received on 16 October 2012	6,000

Required:

Calculate Bright Ltd's corporation tax liability in respect of the 15 month period ended 31 December 2012.

Answers to Self Examination Questions

Answer to SEQ 1

	A Ltd £	C Ltd £	D Ltd £	B Ltd £
Taxable total profits	165,000	5,000	1,800,000	295,000
Franked investment income (Dividends + 10% notional tax credits)	10,000	165	0	15,000
Augmented profits	**175,000**	**5,165**	**1,800,000**	**310,000**
Applicable tax rate	20%	20%	24%	24% less marginal relief

	A Ltd £	C Ltd £	D Ltd £	B Ltd £
Taxable total profits	165,000	5,000	1,800,000	295,000
Corporation tax liability				
£165,000 x 20%	33,000			
£5,000 x 20%		1,000		
£1,800,000 x 24%			432,000	
£295,000 x 24%				70,800
Less: Marginal relief (W1)				(11,324)
Corporation tax liability	**33,000**	**1,000**	**432,000**	**59,476**

Note: in each case the franked investment income is considered to determine the applicable tax rate. But actual tax liability is calculated on profits without considering franked investment income.

Working

W1 Marginal relief = Fraction x (U - A) x N/A
=1/100 x (£1,500,000 – £310,000) x £295,000/£310,000
= £11,324

Answer to SEQ 2

	Year ended on 30-Sep-12 £	3 months period ended on 31-Dec-12 £
Trading profits (12:3) (Note 1)	176,000	44,000
Capital gain	-	26,000
Taxable total profits	**176,000**	**70,000**
Franked investment income	-	6,000
Augmented profits	**176,000**	**76,000**
Corporation tax liability (Note 2)		
Financial Year 2011 (Note 3)		
(£176,000 x 6/12) = £88,000 at 20%	17,600	
Financial Year 2012		
(£176,000 x 6/12) = £88,000 at 20%	17,600	
(£70,000 at 24% less marginal relief) (Note 4)		14,046
Corporation tax liability	**35,200**	**14,046**

Notes

1. Trading profits are allocated on a time basis: £176,000 (£220,000 x 12/15) to the year ended 30 September 2012 and £44,000 (£220,000 x 3/15) to the 3 month period ended on 31 December 2012.

2. Franked investment income is considered to determine the applicable tax rate. But actual tax liability is calculated on profits without considering franked investment income.

3. As the accounting period of the company for the year ended 30 September 2012 straddles 31 March 2012, the accounting period is to be divided according to the financial year. The period from 1 October 2011 to 31 March 2012 (6 months) will fall in the financial year 2011 and the period from 1 April 2012 to 30 September 2012 (6 months) will fall in the financial year 2012. The corporation tax rates will be applied accordingly.

4. The augmented profits for the 3 month period ended 31 December 2012 are above the lower rate limit of £300,000. The lower and upper rate limits are calculated as follows:

The lower limit for 3 month period is: £300,000 x 3/12 = £75,000
The upper limit for 3 month period = £1,500,000 x 3/12 = £375,000

Hence, the tax rate applicable for this 3 month period is 24% less marginal relief.

	£
Corporation tax (£70,000 x 24%)	16,800
Less: Marginal relief	
(1/100 x (£3,75,000 – £76,000) x £70,000/£76,000	(2,754)
Corporation tax liability	**14,046**

SECTION D

CORPORATION TAX LIABILITIES

D4

STUDY GUIDE D4: THE EFFECT OF A GROUP CORPORATE STRUCTURE FOR CORPORATION TAX PURPOSES

Get Through Intro

In today's global economy, many companies operate as a **group** where one main entity controls the operations of many other entities. **The financial position of the group as a whole** is relevant for the purpose of **calculating** the **tax liability of the individual companies that form the group.**

The group relief provisions enable the **losses** made by member companies to be **set off** against the **profits** of any other member companies of the group. These losses should be set off in a manner which will **minimise the tax liabilities** of all the individual member companies.

In this Study Guide we shall discuss the effect of a group corporate structure for the purpose of determining corporation tax, and introduce you to the group relief provisions which help in effective tax planning. It also deals with the principles of transfer pricing.

Learning Outcomes

a) Define an associated company and recognise the effect of being an associated company for corporation tax purposes.
b) Define a 75% group, and recognise the reliefs that are available to the members of such a group.
c) Define a 75% capital gains group, and recognise the reliefs that are available to members of such a group.
d) Compare the UK tax treatment of an overseas branch to an overseas subsidiary.
e) Calculate double taxation relief.
f) Explain the election for the exemption of profits from overseas branches.
g) Explain the basic principles of the transfer pricing rules.

Introduction

Case Study

Merlin Ltd holds 80% of the shares in Marvin Ltd. Marvin Ltd sold one of its major assets during the year and made a large chargeable gain.

Merlin Ltd had excess funds and it wanted to invest those funds in assets to increase the productivity of the company.

The managements of both the companies want to know whether there are any provisions whereby the tax on chargeable gains of Marvin Ltd can be minimised.

In this Study Guide, we will discuss the various provisions relating to groups of companies and try to find out whether there is any solution to this problem.

1. Define an associated company and recognise the effect of being an associated company for corporation tax purposes.[2]

[Learning Outcome a]

Diagram 1 : Associated companies

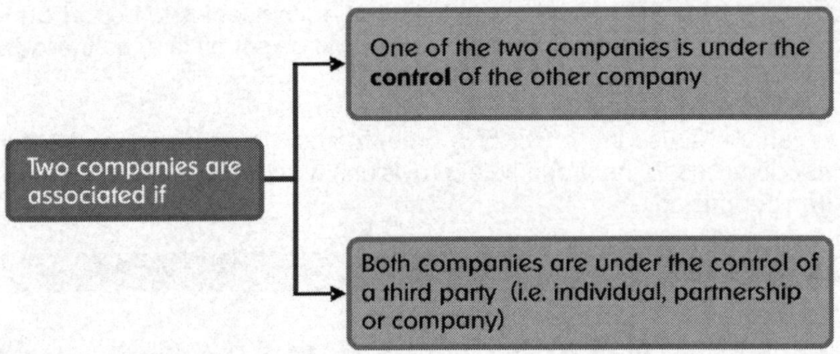

In other words, companies are associated when a person or group of persons can control both, either personally, or via their interests in other corporate shareholdings.

1.1 A company is said to be under control if any of the following conditions are fulfilled:

1. Ownership of over 50% of the company's issued share capital
2. Ownership of over 50% of the company's voting rights
3. Entitlement to over 50% of the company's income, if it were all distributed.
4. Entitlement to over 50% of the company's assets, if the company were wound up.

1.2 Effects of being an associated company for corporation tax purposes

1. To determine the corporation tax rate applicable, the upper and lower limits of £300,000 and £1,500,000 are **divided by the number of associated companies.**
2. Only **one annual investment allowance (AIA)** upto £25,000 is available for a group.
3. For calculating the company's profits, **inter group dividends are not considered as FII**.

These provisions are inserted as an anti-avoidance measure to restrict the separation of a big company into several smaller ones to take advantage.

Example

Global Ltd has four associated companies. The lower limit, which is £300,000 for FY 2012, will be divided among the five companies (Global Ltd and its four subsidiaries). Therefore each company will have a lower limit of £60,000.The upper limit also will be equally divided among the five members of the group and it will be 1,500,000/5 = 300,000

Important

The chart below makes it clear that the small profits' rate's upper and lower limits are equally divided among all associated companies.

No of companies in group	Small profits' rate's lower limit (for each Co)	Small profits' rate's upper limit (for each Co)
	£	£
1 (for individual company)	300,000	1,500,000
2	150,000	750,000
3	100,000	500,000
4	75,000	375,000
And so on .	. .	. .

1.3 Points to be noted regarding association of the companies

1. An associated company should be considered as such, **even if it is an associated company for only part of an accounting period.**

Example

Bigfoot Ltd prepares its accounts to 31 March every year. It held 60% shares of Lillyput Ltd until 31 December 2012 on which date all shares of Lillyput Ltd were sold. In this case, even though Bigfoot Ltd held shares of Lillyput Ltd for only part of the accounting period, Lillyput Ltd will be considered an associated company of Bigfoot Ltd for the whole of the accounting period ended 31 March 2013.

2. An associated company that is not in any trade or business at any time during that accounting period **(a dormant company) is to be ignored.**

3. Companies are considered to be associated even if they are **associated for different parts of the accounting period.**

Example

Rose Ltd prepares its accounts to 31 December every year. It owns 90% shares in Orchids Ltd. Orchids Ltd purchased 60% shares in Lily Ltd in January 2012. In April 2012, these shares were sold and 70% of Marigold Ltd's shares were purchased.

Therefore, up to April 2012, Rose Ltd has two associated companies: Orchids Ltd (60% shareholding) and Lily Ltd (90% x 60% = 54% shareholding). From April 2012, Rose Ltd has two associated companies: Orchids Ltd and Marigold Ltd (90% x 70% = 63% shareholding).

However, for the accounting period ended 31 December 2012, Rose Ltd is considered to have three associated companies: Orchids Ltd, Lily Ltd and Marigold Ltd. Hence, the upper limit, lower limit and AIA will be divided equally among these four associated companies.

4. When **calculating 'augmented profits'** for the purposes of determining the rate of corporation tax, **dividends from associated companies are excluded.**

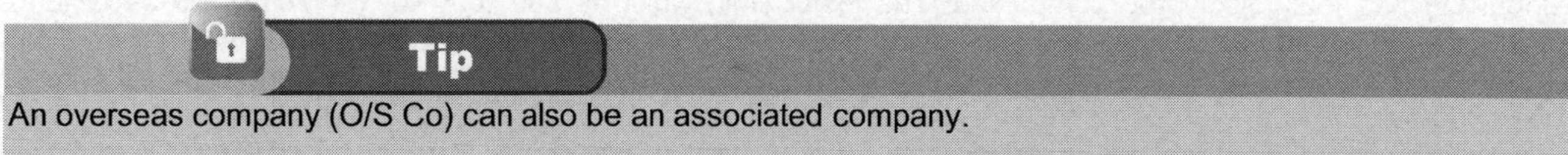

An overseas company (O/S Co) can also be an associated company.

SUMMARY

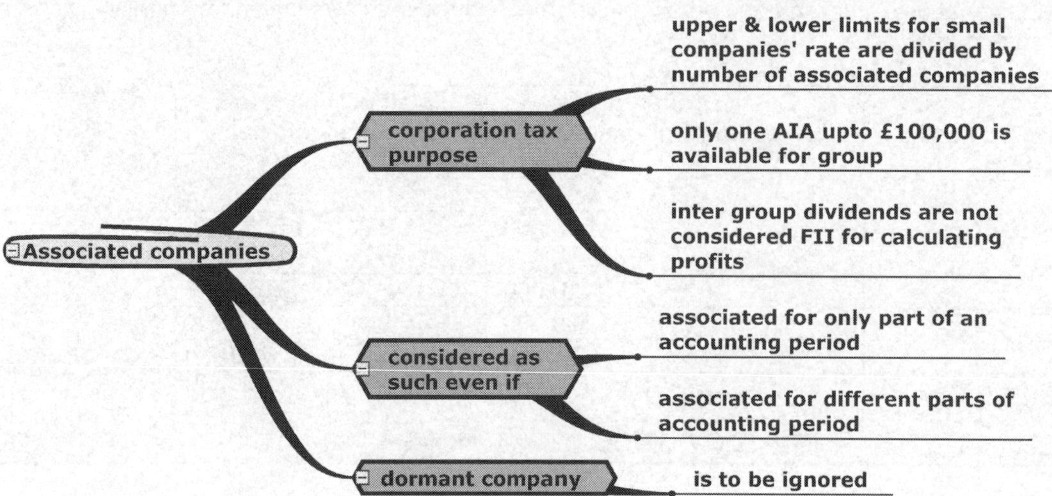

Diagram 2 : Example of associated companies

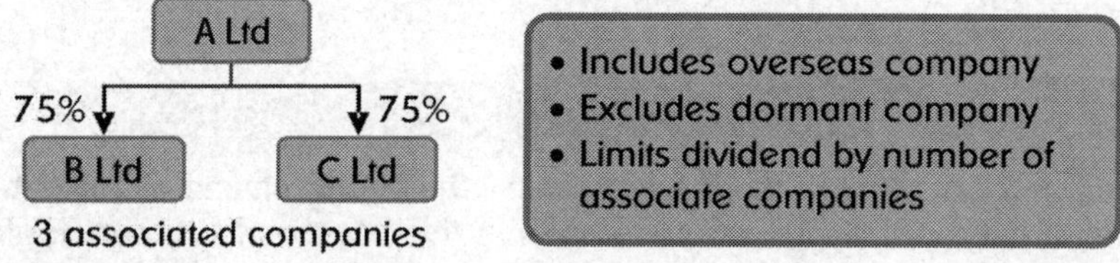

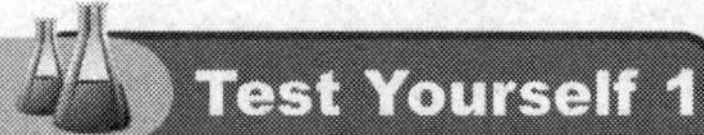

Country Ltd owns 70% of the shares of State Ltd and Division Ltd. State Ltd owns 60% of the shares of City Ltd. City Ld is an overseas company and Division Ltd is a dormant company. Country Ltd purchased shares in State Ltd on 31 December 2012. The accounting period of all the companies is the year ended on 31 March 2013.

Required:

Explain which of these companies are associated with one another in the year ended on 31 March 2013.

King Ltd holds 90% shares of two companies: Giant Ltd and Big Ltd. Big Ltd holds 60% shares of two subsidiaries: Medium Ltd and Small Ltd. Small Ltd is dormant. The chargeable profits of King Ltd are £150,000 for the year ended 31 March 2013 and it has no franked investment income.

Required:

Calculate King Ltd's corporation tax liability for the period.

2. Define a 75% group, and recognise the reliefs that are available to the members of such a group.[2]

[Learning Outcome b]

Diagram 3 : When are the two companies said to be in a group?

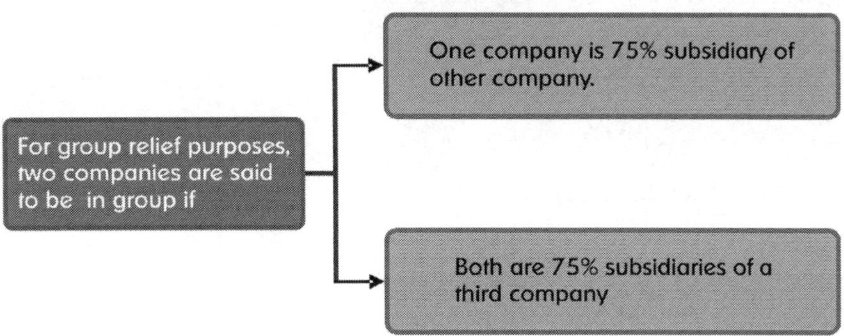

2.1 Members of 75% group

A company is said to be a 75% subsidiary of another company when **all of** the following conditions are fulfilled:

1. At least 75% of the ordinary share capital of the subsidiary company is owned by the holding company **directly or indirectly.**

Example

Direct holding

Saga Ltd owns 85% of the issued share capital of Jana Ltd. As more than 75% shares of Jana Ltd are held by Saga Ltd, Jana Ltd is a 75% subsidiary of Saga Ltd.

Indirect holding

Saga Ltd owns 85% of the issued share capital of Jana Ltd and Jana Ltd owns 95% of the shares of Raga Ltd. Therefore, Saga Ltd indirectly holds 80.75% (85% x 95%) of the shares of Raga Ltd. Hence Raga Ltd is also a subsidiary of Saga Ltd.

2. The holding company is entitled to 75% of the distributable income of the subsidiary company.

Example

Net Ltd and Set Ltd are two companies. Net Ltd owns 80% of the share capital of Set Ltd. It means Net Ltd is entitled to more than 75% of the profit of Set Ltd. This signifies that Set Ltd is a 75% subsidiary of Net Ltd.

3. The holding company is entitled to at least 75% of the net assets of the subsidiary company on the winding up of the subsidiary.

Example

Mark Ltd has a claim to 80% of the assets of The Fine Art Ltd that has been liquidated recently. The major charge to the assets of The Fine Art Ltd is from Mark Ltd hence Mark Ltd exercises control over The Fine Art Ltd. Hence, The Fine Art Ltd is a 75% subsidiary of Mark Ltd for group relief purposes.

4. For the purpose of F6 examination, all the companies in the 75% group must be resident in the UK.

Important

- The effective interest of the holding company must be at least 75% in all the companies in the group whether subsidiaries or sub-subisidiaries.
- The companies which form a group are eligible to claim group relief under group relief provisions.

Tall Ltd holds 80% of the ordinary shares of Medium Ltd and Medium Ltd holds 75% of the shares of Short Ltd.

Required:

Which of these companies form a group to claim group relief ?

Answer

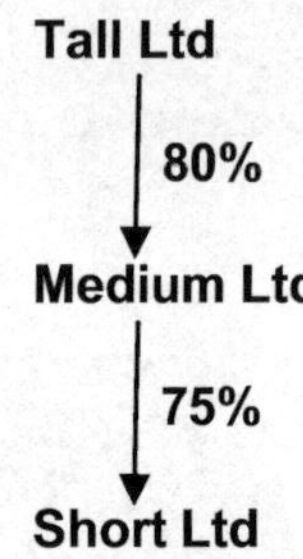

Tall Ltd	Holding
Medium Ltd	80%
Short Ltd	60% (80% x 75%)

Associate companies

Tall Ltd, Medium Ltd and Short Ltd are all associated companies as Tall Ltd (holding company) holds more than 50% shareholding in Medium Ltd and Short Ltd. The AIA limit, lower limit and upper limit will be shared equally among these three members of the group (family).

75% group for loss relief

- **Group 1 (Tall Ltd and Medium Ltd):** Tall Ltd and Medium Ltd are in 75% group but Short Ltd is not in a group with Tall Ltd as the shareholding of Tall Ltd (holding company) in Short Ltd is less than 75%. Therefore losses may be surrendered between Tall Ltd and Medium Ltd but it is not possible for Tall Ltd to surrender losses to Short Ltd and vice-versa.
- **Group 2 (Medium Ltd and Short Ltd):** Short Ltd is a 75% subsidiary of Medium Ltd and hence these two companies can also form a group to claim group relief to surrender their losses. However, Medium Ltd cannot claim group relief from Short Ltd and pass it on to Tall Ltd.

Branch Ltd holds 90% of the shares of Plant Ltd. Plant Ltd holds 90% of the shares of Tree Ltd. Tree Ltd owns 90% of the shares of Farm Ltd.

Required:

Which of these companies form a group to claim group relief?

2.2 Relief Available

1. **Group relief provisions are applicable** to members of a 75% group.
2. By applying group relief provisions, a company which is part of a 75% group can **transfer its trading losses** to other companies within the group. These losses can be set off against the taxable profits of the other companies in the group. Therefore, **the group's overall corporation tax liability reduces.**
3. The company surrendering its trading losses is termed the **"surrendering company"** and the company to whom the losses are surrendered is termed the **"claimant company".**

The main items which may be surrendered are:

a) trading losses
b) property business losses
c) Qualifying charitable payments
d) non-trading loan interest and loan written off (i.e. non-trading loan deficit)
e) excess management charges (in case of companies having only dividend income which are not taxable)

Capital losses realised by any company in the group **cannot be surrendered** for claiming group relief. Excess Qualifying charitable payments have to be surrendered before excess property business losses.

4. A surrender of losses may be from a holding company to a subsidiary company or vice versa or from a subsidiary company to a fellow subsidiary company.
5. Only the surrendering company's **losses for the current period** are **eligible for group relief**.
6. The losses must be **set off against** the **profits** of a **corresponding accounting period**. If the accounting periods of the claimant and surrendering company do not correspond exactly, then both profits and losses respectively have to be apportioned and the result of the overlapping period can only be set off.
7. The **losses surrendered** to a claimant company **cannot exceed the claimant company's taxable total profits** for the **corresponding accounting period (AP)**.

   In other words, the maximum claim is the lower of:

   - the available loss or
   - the available taxable total profits

   Taxable total profits for this purpose is considered after deducting current year and brought forward losses, and Qualifying charitable payments, whether they are actually claimed or not.

Diagram 4: Group of companies

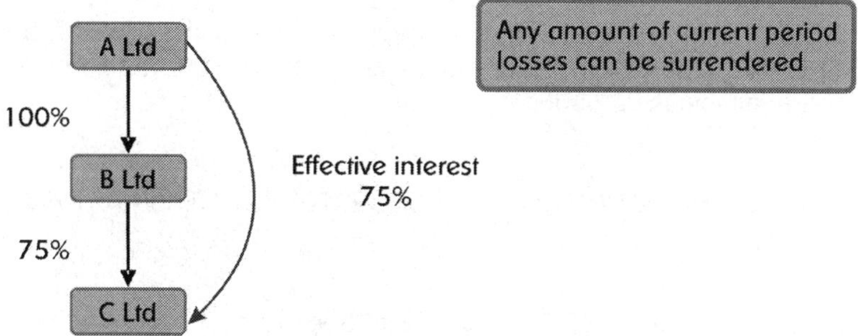

Fortune Ltd prepares its accounts annually to 31st December. It has trading losses of £80,000 for the year ended 31 December 2012. The company also has brought forward trading losses of £26,000.

Its holding company, Destiny Ltd (holding 80% of the share capital in Fortune Ltd) has trading profits of £95,000 for the year ended 31 December 2012 and brought forward trading losses of £32,000.

Required:

What is the amount of group relief that may be claimed?

Answer

As the accounting periods of Fortune Ltd and Destiny Ltd are same, the maximum group that can be claimed is the lower of:

- the available loss or
- the available taxable total profits

As only the current period losses can be surrendered, the available loss is £80,000 of Fortune Ltd.

The available taxable total profit of Destiny Ltd is £63,000 (£95,000 - £32,000) after deducting b/f trading losses.

Hence, the maximum group relief that can be claimed is £63,000, i.e. lower of available loss or available taxable total profits.

Fortune Ltd's unrelieved current year trading loss of £17,000 (£80,000 - £63,000) and brought forward trading loss of £26,000 can be carried forward to claim against the first available trading profits of the company.

Example

Cream Ltd prepares its accounts annually to 31st December. Its holding company, Cake Ltd (holding 80% of the share capital in Cream Ltd), prepares its accounts annually to 31st March. Their trading results are:

Cream Ltd

Loss up to 31/12/2012 £30,000

Cake Ltd

Profits up to 31/03/2012 £20,000
Profits up to 31/03/2013 £45,000

Required:

What is the amount of group relief that may be claimed?

As the accounting periods of Cream Ltd and Cake Ltd do not correspond, the profits and losses are required to be apportioned on a time basis:

	01/01/2012 to 31/03/2012 **£**	**01/04/2012 to 31/12/2012** **£**
Available loss of Cream Ltd (W1)	7,500	22,500
Available taxable total profits of Cake Ltd (W2)	5,000	33,750

The group relief available in each period is the lower of available loss or available taxable total profits. Hence, for the period 01/01/2012 to 31/03/2012 the group relief available is £5,000 and for the period 01/04/2012 to 31/12/2012, the group relief available is £22,500.

W1 Cream Ltd

Total losses for twelve months from 01/01/2012 to 31/12/2012 are (£30,000). Hence, monthly losses are (£30,000)/12 = (£2,500).
Therefore, losses from:

01/01/2012 to 31/03/2012 (three months) = £2,500 x 3 = £7,500
01/04/2012 to 31/12/2012 (nine months) = £2,500 x 9 = £22,500

W2 Cake Ltd

Total profits for twelve months from 01/04/2011 to 31/03/2012 are £20,000. Therefore, profits from:

01/01/2012 to 31/03/2012 (three months) = £20,000 x 3/12= £5,000

Total profits for twelve months from 01/04/2012 to 31/03/2013 are £45,000. Therefore, profits from

01/04/2012 to 31/12/2012 (nine months) = £45,000 x 9/12 = £33,750

---

8. The surrender of losses **can be in part or in full.** Similarly, losses can be surrendered to other companies in the group even though there are sufficient profits available to set off against the company's own profits for that accounting period.

9. A group relief **claim is normally made on the claimant company's tax return**. However, a notice of acceptance is required to be given by the surrendering company.

10. **Effective use of group relief:** to avail the maximum group relief, it is advisable to claim it in the following order:

a) first surrender **to companies which pay corporation tax at a marginal rate** of 25% (in order to bring profits to the small profits rate's limit)

b) then surrender **to companies paying tax at main rate of 24%**

c) finally surrender to companies paying tax at **20%**

Diagram 5: Order of relief

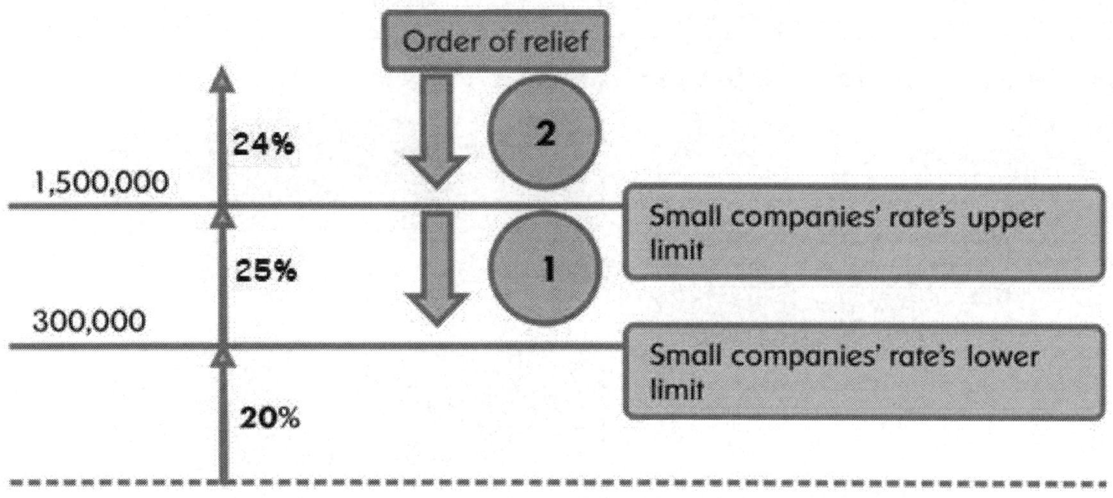

SUMMARY

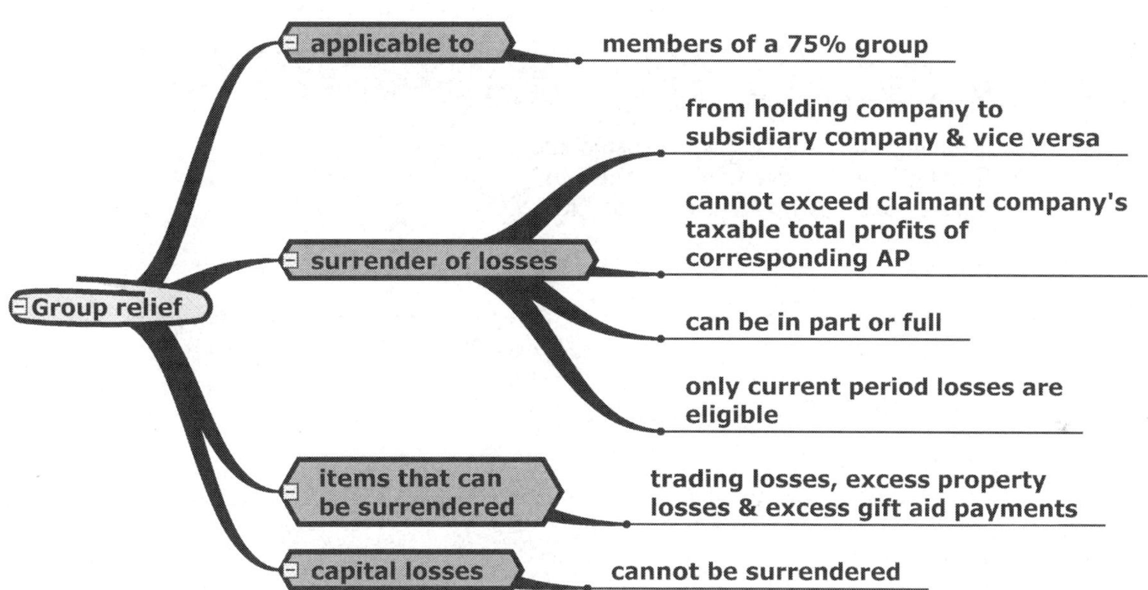

Test Yourself 4

Amanda Ltd owns 100% of the ordinary share capital of Baron Ltd. Their results for the year ended 31 March 2013 are as follows:

	£
Amanda Ltd	
Trading loss	(80,000)
Capital loss	(15,000)
Property income	45,000
Baron Ltd	
Trading profits	90,000
Income from loan relationship	35,000

Amanda Ltd has a trading loss brought forward on 1 April 2012 of £12,000.

Required:

What is the amount of loss that Amanda Ltd may surrender to Baron Ltd?

3. Define a 75% capital gains group, and recognise the reliefs that are available to members of such a group.[2]

[Learning Outcome c]

Diagram 6 : When is a company said to be a member of a 75% capital gains group?

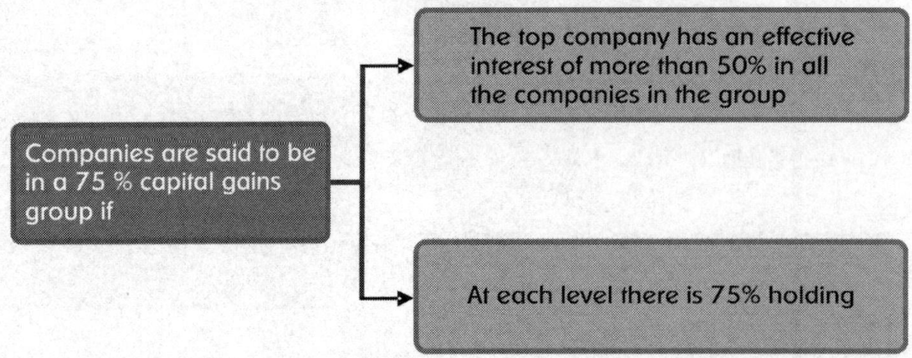

A company cannot be a part of two capital gains groups at the same time. A capital gains group is determined by starting with the top company and then working down according to the two conditions mentioned in the diagram.

State Ltd holds 90% of the issued share capital in District Ltd.
District Ltd holds 75% of the issued share capital in City Ltd.
City Ltd holds 50% of the issued share capital in Home Ltd.

Which of the above companies are members of a 75% capital gains group?

State Ltd ——90%——> **District Ltd** ——75%——> **City Ltd** ——50%——> **Home Ltd**

State Ltd	Holding Company
District Ltd	90%
City Ltd	67.5% (90% x 75%)
Home Ltd	33.75 % (90% x 75% x 50%)

Associated Companies

State Ltd, District Ltd and City Ltd are associated companies as holding company (State Ltd) owns more than 50% shareholding in other two companies The AIA limit, lower limit and upper limit will be shared equally among these three members.

75% group for loss relief

Group 1 (State Ltd and District Ltd): State Ltd and District Ltd are in 75% group but City Ltd is not in a 75% group with State Ltd as the shareholding of State Ltd (holding company) in City Ltd is less than 75%. Therefore losses may be surrendered between State Ltd and District Ltd but it is not possible for State Ltd to surrender losses to City Ltd.

Group 2 (District Ltd and City Ltd): City Ltd is a 75% subsidiary of District Ltd and hence these two companies can also form a group to claim group relief to surrender their losses. However, District Ltd cannot claim group relief from City Ltd and pass it on to State Ltd.

75% capital gains group

1. At each level, there is a 75% holding between State Ltd, District Ltd and City Ltd. But City Ltd does not have a 75% holding in Home Ltd, hence Home Ltd is not a member of the 75% capital gains group.
2. The top company i.e, State Ltd. has an effective interest of more than 50% in District Ltd and City Ltd, but not in Home Ltd.

Therefore, State Ltd, District Ltd and City Ltd are in a 75% capital gains group.

3.1 Reliefs available to members of a 75% capital gains group

Special reliefs are available for companies in a capital gains group (75% direct holding, and more than 50% effective holding in all the companies). These are as follows:

1. **Transfer of chargeable assets without any gain / loss**

- Transfer of chargeable assets between the members of a 75% capital gains group takes place **without giving rise to any chargeable gain or allowable loss**.
- Deemed proceeds for the transferor company on transfer of chargeable assets is the original cost of the assets plus indexation allowance.
- On the subsequent disposal by the company acquiring the asset, the same figure is treated as the deemed cost for the acquiring company.
- The company recieving the asset must remain as a member of the 75% capital gains group for six years. If the holding company sells its controlling interest in the subsidiary company within the period of six years from the date of transfer of the asset, the gain at the time of transfer will arise on the subsidiary company which recieved and is still holding that asset.
- This treatment **is automatic and there is no need to claim it.**

Example

In February 2003 (RPI 179.3) Rise Ltd purchased an office building for £200,000. In May 2007 (RPI 206.2), Rise Ltd transferred the building to Climb Ltd, its wholly owned subsidiary company, for £325,000. The market value of the office building at the time of disposal was £400,000.

In March 2012 (RPI 240.8), Climb Ltd sold the office building for £527,000.

As Rise Ltd holds more than 75% of the shares in Climb Ltd, they both form a 75% capital gains group. When there is a disposal between members of a 75% capital gains group, neither a chargeable gain nor an allowable loss arises.

Deemed proceeds for Rise Ltd will be the original cost of the office building plus indexation allowance.

	£
Cost	200,000
Indexation allowance	
£206.2 - £179.3 = (0.150) x £200,000	30,000
£179.3	
Deemed proceeds	**230,000**

Calculation of chargeable gain on the disposal of office building by Climb Ltd is as follows:

	£
Disposal consideration	527,000
Less: Allowable deductions	
Deemed cost	(227,600)
Unindexed gain	299,400
Less: Indexation allowance	
£240.8 - £206.2 = (0.168) x £227,600	(38,237)
£206.2	
Chargeable gain	**261,163**

2. **Notional transfer of assets**

- The capital gain realised by one company cannot be transferred to another company to utilise the capital losses realised by another company in the group. However, the companies in a 75% capital gains group can elect to use the provision of notional transfer of assets to utilise their capital losses.
- In a notional transfer, the asset on which the gain is realised can be treated as if it had been transferred to another company in the group (having capital losses) before the asset was sold outside the group.
- This election must be made within two years of the end of the accounting period in which the disposal of the asset took place.
- This election can help to set off the group's capital losses against the gains of any company in the group and helps to ensure that corporation tax is paid at the lowest rate on gains by the companies in the group.
- This election also helps to set off the brought forward capital loss of the group member to whom the asset is being transferred.

Forward Ltd owns 100% of the ordinary share capital of Speed Ltd. In the accounting period ending on 31 December 2012, Forward Ltd sold an asset at a capital gain of £100,000. During the same period, Speed Ltd sold an asset at a capital loss of £70,000.

As both the companies form a 75% capital gains group for group relief purposes, they can utilise the capital losses through the provision of notional transfer of assets. The companies can elect the transfer by Forward Ltd which resulted in a capital gain of £100,000 to be treated as being made by Speed Ltd. This will help to set off the loss of £70,000 made by Speed Ltd and therefore the group will have to pay tax only on the net chargeable gain of £30,000 (£100,000 - £70,000).

Alternatively the companies can also make an election to treat the transfer by Speed Ltd which resulted in a capital loss as being made by Forward Ltd. The overall result will be the same in both the conditions.

However, this election should be made within two years of the end of the accounting period in which the disposal of the asset took place, i.e. before 31 December 2014.

---

3. **Group rollover relief**

- All the companies in the 75% capital gains group are treated as one for rollover relief.
- According to the group rollover relief provisions, if one company disposes of an asset eligible for capital gains rollover, and another group member purchases a new qualifying asset within the time limit for reinvestment (i.e., in the period of one year before and three years after the disposal of the old qualifying asset), the gain for the first company can be rolled over into the cost of the new asset purchased by the second company.

Diagram 7: Group rollover relief

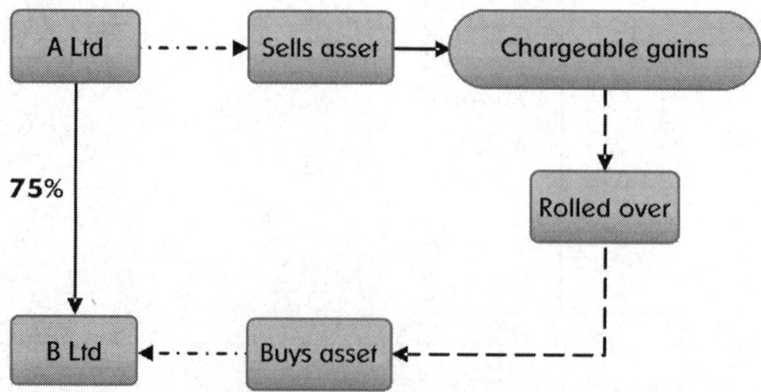

Giant Ltd owns 100% of the ordinary shares of both Big Ltd and Small Ltd. The following information for each company is available for the year ended 31 March 2013:

	Giant Ltd £	Big Ltd £	Small Ltd £
Trading profit (loss)	(135,000)	660,000	140,000
Capital gain (loss)	166,000	(6,000)	-

Giant Ltd's capital gain arose from the sale of property on 1 May 2012 for £396,000. Small Ltd purchases a warehouse for £260,000 on 31 December 2012.

Required:

a) How should the group relief be allocated between the companies to maximise the benefit from group relief?

b) Calculate the corporation tax liability of the three companies for the year ended 31 March 2013 assuming reliefs are claimed in the most favourable manner.

---

4. Compare the UK tax treatment of an overseas branch to an overseas subsidiary.[2]
5. Explain the election for the exemption of profits from overseas branches. [2]
[Learning Outcome d and f]

A company is said to be resident in the UK for tax purposes if it is incorporated in the UK or in the case of a foreign company if its control and management is exercised from within the UK.

The companies which are resident in the UK are liable to corporation tax on all the profits and chargeable gains arising worldwide. A UK resident company can decide to extend its business overseas through either a subsidiary or a branch. Tax treatment of an overseas subsidiary and an overseas branch is different.

Tax treatment of Overseas Branch

A branch is an extension of the structure of the overall company. A UK resident company can extend its business overseas through a branch in which case all the profits from the branch will be assessed to UK corporation tax. Whether the profits are remitted to the UK or not is irrelevant. Similarly, UK capital allowances are also available to the overseas branch on capital assets.

Where the profits of the branch are taxed overseas also, then the double taxation relief is given to reduce the tax burden (double taxation relief is discussed in detail later in this Study Guide).

However, the Finance Act 2011 has given an alternative and simple option for this treatment. Now, a company can opt to treat its profits from an overseas branch as exempt from the UK corporation tax. If an election is made it is for all of a company's overseas branches and becomes irrevocable. This election must be made before the beginning of the accounting period.

If a company has a loss making overseas branch, it should not make a election as it wont be beneficial. Trading loss of an overseas branch is not relieved while calculating the taxable total profits.

If a company sees that the double taxation relief gives very little or no UK corporation tax liability with respect to the branch profits then the company will not make an election until the branch makes a lost in the future.

Important

The examiner has stated that since the rules regarding exemption of overseas branch profits are quite complex especially where small companies are concerned, it will not be examined from the June 2013 exams onwards. It is therefore assumed that for all the overseas branches the exemption option is available.

Tax treatment of Overseas Subsidiary

All profits from the overseas subsidiaries are exempt from UK corporation tax. Previously, the dividends remitted to the UK from overseas subsidiaries were assessed to UK corporation tax as overseas dividend income but from FY2009, overseas dividends are also exempt from corporation tax. Relief is not available to the overseas subsidiary company in the UK for any trading losses incurred. UK capital allowances are also not available to overseas subsidiary companies on its capital assets.

The disadvantage of the overseas subsidiary is that if it is an associate of the UK company, then the small profits rate's lower and upper limits will be reduced, thus increasing the rate of corporation tax.

Jelly Co is a UK resident company and has branches in Nairobi and India. The trading profits for the year ended 31 March 2013 are as follows:

	£
Jelly Co	400,000
India Branch	120,000
Nairobi Branch	(80,000)

Overseas corporation tax was paid on the profits made by the India Branch of £10,000. Jelly Co has not opted to make an election for exemption of the profits of the overseas branches.

The corporation tax liability of Jelly Co would be calculated as follows:

		UK £	India Br £	Nairobi Br £	Total £
Trading profits		400,000	120000	**(80,000)**	**440,000**
Taxable total profits		**400,000**	**120,000**	**(80,000)**	**440,000**
Corporation tax @ 20%		80,000	24,000		88,000
Less: DTR lower of:					
1. Overseas Tax paid	£10,000		(10,000)		(10,000)
2. UK tax on overseas income	£24,000				
Corporation tax due		**80,000**	**14,000**	**0**	**78,000**

If Jelly Co had opted for the exemption of the profits of its overseas branch before 1 April 2012, the corporation tax liability would have been calculated as follows:

	Total £
Trading profits	**400,000**
Taxable total profits	**400,000**
Corporation tax @ 20%	80,000
Corporation tax due	**80,000**

This shows that if Jelly Co would have made an election for exemption, it would not have been beneficial for the company as it would have had to pay £80,000 towards corporation tax as against £78,000 (i.e. the amount of tax payable if it did not make the election).

A summary of the difference between the tax treatment of overseas branch and overseas subsidiary is as follows:

		Overseas Branch	Overseas Subsidiary
1	**C** = Capital allowances		X
2	**L** = Loss relief		X
3	**A** = Associated company	X	
4	**P** = Profit taxed in UK		X

Remember **CLAP**

Tip

According to the Finance Act 2009, overseas dividends which are received on or after 1 July 2009 are exempt from UK corporation tax. However, according to the examiner, the treatment of overseas dividends received before this period will not be examinable.

Example

Nice Ltd has profits of £210,000 chargeable to corporation tax for the year ended 31 March 2013. Dividends received from overseas resident company, Fair Ltd, in December 2012 were £36,000. Nice Ltd holds 52% shares of Fair Ltd. Nice Ltd has no other associated companies.

Required:

Calcuate the taxable total profits and the rate of corporation tax applicable to Nice Ltd.

Answer

Fair Ltd will be considered an associated company of Nice Ltd as Nice Ltd holds more than 50% shares of Fair Ltd.

Fair Ltd is an overseas resident company and dividends received from overseas resident companies on or after 1 July 2010 are exempt from UK corporation tax.

Hence, taxable total profits of Nice Ltd for the year ended 31 March 2013 are £210,000 as dividends are exempt from corporation tax.

Augmented profits of Nice Ltd are also £210,000 as dividends received from associated companies are not included in FII.

Small profits rate upper limit and lower limit will be divided between both the companies as both are associated companies. Hence,
Small profits rate lower limit will be = £300,000/2 = £150,000
Small profits rate upper limit will be = £1,500,000/2 = £750,000

As profits of £210,000 fall between the small profits rate's upper limit and lower limit, the corporation tax rate applicable for Nice Ltd will be 24% less marginal relief.

6. Calculate double taxation relief.[2]

[Learning Outcome e]

The situation may arise where a UK company is taxed both in the UK and overseas on the same profits. The income earned overseas by a UK resident company is taxable in the UK and might also be taxed in the country in which the income arises, depending upon that country's taxation laws.

Double taxation relief is granted in such a situations. This relief is granted by providing **tax credit** to the UK resident company. Hence, it is also referred to as a 'credit relief'. Under this method, the income earned overseas by the UK resident company has to be **grossed up** and included gross while calculating its corporation tax liability. A tax credit is then available equal to the lower of the overseas tax suffered **or** the amount of UK tax payable on the overseas income.

Diagram 8 : Double taxation relief

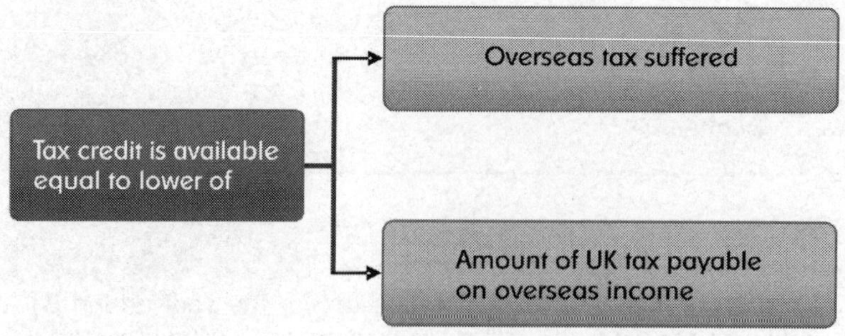

Pro forma for calculation of taxable total profits in respect of overseas income:

Trading income	X
Overseas income (O/S income) (Gross figure)	X
Taxable total profits	**X**
Corporation tax liability (on taxable total profits)	X
Less: Double taxation relief	
Lower of - overseas tax on O/S income	
- UK Corporation tax on O/S income	(X)
Corporation tax payable	**X**

Tip

Double taxation relief is calculated separately for each type of overseas income.

Example

During the year ended 31 March 2013, a UK resident company had UK trading income of £180,000 and received a remittance on account of overseas profits of £85,000 from its overseas branch. The actual profits earned by the branch for the year ended 31 March 2013 are £100,000.These profits were taxed overseas at the rate of 15%.

Required:

Calculate the corporation tax liability for the year.

Answer

Calculation of corporation tax liability

Gross figure needs to be considered while calculating corporation tax liability, therefore £80,000 x 100/80

		UK £	Overseas £	Total £
Trading profits		180,000	100,000	**280,000**
Taxable total profits		**180,000**	**100,000**	**280,000**
Corporation tax @ 20%		36,000	20,000	56,000
Less: DTR lower of:				
1. Overseas Tax (£100,000 x 15%)	£15,000		(15,000)	(15,000)
2. UK tax on overseas income £20,000				
Corporation tax due		**36,000**	**5,000**	**41,000**

Withholding tax

It is the amount of direct tax deducted overseas on any overseas income. Overseas income can be from branch profits, rent and interest. Double taxation relief is always available on withholding tax.

Qualifying charitable payments

Qualifying charitable payments are to be deducted in the appropriate manner to take advantage of double taxation relief. Hence, to increase the amount of double taxation relief, Qualifying charitable payments need to be deducted first from the UK income and then from overseas income. This will increase the amount of UK tax payable on overseas income and thus increase the amount of double taxation relief.

Important

As overseas dividends received on or after 1 July 2009 are now exempt from UK corporation tax, they will not be included in the corporation tax and hence, double taxation relief will not be applicable for this income.

Test Yourself 6

Zeta Ltd's taxable UK trading profits for the year to 31 March 2013 were £786,250. Zeta Ltd had received dividends of £40,000 (net of withholding tax of 20%) from Tetra Inc.

Zeta Ltd had rented a building owned in Switzerland to Spectra SA and received a rental income of £48,000 (net of withholding tax of 40%) during the year ended 31 March 2013.

Both Tetra Inc and Spectra SA are overseas resident companies.

Zeta Ltd had also paid qualifying charitable donation of £15,000 during the year. Zeta Ltd paid no dividends during the year and received no UK dividends.

Zeta Ltd owns 90% of the ordinary shares of Tetra Inc. It has no other associated companies.

Required:

Calculate Zeta Ltd's UK corporation tax liability after double taxation relief.

---

7. Explain the basic principles of the transfer pricing rules.[2]

[Learning Outcome f]

Transfer Pricing

A UK resident company might attempt to reduce its tax liability by transferring goods at artificially low prices to an overseas subsidiary. This would have the result of decreasing the UK resident company's profits and increasing the foreign subsidiary's profits which are not taxable in the UK. The overseas subsidiary may also have a lower tax rate in its own country of domain.

To avoid this situation, "transfer pricing legislation" was brought into existence.

This applies to the transactions between the two companies if one of the two companies is under the control of the other company or both the companies are under the control of a third party (i.e. individual, partnership or company).

According to the provisions of this legislation, the profits of a UK resident company in such circumstances **are to be calculated as if the transaction had been carried out at arm's length prices i.e. the true market price should be substituted for the transfer price and the UK resident company has to make adjustments to its profits accordingly.**

Therefore, companies must self-assess their tax liability under transfer pricing provisions and pay corporation tax due.

Small and medium-sized companies are generally exempt from the transfer pricing legislation.

Answers to Test yourself

Answer to TY 1

Country Ltd is the holding company. The status of the other companies is as follows:

Company	Whether associated or not
State Ltd	Holds more than 50% of the shareholding hence associated for the whole accounting period even though the shares were not owned for the whole year.
Division Ltd	Not associated as it is a dormant company
City Ltd	Not associated as Country Ltd holds less than 50% of the shareholding in City Ltd. It holds only 42% (70% x 60%) of the shareholding.

Hence, the associated companies are only two companies, Country Ltd and State Ltd. The upper limit, lower limit and AIA must be shared equally between these two companies.

Answer to TY 2

King Ltd is deemed to have three associated companies: Giant Ltd, Big Ltd and Medium Ltd (Small Ltd is dormant, hence ignored). The group is as follows:

King Ltd	Holding Company
Giant Ltd	90%
Big Ltd	90%
Medium Ltd	54% (90% x 60%)
Small Ltd	Excluded as it is dormant

Therefore group (family) consist of four members and the limits will be shared equally among these four companies.Therefore, the lower and upper limits are reduced to £75,000 and £375,000 respectively (one fourth of their usual values). The profit of £150,000 falls between these limits, hence, marginal relief is available.

	£
£150,000 @ 24%	36,000
Less: Marginal relief	(2,250)
1/100 (£375,000 - £150,000) x £150,000/£150,000	
Corporation tax liability	**33,750**

Answer to TY 3

Branch Ltd is the holding company and it's effective interest in all the companies should be minimum 75% to claim group relief. The effective interest of Branch Ltd in each of the companies is as follows:

Company	Effective interest	Member of 75% group
Plant Ltd	90%	Yes
Tree Ltd	81% (90% of 90%)	Yes
Farm Ltd	72.9% (90% of 81%)	No

Hence, Branch Ltd, Plant Ltd and Tree Ltd are in a 75% group and can claim group reliefs. However, as effective interest of Branch Ltd in Farm Ltd was less than 75% , it will not be part of the group.

Answer to TY 4

Only current year trading losses may be surrendered. Moreover, there is no group relief for capital losses or. brought forward trading losses. Hence, Amanda Ltd may surrender only the current year trading loss of £80,000 to Baron Ltd.

Answer to TY 5

(a) Allocation of group relief

1. Small Ltd can claim rollover relief for Giant Ltd's capital gain in respect of investment made by it in new the warehouse.

   The excess amount of sales proceeds received by Giant Ltd over the amount invested by Small Ltd (i.e. the amount not re-invested)= (£396,000 - £260,000) = £136,000 cannot be rolled over, and is chargeable immediately.

   The remaining capital gain of £30,000 (£166,000 - £136,000) will be rolled over.

2. If the assets disposed of at a loss by Big Ltd are treated as having been disposed of by Giant Ltd, then the capital loss of £6,000 can be set off against gain of £136,000, leaving chargeable gain to £130,000.

   Giant Ltd should then make a current year loss relief claim to bring its profits down to £100,000.

   The calculation of capital gains roll over relief and capital losses set off among the companies in the group is as follows:

	Giant Ltd £	Big Ltd £	Small Ltd £
Capital gain / (loss)	166,000	(6,000)	-
Less: Roll over relief	(30,000)	-	-
Chargeable gain	136,000	(6,000)	-
Less: Set off of Big Ltd capital loss	(6,000)	6,000	-
Net Chargeable Gain	**130,000**	**Nil**	-

(b) Calculation of corporation tax liability

To maximise the benefits, group relief should be allocated to the company with the highest marginal rate of tax.
As the three companies i.e. Giant Ltd, Big Ltd and Small Ltd are associated companies, the lower limit rates will be divided amongst them. Therefore, the lower limit for each company will be £300,000/3 = £100,000.

Any profit of Giant Ltd and Small Ltd above £100,000 is taxable at the highest marginal rate, which is effectively 25%. Hence group relief should be first allocated to these two companies to bring their profit to £100,000.

Big Ltd bears tax @ 24%, hence the remainder of the relief should be allocated to Big Ltd.

The corporation tax liability of the three companies for the year to 31st March 2013 is calculated as follows:

Remaining loss = £135,000 – £30,000 -£40,000

	Giant Ltd **£**	**Big Ltd** **£**	**Small Ltd** **£**
Trading profits	-	660,000	140,000
Net capital gains	130,000	-	-
	130,000	660,000	140,000
Less: Relief for trading loss under s.37	(30000)	-	-
Less: Group relief	-	(65,000)	(40,000)
Taxable total profits	**100,000**	**595,000**	**100,000**
Tax @ 20%	20,000	-	20,000
Tax @ 24%	-	142,800	-

Answer to TY 6

	UK Trading Income £	Tetra Inc Overseas Dividend Income £	Spectra SA Overseas Rental Income £	Total £
Trading Profits	786,250			786,250
Overseas income (note 1)		-	80,000	80,000
	786,250	**0**	**80,000**	**866,250**
Less: Qualifying charitable donation (note 2)	(15000)	**-**	**-**	(15000)
Taxable total profits	**771,250**	**0**	**80,000**	**851,250**
Corporation tax @ 24% (note 3)	185,100	-	19,200	204,300
Less: DTR (W1)	-	-	(19,200)	(19,200)
Corporation tax liability	**185,100**		**0**	**185,100**

,

Notes

1. Overseas income need to be grossed up while calculating corporation tax liability. Hence,
   Gross dividends received from Tetra Ltd are = £40,000 x 100/80 = £50,000
   Gross rent received from Spectra Ltd is = £48,000 x 100/60 = £80,000
   However, overseas dividends are exempt from UK corporation tax, hence dividends received from Tetra Ltd will not be included in the calculation of CT liability.

2. To take better advantage of qualifying charitable payments, they need to be deducted first from the UK income and then from overseas income.

3. Zeta Ltd and Tetra Inc are associated companies as Zeta Ltd (holding company) holds more than 50% shareholding in Tetra Inc. Hence, upper limit and lower limit will be divided between the two companies as follows:
   Small profits rate's lower limit will be £300,000/2 = £150,000
   Small profits rate's upper limit will be £1,500,000/2 = £750,000

   As Zeta Ltd's profits is above the upper limit, the tax rate applicable will be 24%.

Working

W1 Calculation of double taxation relief

	Tetra Ltd £	Spectra Ltd £
DTR: Lower of		
Overseas tax	10,000	32,000
UK tax on overseas income	-	19,200
	-	**19,200**

Quick Quiz

1. What is an associated company?

2. What is credit relief?

Answers to Quick Quiz

1. In a situation where one company has control over the other company or both the companies are under the control of the same person or persons then the companies are known as associated companies.
2. Tax credit is available equal to the lower of overseas tax suffered or the amount of UK tax payable on overseas income.

Self Examination Questions

Question 1

Briefly explain the following:

(a) What is the group relationship that must exist in order to claim group relief?
(b) What is the group relationship that must exist to form a group for capital gains purposes?
(c) What are the advantages of companies being in a capital gains group?
(d) What is an arm's length price?

Question 2

James Ltd owns 80% of the ordinary share capital of Jolly Ltd. Both companies prepare accounts to 31 March. James Ltd incurs a loss in the year ended 31 March 2013. The company also has a trading loss brought forward on 1 April 2012. Determine the loss to be surrendered to Jolly Ltd in the year ended 31 March 2013.

Question 3

What are the losses that may be surrendered in a 75% group?

Question 4

Sweet Ltd owns 80% of the ordinary share capital of Salty Ltd. Their results for the year ended 31st March 2013 are as follows:

	£
Sweet Ltd	
Trading loss	(160,000)
Property income	25,000
Salty Ltd	
Trading profits	90,000
Chargeable gain	40,000
Qualifying charitable payments	(15,000)

What is the maximum amount of loss of Sweet Ltd that can be claimed by Salty Ltd for group relief?

Question 5

Jimmy Ltd owns 100% of the ordinary share capital of Johnny Ltd. The results of the companies for the year ended 31 March 2013 are as follows:

	£
Jimmy Ltd	
Trading profits	140,000
Property income	15,000
Trading loss b/f under s.45	(23,000)
Qualifying charitable donations	17,000
Johnny Ltd	
Trading profits	(134,000)
Property income	19,000
Qualifying charitable donations	15,000
Trading loss b/f under section 45	(31,000)

Required:

Calculate the maximum group relief that may be claimed for the year by Jimmy Ltd.

Answers to Self Examination Questions

Answer to SEQ 1

(a) The group relationship that must exist to claim group relief needs to meet all of the following conditions:

i. one company must be a 75% subsidiary of the other, or both companies must be a 75% subsidiary of a third company.
ii. the holding company must have an effective interest of at least 75% of the subsidiary's ordinary share capital.
iii. the holding company must have the right to receive at least 75% of the subsidiary's distributable profits and net assets on winding-up.
iv. The companies must all be resident in UK.

(b) The group relationship that must exist to form a group for capital gains purposes are as follows:

i. companies form a capital gains group if at each level in the group structure there is a 75% shareholding.
ii. the parent company must have an effective interest of at least 50% in each group company.

(c) The advantages of companies being in a capital gains group are:

i. the companies in a group can elect to treat any disposal or part of the disposal of the chargeable assets outside the company as if it had been transferred between the companies in the group before the disposal.This can help to set off the group's capital losses against the gains of any company in the group.
ii. gains may be taxed at the lowest marginal rate in the group.
iii. rollover relief is available between group members.

(d) An arm's length price is that price which trading stock can fetch if sold to an unconnected buyer.

Answer to SEQ 2

All of James Ltd's loss in the year ended 31 March 2013 may be surrendered to Jolly Ltd provided Jolly Ltd has the profits to absorb it. The relief is not restricted to the percentage shareholding. Only the current year's losses may be surrendered, not brought forward losses.

Answer to SEQ 3

The losses which may be surrendered in a 75% group are:
i. trading losses
ii. unrelieved property losses
iii. unrelieved qualifying charitable payments

Answer to SEQ 4

Salty Ltd has taxable total profits of £115,000 (£90,000 + £40,000 - £15,000). Hence £115,000 of Sweet Ltd's loss may be surrendered to Salty Ltd.

Answer to SEQ 5

The amount of losses of Johnny Ltd that can be claimed for group relief are calculated as follows:

	£
Trading profits	-
Property income	19,000
Total profits	19,000
Less: Qualifying chargeable donations	(15,000)
	4,000
Less: Current year losses	(134,000)
Losses for group relief	(130,000)

However, Jimmy Ltd has chargeable profits of only £115,000 (£140,000 + £15,000 - £23,000 - £17,000). So, the maximum group relief that may be claimed for the year by Jimmy Ltd is £115,000.

SECTION E

INHERITANCE TAX

STUDY GUIDE E1: INHERITANCE TAX (PART 1)

Get Through Intro

Inheritance tax is mainly a tax due on the value of an individual's wealth when the individual dies and their property is inherited by their heirs.

A charge may also arise during an individual's lifetime when they make a gift either to another individual or to trustees of settled property.

Trustees of settled property may also incur a charge to inheritance tax but not on death, as a trust is a separate legal entity, similar to a company, made up of a body of persons. The charge to trustees arises when they make gifts to beneficiaries or to others on the ten-year anniversary of the creation of the trust.

This Study Guide will explain the concept of inheritance tax, highlight ways of mitigating an inheritance tax charge and set out how you should calculate an inheritance tax liability when it arises.

A question on this topic appears in almost every paper, and so you **must** have a thorough understanding of this Study Guide.

Learning Outcomes

a) Describe the scope of inheritance tax.
b) Identify and explain the persons chargeable.
c) State, explain and apply the meaning of transfer of value, chargeable transfer and potentially exempt transfer.
d) Demonstrate the diminution in value principle.
e) Demonstrate the seven year accumulation principle taking into account changes in the level of the nil rate band.
f) Understand the tax implications of chargeable lifetime transfers and compute the relevant liabilities.
g) Understand the tax implications of transfers within seven years of death and compute the relevant liabilities.
h) Compute the tax liability on a death estate.
i) Understand and apply the transfer of any unused nil rate band between spouses.

1. Describe the scope of inheritance tax.[2]
Identify and explain the persons chargeable.[2]

[Learning Outcomes a and b]

1.1. Scope of inheritance tax

Inheritance tax is paid on 'gifts' or 'transfers' made by chargeable persons. It is usually paid on the transfer of the estate at the time of death of its owner, but it is also applicable to certain transfers made by a person during their lifetime. This is to prevent the person from transferring all of their assets just before their death to avoid inheritance tax.

The person who makes the transfer is termed the donor and the person who receives the transfer is termed the donee.

1.2. Chargeable persons

There are two types of persons to whom a charge to inheritance tax (IHT) will apply. These are:

- individuals; and
- trustees.

For the F6 syllabus, only inheritance tax charge arising on individuals is examinable. The charge arising on trustees is very much a separate subject and is not examinable.

1.3. Domicile

When it comes to inheritance tax, it is an individual's domicile that determines their liability to inheritance tax.

Domicile for inheritance tax purposes has the same meaning as in general law. Stated simply, an individual is domiciled in the country where they have their permanent home. It is only possible to be domiciled in one country at a time.

There are three ways of determining an individual's domicile:

- domicile of origin: acquired at birth from either the father or mother
- domicile of dependency: acquired as a minor when the father or mother change their domicile
- domicile of choice: acquired when aged 16 or over when there is a change in the individual's permanent home

The most important domicile is the one an individual acquires at birth – the domicile of origin. This is generally dependent on the father's domicile at the time of the individual's birth; it is completely irrelevant where the child happens to be born. It is very hard to change an individual's domicile or origin.

An individual domiciled in the UK is liable for IHT in respect of all the assets, whether they are:
- owned and sold in the UK
- owned and sold outside the UK (overseas assets)

A child born in London whilst his Swiss domiciled parents were living there would have a domicile of origin in Switzerland.

A person will always be treated as domiciled in the UK for the purpose of paper F6.

State the three ways of determining an individual's domicile.

2. State, explain and apply the meaning of transfer of value, chargeable transfer and potentially exempt transfer.[2]
Demonstrate the diminution in value principle.[2]
Demonstrate the seven year accumulation principle taking into account changes in the level of the nil rate band.[2]

[Learning Outcomes c, d and e]

2.1 Transfer of value

A charge to inheritance tax arises when there is a transfer of value.

Definition

Transfer of value is defined as a gratuitous disposition made by a person as a result of which, the value of their estate decreases (i.e. diminution in value of that estate).

For individuals making transfers of value, there are two chargeable occasions that may arise:

> The terms 'transfer' and 'gift' can be taken to mean the same!

- Lifetime transfers: transfers of value made during the lifetime of the donor (lifetime transfers); and
- Death estate: transfers of value made on death, for example, when property is left to another person in a will (death estate).

The transfer of value is always calculated as the loss to the donor, not as the gain to the donee.

Tip

Transfer of values should always have a gratuitous intention; that is why poor business deals do not fall within the scope of inheritance tax.

For the purpose of paper F6, transfer of value will be a gift of assets. A gift may be either:
- a chargeable transfer; or
- a potentially exempt transfer.

2.2 Gratuitous intent

Definition

Gratuitous intent is an intention to give or grant a transfer of value without a return or cost or obligation.

Example

Den sells his computers for 50% less cost to his cousin Ben. This is a gratuitous transfer. But if Den sells the computers for 50% less than the original cost due to poor bargaining then there is no gratuitous intent; it would be a business deal.

2.3 Diminution in value principle

The fall in value of the individual's estate, otherwise known as the **loss to the donor**, is worked out by looking at the value of their estate before and after the gift was made. The difference between those two figures is the loss to the donor.

In many cases, the loss to the donor and the gain to the donee will be exactly the same.

Example

Paul gave his son Michael a cash gift of £100,000 to help purchase a property. The loss to Paul's estate is £100,000 and Michael's estate has increased by £100,000.

However, there are situations where the two values are somewhat different.

Example

Paul owned 48,000 ordinary shares for £1 each of Ming Ltd. Ming Ltd is an unquoted trading company having an issued share capital of £60,000. On 17 June 2012, he gifted 12,000 shares to his son, Michael. The following table summarises the value per share for different levels of holdings.

Percentage of holding	Value per share
80%	£15
60%	£9
20%	£5

Paul's transfer of value is as follows:

	£
Value of shares before the transfer (48,000 x £15)	720,000
Less: Value of shares after the transfer (36,000 x £9)	(324,000)
Value of transfer	**396,000**

However, the value of Michael's shareholding (12000/60000 shares x100 = 20%) is 12,000 x £5 = £60,000. It is this loss to the donor of £396,000 that is used for inheritance tax purposes.

2.4 Chargeable transfer

Inheritance tax arises on a chargeable transfer. A chargeable transfer is any transfer of value not covered by an exemption, which could be one of the following:

- **Potentially exempt transfer (PET)**: A transfer made by one individual to another individual is a potentially exempt transfer. Here if the transferor dies within seven years of making the transfer, the value of transfer becomes chargeable. However, if the transferor dies after seven years of making the transfer then the whole amount of transfer i.e. PET will become exempt from tax,

If the donor dies within seven years of making the gift, then the inheritance tax is charged in the year in which the donor dies according to the rates and allowances applicable for that tax year. However, the value on which tax is charged is fixed at the time of transfer.

Example

Tracy gave a gift of £315,000 to her son on 5 December 2004 and also gifted shares to her daughter worth £500,000 on 7 September 2009. Tracy died on 15 February 2012, and the value of the shares on that date was £525,000.

Here, the gift given by Tracy to her son is exempt from inheritance tax (IHT) because she survived more than seven years after giving the gift to her son.

The gift given to her daughter would, however, be chargeable to IHT as soon as Tracy dies as she died within seven years from the date she made the gift. IHT is ignored till Tracy's death. The amount chargeable to IHT is £500,000 and not £525,000 i.e. the amount at which the transfer was originally made. The tax will be charged at the rates and allowances of the tax year in which the Tracy dies, i.e. 2012-13

- **Chargeable lifetime transfer (CLT):** this is a transfer of value made by an individual to a trust and is not effectively a potentially exempt transfer. The transfer of value differs depending on whether the tax is paid by the donor or the donee.

Definition

A trust is an organisation where a person transfers assets or value to a group of people (trustees) to provide service or benefit to the society or other people (the beneficiaries).

A CLT immediately becomes chargeable to IHT at the rate and allowances applicable in that tax year in which the CLT is made irrespective of the death of the donor. However, if the donor dies within seven years of making the gift then an additional charge arises and this charge is calculated according to the rates and allowances prevailing in the tax year in which the donor dies.

Example

Jasmine gifted £310,000 to New Republic Trust on 5 September 2004 and gifted a painting worth £419,000 to Womans Liberation Trust on 11 June 2009. Jasmine died on 24 October 2012 and the value of the paintings as on that date was £425,000 and £500,000 respectively.

The gift of £310,000 to New Republic Trust made on 5 September 2004 immediately becomes chargeable for IHT at the rate prevailing in the year 2004-2005. Since Jasmine died on 24 October 2012, that is more than 7 seven years, no additional charge would be levied on this gift.

However, the CLT made to the Womans Liberation trust on 11 June 2009 becomes immediately chargeable for IHT as soon as the transfer is made at the rate prevailing in the year 2009-10 and since Jasmine died within 7 years of the transfer, an additional charge also arises at the rate prevailing in the year 2012-13.on the original transfer amount of £419,000.

- **Death transfer:** on death, an individual is treated as if they had made a transfer of value of the property in their estate. This is a chargeable transfer to the extent that it is not exempt. A transfer of value on death would not be a potentially exempt transfer.

Test Yourself 2

Define a transfer of value for inheritance tax purposes and state the three occasions when a chargeable transfer would arise.

Test Yourself 3

Chad owns a set of three paintings by Rembrandt. Chad decides to give one of the paintings to his daughter, Olivia. A few months later, Chad decides to give another of his Rembrandt paintings to a local art gallery.

The values of the paintings are as follows:

- Three paintings - £2,000,000
- Two paintings - £1,200,000
- One painting - £500,000

What is the transfer of value made by Chad on each gift?

2.5 Demonstrate the seven year accumulation principle taking into account changes in the level of the nil rate band

Chargeable transfers are taken into account on a **cumulative basis**. The transfers are aggregated over a seven year period, after which they are not included in the **cumulative total**.

The amount of inheritance tax on the latest chargeable transfer is determined by reference to this cumulative total. The chargeable transfer being made is reduced by any exemptions and reliefs available to the transferor. Inheritance tax is then charged, either at the lifetime rate (half the death rate) or the death rate (currently 40%), on the taxable value, which is greater than the transferor's **available inheritance threshold** at the date the chargeable transfer is made.

The transferor's available inheritance tax threshold is the inheritance tax threshold at the date the transfer of value is made, which is £325,000 for 2012/13, less the **cumulative chargeable transfers made in the previous seven years**.

Tip

Only CLT made within seven years, irrespective of the fact that it is made more than seven years before the date of death of the donor, is to be taken into account. PETs that are made more than seven years before the date of death of the donor is completely exempt from IHT.

Example

Harold died on 28 February 2013, leaving behind an estate valued at £750,000. Harold had made the following chargeable transfers in the seven years prior to his death:

- Chargeable transfer of £100,000 to a discretionary trust on 7 April 2010
- Chargeable transfer of £147,000 to a discretionary trust on 18 July 2008

Harold's available inheritance tax threshold at his date of death is as follows:

	£
Inheritance tax threshold – 2012/13	325,000
Cumulative chargeable lifetime transfers in previous seven years	
Chargeable transfer to discretionary trust in April 2010	(100,000)
Chargeable transfer to discretionary trust in July 2008	(147,000)
Available inheritance tax threshold	78,000

Test Yourself 4

Continuing the example of Harold, what would his available inheritance tax threshold be in respect of the gift made to the discretionary trust in April 2010, assuming he did not make any chargeable transfers in the previous seven years?

Note: the inheritance tax threshold limit for the year 2010-11 is £325,000.

Example

On 21 June 2012, Pepper died and her estate was valued at £525,000. On 1 April 2003, she had made a gift of £195,000 to Roadman Trust, and on 1 September 2009, she made a gift of £225,000 to Boatman Trust. The trusts agreed to pay any IHT arising against the gift made to them. The figures mentioned are after availing all the exemptions.

Note: the nil rate band for 2003-04 is £255,000 and for 2009-10, £325,000.

	£	£
Lifetime transfers		
1 April 2003	195,000	
nil rate band £255,000		0
1 September 2009	225,000	
nil rate band balance (£325,000-£195,000) £130,000 at nil%		0
(£225,000-£130,000) £95,000 at 20%		**19,000**
Additional liability on death		
1 April 2003	195,000	
no additonal liability as CLT made more than seven years before Pepper's death		
1 September 2009	225,000	
IHT liability (£325,000 - £195,000) £130,000 at nil%		0
(£225,000 - £130,000) £95,000 at 40%		38,000
IHT already paid		(19,000)
Additional liability		**19,000**
Death estate		
Chargeable estate	525,000	
IHT laibility (£325,000 - £225,000) £100,000 at nil%		0
(£525,000 - £100,000) £425,000 at 40%		**170,000**

Continued on the next page

Note: while calculating IHT, the CLT made on 1 April 2003 is not considered on the death as it is more than seven years before Pepper's death on 21 June 2012. The CLT made on 1 September 2009 is only considered in the calculation and so from the nil rate band of £325,000, only £225,000 is utilised.

Continuing the above example, instead of making the gift to the trust, if Pepper gifts her daughter £225,000 then the IHT calculations would be as follows:

	£	£
Lifetime transfers		
1 April 2003	195,000	
nil rate band £255,000		0
1 September 2009	225,000	
Potentially exempt transfer		0
Additional liability on death		
1 April 2003	195,000	
1 September 2009	225,000	
Potentially exempt transfer		
IHT liability (£325,000 - £195,000) £130,000 at nil%		0
(£225,000 - £130,000) £95,000 at 40%		**38,000**
Death estate		
Chargeable estate	525,000	
IHT laibility (£325,000 - £225,000) £100,000 at nil%		0
(£525,000 - £100,000) £425,000 at 40%		**170,000**

SUMMARY

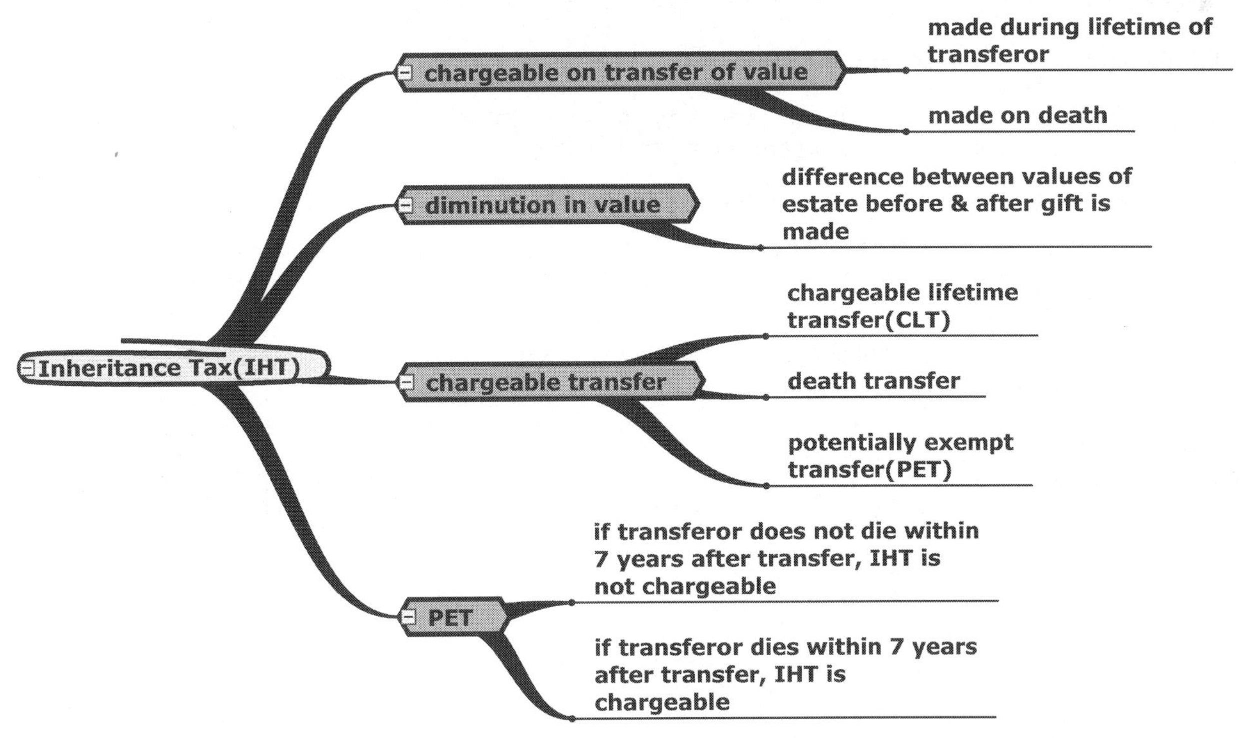

3. Understand the tax implications of chargeable lifetime transfers and compute the relevant liabilities.[2]
Understand the tax implications of transfers within seven years of death and compute the relevant liabilities.[2]

[Learning Outcomes e and f]

There are two aspects to the calculation of tax on chargeable transfers for individuals:

- lifetime tax on chargeable lifetime transfers; and
- additional death tax on chargeable lifetime transfers and on potentially exempt transfers where the donor dies within seven years of making the transfer.

3.1 Chargeable lifetime transfers

The tax rates for the year 2012-13 are given below:

Inheritance Tax	2012 - 13
Nil band	£325,000
Lifetime transfers – lifetime rate	20%
Transfer within 7 years of death – death rate	40%

We have already learnt that a CLT is immediately chargeable as soon as the CLT is made. It is chargeable as above.

Example

Suzie gifts her son cash of £515,000 on 5 September 2004 and dies on 17 October 2008. The gift made by her was initially exempt when she made the gift on 5 September 2004. However, she dies within seven years of making the gift, so it will become chargeable in the tax year 2008-09 when she died.

The first £325,000 is in the nil rate band and the balance amount i.e. £190,000 (£515,000 – £325,000) becomes chargeable at the death rate of 40%.

Inheritance tax is payable when an individual's cumulative chargeable transfers exceed a nil rate band during a seven year period. **The nil rate band for the tax year 2012-13 is £325,000.**

3.2 Lifetime tax on chargeable lifetime transfers

Effectively, this calculation will only arise when transfers of value are made to relevant property trusts e.g. a discretionary trust as they are chargeable lifetime transfers.

Use the following proforma to calculate the inheritance tax due:

	£	£
Chargeable lifetime transfer		X
Inheritance tax threshold	X	
Cumulative chargeable lifetime transfers in previous seven years	(X)	
Available inheritance tax threshold		(X)
Taxable lifetime transfer		X
Inheritance tax @ 20%		X

3.3 Tax at the time of death of a person

The IHT is chargeable on the death of a person at the rate of 40% for the tax year 2012-13 in case of:

a) a death transfer – IHT is calculated on the person's estate

Example

Lucy died leaving behind an estate valued at £585,000 on 5 September 2012.

The IHT liability is calculated as:

	£	£
Death estate		585,000
Inheritance tax threshold	325,000	
Cumulative chargeable lifetime transfers in previous seven years	nil	
Available inheritance tax threshold	325,000	(325,000)
Taxable lifetime transfer		260,000
Inheritance tax @ 40%		104,000

b) on PETs – if the donor dies within 7 years of making the gift

Example

Continuing the above example, suppose Lucy made a gift of £119,000 to her granddaughter on 10 June 2004 (after all the available exemptions)

The IHT liability is calculated as:

	£	£
Death estate		585,000
Inheritance tax threshold	325,000	
Cumulative chargeable lifetime transfers in previous seven years	119,000	
Available inheritance tax threshold	206,000	(206,000)
Taxable lifetime transfer		379,000
Inheritance tax @ 40%		151,600

Tip

Potentially exempt transfers are not subject to inheritance tax at the time of the transfer of value, but will become chargeable at the rate of 40% if the transferor dies within seven years of making the transfer.

c) on CLTs – if the donor dies within 7 years of making the gift for additional tax payable

Chargeable lifetime transfers are chargeable to a maximum of half the death rate of 40% i.e. 20%, when the transfer of value occurs. This is called lifetime tax.

Where the transferor dies within seven years of making the transfer of value, the inheritance tax is recalculated at the death rate of 40%, with any lifetime tax paid being deducted from the death tax liability. Unfortunately, there is no repayment of inheritance tax if the lifetime tax paid is greater than the death tax due.

To clarify, exempt transfers are immediately exempt and do not become taxable even where the transferor dies within seven years of making the transfer of value.

Example

Continuing the above example, instead of Lucy making a gift to her granddaughter, if Lucy had made a gift of £410,000 to a trust on 21 August 2009 after availing all the exemptions, the nil rate band for the tax year 2009-10 would have been £325,000.

The IHT liability is calculated as:

	£	£
Chargeable lifetime transfer - 21 August 2009		410,000
Inheritance tax threshold	325,000	
Less: Cumulative chargeable lifetime transfers in previous seven years	-	
Available inheritance tax threshold		(325,000)
Taxable lifetime transfer on 21 August 2008		85,000
Inheritance tax @ 20%		**17,000**
Additional liability arising on death - 5 Sept 2012		
Chargeable lifetime transfer - 21 August 2009		410,000
Inheritance tax threshold	325,000	
Less: Cumulative chargeable lifetime transfers in previous seven years	-	(325,000)
Taxable lifetime transfer		85,000
Inheritance tax @ 40%	34,000	
Less: IHT already paid	(17,000)	
Additional tax liability		**17,000**
Death estate chargeable	585,000	
Available inheritance tax threshold	nil	
Inheritance tax @ 40%		**234,000**

Note: the whole estate is chargeable at 40% as the nil rate band of £325,000 is fully utilised by the CLT made on 21 August 2009.

Tip

When making potentially exempt transfers and chargeable lifetime transfers as part of any inheritance tax planning exercise with a clean gifts history, creating chargeable lifetime transfers before potentially exempt transfers will usually help to minimise any possible future inheritance tax that could arise on trustees.

Example

Claudia set up a discretionary trust for £369,000 on 5 May 2012. However, she made a chargeable lifetime transfer of £100,000 in September 2005. The trustees agreed to pay any inheritance tax due.

Calculate the lifetime inheritance tax payable by the trustees.

	£	£
Chargeable lifetime transfer		369,000
Inheritance tax threshold	325,000	
Cumulative chargeable lifetime transfers in previous seven years	(100,000)	
Available inheritance tax threshold		(225,000)
Taxable lifetime transfer		144,000
Inheritance tax @ 20%		28,800

Test Yourself 5

Randolph set up a discretionary trust for £517,000 on 13 June 2012. Ralph has made the following gifts in the previous seven years.

- Gift to his son Rupert on 10 April 2012 of £3,000
- Gift to a discretionary trust on 13 September 2009 for £145,000
- Gift to his son Rupert on 8 October 2007 for £120,000

Calculate the lifetime inheritance tax payable where the trustees agree to pay the inheritance tax due.

3.4 Advantages of lifetime transfers

The simplest way of bringing down a person's potential IHT liability is to use lifetime transfers. The implications are:

i. Seven years after a transfer a PET becomes completely exempt from IHT
ii. Seven years after a transfer a CLT will not have any additional IHT liability.
iii. Taper relief will still apply and reduce the IHT payable after three years, if the donor does not survive for more than seven years.
iv. Making gifts of assets whose expected value would increase, e.g. property or shares, is beneficial because the PETs and CLTs are taken at the value the transfer is made and not at the increased value.

3.5 Chargeable lifetime transfers within seven years of death

To summarise a point made earlier, where the transferor dies within seven years of making a lifetime transfer, whether a chargeable lifetime transfer or a potentially exempt transfer, the inheritance tax is recalculated at the death rate of 40% with any lifetime tax paid being deducted from the death tax liability. Again, as stated previously, there is no repayment of inheritance tax if the lifetime tax paid is greater than the death tax due.

However, the longer the transferor survives after making a gift the lower will be the effective rate of death tax.

Taper relief is thus brought in to be fair to the transferor. Where a transferor lives for more than three years, but less than seven years after making a gift, taper relief reduces the amount of tax payable as follows:

Years between transfer and death	Percentage reduction in death tax
3 years or less	0
More than 3 but less than 4 years	20
More than 4 but less than 5 years	40
More than 5 but less than 6 years	60
More than 6 but less than 7 years	80

Note: this table will be given in the exam paper so no need to memorise it.

Death tax on a lifetime transfer is always payable by the transferee, so grossing up is not relevant. Therefore only one calculation is required when calculating the death tax due.

Please note that taper relief may bring down the amount of tax payable but cannot bring down the value of a gift taken for cumulation purposes.

Use the following proforma to calculate the inheritance tax due:

	£	£
Chargeable lifetime transfer		X
Inheritance tax threshold	X	
Cumulative chargeable lifetime transfers in previous seven years	(X)	
Available inheritance tax threshold		(X)
Taxable lifetime transfer		X
Death tax @ 40%		X
Taper relief, if applicable (% basis)		(X)
Death tax due		X
Inheritance tax already paid		(X)
Death tax payable		X

Claudia set up a discretionary trust for £375,000 on 30 September 2007. The trustees agreed to pay any inheritance tax due.

Claudia also made a gift of £250,000 to her daughter Emma on 30 May 2010.

Sadly, Claudia died on 1 July 2012.

Calculate the following inheritance tax liabilities:

a) The lifetime tax payable by the trustees on the transfer to the discretionary trust in September 2007. The threshold limit for the year 2007-08 is £300,000.
b) The death tax payable on the transfer to the discretionary trust in September 2007.
c) The death tax payable on the transfer to Emma in May 2010.

Answer

Gift made to Emma is a potentially exempt transfer; therefore there will be no inheritance tax due at the time of the transfer. However, gift made to the trust is a chargeable lifetime transfer.

a) Lifetime tax payable on gift to trustees – September 2007

	£	£
Chargeable lifetime transfer		375,000
Inheritance tax threshold for 2007-08	300,000	
Cumulative chargeable lifetime transfers in previous seven years	0	
Available inheritance tax threshold	300,000	(300,000)
Taxable lifetime transfer		75,000
Inheritance tax @ 20%		15,000

b) Death tax payable on gift to trustees

	£	£
Chargeable lifetime transfer		375,000
Inheritance tax threshold for 2012-13	325,000	
Less: Cumulative chargeable lifetime transfers in previous seven years	0	
Available inheritance tax threshold	325,000	(325,000)
Taxable lifetime transfer		50,000
Inheritance tax @ 40%		20,000
Less: Taper relief (between 4 to 5 years) 40% of £20,000		(8,000)
		12,000
Less: Inheritance tax already paid		(20,000)
Additional liability		nil

Note: although the additional inheritance liability of £12,000 is lower than the inheritance tax of £20,000, which is already paid, a refund is never made.

c) Death tax payable on gift to Emma

	£
Chargeable transfer	250,000
Inheritance tax @ 40%	100,000
Less: Taper relief (less than 3 years)	0
Inheritance tax liability	100,000

Note: the nil rate band for 2012-13 of £325,000 is already used up by lifetime transfers made to the trust, therefore there is no threshold limit available for the transfer made to Emma.

SUMMARY

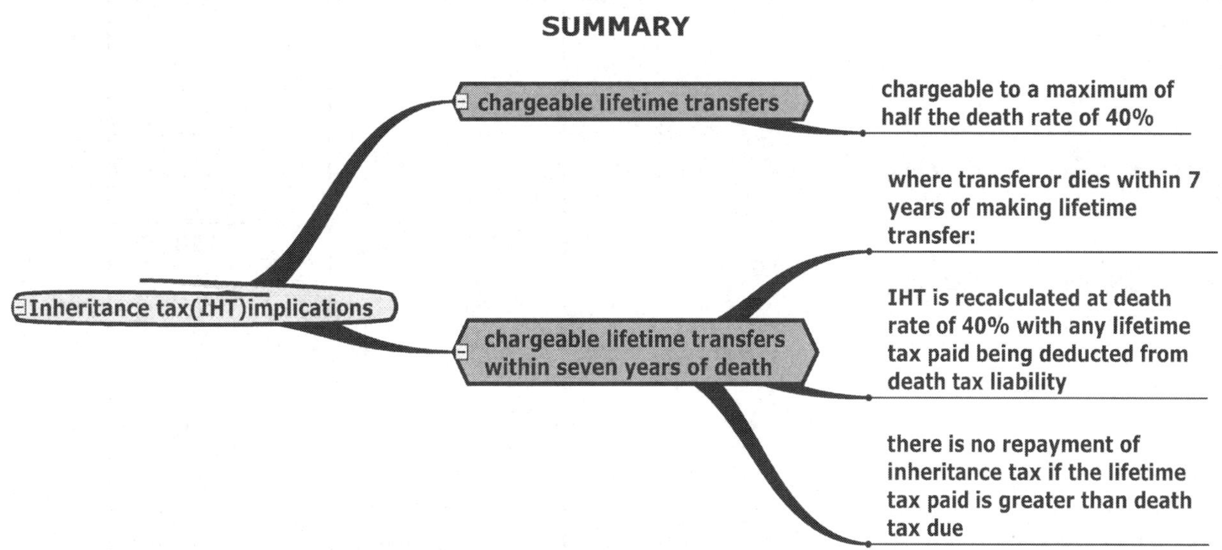

4. Compute the tax liability on a death estate.[2]
Understand and apply the transfer of any unused nil rate band between spouses.[2]
[Learning Outcomes h and i]

4.1 The death estate

When an individual dies, they are deemed to make a transfer of their whole estate, which can be defined as:

- free estate, which includes both realty and property
- property given, subject to a reservation of benefit;
- settled property which is the subject of a qualifying interest in possession.

The death estate would also include anything acquired as a result of death e.g. the proceeds of a life assurance policy, property, shares, motor vehicles, cash and other investments.

Tip

In the calculation of a death estate, the market value of a life assurance policy at the date of death is not considered.

Any outstanding liabilities at the date of death are deducted from the gross estate (unless excluded under anti-avoidance provisions), together with reasonable funeral expenses, mourning expenses and the cost of a headstone.

In addition to the above, the following expenses are permitted:

- amount specifically left by a deceased person to pay a debt that was incurred for a valuable consideration (gambling debts are not allowable)
- mortgages on property: repayment mortgages and interest-only mortgages are allowable but endowment mortgages are not allowed; they are included in the repayment process of the life assurance policy

Example

The following assets were owned by Bernard when he died on 30 October 2012.

- Investments of £37,000
- Shares of £77,000 in Farms and Ferns Ltd
- His bungalow valued at £615,000; this has an interest only mortgage outstanding of £210,000
- A life assurance policy valued at £125,000 as on 30 October 2012

The following are Bernard's liabilities as on 30 October 2012:

- Funeral cost: £3,800
- Cost of headstone: £410
- Verbal agreement to pay legal fees of Rose, his friend: £925
- Credit card bills: £500

The proceeds received from the life assurance policy were £175,000.

	£	£
Free estate		
Personal		
Stocks and shares		77,000
Insurance policy proceeds		175,000
Personal chattels (investments)		37,000
Cash		-
		289,000
Less: Debts due by deceased		
Funeral expenses	3,800	
Cost of headstone	410	
Credit card bills	500	
		(4,710)
Realty		
Freehold property	615,000	
Less: Mortgages	(210,000)	
		405,000
Net free estate		689,290
Settled property		-
Gifts with reservation of benefit		-
Chargeable estate		689,290
Inheritance tax threshold	325,000	
Cumulative transfers made in the previous seven years	-	
Available inheritance tax threshold		(325,000)
Taxable estate		364,290
Inheritance tax at the rate of 40%		145,716

Any reliefs are then applied to certain assets included in the death estate, such as business or agricultural property. Exemptions are also accounted for where assets are left to, say, the spouse or civil partner.

The net estate is then charged to tax, either at the rate of 0% for the value within the available inheritance tax threshold, or 40% for any value greater than the inheritance tax threshold.

As with lifetime transfers, when calculating the available inheritance tax threshold, a deduction has to be made for any chargeable transfers made during the seven years prior to the date of death.

Use the following proforma to calculate the inheritance tax due:

	£	£
Free estate		
Personal		
Stocks and shares		X
Insurance policy proceeds		X
Personal chattels		X
Cash		X
		X
Less:		
Debts due by deceased	X	
Funeral expenses	X	
		(X)
		X
Realty		
Freehold property	X	
Less:		
Mortgages	(X)	
		X
Net free estate		X
Settled property		X
Gifts with reservation of benefit		X
Chargeable estate		X
Inheritance tax threshold	X	
Cumulative transfers made in the previous seven years	(X)	
Available inheritance tax threshold		(X)
Taxable estate		X
Inheritance tax at the rate of 40%		X

4.2 Transferable inheritance tax threshold between spouses

It should be noted that the inheritance tax threshold available to an individual when calculating their death estate, may be greater than the inheritance tax threshold applicable at the time. This is because they may have had some unused inheritance tax threshold transferred to them by their spouse or civil partner following their death.

Since 9 October 2007, you can transfer any unused inheritance tax threshold from a late spouse or civil partner to the second spouse or civil partner when they die. The inheritance tax threshold can only be transferred on the second death i.e. it isn't available during the lifetime of the surviving spouse or civil partner to reduce the inheritance tax liability on chargeable lifetime transfers.

It doesn't matter when the first spouse or civil partner died. Effectively, the outcome of this legislation could increase the inheritance tax threshold of the surviving spouse or civil partner from £325,000 to as much as £650,000 in 2012/13, depending on the circumstances.

Example

Joanie and Chachi are married and have a joint estate worth £800,000. They have three children and have not made any previous lifetime transfers.

Chachi dies first, leaving his entire estate to Joanie. Inheritance tax will not be payable because transfers to UK-domiciled spouses are exempt.

Joanie then dies (and assuming current values and allowances) with her total estate valued at £800,000. The inheritance tax calculation on the second death is:

	£
Value of Joanie's estate	800,000
Joanie's 2012/13 inheritance tax threshold	(325,000)
Chachi's unused inheritance tax threshold	(325,000)
Taxable estate	150,000
Inheritance tax @ 40%	60,000

It should be clarified that the amount of unused inheritance tax threshold transferred on the first death is not the unused amount in monetary terms, but the unused amount as a percentage. This unused percentage is then applied to the inheritance tax threshold applying at the date of death of the surviving spouse or civil partner.

For example, if on the first death the chargeable estate is £150,000 and the inheritance tax threshold is £300,000, 50% of the inheritance tax threshold would be unused. If the inheritance tax threshold when the survivor dies is £325,000, the legislation allows this to be increased by 50% to £487,500 (£325,000 + 50% of £325,000.

The use of a percentage rather than a monetary amount allows for any growth arising on the transferred wealth.

Personal representatives will not have to claim for any unused inheritance tax threshold to be transferred at the time of the first death. All claims will need to be made by the personal representatives of the estate of the second spouse or civil partner to die.

The deadline for the claim will be the later of:

- two years from the end of the month in which the surviving spouse or civil partner dies; or
- three months from the date on which the personal representatives first act; or
- such longer period as the Commissioners for Her Majesty's Revenue and Customs may specify.

If the personal representatives do not make a claim, a claim can be made by any other person liable to tax chargeable on the death of the surviving spouse or civil partner within such later period as an officer of the Revenue may allow in a particular case.

Example

Maggie died on 23 March 2012 and left behind an estate valued at £925,000. She had used only 50% of her husband's nil rate band when he died on 19 August 2002.

Maggie had made a gift of £315,000 to her son on his birthday, i.e. 27 July 2009, after deducting all the exemptions.

The nil rate band for the tax year 2009-10 is £325,000.

Continued on the next page

	£	£
Lifetime transfer on 27 July 2009		315,000
Potentially exempt transfer		
Additional liability arising on death 23 March 2012		315,000
Potentially exempt transfer		
Death estate		
Chargeable estate		925,000
Inheritance tax threshold for 2012-13 - Maggie	325,000	
Inheritance tax threshold for 2012-13 - Maggie's husband	162,500	
Available inheritance tax threshold	487,500	
Cumulative transfers made in the previous seven years	(315,000)	
Available inheritance tax threshold	172,500	
Taxable estate		172,500
Inheritance tax at the rate of 40%		69,000

Note: Maggie's personal representative can claim her husband's unused nil rate band of 162,500 (325000 x 50%). The nil rate band is 487,500 (325,000 + 162,500), i.e. the total of Maggie's and her husband's nil rate band. The PET made to her son is utilised from this nil rate band on 27 July 2009.

4.3 Chargeable lifetime transfer preceded by potentially exempt transfer that becomes chargeable

We have already worked out some examples where the CLT is made before a PET. Here, we will see the treatment of inheritance tax where there is a reversal in the sequence of gifts made and where PET uses some or all of the nil rate band.

Solomon made a gift of £420,000 to his son on 29 June 2009. He also made a gift of £310,000 to a trust for animal care on 15 February 2010. Both gifts were made after availing all the exemptions. Solomon died on 9 April 2012.

The nil rate band for the tax year 2009-10 and 2010-11 is 325,000.

	£	£
Lifetime transfer		
on 29 June 2009 Potentially exempt transfer	420,000	
on 15 February 2010 Chargeable lifetime transfer	310,000	
No lifetime IHT is payable as the CLT is less than the nil rate band for 2010-11		0
Additional liabilities on death		
29 June 2009 Potentially exempt transfer	420,000	
Inheritance threshold for 2011-12	(325,000)	
Available inheritance tax liability	95,000	
Inheritance tax at the rate of 40%		38,000
15 February 2010 Chargeable transfer	310,000	
Inheritance threshold for 2010-11	0	
Available inheritance tax liability	310,000	
Inheritance tax at the rate of 40%		124,000
PET made on 29 June 2009 has fully utilised the nil rate band for 2011-12		

Answers to Test Yourself

Answer to TY 1

The three ways of determining an individual's domicile are:

- domicile of origin: acquired at birth from either the father or mother
- domicile of dependency: acquired as a minor when the father or mother change their domicile
- domicile of choice: acquired when aged 16 or over when there is a change in the individual's permanent home

Answer to TY 2

A transfer of value is a gratuitous disposition made by a person which results in the value of their estate decreasing.

A chargeable transfer will arise on the following three occasions:

- Chargeable lifetime transfer
- Death estate
- Potentially exempt transfer where the transferor has died within seven years of making the transfer

Answer to TY 3

Chad's transfers of value are as follows:

Gift to Olivia - £800,000 (£2,000,000 less £1,200,000)

Gift to local art gallery - £700,000 (£1,200,000 less £500,000)

Answer to TY 4

Harold's available inheritance tax threshold in respect of the gift made to a discretionary trust in April 2009 is as follows:

	£
Inheritance tax threshold – 2010/11	325,000
Cumulative chargeable lifetime transfers in previous seven years	
- Net chargeable transfer to discretionary trust	(100,000)
Available inheritance tax threshold	225,000

Answer to TY 5

The lifetime inheritance tax payable by the trustees in respect of the gift made by Randolph is as follows:

	£	£
Chargeable lifetime transfer		517,000
Inheritance tax threshold – 2012/13	325,000	
Cumulative chargeable lifetime transfers in previous seven years	(145,000)	
Available inheritance tax threshold		(180,000)
Taxable lifetime transfer		337,000
Inheritance tax @ 20%		67,400

Note: gift to individuals are not chargeable lifetime transfers as they are potentially exempt transfers. That is why gift to the son is not included in the above computation.

Self Examination Questions

Question 1

John died on 18 December 2012. He had made the following lifetime transfers:

i. A gift of £530,000 was made to a trust on 15 October 2007. The inheritance tax arising from the transfer was paid by the trust.
ii. A gift of £430,000 was made to his daughter on 25 July 2009.

Note

(a) The above amounts are net of exemptions.
(b) The nil rate band for the year 2007-08 is £300,000 and for the year 2009-10 is £325,000.

Required

Compute the following:

i Inheritance tax which arises on 15 October 2007,
ii Inheritance tax which arises on 25 July 2009 and
iii Inheritance tax which arises on 18 December 2012

Question 2

Anna died on 13 December 2012. She had made the following lifetime transfers:

i Gift of £400,000 to her daughter on 14 September 2005.
ii Gift of a house valued at £730,000 to her brother on 15 July 2010. By 13 December 2013, the value of the house had increased to £755,000.

Required

Discuss whether these gifts fall within the purview of inheritance tax.

Question 3

Mark set up a discretionary trust for £500,000 on 24 September 2012. However, Mark made a chargeable lifetime transfer of £200,000 in August 2006. The trustees agreed to pay any inheritance tax due.

Calculate the lifetime inheritance tax payable by the trustees.

Answers to Self Examination Questions

Answer to SEQ 1

i. Inheritance tax which arises on 15 October 2007,

	£	£
Chargeable lifetime transfer		530,000
Inheritance tax threshold for 2007-08	300,000	
Cumulative chargeable lifetime transfers in previous seven years	(NIL)	
Less: Available inheritance tax threshold		(300,000)
Taxable lifetime transfer		230,000
Inheritance tax @ 20%		46,000

ii. **Inheritance tax which arises on 25 July 2009**

Transfer made to daughter is a potentially exempt transfer, it will not be taxable at the time of transfer. However, if the transferor dies within seven years of transfer, then it will become chargeable. Therefore, no inheritance tax will arise on 25 July 2009.

iii. Inheritance tax arising on 18 December 2012

	£	£
Chargeable lifetime transfer - 15 October 2007		530,000
Inheritance tax threshold for 2012-13	325,000	
Less: Cumulative chargeable lifetime transfers in previous seven years	(nil)	
Available inheritance tax threshold		(325,000)
Taxable lifetime transfer		205,000
Inheritance tax @ 40%		82,000
Less: Taper relief of 60%(as the gift is made between 5 to six years of John's death)		(49,200)
		32,800
Less: Inheritance tax already paid		(46,000)
Additional liability		**nil**
Potentially exempt transfer (PET) - 25 July 2009		430,000
Inheritance tax: £430,000 at 40%		172,000
Less: Taper relief (less than 3 years) : 20% of £172,000		(34,400)
Additional tax liability		**137,600**

Tip

Although the inheritance tax liability of £32,800 is lower than the inheritance tax of £46,000 which is already paid, a refund is never made.

Answer to SEQ 2

Any transfer that is made to another individual is a potentially exempt transfer (PET). If the donor survives for seven years after making the gift, the PET becomes exempt from inherent tax. On the other hand, the PET becomes chargeable to inheritance tax if the donor dies within seven years of making the gift.
Therefore the following is the treatment of the gifts given by Anna:

(i) The gift to her daughter was given more than seven years prior to her death. Therefore the transfer is exempt from inheritance tax.
(ii) The gift to her brother was given less than seven years before her death. Therefore it is chargeable to inheritance tax. However, the value of the PET is fixed at the time the gift is made. Furthermore, tax is charged according to the rates and allowances applicable to the tax year in which the donor dies. Thus £730,000 is chargeable to inheritance tax based on the rates and allowances for 2012-13.

Answer to SEQ 3

	£	£
Chargeable lifetime transfer		500,000
Inheritance tax threshold	325,000	
Cumulative chargeable lifetime transfers in the previous seven years	(200,000)	
Available inheritance tax threshold		(125,000)
Taxable lifetime transfer		375,000
Inheritance tax @ 20%		75,000

SECTION E

INHERITANCE TAX

E2

STUDY GUIDE E2: INHERITANCE TAX (PART 2)

Get Through Intro

Inheritance tax is only due if your estate - including any assets held in trust and gifts made within seven years of death – exceeds the current Inheritance Tax threshold (£325,000 for 2012-13). The tax is payable on the amount over this threshold.

Inheritance Tax is usually paid on an estate when the owner dies. It is also sometimes payable on trusts or gifts made during a person's lifetime. While calculating the threshold amount of £325,000, certain amounts are to be excluded. Knowledge of these exemptions will help you in calculating the correct value of taxable inheritance.

The executor or personal representative usually pays the tax from the deceased's estate. The trustees usually pay the tax on trust assets. Furthermore, certain time limits have been laid down for payment, which in most cases, is 6 months. This Study Guide will help you in understanding these principles

Learning Outcomes

a) Understand and apply the following exemptions:
   i. small gifts exemption
   ii. annual exemption
   iii. normal expenditure out of income
   iv. gifts in consideration of marriage
   v. gifts between spouses.
b) Identify who is responsible for the payment of inheritance tax.
c) Advise on the due date for payment of inheritance tax.

1. Understand and apply the following exemptions:
i. small gifts exemption[2]
ii. annual exemption[2]
iii. normal expenditure out of income[2]
iv. gifts in consideration of marriage[2]
v. gifts between spouses[2]

[Learning Outcome a]

1.1 Exemptions

Exemptions may apply to make chargeable transfers, either whole or in part, not chargeable. Some exemptions only apply to lifetime transfers, whilst some apply to both lifetime transfers and the death estate.

1. Exemptions applying to lifetime transfers only

a) Annual exemption

An individual is allowed to make gifts of up to £3,000 each tax year whilst they are alive. Any unused exemption can be carried forward for one year only. However, any unused brought forward exemption cannot be carried forward a second time.

Example

Molly makes the following gifts during her lifetime:

Tax year	Gift	Tax position
2010/11	£2,500	Entirely exempt; £500 carried forward
2011/12	£2,800	Entirely exempt; £200 carried forward
2012/13	£3,700	£3,200 exempt; £500 potentially exempt

Molly has not maximised the use of her annual exemptions. As you will note, the £500 unused exemption from 2010/11 is lost. It would have been better for Molly to have made a gift of £3,500 in 2011/12 and then £3,000 in 2012/13. The same total of gifts would be made overall, and they would all be exempt.

The annual exemption is used strictly in sequence and is given against PETs even though they are not chargeable.

Example

Tobby gifted his daughter Maria £50,000 in cash on 15 July 2007. He also gifted £115,000 to the Children's Movement Association Trust on 20 August 2008. The nil rate bands for the tax years 2007-08 and 2008-09 are £285,000 and £300,000 respectively.

	£	£
Potential exempt transfer	50,000	
Less: Annual Exemptions of 2006-07	(3,000)	
Annual Exemptions of 2007-08	(3,000)	
Value of PET	44,000	
Tobby is still alive so IHT is ignored		NIL
Chargeable lifetime transfer	115,000	
Less: Annual Exemptions of 2008-09	(3,000)	
	112,000	
Inheritance threshold for 2008-09	(300,000)	
Inheritance tax liability		NIL

---

b) Gifts in consideration of marriage or civil partnership

Exemptions for gifts in consideration of marriage or registering of civil partnership are also available. These are applied before the annual exemption, and depend upon how the person giving the gift is related to the person they're giving it to, as shown below:

Relationship to the recipient	Amount £
Parent of either party to the marriage / civil partnership	5,000
Any other ancestor such as grandparent or great-grandparent	2,500
(Prior to marriage / civil partnership) by one party of the marriage / civil partnership to the other	2,500
Anyone else, whether or not a member of the family	1,000

The gift must be made in contemplation of a particular marriage / civil partnership and, in practice, on the occasion of the marriage / civil partnership. You can't make a gift of £5,000 to your daughter on the basis that she'll eventually get married.

Example

Natheline gave a gift of £50,000 to her daughter on her marriage on 2 May 2012. She did not make any other gift till 6 April 2011.

	£
Potential exempt transfer	50,000
Less Annual Exemptions of 2012-13	(3,000)
Annual Exemptions of 2011-12	(3,000)
	44,000
Less Marriage Exemptions 2012-13	(5,000)
Value of PET	39,000

Note: The gift is a PET as Natheline is still alive and so now the gift will be ignored for IHT purposes. But in case of Natheline's death it will become chargeable to IHT. However in this case no IHT will be charged the value of the PET is coming within the nil rate band of £325,000.

---

c) Normal expenditure out of income

Gifts which are made purely out of income as part of a person's normal expenditure are exempt from inheritance tax. The claimant must show that after allowing for the gifts the donor was left with sufficient income to maintain their usual standard of living and that there was an established pattern of giving.

Example

Betty wants to make gifts to her family free from inheritance tax. Betty's annual income and expenditure are shown below:

	£	£
Income		
Salary	100,000	
Dividends	1,000	
Bank interest	200	
		101,200
Expenses		
Tax	30,000	
National insurance contributions	4,000	
Mortgage	12,000	
Council tax	2,000	
Electricity	500	
Gas	500	
Water	350	
House insurance	200	
General DIY expenses	1,000	
TV/satellite	720	
Food and clothes	8,500	
Motor expenses	2,300	
Holiday, Christmas and birthdays	4,000	
		(66,070)
Surplus income		35,130

In this situation, Betty could make an exempt gift of up to £35,130 each year with no charge to inheritance tax and without impairing the lifestyle that she's used to. However, Betty must show a pattern of making such gifts if her claim is to be successful.

Tip

Therefore a person can make regular annual gifts of £2,500 if his annual income is 100,000 and this can be exempt, however if he makes a one off gift of £50,000 then this will not be exempt but would be treated as PET or CLT.

d) Small gifts

The exemption is £250 and will cover any outright gifts to any one person per tax year. Any number of these small gifts can be made if the limit per person isn't exceeded.

The exemption is applied before the annual exemption but isn't available to cover part of a larger gift to the same person.

Example

Harold makes the following gifts during 2012-13

Date of gift	Gift	Tax position
30 April 2012	Birthday gift to nephew of £3,000	Exempt as within 2012/13 annual exemption
12 December 2012	Christmas present to the same nephew of £250	Exempt as a small gift
12 December 2012	Christmas present to niece of £250	Exempt as a small gift
31 January 2013	Christmas present of £5,000 to daughter	Potentially exempt unless normal expenditure out of income applies

2. Exemptions applying to both lifetime gifts and the death estate

Transfer to spouse or civil partner

Transfers between husbands and wives, or civil partners, are completely exempt from inheritance tax no matter what the value, as long as both parties are UK domiciled.

Example

George is considering making a gift to his son who's getting married this year. George hasn't made any gifts previously and can therefore make the following exempt gift to his son:

	£
Annual exemption – 2012/13	3,000
Annual exemption – 2011/12	3,000
Gift on marriage	5,000
Total exempt gift	**11,000**

Although George has surplus income of £7,000, the normal expenditure out of income exemption would not apply as the gift appears to be a one-off thing and not part of a continued stream of giving. If George were to continue making such gifts to his son, it would be possible to make a total exempt gift of £18,000.

Both lifetime gifts and gift transfers on death to spouses / civil partners are exempt from IHT.

Example

On her 50th wedding anniversary (i.e. on 29 December 2008), Delila gifted her husband £325,000 in cash. She died on 5 May 2012 and in her will she had divided her estate equally between her son and husband. The estate was valued at £850,000. The nil rate band for the year 2008-09 is £312,000.

	£
Lifetime transfer	325,000
Less: Exemption transfer to spouse	325,000
Inheritance tax liability	NIL
Death estate	
Value of estate	850,000
Less: Exemption transfer to spouse	(425,000)
Chargeable estate transfer to son	425,000
IHT Liability	
325000 at nil%	NIL
100,000 at 40%	40,000

SUMMARY

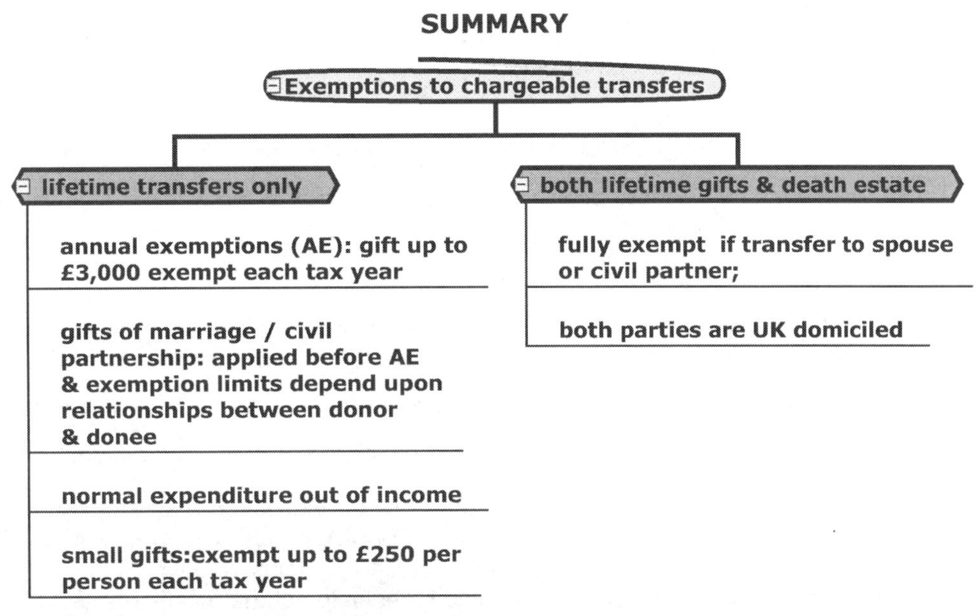

State three exemptions that apply during the lifetime of an individual.

2. Identify who is responsible for the payment of inheritance tax.[2]
Advise on the due date for payment of inheritance tax.[2]

[Learning Outcomes b and c]

2.1 Exceptions to the inheritance tax charge

The following are not chargeable to inheritance tax:

- Transfers where there is no gratuitous intent: for example selling a piece of furniture for £500 which turns out to be worth £25,000. However, the transaction must have been made at arm's length between unconnected persons.
- Transfers made in the course of a trade: for example Christmas gifts to employees
- Expenditure on family maintenance: for example school fees paid for a child
- Waivers of remuneration
- Waivers of dividends provided the waiver is made within the 12 months before the dividend is declared
- Any transfer covered by a specific exemption
- Transfers of excluded property

2.2 The administration of inheritance tax

Inheritance tax is not based on an annual process. Instead, any person who is liable for inheritance tax on a transfer is required to deliver an account giving details of the relevant assets and their values.

However, it is the duty of the personal representatives to provide both full details of the assets in the death estate and of any chargeable transfer made by the deceased person in the seven years before their death.

The personal representatives must deliver an account within 12 months following the end of the month in which death occurred or, if later, three months following the date when they became personal representatives. Where no tax is due, and certain criteria are met, it is not necessary to submit an account. Estates where no account needs to be submitted are called excepted estates.

Similarly, any other account must be delivered within 12 months from the end of the month in which the transfer was made or, if later, within three months from the date liability to tax arose. This would apply on transfers such as chargeable lifetime transfers.

The Revenue also have power to call for documents where they believe inheritance tax is due. There is a right of appeal available to taxpayers where such an information notice is received.

2.3 Liability on death estate

On death, liability for payment of inheritance tax is as follows:

- Tax on the free estate is paid by the personal representatives out of estate assets, with the burden generally falling on the residuary legatee

> The person(s) named in a will to receive any residue left in an estate after the bequests of specific items are made

- Tax on property not in the possession of the personal representatives, having been transferred by the donor subject to a reservation, is payable by the person in possession of the property.
- Tax on potentially exempt transfers that have become chargeable is paid and borne by donees.
- Additional liabilities on chargeable lifetime transfers must be paid and borne by the donees.

However, the Revenue does not simply wait around for the relevant individual to pay. They can in fact look beyond the person primarily responsible for paying the inheritance tax. Generally, it is the personal representatives who will become liable where the inheritance tax remains unpaid. Fortunately, the overall liability the personal representatives will be liable for is limited to the value of the estate assets.

If the personal representatives do not pay inheritance tax due on an estate, the Revenue may collect the tax from beneficiaries under the will to the extent they receive assets under the will.

It is the donor who is primarily liable for the tax due on the chargeable lifetime transfers.

In cases where the donor dies (within seven years of making a CLT gift) and the gift becomes chargeable for additional IHT, then it is the responsibility of the donee to pay the additional IHT.

2.4 Due dates for payment

The normal due dates of payment in respect of inheritance tax are as follows:

Transfer	Due date
Chargeable lifetime transfers between 6 April and 30 September	30 April in following year
Chargeable lifetime transfers between 1 October and 5 April	6 months after end of month in which transfer was made
Death – including additional tax on chargeable lifetime transfers and tax on potentially exempt transfers which become chargeable	6 months after end of month in which death occurs

The personal representatives of a deceased's estate must, however, pay any tax for which they are liable, and which may not be paid in instalments, at the time they apply for probate, even if this is before the due date.

IHT is always paid out of the residual estate that is not exempt.

Andrea made the following lifetime gifts and died on 26 December 2012.

Date of gift	Details of gift
19 August 2011	Gift to her son of £415,000
29 June 2010	Gift to a trust of £525,000
26 December 2012	Willed to her husband £300,000

She left a specific legacy to her brother for £25,000 and the remaining estate was distributed equally among her children. The total value of the estate was £975,000 on 26 December 2012.

For the tax year 2010-11 and 2011-12 the nil rate band is £325,000.

a) Life time transfer

	£
Life time transfer -29 June 2010	525,000
Inheritance tax threshold for 2010-11	(325,000)
	200,000
Inhertiance tax liability (20/80)	50,000
Gross chargeable transfer	575,000
Potentially exempt transfer - 19 August 2011 (intially ignored)	415,000

Continued on the next page

b) Additional liabilities on death

	£
Additional liabilities on death	
Gross chargeable transfer	575,000
Inheritance tax threshold for 2011-12	(325,000)
	250,000
Inheritance tax liability at 40%	100,000
IHT already paid	(50,000)
Additional liability	50,000
Potentially exempt transfer - 19 August 2011	415,000
Inheritance tax threshold available balance	Nil
IHT liability	415,000
IHT liability @ 40%	166,000

The CLT on 29 June 2010 has fully utilised the nil rate band of the inheritance tax threshold.

c) Death estate

	£
Value of estate	975,000
Less: Exemptions to spouse	(300,000)
	675,000
Inheritance tax threshold available	nil
Inheritance tax liability	
Nil rate band	nil
IHT liability	675,000
IHT liability @ 40%	270,000

Due dates for IHT payments to be made

IHT liability	Payable by	Due date
Chargeable lifetime transfers - £50,000	Andrea	30 April 2011
Additonal liability on chargeable lifetime transfer on death - £50,000	Trust	30 June 2013
Additional tax on potentially exempt transfers which become chargeable - £166,000	Andrea's son	30 June 2013
Death estate – £270,000	Andrea's personal representative	30 June 2013

	£
Chargeable estate	675,000
Andrea's husband	(300,000)
Andrea's brother	(25,000)
Residue that the children will inherit	350,000

2.5 Grossing up gifts on death

In all the above explanations and examples, we have assumed that inheritance tax liability was borne by the donee, i.e. the person to whom the transfer or the gift is made. If the transfer is made at the time of death, then clearly the responsibility to pay the tax will be of the donee. However, if the transfer is made during the lifetime of the donor, then the principal responsibility to pay tax will be of the donor and not the donee. In such cases, the donor has to bear the cost of the gift or transfer and also the amount of tax due on it. Therefore to calculate IHT liability, when the tax is paid by the donor, the amount of net gift after deducting available annual exemptions and inheritance tax threshold needs to be grossed up.

The following formula is applied on the chargeable lifetime transfers after deducting annual exemptions and available inheritance tax threshold (nil rate band):

Chargeable amount (in excess of the inheritance tax threshold) x $\frac{20}{80}$

Once the gross figure is calculated, i.e. the amount of net transfer plus IHT liability, all the later calculations arising at the time of death are made on this gross figure.

It is necessary to gross up the net gift to accurately compute the IHT chargeable.
Two important things to note before grossing up

The annual exemptions available need to be first deducted before grossing up.
The amount should be grossed up in excess of the nil rate band

However, specific legacies of foreign property bear their own tax and do not need to be grossed up.

Example

Richard gifted £395,000 to a childcare trust on 20 October 2008 and incurred the IHT arising on this gift. He had not made any other gifts till 6 April 2007. The nil rate band for the tax year 2008-09 is £312,000.

	£	£
CLT made		395,000
Annual exemptions for 2008-09	3,000	
Annual exemptions for 2007-08	3,000	
		(6,000)
Net chargeable transfer		389,000
Inheritance threshold for 2008-09		(312,000)
Taxable transfer		77,000
IHT at 20/80		19,250
Gross chargeable transfer (389000+19250)		408,250

The life time IHT payable by Richard is £19,250. You can cross verify this amount by calculating the IHT on the gross chargeable transfer of £408,250.

IHT liability £312,000 at nil %
£77,000 at 20% = £19,250

The gross chargeable transfer amount is used to calculate all the subsequent calculations.

Tip

CLTs should never be re-grossed on the death of the donor. It should not be re-grossed even when the nil rate band is reallocated because of PET being chargeable.

Example

In continuation with the above example if Richard dies on 10 May 2012, the IHT implications would be:

	£	£
Additional liability on death		
20 October 2008		
Gross chargeable transfer	408,250	
IHT threshold for 2012/13	(325,000)	
Taxable transfer	83,250	
IHT chargeable at 40%		33,300
Less: Taper relief reduction - 20%		(6,660)
		26,640
Less: IHT already paid		(19,250)
Additional liability		**7,390**

Tip

Grossing up is not necessary if the IHT is paid by the done (in this case the trust). So check before you solve a question that involves a CLT – who is paying the IHT.

Test Yourself 2

John and Jo were married for years. Sadly, John died on 13 September 2009 leaving an estate valued at £720,000. John left all of his estate to Jo, except for £200,000 which he left to a discretionary will trust.

Unfortunately, Jo died on 21 May 2012 leaving an estate of £770,000 to her four children. Jo had made a chargeable lifetime transfer of £115,000 in 2007.

Calculate the inheritance tax payable by Jo's personal representatives on the basis that they enter into a claim to transfer John's unused inheritance tax threshold.

Answers to Test Yourself

Answer to TY 1

Three exemptions that only apply during an individual's lifetime are as follows:

- Annual exemption
- Gifts in consideration of marriage or civil partnership
- Normal expenditure out of income
- Small gifts
- Transfer to spouse or civil partner

Answer to TY 2

The following inheritance tax liability arose on Jo's estate:

	£	£
Jo's estate		770,000
Inheritance tax threshold – 2012/13	325,000	
John's unused inheritance tax threshold – 38% @ £325,000	123,500	
	448,500	
Cumulative transfers made in the previous seven years	(115,000)	
Available inheritance tax threshold		(333,500)
		436,500
Inheritance tax @ 40%		174,600

Workings

John's unused inheritance tax threshold

	£
John's inheritance tax threshold – 2009/10	325,000
John's chargeable transfer to a discretionary will trust	(200,000)
John's unused inheritance tax threshold	125,000
Percentage of unused inheritance tax threshold	38%

Self Examination Question

Question 1

Brownie died on 20 February 2012 and made the following lifetime gifts:

2-Feb-04	A gift of £150,000 to a trust
11-Dec-06	A gift of £50,000 to her husband
9-Apr-08	A gift of £150 to her neice
22-May-08	A gift of £200,000 to her son
1-Aug-08	A gift of £250,000 to a trust

Brownie paid the IHT arising from the gifts to the trusts.

The nil rate bands are as follows:

	£
2003-2004	£255,000
2006-2007	£285,000
2008-2009	£312,000

Required:

Calculate the inheritance tax that will be payable as a result of Brownie's death

Question 2

What would be benefit of making lifetime gifts of assets for inheritance tax purposes.

Answer to Self Examination Question

Answer to SEQ 1

(a) The advantages of opting to make lifetime gifts of assets are:

1. A PET gets completely exempt after seven years of making the gift and a CLT will not incur any additional IHT liability
2. Taper relief reduced the amount of IHT payable after three years, though the donor does not survive for seven years.
3. It is beneficial to make gifts of assets that are expected to increase in value as the value of PETs and CLTs are fixed when they are made and so the increased value is not included in the death estate.

(b) Brownie's inheritance tax computation

		£
Lifetime transfers		
2-Feb-04		
Gift to trust		150,000
Annual exemptions 2003-2004 £3000		
2002-2003 £3000		(6000)
Chargeable transfer		**144,000**
No inheritance tax liability as transfer within nil rate band of £250,000		
11-Dec-06		
Exempt as a transfer to spouse		
9-Apr-08		
Exempt as a small gift under £250		
22-May-08		
Gift to her son		200,000
Annual exemptions 2008-2009 £3000		
2007-2008 £3000		(6,000)
Exempt as PET		**194,000**
1-Aug-08		
Gift to a trust		250,000
Inheritance tax threshold (2008-09)	£312,000	
Less: Cumulative transfers in the previous seven years	(£144,000)	
Available inheritance tax threshold		(168,000)
Chargeable transfer		**82,000**
IHT liability £82,000 x 20/80		**20,500**
Gross chargeable transfer (£250,0000 + £20,500)		**270,500**

Notes:

1. The CLT made on 2 February 2004 is less than the nil rate band for 2003-2004 so there is no lifetime IHT payable
2. The annual exemptions for 2008-2009 and 2007-2008 is fully utilised by the PET made on 22 May 2008 and so there is no annual exemption left to be used for the CLT made on 1 August 2008
3. The nil rate band for 2008-2009 is £312,000 but the CLT made on 2 February 2004 is within seven years of the CLT made on 1 August 2008 and thus uses up £144,000 of the nil rate band.

Additional Inheritance Tax on lifetime transfers due to death within 7 years of the transfers

		£	£
2-Feb-04			
Chargeable transfer		144,000	
£144000 at nil%			NIL
22-May-08			
Potentially exempt transfer		194,000	
Inheritance tax threshold	£325,000		
Less: Cumulative transfers made in previous seven years	(£144,000)		
Available inheritance tax threshold		(181,000)	
Chargeable transfer			**13,000**
IHT liability @ 40%			5,200
Less: Taper relief reduction 20%			(1,040)
IHT liability			**4,160**
1-Aug-08			
Gross chargeable transfer		270,500	
IHT liability £270,500 at 40%			108,200
Taper relief reduction 20%			(21,640)
			86,560
IHT already paid			(20,500)
			66,060
Additional liability			**70,220**

Notes:

1. For the PET made on 22 May 2008 the seven year cumulative total is £144,000 so £181,000 (£325,000-£144,000) of the nil rate band for 2011-12 of £325,000 is available.
2. For the CLT made on 1 August 2008, the seven year cumulative total is £338,000 (£144,000 + £194,000) so the nil rate band for 2011-2012 has been fully utilised
3. For the gifts on 22 May 2008 and 1 August 2008 the taper relief reduction is 20% as they were made between three and four years of the date of Brownies death

Answer to SEQ 2

Making a lifetime gifts of assets has the following benefits:

1. A PET is completely exempt after seven years of making the gift and a CLT will not incur any additional IHT liability
2. Use of taper relief will reduce the amount of IHT payable after three years though the donor does not survive for seven years.
3. It is beneficial to make gifts of asset that potentially can increase in their value as PETs and CLTs value are fixed at the time it is made so the increase in the value of the gifts will not be included in the death estate.

SECTION F

NATIONAL INSURANCE CONTRIBUTIONS

F1

STUDY GUIDE F1: NATIONAL INSURANCE: SCOPE AND CLASS 1 AND 1A CONTRIBUTIONS FOR EMPLOYED PERSONS

Get Through Intro

Once an employee's earnings exceed a specific threshold, it becomes mandatory for both the employer and the employee to contribute to class 1 NIC (National Insurance contributions).

In this Study Guide we will discuss the various provisions relating to the employer's and employee's contributions to class 1 NIC, and the tax benefits that they both get from these contributions.

This knowledge will be useful when, as a tax consultant, you need to advise your clients about this threshold for mandatory registration with the National Insurance Contributions Office (NICO).

Examiners often test this knowledge in the first compulsory question.

Learning Outcomes

a) The scope of national insurance
   i. Describe the scope of national insurance.
b) Class 1 and Class 1A contributions for employed persons
   i. Compute Class 1 NIC.
   ii. Compute Class 1A NIC.

Introduction

National Insurance Contributions are used to fund the welfare state and to pay state benefits such as state pensions and unemployment allowance. The contribution goes to a common pool and is disbursed as social security benefits to those who are in need. Therefore it is another form of taxation by the administrative system.

NICs are payable by self-employed persons and employees.

NICs are collected:

- by the National Insurance Contributions Office (NICO)
- from self-employed persons, employees and their employers

NICs are significant factors for the self-employed and employers.

Main classes of NICs

1. Class 1 primary paid by employees
2. Class 1 secondary and Class 1A paid by employers
3. Class 2 paid by the self-employed
4. Class 4 paid by the self-employed

1. Describe the scope of national insurance.[1]

[Learning Outcome a]

1.1 Applicability

Class 1 NICs are payable by all "employed earners" who fulfill the following criteria:

1. the **age** of the employed person is **above 16 years**. He is required to pay for class 1 NIC until he becomes eligible for pension **AND**
2. an employed person **earning more than £146 per week** (£7,606 per annum / 52 weeks) **or £634 per month** (£7,606 per annum / 12 months).

Definition

An employed earner is a person who is paid either as an employee under a contract or as a holder of office.

1.2 Basis

The amount of class 1 NIC payable by the employee is based on a percentage of the employee's earnings during the tax year.

Where a person has more than one job, that person is liable to pay class 1 NIC contributions in respect of **each job.**

An employee's earnings **include gross pay** in the form of:

1. salary, remuneration, wages, commission, bonus
2. all **non-cash vouchers** except those that are exempt under income tax. Examples of non-cash vouchers which are not included in gross pay (so are exempt from tax) are:

   a) **transport vouchers for lower-paid employees** by passenger transport bodies
   b) vouchers to obtain a **parking space for a car / motorcycle or bicycle** etc.
   c) vouchers for meals in the work premises
   d) luncheon vouchers of 15p per day (above this amount is included in gross pay)
   e) vouchers used in connection with sporting or recreational facilities
   f) vouchers for overnight expenses of £5 per night and £10 if the employee is outside the UK

3. amount of employee loan which is written off by the employer (i.e. the employee is not in a position to repay the amount, therefore the employer treats the loan amount as a bad debt, and completes forms P11D and P9D)

4. **employer's contributions to funded unapproved retirement benefit schemes**

5. remuneration in the form of **non-cash assets**, which are readily convertible into cash (examples of non-cash assets are: gold bars, coffee beans, fine wines etc.)

However, an employee's earnings do not include:

a) employee's contribution to approved personal pensions
b) employee's contribution to approved occupational pension schemes
c) employee's contribution to private schemes
d) charitable gifts under the payroll giving scheme
e) tips received directly from customers
f) business expenses paid or reimbursed by the employer

2. Class 1 and class 1A contributions for employed persons
i. Compute Class 1 NIC.[2]
ii. Compute Class 1A NIC.[2]
[Learning Outcome b]

As mentioned previously, both **class 1 and class 1A contributions** are payable in relation to employees who are **above 16 years** old.

Class 1 contributions are calculated on emoluments received in cash and/or which are easily converted into cash.

Class 1A contributions are calculated on benefits in kind received.

2.1 Class 1 primary

1. Paid by employees from age 16 to state retirement age (women 60 years, men 65 years).

2. Charged **on earnings**

3. Earnings **means gross pay (salary and bonus) before deduction** of:
   a) payments into an occupational pension scheme
   b) donations under the payroll deduction scheme
   c) expenses incurred by employee

4. **Exempt from class 1**
   a) Business expenses **reimbursed**
   b) **First £55 per week of childcare vouchers for basic rate taxpayers and £28 per week for higher rate taxpayers and £22 per week for additional rate taxpayers.**
   c) **Tips** from **third parties**
   d) **Mileage allowances** not exceeding the statutory rates
   e) Exempt benefits
   f) Homeworking allowance upto **£**4

5. Employer deducts NICs from **pay via Pay As You Earn (PAYE)**

6. Payable **monthly under PAYE** with income tax, **14 days after the end of the tax month i.e. 19th of the following month.**

7. **Earnings period**
   a) Employees are paid **weekly or monthly** – known as the 'earnings period'.
   b) Class 1 calculated by reference to the earnings paid in the earnings period.
   c) Lower and upper limits apply but all earnings over the lower limit will be subject to some NICs.

8. Class 1 is calculated as follows:

Employee's earnings	Class 1 primary contributions payable
Not exceeding the primary threshold (£7,605 per annum)	Nil
Exceeds primary threshold but does not exceed the upper earnings limit (£42,475 per annum)	(Earnings – Primary threshold) x 12%
Exceeds the upper earnings limit	(Upper earnings limit – Primary threshold) x 12% + (Earnings – Upper earnings limit) x 2%

If earnings are even (i.e. the same amount in each earnings period – no bonus) use the £7,606 figure given in the rates.

If earnings are not even (for e.g. because of a bonus) then calculate NIC by reference to the earnings period.

Tip

The weekly and monthly equivalent of **annual primary threshold** is calculated as follows:

Weekly threshold = (£7,606/52 weeks) = £146 per week
Monthly threshold = (£7,606/12 months) = £634 per month

The weekly and monthly equivalent of the **annual upper earnings limit** is calculated as follows:

Weekly upper earnings limit = (£42,475/52 weeks) = £817 per week
Monthly threshold = (£42,475/12 months) = £3,540 per month

The annual lower and upper limits are given in the exam as follows:

National Insurance Contributions		
		%
Class 1 Employee	£1 – £7,605 per year £7,606 – £42,475 per year £42,476 and above per year	Nil 12.0 2.0

Example

The following information is available for three employees:

Name of employee	Earnings	Period
Tom	£1,260	Monthly
Dick	£180	Weekly
Harry	£4,938	Monthly

The NICs will be calculated as follows:

Name of employee	Workings	NICs
Tom	12% x (£1,260 – £634)	75.12
Dick	12% x (£180 – £146)	4.08
Harry	12% x (£3,540 - £634) + 2% x (£4,938 – £3,540)	376.68

Notes:

1. Tom earns more than the monthly primary threshold of £634.
2. Dick earns more than the weekly primary threshold of £146.
3. Harry earns more than the monthly upper earnings limit.

Test Yourself 1

Calculate the class 1 primary NICs payable by the following employees:

Name of employee	Earnings	Period
Alan	£120	Per week
Alex	£155	Per week
Bob	£1,000	Per month
Cathy	£4,000	Per month

Tip

Dividends paid to employees do not attract NICs.

2.2 Class 1 secondary

1. Paid by **employers and not employees.**
2. **For employees aged over 16** (no upper age limit).
3. Paid on all earnings over the limit of **£7,488 per year. This limit was earlier similar to the primary threshold limit for employees, i.e. £7,606.**
4. **Payable monthly under PAYE with income tax and Class 1 primary, 14 days after the end of the tax month i.e. 19th of the following month.**
5. **Class 1 secondary is deductible as an expense by the employer in computing the trading income of the business.**
6. Class 1 secondary is calculated as follows:

National Insurance Contributions		
		%
Class 1 secondary payable by **employer**	£1 – £7,488 per year	Nil
	£7,489 and above per year	13.8

The weekly and monthly annual secondary threshold is calculated as follows:

Weekly threshold = (£7,488/52 weeks) = £144 per week
Monthly threshold = (£7,488/12 months) = £624 per month

7. If an employee decides to continue to work even after reaching the state pension age (i.e. 60 for women and 65 for men), the employee need not pay his primary contribution but the employer **must continue to pay secondary contributions for these employees.**

The following information is available for three friends:

Name of employee	Earnings (£)	Period
Tom	260	Monthly
Dick	180	Weekly
Harry	2,830	Monthly

Class 1 secondary NICs will be calculated as follows:

Name of employee	Workings	NICs
Tom	-	Nil
Dick	13.8% x (£180 – £144)	4.97
Harry	13.8% x (£2,830 - £624)	304.43

Notes:

1. Tom's earnings do not exceed the monthly primary threshold of £624.
2. Dick earns more than the weekly primary threshold of £144.
3. Harry earns more than the monthly primary threshold of £624.

Calculate the class 1 secondary NICs payable by the following employees:

Name of employee	Earnings (£)	Period
Alan	155	Per week
Bob	1,000	Per month
Cathy	3,000	Per month

2.3 Class 1A NIC

Class 1A NIC is characterised by the following features:

1. **It is paid by employers,** not employees.
2. It is computed on the benefits e.g. living accommodation, assets loaned for private use to the employees / directors who earn £8,500 or more each year. **Note that the figure to be considered here is the same as the one calculated for employment income.**
3. **Benefits exempt** from Class 1A:
   a) workplace **childcare facilities**
   b) first £55 of contracted-for childcare **for basic rate taxpayers and £28 per week for higher rate taxpayers and £22 per week for additional rate taxpayers.**
   c) Homeworking allowance upto £4.
4. It is calculated **annually.**
5. **It falls due on 19 July** following the tax year.

Example

During the tax year 2012-13, Tulip Ltd provided a car for private use to one of the senior managers of the company.
The employer (i.e. Tulip Ltd) is liable to contribute for Class 1A NIC on this benefit given to the employee in kind.
The due date for paying this contribution is 19 July 2013 (i.e. 19 July following the tax year).

---

6. Class 1A is **deductible as an expense by the employer when calculating trade profits for their business.**

7. The contribution is calculated at **13.8%** on the **amount of benefits**.

Example

Jack (whose monthly salary is £500) gets the following benefits from his employer:

1. The chargeable value of living accommodation provided to Jack is £6,000 per annum.
2. Jack's employer also pays his private medical insurance premium of £750 per annum.

The employer's class 1A NIC liability = (£6,000 + £750) x 13.8% = £931.5.

---

8. Class 1A National Insurance Contributions are not payable on benefits if they are:

- exempt from income tax.
- taxable, but specifically exempted from Class 1A NIC liability.
- covered by a dispensation.
- included in a PAYE settlement agreement.
- already included while calculating Class 1 NIC.

Test Yourself 3

In January, Black Ltd purchased a TV system for £18,000. In the same month, the company gave this TV to John for his private use. John's salary is £750 per month.

Required:

Calculate the employer's class 1A NIC liability for the tax year 2012-13.

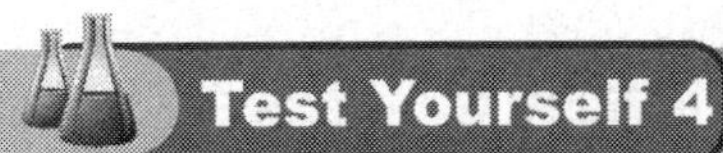

Simon, an employee earning £45,000 per annum, is provided with taxable benefits of £12,520 during 2012-13.

Required:

Calculate:

(a) Class 1 primary NIC
(b) Class 1 secondary NIC
(c) Class 1A NIC

Diagram1: Class 1 NIC

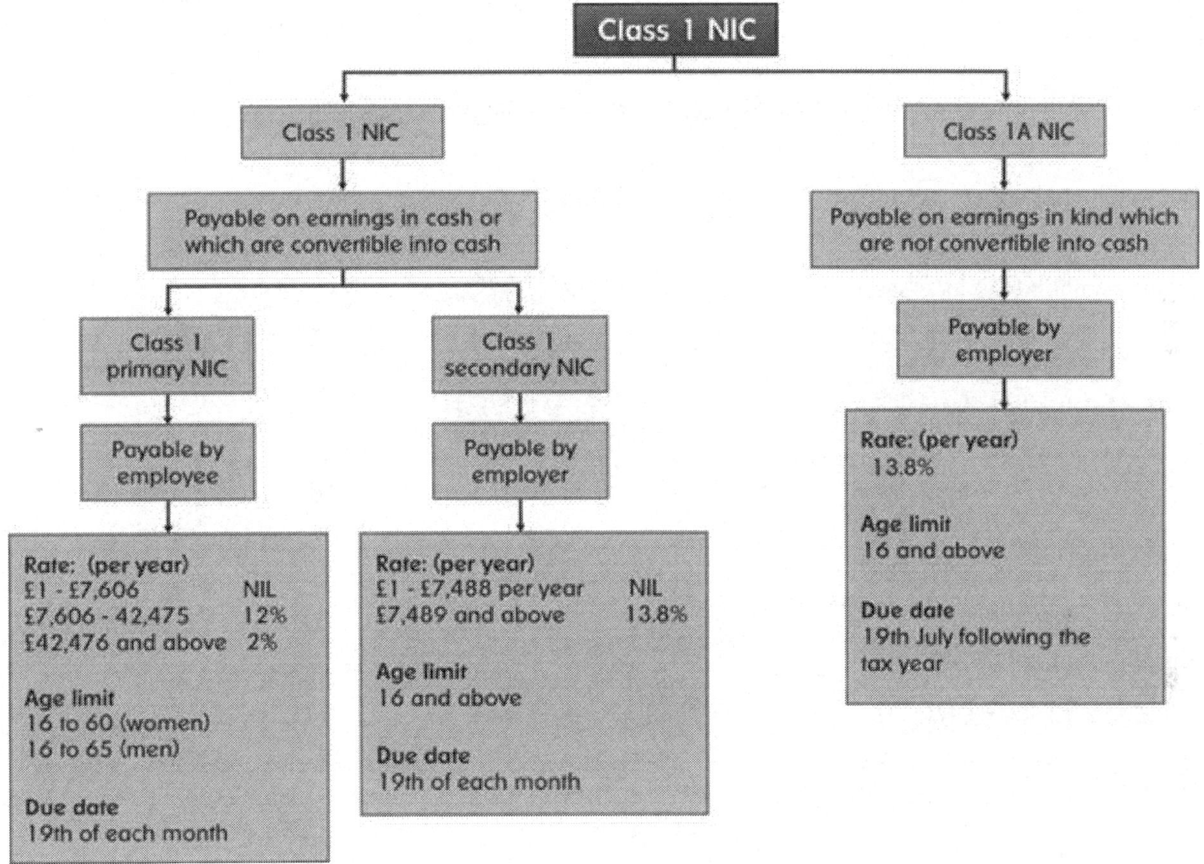

Answers to Test Yourself

Answer to TY 1

1. Alan earns less than the weekly primary threshold of £146. Therefore, he does not have to contribute to NIC.

2. Alex earns more than the weekly primary threshold of £146. Therefore, his contribution to NIC is
   12% x (£155 - £146) = £1.08

3. Bob earns £1,000 per month i.e. his earnings are more than monthly primary threshold of £634.
   Hence he should pay 12% x (£1,000 - £634) = £43.92 as class 1 NIC.

4. Cathy earns £4,000 per month i.e. her earnings are more than the monthly upper earnings limit. Therefore, she should pay the following amount as class 1 NIC:
   = 12% x (£3,540 - £634) + 2% x (£4,000 – £3,540)
   = £348.72 + £9.2
   = £357.92

Answer to TY 2

1. Alan earns more than the weekly primary threshold of £144. Therefore, his weekly class 1 secondary NIC is

   13.8% x (£155 - £144) = £1.52

2. Bob earns £1,000 per month i.e. his earnings are more than the monthly primary threshold of £624. Therefore, his class 1 secondary NIC is:

   13.8% x (£1,000 - £624) = £51.89

3. Cathy earns £3,000 per month i.e. her earnings are more than the monthly primary threshold of £624. Therefore, her monthly class 1 secondary NIC is:

   13.8% x (£3,000- £624) = £327.89

Answer to TY 3

The value of benefit = 20% of the market value of the assets on the date of lending.
(For more details refer to Study Guide B2)

For John, the value of benefit in kind	= 20% x £18,000 = £3,600
Employer's contribution for class 1A NIC	= £3,600 x 13.8% = £496.80

Answer to TY 4

1. **Class 1 primary NIC**

   = (£42,475 - £7,606) x 12% + (£45,000 - £42,475) x 2%
   = £4,184 + £50.5 = £4234.50

2. **Class 1 secondary NIC**

   (£45,000 - £7,488) x 13.8% = £5,176.65

3. **Employer class IA NIC**

   £12,520 x 13.8% = £1727.76

Quick Quiz

Fill in the blanks.

1. Class 1 NIC are payable by a person who is above _________ years of age.
2. Class 1A NIC are payable on benefits received in _________ .
3. Class 1 secondary NIC and Class 1A NIC are payable by _________ .
4. Class 1 primary NIC are payable by _________ .
5. Class 1A contributions are due by _________ following the tax year.

Answers to Quick Quiz

1. 16
2. kind
3. employers
4. employees
5. 19th July

Self Examination Questions

Question 1

The remuneration of various employees is given below. Advise them on their contribution to class 1 NIC.

1. Tom Gulliver is employed with Star Co. His remuneration is £2,500 per month.
2. Joydeep is an employee of Tele Ltd. His weekly remuneration is £885.
3. Irma is a waitress at Red Diamond Hotels Pvt. Ltd. Her monthly remuneration is £650. She also receives tips from customers of around £600 per month.
4. Freda works in a small shop as a sales assistant. Her weekly remuneration is £90.

Question 2

Rimy is a manager at Woodland Ltd. The company pays her a monthly salary of £2,500. In addition to this, the company provides her with a house in Krakow. The company has taken this house on a rental basis. The monthly rental charges are £100.

Required:

Advise Woodland Ltd how much it should pay towards secondary Class 1 and Class 1A NIC.

Question 3

Linda is a 65 year old lady. She works with a watch-making company as a supervisor. She gets a salary of £100 per week.

Required:

Advise her how much she should pay towards class 1 NIC.

Question 4

Marcus is employed with Venus Ltd, earning a salary of £30,000 per annum. He was provided with a new diesel-powered company car on 6 August 2012 with an official CO_2 emission rate of 102 grams per kilometre. The motor car has a list price of £13,500.

Required:

What is the amount of class 1A NIC payable by Venus Ltd?

Question 5

Bell works with Graham Ltd and is paid £45,000 per year, and is provided with the following taxable benefits during the tax year 2012-13:

	£
Company motor car	5,900
Car fuel	4,800
Living accomodation	2,200
	12,900

Required:

Calculate the class 1 primary, secondary and class 1A NIC payable.

Answers to Self Examination Questions

Answer to SEQ 1

1. Tom Gulliver should pay: (£2,500 – £634) x 12% = £223.92 per month as Class 1 NIC.
2. Joydeep's Class 1 NIC contribution is £82 per week calculated as below:
   (£817 - £146) x 12% + (£885 - £817) x 2%
   £80.52 + £1.36 = £81.88
3. An employee's earnings for Class 1 NIC specifically exclude tips directly received from customers. Hence, Irma's contribution towards Class 1 NIC needs to be calculated considering her remuneration of £650. She is required to pay £1.92 per month towards Class 1 NIC calculated as (£650 – £634) x 12% = 1.92
4. Freda's weekly remuneration is less than £146 per week. Therefore, she need not contribute anything towards class 1 NIC.

Answer to SEQ 2

Secondary Class 1 NIC contributions are payable by the employer in relation to the employee, if the employee's earnings in the period exceed the secondary threshold.

Employee's total earnings = Earnings in cash + Earnings readily convertible in cash
= £2,500 + £100
= £2,600

As Rimy's earnings exceed the monthly primary threshold of £624 per month, Woodland Ltd's total contribution towards:

Class 1 secondary NIC is (£2,500 - £624) x 13.8%	258.89
Class 1A NIC is 100 x 13.8%	13.80

Answer to SEQ 3

Linda does not have to pay any contributions towards class 1 NIC, as she has already reached pension age. If any employee continues to work after reaching the state pension age, they do not need to pay Class 1 NIC.

Answer to SEQ 4

Chargeable value of car = 13,500 x 14% x 8/12
= £1,260

Class 1A NIC payable by Venus Ltd = £1,620 x 13.8%
= £173.88

Notes:

1. The CO_2 emissions are below the base level figure of 100 grams per kilometer so the percentage applicable is 14% (11% plus a 3% charge for a diesel car).
2. The motor car is only available for eight months, so the benefit is multiplied by 8/12.

Answer to SEQ 5

Employee class 1 NIC	£
42,475-7,606 = 34,869 at 12%	4,184
45,000 -42,475 = 2,525 at 2%	51
	4,235

Employers class 1 NIC	£
45,000 - 7,488 = 37,512 at 13.8%	5,177

Employers class 1A NIC	£
12,900 (5,900 + 4,800 + 2,200) at 13.8%	1,780

STUDY GUIDE F2: CLASS 2 AND CLASS 4 CONTRIBUTIONS FOR SELF-EMPLOYED PERSONS

Get Through Intro

In the previous Study Guide we discussed various provisions relating to Class 1 NICs applicable to the employer and employee.

In this Study Guide we will discuss the various provisions of NIC relating to self-employed individuals. We will also discuss the tax benefits a self-employed person gets by contributing to Class 2 and Class 4 NIC.

Although you cannot expect a full question from this Study Guide, you may expect a question from this part of the Study Guide as part of the first compulsory question.

A sound knowledge of this topic is necessary for you to gain full marks in the first question and also to advise your client when it is necessary to notify the Inland Revenue.

Learning Outcomes

a) Compute Class 2 NIC.
b) Compute Class 4 NIC.

Introduction

Jeremy is an employee of a shop situated in London. He is also a good singer. His major income source is his salary from the shop, but he also performs stage shows. His income from the stage shows is not more than £100 per month. As he is an employee, his Class 1 contribution is collected through the PAYE system.

He is under the impression that, as his major source of income is salary; he doesn't have to pay Class 2 and 4 NIC. Claud Chapperon, Jeremy's friend, is of the opinion that Jeremy is liable to contribute towards Class 2 and Class 4 NIC. Jeremy does not accept this.

In this Study Guide we will discuss the various provisions of Class 2 and 4 NIC and decide who is right: Jeremy or Claud Chapperon?

1. Compute Class 2 NIC.[2]

[Learning Outcome a]

1.1 Class 2 NIC

Class 2 National Insurance Contributions set at a fixed weekly amount, regardless of earnings, generally count towards benefits such as basic state pension, maternity leave and bereavement benefit.

Following are the main features of Class 2 NIC:

1. Paid by **self-employed.**
2. Aged **between 16 and the state retirement age. (60 for women and 65 for men)**
3. **Flat weekly rate of £2.65 per week** if earning is **above £5,595 for 2012-13.**
4. Payments start when individual turns 16, and cease when they reach the state retirement age.

Maurice follows 31 December as his annual accounting date. His profits for 2012-13 are £5,610.

His Class 2 NIC liability = £2.65 (per week) x 52 (weeks) = £138

1.2 Registration for Class 2 NIC

1. A self-employed person must register himself for Class 2 NIC with HMRC.

A self-employed person must notify HMRC **within three months** from the date of commencement of self-employment. Failure to do so may give rise to a penalty of £100.

On 20 April 2012, Karen started her new business. In this situation, she is liable to notify HMRC within three months from the date of commencement of her employment i.e. before 20 July 2012.

---

2. In the case of failure to notify HMRC, a person may be liable for a penalty of £100.

1.3 Payment of Class 2 NIC

From the tax year 2012-13 onwards, there are two options for payment of class 2 NIC towards the National Insurance Contributions:

a) it can be paid in two instalments, on 31 January 2013 and 31 July 2013, which are also similar to the self-assessment system.
b) it can be paid on a monthly basis by direct debit.

2. Calculate Class 4 NIC.[2]

[Learning Outcome b]

2.1 Class 4 NIC

1. Paid by **self-employed individuals.**
2. **Start if aged 16** at start of the tax year **and profits exceed the lower earnings limit (£7,606).**
3. No longer payable if individuals **reach the state retirement age at the start of the year. (60 for women and 65 for men)**
4. Class 4 **payable on profits:**

	£
Trading income assessment for the tax year	X
Less: Trading loss relief	(X)
Profits for Class 4 NIC purposes	**X**

2.2 Calculation of Class 4 NIC

Profits	Class 4 NIC payable
Not exceeding the primary threshold (£7,605 per annum)	Nil
Exceeds primary threshold but does not exceed the upper threshold limit (£42,475 per annum)	(Profits – Primary threshold) x 9%
Exceeds the upper threshold limit	(Upper threshold limit – Primary threshold) x 9% + (Profits – Upper earnings limit) x 2%

Tip

The annual lower and upper limits are given in the exam as follows:

National Insurance Contributions		
		%
Class 4	£1 – £7,605 per year £7,606 – £42,475 per year £42,476 and above per year	Nil 9.0 2.0

2.3 Important points to remember

1. Class 4 NIC is payable **along with the income tax under self-assessment.**
2. This payment is to be made to **HMRC.** If the person fails to contribute towards Class 4 NIC in time, then he / she is liable for penal interest.
3. If a person is **self-employed** as well as an **employee**, he / she is **liable to Class 1, 2 and 4** contributions.
4. Each active partner in a partnership firm is individually liable to Class 2 and Class 4 contributions.
5. The following is the list of persons who are **exempt** from Class 4 NIC:

a) Persons **above the pension age** (i.e. male 65, female 60) at the beginning of the tax year.

b) Individuals who are **not resident** for income tax purposes.

c) **Trustees and executors** who are chargeable to income tax on the income they receive on behalf of some other persons (e.g. incapacitated person).

d) **Sleeping partners** i.e. a partner in a partnership firm who supplies capital but is not actively involved in the business activities.

e) **An individual** who is **below 16** at the beginning of the particular tax year.

f) **Divers and diving supervisors** who are working on exploration and exploitation activities on the UK Continental Shelf or in UK territorial waters.

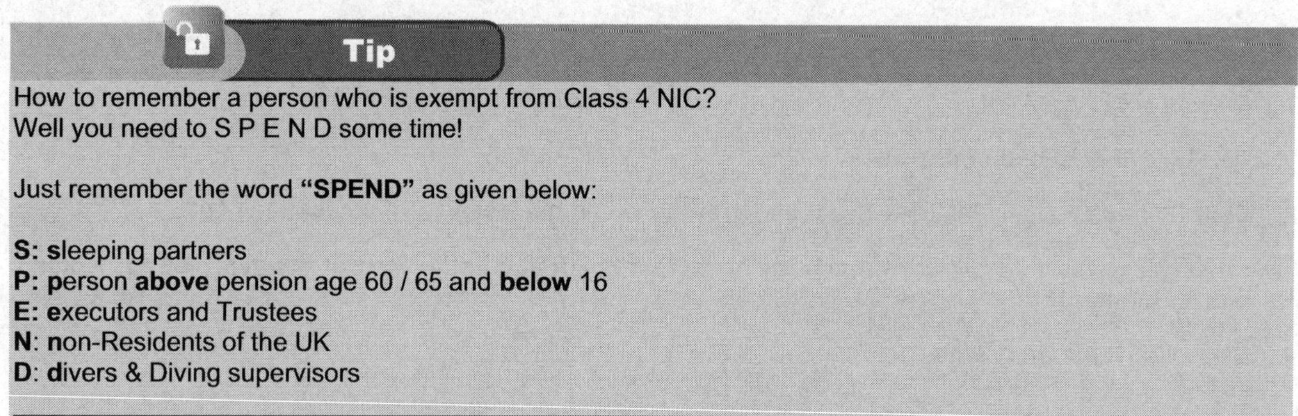

Tip

How to remember a person who is exempt from Class 4 NIC?
Well you need to S P E N D some time!

Just remember the word **"SPEND"** as given below:

S: **s**leeping partners
P: **p**erson **above** pension age 60 / 65 and **below** 16
E: **e**xecutors and Trustees
N: **n**on-Residents of the UK
D: **d**ivers & Diving supervisors

Diagram 1: NIC for the self employed

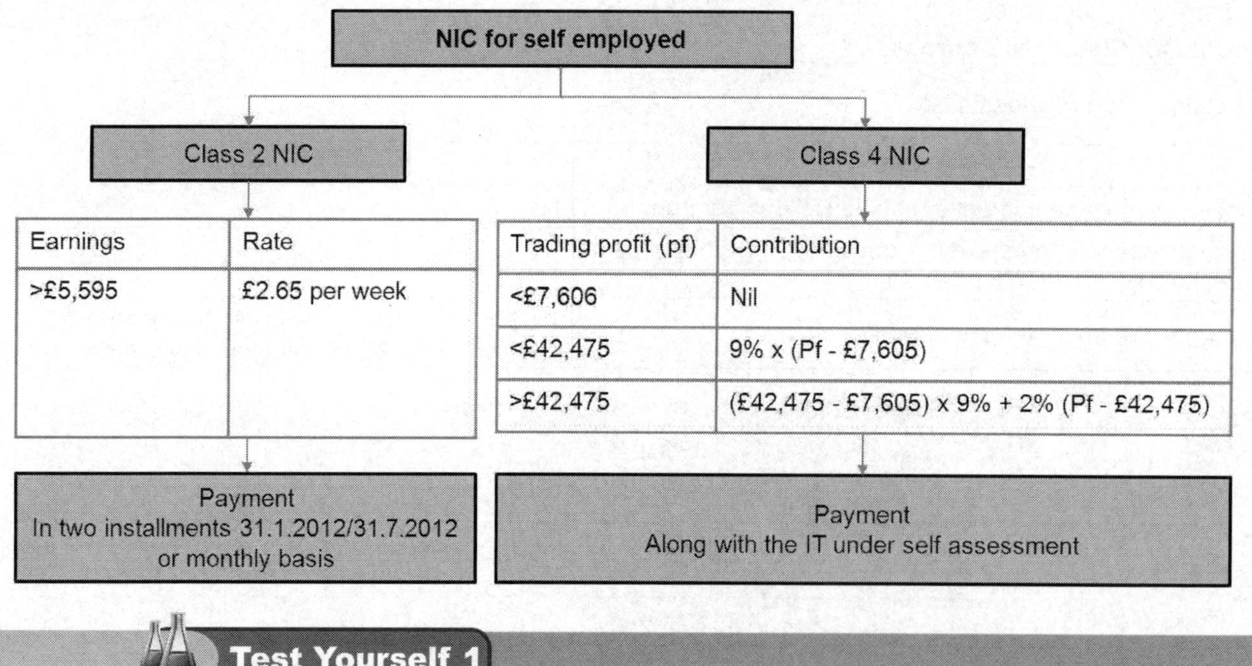

Earnings	Rate
>£5,595	£2.65 per week

Trading profit (pf)	Contribution
<£7,606	Nil
<£42,475	9% x (Pf - £7,605)
>£42,475	(£42,475 - £7,605) x 9% + 2% (Pf - £42,475)

Test Yourself 1

Calculate the Class 4 NICs payable for 2012-13 in the following cases:

1. Ted has trading income for 2012-13 of £15,820.
2. Mary has trade income for 2012-13 of £51,720.
3. Mark has trading income for 2012-13 of £4,820.

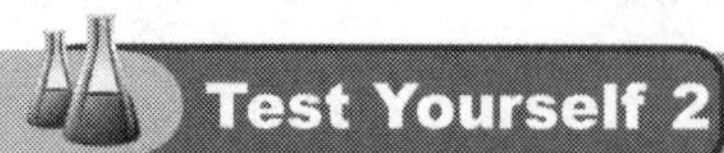

Test Yourself 2

Jack is a self-employed contractor, in this business for many years and prepares accounts on 31 March every year.

His taxable trading profit for the year ended 31 March 2013 is £47,240.

Required:

Calculate Jack's Class 2 and Class 4 NIC liability.

Test Yourself 3

Ann started her own business on 1 October 2010 and prepares accounts to 31 March every year. Her first set of accounts are for the period to 31 March 2011. Her adjusted profits after capital allowances for the first three accounting periods are as follows:

Period to 31 March 2010	£9,490
Year to 31 March 2011	£14,020
Year to 31 March 2012	£19,240

Required:

Calculate Ann's total national insurance contributions for 2012-13.

Answer to Test Yourself

Answer to TY 1

1. 9% x (£15,820 - £7,606) = £739.26

2. 9% x (£42,475 - £7,606) + 2% x (£51,720 - £42,475)
   £3,138 + £185 = £3,323

3. Mark's Class 4 liability for the year is nil, as his profits are less than the lower profit limit (i.e. £7,606).

Answer to TY 2

Calculation of Jack's NIC liability:

	£
1. Class 2 NICs	
(£2.65 x 52 weeks)	137.8
2. Class 4 NICs	
(£42,475 - £7,606) x 9% (maximum)	3,138
(£47,240 - £42,475) x 2%	95
	3,234

Answer to TY 3

Ann's national insurance contributions for 2012-13 are:

		£
Class 2	£2·65 x 52	137.8
Class 4	£(19,240 – 7,606) x 9%	1,047
		1,185

Quick Quiz

Fill in the blanks.

1. The rate for contribution for Class 2 NIC for 2012-13 is __________ per week.

2. Men and women over __________ age are exempt from Class 2 NIC.

3. A self-employed person is liable to Class 4 NIC if his income is above __________ for the year 2012-13.

4. For Class 2 NIC the collection dates are ____________________ and ____________________ for the year 2012-13 if paid in two installments.

Answers Quick to Quiz

1. £2.65 per week
2. State pension
3. £7,606
4. 31 January 2013 and 31 July 2013

Self Examination Questions

Question 1

Ritu is self-employed. She has elected 31 March as the year-end. For 2012-13 her books of accounts showed a profit of £4,000. Does she need to pay Class 2 NIC?

Question 2

Alana is a 63 year old self-employed person. In 2012-13 she earned £5,000.

Required:

Is she liable for any contribution to Class 2 NIC?

Question 3

Stewart has a wholesale stationery business. He prepares annual accounts to 5 April. His trading income from this business for 2012-13 is £3,900. He also owns a toy shop. His income from this business for the year 2012-13 is £4,200.

Required:

How much should he contribute to Class 2 NIC?

Question 4

Bernard is a carpenter. He is working with a company that manufactures furniture. On holidays he also works independently. In the year 2012-13 his monthly salary was £1,900. His income from self-employment was £300 per month.

Required:

Calculate his Class 2 and 4 NIC liabilities for the year 2012-13.

Question 5

Matthew has trading profits of £52,150 for the tax year 2012-13.

Required:

Advise him how much he should pay towards Class 2 and 4 NIC.

Question 6

John is a self-employed tax-consultant for many years. His taxable trading profits for 2012-13 are £60,000.

He is paying a salary of £18,000 p.a. to a full time personal assistant employed by him. This is paid monthly and he also paid a bonus of £6,500 in December 2012.

Required:

Calculate the total NICs payable by John to HMRC for the year 2012-13.

Question 7

Pumi is a constructor and earned 20,500 in the year 2012-13. Whereas Fern is a consultant.and earned 45,225.

Required:

Calculate the Class 4 NIC liabilities.

Answers to Self Examination Questions

Answer to SEQ 1

For 2012-13, a self-employed person whose earnings from self-employment are less than £5,595 need not contribute anything to Class 2 NIC.

Answer to SEQ 2

Class 2 NICs are payable by self-employed persons, who are under the pension age. The pension age for females is 60 years. Therefore Alana, being over 60, need not contribute to Class 2 NIC. However, Alana can voluntarily contribute to Class 2 NIC.

Answer to SEQ 3

Stewart is a self-employed person and his total trading income is £8,100 (£3,900 + £4,200) which is above £5,595. Therefore, for the year 2012-13, he is required to contribute £138 (52 weeks x £2.65) towards Class 2 NIC.

Answer to SEQ 4

Bernard's total earnings are as follows:
Salary income £22,800 (£1,900 x 12)
Trading income £3,600 (£300 x 12)
Therefore total earnings are £26,400.

A self- employed person is liable to Class 2 if his **trading profits** are more than £5,595, and he is liable to Class 4 NIC if his **trading income** is more than £7,606.

However, his earnings from self-employment (i.e. £3,600) are less than the small earning exception limit (i.e. for 2012-13, it is £5,595); Bernard need not pay Class 2 NIC. However, he may contribute voluntarily.

In the same way, his trading income is less than the lower profit limit (i.e. £7,606 for 2012-13,) therefore he need not pay Class 4 NIC.

Answer to SEQ 5

Matthew should pay:

1. £138 (52 weeks x £2.65) towards Class 2 NIC.
2. £3,332 towards Class 4 NIC.

Calculation of contribution to Class 4 NIC is as follows:

	£
Up to first £7,606	-
Next £(42,475 – 7,606) x 9%	3138.2
On remaining amount (£52,150 – £42,475) x 2%	193.5
Total Class 4 NIC contribution	**3,332**

Answer to SEQ 6

John will have to pay the following contributions towards NIC:

1. Flat rate Class 2 contribution in respect of his self employment.

Class 2 NICs

(£2.65 x 52 weeks)	138

2. Class 4 contributions in respect of his self-employed business based on his taxable trading profits as they are more than the primary threshold of £7,606.

Class 4 NICs

	£
(£42,475 - £7,606) x 9%	3,138
(£60,000 - £42,475) x 2%	351
	3,489

3. **Class 1 primary** contributions can be levied on the assistant. But John has to deduct the NIC from the assistant's salary and it should be paid to HMRC.

The assistant is paid £1,500 (£18,000/12) per month for 11 months, and £8,000 (£6,500 + £1,500) in December.

Using the monthly limits i.e. £634 (£7,606/12) and £3,540 (£42,475/12) the Class 1 NICs will be calculated as:

Employee's Class 1 NICs

	£
For 11 months:	
(£1,500 - £634) x 12% x 11 months	1,143
For December:	
(£3,540 - £634) x 12% x 1 month	349
(£8,000 - £3,540)x 2% x 1 month	89
	1,581

The contributions are paid monthly and they are dependent on the monthly wages. Therefore, in the above calculation we compute the contribution due for 11 months of the year and for December 2012 separately.

4. As John is an employer, he will also have to pay **Class 1 secondary** contributions which will be based on his assistant's salary of £18,000 and bonus of £6,500.

By considering the monthly primary threshold as £634 (£7,606/12), the Class 1 secondary NIC paid by the employer will be:

	£
(£1,500 - £634) x 13.8% x 11 months	1,315
(£8,000 - £634) x 13.8% x 1 month	1,017
	2,332

Therefore, total NICs payable by John will be:

	£
Class 2 NIC	137.8
Class 4 NIC	3,489
Class 1 Primary NIC	1,581
Class 1 Secondary NIC	2,332
Total	**7,540**

Answer to SEQ 7

The Class 4 NIC liabilities are as follows:

		£
Pumi	20,500 - 7,606= 12,894 at 9%	1,160
Fern	42,475 - 7,606 = 34,869 at 9%	3,138
	45,225 - 42,475 = 2,750 at 2%	55
		3,193

SECTION G

VALUE ADDED TAX

G1

STUDY GUIDE G1: THE SCOPE OF VALUE ADDED TAX (VAT)

Get Through Intro

VAT is an indirect tax that you pay when you buy goods and services in the European Union (EU), including the United Kingdom. Where VAT is payable it is normally included in the price of the goods or services you buy. However, some goods do not attract VAT.

'Value added tax' – VAT is an important topic of your syllabus for this paper. It is essential that you devote considerable time to this section as a minimum 10 mark question is normally based on this topic.

As the taxation consultant of a big group of companies, you will have to be armed with complete, up-to-date knowledge of the scope, applicability and requirements of VAT.

In this section, **we will take you through the whole syllabus for VAT.**

You will learn about the concept of VAT, all the formalities of VAT registration, calculation of VAT liabilities and payments, filing of VAT returns, assessments and the effect of special accounting schemes.

Learning Outcomes

a) Describe the scope of VAT.
b) List the principal zero-rated and exempt supplies.

Introduction

Value added tax is an indirect tax which means that it is charged on turnover, not profits.

The basic principle of VAT is that tax should be charged at each stage of manufacturing / production as well as at each stage of the whole distribution chain.

The total tax due is ultimately borne by the final consumer of the product i.e. the manufacturer recovers it from the consumer.

The name itself suggests that it is a tax on the value addition put in to the process. The final consumer does not "add value" but consumes the final goods or service, therefore the consumers absorbs the charge to tax.

1. Describe the scope of VAT.[2]

[Learning Outcome a]

The scope of VAT:

- VAT is charged on the **taxable supply** of goods and services in the UK by a **taxable person** in the course of a business run by him.
- VAT is an **indirect tax** in that it is charged **on turnover, not profits**.
- VAT is charged on the consumption of goods and services by the **final consumer**.
- **At each stage** of the manufacturing process, a **trader adds VAT onto his sales** (output VAT), and acts as a collector of taxes for HMRC.
- Each **supplier receives credit for any VAT** he pays **on his purchases** (input VAT).
- The **supplier pays HMRC the difference between the VAT charged and the VAT suffered,** so the supplier does **not suffer VAT** himself.
- The **final consumer suffers the total tax**.

Example

Tasty Ltd manufactures chocolates. The selling price of the chocolates is £60 per packet plus VAT. The cost of the raw materials required to make 1 packet of chocolates is £20 plus VAT of 20%. Mega Ltd is a wholesaler of chocolates. It buys chocolates from Tasty Ltd, wraps them in attractive packaging, and thus adds some value to it.

These chocolates are then sold to various retail outlets for £100 per kg plus VAT. The retail outlets sell the chocolates at £120 per kg plus VAT. Let's see how VAT is accounted for to HMRC at each stage of manufacturing. Ultimately, the final customer will bear the VAT.

	Input		Output			
	Cost £	VAT @ 20%	Net Sales £	VAT on sales @ 20%	VAT payable £	
Manufacturer	20	4	60	12	**8**	**(12-4)**
Wholesaler	60	12	100	20	**8**	**(20-12)**
Retailer	100	20	120	24	**4**	**(24-20)**

Notice that each of the businesses (manufacturer, wholesaler, and retailer) in the chain only account for VAT on the value they are adding. Remember, in accounting for VAT you will have debited the input VAT on purchases to the VAT account while the purchases account has been debited with the purchase value. Similarly the output VAT on sales is credited to VAT account and the sales account is credited only with the sales value.

The final customers are unable to reclaim the VAT that they have paid (£24.00). They suffer the VAT.

1.1 Taxable supply: a taxable supply is a supply of goods or services (other than an exempt supply) made in the UK. A taxable supply is usually either standard rated or zero rated.

1. Standard-rated e.g. supplies of stationery or

2. Zero-rated e.g. supplies of books

However, some supplies are charged at a reduced rate of 5% (e.g. supplies of fuel and power for domestic use).

a) Standard-rated supplies

i. Standard-rated supplies are **taxable at the rate of 20%** (for the tax year 2012-13).
ii. A trader who is registered for VA**T suffers VAT on the purchases (**inputs) which are standard-rat**ed**. The VAT suffered on the purchases is set off against t**h**e output VAT collected on sales at the standard rate. The excess amount collected is paid to HMRC. If the amount suffered is greater than the amount collected, then a refund for the VAT suffered is received.

The examiner has commented that a question **will not be set** involving a VAT period where there is a change of VAT rate.

b) Zero-rated supplies

i. Zero-rated supplies are **taxable at 0%**
ii. A trader whose supplies (output) are zero-rated but whose purchases (inputs) are standard rated will **receive a refund for the VAT suffered** on them.

c) Exempt supplies

i. Exempt supplies are **not chargeable to VAT.**
ii. A trader whose supplies (output) are exempt will not have to charge any VAT but will suffer VAT on purchases (inputs). Such a trader will **not** be able to recover the input VAT.

A person making exempt supplies may not
- **register** for VAT
- **recover VAT** paid on purchases (**inputs**)

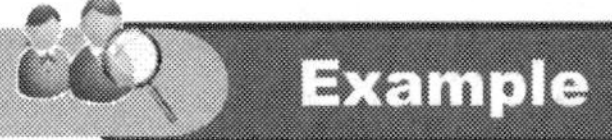

Helen makes standard-rated supplies, Alan makes zero-rated supplies and Acme makes exempt supplies.

The inputs of all the three traders are standard-rated. The following information relates to the quarter ending on 30 April 2012.

	Helen		Alan		Acme	
	£	VAT (£)	£	VAT (£)	£	VAT (£)
Sales	45,000		45,000		45,000	
Output VAT @ 20%		9,000		0		Exempt
Purchases	(35,000)		(35,000)		(35,000)	
Input VAT @ 20%		(7,000)		(7,000)	(7,000)	Exempt
VAT Payable / (Refundable)		2,000		(7,000)		NIL
Net Profits	**10,000**		**10,000**		**3,000**	

The example clearly shows that net profit of standard-rated (Helen) and zero-rated supplies (Alan) is the same, whereas the net profit of exempt supplies (Acme) is lower than the other two. This is because it cannot recover input VAT. In the course of accounting for VAT, the standard rated and zero rated traders can open a VAT account and debit and credit the VAT on purchases and sales. The net amount is either payable or recoverable. On the other hand, the exempt trader who is not registered cannot open a VAT account and therefore the VAT suffered on purchases is a cost to the business.

SUMMARY

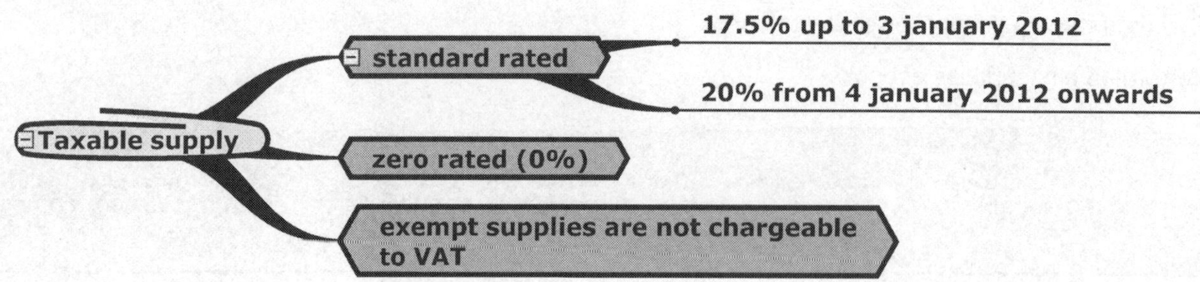

1.2 Taxable persons

A taxable person is a **person making taxable supplies** who **is, or is required** to be, **registered for VAT.**

A person **can be an individual, partnership, limited company, association, charity or club.**

1.3 Supply of goods

1. Supply of goods occurs when:

a) **Ownership** of goods **passes** from one person to another.

b) **Goods are supplied for some consideration**. Consideration can be in the form of money or any other goods (such as in the barter system) but there should be some consideration.

c) **Goods are sold on a hire purchase (HP) basis.**

In general, VAT is charged only when ownership of the goods is transferred. However, in the case of HP contracts, VAT is charged at the time of signing the contract and not when actual ownership is transferred. Furthermore, VAT is charged on the cash price of the goods, rather than on the hire purchase (HP) price.

2. Deemed supplies

The following is a list of transactions that are deemed to be supplies for VAT purposes (i.e. on which VAT must be charged even if there is no consideration):

a) A **gift** of a **business asset**, except gifts amounting to less than £50 made to the same person, in any 12 month period.

Note: From this tax year gifts do not include samples. Samples are **given by the supplier free of cost to his clients. None of the samples are liable for tax even if** two or more identical goods are given to the same person as samples in any 12 month period.

Shine Ltd has a showroom for diamonds. In 2012, the company gave a diamond ring to 50 employees as a New Year gift. Each ring was worth £100.

This gift by the company to its employees is a deemed supply of value for VAT (diamonds are inventory of the company and the cost of the gift is more than £50). Output tax will be due on the total value of the rings gifted i.e. on £5,000.

---

b) Goods on which VAT has been paid and which are removed from the business permanently by the owner or his employee for **private use.**

SUMMARY

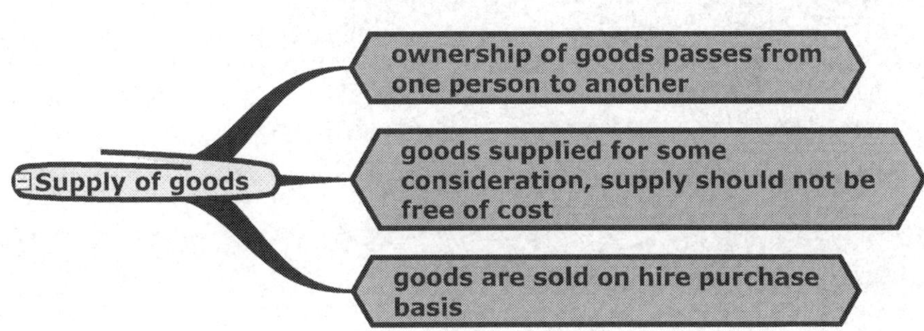

1.4 Supply of services

1. A supply of services takes place when:

a) supply is in exchange for **some consideration.**
b) supply is **not a supply of goods.**
c) goods are **hired** by customers but ownership is not transferred to the customer.

 **Example**

Idea Plc, a leading software company, hired a helicopter on a monthly basis to transport the company's executives. By availing the helicopter on a hire basis, the vendor is supplying services to the company.

In this transaction, even though the ownership of the helicopter is not transferred, the services are liable for VAT.

---

2. Deemed supply of services

The following transactions are deemed to be supplies of services (in respect of goods that were chargeable to VAT when purchased or hired by the owner or employer):

a) when the owner or their employee temporarily makes **private use of goods** owned by the business

 **Example**

A director of Sigma Plc used the company warehouse for six months to store his household furniture while his house was renovated. This temporary use of the warehouse by the director is considered to be a supply of services.

---

b) when the owner or their employee makes **private use of services** supplied to the business

 **Example**

Linda, the CEO of a software company used a helicopter for a weekend with her family, which the company had itself hired. The company paid £450 (plus VAT) for hiring the helicopter.

Here the cost of services for the private usage of helicopter over the weekend by Linda is deemed to be the cost of the taxable supply i.e. £450.

SUMMARY

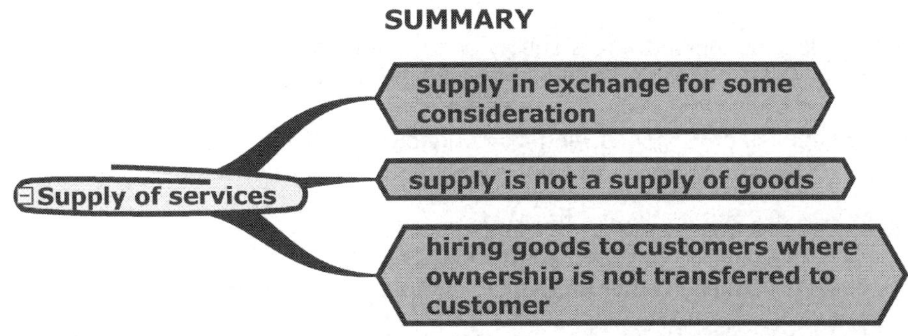

Tip

The use of a business motor car for private purposes by the owner or an employee is not considered to be a taxable supply. Input VAT can be recovered on any business fuel costs but the provision of fuel for private travel will result in a deemed taxable supply based on a fuel scale charge.

Important

The examiner has observed that students find VAT to be the least interesting topic. However, you need to study it well as it forms a significant part of the syllabus.

Test Yourself 1

Acme makes exempt supplies of goods. Its input materials are standard rated. The VAT exclusive value of sales and purchases for the quarter ended 30 November 2012 are £540,000 and £420,000 respectively.

Calculate the net profits of Acme.

2. List the principal zero-rated and exempt supplies.[1]

[Learning Outcome b]

If a supply is not zero-rated or exempt it will be standard rated (unless it falls within the reduced rate category).

2.1 Zero-rated supplies

These are supplies taxable at **zero rates.** The benefit of output supplied at zero rates is that if a supplier's inputs are standard-rated (i.e. taxable @ 20%), then he can reclaim the VAT paid on purchases. As a consequence, the VAT paid on the cost of purchases is reduced to that extent.

Principal categories are

1. Food (for human and animal consumption) except luxury food (e.g. chocolates, ice-cream, alcoholic drinks or food supplied in catering). However, food supplied with catering will not be included.
2. Drugs and medicines prescribed by a practitioner and certain aids to the handicapped
3. Passenger transport (except taxis and hire cars)
4. Books, newspaper, journals etc. (but not stationery and stationery with printed matter)
5. Sale of new buildings by a builder for residential or charitable purposes or an amount payable by tenant for a lease of more than 4 years
6. Children's clothing and footwear
7. Charities
8. Talking books and radios etc. for the blind
9. Exports / International services which are to be performed outside the European Union
10. Sewerage services and water (except for industrial use)
11. Certain caravans and houseboats
12. Bank notes
13. Gold supplied by one central bank to another central bank or member of the London gold market.

To control tax avoidance scheme in relation to standard rated services supplied together with zero rated printed matter, zero-rated supplies specifically do not include goods in circumstances where –

(a) the supply of the goods is connected with a supply of services, and
(b) those connected supply of services and goods are made by one or different suppliers.

And if a single supplier supplies both goods and it's connected services then it is treated as a single supply of service which can be a taxable supply or an exempt supply but NOT a zero rated supply.

2.2 Exempt supplies

Exempt supplies are business supplies other than taxable supplies **on which VAT is not charged.**

Exempt supplies are at par with supplies of a non-registered person. This means that a person making a **supply of exempt output is not allowed to recover VAT paid on input.**

Principal categories are

1. Betting, lotteries and gaming
2. Burial and cremation services
3. Fund-raising events by charities
4. Cultural services
5. Education provided by schools and universities
6. Financial services (e.g. bank charges, stock broking, underwriting)
7. Health and welfare services
8. Insurance
9. Investment gold
10. Land
11. Non profit-making sports competitions etc
12. Postal services provided by post offices
13. Supplies of goods on which input tax is not recoverable
14. Supplies to members by trade unions and professional bodies
15. Disposal of works of art to approved bodies

Answer to Test Yourself

Answer to TY 1

Exempt traders who are not registered cannot open a VAT account and therefore the VAT suffered on purchases is a cost to the business.

Workings

	£	**VAT (£)**
Sales	540,000	
Output VAT @ 20%		Nil
Purchases	(420,000)	
Input VAT @ 20%	(84,000)	Nil
VAT Payable / (Refundable)		**Nil**
Net Profit	**36,000**	

Quick Quiz

1. State whether the following statements are true or false:

   (a) VAT is charged only on goods.
   (b) A 'taxable person' is a person who charges VAT on supplies made by him.
   (c) A person who sells exempt goods but whose purchases are liable to VAT actually bears the cost of the VAT.
   (d) Zero-rated supplies also include those goods the supply of which is connected with the supply of its services by one or different suppliers.

2. State which case is not applicable for VAT and justify your answer.

   (a) Amazon Ltd hired a creative designer as a consultant to design a new product portfolio at a mutually acceptable consideration.

   (b) John, a sole trader of computer hardware, gave an assembled computer to his daughter as a gift. This computer was assembled from his trading stock, on which input VAT had been paid.

   (c) Cleanex Ltd manufactures detergents. The company has introduced a new soap. As a marketing strategy, the company appoints salesmen to distribute the samples of soap across households. The company has decided to give a small soap as sample. Is the company liable for VAT on a sample of soap?

Answers to Quick Quiz

1.

(a) **False.** VAT is also charged on supply of services.

(b) **False.** A taxable person means a person who is registered (or is required to be registered) for VAT.

(c) **True.** A person who sells exempt goods, but whose purchase price includes VAT, cannot register for VAT.

Therefore he cannot reclaim the VAT paid on the purchases. In short, he becomes the last person in the distribution chain and therefore bears the VAT.

(d) **False.** Zero rated supplies do not include goods the supply which is connected with the supply of its services by one or different suppliers to curb tax avoidance by small suppliers. This would come under a standard rated supply or exempt supply

2.

(a) The supply of services is subject to VAT. Services for designing products are not specifically exempt from VAT. If a consultant is a taxable person (i.e. registered for VAT), VAT is chargeable.

(b) If the owner of the business takes business goods (permanently) on which VAT was charged, then this is considered to be a supply of taxable goods. The owner is liable for VAT on the value of the deemed supply.

(c) Vat is not charged on business samples. When one or more than one identical product is given as a sample to the same person without charging for it, then the transaction is VAT-free.

So irrespective of the decision whether Cleanex Ltd wants to give one bar of soap to each customer or more than one, VAT is not chargeable. Hence, Cleanex Ltd need not pay VAT on the free samples distributed.

Self Examination Question

Question 1

Modern Foods makes zero-rated supplies and its inputs are standard-rated. The VAT exclusive value of sales and purchases for the quarter ended 30 April 2013 are £360,000 and £280,000 respectively.

Compute the following:

(a) Output VAT
(b) Input VAT
(c) Net profit

Would VAT be payable or refundable? Calculate the amount.

Answer to Self Examination Question

Answer to SEQ 1

(a) Output VAT is nil as Modern Foods makes zero rated sales.
(b) Input VAT is £56,000 as the inputs are standard rated. Therefore the amount of VAT would be computed on the purchases @20%.
(c) The net profit of Modern Foods would be £56,000 (see working below).
(d) VAT would be refundable as the amount of output VAT is nil.

Workings

	£	**VAT (£)**
Sales	360,000	
Output VAT @ 0% (zero rated)		Nil
Purchases	(280,000)	
Input VAT @ 20% (standard rated)		(56,000)
VAT Payable / (Refundable)		**(56,000)**
Net Profit	**80,000**	

STUDY GUIDE G2: THE VAT REGISTRATION REQUIREMENTS

Get Through Intro

This Study Guide will discuss **when it becomes essential for a person to register for VAT and the advantages of voluntary registration for VAT**. It will also explain when and how a person can **deregister for VAT.**

This Study Guide also introduces you to the concept of recovery of pre-registration input VAT. A thorough understanding of this concept will help you to advise your client as to how voluntary registration for VAT helps to maintain a competitive selling price.

Proper tax planning requires an in-depth knowledge of all the rules and provisions of income tax as well as the VAT Act (Value Added Tax Act 1994).

A thorough study of this Study Guide will enable you acquire this knowledge which will help in your exams as well as in your professional life as a tax consultant.

Learning Outcomes

a) Recognise the circumstances in which a person must register for VAT.
b) Explain the advantages of voluntary VAT registration.
c) Explain the circumstances in which pre-registration input VAT can be recovered.
d) Explain how and when a person can deregister for VAT.
e) Explain the conditions that must be met for two or more companies to be treated as a group for VAT purposes, and the consequences of being so treated.

Introduction

Case Study

Jake and Josh design and manufacture digital flat screen televisions. They are not required to register for VAT as their turnover does not exceed the threshold set by HMRC. They heard from a friend that it may be beneficial for them to register for VAT and are now wondering whether to register. They make taxable supplies of 40 televisions during the quarter ended 30 December 2012 and they retail at £500 each (before VAT). The materials used to produce these taxable supplies cost Jake and Josh £260 each (before VAT).

As Jake and Josh's tax adviser, consider whether they should apply for voluntary registration of VAT.

	If registered £	If not registered £
Sales		
40 x (£500 + 20% VAT)	24,000	
40 x £500		20,000
Less: Output tax		
40 x (£500 x 20%)	(4,000)	-
Sales (excluding VAT)	20,000	20,000
Less: Cost of sales		
40 x (£260 + VAT 20%)	(12,480)	(12,480)
Add: Input tax reclaimed	1,920	
4000 - 40 x (£260 x 20%)		-
Profit	**9,440**	**7,520**

It is advisable to register voluntarily as the profit is higher by £1,920 if the business is registered.

The various advantages of voluntary VAT registration are discussed in this Study Guide.

1. Recognise the circumstances in which a person must register for VAT.[2] [Learning Outcome a]

A person must register for VAT if his taxable turnover exceeds the registration limit of **£77,000 from April 2012 onwards.**

1.1 There are two situations where registration is compulsory:

1. historic test
2. future test

1. Historic test

a) Registration

Registration is **compulsory if,** at the end of any month, the **taxable turnover (excluding VAT) for the last 12 months exceeds £77,000.**

VAT registration is **not required if** taxable supplies in the following 12 months do **not exceed £75,000. A trader may wish to register voluntarily.**

b) Notification to HMRC

Notification to HMRC must be **within 30 days of the end of the month in which the £77,000 limit is exceeded.**

c) Effective registration date

Registration is **effective from the end of the month following the month when the limit was exceeded.**

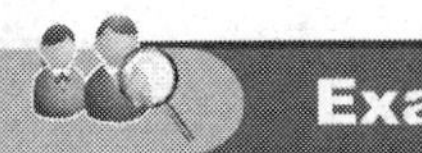

Example

Stephen started his new business in April 2012. His taxable turnover during the first six months of trading is as follows (sales figures provided are individual as well as cumulative):

2012	£	£ (Cumulative)
April	2,000	2,000
May	5,100	7,100
June	12,300	19,400
July	18,000	37,400
August	21,300	58,700
September	22,000	80,700

Taxable turnover exceeds the registration threshold (£77,000) at the end of September 2012. Stephen must notify HMRC by 30 October 2012. (i.e. within 30 days from the end of the month in which the limit is exceeded). The registration will be effective from 1 November 2012.

Test Yourself 1

Adobe Ltd commenced trading on 1 January 2012.It prepares accounts to year end 31 December every year. Its sales are as follows:

	£	Cumulative total (last 12 months)		£	Cumulative total (last 12 months)
Jan-12	6,000	6,000	Sep-12	9,500	59,510
Feb-12	5,500	11,500	Oct-12	11,500	71,010
Mar-12	5,000	16,500	Nov-12	7,600	78,610
Apr-12	6,100	22,600	Dec-12	5,650	84,260
May-12	4,850	27,450	Jan-13	4,050	82,310
Jun-12	6,990	34,440	Feb-13	4,400	81,210
Jul-12	8,770	43,210	Mar-13	4,200	80,410
Aug-12	6,800	50,010			

Required:

(a) When will Adobe Ltd become liable for compulsory VAT registration?
(b) When will it have to notify HMRC?
(c) When will the registration be effective?

2. Future test

a) Registration

Registration is **compulsory if** taxable supplies are **expected to exceed £77,000** during the **next 30 days alone.**

This is **not a cumulative test**; the **taxable turnover in the previous months is not relevant.**

b) Notification to HMRC

Notification to HMRC must be by the end of the 30 day period.

c) Effective registration date

Registration is effective from the beginning of the 30 day period.

Tip

The reason the VAT registration is effective from the beginning of the month is that VAT is immediately chargeable on the £77,000 of expected sales.

Example

Star Ltd commenced trading on 1 September 2012. Sales for the following months are as follows:

		£
2012	September	6,000
	October	7,500
	November	20,500
	December	30,000
2013	January	78,500

1. Star Ltd realised that its taxable supplies for January 2013 would be at least £77,000 when the large order was placed. So, the company is liable for registration from 1 January 2013, being the beginning of the 30 day period.
2. Star Ltd has to notify HMRC by 30 January 2013, being the end of the 30 day period.
3. Registration is effective from 1 January 2013, being the beginning of the 30 day period.

Test Yourself 2

Charmie Ltd started trading on 1 October 2012. The details of orders placed with the company are as follows:

	£
1 November 2012	5,000
1 December 2012	25,000
1 January 2013	78,000

Required:

(a) When will Charmie Ltd become liable for compulsory registration?
(b) When will it have to notify HMRC?
(c) When will the registration be effective?

Tip

Standard and zero-rated supplies are taxable supplies; exempt supplies are not taxable supplies. Therefore registration for VAT is not compulsory for exempt supplies.

Example

Moon Ltd started its business in July 2012. The company considered three alternative types of business that it could operate.

They were as follows:

1. transportation where all the sales will be zero-rated
2. training where all the sales will be standard-rated, and
3. a charitable service, where all the sales will be exempt from VAT.

Sales for each of the above-mentioned alternatives will be £80,000 per month (excluding VAT), and standard-rated expenses will be £15,000 (including VAT).

Zero-rated supplies

In this case, as zero rated supplies are taxable supplies, Moon Ltd will be required to register for VAT.

Output VAT will not be due, but input VAT of £2,500 (£15,000 x 20/120) per month will be recoverable.

Standard-rated supplies

Here, Moon Ltd will be required to register for VAT as it will be making taxable supplies.
Output VAT of £16,000 (£80,000 x 20%) per month will be due (and charged to customers), and input VAT of £2,500 per month will be recoverable. Net VAT payable will be £13,500 (£16,000 – £2,500).

Exempt supplies

Moon Ltd will not be required to register for VAT; in fact, it will not be permitted to register, as it will not be making taxable supplies.

As it is dealing with exempt supplies, output VAT will not be due nor will input VAT be recoverable.

Standard rated expenses are inclusive of VAT. Therefore the value of the supply can be determined using the VAT fraction (which is 1/6 (i.e. 20/120) for the VAT rate of 20%).

Diagram 1: Registration for VAT

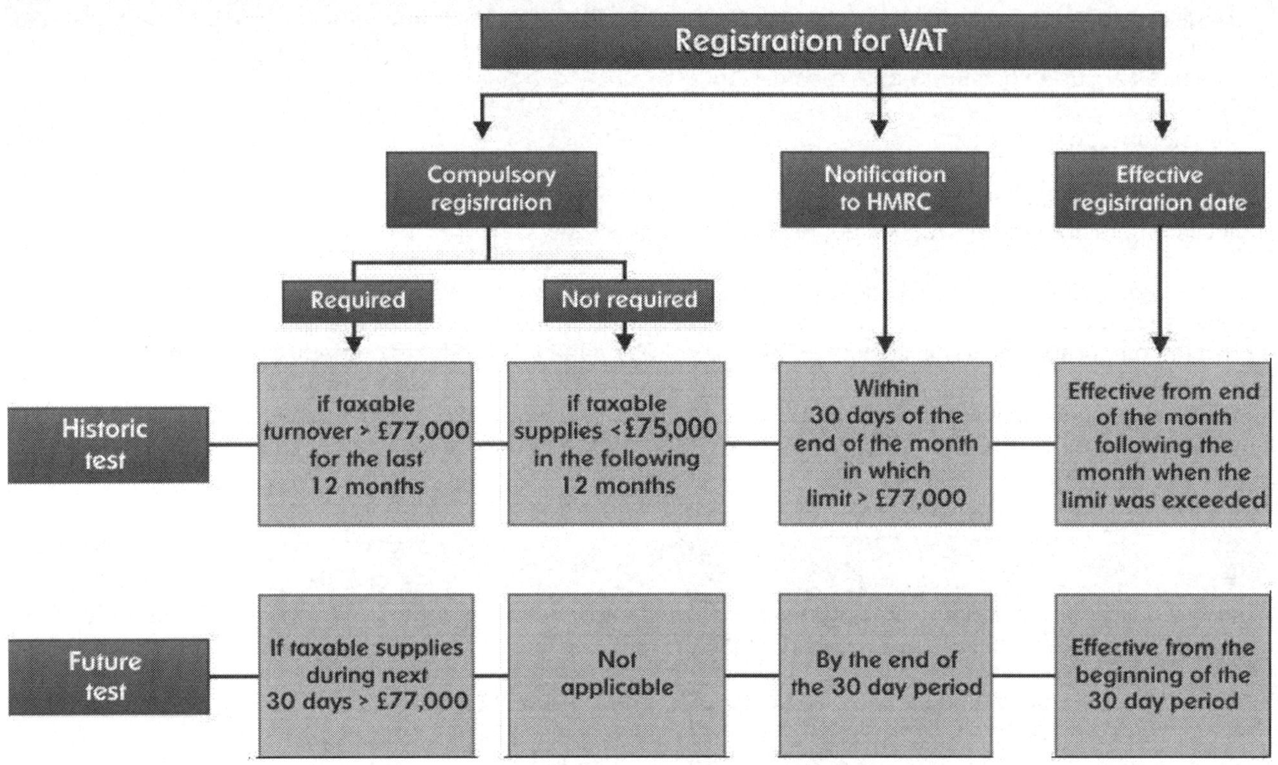

2. Explain the advantages of voluntary VAT registration.[2]

[Learning Outcome b]

A person may become registered for VAT even though his supplies fall below the registration limit.

The individual must then charge output VAT on his supplies and may reclaim input VAT on his purchases.

2.1 Voluntary registration will be beneficial if:

1. The **customers are registered for VAT**. The customers can reclaim the VAT, and the trader should be able to charge VAT on top of the pre-registration selling price.
2. **The supplies are zero-rated**. Output tax is at zero % but input VAT will be recoverable.

Star Ltd commenced trading on 1 September 2012. Sales for the following months were as follows:

		£
2012	September	6,000
	October	7,500
	November	30,500
	December	50,000
2013	January	64,500

The company sales were all standard-rated and were all made to VAT registered businesses.

Assume that input VAT for the period 1 September 2012 to 31 January 2013 was £14,500.

The taxable supplies in a 12 month period exceed the £77,000 compulsory registration threshold in December 2012. Notification must be made to HMRC by 30 January 2013 (30 days after the end of the relevant month). Registration becomes effective from 1 February 2013.

However, the input VAT of £14,500 for the period from 1 September 2012 to 31 January 2013 will not be recoverable if Star Ltd registered for VAT effective from 1 February 2013.

Continued on the next page

If it had registered voluntarily on 1 September 2012 it would have recovered input VAT of £14,500. As all sales were to VAT registered businesses, the output VAT can be passed on to customers without being a real cost to them (as they can reclaim their own input VAT).

2.2 Other advantages

1. Registration lends credibility to the business as it gives the impression that turnover is above the registration limit.
2. Requires accurate and up-to-date records.

2.3 Disadvantages

1. There are additional administration costs and strict compliance rules.
2. If customers are not VAT registered, they cannot recover the VAT.

Voluntary registration will probably not be beneficial where customers are members of the general public. Such customers cannot recover the VAT charged. If a trader is operating in a competitive market, he may not be able to pass the output VAT on to his customers and so he may need to absorb the output VAT himself.

If a trader is currently below the registration limit, and he is offered additional work that will mean the future limit is exceeded, he must consider if the output VAT can be passed on to his customers when making his decision on whether to accept the work or not.

Example

Acme Ltd has been operating a trading business for many years. The company is not registered for VAT. All sales are made to the general public and are standard-rated.

Annual sales of the company are £59,500 at present. It is considering increasing the sales price of its products to a total of £77,500 per year.

Acme Ltd's standard-rated expenses are £7,000 per annum (inclusive of VAT).
Net profit when sales were £59,500 is **£52,500** (£59,500 - £7,000).

When prices go up, sales will increase above the annual VAT registration limit of £77,000. Therefore the company will have to register for VAT from the month in which the taxable supplies in the previous 12 months exceed £77,000.

As sales are made to the general public, Acme Ltd has decided that it cannot further increase its total sale price to the public to reflect the additional VAT cost. It will have to absorb the output VAT.

Revised annual net profit will be as follows:

	£
Revenue (£77,500 x 5/6) (W1)	64,583
Expenses (£7,000 x 5/6)	(5,833)
Net profit	**58,750**

Therefore, we can see that there is an increase in net profit of £6,250 (£**58,750** - £**52,500**).
It is beneficial for the company to raise its prices.

Output VAT of £12,917 (£64,583 x 20%) will be payable, less input VAT recoverable of £1,167 (£5,833 x 20%), giving net VAT payable of £11,750.

W1

This is based on the VAT fraction of 1/6 (assuming a 20% VAT rate)
77,500 is inclusive of VAT , to calculate the net profit we need a figure exclusive of VAT.

Therefore, it would be £77500 x 100/120, i.e. £77,500 x 5/6 = £64,583

The same fraction is applicable for expenses also.

Continued on the next page

Note: you can also consider how this profit figure arose from looking at the VAT inclusive totals. Both give the same answer!

	£
Total Sales (gross)	77,500
Less: Total VAT paid to HMRC	(11,750)
Less: Expenses Incurred (gross)	(7,000)
Net profit retained (as above)	**58,750**

3. Explain the circumstances in which pre-registration input VAT can be recovered.[2] [Learning Outcome c]

Input VAT relating to pre-registration supplies can be **recovered if** the following **conditions are satisfied:**

Goods:

- The goods were supplied for **business purposes.**
- The goods have **not** been **sold or consumed before the date of registration.**
- They were **not acquired more than three years before registration.**
- They include inventory and fixed assets

Services:

- The services were supplied for **business purposes.**
- The services were **not** acquired **more than six months before registration.**

Note: VAT incurred on goods or services for non-business activity by academies especially for free education provided can be recovered by using the procedure currently used by non-VAT registered parish councils.

Example

Gemini Ltd started trading on 1 August 2012, but registered for VAT on 1 December 2012.
For the period 1 August to 30 November 2012, the company had the following inputs:

	August	September	October	November
	£	£	£	£
Goods purchased	2,500	4,500	15,500	28,500
Services incurred	2,200	3,000	4,500	5,000
Fixed assets	70,000			

On 1 December 2012, stock was acquired at a cost of £15,000. All figures are exclusive of VAT.

The stock was acquired within the three years before registration and was not sold or consumed before registration. So, input VAT of **£3,000** (£15,000 x 20%) can be recovered in respect of the stock purchased. This can be reclaimed on 1 December 2012 (the date of registration).

In the same way, input VAT on the fixed assets of **£14,000** (70,000 x 20%) can be recovered.

As the services were supplied in the six months before registration, input VAT on services **£2,940** (£2,200 + £3,000 + £4,500 + £5,000 = £14,700 x 20%) can be recovered.

Total input VAT that can be recovered = £3,000 + £14,000 + £2,940 = **£19,940.**

Bonsai Ltd commenced business as a manufacturer of children's toys on 1 August 2011. Its output and input costs for each of the months from January to April 2012 were as follows:

2012	January £	February £	March £	April £
Output				
Sales	6,000	8,500	41,400	78,510
Input				
Goods purchased	2,500	5,300	21,700	6,400
Services incurred	1,000	2,000	3,000	4,000

The above figures are all exclusive of VAT. Bonsai Ltd's sales as well as inputs are all standard-rated.

On 1 April 2012 Bonsai Ltd realised that its sales for April 2012 were set to exceed £77,000, and therefore the company immediately registered for VAT. On the date of registration, the company had stock that had cost £22,000 (exclusive of VAT), the rest having already been sold.

Required:

Calculate the amount of VAT reclaimable relating to goods purchased and services hired **prior to the registration** of VAT.

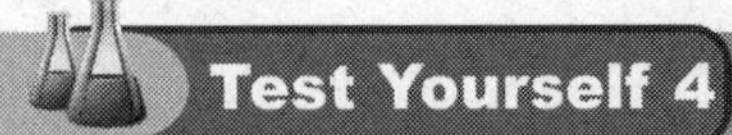

On 5 June 2012, Gary began trading. On 10 November 2012, he voluntarily registered himself for VAT. On 10 July 2012 (i.e. before he had registered his business for VAT) he had hired a lorry to carry machinery for business use and had paid VAT of £300 on the rental cost.

Required:

Can he reclaim the VAT paid on services hired before registration for VAT?

4. Explain how and when a person can deregister for VAT.[1]

[Learning Outcome d]

4.1 Deregistration from VAT

1. Compulsory

a) A registered person must deregister if he **ceases to make taxable supplies.**

Notification to HMRC should be given **within 30 days** of ceasing to make taxable supplies. Failure to do so may lead to a penalty being charged.

b) **Effective deregistration date** is the day taxable **supplies ceased.**

c) Traders who are compulsorily deregistered would have to return to the HMRC the input tax which was wrongly recovered by the trader since the date the trader should have been deregistered.

2. Voluntary

a) A registered person may deregister voluntarily **if taxable supplies in the next twelve months are not expected to exceed £75,000.**

Note: "Taxable supplies" does not include supplies of capital assets and is the figure net of VAT.

b) Notification to HMRC may be made when it appears that the taxable turnover in the next twelve months will not exceed £75,000.

c) **Effective** deregistration **date** is the **date HMRC are notified.**

3. Consequences of deregistration

On deregistration, if there is a deemed supply of business assets (plant, equipment and trading stock) on which input tax was claimed on acquisition, VAT would be chargeable on such supplies, based on the market value at the date of deregistration.

However, the transfer of a business as a going concern (as opposed to piecemeal sale of assets) does not usually give rise to VAT as it is outside the scope of VAT.

Nickle Ltd has been registered for VAT since 2003. It intends to cease trading on 31 March 2013.

It has two options on cessation: option 1: to sell its business assets on a piecemeal basis to individual buyers, or, option 2: to sell its entire business as a going concern to a single purchaser.

The effects on cessation of trading under these two options will be as follows:

Option 1

Business assets sold on piecemeal basis:
- Nickle Ltd's VAT registration will be cancelled on 31 March 2013 as it will cease to make taxable supplies.
- Output VAT will be due on fixed assets on which input VAT has been claimed.
- Notification to HMRC: the company will have to notify HMRC by 30 April 2013, being 30 days after the date of cessation.

Option 2

Business sold as a going concern:
- VAT registration will be cancelled, if the purchaser is already registered for VAT.
- If the purchaser is not registered for VAT, then it can take over the VAT registration of Nickle Ltd. This implies that the purchaser takes over the rights and liabilities of Nickle Ltd as on the date of transfer.
- Output VAT will not be due as sale of a business as a going concern is outside the scope of VAT.

Diagram 2: Deregistration for VAT

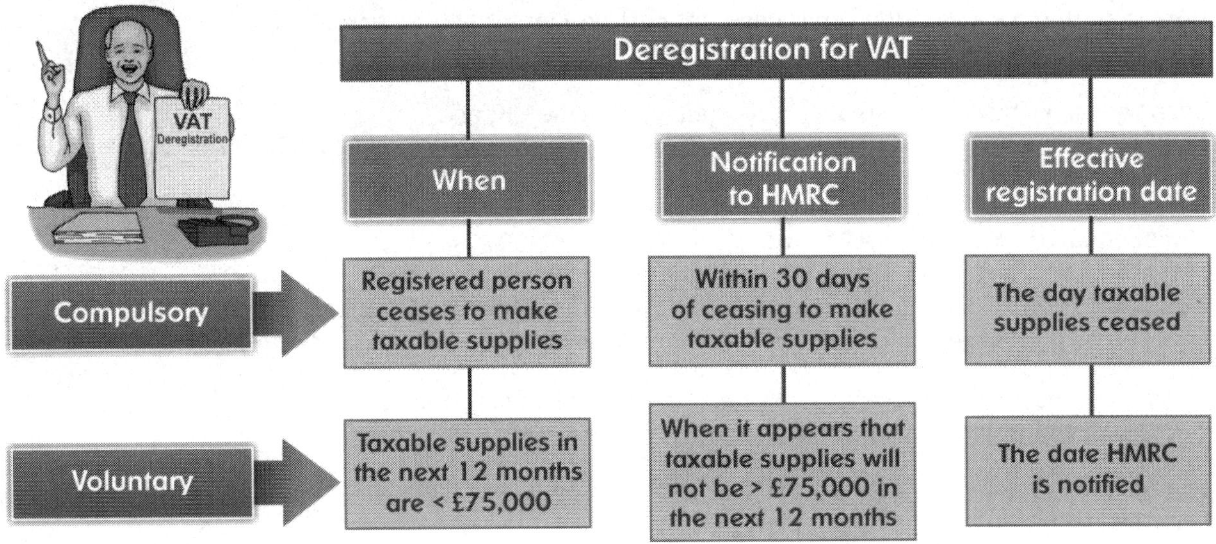

4.2 Other important points

1. When a change in a person's legal status takes place, e.g. a business is taken over by a new owner, the new owner of the business can continue with the existing VAT registration number, provided he agrees to take over all liabilities and rights from the date of transfer of the business. In short, registration under VAT **is in relation to the business and not in relation to the person who owns the business.**

   In effect, on the transfer of business from one person to another, the old registration need not be cancelled just because the ownership has changed.

2. When a person ceases to make taxable supplies, VAT becomes chargeable on all remaining inventory after deregistration and all remaining capital goods on which input tax was claimed previously.

For the last twenty years, Stella has been a manufacturer of calculators. It is her practice to purchase the raw materials for the whole month on the first day of the month. As usual, on 1 July 2012, she purchased raw materials worth £20,000 required for the month of July 2012. She paid input VAT of £3,500 on these purchases.

On 10 July 2012 she sold calculators worth £30,000. She offset the input VAT paid on the raw materials purchased in the month of July against the output VAT payable on the sales.

However, due to a sudden major physical disability, she became incapable of running her business and, on 20 August 2012, she ceased manufacturing. She deregistered her business from the VAT regime. On the date of deregistration, raw materials worth £14,000 remained out of the materials purchased on 1 July 2012.

In this situation, Stella is deemed to have made a supply of £14,000 (i.e. the value of the raw material held in inventory on which input VAT was recoverable). This is additional output VAT and offset against input VAT in the usual way in the final VAT period.

In July 2012, Tim expects that in the current year (i.e. 2012-13) his turnover will not be more than £75,000. He informs HMRC that he wants to deregister himself from the month of September 2012.

Required:

Advise him on whether this is possible.

---

5. Explain the conditions that must be met for two or more companies to be treated as a group for VAT purposes, and the consequences of being so treated.[1]

[Learning Outcome e]

5.1 A VAT group is formed when two or more companies or limited liability partnerships register as a single taxable person. However, the conditions that must be met for two or more companies to be treated as a VAT group are as follows:

- each body must have its principal or registered office in the UK; and
- both the bodies must be under common control i.e. one or more companies should be subsidiaries of a single parent company.

5.2 Consequences of being a VAT group

1. **Registration:** a VAT group is regarded as a single company which has registered for VAT on its own. Group VAT registration must be made in the name of a representative member who is responsible for:

- making VAT payments or receiving VAT refunds on behalf of the group; and
- completing and submitting a single VAT return and making VAT payments.

2. **Goods and services supplied w**ithin the group**:** the group is not required to account for VAT on goods and services that are supplied between group members.

3. **Liability:** the liability for VAT is the joint and several responsibility of the group members.

4. **VAT returns:** the group needs to submit one VAT return for the whole group. Therefore, administrative costs are saved.

5. **Limits relating to various accounting schemes:** limits relating to various accounting schemes such as cash accounting scheme, flat rate schemes (discussed in Study Guide G3) etc. apply to the group as a whole, rather than to the individual companies within the group.

Answers to Test Yourself

Answer to TY 1

1. Adobe Ltd will become liable for compulsory VAT registration when its taxable supplies during any 12 month period exceed £77,000.

   This will happen in November 2012 when taxable supplies will amount to £78,610 (£6,000 + £5,500 + £5,000 + £6,100 + £4,850 + £6,990 + £8,770 + £6,800 + £9,500 + £11,500+ £7,600)

2. Adobe Ltd will have to notify HMRC by 30 December 2012, i.e. **within 30 days of the end of the month in which the £77,000 limit is exceeded.**

3. Adobe Ltd's registration will be effective from 1 January 2013.

Answer to TY 2

1. Charmie Ltd realised that its taxable supplies for January 2013 would be at least £77,000. So, the company is liable to registration from 1 January 2013, being the start of the 30 day period.

2. Charmie Ltd has to notify HMRC by 30 January 2013, being the end of the 30 day period.

3. Registration is effective from 1 January 2013, being the beginning of the 30 day period.

Answer to TY 3

The calculation of VAT amount that can be recoverable is as follows:

	Goods	Services
Value of input	£22,000 (in inventory)	£6,000 (£1,000 + £2,000 + £3,000)
VAT paid at standard rate	20%	20%
VAT recoverable	**£4,400**	**£1,200**

Input VAT paid on goods which are purchased not more than three years prior to the date of registration (i.e., in the case of Bonsai Ltd, goods purchased not before 1 April 2009) can be reclaimed provided the goods remain in inventory on the date of registration. Therefore, Bonsai Ltd can reclaim input VAT on the goods remaining **in inventory (i.e. on £22,000).**

The company can also recover VAT incurred on services from 1 October 2011 to 1 April 2012 (i.e. services hired not more than six months prior to the date of registration).

Answer to TY 4

A registered person can reclaim input tax paid on services purchased prior to registration for VAT if and only if:

1. services are supplied for **business purposes**
2. services are supplied **within 6 months prior to date of registration**

Gary satisfies both these conditions:

(a) he had hired services four months prior to the date of registration for VAT and
(b) the services were hired for business purposes.

He can reclaim the input tax paid on services prior to registration for VAT.

Answer to TY 5

If HMRC is satisfied that taxable turnover will not exceed £75,000 in the next twelve months, HMRC cancels the registration from the date of the taxable person's request.

Tim can request HMRC to deregister him from September 2012.

Quick Quiz

1. Lindsey is a manufacturer. She pays VAT on purchases at the rate of 20% which she cannot reclaim as she is not VAT registered. Her annual turnover is less than 77,000 and, on her output, VAT would be chargeable at 'zero' rate if she were VAT registered. In this situation the VAT paid on purchases is real expenditure and has to be reflected in the price charged to her customers. Hence, the price of the product is not competitive. What action should she take to make her prices more competitive?

2. State with reasons whether the following sentences are correct or not?
   (a) If a supplier expects his taxable turnover to exceed £77,000 within the next 30 days, he must notify HMRC by the end of the next 30 days.
   (b) A person can voluntarily register himself for VAT even if his turnover is below £77,000.
   (c) When a person starts dealing in taxable supplies, he must immediately register for VAT.

3. Humpty is a trader. He has run his business for the last four years. His annual turnover is £100,000 (approximately) so he has registered himself for VAT.

   In April 2012 he admits Dumpty as his partner. Being a VAT registered trader, what are the consequences of changing the legal status of the business (from a sole trader to a partnership)?

Answers to Quick Quiz

1. If Lindsey voluntarily registers herself for VAT, she can reclaim the VAT paid on purchases. This will reduce the cost of purchases. By doing so, she can maintain the profit margin and reduce the selling price.

2.
   (a) **Correct.** If a person believes his taxable turnover during the next 30 days will exceed £77,000, it is his duty to notify HMRC by the end of the 30 day period. The registration will be effective from the beginning of the 30 day period.

   (b) **Correct.** Even if a person's taxable supply is below the prescribed limit (presently £77,000), he can voluntarily register for VAT.

   (c) **Incorrect**. From 1 April 2012, a person must register for VAT if his taxable supplies exceed £77,000 or a person expects his taxable turnover to exceed £77,000 during the next 30 days.

   When a person starts dealing in taxable supplies, if his turnover does not exceed £77,000 or his turnover is not likely to exceed £77,000 within next 30 days, registration for VAT is not compulsory.

3. When there is a change in legal status of a person, compulsory deregistration is triggered. Humpty admitted a partner, so his sole trading business became a partnership. As there was a change in the legal status of a person, HMRC will take steps for compulsory deregistration.

Self Examination Questions

Question 1

Tedtot Plc deals in spare parts for computers. The company started its business on 20 September 2011. In the month of May 2012, the company's turnover exceeded £77,000. In the month of June, the company was registered for VAT. A list of the company's purchases since formation is as follows:

Month	£
October	720
November	8,900
December	7,500
January	10,500
February	12,540
March	17,800
April	17,000

At the time of registration the company had inventory of £32,400 in hand.

Required:

Can the company claim input VAT paid on the inventory after it registers for VAT?

Question 2

Twinkle Ltd's turnover during the last year was £77,000. The company supplies VAT exempt goods to a retail outlet in London. The company pays VAT on its input at standard rates and is considering registering for VAT so that it can reclaim the input tax paid on purchases. Advise the company when it should become registered.

Question 3

In April 2012, Chempco Ltd started its business. In the same month the company took a car on a rental basis. The total bill included VAT of £2,000. In the month of July 2012, Chempco Ltd's turnover was above £77,000 and the company registered for VAT.

Due to poor sales, the goods produced in April were still held in stock until July.

Required:

Can Chempco Ltd offset input VAT paid on the pre registration services against the output VAT on sales?

Question 4

Sibel Ltd started trading on 1 September 2012, and registered for VAT on 1 December 2012.
For the period 1 September to 30 November 2012, the company had the following inputs:

	September	October	November
	£	£	£
Goods purchased	5,600	16,000	30,500
Services incurred	5,000	6,000	7,000
Fixed assets	80,000		

On 1 December 2012, there was inventory of goods costing £25,000.
All figures are exclusive of VAT.

Required:

Calculate the total input VAT that can be recovered.

Answers to Self Examination Questions

Answer to SEQ 1

VAT incurred on purchases before registration for VAT can be treated as input tax only if:

1. Goods are purchased within three years prior to the date of registration.
2. Goods are used for business purposes.
3. The goods have not been consumed or supplied further, before the date of registration or, if at all consumed, final goods are consumed for production of other goods, and final goods are still held as inventory.

In the case of Tedtot Plc, the inventory that was remaining as on the date of registration for VAT was purchased within three years prior to the date of registration. The company can claim input VAT paid on its purchases.

Answer to SEQ 2

The company which supplies only exempt goods / services cannot register for VAT. As a result, the company is not a taxable person and it cannot reclaim input VAT. In short, the company has to treat that input VAT as an additional cost.

Answer to SEQ 3

A taxable person can reclaim VAT paid on services prior to registration, on fulfilment of the following conditions:

1. The services are supplied for the business.
2. The services are supplied six months before the date of registration.

In the given question, Chempco Ltd had paid for services two months before the date of registration. The company can reclaim the VAT paid on these.

Answer to SEQ 4

The inventory of goods was acquired less than three years before registration and was not sold or consumed before registration.
So, input VAT of **£5,000** (£25,000 x 20%) can be recovered on 1 December 2012 on inventory of goods.

In the same way, input VAT on fixed assets **£16,000** (£80,000 x 20%) can be recovered.

As the services were supplied less than six months before registration, input VAT on services **£3,600** (£5,000 + £6,000 + £7,000 = £18,000 x 20%) can be recovered.

Total input VAT that can be recovered = £5,000 + £16,000 + £3,600
= **£24,600**

SECTION G

VALUE ADDED TAX

G3

STUDY GUIDE G3: THE COMPUTATION OF VAT LIABILITIES

Get Through Intro

In this Study Guide we will discuss **how VAT is accounted for and administered and when the tax point emerges**. We will also examine the information that has to be given on a VAT invoice.

This Study Guide also introduces you to the concept of valuation of supplies and the circumstances when input VAT is not deductible. A thorough understanding of this concept will help you to guide your client on how to account for his VAT liabilities.

In addition, this Study Guide explains the various penal provisions relating to VAT.

Proper tax planning requires an in-depth knowledge of all the rules and provisions of income tax as well as the VAT Act.

A thorough study of this Study Guide will enable you to acquire knowledge which will help you in your exams as well as in your professional life as a tax consultant.

Learning Outcomes

a) Explain how VAT is accounted for and administered.
b) Recognise the tax point when goods or services are supplied.
c) List the information that must be given on a VAT invoice.
d) Explain and apply the principles regarding the valuation of supplies.
e) Recognise the circumstances in which input VAT is non-deductible.
f) Compute the relief that is available for impairment losses on trade debts.
g) Explain the circumstances in which the default surcharge, a penalty for an incorrect VAT return, and default interest will be applied.
h) Explain the treatment of imports, exports and trade within the European Union.

Introduction

Case Study

Jones Limited sells luxury products with quarterly sales of £50,000 plus VAT of £10,000 = £60,000.

The cost of making the sales for the quarter is £30,000 plus VAT of £6,000 = £36,000.

The net amount to be paid to HMRC is £10,000 less £6,000 = £4,000. This illustration shows the net amount of VAT to be paid and the simplistic mechanism used to calculate amounts owing or to be repaid.

Case Study

James is the owner of a garden design and landscaping business. On his quarterly VAT return he declares his output tax to be £90,000 and claims input tax of £25,000. With further investigation it was discovered that the output tax was understated by £40,000.

In this case a penalty would not be applied as the amount of understated VAT is less than the determined amount.

The first case study exemplifies the basis of payment of VAT.
The second case study tells us about the penalty provisions and the consequences of non-disclosure to the authorities.

All these concepts are explained in the respective Learning Outcomes.

1. Explain how VAT is accounted for and administered.[2]

[Learning Outcome a]

1. Accounting for VAT

a) The VAT period is a period covered by the VAT return.
b) Normally a VAT return is completed **quarterly** (i.e. for a 3 month period).The VAT period is allocated by HMRC (for example the quarters ending August, November, February and May). The business could ask for VAT periods which fit in with its own accounting year.
c) Return is submitted to HMRC **by the end of the month following the end of the return period.**
d) Return shows total output VAT and total input VAT for the quarter.
e) Return shows **amount payable** (or repayable).
f) Payment should be sent with return.

Tip

For businesses with turnover in excess of £100,000, returns must be filed online and VAT paid electronically for accounting periods that start on or after 1 April 2012.

Example

Cellarage Ltd had an output VAT of £15,000 and an input VAT of £8,000, for the quarter ended 31 December 2012.

The company should submit the VAT return for the quarter ended 31 December 2012 by 31 January 2013.

Payment of VAT is (£15,000 - £8,000) = £7,000. This amount is due on 31 January 2013 when the VAT return is submitted.

2. Monthly VAT accounting

a) Taxable person may **request** to submit monthly returns.
b) Generally, **taxable persons whose input VAT exceeds their output VAT** and are therefore in a repayment situation would **stand to benefit** in terms of improved cash flows.

Example

If some or all of the goods we supply are zero-rated, then the input VAT may be greater than the output VAT which means that HMRC will owe the business money. If the taxable person prepares and submits a VAT return every 3 months, then the repayment will be received every 3 months. However, a monthly VAT return is submitted, then the repayment is monthly which means the money will be received a month earlier. This is good for cash flow.

A disadvantage of monthly VAT accounting is that it increases administration as 12 VAT returns are to be submitted instead of 4 per year.

3. VAT payments on account

If the annual **VAT liability exceeds £2 million,** the taxable person must make payments on account. This is in respect of each quarter. The payment of 1/24 of the total VAT paid in the previous year will have to be paid at the end of each month in the quarter from the second month end. The taxpayer may elect to pay their actual VAT liability instead.

Example

Quarter ended 31/03/2013

Due 28/02/2013 payment on account of 1/24 of the total VAT liability for previous year.
Due 31/03/2013 payment on account of 1/24 of the total VAT liability for previous year.
Due 30/04/2013 balancing payment of balancing amount for the quarter.

Test Yourself 1

Yaan Ltd is liable to make payments on account calculated at £325,000 each for the quarter ended 31 March 2013.

Required:

Calculate the amount of payment or repayment that is due if Yaan Ltd has the following VAT liabilities:

(a) £700,000
(b) £500,000.

---

4. Control visits

a) VAT is self-administered.
b) HMRC make control visits to check the accuracy of VAT returns.

5. Records

A taxable person must keep records for **6 years.**

6. Refund of overpaid VAT

VAT that has been overpaid can be refunded, subject to a **3 year time limit.**

Example

Cuba Ltd has prepared its return for the quarter ended 31 December 2012. The company found that it has not been claiming the input VAT on £545 (inclusive of VAT) that is paid towards the rent of soft-drinks machines for each quarter. The same monthly amount has been paid since 1 January 2007.

A claim for a VAT refund can be made subject to a three-year time limit.

Therefore, Cuba Ltd can claim the input VAT incurred during the quarter ended 31 December 2012 and during the period 1 October 2009 to 30 September 2012.

1.1 Administration of VAT

HMRC is responsible for administering the VAT systems. For the purpose of administration of VAT, the department of HMRC is divided into:

1. Local area office
2. Central unit

1. Local area office

Local area offices deal with local VAT administration. The officers visit the registered person's office in their area. They check the accuracy of the registered person's VAT returns as well as the overall functioning of the VAT system.

2. Central unit

The main functions of the VAT Central Unit are:

a) Maintenance of registration records (every taxable person needs to file a registration form). The registration form is maintained by this department.

b) Collection of VAT returns (i.e. the registered person has to file their returns with this unit) and processing of completed returns. However, from 1 April 2010 many VAT returns are now required to be filed online and from 1 April 2013, this will be applicable for all VAT registered businesses).

c) Collection of VAT due from a registered person and its repayment when it is due.

Diagram 1: Functions of central unit and local area officer

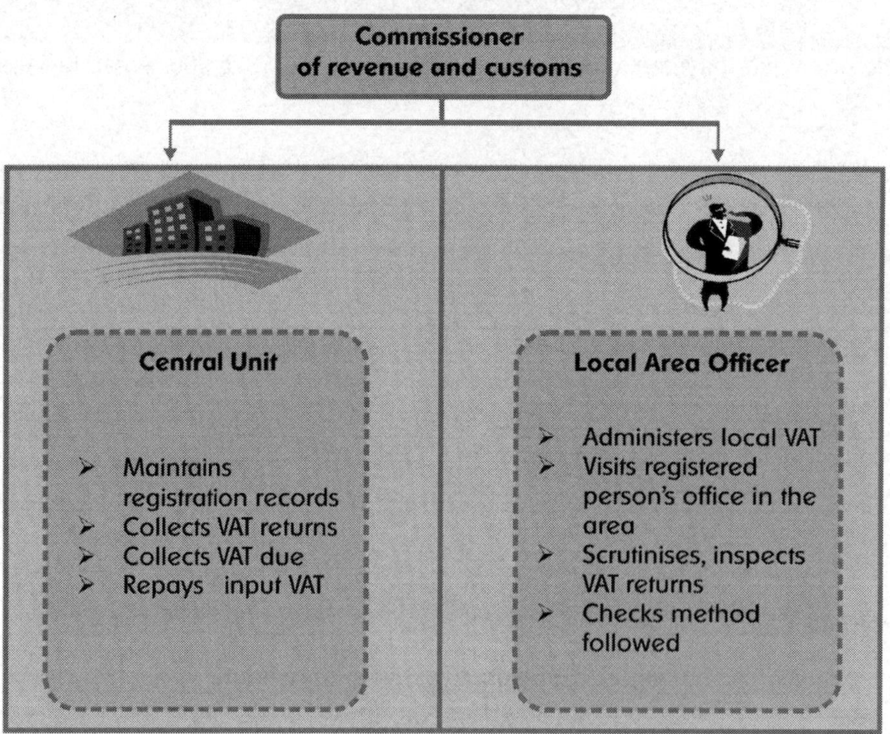

1.2 VAT assessments

VAT is a self-assessed tax, i.e. normally it is not required to make formal tax assessments. However, when any taxable person fails to submit his VAT return or submits a VAT return which is either incomplete or incorrect, HMRC may issue an assessment order.

The normal period for carrying out VAT assessment is three years from the end of the VAT period to which the VAT return relates. However, this period can be extended to 20 years in case of fraud, dishonesty, and unauthorised issue of VAT invoices.

Black Ltd is a wholesaler of shoes. The company's average yearly turnover is £500,000. It was the practice of Black Ltd to issue invoices to registered persons only. During the year 2012-13 Black Ltd raised invoices for only £400,000 and paid output VAT on this amount.

During the year 2012-13, the company also managed not to issue invoices for £90,000 and consequently did not pay output tax on this amount.

As Black Ltd has committed fraud, HMRC can extend the assessment period to 2032-33.

1.3 Appeals

If a taxable person disagrees with the decision made by HMRC, within 30 days from the date of the decision by HMRC, the person may:

- ask a local VAT officer to reconsider the decision or
- make an appeal to a VAT tribunal.

The local VAT officer may:

a) confirm the decision or
b) revise the decision.

A taxable person may **file** an **appeal** to a VAT tribunal provided the **VAT returns** and **amount** shown payable thereon, is paid by the taxpayer. The tribunal can waive payment of the VAT shown in the return before the appeal is heard.

A person must file an appeal with a VAT tribunal within:

- **21 days** from confirmation of decision by a **local officer.**
- **30 days** from the date of decision given **by a central unit** or revised decision of a local officer.

A tribunal's hearings are normally held in public and decisions are published. If a taxable person is dissatisfied with the decision of the tribunal, he may refer the case to the High Court and beyond.

Diagram: 2 Appeal procedures for a person aggrieved with a VAT decision

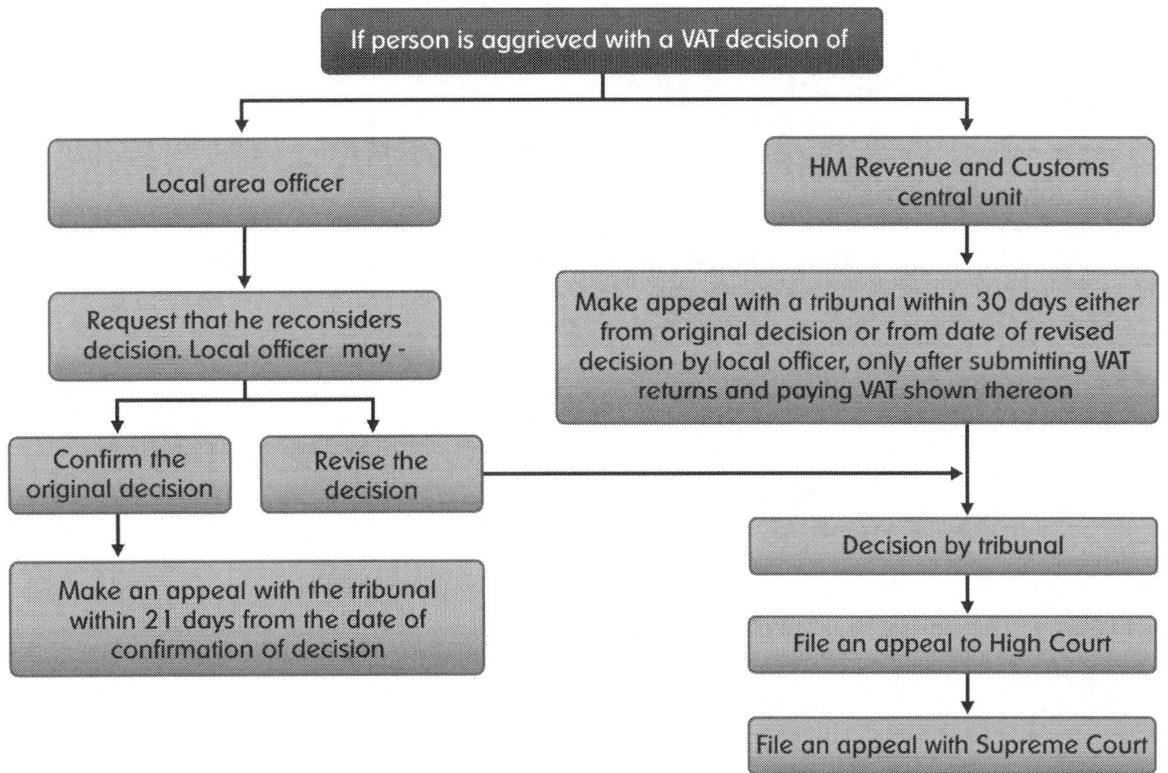

2. Recognise the tax point when goods or services are supplied.[2]

[Learning Outcome b]

VAT is **due at** the **tax point date.** The tax point is the deemed date of supply.

The tax point date determines:

- **the VAT return** in which the VAT must be **accounted** for (i.e. when the output tax is due for payment and the input tax can be recovered); and
- the **rate of VAT** that applies.

Determination of basic tax points

1. The basic tax point is the point when **goods** are **made available** or **services are performed** irrespective of whether the invoice is raised or not.

Example

Eletronica Ltd is a wholesale dealer of electronics goods. On 5 June 2012, Task Ltd made a delivery of 50 music systems to Electronica Ltd. However, the invoice was raised on 10 July 2012.

In this situation, the tax point is taken as the date of delivery of the music systems i.e. 5 June 2012.

---

2. When an invoice is raised before goods are made available or within 14 days from the date of supply of goods or services, the basic tax point is the **date on which the invoice was raised.**

Example

Shine Ltd is a dealer of gold ornaments. On 1 September 2012, Lucy purchased a diamond ring worth £1,000 from Shine Ltd. As she was related to one of the directors of Shine Ltd, the invoice was not raised until 10 September 2012.

The invoice was raised within 10 days of the date of delivery of goods. Therefore, the date of invoice (i.e. 10 September 2012) is taken as the basic tax point.

---

3. When **payment is received before the goods or services are supplied or the invoice is raised**, then the **date of receipt of payment** is taken as the **basic tax point.**

Example

Nancy is a manufacturer of pastries and cakes. On 1 April 2012 she supplied 500 pastries to Victory Ltd. As this was a special order, on 29 March 2012 Nancy took £500 as an advance. The invoice was raised on the date of delivery i.e. 1 April 2012.

Here, Nancy took £500 as an advance before the goods were supplied. Therefore the date of the advance (i.e. 29 March 2012) is taken as the tax point.

---

4. When **invoices are raised every month, a monthly tax point** (such as VAT invoice date or the end of the month) **can be adopted consistently.**

Example

Saniya is a tax consultant. She provides tax consultancy to Web Ltd. Every day she works for approximately 3 hours for the company. However, she raises an invoice at the end of each month.

In this situation, the tax point is the date of (monthly) invoice raised.

Example

Choc Chips Ltd sells chocolates to various retail outlets in London. The company supplied chocolates to Infinity Ltd with delivery on 22 May 2012, which were worth £10,000. Due to the chocolates being of a special type, the company received payment of a non-refundable advance of £3,000 on 20 March 2012 (although no invoice was issued). On 3 April 2012, the company issued an invoice to the retail outlet and received the balancing payment on 5 May 2012.

The company files VAT returns quarterly, namely March, June, September and December every year.

1. State Choc Chips Ltd's tax point.
2. How should the company account for VAT?

Answer

Details	Tax point	Accounting of VAT
Advance of £3,000	20 March as it is the earliest of: ➢ the payment date (20 March), ➢ the invoice date (3 April) and ➢ the date of delivery (22 May).	➢ VAT due on £3,000 is £600 (£3,000 x 20%). ➢ The company should account for VAT of **£600** in the March 2012 return.
Balance payment of £7,000	3 April as it is the earliest of: ➢ the payment date (5 May), ➢ the invoice date (3 April) and ➢ the date of delivery (22 May).	➢ VAT due on £7,000 is £1,400 (£7,000 x 20%). ➢ The company should account for VAT of **£1,400** in the June 2012 return.

Test Yourself 2

Sun Ltd sells electronic items to various retail dealers. To produce these items, Sun Ltd requires a high quality machine. The machine is ordered from High-tech Ltd on 5 June 2012. The cost of the machine is £10,000.

The company is in urgent need of the machine so it pays a non-refundable deposit of £1,000 on 10 June 2012 and receives delivery of the machine on 20 June 2012. However, the invoice is issued by High-tech Ltd on 2 July 2012.

The balance of £9,000 is paid on 4 July 2012.

Required:

(a) What are the different tax points of this transaction?

(b) How will the company account for VAT?

3. List the information that must be given on a VAT invoice.[1]

[Learning Outcome c]

3.1 VAT invoices

When a taxable person supplies taxable goods to another taxable person then he **must issue a tax invoice** to the **buyer** within **30 days**.

1. **No invoice** is required **if the supply is zero-rated.**
2. The **supplier** must **keep one copy** for himself **as documentary evidence.**
3. The tax invoice must show the following details:
    a) identifying serial **number**
    b) **date** of supply
    c) **time of supply or date of issue** of document
    d) **name, address and registration number** of **supplier**
    e) name and address **of person to whom** the goods or services are **supplied**

f) a **description** sufficient to identify the goods or services supplied, and for each, the **quantity** of the goods or the extent of the services, the **rate of VAT** and the **amount payable, excluding VAT** expressed **in** any **currency**
g) the **gross amount payable**, excluding VAT
h) rate of any **cash discount** offered
i) the **total amount of VAT charged**, expressed in sterling
j) the unit price; and
k) the reason for any zero rate of exemption.

4. A taxable person may issue a less detailed invoice where value of supplies including VAT is less than **£250** (e.g. invoice for telephone calls, car park fees). In such situations a taxable person can claim input tax **without VAT invoice**.

A less-detailed VAT invoice must contain

a) **name address and registration number** of the **retailer**
b) the date **of the supply**
c) a description sufficient to identify the **goods or services supplied**
d) for each VAT rate applicable, the total **amount payable including VAT, shown in sterling**
e) the **rate of VAT** in force at the time of the supply

This VAT invoice must exclude exempt supplies!

5. Every VAT registered dealer must retain this tax invoice for **6 years.** It may be kept **on paper, computer or on microfilm,** provided the entity has adequate facilities to:

➢ produce it easily to the office of HMRC when required; and
➢ also allow the HMRC officials to view the invoice when required.

6. If a customer returns any goods after issuing the tax invoice to him then, a credit note must be issued on a customer. This credit note must contain the number and the date of the original VAT invoice.

A typical example of a VAT invoice

Sales Invoice No. 199			
From: Bean Ltd Enterprise House Victoria Road Chesterfield SE1 7RU		VAT Reg. 938 2583 45	
To: Pea Ltd Carbuncle Drive Wither Sea North Yorkshire NY1 8WE			Date of Invoice 05/07/12 Date of Supply 30/06/12 Tax Point 05/07/12
	Quantity	**Description**	**Net Amount**
	10	Desk Teak £30.00	£300.00
		Less:	
		Cash Discount @2%	(£6.00)
		Total	£294.00
		Add:	
		VAT @20%	£58.80
		Total Net	£294.00
		Total VAT	£58.80
		Total to Pay	**£352.80**

This amount is payable in full 30 days from the date of issue of this invoice.
All goods remain the property of Bean Ltd until payment in full is received.
All cheques should be made payable to Bean Ltd.

Test Yourself 3

The following is a sample of the new sales invoice that Tara-rum-Pam Ltd is going to issue to its customers.

SALES INVOICE

Tara-rum-Pam Ltd
121 The West Street
London WC1 2AB

Customer Address:

Ding-Dong Plc
90, The LS Road

Glasgow G1 2CD

Telephone 0208 100 1234

Invoice Date and Tax Point: 1 March 2012

Item description	Quantity	Price
Music system	5	125
Amplifier	2	75
Total amount payable (Including VAT)		**200**

Directors: Tara & Pam
Company Number: 1234666
Registered Office: 121 The West Street, London WC1 2AB

Several customers have recently defaulted on the payment of their debts. In order to encourage prompt payment, Tara-rum-Pam Ltd is considering offering all of its customers a 5% discount if they pay within one month of the date of the sales invoice.

No discount is currently offered.

Required:

State what alterations Tara-rum-Pam Ltd will have to make to its new sales invoices in order for them to be valid for VAT purposes.

---

4. Explain and apply the principles regarding the valuation of supplies.[2]

[Learning Outcome d]

As we have seen in the previous Study Guide, goods and services which are liable to VAT either at the standard, reduced or zero rate are called 'taxable supplies'. The total value of these supplies is called 'taxable turnover'.

4.1 What is the value of supply?

Output VAT is charged on the value of supply, which is usually the **price charged by the taxable person when the supply is of goods or services**.

The amount of VAT is calculated as follows:

VAT = Value of supply x VAT rate

The tax value of a supply depends on what is received by a supplier in exchange for the supply. This something in exchange is called the **consideration**. The consideration for supply is the total value paid by the buyer to the seller. This also includes VAT.

Twinkle is a wholesaler of cosmetics. On 2 April 2012, she supplied 300 bottles of perfume to Casuals (an exclusive boutique in south London). Each bottle was worth £10. The VAT amount and total consideration is calculated as follows (assume perfumes are liable to VAT at standard rate):

	£
Value of supply (300 x £10)	3,000
Add: VAT (@ 20% (£3,000 x 20%)	600
Total consideration	**3,600**

The VAT portion included in the total consideration can be calculated separately from the total consideration if you know the VAT rate.

The formula below will make it easy to calculate the VAT portion.

$$\text{VAT} = \frac{\text{Rate of tax}}{100 + \text{Rate of tax}} \times \text{Total consideration}$$

Continuing the above example of Twinkle

The total consideration of £3,600, VAT is calculated as follows:

$$\text{VAT} = \frac{\text{Rate of tax}}{100 + \text{Rate of tax}} \times \text{Total consideration}$$

$$\frac{£20}{£100 + £20} \times £3,600$$

$$= \frac{£1}{£6} \times £3,600$$

$$= £600$$

For a 20% VAT rate, the fraction is 1/6. This **1/6** is called a **VAT fraction**. The VAT fraction varies according to the rate of tax chargeable.

Test Yourself 4

Vince Ltd supplies goods worth £220. The VAT rate applicable to supplies is the standard rate. Calculate the VAT charged and the total consideration that Vince Ltd receives.

Judo Ltd receives consideration of £17,390 against the supplies of goods. What amount of VAT is included in the consideration? (The VAT rate is standard).

SUMMARY

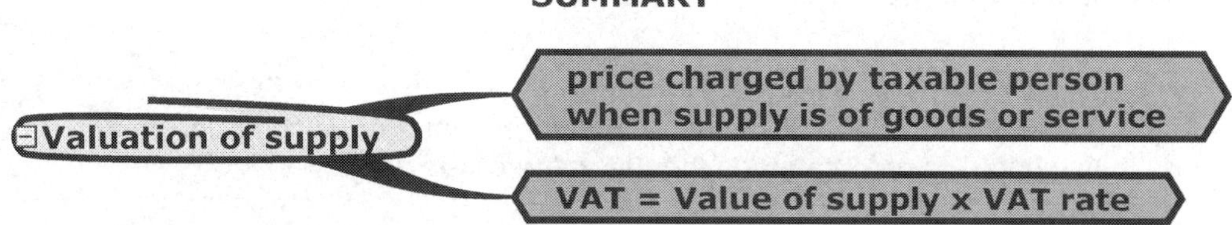

4.2 Exceptional cases where the value of supply is the deemed price of goods / services

a) Where supply includes the value of a business asset given as a gift

If a business asset is given as a gift, then the taxable person has to pay VAT on the value of the asset. In this situation, the value of supply is the value of identical goods that one can purchase on the open market.

Example

Luxury Car Ltd is involved in the production of gear boxes for sports cars. Luxury Car Ltd receives a gift of equipment (a machine used for making gear boxes) from Car-point Plc (both the companies are owned by Jim Bonds). The market value of this equipment at the time of the gift was £10,000.

Car-point Plc gave the equipment to Luxury car Ltd as a gift. In this situation, Car-point Plc must include the market value of the equipment on the date of gift (£10,000) as its taxable supply, and account for VAT on this value.

---

b) Temporary use of business asset

If at any time the employee or owner of a company uses a business asset for his personal use, then this results in supply of services. In this situation, the value of the service provided is equal to the amount by which the asset depreciates.

Example

Rosy is an accountant in Red Ltd. With the permission of the company, Rosy used the company's car for private purposes. Rosy used this car for one month. During the tax year the company claimed capital allowances of £3,000 on this car.

In this situation, Red Ltd has to pay VAT assuming that the company has given Rosy the car on a hire basis. The value of services is calculated as follows:

Value of services = Depreciation that Red Ltd would have claimed for one month.
= £3,000/12
= £250.

---

c) Private use of services

If an employee / owner uses a service provided to the business for his private purposes, then it is considered that the business has provided those services to the employee or the owner. In this situation the value of the resulting services is equal to the **proportionate cost of supplies to the business.**

Example

Octopus is a manager in Sea Ltd. Sea Ltd has hired a small boat to transport goods to the sea shore. For this boat, the company pays a monthly rental of £3,000. During the Christmas vacation, Octopus used the boat (which is hired by the company) for one week.

Here, it is assumed that Sea Ltd gave the boat to Octopus on a rental basis. The value of service is calculated as follows:

Value of service = monthly rental charges/4 weeks (on average, there are 4 weeks in a month)
= £3,000/4
= £750.

4.3 Special situations of output VAT

a) Discount

If the supplier of the goods offers a trade discount (quantity discounts) or discount for prompt payment to the buyer of the goods then the **VAT** is **calculated** on the **net value of the supply**.

Net value = sales price less discount

Even though the customer does not actually take advantage of the discount, VAT is calculated on the net value of the supply.

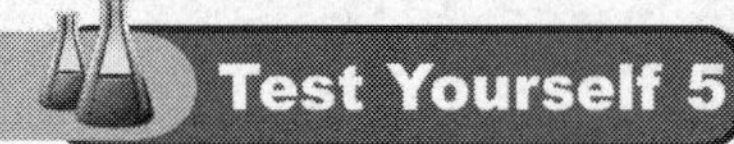

Morgan is a wholesaler of plastic goods. She offered a 2% discount to any customer who pays within 20 days of the date of delivery of goods. On 14 June 2012, she supplied goods worth £40,000 to Sargon who runs a retail shop.

Required:

Assuming the VAT rate as 20%, calculate the VAT charged on the supply and value of supply in the following situations:

(a) Sargon pays within 20 days.
(b) Sargon does not pay within 20 days.

b) Motor expenses

i. Input VAT can be recovered even when the owner of the business or the employee uses the fuel for private mileage. If the business pays for both private and business fuel used in a car, a fixed VAT charge is applicable based on the cubic capacity of the engine and fuel type. This is called the fuel scale charge.

ii. This simplification method allows the business to reclaim VAT on both the business and private elements of the fuel.

For VAT purposes, home to office journeys are not treated as business mileage.

Student Note: During the exam, students must take care to check whether the examiner has given scale rates either inclusive or exclusive of VAT.

If the rates are **inclusive** of VAT then calculate output tax as follows:

VAT = Fuel scale charge x 1/6 (i.e. VAT fraction as we have seen previously)

If the fuel rates are **exclusive** of VAT then calculate output tax as follows:

VAT = Fuel scale charge x VAT rate (i.e. 20%)

The scale charge will be given to you in the examination.

iii. Input VAT can be **fully recovered** for **repairs and maintenance** to a motor car provided the car is put to some business use. However, if a vehicle is used **solely for private motoring**, you cannot recover the VAT on repairs and maintenance.

iv. If a car is used only for business purposes (e.g. a driving school vehicle), VAT may be reclaimed. However, a taxable person then needs to account for VAT when he sells a car.

v. If a car is purchased in order to give it out on a lease basis, the lessor can claim the VAT paid when the car was purchased. Normally the lessee also can reclaim the VAT paid on the cost of hire charges.

However if the lessor has reclaimed input charges and the lessee makes private use of a car, the lessee can recover only **50%** of the input tax paid on lease charges.

Output VAT must be accounted for, based on the scale charge if input VAT is claimed in respect of fuel provided for private use without the cost of that fuel being fully reimbursed.

Rent-a-car Plc is a company which provides cars on lease. During the year 2012-13, the company purchased two cars and paid VAT of £2,000. The company has adjusted this VAT while making payment of output VAT on lease charges.

During the year, Fun Ltd took a car from Rent-a-car Plc on lease for business purposes. The total lease charges paid by Fun Ltd during the year were £500 and VAT of £100 (£500 x 20%). However, Fun Ltd's director also used the car for private purposes.

In this situation, Fun Ltd can claim only 50% of the VAT paid on lease charges i.e. £50 (£100 x 50%).

Diagram 3: Motor car expenses

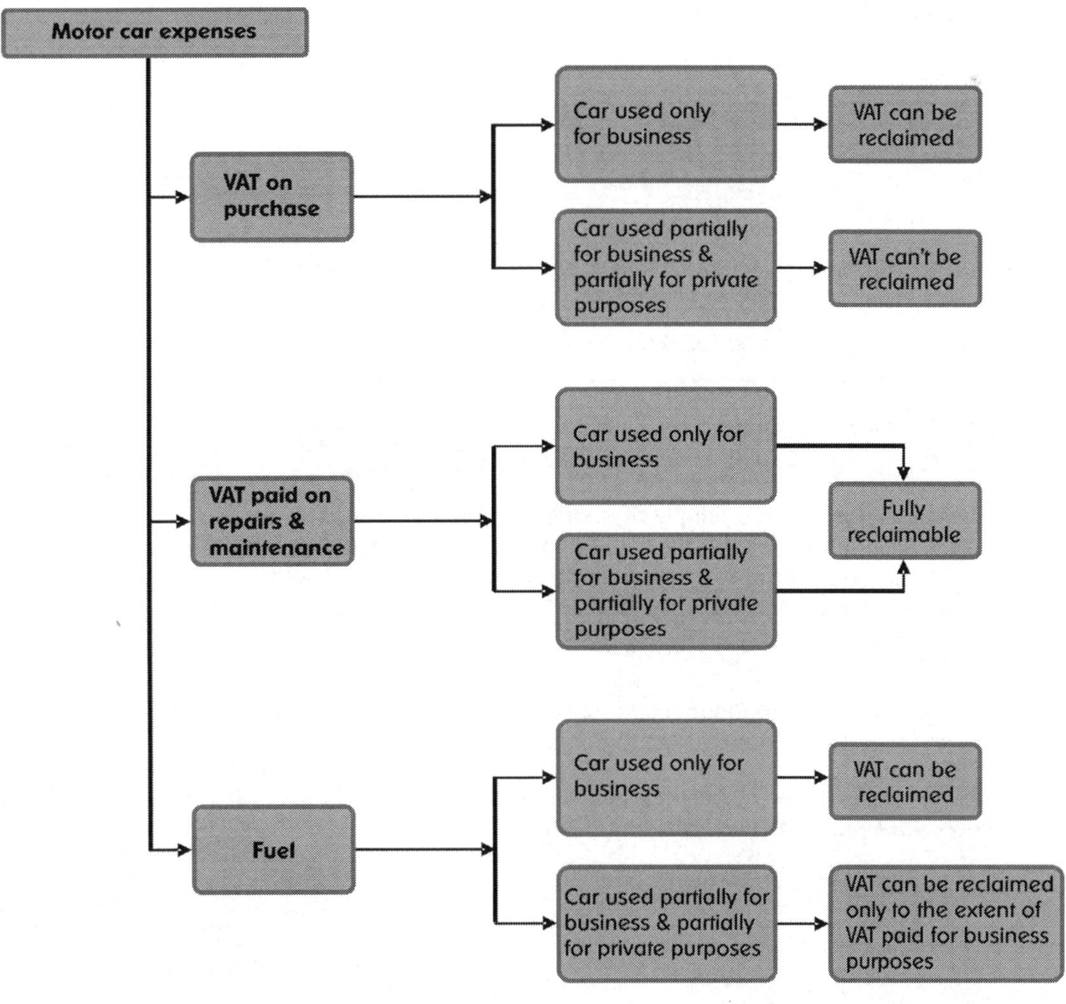

c) Transfer of a business as a going concern

No VAT is due on the sale of a business, provided:

i. all of the business is transferred as a going concern
ii. the purchaser is, or will become, registered for VAT

d) Mixed supplies

Mixed supplies are said to be made when a supplier charges a single inclusive price for a number of separate supplies of goods or services. In other words, more than two goods or services are invoiced in a single invoice at a single inclusive price.

With mixed supplies, the VAT rates applicable to the goods or supplies vary; some are chargeable at standard rates, some may be at a zero rate and so on.

In a mixed supply, the supplier of the goods charges VAT **separately** for each element of the supply by applying the appropriate rate of VAT by notionally apportioning the total value. The supplier can split the total invoice price between the different elements by applying any one of the below-mentioned methods:

i. considering cost to the supplier as a base or
ii. taking open market value as a base

There are no strict rules as to how the total value is apportioned; only that any apportionment must be fair.

Example

A VAT exclusive price of a mixed supply is £600. One of the goods supplied, which cost the supplier £200, is standard-rated and the other, which cost the supplier £50, is exempt from VAT.

In this situation, based on the available information, apportionment of the price of the mixed supply across the standard-rated and exempt goods is done on the basis of the cost of the product.

The value of the standard-rated supply is calculated as follows:

$$\text{Total value of the mixed supply x} \frac{\text{Cost of standard - rated goods}}{\text{Total cost of the mixed supply}}$$

$$= £600 \text{ x} \frac{£200}{£250}$$

$$= £480$$

The supplier needs to charge VAT on this value. The VAT amount is £96 (£480 x20%). The other goods are exempt from VAT. Therefore, VAT on the total mixed supply is £96.

Therefore total price charged should be £696 (£600 + £96).

Test Yourself 6

A price of £490 is charged for a mixed supply of goods, this price being exclusive of VAT. The goods consist of zero-rated goods of which the market value is £300 and standard-rated goods of which the market value is £400 (excluding VAT). Calculate the VAT due on the mixed supply.

---

e) Composite supplies

Composite supply takes place when goods and/or services are supplied together in such a way that the value of the mixture cannot be segregated into different elements.

Composite supplies are held to be a single supply with ancillary elements being taxed at the same rate as the main supply. In such situations, one VAT rate is applied.

Example

Consider a contract for constructing a warehouse where there is a supply of construction material and labour as well as the production of an architectural plan for construction. If the contractor charges £100,000 for constructing the warehouse (with material), we cannot segregate the value of the construction material used, the value of the labour supply and the professional fees of the architect.

In this situation, VAT is charged at one single rate on all the supplies made.

---

f) Zero-rating: splitting of supplies

Where the supply of printed matter is connected with a supply of services and those connected supplies are made by a single supplier or different suppliers, they would be treated as a single supply of services and would be a taxable supply (other than a zero-rated supply) or exempt supply. This change has been introduced from this tax year from April 2011 with a objective to curb tax avoidance.

Example

Hansel Packaging Ltd supplies packaging services to Gratel Toys Ltd. Hansel packs the toys in boxes which displays the picture of the toy, directions to use, caution, address and other required information. The cost of each box is £2 and Hansel supplies 100 such boxes. To get the matter printed on 100 boxes costs £50, packing the toys cost £10,

	£	Item for VAT	VAT rating per item
Cost of 100 boxes	200	boxes	standard rated @ 20%
£2 x 100			
Cost of Printing	50	Printing	zero rated @ 0%
Cost of Packing	10	Packing	exempt rated
Total	260	Total	standard rated @ 20%
VAT @ 20%	52		
	312		

Note: the total always would be charged at standard rated, reduced rated or exempt rated but not at zero rated.

---

g) Business Samples

Identitical goods given or distributed as free samples to promote business are "VAT -free" i.e. such goods are called business samples and they are not chargeable for VAT from April 2012 onwards. Previously they were included in gifts and only one sample given to a particular supplier in 12 months period was VAT free and all the subsequent samples were chargeable for VAT. Now gifts do not include business samples and all the business samples distributed are VAT free.

Example

Pix Ltd manufacturers shampoo and for its business promotion distributes 100 sachets of the shampoo to each of its suppliers. The market value of the whole pack of 100 sachet is £25 and if sold Pix Ltd will charge 20% VAT on £25. However since it has been distributed as business samples free of cost, no VAT is payable to HMRC.

4.4 Some important points in relation to the valuation of supply

a) When goods are permanently taken out of business for private use, **output VAT** must be paid **on their market value.**

b) When a supplier charges different prices to different customers, depending upon their mode of payment, (e.g. by credit card, cash payment, direct debit to bank account etc.) VAT is calculated on the **full value paid** by the customer.

A trading company is in the business of selling computer spare parts. The charges for a printer are as follows:

1. £45 if a customer pays in cash.
2. £5 extra if customer pays by credit card (the trader needs to pay bank charges)

Hence, calculations of VAT in both cases will be as follows:

a) For cash payment: £45 x 20% **= £9**
b) For card payment: (£45 + £5) x 20% **= £10**

---

c) **Self supply (deemed taxable supply)**

If any trading company uses its own services or goods produced or supplied by it which are otherwise liable for VAT, then output tax on these supplies is due.

However, if this final output is not liable to VAT, (i.e. it is exempt from VAT), a trading company cannot reclaim input tax.

Suppose a company manufactures overalls which it then sells. However, the business also uses some of the overalls for its own staff to wear.

In this situation, output tax on the overalls used by the staff even though these are not sold on the open market.

---

5. Recognise the circumstances in which input VAT is non-deductible.[2]

[Learning Outcome e]

5.1 The following are the circumstances in which input VAT is non-deductible:

1. **Business entertainment**

If VAT is paid on the cost of entertainment, then the entity can recover the input VAT only on those expenses that are allowable for tax purposes. Therefore input VAT cannot be recovered in respect of entertainment expenses, such as client entertainment, that are not allowable for tax purposes. However from Finance Act 2012, input VAT relating to the cost of entertaining overseas customers is now recoverable.

On the other hand, entertainment expenses in respect of employee entertainment are allowable, therefore input VAT on such expenses is recoverable.

Fun Ltd decides to give mobile phones as Christmas gifts to all its major buyers in UK. These gifts to customers are not deductible business expenditure while calculating the company's trading profits. Therefore, VAT paid on the purchase of mobile phones cannot be reclaimed.

---

2. **Purchase of motor car**: input VAT cannot be recovered, unless it is used 100% for business purposes.

A car is not purchased for business purposes if it is purchased for purposes **other than the following:**
a) A car purchased by a car dealer, as **stock in trade**
b) A car purchased for a **driving school**
c) A car acquired totally for business purposes (such as a **leasing** business)

If, after the purchase of a car, accessories (such as a car radio or satellite navigation system for example) are purchased & invoiced separately, then **VAT on such accessories is not reclaimable unless the accessories are themselves used for business purposes.**

Example

Allan is a car dealer. He buys cars and then modifies them according to the customers' choice. He bought five cars of which four were bought for business purposes and one for himself. He then modified all five cars. In this case Allan can reclaim input VAT paid on the purchase of accessories for four cars which were bought for business. But he cannot reclaim input VAT on the purchase of accessories for the car which he bought for himself.

3. VAT paid / payable on **second-hand goods** purchased from a dealer operating the **margin scheme**.

Example

Ram Ltd deals in second-hand cars. The company buys used cars from the public, restores them (if required) and then sells them at some margin. Ram is a dealer operating the margin scheme. He has to account for VAT on the difference between the price paid by him for the purchase of the car and the price at which he sells the car i.e. the margin. However, Ram can reclaim input VAT on business expenses such as overheads.

4. **Domestic accommodation for a director:** VAT paid / payable while making provision for **domestic accommodation for a director** of a company cannot be recovered.
5. **Goods or services not used for business purposes:** input VAT cannot be recovered.
6. **Goods and services used partly for business purposes and partly for private purposes:** only input VAT relating to business use can be recovered. There are two ways of treating input tax for private purposes:

a) the entity may deduct the business proportion of the input tax; or

Example

Shiny is a registered dealer of leather products. During the year 2012-13, her total expenditure on telephone was £4,000 (exclusive of VAT). Out of the total usage, 40% was for private purposes and 60% was for business purposes.

Here, Shiny can claim input VAT on £2,400 (£4,000 x 60%). She **cannot claim input VAT** paid on telephone expenses incurred for **private purposes.**

b) the entity may account for the output tax in relation to the element of private use and deduct all input tax.

Output tax in relation to element of private use is accounted for.

Example

Continuing the above example of Shiny,
Shiny may choose to reclaim input VAT on the total telephone expenditure (i.e. £4,000) and pay output VAT on the telephone expenditure incurred for private purposes (i.e. £1,600 {£4,000 x 40%}).

Tip

Input VAT, which is non-deductible, is included in the cost of purchases as expenditure; whereas deductible input VAT is omitted from the costs. The taxable person may adjust it against output tax payable.

Test Yourself 7

State whether input VAT can be recovered in the following conditions.

(a) Bony has taken domestic accommodation on a rental basis. During the year she paid a total of £2,000 as rent (exclusive of VAT).

Bony sells goods which are liable to VAT at the standard rate. Can she reclaim the VAT paid on domestic accommodation?

(b) Comfort Driving is a dealer of 'Sonata cars'. In December 2012, the entity purchased a total of fifty one cars out of which three cars were for office use and forty eight cars were for sale. Can Comfort Driving claim VAT on all the cars purchased?

7. **Academies:** Where goods or services supplied for non business activity of the academy for e.g. free education, then the input tax borne by the academy to be able to provide such goods or services can be reclaimed from HMRC. The claim must be made before the end of the period of 4 years beginning with the day on which the supply is made. Any academies not VAT registered will make a separate claim along the lines of the procedure currently used by non-VAT registered parish councils.

6. Compute the relief that is available for impairment losses on trade debts. [2]
[Learning Outcome f]

Output VAT is accounted for according **to the tax point.**

Output VAT may have been paid to HMRC before the customer has paid his invoice.

Example

Suppose Cool Ltd wants to make a claim for VAT bad debt relief. It can do so after fulfilling certain conditions. The conditions are as follows:

a) In respect of the debt, output VAT must have been accounted for and paid.
b) In the trader's book, the debt must have been written off as a bad debt.
c) At least six months must have been completed since the time the debt was due for payment.

6.1 Treatment of bad debts

Tip

A bad debt is money owed to you that you can't collect.

1. In the case of a cash accounting system

When a taxable person uses the cash accounting system, output tax on supplies made by him during the tax period is accounted for only when payment is received from a debtor. Therefore, a taxable person following the cash accounting system gets automatic bad debt relief.

Example

Sharon is a wholesaler of toys. Last year, she voluntarily registered for VAT. She follows the cash accounting system for accounting for VAT. Last year (i.e. 2011/12) she sold toys worth £8,000 to Kids Gallery Ltd. However, Kids Gallery Ltd became insolvent. In the current year (2012/13), Sharon wrote off the amount receivable from Kids Gallery Ltd as bad debt.

In this situation, as Sharon follows a cash accounting system, the supply is not recorded as consideration as it is not actually received from Kids Gallery Ltd and hence she has not accounted for the output tax. In effect, she received automatic bad debt relief.

2. In the case of accrual system of accounting

Unlike the cash accounting system, in the accrual system of accounting, it is likely that a taxable person may account for output tax relating to the supply before receiving the consideration for that supply.

In this situation, if any bad debt occurs, then a taxable person can **claim a refund** of VAT lost on the amount of bad debts, **only** on fulfilment of the following criteria:

a) Goods or services are supplied for a consideration of money.

b) The related **output tax** on those supplies has been **accounted for.**

c) The consideration receivable for the supply is **not more than the value of the product / service in the open market.**

d) A minimum of **six months** have passed from the **date of supply and** from the **due date of payment**.

Claims for bad debt relief can be made within **three years** after the expiry of six months from the date **later** of:

i. the date of the supply and
ii. the date on which payment was due

Passion Suppliers is a partnership using the accrual system of accounting for VAT purposes. On 1 December 2012 they made supplies to Fashion Plc. The credit period was ten days from the invoice date. The supply was of £1,150 (inclusive of tax at the rate of 20%).

Five months later, Fashion Plc became insolvent and the amount due from the company could not be recovered.

As Passion Suppliers follows the accrual accounting system, they had already accounted for and paid output tax on the supply made to Fashion Plc. However, the firm is unable to recover the amount of VAT from Fashion Plc.

In this situation, Passion Suppliers may reclaim VAT paid on bad debts (i.e. £958 (1,150 –1,150 x 1/6) after six months from the date when the amount became due (i.e. 10 December 2012).

Bad debt relief is available provided:

- debt is written off in financial accounts.
- Output VAT has been paid to HMRC.

SUMMARY

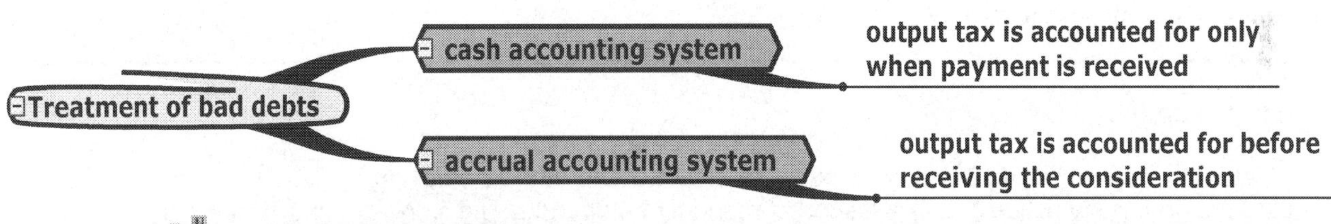

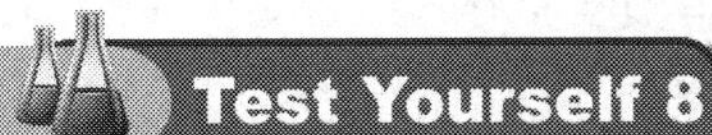

Casuals Ltd is a wholesaler of clothes. On 1 April 2011 the company supplied clothes to For Her Ltd for £20,000 (exclusive of VAT). The credit period was 3 months. However, in spite of reminders by the end of year 2012, For Her Ltd had not made the payment.

In the year 2012-13, Casuals Ltd decided to write off the amount receivable from For Her Ltd.

Required:

Advise Casuals Ltd whether it can claim a VAT refund in respect of this debt. You should assume that Casuals Ltd follows the cash accounting system.

7. Explain the circumstances in which the default surcharge, a serious misdeclaration penalty, and default interest will be applied.[1]

[Learning Outcome g]

7.1 VAT returns

A return is the summarised information of the transactions for each tax period. This return must be submitted to HMRC in **"Form 100"** for each tax period. A VAT return must show details of VAT payable or repayable and other statistical information.

A VAT return must be filed within **one month** of the end of the tax period. This period of one month automatically gets extended by 7 days.

The VAT returns contain the following information:

Box No	Information
1	VAT due on sales and other outputs
2	VAT due from you (but not paid) on acquisitions from other EU countries
3	Total VAT due (total of Box 1 and 2)
4	VAT reclaimable on purchases
5	VAT payable or reclaimable (box 3 less box 4)
6	Total sales excluding VAT
7	Total purchases excluding VAT
8	Total value of goods you supplied to other EU countries
9	The total value of goods you acquired from other EU countries

7.2 Online Filing

It is mandatory that all businesses must file their VAT online and pay their VAT due electronically from 1 April 2012. The VAT online filing and electronic payment must be done within one month and seven days after the end of the VAT quarter.

Example

For the quarter ended 30 June 2012 any business will have to file their VAT return online and also pay the VAT due electronically by 7 August 2012.

7.3 Default surcharge

1. A "default" occurs if the **VAT return is submitted late** or the **VAT is paid late**
2. A surcharge liability notice (SLN) is issued in respect of a default. The SLN remains in force for a period of 12 months from the end of the period in which the default occurred.

Example

Sun Shine Co has quarterly VAT periods to July, October, January and April. During the year 2012-13, Sun Shine Co failed to submit the VAT return on time for the quarter ended January 2013.

In this situation, HMRC will issue a Surcharge Liability Notice (SLN). The notice period will start from 31 January 2013 (i.e. quarter end for which the return was not filed) and will remain in force for one year (i.e. until 31 January 2014).

If, within this period, a further default occurs, the SLN period is extended to 12 months from the end of the period in respect of which the second default arose.

Example

Continuing the above example

Sun Shine Co failed to submit one more return for the quarter ended April 2013. Because of this failure to file a VAT return, the surcharge period will be extended. Now, the original surcharge period will be extended by **one year** from 30 April 2013.

This period will remain effective until 30 April 2014.

---

3. During the surcharge period, if a taxable person in addition to failing to file a return **fails to pay VAT or makes a late payment,** surcharge is levied on the amount of unpaid VAT. The rate of surcharge depends on the number of defaults made in payment of VAT during the surcharge period.

Late payment of VAT during surcharge period	Percentage of surcharge
1st default	0% (only SLN is issued)
2nd default	2%
3rd default	5%
4th default	10%
5th default	15%

The 2% or 5% surcharge will not be collected if the surcharge is less than £400.

Diagram 4: Summary diagram for surcharge

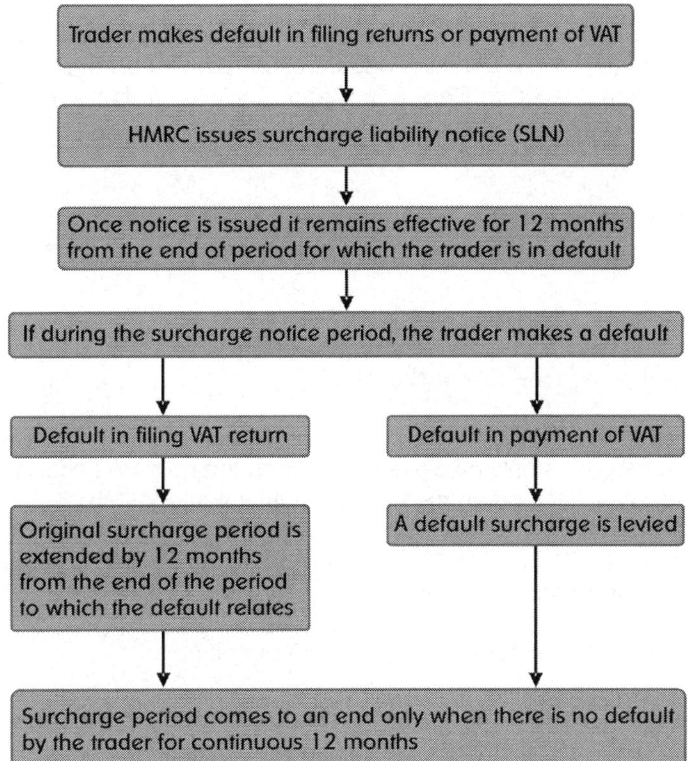

Small Ltd has submitted its VAT returns.
The details of its VAT returns are as follows:

Quarter ended	VAT paid £	Date of submission
30 Jun 2011	3,500	2 Sep 2011
30 Sep 2011	12,000	5 Dec 2011
31 Dec 2011	15,000	24 Feb 2012
31 Mar 2012	8,500	25 Apr 2012
30 Jun 2012	2,000	26 Jul 2012
30 Sep 2012	4,000	26 Oct 2012
31 Dec 2012	7,500	15 Jan 2013
31 Mar 2013	10,000	28 Apr 2013

VAT is paid on the date it is due. The VAT returns were duly submitted by Small Ltd.

The implications of the late submission are as follows:

Continued on the next page

1. For the quarter ended 30 June 2011, the late submission of the VAT return will result in issuance of surcharge liability notice by HMRC mentioning a surcharge period to 30 June 2012.

2. For the quarter ended 30 September 2011, the late payment of VAT will result in a surcharge of £240 (12,000 x 2%). However as the surcharge is less than £400 it will not be levied. Period of surcharge will have been extended to 30 September 2012.

3. For the quarter ended 31 December 2011, the late payment of return and VAT will result in a surcharge of £750 (15,000 x 5%). This will be liable for surcharge as it is more than £400. Period of surcharge will have been extended to 31 Dec 2012.

4. The company has submitted another four returns on time. These are the returns for the quarters ended 31 March 2011 to 31 Dec 2012.

5. For the quarter ended 31 March 2013, the late submission of the VAT return will result in issuance of a surcharge liability notice by HMRC applying a surcharge period to 31 March 2014.

Test Yourself 9

Music Ltd fails to submit a VAT return for the first time, for the quarter ended 31 March 2012. Due to financial crisis, during the second quarter ended 30 June 2012, the company was unable to pay VAT of £2,000.

In the third quarter (i.e. the quarter ended 30 September 2012), Music Ltd paid VAT and filed a return two months late. During the third quarter the VAT liability was £7,000. In the fourth quarter (i.e. the quarter ended 31 December 2012) the company again failed to file a return and pay VAT in time. This time the VAT liability was £5,000.

Required:

Show the calculation of the surcharge liability.

7.4 Errors in a VAT return

When an error is made in a VAT return, the consequences are in the form of either misdeclaration penalty or default interest or both depending upon the circumstances.

1. Where the net error is less than £10,000 or 1% of turnover for the period (whichever is higher) subject to a maximum of £50,000, one can voluntarily disclose the error on the next VAT return.
   There will not be any serious misdeclaration penalty or default interest.

2. Where the net error is more than £10,000 or 1% of turnover for the VAT period (whichever is higher) subject to a maximum of £50,000, one can voluntarily disclose, but the disclosure must be separately made to HMRC.
   There will be default interest, but no serious misdeclaration penalty.

3. Where errors are discovered as a result of a control visit, there can be both serious misdeclaration penalty and default interest.

7.5 A penalty for an incorrect VAT return

The amount of penalty is determined according to the common penalty regime introduced for incorrect returns. This applies to incorrect self assessment tax returns, self assessment corporation tax returns and where a misdeclaration has been made on a VAT return (although the new penalty regime is not yet in force for all taxes).

The amount of penalty is based on the amount of tax understated, but the actual penalty payable is linked to the taxpayer's behaviour, as follows:

- There will be no penalty where a taxpayer simply makes a mistake
- There will be a moderate penalty (up to **30%** of the understated tax) where a taxpayer **fails to take reasonable care.**
- There will be a higher penalty (up to **70%** of the understated tax) if the error is **deliberate but not concealed**,
- and an even higher penalty (up to **100%** of the understated tax) where there is a **deliberate and concealed** error.

However, the penalty will be substantially reduced where a taxpayer makes disclosure, especially when this is unprompted disclosure of an incorrect return following a failure to take reasonable care, the penalty could be reduced to nil.

Example

Venus Ltd has submitted the VAT return for the quarter ended 31 December 2012.

Mac, the tax consultant of Venus Ltd, was appointed by the company after the submission of the December quarter return. While going through the past records, he found some errors in the VAT return already submitted by the company. In such a situation, Venus Ltd can voluntarily disclose the error in the next quarter ended VAT return i.e. 31 March 2013, if the net error total is less than £10,000 or 1% of the turnover for the period (whichever is higher) subject to a maximum of £50,000.

If the total net error is more than £10,000 or 1% of turnover (whichever is higher) subject to a maximum of £50,000, then the company can voluntarily disclose the error, but the disclosure must be made separately to HMRC. Moreover, the default interest will be charged only if the net errors total more than the higher of £10,000 or 1% of the turnover for the VAT period, and not if they are less than the higher of £10,000 or 1% of turnover for the VAT period.

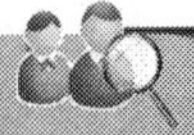

Example

HMRC makes a control visit to the premises of Mars Ltd.

The **purpose** of such a visit is to give HMRC an opportunity to check the accuracy of the VAT returns of Mars Ltd.

The **circumstances** in which the discovery of the understatement of output VAT results in a serious misdeclaration penalty are as follows:

1. If Mars Ltd's VAT return includes a large misdeclaration
   A misdeclaration is said to be large when it is 30% or more of the total output VAT and input VAT for the relevant VAT return.

2. If Mars Ltd cannot convince HMRC that there was a reasonable excuse for the misdeclaration.

7.6 Penalty for late registration

Where a taxable person makes late notification of his liability to register, he is liable for a penalty. The penalty is calculated on the amount of **tax due between the date** on which a person **becomes liable to get registered under VAT** and the **actual date of VAT registration.** The percentage of penalty is as follows: For businesses that fail to register for VAT on time, and should have been VAT registered on 1 April 2011 or later, the fine for late registration is now **up to 100%** of the tax due. The table below sets out the penalty tariff, and this compares very unfavourably with the old regime where the maximum penalty, except in cases of fraud, was 15% of the tax due.

Failure to notify	Disclosure	Min penalty	Max penalty
Reasonable excuse		No penalty	No penalty
Not deliberate	Unprompted	0% within 12 months of tax being due, otherwise 10%	30%
	Prompted	10% within 12 months of tax being due, otherwise 20%	30%
Deliberate	Unprompted	20%	70%
	Prompted	35%	70%
Deliberate and concealed	Unprompted	30%	100%
	Prompted	50%	100%

In June 2011, Miranda started her own business manufacturing soft drinks. In a few months time, she captured a market. By the end of December 2011, her total turnover was £60,000 and by the year end i.e. March 2012, her turnover was £90,000. She had paid input tax of £6,850 on purchases.

However, due to lack of knowledge she did not register for VAT. If Miranda had registered for VAT, her output liability would have come to £18,000. (i.e. £90,000@20%) In the month of March, Miranda registered herself for VAT.

In this situation, the penalty for late registration for VAT is calculated as follows:

Miranda registered for VAT 3 months late. As this was within 12 months, the applicable penalty rate is 0% - 30%.

Penalty = Total tax due until the actual date of VAT registration x say, 5%
= (£18,000 - £6,850) x 5%
= £558.

The actual level of the penalty is at the discretion of HMRC and will take into account all relevant circumstances.

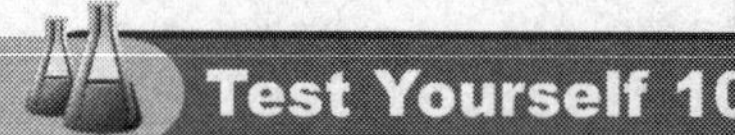

In January 2011, Arnold started a beauty hair salon. As he was very good at his job, his turnover within twelve months exceeded £70,000. He was aware of VAT registration provisions but did not register for VAT as he felt that after VAT registration he may be forced to increase the prices.

During these three months, he paid VAT on purchases. The amount of input VAT was £2,000. Arnold wanted to recover VAT paid on purchases so eventually, on 10 May 2013, he registered for VAT. On the day of registration total turnover was £80,000. The VAT rate applicable to him is 20%.

Can HMRC charge him a penalty? What is the amount of the penalty?

Mango Ltd is a manufacturer of fruit jams. Mango Ltd has submitted a VAT return for the quarter ended 30 June 2012. The turnover in the VAT period is £256,000. The figures disclosed in the return were as follows:

	£
Output tax	100,000
Input tax	(10,000)
Net VAT payable	**90,000**

After the VAT assessment was over, the output VAT liability arose to £150,000. Do you think a misdeclaration penalty will apply? State the amount of penalty if HMRC has discovered that Mango Ltd is liable for the maximum moderate penalty.

7.7 Repayment Supplements

Repayment supplement is paid in the case of tax overpaid by the taxpayer. It is paid subject to certain conditions. If these conditions are fulfilled a taxable person will get a supplement of the higher of:

1. £50
2. 5% of the amount due

The conditions to satisfy for repayment supplement are:

a) Taxpayer must have submitted the VAT return within the due date.
b) The return should not show the amount repayable by more than the greater of:
   - £250 and
   - 5% of the amount due
c) HMRC has unnecessarily delayed the repayment.

The repayment supplement is in addition to interest paid on overpaid VAT.

Example

Butterfly Ltd filed its VAT return for the quarter ended on 30 June 2012 The Company had claimed a VAT refund of £730. However, HMRC wrongly issued a refund of £370.

Here, Butterfly Ltd has filed its quarter end return in time. The amount shown on the return is also correct. However, HMRC wrongly issued a refund cheque for the wrong amount.

As HMRC failed to repay the correct amount of VAT return within 30 days from the receipt of the return, it will pay the repayment supplement. The taxable person is entitled to get a supplement of the higher of the following:

1. £50
2. 5% (£730 - £370) = £18

Butterfly Ltd will get a supplement of £50 (greater of £50 and £18).

Example

Raddle filed his tax return for the quarter ended 31 March 2012, in time. He had claimed a refund of £1,000. HMRC completed the assessment and issued a written instruction for the repayment of a VAT amount of £440. HMRC's instruction was issued 50 days after receipt of the return.

In this situation, Raddle can get repayment supplement if the difference between the refund according to the return and the correct amount according to HMRC's assessment (i.e. £1,000 – £440 = £560) is not more than the higher of the following:

1. £250
2. 5% of (correct refund) (i.e. 5% x £560= £28)

Greater of the above is £250

As the difference is greater than £250, Raddle is not entitled for a supplement refund.

Test Yourself 12

Cluppins filed his VAT return for the quarter ended 30 June 2012 on time. He had made a claim for a refund of £2,450. Within 10 days, HMRC sent him a written instruction for the repayment of £1,200.

He did not get any supplement repayment with this amount.

Required:

Advise Cluppins as to whether he is entitled for supplement repayment.

---

8. Explain the treatment of imports, exports and trade within the European Union.

[Learning Outcome h]

8.1 Transactions within EU

1. Acquisitions

a) Meaning

Goods acquired in the UK by a VAT registered person from another EU state are known as acquisitions.

b) VAT rates

The VAT rates discussed in Study Guide G1(i.e. either standard rated, zero rated or exempt) are applicable to acquisitions also.

c) Value of supplies

The value of supplies is similar to the value of VAT for the goods had they been supplied by a UK supplier.

d) Tax point

VAT is due at the tax point date, which could be earlier of the following:

- the date of issue of invoice; and
- the fifteenth day of the month following the acquisition.

e) Input VAT

The entity making acquisitions can claim input VAT, just like procurement of goods from a UK supplier. The VAT charge is also disclosed on the VAT return as output VAT. This in turn implies that there is no VAT cost. However, entities which make exempt supplies cannot reclaim input VAT, therefore the VAT cost is a cost to the company.

2. Sales (dispatches)

a) Meaning

Goods sold to another EU member state are known as dispatches.

b) VAT rates

The supplies are treated as zero- rated provided:

- the seller is VAT registered;
- the invoice contains the VAT registration number of the customer; and
- the seller retains evidence of sale made to another member state.

In the absence of the above conditions, the VAT rules relating to such transactions would be treated as a sale within the UK.

3. Distance selling

a) Meaning

When a registered entity from the EU (countries outside the UK) supplies and delivers services to a customer (who is not registered for VAT) in the UK, the transaction is referred to as distance selling. The most common example of distance sales is mail order sales. Distance selling only involves goods, not service.

b) Registration

Entities involved in distance selling may be required to register themselves under the provisions of VAT. Registration is dependent upon the total value of distance sales made in the UK.

c) VAT registration threshold

The threshold limit for registration is £77,000. The following table summarises the registration requirements:

Threshold	Implication
If the annual value of distance sales to the UK is less than £77,000	➢ VAT is charged on taxable supplies at the rates which apply in the country of the supplier of goods. ➢ VAT is accounted for in the country of the supplier of goods.
If the annual value of distance sales to the UK is more than £77,000	➢ The supplier of goods would have to register under the UK VAT; and ➢ VAT will be charged on taxable supplies at the rates which apply in the UK.

SUMMARY

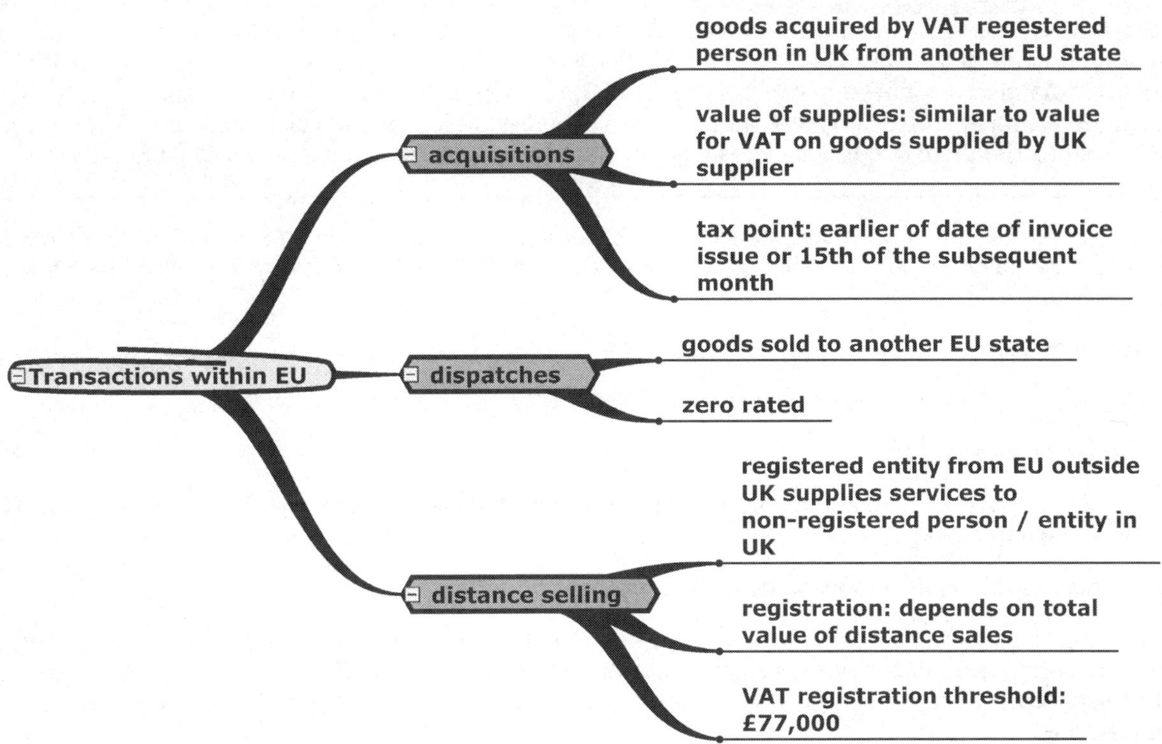

8.2 Transactions with non-EU persons

1. Imports

a) **Purchase of goods from non- EU persons (**i.e. persons from countries outside the European Union) are **called imports.**

The conditions relating to the applicability of VAT and the rates which apply for VAT on the purchase of goods in the home market (discussed in Study Guide G1), are applicable to imports. However, certain works of art and antiques which are imported are subject to an effective VAT rate of 5% on the full value.

b) Value of supplies

VAT is charged on the value of supply, which is usually the **price charged or the invoice value**.

It includes:

- all shipping costs, customs duty and excise duty on imports into the UK;
- incidental costs such as packing, transport, insurance etc. incurred up to the place of the goods' first destination in the UK;
- transportation costs, if incurred to transport the goods to a further destination in the UK (provided this destination is known when the goods are imported).

c) Tax point

VAT is due at the tax point date i.e. the date of entry into the UK.

d) Input VAT

The importer can account for imports at the tax point date and recover the VAT paid on imports in the next VAT return. However, the importer can recover input tax only if it is supported by the certificate in form C79 (issued by HMRC) for the VAT paid. Therefore the evidence of imports needs to be retained.

Xeta Plc is a UK based company. It purchased goods costing £2,000 from Beta Plc, another UK based company. Therefore Xeta paid £2,400 to Beta (£2,000+VAT at 20%) and recovered £400 as input VAT in its VAT return. Xeta also purchased goods costing £2,000 from Gama Plc, a Japanese company. Here Xeta will pay £2,000 to Gama and £400 to HMRC as output VAT. Furthermore, Xeta will also recover £400 as input VAT in its VAT return. Therefore under both the situations, Xeta has paid £2,400 and recovered £400.

Instead of paying VAT on each import transaction, regular importers can set up an account with the HMRC and thereby defer the payment on a monthly basis. However, it would then be necessary to provide the HMRC with a bank guarantee.

e) Supply of services

VAT is charged on standard rated services received in the UK from an overseas supplier.

f) Reverse charge system

The buyer of the services would need to account for the services (instead of the supplier of the services). This is referred to as 'reverse charge'.

Following services are treated as made by the UK recipient:

- certain banking, advertising, professional and freight transport services used for business purposes. This category of recipients may have to register themselves if the deemed services increase the turnover limit.
- other services used by VAT registered recipients for business purposes, provided they are already VAT registered.

Under the reverse charge system, the buyer of the VAT taxable services:

- bears the VAT charge (in the form of output tax); and
- claims it as an input tax.

Thus, the buyer bears no net cost.

2. Exports

a) Sale of goods to non- EU persons, i.e. to countries outside the EU, are called exports. Therefore supplies of services outside the EU are outside the scope of VAT.

b) VAT rates

Exports can be treated as zero rated. For this, it is necessary to retain appropriate evidence that the goods have left the country, as the HMRC officials normally check export evidence by cross checking the VAT records with the invoices. Furthermore, the evidence of export must be obtained within three months from the date of supply.

SUMMARY

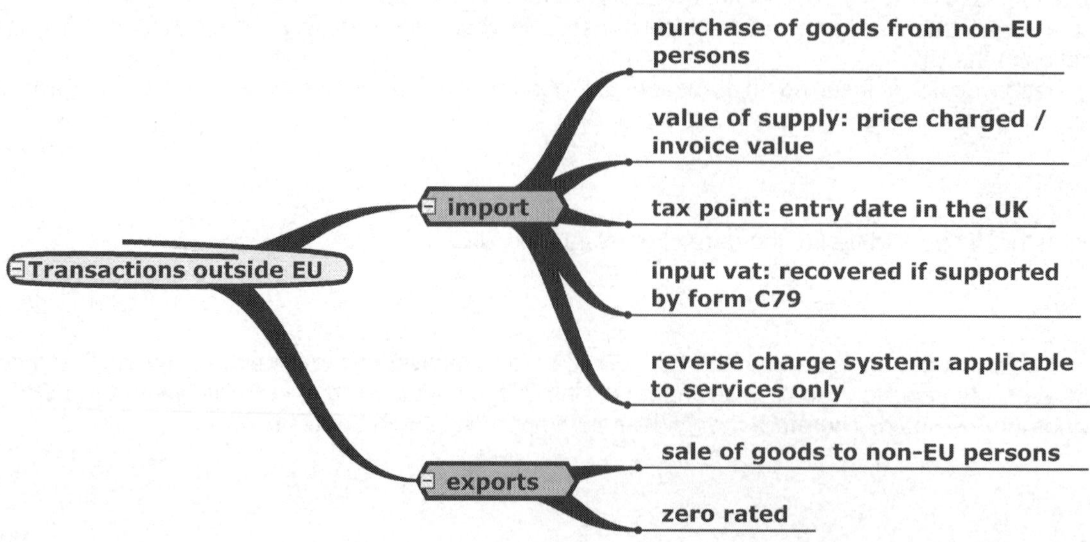

Answers to Test Yourself

Answer to TY 1

1.

28/2/2013	payment of	£325,000
31/3/2013	payment of	£325,000
30/4/2013	payment of	£50,000 to be made with submission of VAT return for quarter

2.

28/2/2013	payment of	£325,000
31/3/2013	payment of	£325,000
30/4/2013		£150,000 to be repaid by customs on submission of return for quarter

Answer to TY 2

1. There are two tax points in respect of this transaction:

(a) The first payment of £1,000 is received before the basic tax point, i.e. before the delivery of the machine. Therefore, the first tax point is the date when the advance of £1,000 is received, i.e. 10 June 2012.

(b) The invoice was raised within 14 days of the basic tax point, i.e. from the date of delivery of the machine until the balance payment of £9,000 is received. Therefore, the second tax point is 2 July 2012, when the invoice was raised.

2. The company should account for VAT as follows:

(a) Advance received on 10 June 2012: the company should account for VAT of **£200 (**£1,000 x 20%) in the June 2012 return.

(b) Delivery was made on 20 June 2012 but invoice was raised within 14 days i.e. on 2 July 2012. The payment of £9,000 was received on 4 July 2012 after invoice was raised on 2 July 2012. Although the delivery date is earlier, it will be replaced by the invoice date as the invoice was raised within 14 days. The company should account for VAT of **£1,800** (£9,000 x 20%) in the quarter ended September 2012 (July – September) return.

Answer to TY 3

The information already given on the invoice is as follows:

1. Name and address of the supplier and the purchaser.
2. Invoice date and tax point
3. Description and the price of the goods
4. Final amount of the invoice

Tara-rum-Pam Ltd is planning to give a discount to its customers. Along with the amount of discount, the company must give following information on the invoice:

1. Invoice number.
2. Tara-rum-Pam Ltd's VAT registration number
3. The rate of VAT for each supply.
4. The VAT-exclusive amount for each supply.
5. The total VAT-exclusive amount.
6. The amount of VAT payable.

Answer to TY 4

1. VAT charge is £220 x 20 % = £44.

Total consideration = Value of supplies + VAT
= £220 + £44
= **£264**

2. Total consideration = £17,390

$$VAT = \frac{\text{Rate of tax}}{100 + \text{Rate of tax}} \text{ x Total consideration}$$

$$= \frac{£20}{£100 + £20} \text{ x } £17,390$$

$$= \frac{£1}{£6} \text{ x } £17,390$$

$$= £2,898$$

Answer to TY 5

Once the supplier **offers** a discount to its customers, VAT is calculated on the net value irrespective of whether the customer takes advantage of the discount or not.

Net value = Sales – Discount
= £40,000 - £800 (i.e. £40,000 x 2%)
= £39,200

In both situations (i.e. whether customer pays within the credit terms or not) for the purpose of calculating VAT, value of the supply will be £39,200.

The VAT amount is **£7,840** (£39,200 x 20%)

Answer to TY 6

The apportionment of the price of mixed supply across the standard-rated and zero-rated goods is made on the basis of the market value of the product. The value of the standard-rated supply is calculated as follows:

$$\text{Total value of the mixed supply x } \frac{\text{Market value of standard - rated goods}}{\text{Total market value of the mixed supply}}$$

$$= £490 \text{ x } \frac{400}{700}$$

= £280

VAT charged on these standard-rated goods is £56 (£280 x 20%). The other product in the mixed supply is charged to VAT at zero rates. Therefore the total VAT due on the mixed supply is £56.
The total price charged should be £546 (£490 +£56).

Answer to TY 7

1. An individual cannot reclaim VAT on costs incurred in relation to the provision of domestic accommodation.

   Bony, therefore, cannot recover VAT paid on costs incurred for the domestic accommodation.

2. Input VAT can be reclaimed on the purchase of the cars if the following conditions are met.

i. Cars are used exclusively for business purposes e.g. a pool car
ii. Cars will be used as taxis
iii. Cars are stock in trade and will be sold by the dealer / manufacturer within twelve months (except second hand cars).

Comfort driving has bought fifty one cars and out of them, three cars are bought for office use. Therefore input VAT can be reclaimed on them. Any subsequent private use of any those cars will attract a liability i.e. the output tax on the current market value of those cars or similar cars.

The input VAT paid on 48 cars can also be reclaimed as they are held as stock in trade provided they are sold within twelve months from the of purchase and those cars are not second hand cars.

Answer to TY 8

A taxpayer can claim a refund of the VAT lost on the amount of bad debts if the following conditions are fulfilled:

1. Goods or services are supplied for a consideration of money.
2. The related **output tax** on those supplies has been **accounted for.**
3. The consideration receivable for the supply is **not more than the value of the product / service on the open market.**

4. A minimum of **six months** have passed since the **date of supply and** since the **due date for payment**.

Claims for bad debt relief can be made within **three years** after the expiry of six months from the **later** of the following dates:

(a) The date of the supply and
(b) The date on which payment was due.

Here, Casuals Ltd supplied garments to For Her Ltd for the consideration of £20,000. A six months period has passed since the date of supply and the due date of payment (due date was 30 June 2011). The company is applying for bad debt relief within three years of the date of supply.

However, Casuals Ltd had not accounted for VAT on this bill (as the company follows the cash accounting system i.e. records bills on the receipt of the bill amount). Therefore, Casuals Ltd cannot reclaim VAT on the bill raised on For Her Ltd.

Answer to TY 9

1. Music Ltd, for the first time, fails to submit a VAT return for the quarter ended 31 March 2012. This being a default, HMRC will issue a SLN. This notice will be effective from the end of the period to which the default relates i.e. 31 March 2012. This notice will remain effective for 12 months i.e. until 31 March 2013.
2. During the surcharge notice period, Music Ltd failed to pay VAT. This being the second default on 30 June 2012 for payment of VAT during the SLN period, surcharge is due at 2% on £2,000, i.e. £40. However as the surcharge is less than £400 it will not be levied. The original surcharge period will be extended to 30 June 2013.
3. By the end of the third quarter, Music Ltd failed to submit a return and to pay VAT in time. Due to this, the original surcharge period is extended by 12 months from the end of the period to 30 September 2013.
4. Therefore the VAT surcharge period is extended to 30 September 2012. As there is second default in payment of VAT, surcharge is calculated at the rate of 5%. Total surcharge liability is £350 (£7,000 x 5%).
5. Again HMRC will not charge surcharge as the applicable surcharge rate was 5% and the surcharge liability was less than £400.
6. By the end of the fourth quarter, Music Ltd again failed to submit a return and to pay VAT in time. This will extend the surcharge period until 31 December 2013. The surcharge is due at 10% and the surcharge liability is £500 (£5,000 x 10%).

Answer to TY 10

When a taxable person makes late notification of his liability to register for VAT, he is liable for a penalty. The amount of the penalty is calculated as penalty rate multiplied by total tax liability.

Arnold registered for VAT **5 months late** and he had **deliberately** delayed registration. However, the registration was not prompted by HMRC. Therefore the applicable penalty rate is 20% - 70%. His total output tax if he had registered for VAT would be £16,000. He had already paid input tax of £2,000. Therefore the total tax liability will be £14,000 (£16,000 – £2,000).

The penalty would be £2,800 - £9,800.

Answer to TY 11

There is an underassessment of £60,000 (£90,000 – £150,000). This underassessment of VAT will attract a penalty if it exceeds the higher of the following:

1. £10,000
2. 1% of turnover for the VAT period (1% x £256,000 = £2,560) subject to a maximum of £50,000.

Higher of the above is £10,000.

The tax lost (£150,000 – £90,000 = £60,000) is more than £10,000.

The amount of penalty is based on the amount of tax understated, but the actual penalty payable depends on the taxpayer's behaviour, as follows

i. If the tax payer has made a simple mistake no penalty will be charged
ii. If the taxpayer fails to take reasonable care there will be a moderate penalty up to 30% of the understated tax
iii. If the error is deliberate a higher penalty up to 70% of the understated tax will be charged, if the taxpayer tries to conceal the error a penalty of up to 100% of the understated tax may be charged.

If the taxpayer makes an unprompted disclosure of an incorrect return the penalty may be reduced to zero even though the taxpayer has failed to take reasonable care.

Mango Ltd is liable to a moderate penalty of 30% of the understated tax.

= 30% of £60,000
= £18,000.

Answer to TY 12

Cluppins was entitled for a VAT refund but there was a difference between the amount of VAT claimed in the return and the correct amount according to the VAT assessment.

HMRC had issued a written instruction for the repayment of VAT amount within 30 days from the receipt of the return.

As a result, Cluppins is not entitled to any repayment supplement.

Quick Quiz

1. Moon Ltd manufactures pens. The company decides on a wholesale price for fountain pens of £5 per pen. The company also decides to give a 2% discount to those who pay within 15 days.

   Advise Moon Ltd on the amount it should charge for VAT and the steps the company should take if a customer does not pay the bill within 15 days.

2. Beauty Ltd sells cosmetics to various retail outlets; its turnover is £28,793,000 for the VAT period. The company declares its output tax liability as £120,000. It claims input tax of £97,000. The company submitted its VAT return for the June 2010 quarter in time. Later it was discovered that input tax was overstated by £50,000.

   Can HMRC apply a penalty order for misdeclaration?

3. Cow Plc supplies milk to retailers in bottles. A VAT-exclusive price of £10 is charged for a bottle of milk. Each milk bottle consists of standard-rated bottles, which cost the company £2 (inclusive of VAT) per bottle and zero-rated bottles which cost the company £5 per bottle. Show the calculation of the output tax due.

4. Décor Ltd makes wooden furniture. Interior Plc owns a furniture shop. Both companies signed an agreement for supply of furniture for the next two years. Being its first dispatch, Interior Plc gave an advance of £20,000 on 10 May 2012, against which an invoice was raised for £30,000 on 10 July 2012.

   The balance amount of £10,000 was paid on 1 August 2012. State Décor Ltd's tax point.

5. Camel Plc, a newly-incorporated company, has entered into a contract with the government to provide car parking on Dessert Street. The company's rates for parking are as follows:

   For 3 hours - £2
   For 5 hours - £3
   For 10 hours - £5
   For 24 hours - £8

   Camel Plc decides that the contents of the invoice to be issued to its customers will be as follows:

   (a) Date and number of invoice.
   (b) Car no.
   (c) Car park fees and VAT on the same.

   The company also decides not to preserve the invoices for more than two years. Can the company do so?

Answers to Quick Quiz

1. Moon Ltd has offered a cash discount for prompt payment. In this situation, the company should charge VAT on the net amount of sales (i.e. sales price less discount offered). The company has to charge VAT on the net sales price only, irrespective of whether or not the customer actually takes advantage of the discount.

   In effect, the company has to charge VAT on £4.90 (£5 – £5 x 2%).

2. Beauty Ltd has overstated the VAT repayable. The company is liable for a misdeclaration penalty if the VAT which would have been lost equals or exceeds the higher of the following:

   (a) £10,000

   (b) 1% of turnover for the VAT period subject to a maximum of £50,000
   = 1% (£28,793,000)
   = £287,930.

   The error of £50,000 is less than £287,930. As this is not large; the company is not liable for a misdeclaration penalty.

3. Cow Plc supplies a mixture of two goods invoiced together under a single inclusive price. Both the items in the mixture are chargeable to VAT at different rates. Hence, to calculate output tax, it becomes necessary for Cow Plc to apportion the price charged between the various ingredients of the mixture.
   As the cost of each item in the mixture is known, this apportionment needs to be done on the basis of the cost of each item to the supplier. However, these costs are inclusive of VAT.

   The value of the supply represented by the standard-rated goods is £10 x 2/7 = £2.86. (Out of total cost of £7, the cost of bottles is £2)

   VAT at standard rate on these bottles is £2.86 x 20% =£0.572

   Therefore, the output tax due per bottle is £0.572.

4. There are two tax points in respect of these transactions between Décor Ltd and Interior Plc.

   (a) In the case of the advance of £20,000, the tax point is the date of advance payment i.e. 10 May 2012. (Being the date of receipt of payment and the date of invoice, whichever is earlier).

   (b) In the case of the balance of £10,000, the tax point is the date of invoice i.e. 10 July 2012 (being the date of invoice and the date of receipt of payment, whichever is earlier).

5. In accordance with the standards prescribed for VAT invoices, each VAT invoice must give the following details:

   (a) **Date** of issue of invoice and invoice number

   (b) **Tax point**

   (c) **Name, address** and **VAT registration number** of the person issuing the VAT invoice.

   (d) Customer's **name** and **address**

   (e) **Descriptions of goods** or **services** supplied for each type of the goods, its quantity, amount and rate of VAT

   (f) **Unit prices** of goods / services supplied

   (g) **Cash discount** if any offered

   (h) **Total VAT** charged

Out of these, Camel Plc gives only three details.

A taxable person who supplies services or goods, of which the value of the supply is less than £250, can issue an invoice with fewer details than prescribed in the standards. Therefore, in the given case, Camel Plc is allowed to issue an invoice with fewer details.

But it is binding on the company to preserve invoices for a minimum of six years.

Self Examination Questions

Question 1

State the VAT rules that determine the tax point in respect of a supply of services.

Question 2

Tardy Ltd registered for Value Added Tax (VAT) on 1 July 2007. The company's VAT returns have been submitted as follows:

Quarter ended	VAT paid/ £	Submitted
30 Sep 2010	18,600	One and half month late
31 Dec 2010	32,200	One and half month late
31 Mar 2011	8,800	On time
30 Jun 2011	3,400	Two months late
30 Sep 2011	(6,500)	One and half month late
31 Dec 2011	42,100	On time
31 Mar 2012	(2,900)	On time
30 Jun 2012	3,900	On time
30 Sep 2012	18,800	On time
31 Dec 2012	57,300	Two months late
31 Mar 2012	9,600	On time

Tardy Ltd always pays any VAT that is due at the same time that the related return is submitted.

Required:

State, giving appropriate reasons, the default surcharge consequences arising from Tardy Ltd's submission of its VAT returns for the quarter.

Question 3

Puzzled Ltd has discovered that a number of errors have been made when preparing its VAT returns for the previous four quarters. As a result of the errors, the company will have to make an additional payment of VAT to **HMRC.**

Required:

Explain how Puzzled Ltd can voluntarily disclose the errors that have been discovered and whether default interest will be due, if the net errors in total are

(a) less than the higher of £10,000 or 1% of turnover for the VAT period or
(b) more than the higher of £10,000 **or 1% of turnover for the VAT period.**

Question 4

Malcolm has filed his VAT return for the quarter ended 31 December 2012. This return represents output tax of £150,000 and input tax of £85,000. Subsequently it was discovered that the output tax was understated by £30,000. The turnover is £456,000 for the VAT period. Is he liable for a misdeclaration penalty?

Answers to Self Examination Questions

Answer to SEQ 1

1. The basic tax point for services is the date on which they are completed.

2. If an invoice is issued or payment is received before the basic tax point, then this becomes the actual tax point.

3. If an invoice is issued within 14 days of the basic tax point, the invoice date will usually replace that in (1).

Answer to SEQ 2

1. If a taxable person fails to file returns in time or to make the payment of VAT in time, HMRC issues a surcharge notice. In the case of Tardy Ltd, the company failed to file two quarter end returns in time.

   This has resulted in HMRC issuing a surcharge liability notice specifying a surcharge period. The surcharge period starts from the end of the period to which the default relates, i.e. 30 September 2010. This notice remains effective until 30 September 2011 (i.e. for 12 months).

2. During a surcharge period, if the taxable person fails to pay VAT or makes late payments, HMRC levies a surcharge. In the case of Tardy Ltd the company has made a late payment of VAT for the quarter ended 31 December 2010.

   This has made Tardy Ltd liable for a surcharge of £644 (£32,200 x 2%) and the surcharge period is extended to 31 December 2011.

3. For the quarter ended 30 June 2011, the company has also failed to pay VAT in time. This has resulted in a surcharge liability of £170 (£3,400 x 5%). However, no surcharge notice will be issued as the surcharge amount is less than £400 and the surcharge period is extended to 30 June 2012.

4. For the quarter ended 30 September 2012 the return is late attracting a surcharge liability of 10% of the tax paid. However in this quarter as there is a refund there will be a surcharge. During the surcharge liability period, if the taxable person fails to file a return in time, this increases the rate of surcharge. Tardy Ltd has failed to file a VAT return in time. Therefore, this will result in a surcharge.

5. During the surcharge liability period, if the taxable person fails to file the return then the original surcharge period will get extended by one year from the date to which the new default relates.

   So, in Tardy Ltd's case, continuous late submission of VAT returns has resulted in the surcharge period being extended to 31 December 2011, then to 30 June 2012 and finally to 30 September 2011.

6. During the period between quarters ended on 31 December 2010 to 30 September 2010, Tardy Ltd has submitted four consecutive VAT returns on time. This has brought the surcharge liability period to an end.

7. Again Tardy Ltd has failed to submit the VAT return for the quarter ended 31 December 2012 in time. Therefore HMRC will again issue a surcharge liability notice specifying a surcharge period running to 31 December 2013.

Answer to SEQ 3

1. If a taxable person makes net errors of which the total is less than the higher of £10,000 or 1% of turnover For the VAT period, he will not be penalised. He can voluntarily disclose the errors by simply entering them on the next VAT return.

2. If the taxable person makes net errors totalling more than the higher of £10,000 or 1% of turnover for the VAT period then he can voluntarily disclose the errors, but disclosure must be made separately to HMRC.

   In this situation a taxable person is not liable for serious misdeclaration penalty if the net errors total more than the higher of £10,000 or 1% of turnover for the VAT period.

Answer to SEQ 4

Misdeclaration penalty is based on the amount of tax understated, but the actual penalty payable is linked to the taxpayer's behaviour as follows:

1. There will be no penalty where a taxpayer simply makes a mistake.

2. There will be a moderate penalty (up to 30% of the understated tax) where a taxpayer fails to take reasonable care.

3. There will be a higher penalty (up to 70% of the understated tax) if the error is deliberate.

4. And an even higher penalty (up to 100% of the understated tax) where there is also concealment of the error.

In Malcolm's case, the error is of £30,000.

1% of £1,456,000 = £14,560. Therefore the higher of £10,000 and £14,560 is £14,560. However the error of £30,000 is more than £14,560. Hence, Malcolm is liable for a misdeclaration penalty. The amount of penalty will depend on the behaviour of Malcolm.

If he has made a mistake unintentionally then no penalty would be charged or would be reduced substantially. However if he has not taken reasonable care then a moderate penalty upto 30% of the understated tax is charged. If he has deliberately made a misdeclaration, then a higher penalty up to 70% of the understated tax is charged and an even higher rate of up to 100% of the understated tax is charged on a deliberate error and its concealment.

STUDY GUIDE G4: THE EFFECT OF SPECIAL SCHEMES

Get Through Intro

To make the correct payment of VAT a taxable person needs to maintain proper accounting records. This Study Guide explains various accounting methods such as the cash accounting scheme, the annual accounting scheme and the flat rate accounting scheme.

In this Study Guide we will also discuss the advantages of these schemes. A thorough understanding of these accounting schemes will help you to advise a client on which accounting method he should follow, depending on the turnover of the business.

Learning Outcomes

a) Describe the cash accounting scheme, and recognise when it will be advantageous to use the scheme.
b) Describe the annual accounting scheme, and recognise when it will be advantageous to use the scheme.
c) Describe the flat rate scheme, and recognise when it will be advantageous to use the scheme.

Introduction

Case Study

Jenny Smith Floral Designs Ltd is a small event company, which specialises in providing exotic flowers for corporate clients. It is owned by two sisters and employs a part-time administration assistant. The company has recently registered for VAT and Jenny and her sister are wondering what the differences are between the various VAT schemes available.

After researching the schemes on HMRC's website Jenny concluded that the Cash Accounting Scheme would be beneficial for the company. It recognises VAT only when the cash has been paid or received, thereby providing considerable cash flow benefits.

Let us consider this decision in this Study Guide and see if Jenny's conclusion is correct.

1. Describe the cash accounting scheme, and recognise when it will be advantageous to use the scheme.[2]

[Learning Outcome a]

1.1 The cash accounting system

The cash accounting scheme allows businesses to account for VAT on a cash receipts basis, rather than an accruals basis.

Under the cash accounting scheme a person accounts for VAT on the basis of **payments received and made**, rather than on invoices issued and received. It simply means that, in the books of accounts, VAT is recorded when actual cash is received or paid.

Under this accounting system, a taxable person need not follow tax points. The **actual date of cash receipt or payment** will determine the return under which the transaction should be covered.

Conditions for joining the cash accounting scheme

1. Value of taxable supplies (excluding VAT) in the next 12 months is not expected to exceed **£1,350,000.**

> Taxable supplies include value of standard and reduced rate items and zero-rated supplies!

2. The company must be **up to date with its VAT returns and payments.**

3. No convictions for VAT offences or assessment penalties for VAT evasion in the preceding 12 months.

4. Businesses using the scheme must cease doing so once the value of taxable supplies in the previous 12 months exceeds £1,600,000.

Conditions for leaving the cash accounting scheme

Entities which leave the cash accounting scheme may have:

- supplies against which collections have not been received from customers; and/or
- unpaid vendor's bills on which input tax is not recovered.

The entity can opt to account for all outstanding VAT either immediately or within a further period of six months.

Example

Edward follows tax periods ending in July, October, January and April. By the end of September 2012, his turnover for the last twelve months was £1,625,000.

In this situation, Edward must withdraw himself from the cash accounting system by the end of the tax period i.e. October 2012. However on 31 October 2012, the entity has an outstanding VAT liability of £2,500.This amount can be paid immediately i.e. on 31 October 2012 or within a further period of six months, i.e. up to 30 April 2013.

1.2 Advantages

1. Where a period of credit is given to customers, VAT is not paid until one month after the return period in which the invoice was paid.
2. Automatic bad debt relief as VAT is only paid to HMRC once the invoice is paid.

Example

On 1 January 2012, Sam sold goods worth £5,000 plus VAT of £250 to Nita. The credit period was 30 days. However, Nita did not pay for the goods on 10 February 2012.

In this situation Sam need not pay VAT to HMRC until the actual date of receipt under the cash accounting basis i.e. 10 February 2012.

1.3 Disadvantage

The recovery of input VAT is delayed until the business has paid for its purchases.

Example

Renaldo uses steel rods in manufacturing spare parts for cars. The spare parts are liable for VAT at the rate of 20%.On 10 May 2012,Renaldo purchased steel rods from James Bond worth £1,000 and paid VAT of £200 on the same. The steel rods were purchased on a credit basis. The credit period was one month. Renaldo paid for these goods on 30 September 2012.

In May 2012, Renaldo used the rods in manufacturing the spare parts. However, while paying VAT on outputs, he cannot set off input VAT until he has paid for the goods. He can therefore set off input VAT only after making the actual payment for the goods (i.e. on or after 30 September 2012).

SUMMARY

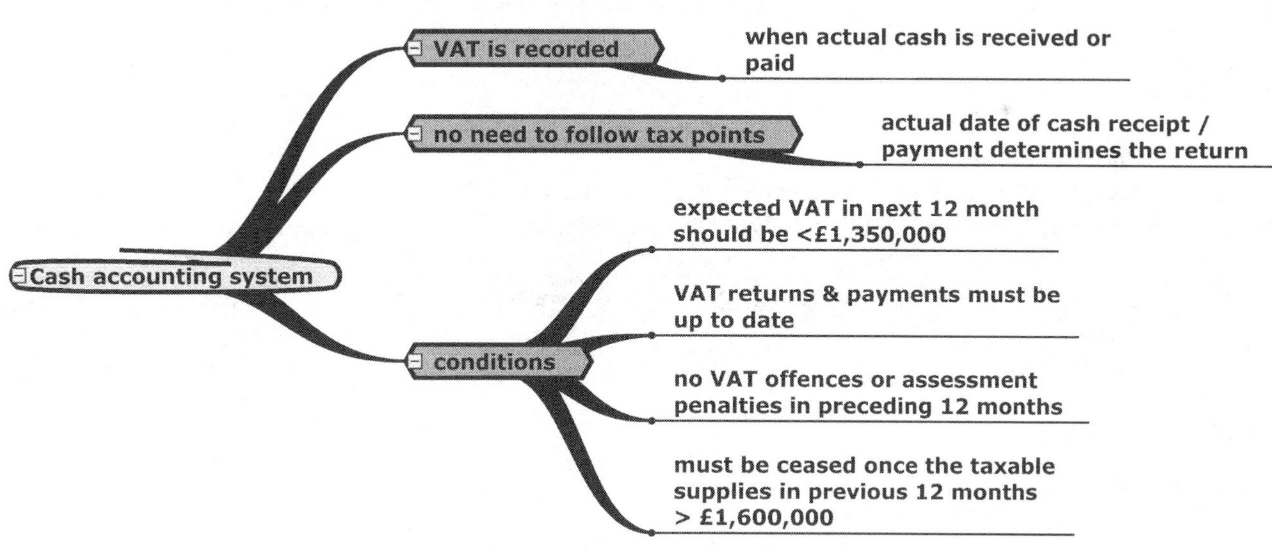

2. Describe the annual accounting scheme, and recognise when it will be advantageous to use the scheme.[2]

[Learning Outcome b]

2.1 Annual accounting scheme

Under the scheme:

1. Only one VAT return is submitted each year, due within two months from the end of the year.
2. VAT dues may be paid by either of the following methods:

- nine monthly payments, each equal to 1/9th of the previous year's VAT payable made on account with the first one being made at the end of the fourth month of the year. This applies to businesses which have been

VAT registered for at least 12 months (if the business has not been VAT registered for 12 months, the instalments are based on the estimated VAT for the next 12 months).

- in three quarterly instalments which fall due at the end of months 4, 7 and 10. Each quarterly payment would be computed as 25% of the previous year's liability.

Example

Peter manufactures furniture. He pays VAT regularly. His year end is March. In the year ended 31 March 2012, his net VAT liability (output VAT – input VAT) was £9,000. If, in the year ended 31 March 2013 he wants to move to the annual accounting system, he must pay VAT of £8,100 (90% of 9,000) during the current year. He can pay VAT by either of the following methods:

(i) £8,100 (90% of 9,000) during the current year. The nine monthly instalments start from the fourth month of the year i.e. July 2012; or

(ii) £6,750 (75% of 9,000) during the current year. The three quarterly instalments must start from the end of the first 4 months of the year i.e. July 2012.

---

3. HMRC **estimates the liability for the year** based on the previous year's liability.

4. Any **balancing payment** must be made with the return.

5. The VAT return should be submitted within two months after the end of the annual accounting period.

2.2 Conditions for joining the annual accounting scheme:

1. Value of **taxable supplies** (excluding VAT) in the next 12 months is **not expected to exceed £1,350,000.**
2. All eligible businesses can join the annual accounting scheme as soon as they register for VAT.
3. Businesses using the scheme **must cease** doing so once the value of taxable supplies in the previous 12 months **exceeds £1,600,000.**

2.3 Advantages

1. **Reduced administration.**
2. Only **one VAT return,** so less chance of incurring a default surcharge.
3. **Payments on account are made**, allowing improved budgeting and cash flow if business is expanding.

3. Describe the flat rate scheme, and recognise when it will be advantageous to use the scheme.[2]

[Learning Outcome c]

3.1 Flat rate scheme

Under this scheme:

> The VAT rate varies between 2% to 13.5%, according to the trade sector.

1. The business issues VAT invoices, charging VAT at either standard or zero rate.
2. **No records** need to be kept of input VAT suffered.
3. VAT payable to HMRC is the flat rate percentage multiplied by the **VAT INCLUSIVE turnover** for the period.

VAT liability = Total turnover (inclusive of VAT) **x Flat rate percentage**

4. **No input VAT is recovered.**
5. There is a reduction of 1% of the normal rate in the first year of registration.

Tip

The flat rate percentage varies according to the type of trade, it will be given in the examination.

3.2 Conditions for joining the flat rate scheme

1. Value of **annual taxable supplies** (excluding VAT) does **not exceed £150,000.**
2. The **annual total turnover,** (including VAT and the value of any exempt and non-taxable income) does **not exceed £187,500.**

For the year ended 31 March 2012, Robert's turnover was £80,000.

In the next 12 months, Robert does not expect his business turnover to exceed £150,000. During these 12 months i.e. during the year ended 31 March 2012 he had planned to sell one of the machines that he owned and used in the business.

He expects that during the year ended 31 March 2013 his total turnover (including the sale proceeds from the sale of the asset) will not exceed £187,500.

In this situation, Robert can join the flat rate scheme.

Alistair expects that, during the next 12 months, his business turnover including VAT will be £130,000. He may dispose of an asset in the business for £60,000. Knowing this, can he join the flat rate scheme?

3.3 Advantages

1. **Simplified** VAT administration
2. Only need to issue VAT invoices to VAT registered customers
3. Business may benefit from paying less VAT to HMRC

3.4 Disadvantages

1. Cannot reclaim input VAT on purchases. However, for purchase of capital items for more than £2,000 per asset (VAT inclusive) VAT can be reclaimed under the capital goods scheme. If later such goods are sold, the sale proceeds are not included in the turnover limits of the flat rate scheme.

As a general rule, businesses that usually receive repayments of VAT should not join the flat rate scheme.

Neptune Ltd registered for VAT with effect from 1 March 2012. The company has annual standard-rated sales of £86,500. These sales are made to the general public. The annual standard rated expenses of the company are £15,000. These amounts are all inclusive of VAT. The relevant flat rate scheme for the company is 10%.

The **conditions t**hat the company must satisfy before being permitted to use the flat rate scheme are as follows:

1. The company's expected taxable turnover for the next 12 months does not exceed £150,000.
2. The company's expected total income (including exempt supplies) for the next 12 months does not exceed £187,500.

Neptune Ltd also gains the following advantages by using this scheme:

1. Simplified VAT administration.
2. On the basis of normal provisions, the VAT liability is calculated as follows:
   £86,500 - £15,000 = £71,500 x 1/6 = **£11,917.**
   If the company uses the flat rate scheme, then, it will have to pay VAT liability amounting **£8,650** (£86,500 x 10%).

There is therefore an annual saving of £3,267 (£11,917 - £8,650).

3.5 Conditions for leaving the scheme

Persons who join the scheme:

- can voluntarily leave the scheme at any time
- are required to mandatorily leave the scheme when their total business turnover (excluding sale of capital assets) exceeds £230,000 (The VAT flat rates need not be memorised. The rates would be provided to you in the exam).
- VAT inclusive turnover would include the turnover of standard rated supplies, zero rated supplies as well as exempt supplies.
- Input VAT on the capital goods scheme needs to be recovered through the VAT return in the normal way, as the flat rate scheme does not permit the recovery of input VAT.

Tip

The above limit of £230,000 is applicable with effect from 4 January 2012. However, there will be no question involving the old limit in the exam.

Test Yourself 2

Ping Ltd is a food shop, which sells mainly ice-creams, a variety of chocolates and fruit drinks. In addition to this, Ping Ltd supplies food such as bread, cake, yoghurt, cheese etc.

Ping's turnover from the sale of chocolates, ice-creams and fruit drinks is around £40,000 (excluding VAT). VAT on all these items is charged at 20%. The turnover of the other food supplies is £11,250. These supplies are zero rated for VAT purposes.

Required:

Calculate the VAT payable by Ping Ltd if it opts for the flat rate scheme. (Flat rate percentage for retailing food is 2%).

Answers to Test Yourself

Answer to TY 1

A person can join the flat rate scheme, provided he fulfils the following conditions for the next 12 months:

1. He does not expect turnover to exceed £150,000, and
2. He does not expect his total turnover (including exempt and non-business income) to exceed £187,500. In Alistair's case he expects his total turnover to exceed £187,500. Hence, even though his expected business turnover is less than £150,000, he cannot join the flat rate scheme.

Answer to TY 2

	Total turnover of Ping Ltd	**£**
1	Turnover of ice-creams, chocolates & fruit drinks	40,000
	Add: VAT @ 20%	8,000
	Gross turnover of ice-creams, chocolates and fruit drinks	**48,000**
2	Turnover of daily required food items	11,250
	Add: VAT – at zero rate	0
	Gross turnover of daily required food items	**11,250**
3	**Total turnover (VAT inclusive) (1 + 2)**	**59,250**

Total VAT payable by Ping Ltd = Total VAT inclusive turnover x flat rate percentage
= £59,250 x 2%
= **£1,185**

Quick Quiz

1. To whom is the cash accounting system advantageous?

2. To whom is the annual accounting system advantageous?

3. To whom is the flat rate system advantageous?

4. Tom has been registered for VAT for the last six years. He expects that, within the next 12 months, his turnover will not exceed £800,000. Can he join the cash accounting system?

Answers to Quick Quiz

1. Under the cash accounting system a taxable person doesn't have to pay tax until the business receives payment of its sales invoice. So, when the goods are sold on a credit basis and the customer does not pay for the same, the trader doesn't have to pay VAT on these supplies (i.e. the supplies which have become bad debts).

   In this way, a trader automatically gets bad debt relief. Hence, the cash accounting system is mainly advantageous to traders who mainly sell goods on a credit basis.

2. The annual accounting system is more advantageous to small traders whose taxable annual turnover will not exceed £1,350,000 in the next 12 months, as they don't have to file tax returns as frequently.

3. Flat rate accounting is mainly advantageous to small businesses. Due to the flat rate accounting system, the supplier doesn't have to maintain records for VAT payable on output or VAT paid on purchases. Small businesses with a small turnover find this convenient as it makes record-keeping easier.

4. The cash accounting system can be followed only if a taxable person expects that, during the next 12 months, his taxable turnover will not exceed £1,350,000. As Tom does not expect his turnover to **exceed** £800,000 in the next 12 months he can join the cash accounting system.

Self Examination Questions

Question 1

Kinte follows the cash accounting system. In the last two years he was irregular in making his VAT payments. What are the consequences of this?

Question 2

Danesh runs the 'Cook & Food' restaurant and has rented out a flat above the restaurant. His total turnover, for the year ended 2012 - 13 is as follows:

(a) VAT inclusive taxable turnover for catering supplies £80,000 at standard rate.
(b) VAT inclusive supplies (takeaway food) £5,000 at zero rate.
(c) Exempt flat rentals £4,000.

Required:

Calculate the total taxable turnover and VAT liable if the applicable flat rate is 12%.

Answers to Self Examination Questions

Answer to SEQ 1

When a registered person who follows the cash accounting system fails to make regular VAT payments, he becomes debarred from the scheme.

Answer to SEQ 2

Under the flat rate scheme, a flat rate percentage is applied on the VAT inclusive of total turnover for the period. Total turnover includes zero rate supplies, low rate supplies and exempt supplies.

Calculation of the total turnover for the year ended 2012-13 is as follows:

VAT inclusive turnover	£
Standard-rated catering supplies	80,000
Zero-rated takeaway food	5,000
Exempt flat rentals	4,000
Total	**89,000**

VAT payable by Danesh under flat rate scheme =Total VAT inclusive turnover x flat rate percentage
= £89,000 x 12% **= £10,680**

SECTION H

THE OBLIGATIONS OF TAX PAYERS AND/OR THEIR AGENTS

H1

STUDY GUIDE H1: THE SYSTEMS FOR SELF-ASSESSMENT AND THE MAKING OF RETURNS

Get Through Intro

In this Study Guide, we will see how a taxpayer is required to self-assess their tax liability. Although HM Revenue & Customs will send the taxpayer (whether an individual or a company) a notice and an appropriate tax form, the responsibility is placed on the taxpayer to inform HMRC about their chargeability to tax in the case of non-receipt of the notice.

As a prospective tax consultant, it is very important that you understand the provisions relating to informing HMRC about tax chargeability, the due dates, exceptions, consequences of not informing HMRC about tax chargeability etc.

Learning Outcomes

a) Explain and apply the features of the self-assessment system as it applies to individuals.
b) Explain and apply the features of the self-assessment system as it applies to companies including the use of iXBRL.

Introduction

What is self-assessment? Does a taxpayer always need to self-assess their tax liability?

Self-assessment is broadly the process by which taxpayers declare:

- taxable income and gains on tax returns
- income tax
- capital gains tax
- class 4 National Insurance Contributions as appropriate

However, HMRC can calculate these liabilities for the taxpayer, provided a tax return is sent by the individual well in advance. **If any taxpayer wants HMRC to calculate their tax liability,** they have to file the tax return by 31 October following the end of the tax year e.g., for the year ended 5 April 2013, the return must be sent to HMRC by 31 October 2013.

Remember, **companies do not have the option of leaving their tax calculations to HMRC.**

1. Explain and apply the features of the self-assessment system as it applies to individuals.[2] [Learning Outcome a]

Most individuals **pay tax** on their earnings or pensions **through PAYE** (**P**ay **A**s **Y**ou **E**arn). Under PAYE, the employer deducts tax on behalf of HMRC. But if a person is **not taxed under PAYE,** and / or is liable to pay additional tax because of other income not taxed through PAYE (e.g. income from property or investments above a certain amount, trading profits etc.), the taxpayer has to **assess himself** to his tax liability. Under the self-assessment system, the **amount of tax** due for the year is **calculated by the taxpayer,** and then checked by HMRC.

1.1 Chargeability to tax

Individuals who HMRC knows are chargeable to income tax are sent a notice of their chargeability to tax. Those who are chargeable to income tax for any tax year, but have not received any notice from HMRC, are required to inform HMRC about their chargeability to tax by sending a notice. This notice is to be given within **six months** from the end of the tax year in which the liability arises.

Example

For the tax year 2012-13, the notice of chargeability by the individual to HMRC should be given before 5 October 2013.

---

a) A taxpayer receives or needs to ask for a self-assessment tax return if:

- he is self-employed and/or a company director
- he gets rent from property that is not accounted for through PAYE
- he gets other untaxed income not accounted for through PAYE
- he realises a chargeable gain

1. **Exception:** generally an individual has to give notice to HMRC about their chargeability to tax, but this is not required if the following conditions are fulfilled:

Diagram: 1 Exception to tax chargeability

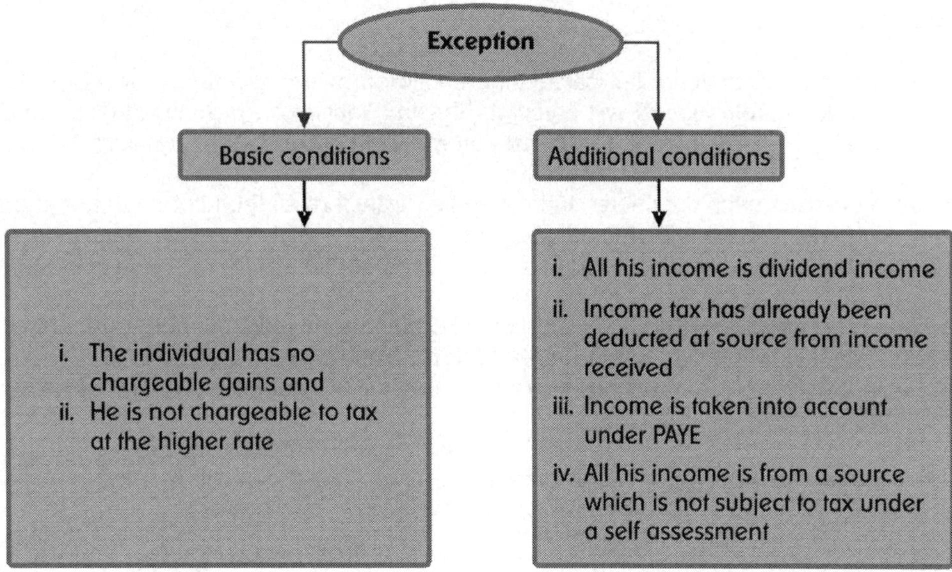

2. **Consequences of not giving notice regarding chargeability**

Where an individual is chargeable to income tax, but fails to give notice of chargeability to HMRC, a penalty **to the extent of 100%** of the tax assessed which is not paid on or before 31 January following the tax year is payable.

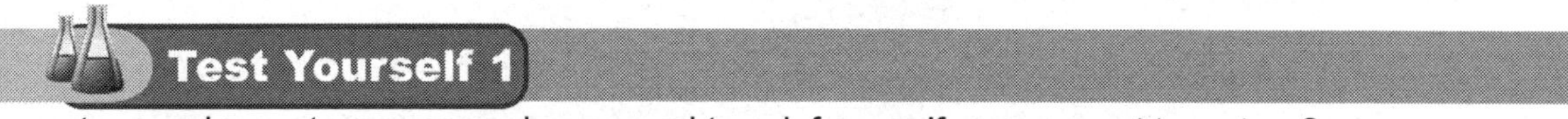

In what circumstances does a taxpayer receive or need to ask for a self-assessment tax return?

1.2 Filing a tax return

HMRC encourages tax payers to file their self-assessment tax returns online by using its website. It has kept two separate filing dates for electronic and non-electronic tax returns which are discussed in detail in Study Guide H2, Learning Outcome 1.

1. **Tax form**

The tax form (along with various supplementary pages relevant to the sources of income declared by the individual) is sent to the individual by HMRC.

a) This tax form is accompanied by a tax guide and various notes relating to the supplementary pages.

b) If the taxpayer has received income from any new source for which supplementary pages are not sent by HMRC, he may have to ask for additional pages.

c) A four-page short tax return is available to taxpayers with simpler tax affairs.

2. **Electronic return filing**

Taxpayers can choose to file their tax return online. Where a taxpayer has filed his income tax return electronically in the previous year, HMRC will send him a notice to file the return, instead of sending him the tax form.

3. Filling in the return

The information related to the tax year just ended is required to be entered on the tax return. The tax return must be submitted in full.

4. Assessment of tax

The main tax return includes an optional tax calculation section in which the taxpayer may calculate their tax liability. If this column is left blank, HMRC will calculate the tax liability on the individual's behalf. If the main return is filed electronically, the tax liability is assessed automatically by computer software.

The Inland Revenue processes each completed tax return i.e., transfers all the information on the taxpayer's tax return form to the computer record with Inland Revenue. Obvious mistakes like calculation errors etc. get corrected in this process, as tax being due or repaid as the case may be.

Once the tax return is processed, each return is then checked by the Inland Revenue. The Inland Revenue can enquire into the completeness and accuracy of any tax return. Enquiry is made on some of the returns, picked out on a random basis. Some returns show an incorrect or incomplete status or amount of tax and are usually picked out for enquiry.

An enquiry can be a request for more information on each item, or a full review on the whole business of the tax payer.

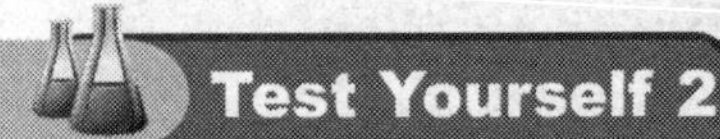

Individuals who are chargeable to income tax for any tax year, but have not received a notice from HMRC are required to notify HMRC about their chargeability.

Required:

(a) What is the time limit for giving this notice?

(b) What are the exceptions to this rule?

---

2. Explain and apply the features of the self-assessment system as it applies to companies, including the use of iXBRL.[2]

[Learning Outcome b]

Self-assessment means that companies are required to **assess themselves** to corporation tax, and **take full responsibility** for that assessment. **If the self-assessment is wrong** due to negligence or recklessness, the company can be liable to **tax-geared penalties.**

1. Chargeability to tax for the first time

Within **three months** from the start of their first accounting period, companies must inform HMRC of their chargeability to tax.

2. Subsequent chargeability to tax

A company, which is chargeable to corporation tax, is sent a notice by HMRC for the filing of a corporation tax return, for the period specified in the notice. However, a company which is chargeable to corporation tax for an accounting period but has not received any notice to that respect from HMRC must notify HMRC about its chargeability to tax within **twelve months** from the end of the accounting period.

3. iXBRL

XBRL (eXtensible Business Reporting Language) is a computer language used to exchange business information. It is web based, and written specifically for the purpose of business reporting. To communicate and exchange business information between business systems, XBRL is the standard based system developed and widely used by regulators who need to maintain a lot of data and statistics. The users of XBRL are thus stock exchanges and securities, banking regulators, business registrars, revenue reporting and tax filing agencies and national statistical agencies.

Countries such as the USA, Japan, Australia, Belgium and the Netherlands have already started using the XBRL form of communicating. Now, HMRC UK require companies to use XBRL to file their tax returns and self-assessment forms.
The XBRL specifications are developed and published by XBRL International, Inc.

4. HMRC's requirement for the use of iXBRL

XBRL defines and exchanges financial information in a computer language and transfers it from one business system to another. HMRC has decided to use XBRL to record the online filing of tax returns to tag all Corporation Tax Returns and company account numbers.

The tags used would be descriptions predefined by HMRC and the UK GAAP/IFRS Taxonomy. The tagged electronic files are submitted through the Government Gateway.

This information will be stored in a database format and will enable HMRC analysts to generate comparison charts for each year and also for interim periods which can be instantly run for individuals as well as for companies within a particular sector of business .
This will increase the efficiency of HMRC to carry out its tax inspections and verifications effectively and make valuable enquiries.

All limited companies need to file their self-assessment corporation tax returns online and pay the corporation tax payable electronically. The deadlines of submission remains the same and the return should be submitted along with the self assessment of the corporation tax payable. If this is done using the software provided by HMRC, it is calculated automatically by the software.

Companies with accounting periods ending after 31 March 2011 are required to submit their corporation tax returns and company accounts online in an XBRL electronic format by the end of the following accounting period.

Rennocks prepares its accounts to 30 September 2011 every year, so it will have to file its company accounts and corporation tax in an XBRL format by 30 September 2012.

HMRC has updated its website with all the relevant information for using the XBRL format. You can access it on the below mentioned link:

http://www.hmrc.gov.uk/ct/returns/online.htm

Companies will have to re-develop the accounting processes that they are currently using and make these systems capable of producing company accounts in XBRL formats.

If companies fail to comply with this requirement then HMRC will reject their submission.

The information required is very detailed; all the financial reporting statements and other documents of the company are required to be submitted. Each and every field needs to be filled in so that the purpose of implementing the XBRL format is achieved.

Companies that come under SMEs with simple accounts can use HMRC's software and take advantage of the accounts and tax computations automatically produced by the software in their appropriate formats.

Companies other than SMEs can use:

- softwares that automatically produce accounts and tax computations in accordance with iXBRL
- any tagging service that applies all the appropriate tags to accounts and computations.
- a software that provides all the appropriate tags that can be added to accounts and the relevant tax computations.

What are tags?

Tags are included in dictionaries known as taxonomies, with different taxonomies for different purposes. It is based on the corporation tax computation according to taxonomy which has above 1,200 relevant tags. The returns that are filed after 1 April 2012 where an accounting period ends after 31 March 2011, these tags have to be considered.

Answers to Test Yourself

Answer TY 1

A taxpayer receives or needs to ask for a self-assessment tax return if:

1. He is self-employed and/or a company director.
2. He gets rent from property that is not accounted for through PAYE.
3. He gets other untaxed income not accounted for through PAYE.
4. He has substantial income from savings and investments.
5. He makes gains (profits) on the sale of shares or other assets above the capital gains tax (CGT) reporting limits.

Answer TY 2

1. Those who are chargeable to income tax for any tax year but have not received a notice from HMRC are required to inform HMRC about their chargeability by sending a notice. This notice is to be given within **six months** from the end of the period.

2. **Exception:** it is not required if the following conditions are fulfilled:

Basic conditions

a) The individual has no chargeable gains.

b) He is not chargeable to tax at the higher rate.

Additional conditions

i. All his income is dividend income.
ii. Income tax has already been deducted at source from income received.
iii. Income is taken into account under PAYE.
iv. All his income is from a source which is not subject to tax under a self assessment.

Quick Quiz

State whether true or false.

1. Notice is normally sent by HMRC to individuals who are chargeable to income tax.

2. Information relating to the current year is filled in the tax return.

3. Companies that are chargeable to tax for the first time must inform HMRC of their chargeability to tax within three months from the **start** of their first accounting period.

4. Companies with accounting periods ending after 31 March 2011 are required to submit their corporation tax returns and company accounts online in an XBRL electronic format by the end of the following accounting period.

Answers to Quick Quiz

1. **True**, however, those who are chargeable to income tax for any tax year, but have not received any notice from HMRC are required to inform HMRC about their chargeability to tax by sending a notice.

2. **False,** the information related to the **year just ended** is required to be entered on the tax return.

3. **True.**

4. **True.**

Self Examination Questions

Question 1

Ambika has been trading for many years, preparing accounts to 31 December. Which accounts will be assessed in 2012-13?

Question 2

Jojoba Ltd prepares its first accounts for a 15 month period ended 31 March 2013. When should notice be sent to HMRC regarding its chargeability to tax?

Question 3

What is HMRC's objective in using XBRL formats for submission of online tax returns and company accounts?

Answers to Self Examination Questions

Answer to SEQ 1

The information related to the year just ended is required to be entered on the tax return. Therefore, accounts relating to the year ended 31 December 2012 will be assessed in 2012-13.

Answer to SEQ 2

Companies that are chargeable to tax for the first time must inform HMRC of their chargeability to tax within three months from the start of their first accounting period. As Jojoba Ltd prepared its first accounts for a 15 month period, and the period of 15 months ended on 31 March 2013, it indicates that Jojoba Ltd started business on 1 January 2012 (1/1/2012 to 31/3/2013 = 15 months). Hence, Jojoba Ltd must inform HMRC on or before 31 March 2012 i.e. within three months from the start of their first accounting period.

Answer to SEQ 3

The XBRL format will enable HMRC to store a large number of databases that can be used for various kinds of analyses as it will instantly give out any amount and any type of comparison charts - between different periods and different sectors of businesses, geographical distribution to income distribution etc.

With these comparative charts and analyses based on them, HMRC can direct and address many questions and implement more effective and efficient tax planning for each section of the society, business and economy.

SECTION H

THE OBLIGATIONS OF TAX PAYERS AND/OR THEIR AGENTS

H2

STUDY GUIDE H2: THE TIME LIMITS FOR THE SUBMISSION OF INFORMATION, CLAIMS AND PAYMENT OF TAX, INCLUDING PAYMENTS ON ACCOUNT

Get Through Intro

While dealing with HMRC, following the due dates is very important as any delay in filing returns and paying tax can lead to heavy penalties.

This Study Guide discusses in detail the due dates for tax payments and return filing as well as interest and penalties applicable. It also explains how HMRC can inquire into a person's self-assessment return.

As a tax consultant, you will need this information to advise clients on how to minimise penalties. A thorough understanding of this topic is important for your examination, as well as in your professional life.

Learning Outcomes

a) Recognise the time limits that apply to the filing of returns and the making of claims.
b) Recognise the due dates for the payment of tax under the self-assessment system.
c) Compute payments on account and balancing payments / repayments for individuals.
d) Explain how large companies are required to account for corporation tax on a quarterly basis.
e) List the information and records that taxpayers need to retain for tax purposes.

Introduction

Case Study

Julian was a dealer of electrical goods. He always filed his income tax return well in advance so that HMRC could prepare a self-assessment form on his behalf.

In May 2012, Julian and two of his friends in a similar line of business formed a private limited company. Julian was under the impression that HMRC would prepare a self-assessment form for this company too.

In this Study Guide, the various provisions regarding the filing of returns, what the due dates are, whether HMRC can prepare self-assessment forms on behalf of taxpayers etc. are explored.

1. Recognise the time limits that apply to the filing of returns and the making of claims.[2] [Learning Outcome a]

1.1 For individuals

HMRC encourages taxpayers to file their self-assessment tax returns online by using its website. It has kept two separate filing dates for electronic and non-electronic tax returns, which are as follows:

Sr No	Mode of filing	Deadline
1.	Electronic	31 January following the tax year. For 2012-13, the deadline would therefore be 31 January 2014.
2.	Non-electronic	31 October following the tax year. For 2012-13 the deadline would therefore be 31 October 2013.

There are two exceptions to the above stated deadlines:

Sr No	Nature of exception	Mode of filing	Deadline
1.	If HMRC issues a notice to file a tax return between 31 July and 31 October of the following year	Electronic	31 January following the tax year
		Non-electronic	The end of three months from the date of notice.
2.	If HMRC issues a notice to file a tax return after 31 October of the following year	Electronic as well as non-electronic	The end of three months from the date of notice.

If a taxpayer wants HMRC to prepare a self-assessment on his behalf by the traditional method and calculate his tax for him, then the deadline for the return would be 31 October (previously it was 30 September) following the tax year. This means that all taxpayers who file their returns using the traditional paper based method by the 31 October will have the option of HMRC preparing a self-assessment on their behalf. Online tax returns are automatically provided with a self-assessment tax calculation as a part of the filing process.

However, in this case if HMRC issues a notice to file a tax return after 31 August of the following year, the deadline would be the end of two months from the date of notice. For example for 2012-13, if the notice is issued on 2 September 2013 and the taxpayer wants HMRC to prepare a self-assessment on their behalf, then the deadline for the return would be 1 November 2013.

HMRC issued a tax return for the tax year 2012-13 to Trish on 15 November 2013. Therefore, the due date for her to submit her tax return (online filing of return) is **the later of**:

- within three months from 15 November 2013 i.e. 15 February 2014
- 31 January 2014

Therefore, the due date is 15 February 2014.

HMRC has issued a notice dated 1 August 2013 to Shan asking him to file his tax return for the tax year 2012-13.

Required:

(a) What would be the deadline for Sam to file his returns, if Sam files his returns through the internet?

(b) What would be the deadline for Sam to file his returns, if Sam files his returns in paper form?

1.2 For companies

1. Filing of return

On receiving a notice from HMRC, a company must file a corporation tax return for the period **specified in the notice.** The return is in form CT600 with the relevant supplementary pages. The supporting accounts and calculations must be attached along with the return.

Companies do not have the option of leaving the tax calculations to HMRC.

2. Due dates for filing returns with HMRC

The return has to be filed **on or before the due date.** The due date for filing the return is the **latest** of:

a) **twelve months after the end of the period covered** by the return i.e. the period specified in the notice by HMRC

b) **twelve months after the end of the period of accounts** if the **period of accounts is less than eighteen months**

c) **thirty months from the start of the period of accounts** if the period of accounts is **more than or equal to eighteen months**

d) **three months after** the issue of notice

Diagram 1: Time limits for filing returns for individuals and companies

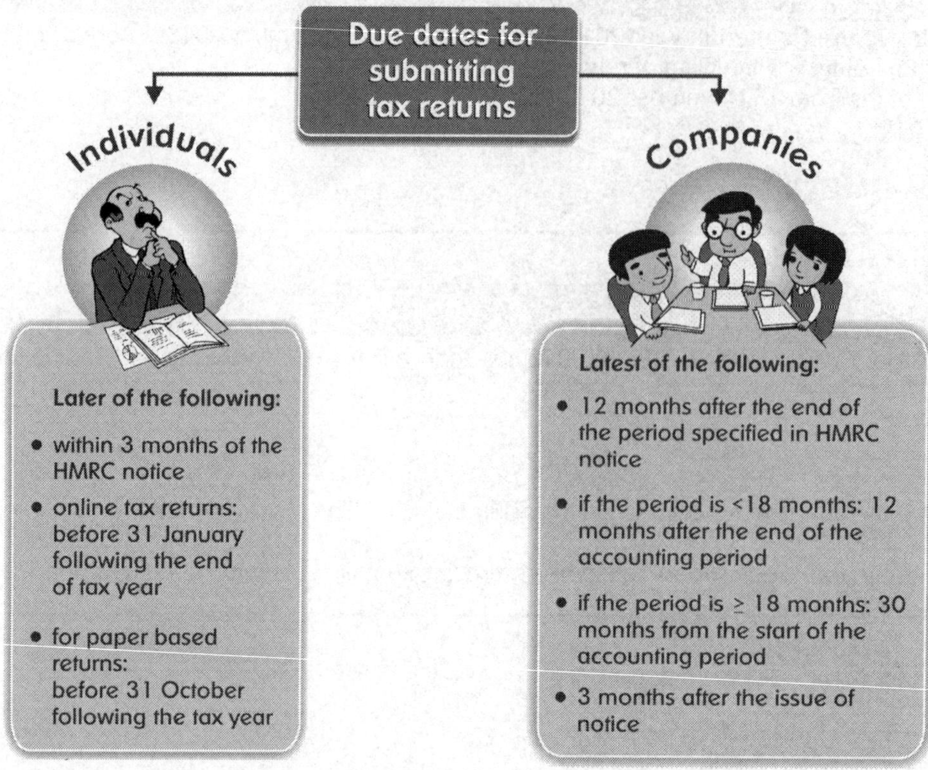

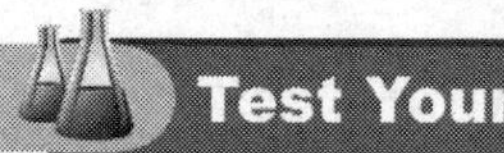

Test Yourself 2

State the date of filing the return by Turbo Ltd if it prepares its accounts for:

(a) 15 months to 31 March 2013. Notice was issued by HMRC on 15 May 2013.
(b) 18 months to 31 May 2013. Notice was issued by HMRC on 1 July 2013.
(c) 9 months to 31 December 2013. Notice was issued by HMRC on 12 February 2014.

The required filing date is normally **twelve months after** the **end** of the **period of account** since the majority of companies prepare their accounts to the same date each year. Notices are usually issued within a few weeks of the end of each period of account.

Test Yourself 3

State the date that CompuServe Ltd's self-assessment corporation tax return for the year ended 31 December 2012 should be submitted.

The time limit for making claims under income tax and corporation tax is four years from the end of the tax year. For example, for the tax year 2012-13, the claim can be made by 5 April 2017.

2. Recognise the due dates for the payment of tax under the self-assessment system.[2] [Learning Outcome b]

2.1 For individuals

Payment of tax: tax due for self-assessment is payable in three parts as follows:

1. A first payment on account is due on **31 January in the tax year** to which the self-assessment relates.

2. 2. A second payment on account is due on the following **31 July.**

3. A final **balancing payment** is due on **31 January** following the end of the tax year to which it relates.

Payment	Due date
1st payment on account	31 January **in** the tax year
2nd payment on account	31 July **following** the tax year
Final payment to settle the remaining liability	31 January **following** the tax year

Example

Simi made her accounts up to 31 December 2012 (falling in tax year 2012-13). Payment of self-assessment tax is due as follows:

1. First payment on account is due on 31 January **2013** (this date **falls in the tax year 2012-13).**
2. Second payment on account is due on 31 July 2013 (31 July following the tax year 2012-13).
3. Final payment to settle remaining liability (if any) is due on 31 January 2014 (31 January following the tax year 2012-13).

2.2 For companies

Due date for payment of tax

A company's corporation tax liability for a particular accounting year is generally payable in a **single payment**. The **due date** for the actual payment of tax is generally **nine months and one day** after the end of the concerned accounting period. Different rules are applicable to large companies, which will be discussed later in this Study Guide.

Example

Zen Ltd has taxable total profits of £690,000 for the year ended 31 March 2012. The due date for payment of corporation tax is 1 January 2013 (nine months and one day after the end of the accounting period).

SUMMARY

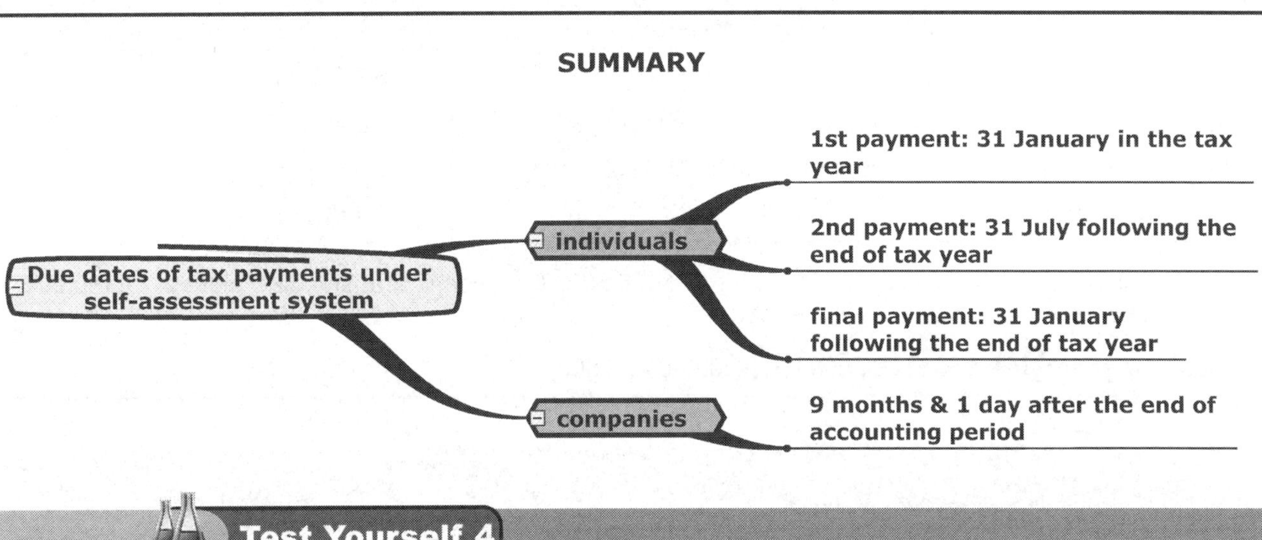

Test Yourself 4

Sasha made her first accounts up to 30 June 2012. When are payments on account due?

---

3. Compute payments on account and balancing payments / repayments for individuals.[2] [Learning Outcome c]

3.1 Payment on account

Payments on account are normally fixed by reference to the previous year's tax liability. The payment on account **on each instalment** is equal to **50% of the relevant amount for the previous year.** If the current year's tax and Class 4 NIC liabilities are more than the previous year's tax liability, then the excess portion is paid by way of a **balancing payment** payable on **31 January following the end of the current tax year.**

Example

Simi's income tax liability for **2011-12** (previous year) excluding tax deducted at source was £10,000. Her tax liability for the tax year **2012-13** is £14,500.

The payments on account for 2011-12 are as follows:

Date		£
31/01/2013	1st **payment on account** (50% of previous year 2011-12 liability)	5,000
31/07/2013	2nd **payment on account** (50% of previous year 2011-12 liability)	5,000
31/01/2014	**Balancing payment** to settle the remaining liability (current year 2012-13 tax liability less sums already paid)	4,500
	Total	**14,500**

Note: there will also be a payment on 31 January 2014 of £7,250, the first instalment of the tax year 2013-14 (50% of the 2012-13 liability).

1. Payment on account on each instalment is 50% of the previous year's tax liability. Hence, a situation may arise where a taxpayer may have paid excess tax over the current year's tax liability, by paying on account. In such a case, the taxpayer is entitled to a **balancing repayment** (i.e. a refund of the excess tax paid by him).

Example

Roma's income tax liability for **2011-12** (previous year) excluding tax deducted at source was £10,000. Her tax liability for **2012-13** is £8,500.

The payments on account for 2012-13 are as follows:

Date		£
31/01/2013	1st **payment on account** (50% of 2011-12 liability)	5,000
31/07/2013	2nd **payment on account** (50% of 2011-12 liability)	5,000
	Total	**10,000**

However, Roma's total tax liability for 2012-13 is only £8,500. This means that she paid more tax through the payments on account than was due for the year.

The **balancing repayment** due is £1,500 i.e. (£10,000 - £8,500).

Test Yourself 5

Ted's tax liability for **2012-13** is £18,300. Calculate payment on account and balancing payment / repayment due, assuming his income tax and class 4 NIC liability for **2011-12** excluding tax deducted at source was:

(a) £12,300
(b) £21,800

2. Capital gains tax is **not** subject to payments on account as capital disposals are unlikely to be the same from year to year. Any capital gains tax payable on 31 January following the tax year (i.e. for 2012-13) will be paid on or before 31 January 2014. The Class 2 NIC (for self-employed persons) is paid on a monthly basis (in the case of direct debit and quarterly by billing) and therefore not required to be included in the computation for payment on account.

Example

Julie is a self-employed musician. Her tax liability for 2011-12 and 2012-13 is as follows:

	2011-12 **£**	**2012-13** **£**
Total amount of income tax charged	12,500	15,000
This included:		
Tax deducted on savings income	6,200	
She also paid: Class 4 NIC	2,800	
Capital gains tax	6,100	2,000

Payments on account for 2012-13 are calculated as follows:

	£
Income tax	
Total income tax charged for 2011-12	12,500
Less: Tax deducted	(6,200)
	6,300
Add: Class 4 NIC	2,800
Self-assessment tax and Class 4 NIC	**9,100**

Payments on account for 2012-13:

Date		**£**
31/01/2013	1st payment on account (50% of £9,100 i.e. 2011-12 liability)	4,550
31/07/2013	2nd payment on account (50% of £9,100 i.e. 2011-12 liability)	4,550
31/01/2014	Final balancing payment to settle the remaining liability (2012-13 less sums already paid)	5,900
	Chargeable gains of 2012-13	2,000
	Total	**17,000**

Notes:

1. Class 2 NIC is not paid through the self-assessment system, but is paid directly to contributing agencies. Therefore, no question of payment on account arises.
2. There is **no requirement** to make payments on account of **capital gains tax. It is all paid on balancing payment.**

---

3. Taxpayers are not required to make payments on account of their income tax (and Class 4 National Insurance) liability if:

a) **more than 80%** of the previous year's liability was covered by PAYE, tax deducted at source and dividend tax credits; or
b) the previous year's tax (and Class 4 National Insurance) liability was less than £1,000.

Helen's total liability to income tax and Class 4 NIC for 2011-12 **was £22,500. Out of** this, she had paid £19,900 by deduction at source. Her total liability for 2012-13 is £25,000, of which £22;000 is paid by deduction at source.

Helen's total liability to income tax	£22,500
Tax deducted at source	£19,900

More than 80% of Helen's total **liability for 2011-12** (£22,500) was **paid by deduction at source**. Therefore, **no payments on account are required** for **2012-13.**

Her 2012-13 liability of £3,000 i.e. (£25,000 – £22,000) is payable on 31 January 2014.

Victor's total liability to income tax and Class 4 NIC for 2011-12 was £750. His total liability for 2012-13 is £5,000 of which £2,800 is paid through deduction at source.

Victor's previous year's tax and Class 4 National Insurance liability was **less than £1,000.** Therefore, **no payments on account are required** for **2012-13.**

His 2012-13 liability of £2,200 i.e. (£5,000 – £2,800) is payable on 31 January 2014.

---

4. Those taxpayers who are required to make payments on account, but who believe that the liability for that year will be less than the liability for the previous year, **may make a claim to** reduce or eliminate payments on account by 31 January following the end of the tax year.

A taxpayer can apply to reduce his payments on account if he knows that his income has decreased from the previous year.

Alan's liability for tax and Class 4 NIC for the tax year 2011-12 was £15,600. Unfortunately, he had an accident in June 2012 and was in hospital for three months. As he was advised to take full rest, he was not able to run his business until December 2012. Therefore his income decreased by more than 70% from that of the previous year.

Alan can apply to reduce his payments on account, as his income has gone down from the previous year, and therefore his tax liability for 2012-13 will be less than the liability for the previous year (2011-12).

The claim may be made on form SA303, on the tax return itself, or by way of a letter giving the reasons for the claim.

A taxpayer needs to be careful about reducing payments on account. If the payments are reduced, then his income increases so that the tax for the year is as much, or more than the original payments on account. In this case, he will have to pay interest from the date the payment on account was due.

Interest is charged if payments on account following the claim are too low, and penalties may be charged for fraudulent or negligent claims.

SUMMARY

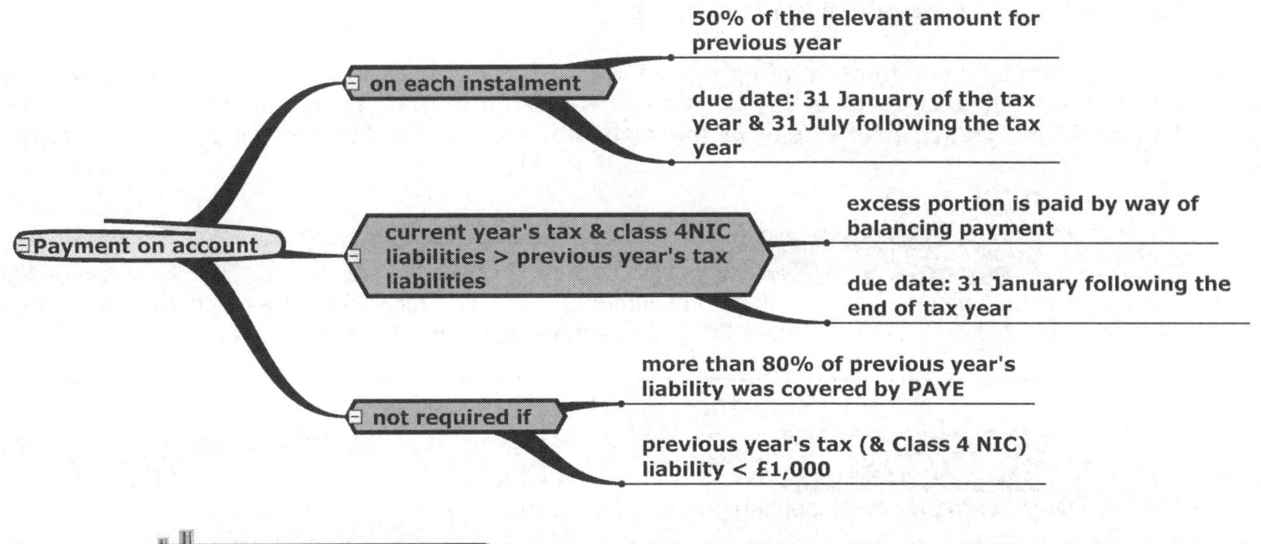

Test Yourself 6

Judy's total liability for income tax and Class 4 NIC for 2011-12 was £20,100. Out of this, she paid £7,500 through deduction at source.

Her total tax and Class 4 NIC liabilities for 2012-13 are £22,800 out of which £2,000 is paid by deduction at source.

Required:

What are the dates when Judy needs to pay her income tax and Class 4 NIC for the tax year 2012-13? Also, calculate the amount payable on each date.

---

4. Explain how large companies are required to account for corporation tax on a quarterly basis.[2]

[Learning Outcome d]

4.1 What is a large company?

A company that pays corporation tax at the main rate (26%) without deduction of marginal relief is categorised as a large company. The augmented profits of such companies are more than the upper limit (i.e. £1,500,000 for FY 2012).

4.2 Method of payment of corporation tax

Large companies have to pay their corporation tax in **instalments.**

However, a large company is **not required to pay** its corporation tax liability by **instalments** for each quarter in the following cases:

1. if the chargeable profits of the company are £10 million or less for the accounting period **and** the company was not a large company in the twelve months preceding that period

2. if the company has a tax liability of less than £10,000 for the period, but still pays tax at a full rate, either because of dividend income, or because it has a number of associated companies

4.3 When are quarterly instalments due?

1. If a company's accounting period is 12 months long

A large company **with a 12 month accounting period** will pay tax in four equal instalments, **starting with the 14th day of the seventh month, then the 14th day of the tenth month, after that, the 14th day of the thirteenth month and lastly, the 14th day of the sixteenth month** from the beginning of the accounting period.

Example

If a company's accounting period is of 12 months starting on 1 January 2012, then quarterly instalment payments are due on 14 July 2012, 14 October 2012, 14 January 2013 and 14 April 2013.

Test Yourself 7

Excellent Ltd is a large company. Its accounting period is for 12 months starting on 1 June 2012.

Required:

When will the quarterly instalment payments be due?

2. If a company's accounting period is less than 12 months long

If a company's **accounting period** is less than 12 months long, then the instalments are due at **three monthly intervals**. The **first instalment must fall** on the 14th day of the seventh month (i.e. six months and 14 days) and the last instalment should fall due on the 14th day of the **fourth month of the next accounting period.** The second instalment is due on the usual quarterly date i.e. on the 14th day of the tenth month.

Example

If a company's accounting period is for 8 months to 30 June 2012, then quarterly instalment payments are due on:

- 14 May 2012 (14th day of the seventh month from 1 November 2011)
- 14 August 2012 (usual quarterly instalment date)
- 14 October 2012 (final payment must fall in the fourth month of the next accounting period)

Test Yourself 8

Well Done Ltd is a large company. Its accounting period is for 10 months to 31 October 2012.

Required:

State when the corporation tax liability will be due for payment.

4.4 Estimation of tax liability by a company

A company has to pay tax for the current year on an instalment basis, and so it is required to estimate its corporation tax liability in advance for the current period. Failure on the part of the company to estimate its tax liability with a reasonable degree of accuracy can result in heavy penalties. Therefore, it is imperative to estimate the tax liability carefully.

Tip

Instalments of corporation tax are based on the estimated corporation tax liability for the current year and not the previous year as in the case of individuals.

How to calculate the amount of instalments

1. Estimate the tax liability.
2. If the accounting period does not equal 12 months, then **perform** the calculation:

$$3 \times \frac{\text{Estimated Corporation Tax}}{\text{No. of months in the period}}$$

3. This procedure is repeated for the next instalments until the amount allocated is equal to the corporation tax liability.

Tip

In practice, most companies prepare management accounts and base their estimated tax liability on those. If the estimated profits change during the year then it may be necessary to increase or decrease the instalment payment.

Example

Tempo Ltd has a corporation tax liability of £990,000 for the 9 month period to 31 October 2012. Accounts had previously always been prepared to 31 December.

The amount of each instalment is calculated as follows:

$$\text{The amount of each installment} = 3 \times \frac{\text{Estimated Corporation Tax}}{\text{No. of months in the period}}$$

$$= 3 \times \frac{£990{,}000}{9\ \text{months}}$$

$$= £330{,}000$$

The due dates and amount payable on each instalment:

14 August 2012	£330,000
14 November 2012	£330,000
14 February 2013	£330,000

SUMMARY

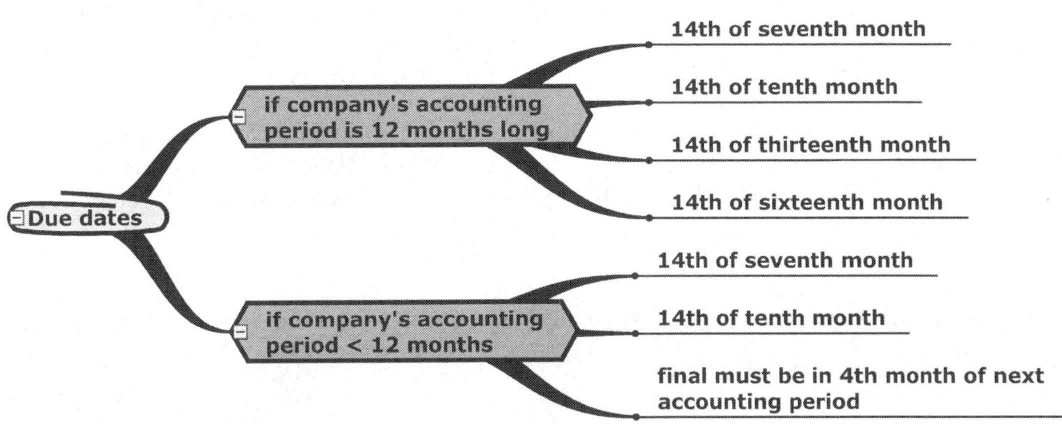

Test Yourself 9

Tick-tock Ltd has taxable total profits of £2,400,000 for the year ended 31 December 2012.

Required:

Show how the liability for the year ended 31 December 2012 will be settled.

5. List the information and records that taxpayers need to retain for tax purposes.[1]

[Learning Outcome e]

Information and records to be kept by employees and directors

- Details of payments made for business expenses (e.g. receipts, credit card statements etc.)
- Share options awarded or exercised
- Evidence of any deductions and reliefs claimed
- Interest and dividend certificates
- Tax deduction certificates
- Dividend vouchers
- Qualifying charitable donation payment receipts
- Personal pension plan certificates
- Personal financial records which support any claims based on amounts paid e.g. certificates of interest paid

Information and records to be kept by businesses

- Invoices, bank statements and paying-in slips
- Invoices for purchases and other expenses
- Details of personal drawings from cash and bank receipts

Important points to remember

1. **All the records** relevant to a taxpayer's return must be kept until 31 January of the sixth year from the end of the tax year.

2. If the taxpayer has income from a business or from **letting a property**, he has to keep records until 31 January of the sixth year from the end of the tax year.

3. If a **formal enquiry** into the return is commenced by HMRC before the expiry of the time limit specified for such an enquiry, then the **records must be kept until that enquiry has been completed.**

4. A taxpayer can **keep records on a computerised system,** provided they can be produced in legible form whenever required.

5. **A penalty of up to £3,000** is chargeable **when** the required **records are not kept** in respect of any tax year.

Answers to Test Yourself

Answer to TY 1

(a) When HMRC issues a notice to file a tax return between 31 July and 31 October of the following year, the return must be filed by 31 January following the tax year, if the taxpayer files his return electronically. Therefore, the deadline for Sam to file his return online is 31 January 2014.

(b) When HMRC issues a notice to file a tax return between 31 July and 31 October of the following year, the return must be filed by the end of three months from the date of notice, if the taxpayer files their return non-electronically. Therefore, the deadline for Sam to file his return in paper form is 31 October 2013.

Answer to TY 2

1. As a fifteen month period is covered while preparing the accounts, Turbo Ltd has to file two tax returns:

(a) one for the year ended 31 December 2012

(b) one for the three months ended 31 March 2013.

The filing date is the **latest among the following three dates:**

i. 12 months from the end of the period covered by the return i.e. 31 December 2013 for the first return and 31 March 2014 for the other return.

ii. 12 months from the period of accounts i.e. 31 March 2014.

iii. 3 months from the date on which the notice was issued by HMRC i.e. 15 August 2013.

Hence the filing date is 31 March 2014.

2. As an eighteen month period is covered while preparing the accounts, ABC Ltd has to file two tax returns:

(a) one for the year ended 30 November 2012
(b) one for the six months ended 31 May 2013.

The filing date is the **latest among the following three dates:**

i. 12 months from the end of the period covered by the return i.e. 30 November 2013 for the first return and 31 May 2014 for the other return.

ii. 12 months from the period of accounts i.e. 31 May 2014.

iii. 3 months from the date on which the notice was issued by HMRC i.e. 1 October 2013.

Hence, the filing date is 31 May 2014.

3. The filing date is the **latest among the following three dates:**

i. 12 months from the end of the period covered by the return i.e. 31 December 2014;

ii. 12 months from the period of accounts i.e. 31 December 2014; or

iii. 3 months from the date on which the notice was received from HMRC i.e. 12 May 2014.

Hence, the filing date is 31 December 2014.

Answer to TY 3

31 December 2013, i.e. within 12 months from the end of the period of account

Answer to TY 4

The accounting date 30 June 2012 falls in the tax year 2012-13. Therefore, due dates for the payment of tax are as follows:

1. First payment on account is due on 31 January 2013.
2. Second payment on account is due on 31 July 2013.
3. Final payment to settle the remaining liability (if any) is due on 31 January 2014.

Answer to TY 5

1. Assuming Ted's income tax and Class 4 NIC liability for 2011-12 was £12,300

The payments on account for 2012-13 are as follows:

Date		£
31/01/2013	1st payment on account (50% of £12,300)	6,150
31/07/2013	2nd payment on account (50% of £12,300)	6,150
31/01/2014	Balancing payment (£18,300 - £12,300)	6,000
Total		**18,300**

Note:

There will also be a payment of £9,150 on 31 January 2014, the first instalment of the tax year 2013-14 (50% of the 2012-13 liability of £18,300).

2. Assuming Ted's income tax and Class 4 NIC liability for 2011-12 was £21,800

The payments on account for 2012-13 are as follows:

Date		£
31/01/2013	1st payment on account (50% of £21,800)	10,900
31/07/2013	2nd payment on account (50% of £21,800)	10,900
Total		**21,800**

However, Ted's total tax liability for 2012-13 is only £18,300. This means he paid excess tax on payment on account.

Hence the **balancing repayment** due is £3,500 i.e. (£21,800 - £18,300).

Answer to TY 6

Judy's payments on account for 2011-12 are as follows:

Date		£
31/01/2013	1st payment on account (50% of (£20,100 - £7,500))	6,300
31/07/2013	2nd payment on account (50% of (£20,100 - £7,500))	6,300
31/01/2014	Balancing payment (£22,800 - £2,000 - £6,300 - £6,300)	8,200

Note: there will also be a payment of £10,400 on 31 January 2014, the first instalment of the 2013-14 tax year (50% of (£22,800 - £2,000)).

Answer to TY 7

Excellent Ltd is a large company. Therefore, the due dates are as follows:

- 14 December 2012 (14th day of the seventh month i.e. from 1 June 2012)
- 14 March 2013 (14th day of the tenth month)
- 14 June 2013 (14th day of the thirteenth month)
- 14 September 2013 (14th day of the sixteenth month)

Answer to TY 8

The due dates are:

- 14 July 2012
- 14 October 2012
- 14 February 2013 (the final payment must fall in the fourth month of the next accounting period)

Answer to TY 9

The corporation tax liability of Tick-tock Ltd is £624,000 i.e. (£2,400,000 x 26%).

Tick-tock Ltd is a large company (as its profits exceed £1,500,000).

Corporation tax is payable in quarterly instalments of £156,000 i.e. (£624,000/4) on 14 July 2012, 14 October 2012, 14 January 2013 and 14 April 2013.

Quick Quiz

Fill in the blanks.

1. A first payment on account is due on _________ in the tax year to which the self-assessment relates.

2. The final payment made on 31 January following the end of the tax year to settle the balance income tax and Class 4 NIC liability is known as __________.

3. Taxpayers are not required to make payments on account of their income tax and Class 4 National Insurance liability if more than ___________ of the previous year's liability was covered by tax deducted at source.

4. Payment on account on each instalment is _________ of the previous year's tax liability.

5. When a taxpayer receives an amount of money because they paid an excess amount in the previous year, it is known as a _________ .

Answers to Quick Quiz

1. 31 January
2. balancing payment
3. 80%
4. 50%
5. Balancing repayment

Self Examination Questions

Question 1

What are the normal dates for tax payment by individuals under self-assessment?

Question 2

State the date of filing self-assessment corporation tax returns for the following period of accounts:

(a) YL Ltd prepared its accounts for twenty months to 31 January 2012. It received notice from HMRC on 15 April 2012 for this period.

(b) AS Ltd prepared its accounts for the year ended 30 April 2012.

(c) TR Ltd made up its accounts for the year ended 31 March 2012. It received notice for this period from the Inland Revenue on 1 July 2012.

(d) BK Ltd prepared its accounts for thirteen months to 31 December 2012.

Question 3

A company has an accounting period with a year end of 31/12/2012. Show the due dates for quarterly payment of tax.

Question 4

Jolly Good Ltd has a corporation tax liability of £770,000 for the 7 month period to 30 November 2012.

Required:

Show when the corporation tax liability is due for payment. Also, calculate the liability on each due date.

Answers to Self Examination Questions

Answer to SEQ 1

Tax due on self-assessment is payable as follows:

1. A first payment on account is due on **31 January** in the tax year to which the self-assessment relates.
2. A second payment on account is due on the following **31 July.**
3. A final balancing payment is due on **31 January** following the end of the tax year.

Answer to SEQ 2

(a) As the period of account of YL Ltd is twenty months, it has to be divided into two accounting periods. Two tax returns have to be filed:

- one for the year ended 31 May 2011.
- one for the eight months ended 31 January 2012

The filing date is the later among the following three dates:

(i) 12 months from the end of the period specified in the notice i.e. 31 May 2012 for the first return and 31 January 2013 for the other return
(ii) 30 months from the start of the period of accounts i.e. 30 November 2012
(iii) 3 months after the issue of the notice i.e. 15 July 2012

The date of filing the return for YL Ltd is 31 January 2013.

(b) The due date for AS Ltd is 12 months from the end of the period of accounts, i.e. 30 April 2013.

(c) The filing date is the **later** among the following two dates:

1. Twelve months from the end of the period covered by the return i.e. 31 March 2013

2. Three months from the issue of the notice i.e. 1 October 2012.

The date of filing the return for TR Ltd is 31 March 2013.

(d) The due date for filing the return is the **later** of:

- twelve months from the end of the period covered by the return i.e. the period specified in the notice by HMRC: information is not given
- twelve months from the end of the period of accounts: i.e. 31 December 2013 as the period of accounts is less than eighteen months
- three months from the issue of notice: this information is not given

Therefore, the date of filing the return for BK Ltd is 31 December 2013.

Answer to SEQ 3

The tax will have to be paid as follows:

1st instalment	14th day of seventh month from the beginning of the accounting period	14/07/2012
2nd instalment	14th day of tenth month from the beginning of the accounting period	14/10/2012
3rd instalment	14th day of thirteenth month from the beginning of the accounting period	14/01/2013
4th instalment	14th day of sixteenth month from the beginning of the accounting period	14/04/2013

Answer to SEQ 4

The amount of each instalment is calculated as follows:

$$\text{The amount of each installment} = 3 \times \frac{\text{Estimated Corporation Tax}}{\text{No. of months in the period}}$$

$$= 3 \times \frac{£770{,}000}{7 \text{ months}}$$

= **£330,000**

The due dates and amount of each instalment:

14 November 2012	£330,000
14 February 2013	£330,000
14 March 2013	£110,000 (balance)

SECTION H

THE OBLIGATIONS OF TAX PAYERS AND/OR THEIR AGENTS

H3

STUDY GUIDE H3: THE PROCEDURES RELATING TO COMPLIANCE CHECKS, APPEALS AND DISPUTES

Get Through Intro

This Study Guide covers the various compliance checks that HMRC can make on self-assessment returns. To ensure that the tax system is operating smoothly and all its customers are paying the right amount of tax at the right time, HMRC makes compliance checks on certain returns. These enquiries are known as **'compliance checks'**.

When HM Revenue & Customs start a compliance check it doesn't necessarily mean that the return is incorrect. Sometimes, HMRC routinely checks a portion of tax returns to make sure that they are correct, or looks for tax returns with a particular type of entry on them, such as chargeable gains.

However, most compliance checks arise with the Revenue because there is something they don't understand or they have some information which makes them think that the tax return or claim might be wrong. Perhaps the return filed is considerably different than those filed in the past or the income may be considerably less than in the past.

Understanding these compliance checks is extremely important for tax professionals, who frequently have to deal with HMRC in responding to compliance checks, appealing decisions etc.

Understanding these concepts will help you to successfully attempt the questions in the exam.

Learning Outcomes

a) Explain the circumstances in which HM Revenue and Customs can make a compliance check into a self- assessment tax return.
b) Explain the procedures for dealing with appeals and disputes.

Introduction

Some of the possible outcomes of a tax compliance check could be as follows:

If nothing is wrong

You will receive a letter from HMRC informing you that the compliance check has finished. No changes will be made to the tax return or claim.

If you've paid too much tax

Your return will be changed by HMRC to reflect the lower figures. HMRC will also pay you interest from the date of your incorrect payment until the date you receive a repayment.

If you've paid too little tax

HMRC will discuss any changes with you and a final figure will be agreed upon (this is often done by way of letter). You will receive a closure notice confirming the changes and will then have 30 days in which to pay the tax due.

If you are unable to pay the full amount immediately, you may be allowed to pay in instalments. If the amount owed is small, you may be able to increase your self-assessment 'payments on account' for the following year.

You will usually be required to pay interest on underpaid tax, depending on the circumstances. Other surcharges for late or non-payment of tax after issue of a closure notice will also apply.

1. Explain the circumstances in which HM Revenue and Customs can make a compliance check into a self- assessment tax return.[2]

[Learning Outcome a]

1.1 Revision of returns

Individuals

The last date for amending a tax return regardless of whether it is paper-based or filed online will be the later of:

- 12 months from the normal due date of submitting tax returns, i.e. 31 January following the tax year; or
- three months from the notice to file a return was issued.

For example, for 2012-13 the deadline for amending a tax return will be 31 January 2015.

Example

Angelina prepares her accounts for twelve months ended 31/03/2013 and files her return online on 15 August 2013. The **deadline for filing the return in this case is however 31/01/2015**. So Angelina can amend her tax return any time up to 31/01/2015.

If Angelina wants to amend the tax return after twelve months of the required filing date for that return, then she may be able to make an "error or mistake" claim to recover any excess tax paid within six years from the end of the relevant accounting period.

Companies

The last date for amending a tax return will be within 12 months of the normal due date for return filing (not the actual date of return filing). For example for an accounting year ending on 31 March 2013, the normal due date for filing the return is 31 March 2014 and so the company can amend its return until 31 March 2015.

1.2 Correction of errors or omissions by HMRC

HMRC has the right to rectify any obvious errors or omissions in the return including anything else that an officer has reason to believe is incorrect in the light of the information available to them, **within nine months from the date the return was filed** by the company. If the company itself notices an error and makes a rectification by filing an amended return, HMRC has 9 months from this date to make the rectification.

Example

Tweety Ltd filed its return on 12 June 2012. It then revised the return on 23 August 2012. Within what date can HMRC make any rectification to Tweety Ltd's return?

HMRC has the right to rectify errors or omissions appearing in the return. It can make such a rectification within nine months from the date the return was filed / amended by the company. The return was amended by the company on 23 August 2012. The time limit for rectification of return by HMRC is **nine months** starting from 23 August 2012 i.e. 22nd May 2013.

1.3 Compliance checks by HMRC

HMRC has the right to make compliance checks into the completeness and accuracy of any tax return. This right covers all compliance checks, from straightforward requests for further information on individual items through to full reviews of a company's business including examination of the company's records.

For conducting such a compliance check, a written notice must be issued to the company, by the later of:
- 12 months from the date that a corporation tax return is received by HMRC, i.e. the actual submission date of the return; and
- 12 months from 31 January, 30 April, 31 July or 31 October (the "quarter date") – whichever comes first, following the actual date of submission of the return, if the return is filed after the due date.

Tip

HMRC can raise only one compliance check in respect of any one return or amendment.

Example

Sun Ltd prepares its accounts to 31 March 2012. Sun Ltd filed its return on 12 January 2013 (i.e. before the submission date). HMRC can open a compliance check on Sun Ltd's return provided a written notice is issued to the company within a period of 12 months from the date that a corporation tax return is received by HMRC i.e. on or before 11 January 2014.

1.4 Time limit for a compliance check by HMRC

After the end of **twelve months** from the required filing date (or the date of receipt of the return for income tax purposes), so long as full disclosure has been made on the tax return then no compliance check can be opened by HMRC. The tax return is usually regarded as finalised after the expiry of this twelve month period.

Example

A company has filed its return for the period of twelve months ended 31 March 2012 on 2 June 2012. In this case, if no compliance check is done by HMRC by 1 October 2013 (i.e. after the end of **twelve months** from the required filing date) then it cannot start a compliance check in the case of this return.

However, HMRC can make a **discovery assessment** even after twelve months from the required filing date. This is discussed in section 1.7 below.

1.5 Procedure for the compliance check

HMRC may amend a self-assessment at any time during a compliance check if it is found that:
1. less tax is paid than required
2. no tax is paid at all
3. revenue of HMRC is lost in any other way

The company may appeal against such an amendment within **thirty days.**

1.6 Result of a compliance check

A compliance check ends when HMRC gives notice that the compliance check is complete. A company has to amend its self-assessment return within thirty days of receiving HMRC's conclusions. If HMRC is not satisfied with the amendments made by the company, it can amend the self-assessment within the next thirty days. The company then has another thirty days in which it may appeal against the HMRC amendments.

Example

Zigzag Ltd received a notice from HMRC of the completion of the compliance check on 12 June 2012. The tax assessed by HMRC as a result of the compliance check was £15,500. Zigzag Ltd has to file the amended return within a period of thirty days from receiving HMRC's conclusions i.e. on or before 12 July 2012 (30 days from 12 June 2012).

If HMRC is not satisfied with the amendments made by the company, it can amend the self-assessment within the next thirty days i.e. on or before 11 August 2012 (30 days from 12 July 2012).
If the company wants to appeal against the amendment made by HMRC in the company's return, such appeal can be made on or before 10 September 2012 (30 days from 11 August 2012).

1.7 Discovery assessment by HMRC

However, if after the expiry of twelve months from the required filing date, HMRC discovers that the company has been assessed to insufficient tax then it can raise a "**discovery assessment**".

The time period for a discovery assessment depends upon the behaviour on the part of the company or persons representing the company. The time limits for discovery assessments therefore are as follows:

Understatement of tax	Period
Not due to deliberate or careless behaviour (i.e. not due to fraud or negligence on the part of the company)	4 years
Due to careless behaviour (negligence)	6 years
Due to deliberate behaviour (fraud)	20 years

These time limits run from the end of the accounting period of the company. The same time limits are applicable in case of discovery assessment for income tax, CGT and VAT liabilities.

Tip

HMRC can only raise a discovery assessment if it "discovers" a reason to believe that insufficient tax has been assessed. Provided that the taxpayer makes full disclosure of all relevant facts on their tax return, they will not usually be exposed to this longer compliance check window.

Test Yourself 1

Zatac Ltd prepares its accounts up to 31/03/2012. Zee is the director of Zatac Ltd. Zatac Ltd purchased a new office and let out the old office to another company for a monthly rent of £700. It was also decided that the tenant company would pay this £700 directly to Zee as directorial remuneration. Zatac Ltd ignored this income of £8,400 as it was given directly to the director, Zee. Zee in his personal return, disclosed this income from Zatac Ltd as director's remuneration.

Required:

What actions can be taken by HMRC?

1.8 Determination of the tax amount by HMRC

If a company fails to file a tax return before the required filing date, HMRC may make a determination of the amount of tax due. Such determination can be displaced only if the company delivers the required return. There is no right of appeal against a determination.

1.9 Preservation of records by the company

A company is required to preserve all the records and accounts including contracts and receipts (on the basis of which a tax return is filed) and other relevant records until the latest of:

1. six years after the end of the concerned accounting period
2. the date compliance checks started by HMRC are completed
3. the date after which compliance checks may not be commenced

HMRC do not usually insist on keeping original records. However, in the following cases, original records must be kept:

a) qualifying distributions and tax credits
b) gross and net payments and tax deducted for payments made net of tax
c) details of foreign tax paid

2. Explain the procedures for dealing with appeals and disputes.[1]

[Learning Outcome b]

2.1 Appeals

Appeal against decisions: if a taxpayer is not satisfied with any of the decisions of HMRC, they can file an appeal against the decision. The main classes of appeal are:

a) imposition of a penalty
b) imposition of a surcharge
c) appeal against the order requiring submission of records and documents
d) appeal against the amendment made to self assessment as a result of compliance check
e) appeal against the existence of relevant grounds for making of discovery assessment
f) appeal against a discovery assessment

Diagram 1: The order of authorities to whom the appeal can be made

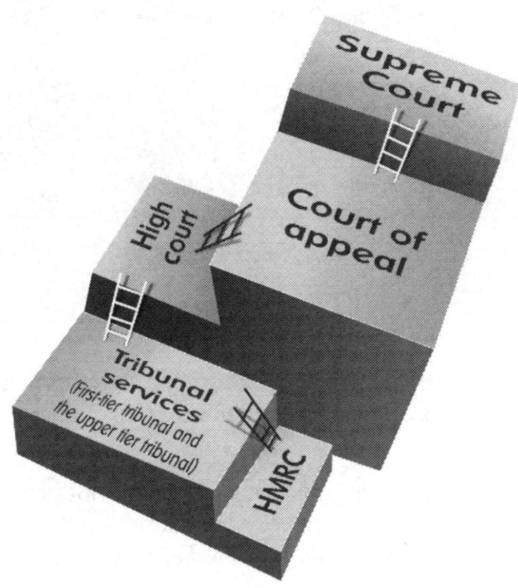

2.2 Procedure of appeal

1. Internal review process

a) When any taxpayer wishes to appeal against an order issued by HMRC, they have to make the appeal for **internal review** in **writing** to HMRC within **thirty days** of the relevant HMRC decision along with the reasons for appeal.

b) A taxpayer may appeal for postponement of a tax payment if the appeal is against the amount of tax assessed.

c) A taxpayer can be represented by their agent during the hearing of the appeal.

d) An appeal is settled by means of **informal discussions** between HMRC and the taxpayer or their agent, therefore this is a comparatively cost effective method.

e) Most of the appeals are generally settled by agreement with HMRC in the internal review process without the need for a Tribunal hearing.

f) A review of the appeal decision is carried out by an officer who has not previously been involved in the decision relating to the appeal. The review is generally completed within 45 days.

g) Requests to third parties for information must normally either be agreed by the taxpayer or approved by the first-tier tribunal. These powers have now been extended to third party bulk data gatherers such as banks and stockbrokers.

h) Appeal to tribunal: taxpayers who disagree with the decision taken in the review process can appeal to an independent Tribunal. The appeal must be made within 30 days from the review conclusion letter.

2. Appeals to Tribunal

Appeals that are not settled by internal review are heard by the Tribunal.

The Tribunal service is divided into two: the First-tier Tribunal and the Upper Tribunal.

- **First-tier Tribunal: i**t deals with most of the appeals.
- **Upper Tribunal:** relatively complex appeals are handled by the Upper Tribunal. It also deals with appeals against decisions of the First-tier Tribunal.

The cases are allocated to any one of the following four tracks on the basis of the differences and the amount of tax involved:

a) Paper track: these involve the most simple and uncomplicated cases and are usually settled without any hearing. For example, fixed penalties in the case of late filing of returns.

b) Basic track: these are usually settled on informal basis, but after a hearing. The requirement for exchange of documents is kept at a minimum. For example, appeal for the postponement of tax.

c) Standard track: it includes most of the other matters which are not covered in the paper track and basic track. These are dealt with on a more formal basis and involve detailed case management. These cases are settled after proper exchange of documents and evidence before the hearing.

d) Complex track: these cases involve lengthy and complex principles of law or issues and a large sum of money. They require lengthy hearing; therefore they can be directly heard by the Upper Tribunal.

If the taxpayer or HMRC are not satisfied with the decision of a tax tribunal, they may appeal further, first to the High Court, then to the Court of Appeal and finally to the Supreme Court (the court that replaced the House of Lords in 2009).

In general, the First Tier Tribunal tends to deal with factual disputes, and the Upper Tier Tribunal deals with disputes involving technical matters.

Answer to Test Yourself

Answer to TY 1

HMRC can make a compliance check from the **required filing date** for that return. The required filing date for Zatac Ltd is 31/03/2013. Hence HMRC can start a compliance check on Zatac Ltd's return at any time up to 31/03/2014.

However, in this case, Zatac Ltd has assessed insufficient tax. It has not disclosed its income of £8,400 due to negligence, i.e. careless behaviour. Therefore, a discovery assessment can be raised by HMRC up to **six years after** the end of the accounting period to which it relates. HMRC can start a compliance check on Zatac Ltd's return at any time up to 31/03/2018 (6 years from 31/03/2012).

Quick Quiz

Fill in the blanks.

1. A company can amend a tax return filed by it within twelve months from the ________ for that return.
2. If any omission or errors are noticed by HMRC in the return filed by the company, then HMRC has the right to rectify such errors within _________from the date the return was filed by the company.
3. HMRC can start a compliance check into a company's tax return at any time before the end of ________from the required filing date for that return.
4. No compliance check can be made by HMRC after the end of ___________from the required filing date, except in the case of a discovery assessment where a compliance check can be raised by HMRC in normal circumstances up to ________ after the end of the accounting period to which it relates.
5. The appeal commissioners may confirm,________ or increase a disputed assessment.

Answers to Quick Quiz

1. required filing date
2. nine months
3. one year
4. twelve months, four years
5. reduce

Self Examination Question

Question 1

For how long is a company required to preserve its records and accounts?

Answer to Self Examination Question

Answer to SEQ 1

A company is required to preserve all the records and accounts (on the basis of which a tax return is filed) and other relevant records until the latest of:

1. six years after the end of the concerned accounting period
2. the date compliance checks started by HMRC are completed
3. the date after which compliance checks may not be commenced

In the following cases, original records must be kept:

(a) qualifying distributions and tax credits
(b) gross and net payments and tax deducted for payments made net of tax
(c) details of foreign tax paid.

SECTION H

THE OBLIGATIONS OF TAX PAYERS AND/OR THEIR AGENTS

H4

STUDY GUIDE H4: PENALTIES FOR NON-COMPLIANCE

Get Through Intro

During the tax year (6 April of one year to 5 April of the next) there are key dates by which taxpayers need to send in their tax returns and/or make certain payments. It is important to be aware of these dates - HM Revenue & Customs (HMRC) may impose penalties and surcharges if they are missed.

The penalties regime is in the process of being updated to apply the same rules to all of the taxes. The new rules have been published in the Finance Act 2009 and are gradually being brought into effect. The difficulty facing tax consultants is that clients may suffer penalties if they miss any dates for filing returns or paying taxes or if they pay inadequate taxes. As the new rules are being brought into effect gradually it is very easy to miss a deadline as it is not easy to identify which penalty regime applies to your clients.

This Study Guide explains the penalties a taxpayer might have to pay for various infringements of the rules.

Learning Outcomes

a) Calculate late payment interest.
b) State the penalties that can be charged.

Introduction

Case Study

Energetic Ltd is an oil refining and marketing company. John, the company tax accountant, assumed that the profits would remain constant and did not forecast the large increase in turnover due to the launch of a number of new petrol filling stations.

As a result, Energetic Ltd's estimated profits were grossly understated when calculating the quarterly instalment payments, resulting in the company owing HMRC a considerable amount of tax for the year.

In this Study Guide we shall see the way in which HMRC apply penalties by way of interest and surcharges on overdue payments.

1. Calculate late payment interest.[2]

[Learning Outcome a]

1.1 Underpaid tax

A taxpayer has to pay interest on underpaid corporation tax for the period beginning **on the date** on which the tax **should have been** paid, up to the date on which it is **actually paid.**

Tip

For the June and December 2013 sitting, the assumed rate of interest on underpaid tax is 3.0%.

1.2 Overpaid tax

If a taxpayer has paid excess tax, HMRC pays interest to the taxpayer on the excess tax amount for the period beginning on the date on which the tax was paid, up to the date on which the excess tax is refunded to the taxpayer.

Tip

The rate of interest is in line with the base rate of tax. Hence, it increases or decreases in accordance with the prevailing base rate of tax. **For the June and December 2013 sitting, the assumed rate of interest on overpaid tax is 0.5%.**

For interest calculation purposes, as a general practice:

a) HMRC uses a denominator of **366** for calculating interest on underpaid tax.
b) HMRC uses a denominator of **365** for overpaid tax on which it pays interest.
c) HMRC follows the same practice of applying 366 and 365 denominators for underpaid and overpaid tax respectively, even if the year under consideration is a leap year.

Example

Alpha Ltd prepares its accounts up to 30 September 2012. For this year, it has calculated a corporation tax liability of £40,000 and paid this amount on 1 July 2013. However, eventually it turns out that the correct liability was only £23,000. The refund of excess tax of £17,000 was made on 12 September 2013. Calculate the interest payable to Alpha Ltd by HMRC.

The overpaid tax of £17,000 was repaid on 12 September 2013 i.e. 72 days later. So the interest payable to Alpha Ltd is:

£17,000 x 0.5% x 72/365 = **£17**

Note:

It is necessary to count the number of days.

Test Yourself 1

In the above example, assume that the tax liability was £40,000 and tax paid was only £23,000, the other information remaining the same. Calculate the interest payable by Alpha Ltd to HMRC.

Tip

- **If** an **individual receives / pays interest to / from HMRC,** it is **not chargeable / deductible. However, for companies, interest paid / received** on underpaid / overpaid corporation tax is **dealt with under income from loan relationship** as interest paid / received on a **non-trading loan relationship.**
- **Rates** of interest are the **same** for **individuals and companies**.

2. State the penalties that can be charged.[2]

[Learning Outcome b]

Penalties are payable in addition to the interest and surcharges. Penalties are charged if an individual or company does not file its tax return, together with the supporting accounts and calculations, by the required date.

2.1 Penalty for failure to submit the return on time for companies

Diagram 1: Penalty for failure to submit the return on time

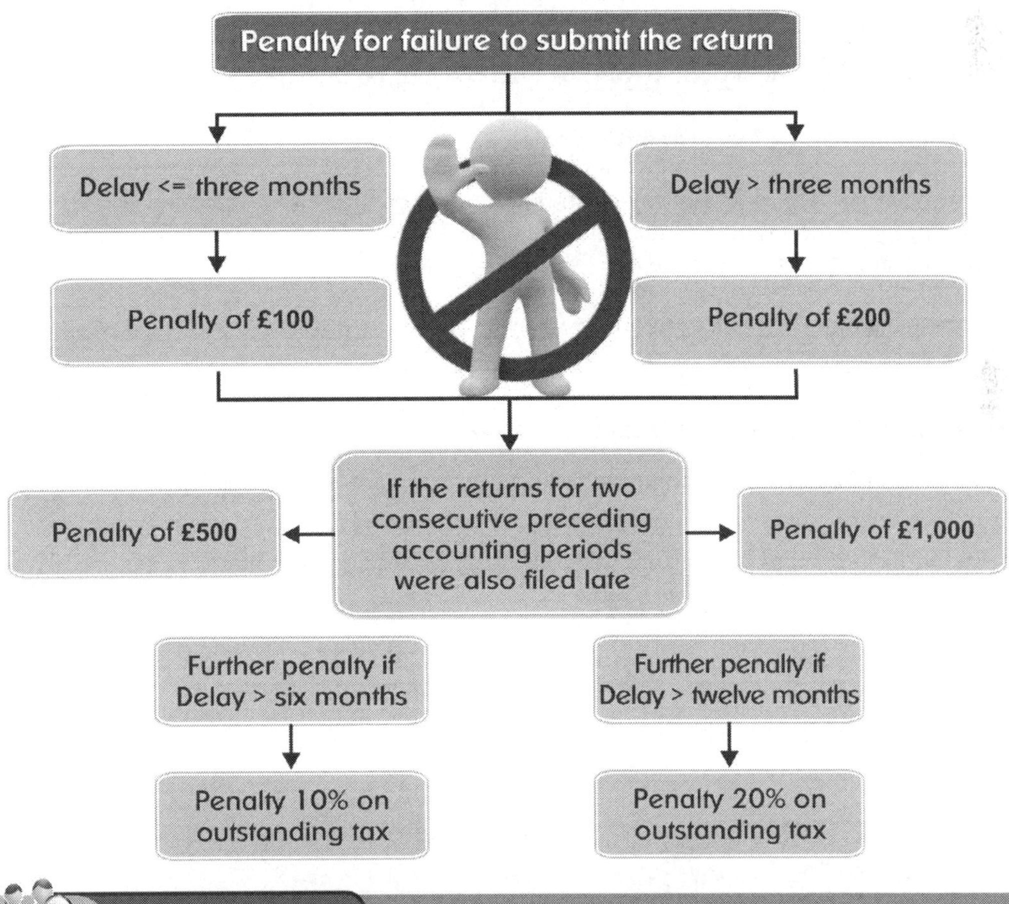

Example

Yoyo Ltd prepares its accounts for twelve months ended 31/03/2012. The due date for filing the tax return was 31/03/2013. Calculate the amount of penalty of Yoyo Ltd:

1. Files the return on 5 May 2013 and during the preceding two years the return was filed on time
2. Files the return on 12 June 2013 but the return was also filed late during the preceding two years
3. Files the return on 28 April 2013 but the return was also filed late during the preceding year
4. Files the return on 5 July 2013 and during the preceding two years, the return was filed on time
5. Files the return on 12 August 2013 but the return was also filed late during the preceding two years
6. Files the return on 28 September 2013 but the return was also filed late during the preceding year

Continued on the next page

Answer

	Date of filing return	Period of delay	Delay for preceding two years	Penalty £
1	05/05/2013	Less than three months	No	100
2	12/06/2013	Less than three months	Yes	500
3	28/04/2013	Less than three months	No	100
4	05/07/2013	More than three months	No	200
5	12/08/2013	More than three months	Yes	1,000
6	28/09/2013	More than three months	No	200

2.2 Penalty for failure to submit the return on time for individuals

A new penalty regime has been introduced for late filing of returns for the individual, which is as follows:

	Amount of penalty
1. Self assessment tax return is filed after the due date	£100
2. If delay in return filing is more than 3 months	£10 per day (up to a maximum of 90 days)
3. If delay in return filing is more than 6 months	5% of the tax due (minimum penalty £300)
4. If delay in return filing is more than 12 months	Additional 5%
Note: if the failure is deliberate, a penalty higher than 5% can be charged.	

2.3 Penalties for late payment of tax: for individuals

In addition to the above penalty, a further tax-geared penalty is charged if tax remains unpaid. This penalty is charged as a percentage of the amount of tax outstanding and replaces the old surcharge regime for individuals (to be introduced for companies at a later date).

Various rates at which a penalty is charged are as follows:

	Amount of penalty
1. Tax remains unpaid for less than one month after the due date	0%
2. Tax remains unpaid for more than one month but up to six months after the due date	5%
3. Tax remains unpaid for more than six months but up to twelve months after the due date	Additional 5%
4. Tax remains unpaid for more than twelve months after the due date	Additional 5%

It is important to note that these rules apply only to balancing payments and not to late payments on account.

Legislation has been introduced regarding the late filling of VAT returns and the late payment of VAT, HM Revenue and customs have yet to introduce the changes. Therefore, for June and December 2013 sittings the changes will not be examined.

2.4 Penalties for incorrect returns – companies and individuals

If an individual or a company **fraudulently or negligently** submits an incorrect return or fails / delays to notify HMRC of a new taxable activity, a new penalty regime will apply, which is as follows:

The amount of penalty is based on the amount of tax understated as a result of incorrect return or failure to notify HMRC, but the actual penalty payable is linked to the taxpayer's behaviour, as follows:

- There will be **no penalty** where a taxpayer simply makes a **mistake**.
- There will be a **moderate penalty** (up to **30% of the understated tax**) where a taxpayer **fails to take reasonable care.**
- There will be a **higher penalty** (up to **70% of the understated tax**) if the **error is deliberate**, and an even higher penalty (up to **100% of the understated tax**) where there is also **concealment of the error**.

However, a penalty will be substantially reduced where a taxpayer makes a disclosure, especially when it is an unprompted disclosure of an incorrect return following a failure to take reasonable care. In such cases, the penalty could be reduced to nil.

Example

The dates of payment made and to be made by McMilan are given. Calculate the amount of surcharge to be imposed, wherever applicable.

Actual Date of Payment	Amount	Due Date of Payment	Amount
31/01/2013	15,000 (POA)	31/01/2013	15,000
01/09/2013	15,000 (POA)	31/07/2013	15,000

Answer

1. As the first POA is paid in full and on time, no penalty is imposed.
2. There is an exception to the penalty rule, that POAs do not attract surcharges, although the second POA is paid 32 days late.

Test Yourself 2

A taxpayer completes a self-assessment tax return for 2011-12 showing a total tax liability of £11,000. Payments on account are paid on time. The balancing payment due on 31 January 2012 is £3,750.

State the amount of penalty if the balancing payment of tax was made on:

(a) 28 February 2012
(b) 31 August 2012

Answer to Test Yourself

Answer to TY 1

The underpaid tax of £7,000 was repaid on 12 September 2013, i.e. 72 days later. So the interest payable by Alpha Ltd to HMRC is:

£17,000 x 3.0% x 72/366 = **£100**

Answer to TY 2

1. If the balancing payment is made on 28 February 2012, the amount of penalty will be: = (£3,750 @ 5%) = £187.5

2. If the balancing payment is made on 31 August 2012, a further additional penalty of £187.50 is due again (£3,750 @ 5%).

Self Examination Questions

Question 1

What is the penalty charged if the income tax self assessment return is submitted late?

Question 2

The corporation tax liability of Soho Ltd was £65,000 for the year ended 30 September 2012. It paid the tax on 30 September 2013. For what period will interest be due on the corporation tax?

Question 3

State the date from which interest due from HMRC will be incurred in the following cases:

1. Poppins Ltd paid corporation tax of £47,000 for the year ended 31 December 2012 on 1 August 2013. The actual liability came to £37,000.
2. Mangola Ltd paid corporation tax of £54,000 for the year ended 30 September 2012 on 1 August 2013. The liability was finally agreed upon as £45,000.

Answers to Self Examination Questions

Answer to SEQ 1

If the delay in filing the return is up to three months, an initial fixed penalty of £100 is charged. The penalty increases to £10 per day if the return is more than three months late, up to a maximum of 90 days. In addition to this, a tax-geared penalty is charged at 5% of the tax outstanding (subject to a minimum of £300) if the return is more than six months late, or an additional 5% if the return is more than twelve months late. Moreover, the rate of 5% can be increased in the case of deliberate failure in return submission.

Answer to SEQ 2

Interest will be due for the period from the due date (i.e. nine months and one day, as it is a small company) to the date the tax was actually paid i.e. from 1 July 2013 to 30 September 2013.

Answer to SEQ 3

1. Interest will run from the **later of**:

(a) the due date: 1 October 2013 (9 months + 1 day after the end of the accounting period)
(b) the date tax was actually paid: 1 August 2013

Hence, interest is due from 1 October 2013.

2. The interest will run from the **later of**:

(a) the due date: 1 July 2013 (9 months + 1 day after the end of the accounting period)
(b) the date the tax was actually paid: 1 August 2013.

Hence, interest is due from 1 August 2013.

INDEX